The **Rough Guide** to

Slovenia

written and researched by

Norm Longley

D0813169

NEW YORK • LONDON • DELHI

www.roughguides.com

Contents

Subterranean Slovenia
colour section following
p.112

The Great Outdoors
colour section following
p.240

◁◁ Piran ◁ Ranjska Gora, Gorenjska

Budapest ◀   Budapest ◀

HUNGARY

CROATIA

Zalaegerszeg

Nagykanisza

Lenti

Lendava

Čakovec

Murska
Sobota

Ljutomer

Ormož

Varaždin

Krapina

Zagreb

Karlovac

Maribor

Ptuj

Rogaška
Slatina

Brežice

Strass

Pragersko

Rogla

Pohorje
Massif

Slovenske
Konjice

Celje

Laško

Olimia

Zidani Most

Šmarješke
Toplice

Kostanjevica
na Krki

Črnomelj

Metlika

Wolfsberg

Dravograd

Slovenj Gradec

Velenje

Novo
Mesto

Dolenjske
Toplice

Kočevje

Graz & Vienna ◀

Graz ◀

V lkermarkt

Ferlach

Savinje Alps

Kamnik

Žužemberk

Ribnica

Cerknica

AUSTRIA

Klagenfurt

Tržič

Kranj

LJUBLJANA

Lake
Cerknica

Mt. Snežnik

Jesenice

Bled

Radovljica

Kropa

Škofja Loka

Cerkno

Idrija

Postojna

Pivka

Villach

Kranjska
Gora

Triglav

Lake
Bohinj

Julian Alps

Most na Soči

Tolmin

Nova
Gorica

Vipava Valley

Štanjel

Divača

Škocjan
Caves

Bovec

Kobarid

Brda

Soča

Trieste

Koper

Hrastovlje

ITALY

Udine

Palmanova

Izola

Piran

Portorož

Adriatic
Sea

Rijeka ▶

Pula ▶

Pula ▶

Venice ▶

Metres							
3000	2000	1500	1000	500	200	100	0

40 km

0

N

Introduction to
Slovenia

**Roughly the size of Wales and with a population of less
than two million, Slovenia sports a geographical diversity
unmatched in many countries twice its size – imperious
white limestone mountains, spectacular underground
curiosities, sweeping vineyards, and a craggy coastline
punctuated by historic coastal resorts are just some of the
attractions packed cheek-by-jowl into this tiny country.**

**And with distances so small, in a
single day you could be hiking in
the Alps in the morning, downing
a few glasses of wine in a local
cellar over lunch, and relaxing by
the beach at the end of the day.**

Dominated by Germanic and, to a lesser extent, Hungarian and Italian
influences from the Middle Ages until the end of World War I, Slovenia
spent the best part of the next seventy years locked into a less than harmoni-
ous **Yugoslav federation**. When the federation began to fracture in the late
1980s, Slovenia was the first to secede; save for the so-called **Ten-Day War**
of independence in the summer of 1991, the country emerged more or less
unscathed from the bloodbath that tragically engulfed Croatia and Bosnia.
Slovenia was by far and away the most **liberal** and **progressive** of Yugoslavia's
erstwhile republics, which partly accounted for its relatively painless transition from one-party rule to multiparty democracy, and from communist to
market economy, following independence.

In 2004, the country finally achieved its long-desired goals of NATO and
European Union membership, and in 2007 it became the first of the ten

5
■

▽ Main Square, Maribor

new EU member states to introduce the **euro**, thus cementing its place within the wider international community. While this appears to have made little tangible difference to the lives of most Slovenes, it has helped raise the country's profile in a big way. Prior to the dismemberment of Yugoslavia, Slovenia, along with Croatia, could always boast the lion's share of the federation's tourist traffic, though this was almost completely decimated during the troubles of the 1990s. It is only in recent years that the country has managed to re-establish itself, and visitors today will be struck by the quality of the **tourist facilities** on offer, be it a tourist farm, ski centre, or one of the country's burgeoning number of spa resorts.

As appealing as many of Slovenia's towns and cities are, especially the enchanting capital Ljubljana, the country's greatest asset is its magnificent, and astonishingly varied, natural heritage; as one of Europe's greenest nations – over half the country is forested – there are limitless opportunities for **outdoor pursuits**: skiing, climbing and hiking in the Alps, white-water rafting, kayaking and canyoning on the country's many rivers, cycling through rolling hills and forests, or riding cross-country on a Lipizzaner, to name but a few.

Where to go

Most visitors to Slovenia begin with a trip to the country's sophisticated capital, **Ljubljana**, whose engaging blend of Baroque and Habsburg architecture, and river cafés and restaurants, could quite happily detain you for a few days. From here it is customary to make a beeline for the stunning alpine lakes and mountains northwest of the capital, namely **Lake Bled**, with its fairytale island church and cliff-top castle, and the even more beautiful **Lake Bohinj**, less than 40km to the west. Both lakes lie on the fringe of the **Julian Alps**, whose magisterial peaks are as popular with climbers and hikers in the summer as they are with skiers in the winter. Most of the Alps are contained within **Triglav National Park**, which extends south

▽ Kayaking on the Soča River

Fact file

• With an area of less than 21,000 square kilometres (roughly the size of Wales), and a population of just two million, Slovenia is one of Europe's smallest nations. Forty percent of the country is mountainous, around a quarter of which is alpine, with three major mountain groups: the Julian Alps, the Kamniške-Savinja Alps and the Karavanke mountains. The highest peak is Triglav (2864m) in the Julian Alps. The remainder of the country is comprised of subalpine hills, karst plateaus, forests and flat plains, whilst the coastline, facing the Adriatic, is just 47km long.

• The country is divided into eight geographical regions – Bela Krajina, Dolenjska, Gorenjska, Koroška, Notranjska, Prekmurje, Primorska and Štajerska – the boundaries of which are very fluid.

• On June 25, 1991, Slovenia became an independent republic for the very first time. The 1991 constitution set in place a parliamentary system of government, elected every four years, with the prime minister at its head. The head of state, the president, is elected every five years. Slovenia became a full member of the EU in May, 2004.

• Tourism is one of the fastest growing sectors of the Slovenian economy, with alpine, coastal and health-spa resorts absorbing the bulk of the country's tourist traffic. Slovenia's most important exports are vehicles, electrical appliances and pharmaceutical goods, and its main trading partners are Germany and Italy.

to the imperious **Soča Valley**, whose eponymous river draws adventure sports enthusiasts to its foaming waters each summer.

South of the Soča Valley, beyond the enchanting **Goriška Brda** and **Vipava Valley** wine-growing regions, you'll find the **Karst**. This rugged limestone plateau is scattered with ancient stone villages, such as **Štanjel**, but is famed above all for its dramatic underground rivers, streams and depressions, manifested most spectacularly in the **Škocjan Caves**. The Karst is also home to the world-famous **Lipica stud farm**, the original home of the Lipizzaner.

Although just 47km long, the Slovenian **coast** packs in a multiplicity of little resorts, the most enjoyable being **Piran**, a town brimming with Venetian architecture, and **Portorož**, the country's major beach resort. A short way north of these is the workaday port town of **Koper**, which conceals an appealing medieval centre.

Returning inland, there are more subterranean wonders to explore, few of which can hold a candle to the breathtaking **Postojna Caves**, which lie within striking distance of another of Slovenia's remarkable natural phenomena, the "disappearing" **Lake Cerknica**. South of here, the dark forests and deep river valleys ranged along the Croatian border offer further possibilities for outdoor pursuits, whilst those seeking cultural diversions can take their pick from a rich tapestry of historical sites – churches, castles and ancient monasteries.

▽ Haymaking, Gorenjska

Slovenian wine

Slovenian wine (*vino*) is little known beyond the country's borders, yet vineyards here cover roughly the same area as the Bordeaux region in France and produce about half the quantity of wine of that region, much of which is of extremely high quality. Slovenia has three distinct wine-producing regions, each of which is subdivided into separate districts (there are fourteen in total): the largest of these regions is **Podravje** in the northeast, where white wines such as Laški Rizling, Sauvignon and Šipon predominate; whereas the **Posavje** region in the southeastern corner of the country is known for its reds, in particular the rich and velvety Metliška črnina from Bela Krajina, and the blended, juice-like **Cvicek** from Dolenjska. The Primorje, or coastal, region yields a prolific number of both red and white wines, foremost of which are the excellent Merlot, the straw-yellow Zlata ("Golden") Rebula, and the dry Tokaj, all of which emanate from the gorgeous Goriška Brda hills bordering Italy. Meanwhile, no visit to the Karst region is complete without a drop of the full-blooded, ruby-red **Teran** wine.

By far the most enjoyable place to sample wine is in one of the many **wine cellars** (*vinska klet*) that abound along the country's twenty or so **wine roads** (*vinske ceste*). Alternatively, most towns and cities have a *vinoteka* (wine shop), where you may be offered tastings, and most decent restaurants will have a healthy complement of Slovenian wines.

By comparison, the eastern part of the country is much less visited, and though it might not possess the clear-cut attractions of other regions, there are some hugely rewarding places to visit. Chief amongst these is the country's most historic, and prettiest town, **Ptuj**, which is also the setting for the marvellous Pust carnival, Slovenia's most exuberant annual event. Just a short ride away is the country's second city, **Maribor**, and the sprawling **Pohorje Massif**, a major summer and winter recreational resort. Eastern Slovenia abounds in **spas**, the most popular of which are **Rogaška Slatina** and **Čatež**, two of the largest in the country. Moving further east, across the Mura River and towards the Hungarian border, the undulating hills of the **Podravje** wine-growing districts give way to the flat plains of **Prekmurje**, a lovely, rural region of smooth fields interspersed with pretty villages distinguished by Hungarian-style farmhouses and little white churches.

9

When to go

Most visitors come to Slovenia in summer, when the weather is at its most reliable, the full range of sights are open, and the country's numerous festivals are in full swing. However, many of Slovenia's attractions, including the capital, Ljubljana, are just as enjoyable outside the peak summer months, and in particular during spring and autumn, when the countryside colours are at their most resplendent, hotel prices (at least in the resort areas) are slightly lower and the crowds are a little thinner. Slovenia's climate follows three distinctive patterns: in the northwest, an Alpine climate predominates, characterized by very cold winters, often with heavy rainfall and snow, and moderately warm summers, occasionally interspersed with short, violent storms. However, with the wide range of pursuits on offer here – skiing between December and March, and climbing, hiking and adventure sports between April and September – a visit to the mountain regions can be enjoyed at pretty much any time of the year. Aside from Kranjska Gora in the winter, and Lake Bled and Lake Bohinj in the height of summer, few resorts get so

▽ Lake Cerknica

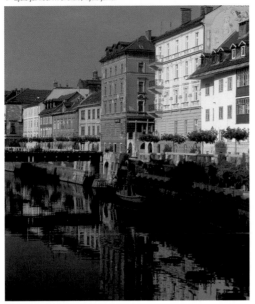

▽ Ljubljanica riverside, Ljubljana

full that finding accommodation becomes a problem.

The Primorska region (from the Soča Valley down to the coast) has a typically **Mediterranean** climate – very warm summers with consistent sunshine, and pleasantly cool winters; this is the one part of the country that can feel a little pressured by crowds, particularly in August when hordes of vacationing Italians arrive from just across the border. Booking accommodation around this time is therefore recommended. Whatever the season, there's a good chance you'll experience the infamous *burja*, a vicious wind that whips down through the Karst on its way to the Bay of Trieste.

The remainder of the country subscribes to a **continental** climate of hot, dry summers – particularly in the south and east of the country – and bitterly cold winters.

Average temperatures

	Jan	Feb	Mar	Apr	May	Jun	Jul	Aug	Sep	Oct	Nov	Dec
Črnomelj												
Temp. °C	1	4	7	11	16	19	21	20	16	11	6	2
Temp. °F	34	40	46	52	61	66	70	68	61	52	43	36
Koper												
Temp. °C	5	6	9	12	17	20	23	23	20	16	10	7
Temp. °F	41	43	48	54	62	68	74	74	68	61	50	46
Ljubljana												
Temp. °C	-1	0	5	9	14	17	19	19	15	10	4	0
Temp. °F	30	33	41	48	57	62	66	66	60	50	40	33
Marlbor												
Temp. °C	-3	-1	4	9	14	17	19	18	14	9	3	-1
Temp. °F	26	30	40	48	57	62	66	64	57	48	37	30

things not to miss

It's not possible to see everything that Slovenia has to offer in one trip – and we don't suggest you try. What follows is a selective taste of the country's highlights: outstanding architecture, natural wonders, historic sites and great food. They're arranged in five colour-coded categories, which you can browse through to find the very best things to see and experience. All highlights have a page reference to take you straight into the guide, where you can find out more.

01 Piran Page **204** • An atmospheric coastal resort strewn with gorgeous Gothic–Venetian architecture, pretty little churches and quaint squares.

02 Lake Bled Page **121** • Fairytale lake complete with island church and atmospheric castle – take a dip, a stroll or just kick back on a gondola.

03 Škocjan Caves Page **193** • Carved out by the thrashing Reka River, the world's largest underground canyon is Slovenia's most amazing natural wonder.

04 Planica ski-jumping Page **144** • Enjoy daring feats, beer and music at one of the world's great ski-jumping venues.

05 Predjama Castle Page **224** • Dramatically sited castle with a labyrinth of rooms, secret passages and underground caves.

07 Cycling Pages **123, 284 & 317** • From the tough-going mountain climbs of the Julian Alps and Koroška to the less demanding trails in Dolenjska and Prekmurje, Slovenia's countryside presents endless cycling possibilities.

06 Ptuj Page **303** • Slovenia's oldest and most appealing town is run through with over two thousand years of history.

08 Lake Bohinj Page 129 • Encircled by
majestic mountains, Bohinj is the pearl of the Alpine lakes, less visited and more serene than Lake Bled.

09 Beekeeping Museum, Radovljica Page 113 •
Fascinating exposition on one of Slovenia's most cherished customs, the highlight of which are the wonderfully expressive beehive panels.

10 Adventure sports on the Soča Page 157
• This fabulous, foaming river is a first-rate venue for any number of adventure sports, from white-water rafting, kayaking and canoeing to hydrospeeding.

11 Logar Valley Page 285 • Impossibly picturesque glacial valley, carpeted with
meadows and forests and hemmed in by the raw peaks of the Kamniške-Savinja Alps.

12 **Potica** Page **32** • Walnut and spice-filled rolled sweet bread – delicious at any time of the day.

14 **Soča Valley** Page **155** • Snow-dusted peaks, a magical river and a raft of historical sites combine to make this a truly memorable place.

13 **Wine** Page **9** • From the sunny Goriška Brda hills in the west to the beautiful Ljutomer–Ormož vineyards in the east, Slovenia possesses some terrific wine-growing regions.

15 **Hiking in the Julian Alps** Page **136** • One of Europe's most stunning and least spoilt mountain ranges, these mountain wilds are Slovenia's prime hiking region, with trails to suit walkers of all abilities.

16
Prekmurje
Page **314** • Lush green fields, picturesque villages, and storks characterize Slovenia's easternmost region.

ACTIVITIES | CONSUME | EVENTS | NATURE | SIGHTS |

17 Kurent Page 310 • Slovenia's most vibrant and entertaining winter spectacle, featuring spooky masked figures dressed in chunky costumes parading through town.

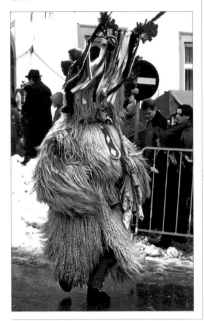

18 Ljubljana's Old Town Page **63** • Enjoy fabulous Baroque and Habsburg architecture, a hilltop castle and leafy riverside cafés in the enchanting Slovene capital.

19 Skiing Page 140 • Take your pick from over twenty ski resorts, with slopes and facilities to suit all abilities.

16

20 The Karst Page **188**. Explore dry-stone villages and a mysterious subterranean world of rivers, streams and caverns.

Basics

Basics

Getting there

Flying is the easiest way to reach Slovenia, with several airlines now flying direct from airports in the UK. Flying from Ireland, North America, Australia or New Zealand will entail one or more changes. Travelling overland from Britain is a rather long, though not unattractive haul. You'll save little, if anything, by taking the train; however, with a rail pass you can take in Slovenia as part of a wider European trip. Bus trips are a reasonably cheap alternative, but can be hard-going. The final option is driving, a journey of some 1500km from Britain, which is best covered slowly over a couple of days.

Air fares always depend on the season, with the highest being around June to August; fares drop during the "shoulder" seasons – March to May & Sept to Oct – and you'll get the best prices during the low season, November to February (excluding Christmas and New Year when prices are hiked up and seats are at a premium).

You can often cut costs by going through a **specialist flight agent** – either a consolidator, who buys up blocks of tickets from the airlines and sells them at a discount, or a **discount agent**, who in addition to dealing with discounted flights may also offer special student and youth fares and a range of other travel-related services such as travel insurance, rail passes, car rentals, tours and the like. Some agents specialize in **charter flights**, which may be cheaper than scheduled flights, but often have fixed departure dates and high cancellation penalties.

Many airlines and discount travel websites offer you the opportunity to book your tickets, hotels and holiday packages online, cutting out the costs of agents and middlemen; these are worth going for, as long as you don't mind the inflexibility of non-refundable, non-changeable deals. There are some bargains to be had on auction sites too, if you're prepared to bid keenly. Almost all airlines have their own websites, offering flight tickets that can sometimes be just as cheap, and are often more flexible.

From the UK and Ireland

Flights

Flying to Slovenia from the UK takes approximately two hours. There are currently three airlines flying from the UK to the Slovenian capital, Ljubljana. Of these, two are low-cost airlines: easyJet, and WizzAir – fares for either of these can be obtained for as little as £40 return, including tax. The Slovenian national carrier, Adria Airways, has economy-class return fares starting from around £120 in low season and £180 in high season.

If you're struggling to get a direct flight, there is the option to fly into one of the neighbouring countries with Ryanair or easyJet – in fact this can actually work out more conveniently, depending upon which part of Slovenia you are intending to visit (see "overland from neighbouring countries" p.20)

By rail

Travelling by train, the shortest journey from London to Ljubljana takes about eighteen hours, but is more expensive than flying. However, stopovers on the way are possible, and prices are more attractive if you're a student, under 26 or over 60.

A standard second-class return ticket, incorporating Eurostar, will cost around £260. Arriving in Paris, you take a train to Venice and change there for the final leg to Ljubljana. Tickets are usually valid for two to three months and allow for unlimited stopovers (as long as you stick to the prescribed route), unless that is, you travel the London–Paris part by Eurostar, in which case you'll have to commit yourself to reservations on specific services on this leg to qualify for the cheapest tickets.

By bus

Although much cheaper than train, the **bus** journey from London to Maribor – there is no bus to Ljubljana – is a stamina-sapping thirty hours, with one change in Frankfurt. A standard return fare costs around £120 (valid for six months), but regular promotional offers can bring the cost down considerably.

By car

If you have the time and inclination, driving to Slovenia, a distance of 1500km from London, can be a pleasant proposition. However, it's really only worth considering if you are planning to travel around Slovenia extensively – another very attractive proposition in itself – or want to take advantage of various stopovers en route.

Once across the channel, the most direct route to Ljubljana (around 30 hours at a leisurely pace with plenty of stops) is via Brussels, Stuttgart, Munich and Salzburg before crossing into Slovenia at the Karavanke Tunnel border. Detailed printouts of the route can be obtained from the websites of the AA (ⓦwww.theaa.com), or RAC (ⓦwww.rac.co.uk). See p.26 for details of driving within Slovenia.

There are numerous ferry services between Britain and Ireland, and between the British Isles and the European mainland. Which service you use will depend on where exactly you are coming from and which part of Europe you are aiming for.

. You could also travel via the Eurotunnel (ⓣ0870/535 3535, ⓦwww.eurotunnel.com), which operates drive-on drive-off shuttle trains through the Channel Tunnel for vehicles and their passengers only.

From the US and Canada

There are no direct flights from either Canada or the USA to Slovenia, so you'll have to rely on using one of the bigger European airlines to fly you into their home hub, from where you can continue the journey. Another alternative is to fly into the capital city of one of the neighbouring countries, such as Budapest in Hungary, or Vienna in Austria, from where there are onward train connections into Slovenia. Malev, the Hungarian carrier, flies direct from New York's JFK to Budapest, with fares from around $550 low season and $800 high season, whilst they also schedule direct flights from Toronto, with fares from around Can$900 low season and Can$1300 high season.

From Australia and New Zealand

There are **no direct flights** to Slovenia from Australia or New Zealand, so you'll have to change airlines, either in Asia or Europe, although the best option is to fly to a Western European gateway and get a connecting flight from there. A standard return fare from eastern Australia to Ljubljana, via London, with Qantas, is around Aus$2200 low season and Aus$2700 high season. The same routes apply for flights from New Zealand, with a standard return fare from around NZ$3300.

From South Africa

There are **no direct flights** to Slovenia from South Africa, so you'll have to change airlines at one of the main European gateways. A standard return fare from Johannesburg to Ljubljana, via Frankfurt or Vienna (with South African Airways or a leading European airline), is around ZAR9500 low season and ZAR11500 high season.

Overland from neighbouring countries

Slovenia is conveniently placed for easy access from a number of neighbouring countries. Travellers from the UK (or Ireland) on a low-cost flight (to Budapest, Graz, Trieste, or Venice) can continue the onward journey by bus or train. Travellers from North America or Australia/New Zealand are likely to fly into one of the European gateway cities (for example Paris or Frankfurt), also necessitating an onward journey to Slovenia by train or bus.

From Graz six trains a day make the short one-hour journey to Maribor, two of which continue on to Ljubljana. From Venice there are three daily trains to Ljubljana, all of which stop in the border town, Villa Opicina. Alternatively there are regular buses from Trieste

Fly less – stay longer! Travel and climate change

Climate change is a serious threat to the ecosystems that humans rely upon, and air travel is among the fastest-growing contributors to the problem. Rough Guides regard travel, overall, as a global benefit, and feel strongly that the advantages to developing economies are important, as is the opportunity of greater contact and awareness among peoples. But we all have a responsibility to limit our personal impact on global warming, and that means giving thought to how often we fly, and what we can do to redress the harm that our trips create.

Flying and climate change
Pretty much every form of motorized travel generates CO_2 – the main cause of human-induced climate change – but planes also generate climate-warming contrails and cirrus clouds and emit oxides of nitrogen, which create ozone (another greenhouse gas) at flight levels. Furthermore, flying simply allows us to travel much further than we otherwise would do. The figures are frightening: one person taking a return flight between Europe and California produces the equivalent impact of 2.5 tonnes of CO_2 – similar to the yearly output of the average UK car.

Fuel-cell and other less harmful types of plane may emerge eventually. But until then, there are really just two options for concerned travellers: to reduce the amount we travel by air (take fewer trips – stay for longer!), and to make the trips we do take "climate neutral" via a carbon-offset scheme.

Carbon offset schemes
Offset schemes run by climatecare.org, carbonneutral.com and others allow you to make up for some or all of the greenhouse gases that you are responsible for releasing. To do this, they provide "carbon calculators" for working out the global-warming contribution of a specific flight (or even your entire existence), and then let you contribute an appropriate amount of money to fund offsetting measures. These include rainforest reforestation and initiatives to reduce future energy demand – often run in conjunction with sustainable development schemes.

Rough Guides, together with Lonely Planet and other concerned partners in the travel industry, are supporting a **carbon offset scheme** run by climatecare.org. Please take the time to view our website and see how you can help to make your trip climate neutral.

Ⓦ **www.roughguides.com/climatechange**

to Koper, which is well connected to the capital by bus and train. From Budapest (Keleti and Deli stations) there are half a dozen trains a day to Ljubljana, with a journey time of around nine hours. Heading south from Slovenia into Croatia, there are currently eight trains a day from Ljubljana to Zagreb (two hours thirty minutes), three of which continue to Belgrade, in Serbia (nine hours).

Airlines, agents and operators

Online booking

Ⓦwww.expedia.co.uk (in UK), Ⓦwww.expedia.com (in US), Ⓦwww.expedia.ca (in Canada)
Ⓦwww.lastminute.com (in UK)

Ⓦwww.opodo.co.uk (in UK)
Ⓦwww.orbitz.com (in US)
Ⓦwww.travelocity.co.uk (in UK), Ⓦwww.travelocity.com (in US), Ⓦwww.travelocity.ca (in Canada), Ⓦwww.zuji.com.au (in Australia), Ⓦwww.zuji.co.nz (in New Zealand).

Airlines

Adria Airways US ☎718/733-6900, UK ☎020/7734 4630 or 7437 0143, Australia ☎0293/271 001, Ⓦwww.adria-airways.com. **easyJet** UK ☎0905-8210905, Ⓦwww.easyjet.com. **Malev Hungarian Airlines** US ☎1-212/566-9944, Canada ☎1-800 665-6363, UK ☎0870/909 0577, Republic of Ireland ☎01/844 4303, Ⓦwww.malev.hu.

21

Ryanair UK ☎0871/246 0000, Republic of Ireland ☎0818/30 30 30, ⊛www.ryanair.com.
WizzAir ⊛www.wizzair.com

Agents and operators

ebookers UK ☎0800/082 3000, Republic of Ireland ☎01/488-3507, ⊛www.ebookers.com. Low fares on an extensive selection of scheduled flights and package deals.
Flightcentre UK ☎0870/890 8099, ⊛www .flightcentre.co.uk. US ☎1-866/WORLD-51, ⊛www.flightcentre.us, Canada ☎1-888/WORLD-55, ⊛www.flightcentre.ca. Australia ☎13 31 33, ⊛www.flightcentre.com.au, New Zealand ☎0800 243 544, ⊛www.flightcentre.co.nz. Rock-bottom fares worldwide.
North South Travel UK ☎01245/608 291, ⊛www.northsouthtravel.co.uk. Friendly, competitive travel agency, offering discounted fares worldwide. Profits are used to support projects in the developing world, especially the promotion of sustainable tourism.
STA Travel US ☎1-800/781-4040, Canada ☎1-888/427-5639, UK ☎0870/163 0026, Australia ☎1300/733 035, New Zealand ☎0508/782 872. Worldwide specialists in independent travel; also student IDs, travel insurance, car rental, rail passes, and more. Good discounts for students and under-26s. ⊛www.statravel.com.
Trailfinders UK ☎0845/058 5858, Republic of Ireland ☎01/677 7888, Australia ☎1300/780 212, ⊛www.trailfinders.com. One of the best-informed and most efficient agents for independent travellers.
Travelbag UK ☎0870/890 1456, ⊛www. travelbag.co.uk. Discount deals worldwide.
Travel Cuts US ☎1-800/592-CUTS, Canada ☎1-888/246-9762, ⊛www.travelcuts.com. Popular, long-established student-travel organization, with worldwide offers.
USIT Northern Ireland ☎028/9032 7111, ⊛www .usitnow.com, Republic of Ireland ☎0818/200 020, ⊛www.usit.ie. Specialists in student, youth and independent travel – flights, trains, study tours, TEFL, visas and more.
World Travel Centre Republic of Ireland ☎01/416 7007, ⊛www.worldtravel.ie. Excellent fares to Europe.

Tour operators

Adventure Center ☎1-800/228-8747 or 510/654-1879, ⊛www.adventurecenter.com. Eight- to ten-day tours of the mountains and lakes; eight-day white-water activity break; or a sixteen-day tour combined with a cruise along the Croatian Dalmatian coast.
Balkan Holidays ☎0845/130 1114, ⊛www .balkanholidays.co.uk. Southeastern Europe specialists, offering weekly package deals to Bled,

Kranjska Gora and Portorož. Ski package and flight-only deals available too.
Cross-Culture ☎1-800/491-1148 or 413/256-6303, ⊛www.crosscultureinc.com. Eight-day cultural tour of the Julian Alps and Adriatic coast.
Crystal Holidays ☎0870/166 4951, ⊛www .crystalholidays.co.uk. Summer and winter (ski) package deals to Bled, Bohinj, Bovec, Kranjska Gora and the Adriatic Coast. Flight-only deals too.
Eastern Eurotours Australia ☎1800/242 353 or 07/5526 2855, ⊛www.easterneurotours.com.au. Several excellent week-long escorted tours throughout the country, including the Alps and Slovenian Castles.
Exodus ☎0870/240 5550, ⊛www.exodus.co.uk. Wide range of eight-day tours, including multi-activity (white-water adventure sports on the Soča River) and trekking/climbing (including an ascent of Mount Triglav), both from around £550.
Explore Worldwide ☎0870/333 4001, ⊛www .explore.co.uk. Eight-day Alpine Lakes tour taking in Ljubljana, the Julian Alps, Škocjan Caves and the Adriatic coast (£555); and same-length cycling tour (Villages and Vineyards) through Dolenjska and Bela Krajina (£600).
Inghams ☎020/8780 4400, ⊛www.inghams .co.uk. Seven- to fourteen-day summer (lakes and mountains), and winter (skiing) package tours.
Inntravel ☎01653/617949, ⊛www.inntravel. co.uk. Seven-day walking trips of the Karst and Coast (from £700), and the Lakes and Alps (from £800).
Insight International Tours ☎1-800/582-8380, ⊛www.inusa.insightvacations.com. Ljubljana as part of a fourteen-day multi-country tour (Austria, Hungary and Croatia).
Just Slovenia ☎01373/814230, ⊛www. justslovenia.co.uk. UK's premier Slovenia specialist, offering tailor-made holidays, including fights, accommodation (including tourist farms), sports and activities/recreational pursuits, and car hire.
Naturetrek ☎01962/733051, ⊛www.naturetrek. co.uk. Eight-day botanical and natural history walking tour in the Julian Alps, based in Bohinj; £985.
Peakland Walking Holidays ☎01298/872801, ⊛www.walkingholidays.org.uk. Week-long walking tours in the Julian Alps (£899), running concurrently with a Natural and Local History week (£850); they also organize a couple of long weekends each year (£399).
Ramblers Holidays ☎01707/331133, ⊛www .ramblersholidays.co.uk. Fifteen-day hikes between June and August in the Julian Alps (moderate/difficult), based in two centres, Bohinj and Jezersko; £685.
Russian Gateway Tours Australia ☎02/9745 3333, ⊛www.russian-gateway.com.au. Russian specialists who also organize seven-day summer and winter trips to Slovenia; can also help arrange any aspect of your trip to Slovenia.

Skedaddle ☎0191/265 1110, ⓦwww.skedaddle.
co.uk. Eight-day cycling tour of the Julian Alps, based
in the Soča Valley; £725.
Thermalia Travel ☎0870/165 9420, ⓦwww
.thermalia.co.uk. Spa holiday specialists offering
a range of four-, seven- and ten-day treatment
programmes at the Laško, Rogaška Slatina and
Šmarješke Toplice spas.
Vamos Travel ☎0870/762 4017, ⓦwww
.vamostravel.com. Central and Eastern Europe
specialist offering tailor-made city break tours to
Ljubljana.
Wilderness Travel US ☎1-800/368-2794,
ⓦwww.wildernesstravel.com. Thirteen-day hiking
trip through Slovenia, also visiting Ptuj, Ljubljana, and
Piran; begins in Vienna and ends in Venice.

Rail contacts

CIT World Travel Australia ☎02/9267-1255 or
03/9650-5510, ⓦwww.cittravel.com.au.
DER Travel US ☎1-888/283-2424, ⓦwww
.dertravel.com/rail. Eurail and many individual
country passes.
Europrail International Canada ☎1-888/667-
9734, ⓦwww.europrail.net. Eurail and many
individual country passes.
Eurostar UK ☎0870/518 6186, ⓦwww.eurostar
.com.
International Rail UK ☎0870/751 5000, ⓦwww
.international-rail.com.

Rail Europe US ☎1-877/257-2887, Canada ☎1-
800/361-RAIL, UK ☎0870/837 1371, ⓦwww
.raileurope.com/us. Discounted rail fares for under-
26s on a variety of European routes; also agents for
Inter-Rail, Eurostar and Eurodomino.
Rail Plus Australia ☎1300/555 003 or 03/9642
8644, ⓦwww.railplus.com.au; NZ ☎09/377 5415,
ⓦwww.railplus.co.nz. Sells Eurail passes.
ScanTours US ☎1-800/223-7226 or 310/636-
4656, ⓦwww.scantours.com. Eurail and European
country passes.
Trailfinders UK ☎0845/058 5858, Republic of
Ireland ☎01/677 7888, Australia ☎1300/780 212,
ⓦwww.trailfinders.com.

Bus contacts

Eurolines UK ☎0870/5 80 8080, Republic of
Ireland ☎01/836 6111, ⓦwww.nationalexpress
.com/eurolines.

Ferry contacts

Hoverspeed UK ☎0870/240 8070, ⓦwww
.hoverspeed.co.uk. Dover to Calais.
P&O Ferries UK ☎0870/600 0600, ⓦwww
.poferries.com. Dover to Calais.
SeaFrance UK ☎0870/571 1711, ⓦwww
.seafrance.com. Dover to Calais.
Stena Line Britain ☎0870/400 6798, Northern
Ireland ☎028/9074 7747, ⓦwww.stenaline.co.uk,
Republic of Ireland ☎01/204 7777, ⓦwww
.stenaline.ie. Harwich to Hook of Holland.

Getting around

Travelling around Slovenia is wonderful, and whether you travel by train, bus or
car, any journey you undertake will rarely be anything other than extremely scenic;
moreover, the country's tiny scale means that you'll never have to travel long distances. On the whole, both trains and buses are clean, reliable and inexpensive;
although trains are cheaper, buses do cover a far greater number of destinations.
Driving brings the obvious advantages of allowing you to visit pretty much anywhere you please, and in your own good time. Approximate times and frequencies
are given in the "Travel Details" section at the end of each guide chapter.

By rail

Slovene railways (*Slovenske železnice*) run
a smooth, efficient and inexpensive service
covering a modest 1200 kilometres, almost
half of which is electrified. All the key lines,

as well as international trains, run through
Ljubljana, but even if you're not intending to
travel to the capital, you'll often save yourself
a lot of hassle by heading to Ljubljana first
and changing there, instead of messing

Useful timetable publications

The red-covered *Thomas Cook European Timetables* details schedules of over 50,000 trains in Europe, as well as timings of over 200 ferry routes and rail-connecting bus services. It's updated and issued every month; main changes are in the June edition (published middle-end of May), which has details of the summer European schedules, and the October one (published middle-end of Sept), which includes winter schedules; some have advance summer/winter timings also. The book can be purchased online (which gets you a ten percent discount) at ⓦ www.thomascookpublishing.com or from branches of Thomas Cook (see ⓦ www.thomascook.co.uk for your nearest branch), and costs £10.50. Their useful Rail Map of Europe can also be purchased online for 25 percent off the normal retail price of £7.95.

about changing at a host of small regional stops.

Trains (*vlaki*) are divided into **slow trains** (*potniški*), which stop at every halt, **Intercity** trains ("IC") which are faster, more comfortable, and stop at fewer stations, and the relatively new, and very fast, **Inter City Slovenia** ("ICS"), three-carriage tilting trains which run between Maribor and Ljubljana, stopping at Pragersko, Celje and Zidani Most and covering the journey in just one hour forty-five minutes; these trains are air-conditioned, have catering and are wheelchair accessible. For information on the car (Bohinjska Bistrica to Most na Soči) and museum (Jesenice to Most na Soči) trains see p.129 and p.169. There are no domestic overnight trains in operation.

Although there are no special carriages, **bicycles** (*kolo*) can be carried on all trains (except the ICS), for which you have to pay an extra €3.

Most timetables (*vozni red*) have explanations in English; the yellow boards with *Odhodi* are departures, the white boards with *Prihodi* arrivals. Timetable leaflets, which only indicate routes that trains from that station take, are sometimes available from counters, but if you're planning to travel extensively on the railways you might want to invest in a national timetable (*Vozni Red Slovenske Železniške*; €5), available from most stations. You can also check train information on the website ⓦ www.slo-zeleznice.si, which has good English explanations. There are left-luggage lockers (*garderoba*; typically €2 for 24hr) at the following stations: Celje, Divača, Koper, Ljubljana, Maribor, Nova Gorica, Postojna and Sežana.

Tickets

Tickets for domestic train services can be bought at the station (*železniška postaja*) on the day of departure and up to two months

Driving distances (km)

	Bled	Bovec	Celje	Čronmelj	Koper	Kranj	Kranjska Gora	Ljubljana	Maribor
	---	99	114	164	162	23	35	53	162
		---	187	216	166	122	44	125	243
			---	130	194	82	161	77	68
				---	185	117	202	91	188
					---	143	198	117	250
						---	58	26	138
							---	88	221
								---	133

Bus Timetables

Bus timetables can be difficult to comprehend, as there's often little by way of English explanation. However, the following letters indicate those days that buses operate: V (every day); D (Mon–Fri); D+ (Mon–Sat); SO (Sat); N (Sun); NP (Sun & holidays); ŠP (school days).

in advance. If you enter a train without a ticket (for a good reason) you will have to pay a supplement of around €2 on top of the ticket price. Otherwise, fare dodging (not advised) could cost you anything up to €40. Most town and city stations now accept payment by credit card (Visa and Eurocard only) for both domestic and international tickets.

Fares are calculated by distance travelled, with a return ticket (*povratna vozovnica*) exactly double that of a single (*enosmerna vozovnica*). To give you some idea, a journey of 50km costs around €4 (€6 first class), a journey of 100km, €6 (€9 first class), and a journey of 200km, €10 (€15 first class). ICS trains, however, are more expensive; the second class fare for the journey between Ljubljana and Maribor (156km) currently costs around €13. **Concessionary fares** on domestic services are available for children under the age of 6 (free), and for children aged between 6 and 12 (half-price).

Seat reservations (*rezervacije*; €1.5) are obligatory for services marked on a timetable

with a boxed R (in effect all ICS trains and some international services), and optional for those designated by an R. Slovenian railways do not issue any passes for travel within the country. However the country is included in Group G under the Inter-rail system, is part of the Eurail Selectpass scheme and falls under the Eurodomino pass coverage.

By bus

Slovenia's **bus network** consists of a slightly confusing, but generally well-coordinated, array of small local companies. On the whole, buses are clean, reasonably comfortable, and, except for some departing on a Friday evening, rarely crowded. They also have the advantage of being able to reach significantly more destinations than trains; moreover, services tend to be more frequent. That said, services, particularly those on rural routes, are dramatically reduced (or even nonexistent) at weekends, and especially on Sundays.

Towns such as Ljubljana, Maribor and Koper have large bus stations (*avtobusna postaja*) with computerized booking facilities where you can buy your tickets hours (if not days) in advance – recommended if you're travelling between Ljubljana and the coast in high season. Otherwise, simply pile onto the bus and pay the driver or conductor. If you need to store items of baggage in the hold you'll be charged a little extra. Like trains, **fares** are calculated according to distance travelled; typical fares are around €6 for 50km and €12 for 100km.

Murska Sobota	Nova Gorica	Novo Mesto	Postojna	Ptuj	Slovenj Gradec	
291	159	127	102	165	143	Bled
299	76	198	121	246	215	Bovec
103	165	100	130	59	49	Celje
232	173	37	121	179	179	Čronmelj
306	90	181	64	253	223	Koper
194	102	99	79	141	108	Kranj
281	120	157	140	216	187	Kranjska Gora
191	113	73	53	136	114	Ljubljana
56	224	139	186	26	71	Maribor
---	268	195	242	54	126	Murska Sobota
	---	161	62	224	194	Nova Borica
		---	111	148	130	Novo Mesto
			---	189	161	Postojna
				---	74	Ptuj
					---	Slovenj Gradec

By car

All things considered, driving in Slovenia is a joy. Despite the country's high level of car ownership, Slovenia's well-surfaced roads often seem blissfully traffic-free, and you'll be endlessly distracted by the scenery. Neither is driving likely to tire you out, such are the (very short) distances between destinations. If driving in the mountainous regions, bear in mind that some of the higher passes, such as the Vršič Pass in the Julian Alps, are often closed for days or weeks at a time during periods of heavy snowfall. To drive in Slovenia you'll need your **driving licence** and **third-party insurance**.

Hitchhiking is widely practised by Slovenes, and you'll often see queues of students lining roadsides on the outskirts of Ljubljana and other towns on a Friday evening in a quest to get home. Avoid these places at these times and you shouldn't have too much of a problem getting a ride with someone. As anywhere, however, it's not a foolproof pursuit, so caution should be exercised.

Roads and services

The country is crossed by two **motorway** corridors (*avtocesta*), the A1 which runs in an east–west direction from Šentilj, just north of Maribor, down to Koper on the coast (there's also a short stretch from Postojna up to Nova Gorica, the H4), and the A2 which runs north-south from the Karavanke Tunnel on the Austrian border to Obrežje on the Croatian border (and continuing down to Zagreb) – there are, though, still incomplete sections on the latter route; both these motorways pass through Ljubljana. **Tolls** are payable on each stretch: some typical costs are: on the A1, Ljubljana to Postojna €2, and Ljubljana to Videž, near Koper €5; and on the A2, Ljubljana to Kranj (en route to Jesenice and Austria), €1.5. Lesser **highways**, linking the major centres, are numbered with a single digit link, whilst secondary or tertiary roads are identified by two or three digit numbers.

Petrol stations (*Bencinska črpalka*) can be found everywhere, even in the most rural backwaters. Whilst most open from around 7am to 9 or 10pm, there are now quite a few 24-hour service stations, usually located on the outskirts of larger towns and cities, and around resort areas. Lead-free fuel (*neosvinčen bencin*), which costs around €0.90 per litre, is the most commonly used. Credit cards are accepted at most stations.

In cities, **parking** in white zones (marked with white lines) is permitted for up to one hour (€0.50), whilst you can stay in a "blue zone" for up thirty minutes (free). *Brezplačno* means free parking. Parking in car parks normally costs around €1 per hour.

For information on any aspect of driving within Slovenia, you can contact the Automobile Association of Slovenia (Avto-moto zveza Slovenije or AMZS), based in Ljubljana at Dunajska 128 (☏01/530-5100). Their information centre (daily 5.30am–11pm; ☏01/530-5300) provides information and assistance, whilst their website (ⓦwww.amzs.si) tells you all you need to know about driving in Slovenia and provides up-to-the-minute information on road traffic conditions. They also publish a 1:270,000 tourist road map of Slovenia (€6).

Rules & regulations

Traffic drives on the right and **speed limits** for vehicles are 130kph on motorways, 100kph on secondary and tertiary roads, and 50kph in built-up areas. Otherwise, the most important **rules** are the prohibitions against sounding the horn in a built-up area (unless to avert accidents) and using a hand-held mobile whilst driving. It is compulsory for driver and passengers to wear seatbelts; to use dipped headlights when travelling on all roads at all times of the day; and to keep a triangular breakdown sign in the car. Between mid-November and mid-March you're required to carry snow chains.

Random stops by the police are common and if you are stopped – you'll see plenty of police vehicles on approaches to villages and built-up areas – you'll be required to show all your documents, so make sure you have them in the car at all times. The police are extremely hot on road traffic violations and any offence committed (speeding, not wearing a seatbelt, illegal parking and the like) is subject to an on-the-spot **fine**, which can be anything between €40 and €250, depending upon the offence. It goes without saying that **drinking and driving** do not go hand in hand; the permitted blood-alcohol level for drivers is 0.05mg per 100ml of blood, although you may still be liable to a €130 fine if caught with this amount. Any amount over this means a fine of anything up to €500 and the confiscation of your licence.

Accidents and emergencies

In the event of a **breakdown**, call AMZS's Assistance-Information Service (SPI) on the 24-hour emergency number ☎1987. There are 24-hour technical centres in Celje, Koper, Kranj, Ljubljana, Maribor, Otočec and Posto-jna, with **technical units** (open 7am–8pm) in the other major towns; the addresses and telephone numbers of all centres can be found on the AMZS website (see opposite). All accidents should be reported to the police on ☎113.

Car rental

Renting a car is simple enough, provided you are 21 or older, and hold a valid national driving licence. You can order a car through rental agencies in your own country (see box below), which sometimes works out cheaper. Once in Slovenia, the most convenient place to rent a car is at Brnik airport, where all the major companies have an outlet, or in downtown Ljubljana (see p.85); some companies have branches in other major towns and cities.

Car rental **costs** are not especially cheap and there's little difference in price amongst the major companies; for a group A car expect to pay around €50 upwards for a day's hire (unlimited mileage) and €260 upwards for a week. You may find that local companies, such as ABC Cars in Ljubljana, offer better deals, so it's worth looking around before deciding upon which company to use. Credit cards are usually required for a deposit. Before signing, check on any mileage limits or other restrictions, extras, and what you're covered for in the event of an accident. You should normally be able to take the car into neighbouring countries, although some companies may balk (or just charge you a little more) at the thought of you driving into Hungary or Croatia; in any case, should you have any intention of leaving the country, check with the car rental company first.

Car rental agencies

ABC Cars SLOVENIA ☎01/518 7558 or 04/206 1684, ⓦwww.europcar.si.

Avis UK ☎0870/606 0100, ⓦwww.avis.co.uk. Northern Ireland ☎028/9024 0404, Republic of Ireland ☎021/428 1111, ⓦwww.avis.ie. US ☎1-800/230-4898, Canada ☎1-800/272-5871, ⓦwww.avis.com. Australia ☎13 63 33 or 02/9353 9000, ⓦwww.avis.com.au. NZ ☎09/526 2847 or 0800/655 111, ⓦwww.avis.co.nz.
Budget UK ☎0800/973 159,ⓦwww.budget .co.uk. Republic of Ireland ☎09/0662 7711, ⓦwww .budget.ie. US ☎1-800/527-0700, Canada ☎1-800/472-3325, ⓦwww.budget.com. AU ☎1300/362 848, ⓦwww.budget.com.au. NZ ☎09/976 2222 or 0800/652 227, ⓦwww.budget.co.nz.
Cosmo Thrifty Northern Ireland ☎028/9445 2565, ⓦwww.thrifty.co.uk.
Dollar US ☎1-800/800-3665, ⓦwww.dollar.com.
Europcar UK ☎0870/607 5000, ⓦwww.europcar .co.uk. Northern Ireland ☎028/9442 3444, Republic of Ireland ☎01/614 2888, ⓦwww. europcar.ie. US & Canada ☎1-877/940 6900, ⓦwww.europcar.com. AU ☎1300/131 390, ⓦwww.deltaeuropcar.com.au.
Hertz UK ☎0870/844 8844, ⓦwww.hertz.co.uk. Republic of Ireland ☎01/676 7476, ⓦwww .hertz.ie. US ☎1-800/654-3001, Canada ☎1-800/263-0600, ⓦwww.hertz.com. AU ☎13 30 39 or 03/9698 2555, ⓦwww.hertz.com.au. NZ ☎0800/654 321, ⓦwww.hertz.co.nz.
Holiday Autos UK ☎0870/400 0099, ⓦwww .holidayautos.co.uk. Republic of Ireland ☎01/872 9366, ⓦwww.holidayautos.ie. AU ☎1300/554 432, ⓦwww.holidayautos.com.au. NZ ☎0800/144 040, ⓦwww.holidayautos.co.nz.
National UK ☎0870/536 5365, ⓦwww .nationalcar.co.uk. US ☎1-800/962-7070, ⓦwww. nationalcar.com. AU ☎13 10 45, ⓦwww .nationalcar.com.au. NZ ☎0800/800 115 or 03/366 5574, ⓦwww.nationalcar.co.nz.
SIXT Republic of Ireland ☎1850/206 088, ⓦwww .irishcarrentals.ie.
Suncars UK ☎0870/500 5566, ⓦwww.suncars .com.
Thrifty UK ☎01494/751 600, ⓦwww.thrifty.co.uk. Republic of Ireland ☎1800/515 800, ⓦwww. thrifty.ie. US & Canada ☎1-800/847-4389, ⓦwww .thrifty.com. AU ☎1300/367 227, ⓦwww.thrifty .com.au. NZ ☎09/309 0111, ⓦwww.thrifty.co.nz.

Cycling

Slovenia's wonderfully varied topography presents endless opportunities for cyclists. From the tough mountain climbs in Triglav National Park to the iron-flat landscapes of Prekmurje, there are a number of well-organized recreational routes and trails all over the country. Otherwise, cycling is permitted on all roads except motorways. Most urban centres have, to a greater or lesser degree, well-integrated cycle lanes or paths, though the traffic in towns and cities is rarely threat-

ening. On a practical note, bikes can be taken onto trains, except ICS, for a small fee, whilst some buses might allow you to store your bike in the luggage compartment.

Accommodation

Finding somewhere to bed down, even in the busiest resorts during high season, is unlikely to be a problem; hotels abound and there are an increasing number of good-value pensions to choose from. For those with less cash to spend, there are plenty of private rooms to go around, particularly in the more well-touristed areas such as Bled, Bohinj and the coast, whilst a stay on a tourist farm provides an attractive, affordable, and peaceful alternative. There's a good spread of decent campsites across the country, though hostels are few and far between.

Reservations for all types of accommodation are advisable during high season in the capital and more popular places (June–August & December–February in the ski resorts), or if you're bound for somewhere with limited possibilities. Details of all Slovenia's hotels, private rooms, tourist farms and campsites are listed in booklets available from the Slovenia Tourist Board; you can view the same contents online at ⓦ www.slovenia.info.

Hotels and pensions

Slovenian hotels use the traditional **five-star grading** system for classification, although in many cases this only gives a vague idea of prices, which can vary dramatically according to the locality and season. Generally speaking, prices in the capital, along the coast and in the major resorts, such as Bled, Bohinj and Kranjska Gora, are higher

than elsewhere. Moreover, the ratings are not always indicative of the quality of a place – for example, three-star places can, and do, vary appreciably from one place to another.

Unfortunately, many of Slovenia's city **hotels** are heavily geared towards the business traveller – in Ljubljana, for example, budget or medium-priced hotels are few and far between, a situation common to other places like Maribor, Celje and Nova Gorica. Many of the hotels in key resorts such as Bled, Bohinj or Portorož are aimed squarely at the package-tourist – the same goes for the ever-growing number of spa hotels in Slovenia. That said there are an increasing number of **family-run hotels** and **pensions** (*penzion*) which, in most cases, offer much better value than a hotel of a similar price and invariably come with a more personal touch. Some pensions are more commonly known as **gostišče**, not to be confused with

Accommodation price codes

Accommodation in this guide is graded according to the price bands below. Note that prices refer to the **cheapest available double room in high season**. For hostels and dormitories, the price per bed has been given.

❶ under €25
❷ €25–34
❸ €35–44

❹ €45–57
❺ €58–69
❻ €70–83

❼ €84–94
❽ €95–110
❾ over €110

a *gostilna* (which is an eating establishment), but these are usually found in smaller towns and more rural areas.

Slovenia can count less than a handful of five-star establishments, a couple of which are in Ljubljana and Maribor, whilst the others have been incorporated into historic buildings, for example at Mokrice and Otočec castles. Most four-star hotels have all the luxuries you'd expect, with modern, and in many cases, renovated, rooms, satellite TV, minibar and Internet access. The vast majority of the country's hotels are in the three-star category, and this is where standards can vary. However, in most cases the rooms are reliably comfortable and come with TV and minibar. More predictably, one- and two-star hotels – of which there are actually very few – can be tatty, soulless places (and sometimes come without private bathroom) but are usually clean and bearable. Most hotels include **breakfast** in the price, but this is not always clear and it's worth checking.

Private rooms and apartments

Hostels aside, taking a **private room** (*zasebne sobe*) is the cheapest option available, particularly if there are two of you sharing. Few towns and cities are well stocked with private rooms, but you'll find that there are plenty to go around in the busier lake and coastal resorts. Rooms are **categorized** from one to three stars; a one-star place is very basic and comes with shared shower and toilets, a two-star usually has private shower and toilet, and a three-star comes with plusher furnishings and sometimes a television.

As a rough guideline, **prices** start at around €18 for a double room in a catego-

ry-one place, €25 for a category-two place, and €30 for a category-three place. Not included in the price is tourist tax, which is usually around €2 per person; nor is breakfast included. Moreover, in most places, prices are subject to a thirty percent surcharge if you stay fewer than three nights. Rented out in the same way as private rooms, **apartments** (*apartmaji*) are a reasonably cheap alternative, particularly if there are a few of you. A standard four-bed apartment in Bohinj or on the coast will cost in the region of €65, a six-bed place around €80 per night.

With the odd exception (for example in Bohinj) very few tourist offices administer bookings for private rooms; these are usually handled by local agencies, which can be found in most places. Larger agencies such as Kompas or Globtour have branches in several towns and resorts.

Tourist farms

Farm tourism (*turističnih kmetji*) is a thriving sector in Slovenia, and if you're looking for a restful night, then these rural retreats are perfect. Note though that their very isolation means that, unless you have your own means of transport, they can often be quite difficult to reach.

Despite a **classification system** (denoted by apples), there is often little distinction between the highest grade (four apples) and a lower grade most farms offer reasonably sized, modestly furnished rooms with bathroom. That said, farms with four apples invariably have larger, slightly better furnished rooms, sometimes with television. Although there are no hard and fast rules regarding **pricing**, as a guide a double room on a farm with three or four apples will cost around €35, two apples around €32, and one, or unclassified, farms around

€28. All prices include breakfast, which is a wholesome affair, typically consisting of tea, coffee, juice, cereal, home-made bread, jam, cheese and ham; in some places you may also be offered something cooked. Most farms offer a half-board option for about €5 extra, which is exceptional value given that the cooking is invariably superb – many also produce their own wine. Some farms also offer additional activities, such as horse riding, cycling and tennis, whilst others allow you to help out on the farm – from preparing foodstuffs (baking bread or making jam), to milking the cows or feeding the calves.

The excellent *Friendly Countryside* brochure, produced by the Association of Tourist Farms of Slovenia in conjunction with the Slovenian Tourist Board, lists and describes each and every tourist farm in the country. The Association is based in Celje at Trnoveljska 1 (☎03/491-6480, ⓦwww. slovenia-tourism.si/touristfarms).

Mountain huts

There are some 170 **mountain huts** (*Planinarski Domovi*) scattered across Slovenia's hills and mountains, ranging from the most basic refuges with huge dorms and cold running water, to more comfortable alpine villas offering a wider range of cosier rooms, hot water and other amenities. In any case, most huts are convivial places, where hikers share a beer or two and exchange information about trails or the weather before pushing on.

The majority of huts, especially those at higher altitudes, are open between June and September, whilst some are open a month or two longer than this, and a few year round; if you're planning to spend any length of time in the more popular hiking areas, for example around Triglav, you'd be wise to book ahead. Depending upon the type of hut and its location, you'll pay anything between €10 and €20 for a bed; UIAA-affiliated members are entitled to a discount. The useful, if very dated, *Mountain Huts* book, published by the Slovene Alpine Association, lists every hut, together with routes and approaches to the next lodge. For more on mountain huts see the box on p.60.

Hostels and dormitories

Hostels in Slovenia are thin on the ground and most that are touted as such are actually student dormitories (*dijaški dom*). Slovenia's best equipped hostels are those in Bled, Ljubljana (Celica), the Karst (Pliskovica) and Ptuj (Kurent) – uniformly excellent, and with comprehensive amenities, each of these hostels has rooms sleeping between two and six people (those in Celica and Pliskovica also have 14-bed dorms), and charge around €16 per person, including breakfast. All these offer discounts to HI card holders. **Student dorms**, which are generally of a decent standard, are usually only open in July and August once the students have packed up (although quite a few keep some beds aside during the rest of the year, but these are usually available at weekends only); expect to pay around €10–15 for a bed. The website ⓦwww.youth-hostel.si has details on all Slovenia's hostels.

Camping

Slovenia has a good, if rather uneven, spread of **camping grounds** (*kampi*) across the country. Most campsites, whatever their size, are clean and well-appointed places, whilst the better ones (sites are categorized from between one and three stars), such as those in Bled and Bohinj, have excellent amenities – more often than not with restaurants, shops, sports facilities and children's play areas. Nearly all sites have hot water.

Expect to pay around €2–3 for ground rent plus €8–10 per person per night and slightly more at the better sites. Prices are reduced slightly outside July and August. The majority of sites are open from April or May to September or October, with a handful – including the one in Ljubljana – open year-round. Note that **camping rough** is illegal.

If you're planning to do a lot of camping, an **international camping carnet** is a good investment. The carnet gives discounts at member sites and serves as useful identification. Many campsites will take it instead of making you surrender your passport during your stay, and it covers you for third-party insurance when camping. In the UK and Ireland, the carnet costs

£4.50/€6.35, and is available to members of the AA in Ireland or the RAC in Britain (see p.20), or for members only from any of the following: the Camping and Caravanning Club (☎024/7669 4995, ⓦwww.campingandcaravanningclub.co.uk; annual membership £30 plus £5 joining fee), the CTC (☎0870/873 0061, ⓦwww.ctc.org.uk, membership £32), or the Camping and Caravanning Club's foreign touring arm, the **Carefree Travel Service** (☎024/7642 2024), which provides the international camping carnet free if you take out insurance with them; they also book ferry crossings and inspect camping sites in Europe. In the US and Canada, the carnet is available from home motoring organizations, or from Family Campers and RVers (FCRV; ☎1-800/245-9755 or 716/668-6242, ⓦwww.fcrv.org). FCRV annual membership costs $25, and the carnet an additional $20.

Food and drink

Slovenia straddles several culinary cultures, absorbing Austrian, Balkan, Mediterranean and Pannonian influences. That said, and despite the increasing internationalization of restaurants and cafés, there remains a strong native Slovene tradition based on age-old peasant recipes. For a full glossary of food and drink terms, see pp352–355.

Breakfasts, snacks and sandwiches

Breakfast (*zajtrk*) in your average hotel typically consists of bread or rolls with jam or marmalade as an accompaniment, and sometimes cereal and yoghurt – only in the better hotels will you be offered a full buffet complement, with cooked food, pastries or croissants and fresh fruit. Breakfast on a tourist farm is invariably an enjoyable, wholesome affair, with everything from bread and milk to jams and cheeses prepared on the farm.

The best places for **snacks** are *okrepčevalnice* (snack bars) and street kiosks, which dole out *burek*, a flaky and often very greasy pastry filled with cheese (*burek z sirom*) or meat (*burek z mesom*). Sausages come in various forms, most commonly hot dogs, *hrenovke* (Slovene frankfurters), or the much tastier *kranjska klobasa* (big spicy sausages). A popular light lunchtime meal is *malica*, a quick-filling two or three-course meal with drink usually served from 11am or midday until 3pm, and costing around €3–4.

Slovenia's **supermarkets** (*trgovina*) and delicatessens (*delikatesa*) are good places to stock up on sandwich and picnic ingredients, like local cheese (*sir*) and salami. You can buy fresh fruit and vegetables here too but, if possible, try and get your produce from outdoor markets (*tržnica*) or roadside stalls. Bread is best bought from bakeries (*pekarna*), most of which usually sell a decent range of croissants and sandwiches – which makes them the best place to head if you've not been offered breakfast at your hotel or lodging. In a similar vein is the almost impossible to pronounce *slaščičarna* (patisserie), where you can indulge in all sorts of sweet-toothed delights.

Restaurants and meals

The most common type of eating establishment in Slovenia is a **restavracija** (restaurant). These can be found everywhere, though the quality is often variable, from the down-at-heel to the very classy. Although there are plenty of restaurants in the larger towns and cities (Ljubljana and Maribor specifically), you'll often find that choices are extremely limited in smaller towns. Invariably more atmospheric is a **gostilna**, an inn-type place which is usually, but not always, located on the outskirts of town and in more rural areas; along the same lines, a **gostišče** serves food and also has some accommodation available. If possible, don't pass up the opportunity to eat on a tourist farm, where you'll find Slovenian home-cooking at its finest, with ingredients usually harvested on the farm itself.

Generally speaking, **menus** vary little wherever you eat, and are invariably dominated by meat dishes (*mesne jedi*), mostly schnitzels (*zrezek*), beef (*govedina*), pork (*svinjina*) and veal (*teletina*). However, the tasty southern Balkan meats *čevapčiči* (grilled rolls of minced meat) and *sarma* (cabbage stuffed with meat and rice) frequently make their way onto menus. One particularly curious Slovene speciality is horse steak (*žrebičkov zrezek*), and neither are Slovenes squeamish about offal – liver (*jetra*) and grilled or fried brains (*možgani*) are popular standbys in cheaper restaurants. The majority of menus in classier restaurants will often feature game, with Slovenes particularly partial to bear (*medved*), deer (*srna*), pheasant (*fazan*) and rabbit (*zajec*). Soup (*juha*) is a standard **starter** – in Primorska try *jota* (beans and sauerkraut), and in Štajerska, *kisla juha* (pigs' knuckles and head with sour cream); delicious dry-cured ham (*pršut*) from the Karst is another good appetizer. Two of the most traditional Slovene dishes are *žlikrofi*, ravioli filled with potato, onion and bacon; and *žganci*, once the staple diet of rural Slovenes, a buckwheat or maize porridge often served with sauerkraut.

On the coast you'll find plenty of fish dishes (*ribje jedi*), with mussels (*školjke*), shrimps (*škampi*) and squid (*lignji*) particularly prominent. If you're anywhere near the Soča Valley (and in particular Kobarid, which has three of the country's best restaurants), do try the fabulous freshwater trout (*postrvi*) from the local Soča River, the king of which is the superb, and much sought-after, marble trout (*Salmo trutta marmoratus*). Otherwise, Italian pasta dishes appear on many restaurant menus, whilst goulash (*golaž*) is found almost everywhere; *segedin* is goulash with lashings of sauerkraut.

Typical **desserts** include solid Central European favourites such as strudel and *štruklji*, dumplings with fruit filling; the two most traditional Slovene sweets are *potica*, a doughy roll filled with nuts, tarragon and honey; and, from the Prekmurje region, *gibanica*, a delicious layered pastry consisting of poppy seeds, walnuts, apple and cream. For something more straightforward you can't go wrong with *palačinke* (pancakes with a choice of fillings) or ice cream (*sladoled*).

Inevitably, standards of **service** vary depending upon the type of establishment you are dining in, but by and large you'll find waiting staff courteous and friendly; moreover, you'll rarely have trouble making yourself understood as most waiting staff speak a good standard of English. If you think it's merited, a ten percent **tip** would be standard.

Drinking

Daytime drinking takes place in small **café-bars**, or in a *kavarna*, where you might also find a range of cakes, pastries and ice cream on offer. Coffee (*kava*) is usually served black unless specified otherwise – ask for *mleko* (milk) or *smetana* (cream) – and often drunk alongside a glass of mineral water (*mineralna voda*), the most popular of which is *Radenska*, from the spa town Radenci. Cappucinos are a hit-or-miss affair, ranging from good quality to little more than a regular coffee

Vegetarians

Whilst the situation for vegetarians is no longer the disaster zone it once was, the options, except in better restaurants, are usually both meagre and fairly predictable. Aside from the usual salads, vegetable and omelette dishes, Slovenian specialities to look out for are *štruklji* (dumplings with cheese or fruit filling), *ocvrti sir* (cheese fried in breadcrumbs) and *gobova rižota* (mushroom risotto) – the latter is usually excellent; in the better restaurants, you'll find upmarket variations on the above plus, possibly, one or two other dishes.

with a dollop of whipped cream on top. **Tea** (*čaj*) drinkers are in a minority here, although its popularity is growing and there are a couple of fantastic little teahouses (*Čajna hiša*) in Ljubljana and Maribor.

Evening drinking usually goes on in small European-style bars or the more traditional *pivnica* (beer hall) or *vinarna* (wine cellar). **Slovene beer** (*pivo*) is of the Pilsner type and is not bad at all – in fact it was always considered amongst the best of the many beers brewed in any of the ex-Yugoslav republics. The two dominant breweries are Laško, based in the town of the same name and producer of *Zlatorog* (the mythical chamois), and the Ljubljana-based Union; opinion varies as to which is the best though, on balance, the more flavoursome

Laško probably has the edge; both breweries also produce *temno pivo* (literally "dark beer"), a Guinness-like stout.

Although excellent, **Slovenian wine** (*vino*) is little known – it rarely makes it onto the shelves of Western supermarkets – but its reputation is growing. White wine (*belo*) predominates; particularly worth trying are *Beli Pinot* and *Šipon*, and there are some fine reds (*črno*) too, notably Cabernet Sauvignon and Merlot from the Vipava Valley, and the dark, acidic *Kraški teran* from the Karst. For more on Slovenian wine, see the boxes on p.176, p.264 and p.304. You shouldn't leave the country without trying one of the fiery brandies: *slivovka* (plum brandy), *viljamovka* (pear brandy), *sadjevec*, a brandy made from various fruits, and the gin-like juniper-based *brinovec*.

The media

Despite 45 years of communism, the Slovene media always had the most balanced and pluralistic coverage of the ex-Yugoslav republics. Given its size, though, it's not surprising that the country has fewer daily newspapers in circulation than just about any other European nation; its television coverage, meanwhile, differs little from that in any other central-east European country, with foreign cable and satellite television having made huge inroads in recent years.

Television

As in most countries, national TV is a rather bland, often unedifying diet of dull movies, game shows and soaps, although many households now subscribe to satellite channels. The public service broadcaster, RTV Slovenija (Radio-Television Slovenia), transmits on two channels, whilst the chief commercial channels are Kanal A and Pop TV, both of which broadcast the standard diet of foreign movies, soaps, sit-coms and music. RTV Slovenija also broadcasts the country's three major radio channels.

Most hotels have satellite TV, though overwhelmingly most channels are German or Italian, whilst the better-quality hotels will usually have English language channels such as CNN, Sky News and BBC World.

The press

Amongst the five major dailies, the most widely read by the urban population is the mildly pro-government *Delo*, which is also considered the most sophisticated read; this is followed by *Dnevnik* (daily), and the Maribor-based *Večer* (evening). Closest to western tabloids in style is *Slovenske Novice*, full of the usual sensationalist trash stories.

With the exception of some of the major bookshops and more upmarket hotels in Ljubljana, English dailies are difficult (if not impossible) to come by. There are, however, a couple of decent English-language publications worth seeking out: the informative *Slovenia Times* (ⓦ www.sloveniatimes.com), published twice-weekly,

Mladina

Mladina (Youth), which began life as a periodical of the League of Slovene Youth in 1943, is Slovenia's foremost liberal non-party youth magazine. In the late 1970s the magazine's focus changed dramatically from a straightforward cultural-oriented rag to a highly politicized and confrontational publication, renowned for its stinging campaigns against corrupt officials, and fearless reporting of taboo subjects such as the Yugoslav Army, World War II massacres and homosexuality. In 1988 three of the magazine's editors (and an army corporal) were put on trial, and subsequently convicted, by the Yugoslav Federal government for allegedly distributing state secrets. This was dubbed the "Ljubljana Four Trial" (see p.334), an event which sparked Slovenia's final drive towards independence. Despite fewer and less obvious targets since independence, *Mladina* remains an influential and topical political journal.

and the more politically oriented *Slovenia News* (ⓦwww.uvi.si/eng/slovenia/news), published weekly. The bi-monthly *Ljubljana Life* (ⓦwww.ljubljanalife.si) is a more straightforward listings magazine for the capital, with a good entertainments section.

BBC (ⓦwww.bbc.co.uk/worldservice), **Radio Canada** (ⓦwww.rcinet.ca), and **Voice of America** (ⓦwww.voa.gov) list all the world service radio frequencies around the globe.

Festivals

The Slovenian calendar is littered with some marvellous festivals and events. While a good number of these take place in the larger cities such as Ljubljana and Maribor, there's an excellent spread of local events throughout the rest of the country. Neither are these entirely confined to the summer: Slovenia has several strongly rooted seasonal traditions, none more so than the "Pust" in February, which is perhaps the most uniquely Slovenian celebration.

Most cities, and many of the larger towns, stage some form of **Summer Festival**, which invariably incorporates a colourful mix of classical and contemporary music, art and theatrical performances. A great deal of fun are the **Medieval Days Festivals**, which seek to recreate life in the Middle Ages in the form of medieval crafts markets, song and dance, and knights' games; the two highest-profile ones are held in the historic towns of Kamnik and Škofja Loka in June. A number of the country's castles stage classical music concerts on summer evenings.

The country's strong wine-growing tradition is manifest in its many **wine-related events**, which occur throughout the major wine-producing centres, such as Brda and Jeruzalem, between May and September; the main collective wine celebration is St Martin's Day, on November 11. Aside from the main festivals listed below – each of which is covered in greater detail in their respective chapters – there are dozens of other, more local, events taking place across the country, some of which are also described in this guide.

January Snow Castle Festival Črna na Koroškem, last weekend in January. Hugely popular snow castle building competition in the Koroška mountains.

February Kurentovanje Ptuj, Sunday before Shrove Tuesday and Shrove Tuesday. The most famous of Slovenia's pre-Lent carnivals, featuring riotous displays of masked revelry; the other major Pust carnivals take place in Cerkno and Cerknica.

March Ski-jumping World Championships Planica (Kranjska Gora), mid-March. The climax to the World Ski-Jumping Championship at Planica is a high-octane weekend of top-class sport, music and lots of beer.

May Druga Godba Ljubljana, end of May for one week. Alternative/world music festival with a strong line-up of both Slovene and international artists.

June Ana Desetnica Street Theatre Ljubljana, end of June. Colourful and enjoyable street theatre performances in the Old Town and surrounds.

Festival Brežice in Brežice and other venues across Slovenia, end of June to the end of August. Prestigious classical music festival of ancient Baroque music, starring some of Europe's finest singers, orchestras and musicians.

Lent Festival Maribor, end of June for two weeks. Massive gathering of popular and serious music, dance and ballet, street and puppet theatre, and folkloric events down by the Drava River.

Ljubljana Jazz Festival Ljubljana, end of June. Three days of world-class musicians at Slovenia's premier jazz festival.

July Bled Days Bled, mid-July. Weekend fair and crafts stalls down by the lake, culminating in a spectacular fireworks display and thousands of candles on the lake.

Ljubljana Summer Festival Ljubljana, July to mid-September. More than two months of top-notch opera, classical music, ballet and theatre in the capital's key cultural happening.

Mediterranean Festival Izola, July. World, ethno and folk music festival on an open-air stage in Izola's Old Town.

Primorska Summer Festival Izola, Koper and Portorož, July to August. Open-air stage and street theatre performances, some of which take place in unusual locations such as a disused railway tunnel and the Sečovlje saltpans.

Rock Otočec Novo Mesto, first week of July. The country's largest rock festival, with a cool line-up of both Slovenian and international artists.

Soča Reggae Riversplash Tolmin, mid-July. Good-time international festival consistently attracting some of the biggest names in reggae.

August Etno Festival Bled, first weekend in August. International and domestic folk music gathering.

Knights' Tournament Predjama Castle, last Sunday in August. Jousting tournament and large doses of medieval merriment.

Festival Radovljica, mid-August. High-class international festival of ancient classical music.

TrnFest Ljubljana, August. Cracking, small-scale festival with gigs, exhibitions and workshops (some for kids) organized by the KUD cultural centre.

September Kravji Bal (Cow's Ball) Lake Bohinj, second or third weekend in September. Mass booze-up to celebrate the return of the cows from the mountains.

National Costumes Festival Kamnik, second weekend in September. Song, dance and colourful finery from Slovenia's multifarious regions.

November St Martin's Day Countrywide, November 11. Nationwide wine celebrations.

December Christmas Celebrations Countrywide. A month of yuletide celebrations kick off on December 6 (St Nicholas's Day) with the giving of gifts to children.

Sports and the outdoors

Given its size and resources, Slovenia's sporting pedigree is impressive, many of its sportsmen and women having achieved notable successes in a number of sports since the split with Yugoslavia in 1991. The most high-profile sporting event in the Slovenian calendar is the World Ski-Jumping Championships at Planica in March.

The country's finest moment came at the 2000 Sydney Olympics, when it captured its first-ever gold medal courtesy of the rowers Iztok Čop and Luka Špik; indeed, **rowing** has been Slovenia's most prominent summer sport since the times of the former Yugosla-

via, and now, as then, several major regattas are held each summer on Lake Bled. Given the country's excellent facilities, it's little surprise that Slovenia has produced a legion of fine **skiers** and **ski-jumpers** – the Yugoslav national ski team was almost always comprised exclusively of Slovenes – and there's been a healthy measure of Olympic and World Championship success over the past decade.

In popular **team sports** such as basketball, handball and water polo – traditionally very strong sports in the former Yugoslavia – Slovenia has been left somewhat in the slipstream of Serbia and Croatia, but its teams still manage to perform creditably at European level. The current golden girl of Slovenian sport is the outstanding middle distance runner Jolanda Čeplak, holder of several European and world 800/1500-metre records. In spite of a desperately weak domestic league Slovenia's footballers have massively overachieved in recent years, qualifying for both the European Championship Finals in Holland and Belgium in 2000, and then the 2002 World Cup in Japan – the first time it had qualified for either finals.

There are few more active nations in Europe than Slovenia, most of whose inhabitants begin trekking, climbing and skiing from a very early age. The country's mountains, forests, hills, rivers and lakes offer unlimited potential to indulge in a wide range of **outdoor pursuits** – hiking and skiing in the Julian Alps, whitewater rafting or kayaking in the Soča Valley, cycling through the rolling hills of Dolenjska, or riding through the Logarska Dolina Valley, to name just a few. Moreover, just about any of these activities can be done as part of an organized group, usually with gear supplied. Before taking part in any adventure activities, check your insurance cover. For more on all these activities see the "The Great Outdoors" colour insert.

Although a mere 46km long, the Slovene coast offers possibilities to indulge in a number of **water sports**: scuba diving (*pota-*

pljanje) in the waters around Piran, as well as sailing (*jadranje*) and windsurfing (*surfanje*). The coastal waters are perfectly safe for swimming (*plavanje*), but if you fancy something a little bit warmer you should be able to track down a local indoor pool in most towns of a reasonable size. Some of the better hotels, particularly those on the coast, have their own pools that can be used for a small fee by those not staying as guests.

There are currently ten **golf** courses in Slovenia (with more under construction), some of which, like those at Bled and Voljči Potok, can be played out against quite stunning alpine backdrops. You can find **tennis** courts in most places.

Working and studying in Slovenia

Opportunities for working in Slovenia are few and far between, especially in the most traditional form of work abroad, teaching English. International House, in Ljubljana, is the only international school in the country, though there are a few small private schools in the capital and Maribor. There is also an excellent voluntary work programme, and, for those keen to pick up a new language – or brush up on existing skills – there's a well-established language centre at Ljubljana University.

Study and work programmes

The Centre for Slovene as a Second Foreign Language, at Ljubljana University's Faculty of Arts Department, runs a summer **language course**. The courses, available at all levels from beginners to advanced, and covering a range of topics including Slovene literature and culture, business Slovene and theatre workshops, run for either two (€470) or four (€780) weeks throughout July. The course also incorporates a varied social programme, which may include, for example, a two-day mountain trip, local workshops, and evening entertainment. Registration is required by the end of May for participation that summer; accommodation can also be arranged. They also offer a two-week winter course at the end of January (€470), while there are a number of more straightforward language courses at the university available throughout the year, lasting from two weeks up to a year. For more information contact the centre at Kongesni trg 12 (☏01/241-8648; ⊛www. centerslo.net).

An organization called Voluntariat, working in conjunction with local organizations, coordinates around a dozen **work camps** throughout Slovenia, with projects as varied as working with Roma, in Prekmurje, to working on the saltpans near Portorož. In theory these programmes, which can last from two weeks to several months, are available year-round, but most volunteers work in the period between May and September. The only cost involved is a participation fee (around €80), payable upon registration; thereafter all board and lodgings are paid for.

If you are involved in a longer-term project (several months), you may also receive pocket money. To find out more contact Voluntariat at Breg 12, Ljubljana (☏01/241-7620, ⊜placement@zavod-voluntariat.si).

Useful publications and websites

A good pre-planning strategy for working abroad, whether teaching English or otherwise, is to get hold of one of the books on summer jobs abroad and how to work your way around the world published in the UK by Vacation Work; call ☏01865/241 978 or visit ⊛www.vacationwork.co.uk for their catalogue. Travel magazines like the reliable *Wanderlust* (every two months; £3.80) have a Job Shop section which often advertises job opportunities with tour companies. ⊛www.studyabroad.com is a useful website with listings and links to study and work programmes worldwide.

UK and Ireland

British Council ☏0161/957 7775. Produces a free leaflet which details study opportunities abroad. The Council's Central Management of Direct Teaching (☏020/7389 4931) recruits TEFL teachers with degrees and TEFL qualifications for posts worldwide (check ⊛www.britishcouncil.org/teacherrecruitment. htm for a current list of vacancies), and its Education and Training Group (☏020/7389 4169) runs teacher exchange programmes and enables those who already work as educators to find out about teacher development programmes abroad.
Erasmus EU-run student exchange programme enabling students at participating universities in Britain and Ireland to study in one of 26 European countries. Mobility grants available for three months to

a full academic year. Anyone interested should contact their university's international relations office, or check the Erasmus website ⓦ www.europa.eu.int/comm/ education/programmes/mundus/index_en.html. **International House** ☎ 020/7518 6999, ⓦ www. ihlondon.com. Head office for reputable English-teaching organization which offers TEFL training leading to the award of a Certificate in English Language Teaching to Adults (CELTA), and recruits for teaching positions in Britain and abroad.

The US

Bernan Associates ☎ 1-800/274-4888, ⓦ www .bernan.com. Distributes UNESCO's encyclopedic *Study Abroad*.
Council on International Educational Exchange (CIEE) ☎ 1-800/40STUDY, ⓦ www. ciee.org. The non-profit parent organization of Council Travel, CIEE runs summer, semester and academic-year programmes, as well as volunteer projects, throughout Europe. Also publishes *Work, Study, Travel Abroad* and *Volunteer! The Comprehensive Guide to Voluntary Service in the US and Abroad*.
Earthwatch Institute ☎ 1-800/776-0188 or 978/461-0081, ⓦ www.earthwatch.org.

International non-profit organization with offices in Boston, Oxford, England, Melbourne, Australia and Tokyo, Japan. 50,000 members and supporters are spread across the US, Europe, Africa, Asia and Australia and volunteer their time and skills to work with 120 research scientists each year on Earthwatch field research projects in over 50 countries all around the world.
Harper Collins Perseus Division ☎ 1-800/242-7737, ⓦ www.harpercollins.com. Publishes *International Jobs: Where They Are, How to Get Them*.
Volunteers for Peace ☎ 802/259-2759, ⓦ www .vfp.org. Non-profit organization with links to a huge international network of "workcamps", two- to four-week programmes that bring volunteers together from many countries to carry out needed community projects. Most workcamps are in summer, with registration in April–May. Annual membership including directory costs $20.

Australia and New Zealand

Australians Studying Abroad ☎ 03/9822 6899, ⓦ www.asatravinfo.com.au. Study tours focusing on art and culture; AUS$500 deposit.

Travel essentials

Costs

Although Slovenia can by no means be classified as a bargain destination, it's still very good value on the whole, though prices in the capital, as well as in some of the more popular destinations, are invariably higher than the rest of the country.

As with most destinations, your biggest expenditure will be on accommodation; outside Ljubljana and the coast, the average three-star hotel (in high season) comes in at around the €60–70 mark for a double, whilst for a private room, a night on a tourist farm, or a hostel bed, expect to part with around €15–20 per person. Eating out in a decent restaurant will set you back €10–15, including drinks, whilst you can get a more basic,

but no less substantial meal for around €7 in most places. You'll find foodstuffs in supermarkets and convenience stores on a par with western European prices.

Museum admission charges vary between €2 and €4, but you'll pay considerably more for star attractions such as the Postojna or Škocjan Caves.

Crime

Slovenia has a very **low crime rate** and it's extremely unlikely that you'll have any problems; violent crime against tourists is almost nonexistent and petty crime rare. That said, the usual common-sense precautions apply: watching where you walk late at night, keeping an eye on valuables, particularly in crowded buses, and locking your car at all times when unattended.

In the unlikely event of any dealings with the police (*policija*), you'll generally find them easy-going, approachable and likely to speak some basic English. The only time you may be asked to provide some form of identification is if stopped whilst driving. If you do have anything stolen while in Slovenia, you'll need to go to the police and file a report, which your insurance company will require before paying out for any claims made on your policy. Should you be arrested or need legal advice, ask to contact your embassy or consulate in Ljubljana (see listings p.85). To call the police dial ☎113.

Culture and etiquette

Although **tipping** is not obligatory, it is polite to round the bill up to a convenient figure in restaurants and when taking a taxi. In common with all those countries from the former Yugoslavia, **smoking** is commonplace and many restaurants still allow smoking throughout. However, an increasing number do have no-smoking sections, and it's always worth asking to see if that's the case.

Public toilets (*javno stranišče*), which can be found in most train and bus stations, are, on the whole, clean, though you'd do well to carry your own paper; most charge around €0.20. *Moški* means men and *Zenske* means women.

Disabled Travellers

Although progress is being made, Slovenia remains dreadfully slow in acknowledging the needs of the disabled traveller, and you shouldn't expect much in the way of special facilities.

Few places are well equipped, or have facilities, for disabled travellers and, aside from the better ones, access to hotels and public buildings is generally poor, even in Ljubljana. Public transport is little better, although the Inter City Slovenije trains between Maribor and Ljubljana do have wheelchair facilities and specially adapted toilets, whilst an increasing number of train stations provide ramps for access to platforms. Similarly, most museums are ill equipped to deal with wheelchair users. The Slovene Disabled Association (Zveza Paraplegikov Slovenije) at Štihova ulica 14 (☎01/432-

7138; ⓦwww.zveza-paraplegikov.si) can assist with any specific queries you may have about travelling in Slovenia.

Electricity

Wall sockets in Slovenia operate at **220 volts** and take round, two-pin plugs. A standard continental adaptor allows the use of 13-amp, square-pin plugs.

Entry requirements

Citizens of the EU, Australia, Canada, New Zealand and the USA can enter Slovenia with just a passport and may stay in the country for up to ninety days, whilst citizens of some neighbouring countries, such as Italy and Austria, require only an identity card. All the latest information can be obtained from the Slovene Foreign Ministry website at ⓦwww. mzz.gov/si.

Assuming that you do require a **visa**, applications can be made to any Slovenian consulate abroad in person, or by post. Ninety-day stay tourist visas, with the option of single, double or multiple entry, currently cost £25/€35; transit visas, valid for five days, cost £10/€15.

Slovenian embassies and consulates abroad

Australia Embassy: Level 6, Advance Bank Centre, 60 Marcus Clarke Street, Canberra ACT 2601 ☎02/6243 4830, @vca@mzz-dkp.gov.si; Consulate: 86 Parramatta Road, Sydney NSW 2050 ☎02/9517 1591.
Britain 10 Little College Street, London, SW1P 3SH ☎020/7222 5400, @vlo@mzz-dkp.gov.si
Canada Embassy: 150 Metcalfe Street, Suite 2101, Ottawa, Ontario K2P 1Z1 ☎613/565-5781; Consulates: 747 Browns Line, 2nd Floor, Etobicoke, Toronto, Ontario M8W 3V7 ☎416/201-8307.
Ireland Embassy: Morrison Chambers, 2nd Floor, 32 Nassau Street, Dublin 2 ☎01/670 5240, @vdb@mzz-dkp.gov.si
New Zealand Consulate: PO Box 30247, Eastern Hutt Road, Pomare, Lower Hutt, Wellington ☎04/567 0027.
USA Embassy 1525 New Hampshire Avenue NW Washington DC 20036 ☎202/667-5363, @vwa@mzz-dkp.gov.si; Consulate: 600 Third Avenue, 21st Floor, New York, NY 10016 ☎212/370-3006.

Rough Guides Travel Insurance

Rough Guides has teamed up with Columbus Direct to offer you travel insurance that can be tailored to suit your needs. Readers can choose from many different travel insurance products, including a low-cost backpacker option for long stays; a short-break option for city getaways; a typical holiday package option; and many others. There are also annual multi-trip policies for those who travel regularly, with variable levels of cover available. Different sports and activities (trekking, skiing, etc) can be covered if required on most policies.

Rough Guides travel insurance is available to the residents of 36 different countries with different language options to choose from via our website – ⓦwww .roughguidesinsurance.com – where you can also purchase the insurance.

Alternatively, UK residents should call 0800 083 9507; US citizens should call 1-800 749-4922; Australians should call 1 300 669 999. All other nationalities should call +44 870 890 2843.

Gay and lesbian travellers

Slovenia was always the most tolerant of the ex-Yugoslav republics, with an active gay and lesbian movement in existence since the mid-1980s, though that's not to say gays and lesbians have had an easy time of it. Although attitudes have softened slightly in recent years, the majority of the population remains largely unsympathetic towards the gay and lesbian community.

Not surprisingly, Ljubljana is the centre of the gay and lesbian scene in Slovenia, and manifestations of gay life beyond the capital are almost nonexistent. A number of events and happenings now take place in Ljubljana, the most prominent of which are the annual **Gay Pride Parade** (late June or early July) – first organized in 2001 and now an established fixture in the capital's festival calendar – and the **Gay and Lesbian Film Festival** at the beginning of December, which has been running for the best part of two decades.

Both of these events are organized by the proactive gay association **Roza Klub**, itself just one wing of the autonomous, alternative cultural society Škuc, based at Kersnikova 4 (☏01/430-4740, ⓦwww.ljudmila .org/siqrd). Roza Klub also runs Galfon, a gay and lesbian advice line (☏01/432-4089; daily 7–10pm), organizes club nights, and publishes several magazines and fanzines. The group **Out in Slovenia,** at Kašeljska 121 (☏041/562-375, ⓦwww. outinslovenija.com), organizes numerous sport and recreational activities – hiking,

cycling, skiing and the like – for gays and lesbians.

Health

Travelling in Slovenia should present few problems: the country has high standards of hygiene and health care, inoculations are not necessary and tap water is safe everywhere. Most problems tend to be weather-related; summers can be blisteringly hot, particularly in central, southern and eastern regions, so a high-factor sun cream is a useful aid. Conversely, inclement weather in the mountainous regions, particularly at higher altitudes, can present potentially serious dangers – hence the usual provisos apply, namely, suitable clothing, sufficient provisions and equipment, and a watchful eye on the forecast. If you're planning to spend time in the mountains or forested areas, you may wish to consider being inoculated against tick-borne encephalitis.

All towns and most villages have a **pharmacy** (lekarna), with highly trained staff, most of whom invariably speak a good standard of English. Opening hours are normally from 7am to 7 or 8pm; signs in the window give the location or telephone number of the nearest all-night pharmacy (dežurna lekarna). In emergencies dial ☏112 for the ambulance service, who will whisk you off to the hospital (bolnica) where you should be attended to fairly rapidly.

Insurance

Even though EU health-care privileges apply in Slovenia, you'd do well to take out an insurance policy before travelling to cover against theft, loss, and illness or injury. A typical travel insurance policy usually provides cover for the loss of baggage, tickets and – up to a certain limit – cash or cheques, as well as cancellation or curtailment of your journey. Most of them exclude so-called dangerous sports unless an extra premium is paid: in Slovenia this could mean, for example, skiing, scuba diving, white-water rafting, and trekking, though probably not activities such as canoeing or kayaking.

Internet

Although you can find an Internet café in most towns of any decent size in Slovenia, there remain surprisingly few places where you can log-on – when you do find one expect to pay anywhere between €1–3 for one hour. That said, an increasing number of tourist offices now offer free use of a terminal, while another option is the local library, although these are usually closed at weekends and connections can be infuriatingly slow. Some of the more upmarket hotels have an ISDN line.

Kids

From a practical point of view travelling with children in Slovenia will present no obvious problems. Most of the better-quality hotels are well disposed to catering for children, whilst most restaurants (at least those of a decent standard) should be able to provide highchairs for younger children and babies. Most car-rental firms provide child or baby seats for a small extra charge. All supermarkets, and many smaller shops, are well stocked with the requisite nappies, baby food and so on.

Your biggest challenge will be keeping the kids entertained; bar the odd zoo there are few attractions specifically targeted at children, even in Ljubljana. The most obvious destinations are the **beaches** along the coast which, on the whole, are clean and safe (most bathing areas are roped off), whilst some have grassy areas with sporting and play facilities.

Another thing that might appeal to adults as well as kids is **puppetry**, a popular and well-regarded form of entertainment in Slovenia; there are particularly good theatres in Ljubljana and Maribor, details of which are given in the relevant sections.

Beyond this, you'll find that some of the country's **festivals** also incorporate elements specifically designed with children in mind; foremost amongst these is the excellent TrnFest, which takes place in Ljubljana in August, and the Pippi Longstocking Festival in Velenje in late September, featuring music, cinema, theatre, and dozens of workshops for kids.

Laundry

Self-service laundries (*pralnica*) are nigh-on impossible to find in Slovenia, even in the larger towns and cities. Your options are, therefore, limited to hotels, some hostels and campsites.

Mail

The Slovene postal service (*Pošta Slovenije*) is a well-run, efficient organisation. **Post offices** (*pošta*), rarely crowded, are orderly affairs and are usually open Monday to Friday 8am to 6 or 7pm and until noon or 1pm on Saturday, although in Ljubljana and some of the coastal resorts you'll find that the main post offices keep longer hours. **Stamps** (*znamke*) can be bought at the post office and at newsstands.

Money

On January 1, 2007, Slovenia officially changed over from the tolar to the **euro**. The euro is split into 100 cents. There are seven euro **notes** – in denominations of 500, 200, 100, 50, 20, 10, and 5 euros, each a different colour and size – and eight different **coin** denominations, including 2 and 1 euros, then 50, 20, 10, 5, 2, and 1 cents. Euro coins feature a common EU design on one face, but different country-specific designs on the other.

As a rule you're best off **changing money** in banks (*banka*), which you can find in all but the smallest towns, and which are generally open 8.30am–12.30pm and 2–5pm weekdays, and 8.30–11am or noon on Saturdays. Otherwise, you can change money at numerous small exchange offices (*menjalnice*), tourist offices, tourist agencies, post offices and hotels, though you may end up paying considerably more in commission. Changing travellers' cheques is a relatively painless process, although some banks do insist on seeing your passport and issuing receipt in order for the transaction to go ahead.

Credit cards are now accepted in most hotels, restaurants and shops, and you'll have little trouble finding **ATMs** (bančni avtomat), even in the smallest towns. Remember that all cash advances are treated as loans, with interest accruing daily from the date of withdrawal; there may be a transaction fee on top of this. However, you may be able to make withdrawals from ATMs in Slovenia using your debit card, which is not liable to interest payments. Make sure you have a personal identification number (PIN) that's designed to work overseas.

If carrying **travellers' cheques**, then by far the most recognized are American Express, either sterling or dollars. In the event of lost or stolen cheques, report the loss forthwith to the American Express office in Ljubljana, which is opposite the train station at Kolodvorska 16 (Mon–Fri 8am–5pm; ☎01/430-7720); lost or stolen cheques can usually be replaced within 24 hours.

A compromise between travellers' cheques and plastic is **Visa Travel Money**, a disposable prepaid debit card with a PIN which works in all ATMs that take Visa cards. For more information, check the Visa Travel-Money website at ⦿usa.visa.com/personal/cards/visa_travel_money.

Opening hours and public holidays

Most **shops** open Monday to Friday from 8am to 7pm and on Saturdays from 8am to 1pm, with some (usually the mall-type places in bigger towns and cities) open on Sundays between 11am and 5pm. There are also an increasing number of 24-hour food shops open throughout the country.

Post offices open Monday to Friday 8am to 6 or 7pm and until noon or 1pm on Saturday; **banks** generally open 8.30am to 12.30pm and 2 to 5pm weekdays, and 8.30 to 11am or noon on Saturdays; and **pharmacies** 7am to 7 or 8pm.

Inevitably, **tourist office** opening times vary greatly, depending upon both their location and the season; some keep impossibly convoluted hours, but as a rule you'll find most open between 9am and 6 or 7pm (til 8 or 9pm in more touristed areas) over summer. Similarly, tourist agencies' opening hours vary enormously, depending upon the time of year; during high season, some stay open as late as 10pm, though some are prone to closing an hour or so earlier, or later, than the scheduled time, depending upon custom.

Museums are generally open Tuesday to Sunday 9 or 10am to 5 or 6pm, with shorter hours in winter, whilst some close down altogether during this period; there are, of course, exceptions to the above but in any case all times are detailed throughout the guide.

Public holidays

Slovenia counts no fewer than **fourteen national holidays**, a number of which celebrate important milestones in the country's history. Should any of these fall on a Sunday, then the Monday becomes the holiday. Don't expect much to be open on the following days.

January 1 & 2 New Year
February 8 Day of Slovene Culture (Prešeren Day)
Easter Monday
April 27 Resistance Day
May 1 & 2 Labour Day Holidays
June 25 Day of Slovene Statehood
August 15 Assumption Day
October 31 Reformation Day
November 1 All Saints' Day
December 25 Christmas
December 26 Independence Day

Phones

Public phone boxes, found just about everywhere, use **phonecards** (*telekartice*), which currently come in denominations of €3, €4 and €7; you can buy these from post offices, newspaper kiosks and tobacco shops. If making long-distance and international calls it's usually easier to go to the post office, where you're assigned to a cabin and given the bill afterwards. All Slovenian land line numbers are seven-digit, and are preceded by two-digit **regional codes** – of which there are six (℡01 for Ljubljana, up to ℡07, but no ℡06). To make a direct call to somewhere outside the area you are in, you must use the regional code.

Slovenian **mobile phone** numbers have nine digits, including one of these prefixes, ℡031, ℡041, ℡051, or ℡040. Calling a mobile from a public or private phone you must dial all the numbers; when calling from abroad drop the 0.

If you want to use your mobile phone abroad, you'll need to check with your phone provider whether it will work abroad, and what the call charges are. You are likely to be charged extra for incoming calls when abroad, as the people calling you will be paying the usual rate. If you want to retrieve messages while you're away, you'll have to ask your provider for a new access code, as your home one is unlikely to work. For further information about using your phone abroad, check out ⓦwww.telecomsadvice.org.uk/features/using_your_mobile_abroad.htm.

Shopping

Just about all of Slovenia's cities and bigger towns now accommodate at least one **shopping mall** – invariably incorporated within a multi-purpose entertainment complex – the result being that traditional town centre shopping areas are shrinking. Slovenia's rich **folk art** tradition – manifest most obviously in the paint-

Clothing and shoe sizes

Women's dresses and skirts

American	4	6	8	10	12	14	16	18
British	8	10	12	14	16	18	20	22
Continental	38	40	42	44	46	48	50	52

Women's blouses and sweaters

American	6	8	10	12	14	16	18
British	30	32	34	36	38	40	42
Continental	40	42	44	46	48	50	52

Women's shoes

American	5	6	7	8	9	10	11
British	3	4	5	6	7	8	9
Continental	36	37	38	39	40	41	42

Men's suits

American	34	36	38	40	42	44	46	48
British	34	36	38	40	42	44	46	48
Continental	44	46	48	50	52	54	56	58

Men's shirts

American	14	15	15.5	16	16.5	17	17.5	18
British	14	15	15.5	16	16.5	17	17.5	18
Continental	36	38	39	41	42	43	44	45

Men's shoes

American	7	7.5	8	8.5	9.5	10	10.5	11	11.5
British	6	7	7.5	8	9	9.5	10	11	12
Continental	39	40	41	42	43	44	44	45	46

ed beehive panels, woodenware from Ribnica, lace from Idrija and black pottery from Prekmurje – is a good source of ideas for souvenir gifts; more often than not, such items can be found in museums where they are actually exhibited, though there are occasional shops where you can pick up these things. Whether buying for oneself or as a gift, Slovenia's excellent wine (see p.9) makes a terrific purchase; this is best bought from a *vinoteka* (wine shop) or *vinska klet* (wine cellar). **Flea markets** are few and far between, though the Sunday morning one on the banks of the Ljubljanica, in Ljubljana, is definitely worth a browse, particularly for its communist-era knick-knacks (see p.83).

Time

Slovenia is one hour ahead of GMT, six hours ahead of Eastern Standard Time and nine ahead of Western Standard Time. It is also ten hours behind Australian Eastern Standard Time and twelve hours behind New Zealand.

Tourist Information

A large number of free brochures and special-interest pamphlets are produced by the Slovenian Tourist Board (⊛www.slovenia.info), and distributed by their offices abroad as well as their excellent, and extensive, network of local authority-run tourist offices within Slovenia. Almost without exception the staff, most of whom speak excellent English, are extremely knowledgeable and unfailingly helpful.

The tourist board's main publication is the *Next Exit* booklet, which plots six different routes throughout the country, each of which lists tourist offices, places to eat and sleep and key sites of natural and cultural interest – many off the beaten track. The booklet also contains a range of discount coupons for use in hotels, restaurants and museums. Although there are exceptions, and these are listed throughout the guide, tourist offices do not deal in private accommodation (see p.29); for this you're best off heading to local tourist agencies, which can be found in most towns and cities – again, these are listed where relevant.

In Britain you can contact the Slovenian Tourist Office for more information (☎0870 225 5305, ⊛www.slovenia.info).

Guide

Guide

1

Ljubljana

CHAPTER 1 # Highlights

✳ **Jože Plečnik** Stunning architecture at almost every turn from the nation's greatest architect. See p.62

✳ **Old Town** With Baroque churches, elegant townhouses and cool cafés, the Old Town has charm in spades. See p.63

✳ **Ljubljana Castle** Looming high above the Old Town; climb the clocktower and take in the magnificent views of the Alps. See p.65

✳ **Križanke** Take in a jazz or rock concert at the atmospheric, Plečnik-designed open-air theatre. See p.68

✳ **Trnovo** Roman ruins, Plečnik oddities and riverside cafés in this green and peaceful suburb. See p.71

✳ **Tivoli Park** The city's green heart, affording easy promenade strolls or more exerting hillside walks. See p.74

✳ **Ethnographic Museum** The city's most absorbing museum brings together a terrific array of cultural heritage from both Slovenia and non-European lands. See p.60

✳ **Drinking by the Ljubljanica** Enjoy a beer at sundown in one of the many bars along the willow-fringed banks of the Ljubljanica River. See p.80

△ Mestni Trg, Old Town

Ljubljana

Thrust into the spotlight in 1991 as the capital of a newly self-confident nation, **LJUBLJANA** is one of Europe's brightest and most engaging small cities. Situated in the southern part of the Ljubljana river basin, at the juncture of the Alps and Dinaric mountain ranges, pretty much everything converges here: all major transport links, industry and commerce, culture, politics and power. However, with a population of less than 300,000 – which easily makes it one of Europe's smallest capital cities – Ljubljana retains a distinctly languorous and provincial air.

As the former Yugoslavia imploded in the early 1990s, Ljubljana suffered few of the traumas that befell neighbouring Zagreb, its path smoothed by a relatively sound economic and political infrastructure. A little over a decade later – as capital of one of the European Union's newest member states – Ljubljana is a prosperous, self-assured place, its slick veneer of sophistication masking a disparate number of outside influences – Austrian, Balkan and Mediterranean – subtly absorbed and tinkered with over the years. That said, it is Slovenian through and through, and one of the least ethnically diverse capitals in Europe, which perhaps explains why it suffers relatively few of the ills commonly associated with the big city.

The city's tremendously compact centre lends itself perfectly to discovery by foot and it's unlikely you'll need, or want, to use the refreshingly clean and efficient public transport system. While the city boasts a number of eminently enjoyable museums and galleries – the City Museum, Ethnographic Museum, and National Gallery chief amongst them – its real charms lie outdoors. Ljubljana's central core is a showcase of princely Baroque and Secessionist edifices, while the legacy of magnificent buildings, bridges and pathways bequeathed by Jože Plečnik, Slovenia's greatest architect, is difficult to overestimate, transforming as it did the entire fabric of the city between the two world wars. Its churches too reveal dazzling artistry, from Francesco Robba's extraordinary altar sculptures to Quaglio's resplendent frescoes.

Fundamental to the city's layout and history is the slender **River Ljubljanica**, a once navigable waterway, but now sprinkled with several fine-looking bridges. On both the left and right banks vestiges of the city's Roman and medieval past can be detected, but it's the splendid Baroque townhouses and maze-like streets of the majestic **Old Town**, lorded over by the landmark castle, which exerts the greatest pull. Furthermore, the splashes of greenery – such as **Tivoli Park** – give just a hint of what lies beyond the city's boundaries. Above all though, Ljubljana is a sociable city, a place to come and meet people, dip in and out of its enchanting riverside cafés, and engage in the nightlife.

Owing to both the country's size and the city's central location, it's perfectly feasible to do a day-trip from here to just about any of the country's principal attractions, be it the mountain lakes of Bled and Bohinj to the northwest, the karst and coast to the south and west, or the castles and spas to the east.

Some history

Though sources first mention Ljubljana in 1144, the history of settlement here goes as far back as 2000 BC, when lake-dwellers inhabited the area of the marshes to the south of the city. They were closely followed by the **Illyrians** and **Celts**, though it was the **Romans** who engineered the first major commune, constructing a fortified military encampment on the left bank of the River Ljubljanica around 50 BC. It was given the name **Emona** and inhabited by some five thousand civilians working as artisans, tradesmen and retired officers; remnants of this Roman period can still be seen in the form of several sections of the city walls, as well as archeological sites contained within two gardens in the eastern and southern parts of the city. After repeated attacks by the Huns and Barbarians, Emona was eventually sacked around 450 AD.

Next up were the **Slavs**, who settled here at the tail end of the sixth century and proceeded to establish a settlement on the right bank of the Ljubljanica beneath the castle – what is now Stari trg and Mestni trg. During the twelfth century this evolved into Ljubljana's **medieval** core, and was given the German name Laibach in 1144, before assuming its Slovenian name, Luwigana, in 1146. Aside from Stari trg and Mestni trg, medieval Ljubljana also incorporated Novi trg on the left bank, and by the sixteenth century, this entire district was enclosed by city walls rearing all the way up to the castle. Following their arrival in the thirteenth century, the **Spanheim** family of **Carinthian dukes** granted the municipality city rights, and in 1243 the name **Ljubljana** first appeared; at around the same time, the city became the capital of the Carniola province, before falling under the jurisdiction of the **Habsburgs** in 1335.

A catastrophic **earthquake** in 1511, which left little of the city standing, coincided with Ljubljana becoming the leading centre of the **Reformation** in Slovenia. This period was marked by significant spiritual and cultural progression, thanks largely to leading reformers such as Primož Trubar, who sought to promote literacy among the populace and who successfully published the first Slovene book – the primer, *Abecedarium* – in 1550; at this time the city also gained its first college and public library. The Reformation was successfully snuffed out at the end of the sixteenth century, a period that saw the arrival of the **Jesuits** (1597), who set about reorganizing the city's educational system, as well as establishing many religious buildings. The city's cultural pulse quickened further with the establishment of the Academia Operosorum – the first society of scholars and intellectuals – in 1693, and the Academia Philharmonicorum in 1701, one of the first musical institutions in Europe. Alongside this new Catholic order, a distinct architectural style, **Ljubljana Baroque**, emerged, expressed most sublimely in the city's four principal churches: St James's (1615); the Annunciation (1660); St Nicholas's (1706); and Ursuline (1726), as well as Robba's outstanding Fountain of the Three Rivers.

Between 1809 and 1814, Ljubljana was designated the capital of Napoleon's **Illyrian Provinces**, the city deemed a geographically convenient location for Napoleon in his attempt to prevent the Habsburgs accessing the Adriatic. A few years after his downfall Ljubljana was chosen to host the prestigious **Congress of the Holy Alliance** (in 1821), a gathering of the triumphant monarchy states that had defeated the French. During the mid-nineteenth century, and despite continued political repression, the city experienced something of an **industrial revolution** – the catalyst for which was the completion of the Vienna–Ljubljana–Trieste rail line in 1857. Having been provincialized for the greater part of the century, the city began to emerge from its cultural and political strait-jacket in the 1880s; all its elected mayors were Slovenian, while a raft of cultural institutions, including the Opera House (1892) and National House (1896), were established. In 1895, a second, and equally destructive earthquake necessitated yet more wholesale reconstruction, though this time it was Vienna and the Secessionist school which provided the inspiration – the results of which are particularly outstanding along Miklošičeva ulica.

With the creation of the **Kingdom of Serbs, Croats and Slovenes** in 1918 – recast as the Kingdom of **Yugoslavia** in 1929 – power transferred from Vienna to Belgrade, though this left Ljubljana no better off than when under Habsburg rule. Nevertheless, the founding of the National Gallery (1918), University (1919) and Academy of Sciences and Arts (1938) was confirmation of the city's continuing cultural efflorescence. During this interwar period, the city also experienced an architectural revolution, thanks to **Jože Plečnik**, Slovenia's greatest and most revered urban planner. From stunning new monuments – such as the National University Library and Žale Cemetery – to randomly scattered pillars and pyramids, the great architect completely transformed the city landscape. With every justification, the city was dubbed "Plečnik's Ljubljana". Following **World War II**, a period during which the city was occupied by both Italians and Germans before being liberated by the Partisans, it became the capital of the Republic of Slovenia, one of the six federal republics of the Federal People's Republic of Yugoslavia, and then, in 1963, the Socialist Federal Republic of Yugoslavia.

After Tito's death in 1980, relations between Ljubljana and Belgrade gradually worsened, coming to a head in 1988 with the staging of the **"Ljubljana Four Trial"** (see p.334), a case many at the time regarded as the final denouement in Slovene–Serb relations (and by implication the end of Yugoslavia). At around the same time, Ljubljana was at the forefront of Yugoslavia's intoxicating **alternative cultural scene**, thanks in no small part to the controversial and provocative arts collective Neue Slowenische Kunst (NSK), or New Slovene Art, the core of which was the anarchic rock group Laibach, one of the few bands from the former Yugoslavia to make an impact outside their own country. They, and other alternative movements – styled as New Social Movement groups – were fundamental in stimulating further debate on the social and political issues of the time, prescient given the deepening tensions between Ljubljana and Belgrade.

On June 26 1991, the day after Slovenia had officially declared its **independence**, thousands gathered on Republic Square to celebrate – somewhat prematurely as it turned out – unaware that Yugoslav Army (JNA) tank units were closing in on Brnik airport, just 23km away. However, the subsequent **ten-day war** had little direct effect on the city and on July 7 it was able, finally, to rejoice in its status as the capital of a new **republic**. As Ljubljana now settles down to life as the capital of a fully fledged EU member state, there's little doubt that the city's profile is on the rise, and deservedly so, yet the hope is that it manages to retain the low-key charm which makes it such an enjoyable destination.

Arrival, information and city transport

Ljubljana's **airport**, Letališče, is located in Brnik, 23km north of the city, and connected to the main bus station by a number of buses operated by various companies. The most frequent, but slowest, are public buses (Mon–Fri hourly 5am–8pm; Sat & Sun 7am, then every 2hr between 10am–8pm; 45min; €3.50), which arrive at bay 28 of the bus station from where they also leave (Mon–Fri 5.20am, then hourly 6.10am–8.10pm; Sat & Sun 6.10am, then every 2hr 9.10am–7.10pm). Adria Airways operates nine buses a day from Brnik (7.40am–midnight; 30min; €4.50) to their terminal at the bus station, and the same number in the opposite direction (6.15am–10.30pm). Adria also offer a minibus shuttle service (€8), which operates around the clock and can drop you off anywhere in the city; reservations are required if travelling from the city to the airport (☏041/362-079). A taxi to or from the airport will cost around €25.

The **train** (Železniška postaja) and **bus stations** (Avtobusna postaja) are located next to each other on Trg Osvobodilne fronte, from where it's a ten-minute walk south into the centre. The immaculately clean train station has some good facilities, including a train information office (daily 5.30am–9.30pm), tourist information office (see opposite), exchange desk (daily 5.30am–10pm) and 24-hour left-luggage lockers (€2 per day). The bus station ticket office is open daily 5am–10.30pm.

Information, maps and tours

The excellent **Slovenian Tourist Information Centre (STIC)** at Krekov trg 10 (daily: June–Sept 8am–9pm, Oct–May 8am–7pm; ☏01/306-4576, ✉stic@ljubljana-tourism.si) can assist with information on any aspect of travel within the country, including the capital. The main city **Tourist Information Centre (TIC)** is in the old town on Stritarjeva next to the Triple Bridge (June–Sept Mon–Fri 8am–9pm, Sat & Sun 10am–6pm; Oct–May Mon–Fri 8am–7pm,

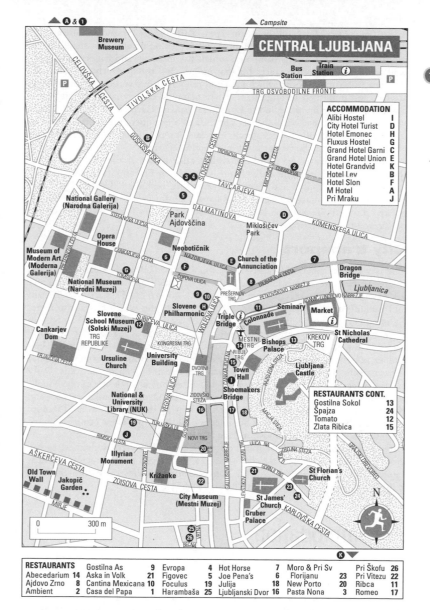

CENTRAL LJUBLJANA

Brewery Museum

Bus Station Train Station ⓘ

TRG OSVOBODILNE FRONTE

ACCOMMODATION	
Alibi Hostel	I
City Hotel Turist	D
Hotel Emonec	H
Fluxus Hostel	G
Grand Hotel Garni	C
Grand Hotel Union	E
Hotel Grandvid	K
Hotel Lev	B
Hotel Slon	F
M Hotel	A
Pri Mraku	J

CELOVSKA CESTA

TIVOLSKA CESTA

GOSPOSVETSKA

SLOVENSKA CESTA

TRDINOVA ULICA

DALMATINOVA

CUFARJEVA

National Gallery (Narodna Galerija)

STEFANOVA ULICA

Park Ajdovščina

Miklošičev Park

KOMENSKEGA ULICA

Opera House

CANKARJEVA CESTA

Neboticnik

NAZORJEVA ULICA

Church of the Annunciation

Museum of Modern Art (Moderna Galerija)

TOMSICEVA

ČOPOVA ULICA

National Museum (Narodni Muzej)

PRESERNOV TRG

TRUBARJEVA CESTA

PETKOVSKOVO NABREZJE

ADAMIC LUNCEVO NABREZJE

Dragon Bridge

Ljubljanica

Cankarjev Dom

Slovene School Museum (Solski Muzej)

SUBICEVA ULICA

Slovene Philharmonic

WOLFOVA ULICA

Triple Bridge ⓘ

Colonnade

Seminary

Market ⓘ

St Nicholas' Cathedral

TRG REPUBLIKE

KONGRESNI TRG

Ursuline Church

University Building

MESTNI TRG

RIBJI TRG

Bishops Palace

KREKOV TRG

Town Hall

Ljubljana Castle

National & University Library (NUK)

VEGOVA ULICA

DVORNI TRG

ZIDOVSKI STEZA

Shoemakers Bridge

MACJA STEZA

RESTAURANTS CONT.	
Gostilna Sokol	13
Špaja	24
Tomato	12
Zlata Ribica	15

RIMSKA CESTA

TURJASKA UL.

NOVI TRG

Illyrian Monument

GALLUSOVO NABREZJE

JULIJA NA

ASKERCEVA CESTA

Old Town Wall

Jakopič Garden

Križanke

ZOISOVA CESTA

City Museum (Mestni Muzej)

KARLOVSKA CESTA

St James' Church

Gruber Palace

GORNJI TRG

St Florian's Church

0 — 300 m

MIRJE

N

RESTAURANTS		Gostilna As	9	Evropa	4	Hot Horse	7	Moro & Pri Sv		Pri Škofu	26
Abecedarium	14	Aska in Volk	21	Figovec	5	Joe Pena's	6	Florijanu	23	Pri Vitezu	22
Ajdovo Zrno	8	Cantina Mexicana	10	Foculus	19	Julija	18	New Porto	20	Ribca	11
Ambient	2	Casa del Papa	1	Harambaša	25	Ljubljanski Dvor	16	Pasta Nona	3	Romeo	17

Sat & Sun 10am–6pm; ☎01/306-1215, ⓦwww.ljubljana-tourism.si). Both of these provide comprehensive information on the city (in several languages, including English), have free, detailed **maps** to give away, and can book private accommodation (see p.54). The office on Stritarjeva also has a ticketing centre, where you can buy tickets for cultural and sporting events, both in the city and throughout the country. There is also an information office at the train station (June–Sept daily

8am–10pm; Oct–May Mon–Fri 10am–7pm; ℡01/433-9475), and an information desk at the airport (daily 11am–5.30pm). Worth picking up at any of these are the monthly *Where To?* events pamphlet, which has museum and gallery listings as well as events and performances for that month, and the quarterly *Ljubljana Life* (Ⓦwww.ljubljanalife.com), which has good restaurant, bar and club listings; both are free and published in English. If you're planning on staying in the city for a few days, consider investing in the **Ljubljana Tourist Card** (€13), which entitles you to unlimited travel on all the city's buses, and offers discounted entrance fees to selected museums, galleries, restaurants and bars; it's valid for three days and can be obtained from all of the city's tourist information centres.

The tourist office offers two-hour **sightseeing tours** of the city, starting at the Town Hall (April–Sept daily 10am; Oct–March Fri–Sun 11am; €7). They can also organize longer and special interest tours, including Baroque Ljubljana, Secessionist Ljubljana and Plečnik's Ljubljana (€35 for groups up to five, €50 for group up to ten). Tickets can be purchased on the spot or from the tourist offices on Krekov trg and Stritarjeva.

City transport

The city **buses**, run by Ljubljanski Potniški Promet (LPP), are clean, cheap and frequent; there are 22 bus lines, the majority of which operate between 5am and 10.30pm, with the most important lines (#1, #2, #3, #6 & #11) starting at 3.15am and running until midnight – each stop clearly indicates which buses stop there. Entering via the front door only, you pay in cash by depositing the exact amount in the box next to the driver (a single journey costs a flat **fare** of €1.25 or by using the slightly cheaper plastic tokens (*žetoni*; €0.80), which are also deposited in the box and are bought in advance from post offices, newspaper kiosks and some shops and supermarkets. Each payment or token is valid for one unbroken journey only. Daily (*dnevna vozovnica*; €3.50) and weekly (*tedenska vozovnica*; €12) tickets can be bought from the LPP kiosks at Trdinova ulica 3 and Bavarski Dvor, Slovenska cesta 55, and the main bus station. It might also be worth picking up the small, fold-up LPP **map**, which clearly denotes the various bus lines and all the stops. These can be obtained from the kiosks mentioned above and the tourist offices.

It's unlikely that you'll have much call for a **taxi**, but if you do, expect to pay around €8 for a ride across the city – these can be flagged in the street or found at ranks by the train station, outside the *Hotel Slon* and near Prešernov Trg – the most reliable company is Rumeni Taxis (℡041/731-831).

Accommodation

For a capital city, even such a modestly sized one, accommodation possibilities in Ljubljana are fairly stark. While the city is reasonably well served with **hotels** at the upper end of the price range, there is an appreciable gap when it comes to mid-range and budget places. There are, though, a growing number of **youth hostels** and **student dorms** around town, while **private accommodation** is another option – if the latter is your preferred choice, head to the tourist office on Stritarjeva, who should be able to arrange something close to the centre. More often than not, rooms (❷) come with shared bathroom facilities and without breakfast. You could also try Tour AS at Mala ulica 8 (℡01/434-2660, Ⓦwww.apartmaji.si); though they deal predominantly with apartments (❺–❽), they have a handful of private rooms too (❸) – discounts are offered for stays of longer than seven days.

The city's one **campsite** is located 4km north of the centre in Ježica (buses #6 or #8), at the Ljubljana Resort (℡01/568-3913, ⓦwww.ljubljanaresort.si). This large, clean and spacious site by the Sava River also has a decent hotel (ⓞ), and fully-furnished, self-catering chalets sleeping up to four people (ⓞ) – the resort's superb facilities include the Laguna water park, a bowling alley, beach volleyball courts, children's play area and restaurant.

Hostels

Ljubljana now has a pretty good selection of **youth hostels** – all centrally located and open year round – in addition to four clean and well-run **student hostels** (Dijaški dom) scattered around the city. These student hostels are only open between mid-June and August, and all are similarly priced: excluding breakfast, expect to pay around €10 per person for a dorm bed and €15 for a bed in a single or double room. Reservations are advised for all these places.

Alibi Hostel Cankarjevo nabrežje 27 ℡01/251-1244, ⓦwww.alibi.si. This colourful and friendly hostel, in a super Old Town location overlooking the Ljubljanica river, has six-, eight- and twelve-bedded dorms (€20), as well as a few double rooms (€30), spread over five floors. Internet access available but breakfast not provided.

Hostel Celica Metelkova 9 ℡01/430-1890, ⓦwww.souhostel.com. Brilliantly original hostel constructed from the remnants of the barracks' former military prison. The twenty colourful cells, individually designed and each with a different theme in mind, sleep two to three people (€19–24) – shower facilities are shared; four- and five-bed rooms (€22) do have shower facilities and there is also one large dorm (€18) sleeping twelve. The hostel's range of facilities includes an information point, small art gallery and library, Internet access and Oriental café.

Dijaški dom Bežigrad Kardeljeva ploščad 28 ℡01/534-2867, ⓔdd.lj-bezigrad@guest.arnes.si. Three- and four-bed rooms in three interconnected buildings, some with shower and toilet. Take bus #6 or #8 to stop Mercator, cross the road and walk back 150m then head through the small park.

Dijaški dom Ivana Cankarja Poljanska 26 ℡01/474-8600, ⓔdd.lj-ic@guest.arnes.si. This hostel, a short way southeast of the centre, has the largest capacity of all, with some 500 beds, including singles, doubles and multi-bedded rooms; all bathroom facilities are shared. Bus #5 to stop Ambrožev trg and it's set back 50m from the main road.

Dijaški dom Poljane Potočnikova 3 ℡01/300-3137, ⓔdd-poljane@guest.arnes.si. A ten-minute walk east of *dom Ivana Cankarja*, this is the smallest of the *Dijaški doms*; four-bed rooms plus a few singles, some with shower. Bus #5 to stop Gornje Poljane then a five-minute walk. Breakfast available. Open mid-June to July.

Dijaški dom Tabor Vidovdanska 7 ℡01/234-8840, ⓔssljddta1s@guest.arnes.si. The most central, and busiest, of the *Dijaški doms*, located just ten minutes' walk southeast of the train and bus stations in a quiet area near the *Hotel Park*. Singles, doubles and multi-bedded rooms with shared toilet and shower facilities. Breakfast available.

Fluxus Hostel Tomšičeva 4 ℡01/251-5760, ⓦwww.fluxus-hostel.com. Small, intimate and bright central hostel with a six- and eight-bed dorm (€20), and one double room (€60).

Hotels

The majority of Ljubljana's **hotels** are at the upper end of the scale, patronized in the main by business people, and with prices that reflect this. There are only a couple of places that could be termed mid-range or budget, a situation unlikely to improve in the short term. Many of these hotels are centrally located and can be easily reached on foot from the train and bus stations. All include **breakfast** in the price.

BIT Center Hotel Litijska 57 ℡01/548-0055, ⓦwww.bit-center.net. Busy and lively sports hotel 2km east of the centre with clean and simple no-frills rooms; fifty-percent discount on use of sporting facilities (squash, badminton and fitness centre) and free use of the adjoining public pool in summer. Buses #5, #9, #13 and #22. ⓞ

City Hotel Turist Dalmatinova 15 ℡01/234-9130, ⓦwww.cityhotel.si. Just a 5min walk from the stations, this extensively renovated, and excessively

overpriced, downtown hotel has a range of differ-
ently sized, smoking and no-smoking rooms; all
have a/c and wi-fi access. ❽–❾

Domina Grand Media Dunajska 154 ☎01/588-
2500, ⓦwww.dominagmljubljana.com. The city's
main congress venue aspires to being one of the
most technologically advanced hotels in the world;
each room possesses a huge plasma screen which,
linked to a central computer system, allows you to
receive free of charge calls to dozens of countries,
access the Internet, and receive on-line video
games and digital movies; the remote also allows
you to control all facilities within the room (locks,
lights, a/c etc); incidentally, the designer furnishings
look fabulous. Wi-fi access throughout hotel. ❾

🏃 **Hotel Emonec** Wolfova 12 ☎01/200-1520,
ⓦwww.hotel-emonec.com. Cracking-value
place in a quiet off-street location in the heart of
town; the blue and white decorated rooms are
simple, but fresh and modern looking, while the
bathrooms are beautifully designed. ❺

Grand Hotel Garni Miklošičeva 9 ☎01/308-4300,
ⓦwww.astralhotel.net. Just 300m south of the bus
and train stations, this hotel is aimed squarely at
the business traveller. The rooms, decorated in a
sunny yellow and green colour scheme, are well
furnished, with stylish and comfortable beds, a little
sofa, minibar, safe and Internet. ❾

🏃 **Grand Hotel Union** Miklošičeva 1
☎01/308-1270, ⓦwww.gh-union.si.
Housed in a splendid Art Nouveau building a few
steps north of central Prešernov Trg, this is actually two hotels in one; the *Executive* is Ljubljana's
most refined and characterful hotel, its generously
sized, a/c rooms magnificently furnished with the
requisite first-class facilities; some have a balcony
with views across to the castle. Rooms in the
adjoining *Business* hotel are similarly furnished,
though the colour scheme is somewhat dowdy. In
addition to the fitness centre and sauna, it's the
only hotel in town with a swimming pool (on the
rooftop). Both ❾

Hotel Grandvid Dolenjska 336 ☎01/360-2200,
ⓦwww.grandvid-hotel.com. Pleasant hotel with
shiny, ultramodern rooms and facilities located
7km southeast of the city centre in the suburb of

Lavrica. The hotel can arrange a taxi (around €10),
or take any bus heading towards Grosuplje (from
bay 20 at the bus station). ❼

Hotel Lev Vošnjakova 1 ☎01/433-2155, ⓦwww.
hotel-lev.si. This gleaming glass high-rise, a 5min
walk west of the bus and train stations opposite
Tivoli Park, is the most expensive hotel in town,
frequented in the main by business groups; the
lavish, but surprisingly modestly sized rooms, have
a/c, smart oak chairs and desks, and Internet. ❾

Hotel Park Tabor 9 ☎01/300-2500, ⓦwww.
tabor.si. High-rise budget place located amidst a
jumble of apartment buildings a few blocks east
of the station. The one-star rooms, with shared
toilet and shower facilities, are grim and bare; the
category-two rooms, with en-suite facilities and TV,
are considerably better and worth paying the extra
amount for. ❹–❻

Hotel Slon Slovenska 34 ☎01/470-1100, ⓦwww.
hotelslon.com. The "Hotel Elephant" is so-named
after Archduke Maximilian who, with elephant
in tow, allegedly stayed at an inn on the current
site of the hotel en route to Vienna in 1552. Glass
doors lead into bright, parquet-floored bedrooms,
furnished with desks and chairs, safe, Internet and
coffee-and tea-making facilities. The hotel houses
two fine restaurants, a magnificent breakfast room,
the *Art Café* (with confectioners) and delicates-
sen. ❾

M Hotel Derčeva 4 ☎01/513-7000, ⓦwww.
m-hotel.si. Though somewhat lacking in character,
this large hotel 2km northwest of the centre has
modern, neat and spacious rooms painted in gentle
blue tones and possesses a pleasant breakfast
terrace. Triples and apartments available too. Buses
#1, #3, #15 and #16 to stop Kino Šiška. ❾

Pension Tavčar Cesta v Šmartno 7 ☎01/546-
6970, ⓦwww.penzion-tavcar.com. Neat, bright,
and very reasonably priced little pension 2km
northeast of the city centre. Take bus #12 to stop
Hrastje, walk back 200m and take a right. ❺

Pri Mraku Rimska 4 ☎01/421-9600, ⓦwww.
daj-dam.si. In a prime downtown location near
Križanke, this enjoyable – though extremely overpriced – pension has warm, exuberantly coloured
rooms with Internet access and safe. ❽

The City

Geographically and socially, the heart of the city is **Prešernov trg**, a small, animated square located on the left bank of the **River Ljubljanica**. Several important
streets converge here while just about all the major sights and points of interest
are within comfortable walking distance. With the exception of **Miklošičeva
ulica** – a street rampant with extraordinary Secessionist architecture – and one or

two other sights around, the commercial district north of Prešernov trg is largely devoid of worthwhile sights.

In any case, most people head straight for the magical **Old Town** on the right bank of the Ljubljanica: strewn with gorgeous Baroque townhouses and stately churches, all wrapped around a regal, **castle-topped hill**, it is easily the most

LJUBLJANA

ACCOMMODATION

BIT Center Hotel	**F**
Hostel Celica	**D**
Domina Grand Media	**B**
Hotel Park	**E**
Pension Tavčar	**C**
Ljubljana Resort	**A**

appealing part of the city. The left bank too has more than its fair share of fine architecture, notably south of the main square **Kongresni trg**, beyond which are the delightful village-like suburbs of **Krakovo** and **Trnovo**.

Most of the city's key museums and galleries are concentrated within a compact area between **Slovenska cesta**, the busy main thoroughfare west of Kongresni trg, and **Tivoli Park**, the city's engaging green pocket and something of a ramblers' paradise. Beyond the central zone, and especially to the north and south, there are a handful of further sights worthy of investigation, including some fabulous churches, a castle and some splendid natural heritage.

Prešernov trg

Flanked on three sides by characterful buildings and busy streets, and on the other by the gently curving sweep of the River Ljubljanica, cobbled **Prešernov trg** (Prešeren Square) is Ljubljana's major point of reference, an atmospheric space where open-air cafés do a cracking trade and street theatre performers and jazz musicians keep the punters entertained during the summer months. Presiding over all this activity, on the east side of the square, is the **monument to France Prešeren**, Slovenia's greatest poet (see box, p.126), after whom the square is named. Designed by Maks Fabiani and Ivan Zajec in 1905, the large, rather scruffy-looking bronze monument has a straight-backed Prešeren standing underneath a naked muse holding a laurel wreath – the circular plinth underneath is a traditional meeting place for locals and tourists alike.

On the north side, a three-part staircase leads up to the Baroque seventeenth-century Franciscan **Church of the Annunciation** (Frančiškanska Cerkev Marijnega oznanjenja; daily 9am–noon & 3–7pm), its striking sandy-red exterior providing a marvellous backdrop to the square. The first church on this site – this is the third – was erected in 1329 by the Augustins, but following the dissolution of the order by Emperor Joseph II in 1784, it was taken over by the Franciscans, who made several significant alterations to the structure and appearance of the church. The centrepiece of a rather gloomy and weary-looking interior is Francesco Robba's eighteenth-century marble high altar, richly adorned with spiral columns and plastic figurines. The illusionist frescoes on the nave and presbytery vaults are by Matevž Langus and Matej Sternen, while the paintings in the side altars have all but disappeared.

A few paces east of the church is the **Urbanc House**, also known as **Centromer-kur**, Ljubljana's oldest department store, built in 1903 by Friedrich Sigmund of Graz. The focal points of this fine Secessionist building are the narrow clamshell-shaped glass canopy shading the entrance and the statue of Mercury, the Roman god of commerce, standing atop the narrow frontage. While the goods now on offer are unremarkable, it's worth having a look inside to view the superb Art Nouveau interior – the elegant staircase and gallery, the allegorical statue representing craft (fabric has long been sold here) and the beautifully polished wood furnishings, most of which are original. On the opposite side of the square, a few steps down Wolfova ulica to the left of the four-storey Secessionist **Hauptman House**, you'll notice a terracotta window framing a relief of Julija Primic, gazing across to Prešeren, her life-long admirer. To the right of the Hauptman House is Čopova ulica, a lively pedestrianized shopping street, but with few shops actually worth venturing into. However, do take a look at the street's one outstanding building, the **City Savings Bank** at no. 3, featuring a fine glass and wrought-iron canopy, either side of which are allegorical statues symbolizing trade and commerce.

Miklošičeva cesta and Slovenska cesta

The main street spearing north from Prešernov trg, **Miklošičeva cesta**, is strewn with a raft of marvellous Secessionist buildings, all of which were designed following the earthquake in 1895. Directly behind the Franciscan church stands Ljubljana's finest hotel, the **Grand Union**, completed in 1905 by the same architect who designed the City Savings Bank, the Croatian Josip Vancaš – hence the striking similarities. Opposite the Grand Union, at no. 8, is the wildly colourful **Cooperative Bank** (Zadružna gospodarska banka). Designed in 1922 by the Slovene Ivan Vurnik, and painted by his wife Helena, the geometric folk-patterned decoration marks this building out as one of the most outstanding in the city; the interior, with a display of national motifs, is no less spectacular. Two hundred metres further on is **Miklošič Park**, laid out in 1899 by Maks Fabiani, a student of Otto Wagner and the Secessionist school of architecture in Vienna. Immediately after the earthquake, Fabiani was assigned the task of reshaping the entire area, a task he accomplished with astonishing speed. Formerly called Slovenski trg, the square was renamed Miklošič Park in 1991 on the hundredth anniversary of the death of the philologist Fran Miklošič.

Built for the well-known Ljubljana printer Otomar Bamberg in 1907, the **Bamberg House** (Bambergova hiša) at no. 16 is one of Fabiani's more restrained pieces of work, featuring a simple, rather plain design, but worth a glance for the ceramic reliefs of several eminent printers along the top. On the opposite side of the road, at no. 20, is another, earlier Fabiani building, the **Krisper House** (Krisperjeva hiša). Built in 1901, it was the first building to be designed within his overall concept of the square, and features garland-like, botanical decoration running along the entire length of the facade and a turret under a bell-shaped roof – note how, with the exception of the Bamberg House, all the buildings standing at the corners of the square have corner turrets, another Fabiani concept. The northern side of the square is consumed by the monumental Neoclassical **Court Building**, from where it's a short walk west to the **Čuden House** (Čudnova hiša) at Cigaletova ulica 3, perhaps the most flamboyant example of Secessionist architecture in the area. Back on Miklošičeva ulica, the street winds up at **Trg Osvobodilne fronte**, a traffic-choked east–west thoroughfare and site of the train and bus stations.

Running parallel to Miklošičeva ulica is the broad slash of **Slovenska cesta**, the city's busy main north–south thoroughfare. Though there's little of note along here, there are a couple of minor landmarks worth checking out if you happen to be passing. At the corner of Slovenska cesta and Štefanova ulica is the chunky seventy-metre-high tower block, **Neobotičnik**, also known simply as "Skyscraper". Commissioned by the Slovenian Pension Fund for the purpose of housing offices and apartments – and built in response to the American Art Deco skyscrapers of that period – it was, at the time of its completion in 1933, one of the highest residential buildings in Europe, and the first multistorey building in the Balkans. The rooftop café and observation deck are now both closed, but you can still take a peek inside at the impressive marble lobby and monumental spiral staircase. A couple of minutes further north along Slovenska, at the junction with Gosposvetska ulica, is the site of the former **Hotel Evropa**, built in 1869 by the Viennese architect Tietz and modelled on the Heinrichshof in Vienna; the hotel is long gone, the premises now occupied by one of the city's most upscale restaurants (see p.79).

Prešernov trg to Metelkova

The area east of Prešernov trg is fairly low-key, but contains one or two sights which make its investigation worthwhile. Due east of the square is **Trubarjeva cesta**, a long, narrow, winding street accommodating an eclectic mix of cafés, bars and shops. Midway down Trubarjeva, shortly after crossing Resljeva cesta, take a left up Vidovdanska cesta towards the *Hotel Park*, and carry on until you hit **Metelkova ulica**. Up on the right-hand side is the barracks complex of the former Yugoslav People's Army (JNA).

Metelkova's history is a fascinating one: up until the moment the JNA withdrew in the autumn of 1991, Metelkova had served as a barracks for over one hundred years, having been initially commissioned by Vienna for the Austro-Hungarian army. In December 1990, on the same day that the plebiscite for independence was held, the Network for Metelkova – an organization born out of several student and cultural movements – was established, their express aim being to convert the barracks into Ljubljana's alternative cultural mecca. However, after three years of frustrating and protracted negotiations with the city authorities, and their subsequent attempt to demolish the premises in September 1993, the Network finally carried out their threats to squat. In the event, and after further crises, various groups and societies gradually established their own territories within the complex, and there now exists, among the still half-wrecked and rubble-strewn buildings, a cosmopolitan gang of bars, clubs, galleries and independent societies, collectively known as Metelkova (see p.81). Located at the entrance to the site is the **Hostel Celica** (see p.55), something of an attraction itself having been converted from the gutted remains of the former military prison. Even if you're not staying here, it's worth a look around (or you can join the free daily tour at 2pm) just to see the wonderful, artistically designed "cells", which now function as rooms; there's a small gallery, neat café and decent restaurant here too.

At no. 2, another superbly renovated building holds the **Ethnographic Museum** (Etnografski muzej; Tues–Sun 10am–6pm; €2; Ⓦwww.etno-muzej.si), which holds a captivating collection of both Slovene and non-Slovene exhibits. The first part of the museum is dedicated to the peoples of Asia, Africa and the Americas, with particularly enlightening expositions on the lives of the Mestizo peoples and the Meso-American Indians, complete with some intriguing archive video footage. The Slovene collection comprises a beautiful assortment of artefacts and treasures, from regional costumes and items representing prominent eighteenth- and nineteenth-century industries – such as pottery, blacksmithing, clockmaking

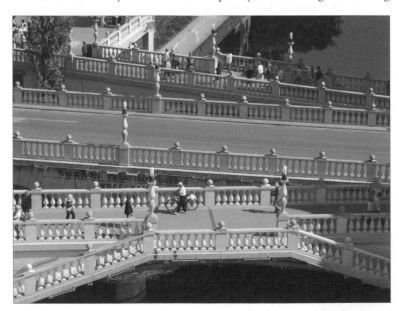

△ Triple Bridge, Ljubljana

and shoemaking – to the ever wonderful, and amusing, beehive panels, as well as masks from the Kurent festival in Ptuj and Laufarija festival in Cerkno.

Two hundred metres beyond the end of Trubarjeva is **St Peter's Church** (Cerkev Sv Petra), built between 1729 and 1733 according to the designs of the Trieste architect Giovanni Fusconi. Its flat, rectangular facade, with two identical bell towers, is enlivened by several beautiful mosaics created by Ivan and Helena Vurnik, including one of St Peter above the main portal. Inside, the central cupola and vaults were beautifully frescoed by the local artisan Franc Jelovšek with scenes depicting the life of St Peter.

Triple Bridge, Marketplace and around
Linking Prešcrnov trg and the right bank of the **River Ljubljanica** is the enchanting **Triple Bridge** (Tromostovje), a brilliant piece of architecture and Ljubljana's most photographed landmark. In 1929, Plečnik decided to broaden the existing central bridge, which dates from 1842, with two lateral footbridges, in order to make access to the Old Town safer and more convenient for pedestrians; to top it off he added the Renaissance balustrades, based on the rising bridges of Venice's waterways, and rows of lamps, all of which gives the bridge a magical appearance at night. Once across the bridge, turn left onto Adamič-Lundrovo nabrežje and you're immediately confronted with another Plečnik masterpiece – the magnificent **Market Colonnade**, an elongated, gently curving pavilion harbouring a galaxy of excellent food shops (see p.77) and a downstairs fish market. The colonnade runs along the length of the riverbank from the Triple Bridge to the **Dragon Bridge** (Zmajski most), a quite beautiful piece of Secessionist architecture completed in 1901 by the Croatian Jurij Zaninovich, another student of the Vienna Wagner School. Sitting atop the chunky pylons located at each corner of the bridge are four carved, spitting, swirly-tailed dragons – the city symbol.

The two squares adjacent to the Colonnade, **Pogačarjev trg** and the much larger **Vodnikov trg**, have been the site of the wonderfully brash and colourful city **market** (Mon–Sat 8am–3pm) for over a century; it's a great place to stock up on fresh produce, particularly on a Saturday morning when it seems that half the city congregates here. On the southern side of Pogačarjev trg stands the Renaissance-style **Bishop's Palace** (Škofijski dvorec), one of the oldest buildings in the city, dating back to 1512. Once a residence for distinguished guests – Napoleon stayed here in 1797, as did Tsar Alexander I in 1821 – its outstanding feature is the Baroque seventeenth-century arcaded courtyard. On the eastern side of the same square is the **Seminary** (Semenišče), built between 1708 and 1714 and still used by theology students from the dioceses of Koper and Ljubljana; the seminary houses the oldest library in the city, a quite stunning union of Baroque oak-wood furnishings and sky-blue ceiling frescoes representing Theology, Faith and Love by Giulio Quaglio. The stone portal on the southern side – by the flower market – is flanked by two lumbering giants carved by Angelo Pozzo. Visits to the library can be made by contacting the tourist information centre.

St Nicholas's Cathedral
Lording it over Pogačarjev trg, the Baroque **St Nicholas's Cathedral** (Stolnica Sv Nikolaja; daily 6am–noon & 3–6pm), easily spotted from all over town due to its enormous twin bell towers and twenty-four-metre-high dome, is Ljubljana's most important and best-preserved ecclesiastical building. Dedicated to St Nicholas, the patron saint of fishermen and sailors – many of whom lived in the suburb of Krakovo – the present building, designed by Andrea Pozzo from Rome and completed in 1706, stands on the site of a thirteenth-century basilica. Entering through the weighty **bronze door**, designed in 1996 to commemorate the pope's visit and

Jože Plečnik

Born on January 23, 1872 in the Ljubljana suburb of Gradišče, **Jože Plečnik** was an architect of world-class stature, transforming Ljubljana into an architectural and urban planning phenomenon. He also completed countless other projects across the country, establishing an immense body of work encompassing churches and their interior furnishings, town squares and parks, public buildings, and a scattering of columns, pillars and obelisks.

After graduating in carpentry and furniture design at secondary school in Graz, Austria, Plečnik enrolled at the School of Architecture at the Vienna Academy of Fine Arts, excelling under the tutelage of his mentor **Otto Wagner**, whom he would later work with for a brief period. For the most part, though, Plečnik worked independently, renovating numerous buildings and concerning himself with interior design projects. Disillusioned with the growing tide of German nationalism, and the increasingly oppressive atmosphere in the Austrian capital – he also clashed with Archduke Franz Ferdinand, who considered Plečnik's style too flamboyant for his own rather conservative leanings – Plečnik moved on to **Prague** in 1911, where his burgeoning reputation was further enhanced following the execution of several key projects in the Czech city, including the Sacred Heart Church in Vinohrady and the restoration of Hradčany Castle, the latter at the request of President Masaryk.

Although settled in Prague, the lure of a professorship in his home town proved too compelling and, in 1921, he accepted an offer from the newly founded **Ljubljana University** to become head of the school of architecture; moreover, his return presented him with the opportunity to map out and implement his grand vision for the city. Over the next twenty years, and with extremely limited financial resources, Plečnik married classical architectural forms with his own richly imaginative ideas to create a series of monumental new buildings (Market Colonnade, National and University Library, Žale Cemetery to name but three), bridges (Triple Bridge, Shoemakers Bridge) and churches (St Francis in Šiška, St Michael on the Marsh). A key component of his blueprint for this new cityscape was the redesign of large segments of the city, including numerous park areas, squares and streets, as well as sections of the Ljubljanica riverbank. The design of the Križanke complex aside, the post-World War II period was a difficult time for the ageing Plečnik; he received no further major contracts and many other projects conceived during the war, including plans for the new Slovene Parliament, went unrealized.

Despite his extraordinary range and output, Plečnik's work was not appreciated by everybody, not least his contemporaries, most of whom were wed to the more traditional, functionalist principles of architecture, and thus had little time for his, then unorthodox, form of modernism. Indeed it wasn't until some thirty years after his death, following a major retrospective exhibition at the Pompidou Centre in Paris in 1986, that he received the recognition his work deserved. Plečnik died on January 7, 1957 and is buried at Žale Cemetery in Ljubljana.

bearing an impressive relief portraying over a thousand years of Slovene Christianity, you're presented with a riot of fine architecture, immaculate carvings and vibrant frescoes. The cathedral really owes its reputation to the **frescoes** painted by Quaglio between 1703 and 1706, but restored in 2006; these supremely colourful paintings illustrate the many sea-bound miracles of St Nicholas, such as the one depicting him steering a ship full of sailors to safety during a particularly nasty storm. Remarkably, Quaglio painted the presbytery vault, showing the scene of the Establishment of the Ljubljana bishopric, in just twelve days. The most impressive **altar** is in the northern wing of the transept, decorated by an oil painting of the Three Magi by Matevž Langus and further embellished with Robba's delightfully sculpted angels and cherubs. In the opposite, southern wing, is a copy of the

Virgin Mary of Brezje (see p.115), held within a magnificent frame. Note too, the fine Baroque choir seats with gilded reliefs of Christ and the Apostles, and the splendid pulpit, whose author is unknown. Inevitably, Plečnik also had a hand in the proceedings, designing the baptismal font and bishop's throne.

East of Vodnikov trg

The area east of Vodnikov trg is fairly nondescript, though there are a couple of buildings that might be of interest, particularly to fans of Plečnik. At the beginning of Poljanska cesta, you'll pass Plečnik's **Flat Iron Building** (Peglezen), so named after its extraordinary tapered shape; originally constructed as a municipal building in 1934, it now accommodates a shop on the ground floor, and dwellings and a winter garden on the floors above. A few minutes further on, take a right turn down Ulica Janeza Pavla II towards the huge neo-Romanesque **St Joseph's Church** (Cerkev Sv Jožefa), completed in 1922 by the Jesuits. The vast interior is remarkably bare and, aside from Plečnik's monumental semicircular altar, there is literally nothing to see – which probably explains why it was used as a film studio from the end of World War II until its return to a monastery in 1996.

The Old Town

Defined by a tangle of narrow streets, handsome orange-and-red-roofed townhouses, and neat rows of compact pavement cafés, Ljubljana's fabulous **Old Town** is for many the most enjoyable part of the city. Heavily fortified in the twelfth century by the Carinthian dukes, the Old Town – cobbled and mercifully free of traffic – extends from **Mestni trg**, across from the Triple Bridge, south down **Stari trg** to **Levstikov trg** and **Gornji trg**; the entire district is wedged between the Ljubljanica to the west and the castle-topped hill to the east.

Mestni trg

After crossing the Triple Bridge and walking to the end of Stritarjeva, you enter elegant **Mestni trg** (Town Square), the first of three medieval squares that form the backbone of the Old Town. Located on the square's northern fringe is Robba's majestic Baroque **Fountain of the Three Carniolan Rivers**, indisputably his most spectacular piece of work. Allegedly modelled on Bernini's Fountain of the Four Rivers in Rome's Piazza Navona (it is strikingly similar), the fountain, completed in 1751, symbolizes the meeting of the rivers Sava, Krka and Ljubljanica, as represented by three muscular tritons grasping oval jugs, with dolphins splashing at their feet. An ongoing debate centres around whether the fountain should be moved to the entrance hall of the National Gallery, so as to protect it from the icy winters, although it's usually encased in perspex during the colder months anyway.

The square's most prominent and important building is the white- and greybrick **Town Hall** (Magistrat) at no. 1, dating from 1719 and one of the most identifiably Baroque buildings in the city. Sporting a gently protruding balcony and impressive clocktower, the building's most interesting features lie within, namely the arcaded inner courtyards adorned with sgraffiti and featuring two sculptures: the fountain of Narcissus by Robba, and a statue of Hercules, which previously stood in a fountain outside the Stična Mansion on Stari trg. Free tours of the town hall, which include viewings of the banquet and wedding halls, and grand council chamber, take place at noon every Saturday between April and September. Of the many other fine buildings on the square, take a look at no. 24, the **Souvan House** (Souvanova hiša), whose frontage is the most beautiful example of Biedermeier to be found anywhere in the city – note the stucco reliefs under the third-floor windows representing agriculture, art and trade. Opposite the town hall a narrow passageway leads to **Ribji trg** (Fisherman's Square), a small, cobbled square where, during the sixteenth century, the fishermen of Krakovo would bring their freshly caught haul from the Ljubljanica to sell to the local inns and houses. Points of interest here include the house (now a restaurant – see p.78) at no. 2, which dates from 1528 (as indicated by its coat-of-arms), making it one of the oldest residences in the city, and the Neoclassical fountain in the centre featuring a gilded statue of a girl pouring water from a pitcher. The square opens up onto **Cankarjevo nabrežje**, an engaging riverside parade quartering some of the city's busiest and most vibrant bars and cafés, and site of the terrific Sunday flea market (see p.83).

Stari trg to Levstikov trg

Mestni trg gradually tapers southwards towards **Stari trg** (Old Square), Ljubljana's oldest medieval square, a slight misnomer for this narrow, gently curving street. With a sprightly assortment of cafés, restaurants and ice-cream parlours, it's the ideal place to re-energize yourself before pressing on with sightseeing.

Shortly after entering Stari trg, take a right down Pod Trančo – formerly the site of a jail ("tranča" means jail) – which opens up onto the expansive **Shoemakers Bridge** (Čevljarski most), so named after a group of local cobblers set up their trading booths here. Prior to their arrival, the bridge was settled by a group of butchers, but so troubled were the locals by the stench that the then emperor, Maximilian I, paid them all off to relocate elsewhere. Remarkably, there has been a bridge of sorts here since the thirteenth century, though this, the second of Plečnik's bridges, was built in 1932.

Back on Stari trg, at no. 11a, is the **Schweiger House**, showcasing a splendid Rococo facade. The stone telamon supporting the wrought-iron balcony above the main portal has a finger raised to his lips in an apparent request for silence – Schweiger, the name of the German owner, meaning "the silent one". The house was later owned by the poet Lily Nova, a bust of whom sits to the left of the main entrance. A few doors down at no. 21 is the **Škuc Gallery** (Tues–Sun noon–8pm; free), a wing of the Škuc Cultural Society, formed in 1978 as a counterpoint to the exhibition policies of the then-dominant state cultural institutions; the gallery hosts imaginative temporary exhibitions by both local and foreign artists.

Beyond the gallery, Stari trg opens up into **Levstikov trg** (Levstik Square), considered to be the true centre of the Old Town and bounded by some notable buildings and monuments. In the centre of the square is the **Hercules Fountain**, a 1991 copy of the original, now in the town hall. A few paces west of the fountain, the **Stična Mansion** (Stiški dvorec), built as a town residence for the abbots of the Stična Monastery in 1630 (which was abolished in 1784) now houses the Academy of Music. During the Counter-Reformation period, the Jesuits settled in and around the square, acquiring a number of houses as well as introducing a grammar school and college here. Their main legacy, however, was **St James's Church** (Cerkev Sv Jakoba), the first Jesuit church in Slovenia, a bright lemon-yellow structure completed in 1615 and festooned with some magnificent sculptures. Retaining only the presbytery from the preceding Gothic church, the present layout is unusual, comprising a Baroque nave with rows of lateral chapels either side, each adorned with colourful Venetian-style stone altars designed by the local stonemason Luka Mislej, the author of most of the altar sculptures. The high altar, another by Robba, is a far more modest take on his other works, but no less impressive – he also made the marvellous sculptures in the Altar of St Anne, the third chapel on the left. The church's most significant addition, the octagonal chapel of St Francis Xavier, was completed in 1670, and features another marble altar with unusual statues of a "White Queen" and "Black King". The church is more often than not closed, so try and visit during daily evening mass (6.30pm) or one of the several Sunday morning services. Next to the church stands the slender column of the Virgin Mary, erected in 1682 in honour of victory over the Turks at Monošter (now Szentgotthard) in Hungary; the pedestal with four saints, underneath the bronze figure of Mary, was added by Plečnik when he redesigned the square between the two world wars.

Across the busy main road is the custard-coloured pile of the **Gruber Palace** (Gruberjeva palača), built by the Jesuit Gabriel Gruber between 1773 and 1781 for the purposes of research into mechanics and hydraulics; it now houses the National Archives of Slovenia. However, its real architectural delights are concealed within, in particular a wonderful Baroque oval staircase with stucco flower plaits, the dome with an allegorical fresco representing trade, craft and technology, and the chapel on the second floor with oil paintings by the Austrian Kremser-Schmidt. Visits, which are free, can be arranged by appointment (T01/241-4256).

Gornji trg

Arching eastwards from Levstikov trg is **Gornji trg** (Upper Square), a lovely, gently inclining street whose dwellings, notwithstanding the Baroque elements, have retained a number of medieval characteristics – three windows, wide with triangular gables, slightly set back from each other and separated by narrow passageways. As you walk along the street, keep your eye out for a number of interesting details, notably the rustic stone relief of St Christopher, thought to date from around 1530, on the front of the house at no. 1; the bronze plaque with a portrait of the historian Baltazar Haquet at no. 4; and, at no. 16, the sign on the portal denoting that the painter Valentin Metzinger once lived here.

Crowning the upper end of the street is **St Florian's Church**, built in 1672 following a fire twelve years earlier that wiped out the majority of houses along here – St Florian is the patron saint of firefighters and protection from fires. Above all else, the church has some intriguing external elements: in the 1930s Plečnik moved the entrance so that the statue of the Bohemian prelate St John of Nepomuk was placed in front of the original, now walled up, portal. Robba's dramatic relief, in the niche under the pedestal, is of St John being thrown from the Charles Bridge into the Vltava River in Prague. Look out too for the built-in head of an Emona citizen, thought to date from 2 AD; the two niches with badly damaged statues of Charles the Great and St Charles of Borromeo; and the fountain with a portrait of a mask from whence water spouts. Beyond the church, the building at no. 27 features a late-Baroque statue of the Virgin and Child; at one stage it was an asylum for orphans, which earned it the rather disdainful slur, "the shitty school". If you're looking for somewhere a little bit more upmarket to dine, Gornji trg contains several of the city's finest restaurants (see p.78).

Ljubljana Castle

Peeking out above lush woodland high above the Old Town on Castle Hill, **Ljubljana Castle** (Ljubljanski Grad; daily: May–Sept 9am–10pm; Oct–April 10am–9pm; free), with its immaculate whitewashed walls and silky, manicured lawns, does little to give the impression of a residence dating back to the twelfth century, although much of what remains today is actually sixteenth-century, following the earthquake in 1511. Its first inhabitants were the Spanheim family of Carinthian dukes who settled here during the twelfth century, before the provincial lords of the Carniolan province, along with the Habsburgs, took over residence in the fourteenth century. Thereafter, the castle was used as a military fortress, a provincial jail and as a refuge for the poor. Crossing the bridge into the castle, you can see, on the right, the remains of the cells where prisoners were held.

In 1905 the castle was taken over by the municipal authorities, with the intention of using it as a cultural centre, although in the event it continued to house convicts, including the writer Ivan Cankar who was imprisoned here for six weeks in 1914. Furthermore, the chronic housing shortage in the city meant that additional tenements had to be constructed, most of which remained occupied until the 1960s. Systematic development has continued ever since, including the excavation of a **lapidarium** (this can only be visited if part of an organized group) and the addition of the excellent **Virtual Museum** (Virtualni muzej; daily: May–Sept 9am–9pm; Oct–April 10am–6pm; €4, which includes entrance to the clocktower); it's not a museum in the conventional sense, but an enlightening twenty-minute 3D visual presentation chronicling the city's urban and architectural development and its cultural and economic growth. Aside from the museum there's not an awful lot to see, though the fifteenth-century Gothic **Chapel of St George** on the western side of the courtyard – one of the oldest remaining parts of the castle – is worth a look for its colourful and remarkably intact coats-of-arms, representing the Carniolan provincial governors. Most visitors, though, come here to climb the landmark **Clocktower**, built in 1848 but subsequently raised, and now affording wide and superlative views of the city and the Kamniške Alps to the north. The vast courtyard, meanwhile, stages many of the city's principal cultural happenings, including a good number of events connected to the International Summer Festival (see box p.82).

If you don't have a car, you can take the **tourist train**, which leaves from Prešernov trg every hour, on the hour (daily 8am–9pm; €2.50 return), or walk. Three paths wind up to the top, each a stiff fifteen-minute climb: south of Vodnikov trg follow the path up Študentovska ulica; on Stari trg follow Reber Way and then Osojna steza; and from St Florian's Church on Gornji trg take Ulica na Grad.

Left Bank of the Ljubljanica

The left bank of the Ljubljanica, defined here as the area between **Kongresni trg** and **Zoisova cesta** to the south, holds more magnificent architectural set-pieces, as well as vestiges from Roman Emona and some of Plečnik's greatest work. Its medieval heritage is most pronounced in **Novi trg**, the second oldest square in the city – it too was once surrounded by ramparts which extended as far south as Zoisova cesta.

Kongresni trg and around

From Prešernov trg, Wolfova ulica leads south to **Kongresni trg** (Congress Square), a popular, grassy park shaded by leafy plane trees and fringed by a number of venerable architectural gems. Also called Zvezda ("Star"), on account of its vaguely star-shaped path design, the square was laid out in 1821 for the staging of the Congress of the Holy Alliance, before which time it was the site of a Capuchin Monastery. Having been present on the site for just over two hundred years, the monastery – though never officially abolished – was converted into a barracks by the French in 1810, before being deserted and the ruins eventually cleared to make way for the congress; all that remains is the **drinking fountain** in the centre of the square. Occupying the northwestern corner of the square is the **Kazina** (Casino), a lovely Classicist mansion built in 1837 by the Kazina Society for the purposes of entertaining the Ljubljana elite, largely in the form of dances, evenings of song and other prestigious social events. Among the society's more distinguished patrons was France Prešeren, who spent many an evening here with his contemporaries; the Kazina is even recalled in several of his poems. The building's present-day functions are somewhat more prosaic, housing a bookshop and dance school. Between the two world wars, the Kazina also accommodated the posh *Café Zvezda* – its rather less refined modern-day equivalent, located a little further down on the northeastern corner, serves up some of the best cakes and desserts in town (see p.81).

Recessed within a row of buildings on the western side of the square (across the road) is the **Ursuline Church of the Holy Trinity** (Uršulinska Cerkev Sv Trojice), completed in 1726 and perhaps the most original Baroque statement in Ljubljana. Its fading coffee-coloured frontage, incorporating six thick columns and a graceful triangular ridged gable containing Gothic arches, is designed in Palladian style – its curved side wings serve as the entrances. The bright, airy interior, unpainted and completely white, is rather less elaborate, the exception being Robba's dazzling high altar; made from multicoloured African marble and adorned with the allegorical figures of Faith, Hope and Charity, it ranks alongside his most distinguished work. Other notable artwork includes the side altar paintings by Metzinger, and the wooden altar of Ecce Homo with a relief of the Virgin and Child, dating from 1638. The pillar of the **Holy Trinity** opposite the church was brought here by Plečnik in 1930 from Ajdovščina, just off Slovenska cesta.

Located next to the church on the corner of Slovenska cesta and Plečnikov trg, the little known **Slovene School Museum** (Slovenski Šolski Muzej; Mon–Fri 9am–1pm; €2) charts the history of Slovene schooling from the Middle Ages to the end of the twentieth century. Housed in the building of the former Ursuline school, its displays, divided by periods, include a diverse selection of educational memorabilia, ranging from books and reports to teaching aids and uniforms, as well as a couple of mock-up classrooms complete with chalkboards and desks. Alas, the absence of English captions makes what would otherwise be an engaging visit somewhat frustrating.

The square's most prepossessing building is the buttermilk-coloured **Slovene Philharmonic Hall** (Slovenska filharmonija), whose orchestra, in its various guises, has been performing on this site for over three hundred years; although this building only dates from 1892, it's one of the oldest musical institutions in Europe. Given its modest size, Slovenia's musical heritage is remarkably strong. The Academia Philharmonicorum, established in 1701, was the forerunner to today's Philharmonic, which subsequently became one of the foremost musical institutions in the Habsburg Empire. Its reputation was further enhanced by a roll-call of distinguished honorary members – Haydn, Beethoven and Mozart to name just three – and it employed Gustav Mahler to conduct here for the 1881/1882 season. For more information on attending a performance, see p.83. Diagonally across from the Philharmonic, the immense neo-Renaissance **University building**, built between 1899 and 1902, has functioned as the main seat of the university since 1919, and today also houses the Faculty of Law. Busts of academic luminaries, including one of Plečnik, form a semicircular sweep around the entrance.

South of Kongresni trg

Vegova ulica, the main street darting southwards from Kongresni trg, was once the westernmost boundary of the medieval city walls. It received its present appearance during the interwar period courtesy of Plečnik, who rearranged the entire street, punctuating it with several of his greatest monuments. The first building of note, on the right-hand side at no. 4, houses the **Faculty of Engineering**, its stately neo-Romanesque facade and thrusting corner towers more than a match for the university building opposite. Across the road is the **Music School** (Glasbena Matica), distinguished by portrait reliefs on the facade, and busts of Slovene musicians – as well as a Croat and a Serb – lining the wall in front of the building; although Plečnik's idea, they were sculpted by his colleague Lojze Dolinar.

Taking five years to complete (1936–41), the **National and University Library** (Narodna in univerzitetna knjižnica; Visiting hours for tourists and non-library members: Mon–Tues & Thurs–Sat 2pm–6pm, Wed 4pm–6pm, Sun 9am–5pm; free; ⓦwww.nuk.uni-lj.si), occupying the entire block between Turjaška ulica and the Križanke, is Plečnik's most lauded piece of work. Located on the site of a former palace, its extraordinary, variegated facade, consisting of rough grey stone quarried from Vrhnika and smooth orange brick from Podpeč is one of the city's most outstanding, and conspicuous, landmarks. Upon entering the building from Turjaška ulica – note the smart bronze horse-head handles on the copper-covered wooden door – you're confronted with a dark staircase ascending to a vestibule lined with black marble columns, the walk up symbolically meant to represent the journey from darkness to light, or, from ignorance to knowledge. Beyond here, and filling the entire width of one wing of the building, is the magnificent reading room, worth visiting for its furnishings, and in particular its "catherine wheel" chandeliers and industrial-style reading lamps.

Vegova ulica winds up at **Trg Francoske revolucije** (French Revolution Square), whose main point of reference is the stern, square-shaped **Illyrian Monument**, designed by Plečnik in 1929 in belated recognition of Ljubljana's short-lived stint as the capital of Napoleon's Illyrian Provinces (1809–13). The obelisk, made from white marble from the island of Hvar in Croatia, is embellished with the Illyrian coat-of-arms – a crescent moon with three stars – and gilded bronze masks of Napoleon and Illyria. Retained within the core of the monument are the ashes of an unknown French soldier, killed in battle in 1813. The **Friedl-Rechar House**, the curved, crumbling building on the western corner of the square, was once a palace accommodating shops and apartments; its ground floor now houses *Le Petite Café*, one of Ljubljana's most frequented and atmospheric haunts (see p.81).

A few paces south of here is the majestic **Križanke**, formerly the monastic complex of the Teutonic knights but now the setting for the city's prestigious International Summer Festival and other major concerts (see box on p.82). Its present appearance dates from the mid-1950s, when Plečnik, in his last great contribution to the city – he was eighty upon its completion – set about transforming the abandoned monastery into an open-air theatre and festival space. The complex's original Gothic details were gradually usurped by Renaissance and Baroque elements, which can be most clearly seen in the main courtyard, which also features shallow archways and exuberantly coloured sgraffiti. Next door, the amphitheatre-like southern courtyard, with its vast retractable canopy, is a superb venue for classical, jazz and rock concerts. Plečnik also designed the **Devil's Courtyard** (Peklensko dvorišče), accessible through the restaurant (in itself nothing special) and spotted with neat rows of weird-looking wall lamps. On the east side of the complex is the modest **Church of Our Lady of Mercy** (Cerkev Marija Pomočnica), built between 1714 and 1715.

The City Museum

Between Križanke and the Ljubljanica the chief attraction is the **Auersperg Mansion** (Auerspergova palača), adjacent to Križanke at Gosposka ulica 15. After residing here for over three hundred years, the Turjak counts, a noble Slovene family with roots going back to the eleventh century, sold the palace to the city authorities who subsequently used the premises to house the **City Museum** (Mestni Muzej; Tues–Sun 10am–6pm; €2). Following a painstaking, decade-long renovation programme, the museum reopened in 2005, and the building itself once again looks fantastic. An impressive stock of archeological remains can be viewed down in the basement, including part of the original Roman road that once linked Emona to the port on the Ljubljanica river, though the greater part of the museum is given over to the lives and the people (ljubljančani) who have inhabited the city over the course of time. Up on the second floor, in the proto-col (or Mayoral) room, take a look at the statues of Adam and Eve, sculpted by Janez Lipec in 1484, and a portrait of Ljubljana's most revered mayor, Ivan Hribar (1851–1941), painted by Slovenia's greatest female artist Ivana Kobilica, more of whose work can be seen at the National Gallery (see p.71). There's a very pleasant café on site too (same times as museum).

Novi trg and around

Continuing along Gosposka ulica, which runs parallel to Vegova ulica, you'll pass the eastern side of the National and University Library – and, above its second entrance, a dramatic sculpture of Moses, by Dolinar – before reaching **Novi trg** (New Square), a rectangular, sloping space extending down to the Ljubljanica. The square is framed by some wonderful seventeenth- and eighteenth-century mansions, the best example of which is the **Lontovž** on the corner at no. 3; built in 1790, it has housed the Slovenian Academy of Arts and Sciences since 1938. In its courtyard stands a beautiful fountain of Neptune, the precursor to Robba's fountain on Mestni trg (see p.63).

By taking a left turn at the bottom of Novi trg, and walking on a few paces, you'll find yourself back at the Shoemakers Bridge, which lies next to another, smaller square, Jurčičev trg. **Židovska steža** (Jewish Lane) and **Židovska ulica** (Jewish Street), immediately west of the bridge, together once comprised Ljublja-na's small Jewish ghetto. Neither the synagogue, which once stood at Židovska steža 4, nor any other original tenements remain, although a new synagogue – Slovenia's third – was opened in 2003; it's located a ten-minute walk southwest of the centre at Tržaška cesta 2. Jews have played little more than a walk-on role in Slovenian history and it remains unclear as to when they first settled in the country, though it is believed that there was a Jewish presence here in the twelfth century. What is known is that following an edict by Emperor Maximilian in 1515, all Jews were banished from Ljubljana, with the majority fleeing to neigh-bouring Italy and Hungary, and some being dispersed to Slovene villages. Today, it is estimated that around three hundred Jews live in Slovenia, most of whom have settled in Ljubljana.

Treasures of the Ljubljanica

The languid, muddy-green waters of the Ljubljanica have for centuries concealed one of Slovenia's most unlikely, and extraordinary, archeological sites. Over the past thirty years or so a remarkable number of ancient artefacts have been retrieved from the riverbed, including Bronze Age sickles and helmets, Iron Age spearheads, 2000-year-old Hallstatt bracelets, Roman pots, and medieval swords and brooches, proof, if any were needed, that the river was a key centre of activity and movement long before its heyday in the seventeenth and eighteenth centuries.

Some of these items, many of which have been superbly preserved owing to centuries of submersion, are held at the National Museum (see p.73), though many more have been gathered up by amateur archeologists, and hence reside in private collections. If you fancy taking a trip along a stretch of the river, there are one-hour guided excursions during the summer, embarking from Ribji trg (April, May & Oct Mon–Fri 5.30pm, Sat & Sun 10.30am and 5.30pm; June–Sept Mon–Fri 6.30pm, Sat & Sun 10.30am & 6.30pm; €7). Tickets are available from the departure point or the tourist information centres.

Turning right at the bottom of Novi trg brings you to **Breg** (Embankment), a river wharf in the fourteenth century when the Ljubljanica was a navigable waterway. Indeed, the river remained the city's principal transport artery, with Breg as its chief port, until the end of the eighteenth century, when the widespread construction of the railways – and in particular the building of the Vienna–Trieste line – spelt its death knell. The boats and ships that used to dock here would sail up from Vrhnika, near its source 20km south of Ljubljana, laden with wood, salt and other goods from the Mediterranean.

Krakovo

A short walk south of Breg is the genteel suburb of Krakovo, reachable from either Emonska ulica – an extension of Vegova ulica – or from Breg, both routes crossing busy Zoisova cesta. During the Middle Ages Krakovo was largely settled by fishermen, many of whom supplemented their income by working as *Pelajhtarji* (light carriers), which entailed escorting the local citizens home late at night from the theatre or the inn. Horticulture is now the prime activity here and one of the first things you'll notice are the strips of magnificently tended vegetable plots, the results of which sustain the daily market on Vodnikov trg.

In parts, the area still retains a wonderful, medieval village-like character and this is especially true of Krakovska ulica, with its handsome, one- and two-storey squat houses; the street was once the haunt of prominent town artists, including the celebrated Slovenian Impressionist painter Rihard Jakopič (1869–1943) who was born at no. 11. Jakopič actually worked a short walk west of Krakovska at Mirje 4, in what is now called the **Jakopič Garden** (Jakopičev vrt), site of some Roman ruins including black and white mosaics and the remains of a complex heating system. If you wish to see the ruins close up – it's only possible to catch a glimpse

△ Gardens in the Krakovo district

of them from the gate – then contact the Cultural Information Centre of the City Museum in advance (℡01/251-4025). West of the garden, across Barjanska cesta and spanning almost the entire length of Mirje, is a reconstructed section of the **Roman city wall** (Rimski Zid), topped with an incongruous looking pyramid – one of Plečnik's less-inspired concepts.

Trnovo

"Trnovo, a place of miserable name", Prešeren once wrote of Krakovo's attractive neighbouring suburb. It can be reasonably assumed that the motive for this mildly apoplectic outburst was an unrequited love affair, for it was here in 1833 that Prešeren met his great love Julija Primic, who, tragically for the poet, never reciprocated his feelings. Prešeren first set eyes on Primic in the towering neo-Romanesque **Church of St John the Baptist**, built in 1855 but radically altered following the 1895 earthquake. The stark, bare interior has few highlights, though the presbytery ceiling frescoes by Matej Sternen are worth a look. The bronze relief plate to the right of the main door features portraits of Plečnik and the parish priest and writer Franc Finžgar. With the exception of Mass, the church is usually closed, so try calling at the priest's door to the right of the church if you wish to have a look. Facing the church is the Plečnik-designed **Trnovo Bridge**, completed in 1932 and incorporating several ungainly stone pyramids, a statue of St John the Baptist and rows of birch trees on either side. Leafy Eipprova ulica, the street running eastwards from the bridge along the Gradaščica canal's southern embankment, is well worth checking out for its delightfully quirky cafés and bars (see p.80).

Directly behind the church at Karunova ulica 4 is **Plečnik's House** (Plečnikova hiša; Tues–Thurs 10am–2pm & 4–6pm, Sat 10am–2pm; €3), where the great man lived from 1921 until his death in 1957. Most of this fascinating and neatly preserved collection of equipment, books, plans and furniture is located in the cylindrical annexe which Plečnik purposely built to house his studio. The house exemplifies Plečnik's extraordinary commitment to modesty, each room practically yet creatively schemed. Among the more interesting rooms are his studio, with desks bearing numerous instruments, plans and models; the spartan-looking bathroom complete with ingenious wood-heated shower; the small reception room, where he would receive friends and colleagues – note the stove with its built-in copper kettle; and the kitchen, containing his special chair that enabled him to eat and work at the same time. Having browsed around the house, it's hard to reconcile such a modest man with the grand structures that have left such an indelible mark on this city.

West of Slovenska cesta

The neatly ordered district west of Slovenska cesta contains some of the city's most significant museums. Heading west along Cankarjeva cesta, you'll pass the horseshoe-shaped, neo-Renaissance **Opera House**, constructed in 1892 and home to the Slovenian National Opera and Ballet companies (see p.83). Within the impressive tympanum above the main entrance are the figures of Poetry and Glory, above which is a statue of Genius; in the niches in the facade either side of the main entrance stand the allegorical figures of Comedy and Tragedy.

The National Gallery

At the end of Cankarjeva ulica is the **National Gallery** (Narodna galerija; Tues–Sun 10am–6pm; €4.5; Sat free admission after 2pm; ⓦwww.ng-slo.si), whose modest but rewarding two-part collection makes this one of the city's more deserving visits. The collection is actually located in two buildings: the exhibition of Slovenian painting is housed in Slovenski Dom (National House), a grandiloquent, Habsburg-era pile facing Cankarjeva ulica, and initially designed to house a range of Slovene cultural institutions. The exhibition of European painting is located in the northern extension, a stark postmodernist building around the corner on Prešernova ulica; the two buildings were connected in 2001 by a walkway and glass-fronted entrance.

The Slovene collection, which presents Slovene art from the Middle Ages through to Impressionism, is located up the stairs and to the right. The collection kicks off with **medieval art** and a superb display of Gothic statuary and frescoes, the most interesting of which are located immediately to the left and right as you enter; the most renowned piece is the exquisite, almost porcelain-like *Standing Madonna* (minus Jesus, who was cut off) from the Ptujska gora workshop, thought to date from around 1410. Other notable pieces here include the tympanum with the relief of *Madonna on Solomon's Throne*, which once stood in Križanke, and the fragment of the fresco of *Madonna and Child*, from the late fourteenth century. From here, you enter the grand main hall containing paintings from the **Baroque** and **Neoclassical** periods. Its highlight is the *Cardplayers* by Almanach, considered to be the most important seventeenth-century group portrait in the country (this Dutch piece is included here, as opposed to in the European section, as Almanach worked extensively in the former Slovene province of Carniola). There is also an impressive clutch of paintings by Valentin Metzinger and Franc Jelovšek, two of the country's foremost exponents of eighteenth-century church painting – the former was principally concerned with oils, whereas Jelovšek was almost entirely devoted to painting wall and ceiling frescoes. Next up after a rather ordinary collection of **Biedermeiers** are the **Realists**, with a superb offering by its leading representatives, Janez and Jurij Šubic, including the fine *Before the Hunt* and the melancholic *Alone*, both by Jurij. One of the more curious pieces here is by Jožef Petkovšek, whose bleak *At Home* is notable for the missing arm and lower body of his mother – it's believed he'd gone mad by the time he painted this. There is also a wonderful collection by Ivana Kobilca (1861–1926), Slovenia's most celebrated female painter; amongst her finest works are the cheeky-looking *Woman Drinking Coffee* and the joyous *Summer*.

After passing through a room of bronze busts and statues, the exhibition finishes on a high, with an outstanding collection of work from Slovenia's highly revered **Impressionist** painters. This distinguished group of four artists was led by Ivan Grohar (1867–1911), renowned for investing great emotion in his dreamlike landscapes, such as the masterful *Sower* and *Škofja Loka in Snowstorm*. Rihard Jakopič, a close colleague of Grohar, was a painter of bolder, more expressionist works, as shown in his paintings *Memories* and *The Green Veil/Girl with Crown*. The third and fourth members of this quartet, Matej Sternen and Matija Jama, produced works of a brighter, more orthodox bent, for example in Sternen's *The Red Parasol* and Jama's *Village in Winter*.

The **European collection** is a less thrilling affair, although there are one or two notable highlights, such as another *Cardplayers* by Almanach – the players in this one considerably more worse for wear. One of the collection's most prestigious paintings is *Empress Maria Theresa* by Martin van Meytens, located in the Central European section.

Museum of Modern Art

Diagonally across from the National Gallery, the **Museum of Modern Art** (Moderna galerija; Tues–Sat 10am–6pm; €3; Ⓦ www.mg-lj.si) takes over from where the National Gallery left off, namely Slovene art from the 1950s onwards.

However, it's a bit of a mixed bag and comes as something of a disappointment after its counterpart. It does, however, stage excellent temporary exhibitions. The highlights from the first hall are the smooth sculptures by Zdenko Kalin and Jakob Savinšek, while the second hall is the most heterogeneous – by virtue of the fact that the work on display spans the 1960s to the 1980s. The most intriguing pieces are Lojze Spacal's wooden sculpture of Downing Street and Rudolf Kotnik's series of oddly shaped canvases interwoven with metal plates and wires. Also worth taking a look at are the exhibits by the retro-avant-garde collective Irwin, who co-founded the controversial and influential Neue Slowenische Kunst or NSK (New Slovene Art) movement in the mid-1980s. The exhibition winds up with a bunch of odd, media-inspired pieces from the 1990s and a more sobering piece of work – a vase created from a mortar shell that fell on Sarajevo.

The National Museum and the Natural History Museum

A short walk southeast of the Museum of Modern Art, at Prešernova 20, lies the **National Museum** (Narodni muzej; Tues–Sun 10am–6pm, Thurs til 8pm; €3; Ⓦwww.narmuz.lj.si), housed in this handsome Rudolfinum building since 1888 and graced at the entrance by four allegorical figures representing Art, History, Natural History and Labour. Inside there's a magnificent double staircase with beautiful sculptures of reclining muses, and ceiling frescoes executed by the Šubic brothers. Much of the museum's rich permanent collection remains under wraps, but its extensive stockpile of archeological treasures is now on show, the most noteworthy item being the Neanderthal flute discovered at the Divje Babe Cave near Cerkno in 1995 (see p.187); there is also a hoard of finds excavated from the unlikely source of the Ljubljanica river (see box on p.69), as well as a tremendous stash of Stone-Age pottery and tools, Copper-age vessels and implements from the Ljubljana Marshes, and Celtic weaponry and jewellery.

Located on the second floor of the building is the **Natural History Museum** (Prirodoslovni muzej; same hours and ticket; Ⓦwww2.pms-lj.si), featuring an almost complete twenty-thousand-year-old skeleton of a mammoth found near Kamnik in 1938, and a two-hundred-million-year-old fossilized fish skeleton found near Triglav. The museum's most impressive assemblage, and one of the most important collections of its kind in Slovenia, is the Zois Collection of Minerals, named after the eminent mineralogist Žiga Zois. To round things off, there is a small multimedia presentation of the extraordinary Proteus Anguinus (aka "The Human Fish"), the largest cave-dwelling vertebrate in the world (see the *Subterranean Slovenia* colour section).

Trg Republike and around

South of the National Museum is the vast concrete car park of **Trg Republike** (Republic Square), the largest and, by some distance the ugliest square in the city, embraced by unsightly postmodern buildings. Shadowing the south side are two towering office blocks, behind which is **Cankarjev Dom**, the country's most capacious cultural and congress centre, named in honour of the great Slovene novelist Ivan Cankar; the centre's two galleries regularly host top-class exhibitions (Tues–Sat 10am–7pm, Sun 10am–2pm; Ⓦwww.cd-cc.si; free). Residing on the north side is the unexceptional **Parliament** building, worth a glance for its portal, framed by blackened statues depicting the working-class family and various industries. It was in front of here, on the night of June 26, 1991, that President Milan Kučan unfurled the new Slovene flag and pronounced "This evening dreams are allowed, tomorrow is a new day" – the thousands celebrating on the square oblivious to the fact that, in a matter of hours, they would be at war (see box on p.335).

Between the two office blocks, across Erjavčeva ulica and behind the primary school, are further **ruins** of Emona. Discovered during excavations in 1969, the finds included part of a baptistry and portico, as well as some lovely mosaics. The gate is likely to be closed but it is possible to see a reasonable amount from a distance. However, if you wish to see it close up contact the Cultural Information Centre of the City Museum (☏01/251-4025). East along Erjavčeva cesta, on the corner of Slovenska cesta, is the muddy-green **Slovene National Theatre** (Narodno Gledališče), also known as the German Theatre – on account of the fact that it was initially intended for German-speaking audiences only, with Slovenian performances taking place in the Opera House.

A five-minute walk southwest of Erjavčeva at Tobačna ulica 5 is the **Tobacco Museum** (Tobačni muzej; first Wed and third Thurs of each month 10am–6pm; free; ⓦwww.tobacna.si), housed in the Ljubljana Tobacco company building. Despite the absence of English captions, it's one of Ljubljana's more enlightening museums, though you'll do well to get a visit in as it's rarely open. The collection, neatly presented in gleaming glass cabinets, documents the processing and use of tobacco from the factory's establishment from 1871 to the present day, as well as the lives of those who worked in the factory. Prior to the introduction of machines at the beginning of the twentieth century, the factory employed mainly women (known as *cigarice* or "cigar ladies") as they were deemed to be more dextrous, a prerequisite for the delicate task of hand-rolling hundreds of cigars each day. Aside from photographs and documents there are some wonderful tobacco products, including a superb display of beautifully crafted pipes, cigar holders and snuff boxes.

Tivoli Park

If you're looking for a bit of peace and relaxation you won't have to go far. To the west of Trg Republike, beyond Tivolski cesta, is Tivoli Park, a lush expanse of greenery carved up by broad promenades and backed by dense woodland and hills; it's also a major recreation centre with the city's principal sporting facilities located here. The park is accessible from a number of routes, though the most direct is via the subway by the Museum of Modern Art. Exiting the subway, head up Jakopič Promenade, laid out by Plečnik and split down the middle by a row of shabby lampposts, towards **Tivoli Castle** (Tivolski Grad). Since being transformed into a mansion by the Jesuits in 1713, it has been used as a military hospital and barracks, and as a residence for city officials. Local rumour has it that the creator of the cast-iron dogs by the staircase, Anton Fernkorn, was so disturbed by omitting their tongues that – in what might be construed as an over-reaction – he shot himself. The mansion is now the permanent home of the **International Centre of Graphic Arts** (Mednarodni Grafični Likovni Center; Wed–Sun 11am–6pm; €2; ⓦwww.mglc-lj.org), an enterprising institution devoted to the promotion and printing of graphic art. Its chief activity, however, is the organization of the International Graphic Arts Biennial, the world's longest-running graphic-arts exhibition – a prestigious, three-month-long event taking place between June and September every odd-numbered year.

Up on the northern edge of the park is the brilliant-white Baroque mansion of the **Sequin Castle** (Cekinov grad), which, since 1951, has housed the enlightening **Museum of Modern History** (Muzej novejše zgodovine; Tues–Sun 10am–6pm; €3, free first Sun of the month; ⓦwww.muzej-nz.si). The collection, much of it presented in multimedia form, is arranged chronologically, each room representing a period of twentieth-century Slovenia. The starting point is World War I, featuring several mock-up shelters and a remarkable display of photos and mementoes from the battlefields. The collection moves swiftly on to the interwar period, and illustrates the struggle to establish the country within the new Kingdom of Serbs, Croats and Slovenes. This first part concludes with World War II and a rapid-fire projection of 1500 photos onto the surrounding walls, accompanied by thunderous sound effects. Among the more interesting exhibits in this room, which includes uniforms from the warring sides, is a chess set made from bread and saliva by a prisoner of war. The following rooms are devoted to war damage reconstruction and daily life in socialist Yugoslavia, with particular emphasis on the Slovenian economy. Of interest to most will be the last room, which documents the events leading up to Slovenia's gaining independence in 1991, including the accompanying Ten Days' War (see box on p.335); exhibits include the remains of a Yugoslav army helicopter shot down and items dumped by the army as they retreated.

Rožnik Hill and the Zoo

Bunched up behind Tivoli Park are a number of modest peaks, sewn together by a network of tidy, well-signposted tracks. The most popular short hike (approx 45min) is up to **Rožnik Hill**, accessible via a number of paths, the best of which begins from behind Tivoli Castle. Having made it to the top, you can take a break and buy some refreshments at the **Cankar Inn**, once periodically the home of Ivan Cankar; opposite is a memorial room (April–Oct Sat & Sun 11am–6pm; free) containing a few of his personal effects and some original furniture. The **Church of St Mary's Visitation**, just down from the inn, was built in 1740 – the high altar has a particularly fine painting by Jurij Šubic (visits during Mass only; May–Sept 10.30am).

Nestling in thick woodland on the southern slope of the hill is the city **Zoo** (Živalski vrt; Tues–Sun: April–Oct 9am–7pm; Nov–March 9am–4pm; €5), an impressively landscaped park, with more than a few steep paths and an exhaustive range of animals, which will at least keep the kids happy. No buses head this way, though the #14 passes through the suburb of Vič, a fifteen-minute walk south (alight at Cesta XV); otherwise, from Tivoli Castle it's a thirty-minute walk around the southern rim of Tivoli Park (along Cesta 27 aprila then Večna pot).

North of the centre

Otherwise unexceptional, the area north of the centre has a few sights worthy of exploration, most of which, inevitably, bear Plečnik's unmistakable stamp. West of the train station, at the intersection of Celovška cesta and Ruska ulica (opposite Tivoli Park) is the **Brewery Museum** (Pivovarski muzej; first Tues of the month by appointment; €3; ☎01/471-7340, ⓦwww.pivo-union.si), located in the old malt-house of the sprawling Union Brewery – founded in 1864 by the cartographer Peter Kosler and one of the two largest breweries in the country. The two-part visit first takes in a tour of the filtration and bottling plants where some sixty thousand bottles are filled each hour, followed by the museum proper, whose exhibits include century-old wooden barrels, carts for carrying crates and a fine collection of beer mugs and tankards. Slovenes consume on average 87 litres of beer a year, which places them in a steady mid-table position in the European league of drinkers.

Close by is the **Railway Museum** (Železniški muzej; Tues–Sun 10am–6pm; €2), which is actually split between two locations. In the roundhouse at Parmova ulica 35 is a marvellous collection of old steam locomotives and rolling stock – sure to get rail buffs misty-eyed – while 300m further south, at Kurilniška ulica 3, there is a more straightforward exhibition presenting the history and development of the Slovenian rail network.

A fifteen-minute walk north of these museums in the suburb of Šiška is the first of the city's two Plečnik-designed churches, the **Church of St Francis of**

Assisi (Cerkev Sv Frančiška Asiškega), Verovškova ulica (bus #22 to Drenikova ulica), distinguished by its double-storey, cylindrical belfry topped with a cone. Completed in 1931, this is the least conventional of Ljubljana's churches, its square main hall with a high, flat wooden ceiling and rows of square windows more redolent of a school gymnasium than your average place of worship. A colonnade of chunky, circular brick pillars forms a kind of inner square, in the centre of which is a pyramid-shaped altar; both this and the chandeliers are classic Plečnik.

From the church, head eastwards along Drenikova ulica, and then Samova ulica, for twenty minutes (or take bus #22 from Drenikova) until you reach Dunajska cesta in the suburb of Bežigrad. On your left is the modestly sized **Central Stadium** (Centralni Stadion), formerly home to the now defunct local football team, Olimpija Ljubljana, but now only used for major rock concerts. It's rare for sports stadiums to be given such a classy touch, but here Plečnik embellished the arena using his favoured motif of columns in both the interior (the elegant pavilion) and the exterior (the colonnade) – unfortunately, you can only catch a glimpse of the pavilion through the gates.

One and a half kilometres east of the stadium is **Žale Cemetery** (Pokopališče Žale), announced by a magnificent entrance in the form of a bright, two-storeyed arcade split by a graceful ceremonial arch – meant to symbolize the border between the city of the living and that of the dead. In the park through the entrance there are a number of funeral chapels dedicated to patron saints, part of Plečnik's overall concept for the entire complex. The cemetery itself is beautifully ordered with lovely gravel walkways and well-tended graves – Plečnik's grave, as modest as the man himself, is to the left of the entrance in Plot 6. From the centre of town, bus #2 stops outside the entrance.

Around the city centre

While it's unlikely you'll be in any hurry to escape the city centre, there are some very enjoyable visits to be had not too far away. Just under 1km south of the centre, and easily reached on foot (along busy Karlovška cesta or, more peacefully, along the banks of the Ljubljanica), are the university's **Botanical Gardens**, at Ižanska cesta 15 (Botanični vrt; daily: April–Oct 7am–7pm; Nov–March 7am–5pm; free; bus #3 to Strelišče). Established in 1810 by the Slovene botanist Franc Hladnik, these colourful gardens hold over fifty thousand species of plants, shrubs and trees, representing every continent.

Covering an area of over 160 square kilometres, the **Ljubljana Marshes** (Ljubljansko barje), 2km south of the Botanical Gardens, originated some two million years ago and are believed to have been the site of the first settlement in the city. The marshes are now a protected area, noted for their tremendously varied flora and fauna, with excellent opportunities for bird-watching, particularly around Kozlerjeva gošča, near the village of **Črna Vas** (Black Village) on the eastern extremes. The marshes are also something of a fertile hunting ground for archeologists, having yielded innumerable objects since extensive research began here soon after World War II; the latest significant find, in 2002, was a wooden wheel believed to be over fifty thousand years old, making it the oldest such wheel ever discovered. In the centre of Črna Vas is Plečnik's **Church of St Michael on the Marsh** (Cerkev Sv Mihaela na Barju), built in 1938 – some ten years later than the Church of St Francis of Assisi (see p.75) but perhaps even more bewitching. The stone-built exterior, bridge-style staircase and detached hollow belfry are all instantly recognizable as Plečnik's work, as is the extraordinary, largely wooden interior, with its cupboard-shaped altar and Turkish-style lamps. The marshy ground necessitated construction on solid eight-metre-long oak piles, while the hall was elevated to the second floor because of the dangers of flooding. To be sure of getting a look-in, try and visit during Mass (weekend mornings at 10am). To get to the church from the centre take bus #19 to the last stop, Barje, walk back across the junction, and it's 500m ahead; to return, take the same bus from the same stop.

Two kilometres east of the centre, in the suburb of Studenec, is **Fužine Castle** (Grad Fužine), a handsome, Renaissance structure dating from the mid-sixteenth century. The castle was named after the old iron foundry near Polje pri Ljubljani – Fužine means "smelter" – and was originally intended to house a glassworks and paper mill, its location on the Ljubljanica ideal for such industries. Over the centuries, and under various owners, it was rearranged, modified and tinkered with, and there is now very little of interest to see, save for the chapel interior which has some fresco remains. In one wing of the castle is the **Architectural Museum** (Arhitekturni muzej; Mon–Fri 9am–3pm, Sat 11am–6pm, Sun 11am–3pm; €3) – a slight misnomer for what is no more than an exhibition of Plečnik's oeuvre, consisting of photos, illustrations and models of some of his projects. The display is actually a condensed edition of a larger exhibition held in 1986 at the Pompidou Centre in Paris, and, interestingly, it includes sketches and photos of his earlier works in Vienna and Prague. To get here take bus #20 to the last stop and it's a five-minute walk; return from the same stop, via the same bus.

Šmarna gora, some 10km northwest of the centre, is an extremely popular outing with Ljubljančani, many of whom come here after work to pound up and down this isolated 669-metre-high hill. At the summit, a partly preserved fifteenth-century wall is evidence that the hill was once a fortified camp providing protection from the rampaging Turks, though in the event it was never conquered. The **Pilgrimage Church of the Holy Mother**, first mentioned in 1314, was built on the old ruins in 1729 and has some lovely frescoes by Matevž Langus, though the only chance you'll get to see these is by visiting during Mass, each Sunday at 11am. Once you've reached the top, which takes around 45 minutes up one of the steep and bumpy tracks, give the bell-rope a sharp tug, partake in a sweet cup of tea, available from the hilltop hut, and take in the terrific views of the city and Sava Plain spread out below. To get to the hill take bus #8 to Brod and it's a five-minute walk to the start of the main trail.

Eating and drinking

As befits its sophisticated image, Ljubljana is able to boast a tight concentration of first-rate **restaurants**, most of which offer excellent value for money. However, beyond the predominantly Slovene and international cuisine, there is still disappointingly little in the way of genuine ethnic food. During the summer al fresco dining is extremely popular amongst Ljubljančani, and many of the restaurants listed offer outdoor seating in the warmer summer months. Although prices here in Ljubljana are slightly higher than in most other places, you can still eat extremely well without having to break the bank: expect to pay around €8–10 for a two-course meal with a glass of wine in an average establishment, and around €18–20 in the most expensive places. Phone numbers are included where booking is advisable.

The best choice for quick-fix **snacks** are those kiosks and stands opposite the stations and at the northern end of Miklošičeva, selling *burek*, pizza, hot dogs and the local *gorenjska* sausages. Plečnik's splendid **Market Colonnade**, curving along the east bank of the Ljubljanica between the Triple Bridge and the Dragon Bridge,

△ Fruit and vegetable stall in the central market

houses dozens of excellent little food shops (Mon–Fri 7am–4pm, Sat 7am–2pm), selling a wide range of breads, cheeses, sandwiches, cakes and confectionery.

The large and colourful outdoor **market** (Mon–Sat 6am–2pm), opposite the Colonnade on Vodnikov trg, is the best place to stock up on fresh produce, and there are fish, meat and dairy products down in the basement of the Seminary building on adjacent Pogačarjev trg. There are also plenty of well-stocked **supermarkets** around town, the most central and largest of which is the one in the basement of the Maximarket shopping centre on Trg Republike (Mon–Fri 9am–7pm, Sat 8am–7pm). Also located down here is an excellent **self-service restaurant** (Samopostrežna Restavracija; Mon–Fri 9am–7pm, Sat 9am–4pm).

Snacks, sandwiches and fast food

Ajdovo Zrno Trubarjeva 7. A convenient spot for lunch, this bright and cheerful vegetarian place, located in an off-street courtyard, has a fresh salad bar, tasty soups, tortillas and tofu. Sit down or takeaway.

Hot Horse Trubarjeva 31. Popular burger bar specializing in horse burgers, though you can also get veggie burgers and salads. One of the few places in town for late night munchies. Daily 8am–1am.

Pasta Nona Gosposvetska 2. Attractive, informal bistro offering a choice of two or three different pasta and soup dishes each day, one of which is usually vegetarian. Daily 10am–5pm.

Ribca Market Colonnade. Terrific fish snack bar located on the lower floor of the colonnade, serving generous plates of grilled and fried squid, sardines and seafood salads. Sit down or takeaway. Mon–Fri 7am–4pm.

Tomato Šubičeva 2. Lively diner-style joint which knocks out cheap and filling sandwiches, rolls and grilled snacks, as well as simple cooked breakfasts alongside fresh juices and pastries. Sit down or takeaway. Mon–Fri 7am–10pm.

Restaurants

Abecedarium Ribji trg 2. Named after the first Slovene book, and located in the former residence of its author, Primož Trubar, this informal café/restaurant combines an interesting selection of regional specialities, such as *bograč* from Prekmurje, *žlikrofi* from Idrija and *polenta* from the Karst, with lots of quality meat dishes (beef, lamb and wild boar), each of which comes with a suggested wine; there's also an appealing breakfast menu. Daily 8am–11pm.

Ambient Čufarjeva 2. Funky, bright orange-decorated bistro whose comfortable, loungey interior and smart outdoor terrace draws a hip lunchtime and evening crowd; the menu, which is continually changed (curry risotto, beef gnocchi and grilled pork ribs are typical dishes), is top-notch, and the service warm; for breakfast try the hot toasted sandwiches or omelettes with truffles alongside a big mug of coffee. Mon–Fri 7am–11pm, Sat 9am–11pm.

Gostilna As Čopova 5 (enter via Knafljev prehod) ☎01/425-8822. A perennial favourite amongst local politicians and bigwigs, *As* is as posh and as expensive as it gets in Ljubljana. The food's not bad either, with seafood and risotto dishes the main staples, complemented by some fine Slovene vintages. The bistro dining area offers simpler, more affordable eating (salads, pizza and pastas). Daily 9am–2pm.

Aska in Volk Gornji trg 4. Wonderfully characterful Bosnian restaurant with Balkan staples likes *čevapčiči* (rissoles of spiced minced meat), *karadjordje* (breaded veal cutlet rolled and stuffed with cheese), *pasulj* (oven-cooked beans), and the best roasted lamb in Ljubljana forming the mainstay of a terrific menu. The restaurant itself looks fantastic; the main room has a large open log fire and peasant paraphernalia dangling from the ceiling and walls, while there are three cosy, vibrantly coloured coves for intimate dining. In warmer weather eat out on the little terrace through the back, adjacent to St Nicholas's Church. Daily 11am–11pm.

Cantina Mexicana Knafljev prehod. Flashy Mexican restaurant just across from *As* in this busy courtyard area – the menu differs little from your average Mexican, but the food is well cooked and presented with style; there's a fancy cocktail bar too. Daily 11am–1am.

Casa del Papa Celovška 54a. A long-standing local favourite, there's decent international food to be had here, in rooms decorated on an Ernest Hemingway theme (Key West room, Cuba room and so on). You can get down to Latino and salsa grooves as the evening wears on. Daily noon–midnight.

Evropa Slovenska 47. Occupying the premises of the old *Hotel Evropa*, this is another of the city's more refined restaurants; furnished with elegant simplicity – chandeliers, smooth wooden tables and brown leather sofas – it boasts a fine à la carte menu with choices like scampi soup, tuna steak and roast beef medallions. Mon–Sat 9am–11pm.

Figovec Gosposvetska 1. Just across the road from *Evropa*, this is a charmingly old-fashioned downtown restaurant specializing in pony steaks, horsemeat goulash and traditional Slovene standards. The terrace is fine, so long as you don't

mind the incessant traffic streaming by. Mon–Fri 10am–midnight, Sat & Sun noon–5pm.

Foculus Gregorčičeva 3. Flamboyantly decorated pizzeria offering an exhaustive range of pizzas in lively surroundings, including a better-than-average vegetarian selection, and a generous salad buffet. Mon–Fri 10am–midnight, Sat & Sun noon–midnight.

Harambaša Okrepčevapnica Vrtna 8. Replicating a traditional Bosnian tavern, with low wooden tables and stools and kitsch knick-knacks splayed across the walls, this Sarajevan-owned restaurant is great fun; the menu, such as it is, features a handful of classic Bosnian dishes such as *pljeskavica* (thick, oversized hamburger) and *čevapčiči* (rissoles of spiced minced meat) served with *kajmak* (creamy cheese) and *lepinja* (a large doughy bread), while you can round things off with a cup of *Turška kava* (Turkish coffee) and a piece of Turkish delight. It's absurdly popular so you may have to wait a bit for a table, as there are no reservations. Mon–Fri 10am–10pm, Sat noon–10pm, Sun noon–6pm.

Joe Pena's Cankarjeva 6. Although not as flash as *Cantina Mexicana*, the food at this breezy, and justifiably popular, Mexican restaurant is no less enjoyable. Mon–Thurs 10am–1am, Fri & Sat til 2.30am, Sun til midnight.

Julija Stari trg 9. A bright, simple eatery in a central Old Town location, with decent salads, pasta, risotto and Mediterranean dishes. During the summer, the tables strung along the cobbled street outside are an enormously popular place to eat. Daily 8am–midnight.

Ljubljanski Dvor Dvorni trg 1. Another of the city's impressive stock of pizzerias, *Dvor* counts some one hundred pizzas, including the best vegetarian choice in town; the expansive patio area overlooking the Ljubljanica, and with views up to the castle, is terrific. Mon–Sat 10am–midnight, Sun 1–11pm.

Moro & Pri Sv Florijanu Gornji trg 20 ☎01/251-2214. Two restaurants in one: the former in the cosy vaulted basement specializes in fine Moroccan cuisine, and though not an extensive menu, the food is exquisite – try the chicken and lamb tagine with couscous or the fish skewer, and top it off with a cup of mint tea; *Florijanu*, the rather more formal restaurant upstairs, offers an interesting choice of exotic dishes such as fillet of deer, beefsteak with truffles, and chicken tandoori. It has good-value daily lunch menus for under €10. Daily noon–midnight.

New Porto Breg 8. This engaging riverside restaurant, featuring a lovely burgundy-painted vaulted interior, is ideal for either a spot of light lunch – salads (beef, spinach, zucchini) and risottos (asparagus, mushroom) – or more substantial evening fare, such as minted lamb, deer fillet and trout. Daily 11am–11pm.

Pri Škofu Rečna cesta 5 ☎01/426-4508. Secreted away in a quiet residential street in Krakovo, this is one of the city's most enjoyable restaurants; the menu changes daily, but if you don't fancy anything on offer, ask for one of the house specialities – gnocchi, black risotto (Črna rižota), black-pepper-encrusted tenderloin medallions (Biftek Škof) or grilled aubergine with white rice and buckwheat (Malančani Damjana). The simple, sunny interior, with its lovely handmade ceramic wall hangings, paintings and table decorations, rounds things off beautifully. Mon–Fri 8am–11pm, Sat & Sun noon–midnight.

Pri Vitezu Breg 18–20 ☎01/426-6058. Pri Vitezu is another of Ljubljana's top-end restaurants, a warm, classy place offering a creditably distinguished Italian/Slovene-fashioned menu including, for appetizers, swordfish, scallops and snails, and for mains, seafood black risotto, duck breast and horse fillets. Mon–Sat noon–11pm.

Romeo Stari trg 6. Located opposite Julija, naturally, Romeo offers a more wide-ranging menu,

though with an obvious slant towards Mexican – tacos, burritos and the like. Good for late-night munchies. Daily 9am–1am.

Gostilna Sokol Ciril Metodov trg 18. As close to a traditional countryside gostilna as you'll get in Ljubljana; the thick wooden bench seating and tables of this labyrinthine establishment provide a congenial setting for very hearty portions of Slovene food culled from the country's various regions – for example, ham and olives from the Karst, trout from Primorska, and Gibanica from Prekmurje. Try, too, a bottle of the domestic Sokol pivo, or a glass of red wine in the downstairs bar. Mon–Sat 7am–11pm, Sun 10am–11pm.

Špajza Gornji trg 28 ☎01/425-3094. Completing the handful of excellent establishments along Gornji trg, the elegant rustic trappings of this homely restaurant complement the beautifully cooked Slovene food superbly. First-class selection of wines too. Expensive. Daily noon–midnight.

Zlata Ribica Cankarjevo nabrežje 5. Occupying one of the best outdoor dining areas in the city, this modest and inexpensive fish restaurant facing the River Ljubljanica, on the corner of Ribji trg, is delightful. Daily 11am–11pm.

Drinking and nightlife

While Ljubljana's **nightlife** cannot match the vibrancy or diversity of larger cities, a drink on a warm summer's evening in one of the many convivial **cafés and bars** strung along the banks of the River Ljubljanica is one of the joys of being in this city. Alternatively, a wander up and down Mestni trg and Stari trg will yield an interesting locale every fifty yards or so, whilst the clutch of energetic bars in Knafljev prehod (the courtyard area between Wolfova ulica and Slovenska cesta) are usually packed to the rafters. Ljubljana's limited, but eclectic, bunch of **clubs** – some of which double up as multicultural, arts-type centres – are more widely dispersed throughout town, although all are within walking distance of the centre.

The city offers a reasonable, if rather Balkan-centric, diet of **live music**, though it does suffer from having few decent **gig venues** to call upon; bigger names play at the Central Stadium or Tivoli Hall, in Tivoli Park, while the two other principal venues are the Cankarjev Dom Congress Centre on Trg republike and the marvellous open-air stage at the Plečnik-designed Križanke complex on Trg francoske revolucije. The monthly Where To? events pamphlet, available from all the tourist offices, lists all events and performances for that month.

Cafés and bars

Café Antico Stari trg 27. Bare wooden floors, high tables and stools, and pastel-vaulted ceiling give this popular Old Town hangout a pleasantly dated ambience; there are a couple of little coves for more solitudinous drinking.

Bi-Ko-Fe Židovska steza 1. Artsy, colourful and chilled-out café with an imaginative range of coffees, as well as teas and alcoholic beverages.

Breg Breg 2. Classy, if rather posey, wine bar, set in a lovely location by the Ljubljanica; excellent selection of wines available, as well as (expensive) tasting sessions. Mon–Sat 9am–1am.

Café Gaudi Nazorjeva 10. A delightful, quirky interior and seductive range of coffees – alcoholic, iced, chocolate – makes this a terrific place for a quick coffee stop.

Čajna Hiša Stari trg 3. Bijou tea-house offering a superb range of teas from around the world, excellent sandwiches and cakes and decent breakfasts. Deservedly one of the most popular places with the locals. Closed Sun.

Cutty Sark Knafljev prehod 1. Opposite *Cantina Mexicana*, this lively, Brit-fashioned pub has a more raucous atmosphere than most places in town, and regularly features live music.

Lepa Žoga Celovška 43. Small sports café-bar near Tivoli Park, with shirts and other paraphernalia of the good and great (mostly foreign sports stars) draped along the walls, and a constant diet of live TV sports, including English football on Sunday afternoons.

Le Petite Café Trg francoske revolucije 4. A small slice of Paris at this eternally popular and wonderfully atmospheric street corner café opposite Križanke; perfect for a large white coffee (*bela kava*) and croissant for breakfast or a glass of wine in the evening.

Maček Krojaška 5. The most popular of the string of hip cafés on the right bank of the Ljubljanica; the place to see and be seen, and consequently always crammed.

Vinoteka Movia Mestni trg 2 ☎01/425-5448. This snug little wine bar next to the Town Hall on Mestni trg is the best place in town to sample Slovenian wine. The friendly, knowledge-able staff can assist with vintages from every Slovene wine-producing region, including those from their own winery in Goriška Brda (see p.176). Mon–Sat noon–midnight; visits outside these times can be arranged.

Patrick's Prečna 6. Up a little side street off Tru-barjeva, the city's token Irish pub is not a bad place at all, though the draught beers (Guinness, Mur-phy's, Kilkenny) are as expensive as you'd expect.

Pločnik Prešernov trg. Permanently crowded sum-mer-only outdoor café on the busy main square, which also has a terrific ice-cream parlour; on the opposite side of the square is *Sladoledni Vrt Poet*, another seasonal hotspot popular for its bewilder-ing array of ice creams and sundaes.

Ragamuffin Krojaška 4. In the first alleyway behind *Maček*, this intimate, reggae-oriented café-bar is an enjoyable chill-out haunt, by day or by night. Good tunes too.

Sax Pub Eipprova 7. The colourful, spray-painted *Sax* is just one of several cool cafés and bars in this idyllic canal-side street five minutes walk south of Breg. Occasional live jazz too.

Slamič Kersnikova 1. Whilst not as atmospheric as *Čajna Hiša*, this pleasant, restful little place has a similarly varied range of teas, in addition to coffee and ice cream.

Zlata Ladjica Jurčičev trg 1. Fun, energetic pub next to the Shoemaker's Bridge on the left bank of the Ljubljanica; if you're here during winter, try the delicious mulled wine.

Zvezda Wolfova 14. Named after the eponymous pre-World War II café in the Kazina building further up on Kongresni trg, this is the place to come for ices and pastries.

Clubs and discos

Bachus Kongresni trg 3. Swanky three-in-one club (Tues–Sat 9pm–4am), lounge bar (Mon–Sat 8am–1am) and restaurant; the banging club features different music on different nights of the week (Thurs disco, Fri hip-hop, Sat R&B), while the lounge bar suffices equally for a daytime coffee or shake, or an evening beer.

Global Slovenska (top of the Nama department store). Lots of spangly silver and gold decor in the city's most straightforward disco venue, with a different musical theme for each night of the week (Tues student night, Wed R&B, Fri House/Dance, Sat 1970s disco). Access is via a glass lift on the street. Mon–Sat 9pm–5am.

Jazz Club Gajo Beethovnova 8. Refined late-night jazz club with regular quality offerings by both domestic and foreign acts. Jam sessions on Mondays from 9pm. Between mid-May and September the club has performances at a fabulous outdoor garden on Cankarjeva cesta, across from the National Gal-lery. See ⓦ www.jazzclubgajo.com for programme.

K4 Kersnikova 4. Stalwart of Ljubljana's alternative scene, offering some of the best music in the city – mainly electronic, but also rock, jazz, hip-hop and folk, plus gay night on Sundays. Student parties and performance art too. Look out for flyers or check ⓦ www.klubk4.org.

KUD Prešeren Karunova 14. Superb, long-standing gig venue in the Trnovo district that also organizes regular literary events, workshops (including some for kids) and art exhibitions. There's a fine little café here too. Also stages the excellent *Trnfest* festival in August (see box on p.82). Daily 11am–1am.

Metelkova mesto Metelkova cesta. Ljubljana's legendary alternative cultural mecca, consisting of a cosmopolitan gang of clubs, bars and NGOs (collectively entitled Metelkova), is located in the former army barracks near the Hostel Celica; ven-ues include Channel Zero (dance), Gala Hala (punk/metal), Mizzart (low-fi), Klub Monokel (lesbian only), Tiffany (gay) and Gromki (performance).

Orto Bar Grablovičeva 1. This good-time haunt a couple of blocks east of the train station has regular late-night disco evenings; it's also the city's main small live-rock venue, and you can bank on at least a couple of gigs a week here. Daily 8pm–4am.

Entertainment

For a relatively small city, Ljubljana offers a surprisingly rich diet of **classical culture**, with well-established orchestral, operatic and theatrical companies, and there's a good chance you'll catch something whatever time of the year you're here; although most of these institutions close down in July and August, by way of compensation there's plenty going on as part of the city's International Summer Festival (see box below).

Classical music, ballet, opera and theatre

Cankarjev Dom, the enormous arts and convention centre on Trg Republike, is the scene of major orchestral and theatrical events, folk and jazz concerts and all manner of art exhibitions (the box office is in the nearby Maximarket shop-

---

Festivals and events: the Ljubljana year

Ljubljana puts on a wonderfully diverse range of festivals throughout the year, many of which attract a distinguished roster of artists and performers. The festival year kicks off in Spring with **Slovenian Musical Days**, four or five days (usually at the end of March) of concerts performed principally by the Slovene Philharmonic and RTV Symphonic orchestras. One of the year's most enjoyable music events is the ethno-alternative music festival **Druga Godba** ('The Other Music'), held at the end of May in the wonderful surrounds of Križanke, and featuring a terrific line-up of both domestic and foreign musicians and bands.

The key festival months are those between June and September; taking place between July and mid-September, the **International Summer Festival** has been the city's major annual event for over fifty years, comprising orchestral and chamber music, theatre and dance – the main venues are Križanke and the Ljubljana Castle courtyard, with additional concerts at Cankarjev Dom and the Slovene Philharmonic Hall. Also staged at Križanke (at the end of June) is the **Ljubljana Jazz Festival**, three days of world-class jazz concerts. Otherwise, the end of June offers the **Ana Desetnica Festival of Street Theatre**, in which the streets of the Old Town and thereabouts are the setting for a varied programme of wonderful and often wacky street performances; and the **Viticulture and Winegrowers Fair**, staged at the Ljubljana Exhibition Grounds behind the train station, which might appeal, particularly if you're unable to get to any of Slovenia's wine regions – there's plenty of tasting to be had.

The city's foremost artistic event (albeit taking place every odd-numbered year) is the **International Biennial of Graphic Arts**, held between June and September at Tivoli Castle, a prestigious affair rated as one of the premier exhibitions of its kind in Europe. **Trnfest**, a smaller-scale summer festival organized by the KUD cultural centre, takes place throughout August, with gigs, exhibitions, workshops and video screenings – there's a good programme for kids here too.

Rounding off the year is the **City of Women International Festival of Contemporary Art**, ten days of female artists' exhibitions, as well as theatre and performance, taking place in the middle of October. The **Ljubljana International Film Festival (LIFFe)** presents a wide selection of primarily European films for two weeks during November at Cankarjev Dom.

Christmas celebrations start in earnest at the beginning of December with a procession by Santa Claus, followed by a month of festive events for both adults and children, most of which take place in and around the Old Town and along the banks of the Ljubljanica; the month's festivities conclude with a spectacular New Year's Eve fireworks display from the castle. Advance information on all these events can be obtained from any of the tourist information centres (see p.52).

ping centre Mon–Fri 11am–1pm & 3–8pm, Sat 11am–1pm; also 1hr before each performance; ☎01/241-7299, ⓦwww.cd-cc.si). Ljubljana's energetic and highly regarded **symphony orchestra**, the Slovenska Filharmonija, performs at the Philharmonic Hall on Kongresni trg (☎01/241-0800, ⓦwww.filharmonija.si), while the republic's **opera and ballet** companies are housed in the National Opera and Ballet Theatre, Župančičeva 1 (ticket office Mon–Fri 1–5pm, Sat 11am–1pm; also 1hr before each performance; ☎01/241-1764). **Theatrical** productions take place at the Slovene National Theatre (Narodno Gledališče), just off Slovenska cesta at Erjavčeva 1 (☎01/252-1511), whilst the extremely popular **puppet theatre** (Lutkovno Gledališče), Krekov trg 2 (ticket office Mon–Fri 4–6pm, Sat 10am–noon; also 1hr before each performance; ☎01/300-0970), puts on a regular programme of shows throughout the year.

There's an outstanding programme of domestic and international classical and orchestral concerts as part of the **International Summer Festival** (see box opposite) taking place between July and mid-September; venues include the Križanke Theatre, Cankarjev Dom and castle (the festival box office is at Križanke: Mon–Fri 10am–1.30pm & 4–8pm, Sat 10am–1pm; also 1hr before each performance; ☎01/241-6026, ⓦwww.festival-lj.si). The monthly English-language *Where To?* events pamphlet, available free from the tourist information centres, has complete listings of concerts and events.

Cinema

The majority of **cinema**-(*kino*) goers now make the trek out to the **Kolosej multiplex** at the BTC shopping complex 1.5km east of the centre on Šmartinska cesta (bus #2 or #7). The best of the few remaining downtown cinemas are the excellent art cinema, Kinodvor, across from the train station at Kolodvorska 13; Kinoteka, at Miklošičeva 28, which screens premieres, cult classics and retrospectives, and Komuna, at Cankarjeva cesta 1; tickets for all cinemas cost around €4. There are occasional screenings at Cankarjev Dom (see p.73), which is also the principal venue for the two-week **Ljubljana International Film Festival** (LIFFe) in November (see box opposite).

Shopping

There are few **shopping areas** of note within the city centre itself, although a wander up and down Čopova ulica, Trubarjeva cesta or Mestni trg might yield the odd find. Otherwise, most of the city folk do their shopping out at the enormous and ever-expanding BTC shopping complex (Mon–Sat 9am–8pm), 1.5km east of town on Šmartinska cesta; this is also the location for the Kolosej multiplex (see above). A great place to browse on a Sunday morning is the **flea market** along the right bank of the Ljubljanica, between the Triple Bridge and the Shoemakers Bridge; here you can find just about anything and everything, from old records, books and stamps to furniture, musical instruments and Tito-era memorabilia.

There are several excellent **bookshops** in town, all of which stock a wide-ranging selection of English-language books: the two best ones are Mladinska at Slovenska 29 (Mon–Fri 9am–7.30pm, Sat 9am–2pm), and the smaller Novak at Wolfova 8 (Mon–Fri 10am–10pm, Sat 10am–2pm). For **maps**, try Kod & Kam, just down from Križanke at Trg francoske revolucije 7 (Mon–Fri 9am–8pm, Sat 8am–1pm), or Geonavtik, at Kongresni trg 1 (Mon–Fri 8.30am–8.30pm, Sat 8.30am–4pm). If you're on the lookout for **music** head to Big Bang or Mueller, next to each other on Čopova ulica (both also have stores at BTC – see above), though Music Box, at Levstikov trg 4a (Mon–Sat 10am–10pm, Sun 4–8pm), has the best selection of music from both Slovenia and the other ex-Yugoslav republics.

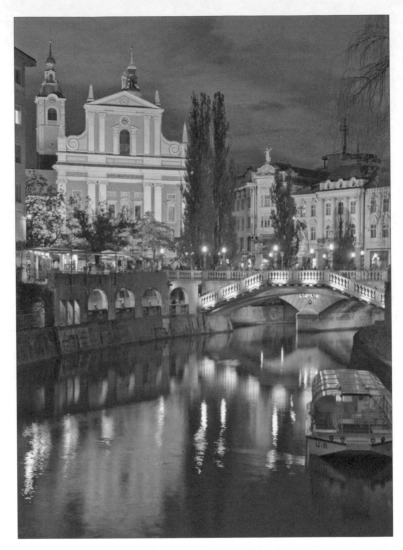

△ Ljubljanica River and the Church of the Annunciation

Ljubljana listings

Airlines Adria, Gosposvetska 6 ⊕01/231-3312; Austrian Airlines, Dunajska 58 ⊕01/436-8566; British Airways, Trg Republike 3 ⊕01/241-4000; Lufthansa, Gosposvetska 6 ⊕01/434-7246. **Banks and exchange** Money can be exchanged at all banks, and the post offices (see opposite),

while the exchange office in the train station is useful if arriving early or late (daily 5.30am–10pm). There are several exchange bureaus (*menjalnica*) throughout the city, most of which offer good rates – one of the best is on Pogačarjev trg (Mon–Fri 7am–7pm, Sat 7am–2pm).

Bicycles From May to October the excellent "Ljubljana Cycle" programme offers cheap bike rental (€1 for 1hr, €4 for the day); bikes, which must be returned by 8pm, can be rented from a number of locations, including the Slovenian Tourist Information Centre, the *TIR* café bar at the railway station and Hostel Celica.

Car rental ABC/Europcar, Dalmatinova 15 (*City Hotel Turist*) ☎01/510-4330, and airport ☎04/206-1684, are an excellent local company with very competitive rates; Avis, Čufarjeva 2 ☎01/430-8010, and airport ☎04/236-5000; Budget, Miklošičeva 3 (*Grand Hotel Union*) ☎01/421-7340 and airport ☎04/201-4300; Golf-tourist, Trdinova 4 ☎01/430-6780; Hertz, Tivolska 44 ☎01/239-6010; National Car Rental, Baragova 5 ☎01/588-4451, and airport ☎04/238-1020.

Embassies and consulates Australia, Trg republike 3/XII ☎01/425-4252; Canada, Miklošičeva 19 ☎01/430-3570; Ireland, Poljanski nasip 6 ☎01/300-8970; UK, Trg republike 3/IV ☎01/200-3910; USA, Prešernova 31 ☎01/200-5500.

Emergencies Ambulance ☎112; police ☎113; fire service ☎112.

Hospitals The main hospital is at Bohoričeva 4 ☎01/232-3060, while emergency treatment is also available from the Klinični center at Zaloška cesta 2 ☎01/522-5050. There is also a dental clinic (Stomatološka klinika) here ☎01/431-3113.

Internet access Slovenian Tourist Information Centre, Krekov trg 10 (daily June–Sept 8am–9pm, Oct–May til 7pm; eight terminals); the British Council, Tivolska 30 (Mon–Thurs 10am–6pm, Fri 10am–4pm, closed Aug; six terminals); *Cyber Café Xplorer*, Petkovškovo nabrežje 23 (Mon–Fri 10am–10pm, Sat & Sun 2–10pm); *Kiber Pipa*, in the student centre at Kersnikova 6 (Mon–Fri 10am–10pm; free); three terminals inside the bus station ticket office; and the small library in the train station underpass (Mon–Fri 7am–7pm) which allows just 15 minutes surf time, but at no cost.

Laundry Chemo-express, Wolfova 12 (service washes only; Mon–Fri 7am–6pm; ☎01/251-4404).

Left luggage Lockers at the train station (open 24hrs; €2).

Petrol Several petrol stations open 24hrs; Celovška 226; Dunajska 130; Tivolska 43; Tržaška 130; Šmartinska 130.

Pharmacies Lekarna Ljubljana, Prisojna 7 ☎01/230-6230, has a 24hr duty service.

Police For accidents and emergencies go to Trdinova 10 ☎01/432-0341.

Post office The main office/poste restante is at Slovenska 32 (Mon–Fri 8am–7pm, Sat 8am–1pm), though the office at Trg Osvobodilne fronte, next to the train station, keeps longer hours (Mon–Fri 7am–8pm, Sat 7am–6pm).

Telephones International calls can be made from any phone box on the street, or from booths inside the two post offices (see above).

Travel agencies Specializing in travel for those under 27, the friendly Erazem agency, Miklošičeva 26 (☎01/430-5537, ⑯www.erazem.net), make hotel and hostel reservations, issue ISIC and hostel cards, and sell domestic and international tickets (for all forms of transport); Mladi Turist, Salendrova 4 (☎01/425-9131), also make reservations for hostels throughout the country, and issue plane and train tickets; outdoor pursuits specialists Trek-Trek, Bičevje 5 (☎01/425-1392, ⑯www.trektrek. si), offer a wide range of adventure-sports activities in the Julian Alps.

Travel details

Trains

Ljubljana to: Bled-Lesce (hourly; 45min–1hr); Brežice (7–13 daily; 1hr 45min–2hr); Celje (every 30min–2hr; 1hr–1hr 40min); Črnomelj (5–9 daily; 2hr 10min–2hr 45min); Divača (every 40min–1hr; 1hr 30min); Kamnik (hourly; 50min); Koper (3–5 daily; 2hr–2hr 30min); Kranj (hourly; 25–35min); Litija (every 30min–2hr; 30min); Maribor (every 30min–2hr; 1hr 45min–2hr 45min); Metlika (5–9 daily; 2hr 30min–3hr); Novo Mesto (7–13 daily; 1hr 20min–2hr); Postojna (every 40min–1hr; 1hr); Sežana (hourly; 1hr 40min–2hr); Ptuj (5–9 daily; 2hr 30min–3hr); Zidani Most (every 30min–1hr; 45min–1hr).

Buses

Ljubljana to: Bled (hourly; 1hr 20min); Brežice (Mon–Fri 6 daily, Sat & Sun 3 daily; 2hr 30min); Celje (every 1–2hr; 1hr 35min); Idrija (Mon–Fri every 2hr, Sat & Sun 6 daily; 1hr 15min); Ivančna Gorica (hourly; 50min); Kamnik (every 15–30min; 35min); Kočevje (hourly; 1hr 30min); Koper (Mon–Fri 9 daily, Sat & Sun 5 daily; 2hr 20min); Kranj (every 30min–1hr; 40min); Kranjska Gora (hourly; 2hr); Maribor (6 daily; 2hr 20min–3hr 10min); Murska Sobota (2 daily; 3hr 30min); Nova Gorica (Mon–Fri hourly, Sat & Sun 2 daily; 2hr 30min); Novo Mesto (Mon–Fri 10 daily, Sat & Sun 6 daily;

1hr 10min); Piran (Mon–Fri 6 daily, Sat & Sun 4 daily; 2hr 40min); Postojna (every 30min–1hr; 1hr); Ribčev Laz (Lake Bohinj) (hourly; 2hr); Škofja Loka (every 30min–1hr; 40min).

International trains

Ljubljana to: Belgrade (3 daily; 8hr 30min); Budapest (3 daily; 8hr 45min); Munich (2 daily; 6hr 30min); Rijeka (2 daily; 2hr 35min); Trieste (2 daily; 3hr); Venice (2 daily; 6hr); Vienna (1 daily; 6hr 15min); Zagreb (6 daily; 2hr 15min).

International buses

Ljubljana to: Rijeka (1 daily; 2hr 30min); Trieste (1 daily; 2hr 30min); Zagreb (3 daily; 2hr 50min).

Northwest Slovenia

CHAPTER 2 # Highlights

✳ **Velika Planina** This alluring highland plain is spotted with shepherd's huts, and offers great walking opportunities. See p.95

✳ **Škofja Loka** Compact and elegant Škofja Loka is one of Slovenia's most beautifully preserved medieval towns. See p.97

✳ **Beekeeping Museum, Radovljica** This most cherished of Slovene customs is explored in this engaging exposition. See p.113

✳ **Lake Bled** This fairytale lake comes complete with a romantic island church and cliff-top castle. See p.121

✳ **Lake Bohinj** Fish, swim, take a boat ride, or just stroll around Slovenia's most stunning lake. See p.129

✳ **Hiking in the Julian Alps** Superb hiking and climbing including, for the more adventurous, Mount Triglav, the country's highest peak. See p.136

✳ **Vršič Pass** Slovenia's most spectacular mountain pass incorporates nearly fifty hairpin bends, with dozens of attractions along the way. See p.145

△ Julian Alps

Northwest Slovenia

With by far the highest profile of any of the country's eight regions, **Gorenjska**, Slovenia's northwestern province, offers an outstanding synthesis of natural and cultural heritage, from dramatic alpine mountains, valleys and lakes to startlingly pretty medieval towns and villages. The defining feature of the region is the **Julian Alps**, a majestic limestone range packed with sawtoothed peaks, fantastically shaped gorges and ravines, deep mountain lakes, and dozens of waterfalls. Most of the Slovene part of the Julians – a small portion spills over into neighbouring Italy – fall within **Triglav National Park**, Slovenia's only designated national park, at the heart of which is **Mount Triglav**, the country's highest and most exalted peak. Bordering Austria to the north are two further mountain ranges: the slender **Karavanke** chain, and, east of here, the **Kamniške Alps**, whose gloriously tapered peaks strongly resemble the Julians in parts. The tangle of well-worn paths furrowed across these three ranges heaves with hikers during the summer, though the crowds, rarely oppressive, are easily avoided. Hiking aside, the region present stacks of opportunities for adrenaline-fuelled activities – typically, rafting, canyoning, hydrospeed and paragliding – as well as more traditional pursuits such as cycling, horse riding, fishing and swimming. Moreover, Gorenjska possesses the country's densest concentration of ski resorts, the largest and most popular of which is in **Kranjska Gora**, squeezed up against the Italian and Austrian borders in the extreme northwestern corner of the country. Located at the tail end of the Alps are Slovenia's celebrated alpine resorts, the most known and visited of which is **Bled**, a once fashionable health resort whose enchanting lake now ranks as one of the country's premier sites. For many though, Lake Bled is surpassed by the fjord-like **Lake Bohinj**, a majestic body of water settled amidst gorgeous mountain scenery and bound by a huddle of sleepy villages.

Gorenjska is also sprinkled with a few, albeit small, urban towns: the most engaging of these are the medieval towns of **Kamnik**, sheltered under the Kamniške Alps a short way north of Ljubljana, and **Škofja Loka**, located west of Ljubljana on the fringe of some delightful, rolling countryside; meanwhile, **Kranj**, Gorenjska's largest city and its key commercial and industrial centre, though initially uninviting, masks a surprisingly endearing old core. Pushing on towards the mountains – as most travellers are apt to do as quickly as possible – the towns of **Tržič** and **Radovljica** are both worthy of a brief stop-off, especially the latter, whose fascinating Beekeeping Museum is one of the region's best. Just beyond are the exquisite villages of **Kropa** and **Begunje**, both of which offer a couple of excellent museums, and **Brezje**, the site of Slovenia's most important pilgrimage church.

Just about all of these places can be reached from Ljubljana with minimum fuss and, with the exception of the park interior, **getting around** the region is easy. Although trains serve most places – and there is the useful **car train** (see p.129), which runs between Bohinj Bistrica and Most na Soči – you're best off sticking to buses, which offer faster and more frequent connections. Save for a couple of key roads, most notably the serpentine **Vršič Pass**, which forges a spectacularly scenic route across the mountains between Kranjska Gora and Bovec (in the Soča Valley), motorized access within Triglav Park is fairly limited. However you'll have few problems reaching the major attractions if you have your own transport. There are also quick and easy crossings into Italy and Austria, the former reached via the main road that bypasses Kranjska Gora, and the latter via the Karavanke tunnel, under the mountains near Jesenice, and the Ljubelj tunnel north of Tržič.

Kamnik and around

In many ways the tract of land northwest of Ljubljana is a gentle teaser for what lies beyond. It's an area of hugely varied topography, a blend of flatlands, twisting, wooded valleys and sharp mountain peaks, all of which present great opportunities for rambling, cycling, skiing and other leisurely pursuits.

Hemmed in by thick forests at the foot of the Kamniške Alps, **KAMNIK** – 23km north of Ljubljana – is one of Slovenia's prettiest medieval towns and a major staging post for hikers and skiers heading onwards to the nearby alpine resorts. A market borough in the thirteenth century, the town established itself as a key trade and crafts centre during the Middle Ages, though the later creation of alternative routes left the town somewhat out on a limb. Industrialization and the construction of the Ljubljana–Kamnik railway in the nineteenth century played a part in its revival, as did the popularity of its thermal spas, frequented by both Ljubljančani and Austrians. Nowadays, Kamnik is a sleepy, old-fashioned place which really only ever comes alive during the staging of the town's three major festival. Nevertheless, its spruce, neatly preserved medieval core, castles and museums warrant a trip any time.

Each year the town plays host to three very colourful festivals. **Medieval Days**, taking place on the first or second weekend of June, involves a mock medieval market, trades and crafts shows and medieval sports such as sword fighting and archery. **Kamfest**, in August, constitutes three weeks of music and dance centred on Mali Grad, while the **National Costumes Festival**, on the second weekend of September, sees groups from Slovenia's multifarious regions dress up in their most colourful finery. Naturally, there is much merriment at all three.

Arrival, information and accommodation

The town's main **train station** is on Kranjska cesta, a five-minute walk south of the main street, Šutna, but you're better off alighting at the next stop, Kamnik-Mesto, a short stroll west of Glavni trg (main square) on Kolodvorska ulica; Kamnik-Graben, a couple of minutes' further down the line, is the last stop. From the **bus station** on Maistrova ulica, it's a five-minute walk to Glavni trg and the **tourist office** at no. 2 (July & Aug Mon–Fri 9am–7pm, Sat & Sun 9am–2pm; Sept–June Mon–Fri 8am–4pm, Sat 8am–noon; ℡01/839-1470, ⓦwww.kamnik. si). The **post office** is at Glavni trg 27 (Mon–Fri 8am–7pm, Sat 8am–noon).

Of the town's three, almost identically priced **pensions**, the best value is the *Kamrica*, beneath Mali Grad at Trg svobode 2 (℡01/831-7707, ℉831-7706; ❺). Similarly furnished, but with smaller, more functional rooms, are *Prenočišča špenko*, right by the bus station at Prešernova ulica 14c (℡01/831-7330, ℉834-1753; ❹); and the *Pri Cesarju*, a five-minute walk north of Glavni trg at Tunjiška cesta 1 (℡01/839-2917, ℉839-1196; ❺), and which also has a few triples. The crowns on the doors are in tribute to the time when Emperor Franz Jozef allegedly stayed here. The very small and basic **campsite** (℡01/831-7314; May–Sept) is located on Maistrova ulica, a ten-minute walk northeast of the bus station next to the outdoor public swimming pool.

The Town

Most of Kamnik's attractions lie east and south of **Glavni trg** (Main Square), part square, part street, and the town's focal point. On the east side of the square, at no. 2, is the **Miha Maleš Gallery** (Tues–Sat 8am–1pm & 4–7pm; €2.5), named after the celebrated graphic artist but actually hosting temporary exhibitions by other local artists. A short walk west of Glavni trg is the **Franciscan Monastery** (Frančiškanski samostan), dating from 1495, whose library holds a fine collection of manuscripts and incunabula (contact the tourist office if you wish to visit). Adjoining the monastery is the **Church of St Jacob** (Cerkev Sv Jakoba), also built in the fifteenth century but redesigned in Baroque style; otherwise unexceptional, the church is a must-see for Plečnik's extraordinary **Chapel of the Holy Grave**, positioned to the right of the high altar – charged with images of war, the great architect (see p.62) cast the altar in the shape of a bullet, lined the walls with rows of studded lights (meant to represent helmets), and shaped the door-knob into a dove's head, to symbolize peace.

Mali Grad

Occupying a hillock south of Glavni trg is **Mali Grad** (Little Castle), the town's most evocative and identifiable building. At the summit, on the eastern tip of the ruins, is the whitewashed, two-storey **Romanesque chapel and crypt** (daily: June–Aug 9am–7pm; €1.5), parts of which date from the eleventh century, making it one of Slovenia's oldest surviving ecclesiastical monuments. The exquisite chapel, much strengthened and remodelled, contains remnants of some superb fifteenth-century late-Gothic frescoes illustrating several venerated saints, as well as paintings by Janez Potočnik. Step outside onto the balcony and there are some fantastic views of the Alps.

Three decades of ongoing research have revealed some intriguing finds around the castle site, including the remains of a **Stone Age settlement** and some 27 graves from an Old Slavic burial ground believed to date from the tenth century – some of the finds are on display at the Kamnik Museum (see below). According to local myth the castle is home to **Countess Veronika**, half-woman, half-snake, who is said to jealously guard the castle's hidden treasures. Whatever the truth, her legend lives on in the town seal, and each year she's brought back to life during the Medieval Days festival (see p.92).

From Sutna to the Stari Grad

From the bottom of the castle continue south along **Šutna**, the town's attractive, crescent-shaped main street, which is lined with neat two-storey Baroque buildings variously housing shops, living quarters and the odd café. Midway along the street, the **Parish Church of the Annunciation**, along with its enormous detached Gothic belfry, looms into sight. Preceded by two earlier churches, this eighteenth-century building features a Renaissance-style altar by Ivan Vurnik – well known for his decorative work in Ljubljana – while the frescoes on the presbytery walls, illustrating various feast days, are by Matija Kozelj who also painted the nave and chapels. Note too the intricately cut relief above the portal entrance, which depicts a lamb with vine leaves.

A little further down at no. 33 is the **Sadnikar Collection** (Sadnikarjeva muzejska zbirka), a wonderful assemblage of antique furniture, porcelain, weapons and sacral art, amassed by local veterinarian Dr Josip Nikolaj Sadnikar (1863–1952), the man who discovered the woolly mammoth skeleton now residing in Ljubljana's Natural History Museum. Among its many priceless items are paintings by Metzinger and Tintoretto (the latter one of only two in the country), and a bust by Ivan Mestrovič, Croatia's greatest sculptor. Take a close look at the magnificent carved wooden door leading into the main room, inscribed with the date August 12, 1936, to commemorate the day the King of Yugoslavia came to the house. Visits must be arranged through the tourist office (€2 per person).

Two hundred metres south of here, on a gently sloping hillside across the rail tracks, is the sixteenth-century **Zaprice Castle** (Grad Zaprice), later renovated into a Baroque mansion and now housing the occasionally stimulating **Kamnik Museum** (Tues–Sat 9am–noon & 4–6pm, Sun 10am–1pm; €2). It's particularly worth visiting for its exhibition on the recent excavations at Mali Grad (see p.93), which includes an old Slavic skeleton discovered in 1990 and various other prehistoric relics. Rather less stirring is the exhibition of Bentwood furniture, whose pioneer, Michael Thonet, was the first to use wood-bending techniques for the purpose of crafting chairs and tables, and an exhibition on Kamnik bourgeois life in the nineteenth century. On the overgrown lawn in front of the museum are four one- and two-cell *kašče* or **granaries** – squat, thatched-roof structures which served as storehouses for alpine herdsmen as they went about their work in the mountain valleys. Prevalent in the nearby Tuhinj Valley (from where these are taken), this particular form of peasant architecture is common throughout the country.

Atop the 585-metre-high Bergantov Hill, east of the Kamniška Bistrica river, is **Stari Grad** (Old Castle), dating from the twelfth century but abandoned in the sixteenth century. Although there's now little to see except a desolate heap of ruins and a rather downbeat restaurant, the reward for the tough little walk to reach them – which begins 100m south along the main road opposite the bus station – is some fine **views** of the town and Alps. You can also reach the castle by car, taking the road beginning in the suburb of Novi Trg.

Eating and drinking

The choice of places to **eat** in Kamnik is very limited. Best bets are the colourful and characterful *Napoli Pizzeria*, on the south side of Mali Grad at Sadnikarjeva 5, and in the same vein, *De Cecco* at Šutna 68, which also offers a number of fondues. Alternatively, *Pri Podkvi*, next to the *Pension Kamrica* at Trg Svobode 1 (closed Sun), has a largely steak-based menu, with dishes that change daily. *Kavarna Veronika*, located in a fabulous spot underneath Mali Grad, on the corner of Glavni trg and Japljeva ulica, is, day or night, the town's premier meeting place, serving up the full range of **coffees** and **beers** as well as a tempting selection of cakes.

Volčji Potok and the Snovik Thermal Spa

Four kilometres south of Kamnik, near the village of Radomlje, is the **Volčji Potok Arboretum** (daily 8am–6pm, until 8pm in summer; €5, free in winter; ⓦ www.arboretum-vp.si), Slovenia's largest and most important horticultural park. Volčji Potok, meaning "Wolf's Brook", had a number of proprietors over the centuries, before the aristocratic Souvan family bought the estate in 1882. They nurtured extensive parklands around the Baroque mansion house, which was subsequently destroyed during World War II. Following Leo Souvan's death in 1949, the estate was turned over to the government, though it was under the auspices of Ljubljana University that the park was conceived, in 1952.

The great Slovene polymath Janez Vajkard Valvasor (see p.242) once described the park as "a great and fertile place, boasting superb meadows and most fruitful fields". It is no less appealing today, home to over three thousand species of plants, shrubs and trees, all sensitively assimilated into the surrounding woodland. However, it's the neatly manicured **French Garden** that most people make a beeline for, though just as lovely is the landscaped **English Park**, with its silky, perfectly trimmed lawns, and the **beech forests** are ideal for a gentle ramble. Although a beautiful place to visit any time of year, the best time to come is in spring, when the daffodils and tulips are in full bloom. The bizarre (and, quite frankly, useless) bus schedule has five buses a day making the trip from Kamnik on weekdays (6am, 8am, 1.15pm, 2.45pm & 7.10pm), but only one on Saturdays (4.50pm) and Sundays (4pm). Coming back, there are just two a day on weekdays (7.35am & 5.55pm), with one on Saturdays (9.45am), and on Sundays (9.35am). The fantastically scenic **Golf Course Arboretum**, located right next to the park, is a very tight eighteen-hole course, guaranteed to satisfy even the most demanding of golfers – expect to pay around €35 per round (☏01/831-8080, ✉igrisce@golfarboretum.si).

If you fancy something slightly more relaxing, head to the **Snovik Thermal Spa** (☏01/834-4100, ✉terme-snovik@zarja-kovis.si), located in a peaceful spot 9km east of Kamnik out on the road towards Celje. Slovenia's newest spa incorporates indoor and outdoor pools (Mon–Thurs 9am–8pm, Fri–Sun til 10pm; €7 for 2hr, €10 day ticket), saunas and steam baths; if you wish to stopover, there are apartments sleeping two- to- five people (❻–❽) – the price includes entry to the spa. From Kamnik there are just two buses a day on weekdays (10.30am & 12.30pm) and one on Saturdays and Sundays (10.30am), with two return buses Monday to Saturday (1.20pm & 4.15pm) and one on Sundays (4.15pm).

Velika Planina

Velika Planina, a broad alpine plateau comprising grassy slopes, sinkholes and clusters of dwarf pines, is one of Slovenia's prime dairy farming regions as well as a hugely popular destination for skiers and walkers. Touching a height of 1666m, the plain, also known as the Great Highlands, was once a heavily forested area

– as evidenced by the remaining clumps of trees scattered across the terrain – but is now given over to a group of small settlements (Velika Planina, Mala Planina, Tiha Dolina and others), distinguished by dozens of silvery-grey wooden huts, unique for their conical, shingled roofs which extend like witches' hats almost all the way down to ground level. Though popular with skiers during the winter, the plateau is at its busiest during the summer months, when walkers, loaded with picnic supplies, trek the well-worn, marked paths between settlements, occasionally stopping off to buy cheese or milk from the shepherds. There are three mountain huts on Mala Planina; *Jarški Dom* (☏041/676-254; open all year), *Črnuški Dom* (☏041/843-172; June–Sept daily; Oct–May Sat & Sun), and *Domžalski Dom* (☏051/340-730; June–Sept daily; Oct–May Sat & Sun), all of which have **accommodation** in multi-bedded rooms, and offer hot food – see box on p.146 for more information on mountain huts.

The most satisfying way to visit Velika Planina is to hike up and take the **cable car** down. The cable car (*žičnica*; June to mid-Sept: hourly Mon–Thurs 8am–6pm, Fri–Sun 8am–8pm; mid-Sept to May: hourly Mon–Thurs 8am–4pm; Fri–Sun 8am–6pm; €8 return) is located 11km north of Kamnik and ascends to 1407m, from where there are chairlifts up to the top of the plateau – the area known as **Gradišče**; alternatively, or if the chairlift is not operational, you can walk, though it is a steep and gruelling climb. You will be rewarded, however, by the presence of the *Zeleni Rob* snack bar at the top (June–Aug daily, Sept–May Sat & Sun). The main trail begins at the village of **Stahovica**, 5km north of Kamnik and 6km south of the cable car station, a most enjoyable hike which takes around three hours at a steady pace; after about an hour, a sign diverts you to the fifteenth-century **Church of St Primoz** (Cerkev Sv Primoz), a convenient spot to pause and take in the glorious views, before pushing on towards Mala Planina.

There's a small **campsite** next to the cable car station (☏01/832-5566; June–Sept), and **bikes** for hire (€11 for the day) from the same spot; these can be taken on the cable car, which is useful as there is a good, and fairly demanding, cycle track on Velika Planina itself – a cycle map detailing a number of routes in the region can be obtained from the tourist office in Kamnik (see p.93).

Kamniška Bistrica

Three kilometres north of the cable car station is the tiny settlement of **KAMNIŠKA BISTRICA**, an idyllic recreation spot lying at the head of the Kamniške Alps and a key starting point for **hikes** up into the central tract of the mountains. Note that the following routes are all one way. The two most popular hikes from here, which should suit walkers of all abilities, are **Kamniško Sedlo** to the north (1884m; 3hr 30min) and **Kokrško Sedlo** to the northwest (1793m; 3hr 30min) – both have mountain huts open between June and mid-October. There are several longer and more demanding hikes just over a kilometre back down towards the cable car station, beginning at a track just before the stone bridge; the track, which heads eastwards up the **Kamniška Bela Valley** (you must also cross the brook, which may be tricky if there has been rain), leads to **Presedelj** (1613m; 3hr), **Korošica** (1910m; 4hr 45min) – there's a hut here open between June and September – and **Ojstrica** (2350m; 6hr). If you don't fancy one of these hikes, take the same path for about 25 minutes until you come to a fork – the rocky path to the left will shortly bring you to the **Orglice Waterfall** (Slap Orglice), partly concealed but still an impressive sight. Back in Kamniška Bistrica, **refreshments** can be taken at the *Dom v Kamniški Bistrici*, which also offers dorm **accommodation** (☏01/832-5544; May–Oct daily; Nov–April Sat & Sun only). From Kamnik to Kamniška Bistrica, there are three **buses** a day on weekdays (7am, 11.30am & 4.35pm) and two on Saturdays (7.20am & 4.45pm) and Sundays (7.50am &

4.55pm). The return buses are: weekdays (7.35am, 12.05pm & 5.10pm); Saturdays (8.25am & 5.20pm); and Sundays (8.30am & 5.30pm).

Škofja Loka and around

Not to be outdone by Kamnik, **ŠKOFJA LOKA** (Bishop's Meadow), 19km northwest of Ljubljana, lays fair claim to being one of the oldest and loveliest settlements in Slovenia. Lying at the confluence of the two branches of the Sora River, Škofja Loka was first documented in 973 AD, when the settlement of Stara Loka, along with the Selška Dolina and Poljanska Dolina valleys, was conferred upon the bishops of Freising, who would oversee town rule for the next eight centuries. During the early fourteenth century the town was fortified with a five-gate wall – parts of which can still be seen – while the ancient core was "parcelled" into segments. However, despite being pillaged by both the counts of Celje and the Turks, the town layout has changed remarkably little.

For such a modestly sized town, its sights are reasonably well dispersed, from Mestni trg and the handsome town castle in the centre to Stara Loka in the north, and the suburb of Puštal to the southeast. Beyond here, in **Crngrob** and **Suha**, are two of the finest frescoed churches in Slovenia. Škofja Loka could easily be done as a half- or full-day trip from Ljubljana – accommodation is almost non-existent and the nightlife won't detain you – or alternatively en route to Bled or Bohinj via Kranj.

△ Velika Planina

▲ Selška Valley, Stara Loka, Crngrob & ❶

CESTA TALCEV

KIDRIČEVA CESTA

N

Train Station ▶

Capuchin Monastery

Church of St Anne

KAPUCINSKI TRG

Bus Station

STARA CESTA

Suha & Church of St John Baptist ▶

Capuchin Bridge

River Selščica ◀

Church of St James

❸ Granary & France Mihelič Gallery

CANKARJEV TRG ❷

NAZLJA ULICA

Church of St Mary

❹ MESTNI TRG

KLOBOVSOVA ULICA

Homan House

SPODNJI TRG

Spital Church

STUDENEC

SORŠKA CESTA

Town Castle

Town Hall

(i)

Sora River

Martin House

GRABENK POT

POLJANSKA CESTA

KGZ

FUŽINSKA ULICA

ACCOMMODATION
Mini-hotel   **A**

Puštal Castle

Church of Holy Cross

PUŠTAL

RESTAURANTS & CAFÉS
Homan	**4**
Jesharna	**2**
Kašča	**3**
Pr' Starman	**1**

Devil's Footbridge

0   100 m

ŠKOFJA LOKA

▼ Žiri & Poljanska Valley   ▼ Nace's House   ▼ Nace's House

The town's major annual happening, at the end of June, is the **Medieval Days Festival**, a week of medieval-themed events similar to those which take place in Kamnik.

Arrival, information and accommodation

The **train station** is located 3km northeast of town and connected to the centre by hourly buses (none Sun). Far more conveniently, the **bus station** is on Kapucinski trg, just a few paces from the old town across the river; it has a left-luggage office (daily 6am–6pm; €1.5). The main **tourist office** is a five-minute walk east of the bus station at Kidričeva cesta 1a (May–Sept Mon–Fri 8am–7pm, Sat & Sun 9am–2pm; Oct–April Mon–Fri 8am–4pm, Sat 9am–2pm; ℡04/517-0600; ⊛www.skofjaloka.si) There's another, less useful one, at Mestni trg 7; June–Sept Mon–Fri 8.30am–7.30pm, Sat & Sun 8.30am–12.30pm & 5–7.30pm; Oct–May Mon–Fri 8.30am–7pm, Sat 8.30am–12.30pm; ℡04/512-0268) – they do, however, have **bikes** for hire here (€8 for half a day, €15 for a full day). The **post office** is located next to the bus station (Mon–Fri 8am–7pm, Sat 8am–noon).

The only **accommodation** in town is the *Mini-hotel*, 1.5km west of the centre at Vincarje 47 (℡04/515-0540, ✉metka@minihotel.si; ❺), whose ultra-clean, comfortably furnished rooms have fabulous views of the Alps; the hotel also has tennis and squash courts (free to guests), sauna and fitness facilities. To get here from the bus station, cross the Capuchin Bridge, take a right turn and continue along the road. Another possibility, if you don't mind staying a little further out, is accommodation on a **tourist farm** (❷), which can be booked through the tourist office.

The Town

The best place to start a tour of the town is Kapucinsksi trg on the north bank of the River Selščica. On this square, and a few paces west of the bus station, is the modest little **Church of St Anne**, consecrated in 1713. More interesting is the adjoining **Capuchin Monastery**, and its library, whose priceless collection of medieval manuscripts includes a copy of the celebrated *Škofjeloški Pasjon* (Škofja Loka Passion), the oldest written dramatic text in the Slovene language, dating from 1721 (see box below). If you want to see this, as well as other works in the library, contact the tourist office or the monastery (☎04/512-0970). From the monastery proceed south across the narrow **Capuchin Bridge** (Kapucinski most), whose stunning stone arch is reminiscent of the Mostar Bridge in Bosnia, which was blown up in 1993 during the Bosnian war. It was built upon the orders of Bishop Leopold in the fourteenth century, making it one of the oldest of its type in Europe, and later named after the Capuchin friars who settled here in the eighteenth century. Some years later, in a cruel twist of fate, the bishop plunged headlong into the river whilst riding across the bridge on his horse – an incident that probably would not have occurred had he also erected iron balustrades of the type that now line either side of the bridge. Perched on a pedestal in the centre of the bridge is a statue of a wistful looking St John Nepomuk.

Passing through the arch that once served as the town gate, you enter the old town. The first site of note is the **Convent Church of St Mary**, whose Baroque design came about as a result of a fire in 1669 that destroyed much of the original 1358 building. A short walk east of the church is Cankarjev trg, a nondescript square partly redeemed by the late-Gothic **Parish Church of St James** (Cerkev Sv Jakob), most of which dates from 1471. Its untidy grey exterior contrasts sharply with the interior, which, though eerily dark, features a magnificent stellar rib-vaulted ceiling embellished with bosses showing portraits of church patrons and

Škofja Loka Passion Play

Performed for the first time in over 270 years in 1999, the **Skofjeloški pasijon** (Škofja Loka Passion Play) is one of Slovenia's most remarkable, albeit rarely seen, spectacles. Written by Friar Romauld Marušič in 1721, it was the first dramatic text in the Slovenian language, a form of medieval and Baroque theatre comprising biblical stories or allegories pertaining to the suffering of Christ – hence its staging around the Good Friday period.

The tone of the play (it's actually more of a procession) is set by the Starbearer – dressed in a red habit to symbolize the impending, bloody agony – followed by Death, Hell and a total of seventeen other scenes, or tableaux, such as the Last Supper, Judgement Day and the Crucifixion. Aside from its slight contemporary twist, and the introduction of a musical element, the play has otherwise remained faithful to its original eighteenth-century production, based on a similar order of events, an almost identical text, and use of the original language.

Such is the organization and finance involved – some six hundred amateur actors, eighty horses, and carefully constructed stage sets at various locations around town are required – that the event is staged only every few years; there are no definite plans for the next one, so it's best to check with the tourist office for details.

the town guilds. Other notable works include the black marble Renaissance altars dating from 1694, and the chandeliers and baptismal font by Plečnik. Note too the splendid late-Gothic tympanum above the main entrance. Behind the church is the **School**, which has existed here in some form or other since the sixteenth century; the stone tablet on the crumbling facade identifies the founder as Mihael Papler, the owner of Loka Castle.

Mestni trg and Spodnji trg

From Cankarjev trg the street narrows before opening up into **Mestni trg** (Town Square), the town's old medieval market place, an atmospheric, rectangular space framed by many-coloured three-storey burgher houses, almost every other one marked with a plaque denoting its historical significance. Occupying a prime spot at the square's north end is the **Homan House** (Homanova hiša), an exceptional amalgam of Gothic and Renaissance styles, featuring a turret-like corner projection and sixteenth-century frescoes of St Christopher and the bottom half of a warrior, only discovered in 1970. Its outdoor **café**, shaded by a magnificent linden tree, is the most popular meeting place in town; Ivan Grohar, the great Impressionist painter, was a regular at the inn and completed his celebrated *Loka in Snow*, now hanging in the National Gallery in Ljubljana, from here. Further Baroque frescoes were revealed in 1972 on the facade of no. 35 – the former **town hall** (Rotovž) – which also possesses a fine Gothic portal and Renaissance-style arcaded courtyard. Opposite the town hall is the **Plague Pillar**, erected in 1751 by the townspeople in gratitude for their deliverance from fire and plague. Heading down through the square, other buildings worth a glance include the **Žigon House** (Žigonova hiša) at no. 15, formerly a sixteenth-century residential and trade house, and the **Martin House** (Martinova hiša), the last house on the right at no. 26, which was built on top of a section of the old town walls.

Running parallel to Mestni trg to the east is **Spodnji trg** (Lower Square), formerly a residential area for the poorer townsfolk, but now a downtrodden, traffic-filled thoroughfare. At its extreme northern end is the **town granary** (Kašča), a sturdy old building used during the Middle Ages for collecting taxes, which usually took the form of grain or cheese; the granary now houses a good restaurant (see p.102) and the **France Mihelič Gallery** (Galerija Franceta Miheliča; Tues–Sun noon–5pm; €2), featuring a superb exhibition of the artist's work from the 1970s. His apocalyptic themes of disintegration, decay and disappearance are embodied in a series of disturbing, surrealist paintings of dismembered bodies and rotting organisms; of particular interest are his paintings of scenes from the Ptuj Kurent (see box on p.310). Midway down the street is the **Špital Church**, a shabby-looking Baroque structure rebuilt in 1720 after the previous church burnt down.

Škofja Loka Castle

Mounted on a low grassy hill to the west of Mestni trg is Škofja Loka's majestic medieval **town castle** (Loški Grad), first mentioned in 1215 as "castrum firmissimum Lonca" – meaning "strongly fortified castle" – though most of what you see today dates from the beginning of the sixteenth century, following the earthquake of 1511. The main reason for visiting the castle is its **Town Museum** (Loški Muzej; April–Oct Tues–Sun 9am–6pm; Nov–March Sat & Sun 9am–5pm; €2.5), which holds a comprehensive, and occasionally enlightening, collection of local and regional exhibits. Before entering the museum proper, pop into the **castle chapel**, which holds four spectacular Baroque gilded altars rescued from the church in the village of Dražgoše, near Železniki, which was destroyed by the Germans during World War II.

The first three rooms, given over to the dominion of Škofja Loka, are unspectacular, save for a superb votive oil painting depicting the great town fire of August 19, 1698. The next room charts the rise of the town craftsmen and their **guilds**, set up in and around Škofja Loka in the fifteenth century in order to protect the interests of blacksmiths, tanners, tailors and other trades from both local and foreign competition; the assemblage of deeds, chests and banners is very impressive. Guilds were eventually abolished in 1859, owing to a combination of increased free-marketing practices and the French Revolution, although many of their customs were preserved until World War II in the form of guild fraternities. Elsewhere on the ground floor, look out for some possessions of the acclaimed Slovene writer Ivan Tavčar, and painted peasant furniture belonging to the Kalan family, whom Tavčar wrote about in his celebrated novel *Visoška kronika* (Visoko Chronicle; see p.106).

Heading upstairs, bypass the dull natural history and archeological sections and make for the excellent **ethnographical collection**, which illustrates the traditional ways and means of peasant living before industrialization, with a fine display of agricultural tools and objects, models of buildings indigenous to the Loka region, and a mock-up of a typical "black" kitchen (a superb real-life example of which can be seen in Nace's House; see below). The remaining rooms catalogue the importance to the region of crafts such as lace-making, millinery and dyeing, many of which have long since disappeared. The last room is dedicated to the art of making honey bread using ornate wooden moulds, a practice known as "Mali Kruhek" ("Small Loaves"); on display is a collection of the types of moulds – typically made from pear- or plum-tree wood and featuring motifs of a secular or figural design – used to shape the bread, traditionally baked for holidays and religious feasts. The castle is reachable via two footpaths: from Klobovsova ulica just to the west of the Homan House, or from the path at the southern end of Mestni trg.

Stara Loka

The suburb of **Stara Loka** (Old Loka), a short walk north of Kapucinski trg, stakes its claim to be one of the oldest localities in Slovenia, with origins dating from 973 AD. In the centre of the district is the lesser-known **Old Loka Castle**, thought to have evolved from the Bishop's Palace around the beginning of the fifteenth century, but which, save for the round towers, has retained few of its original features. One part of the castle houses the **Museum of Post and Telecommunications** (Muzej pošte in telekomunikacij; Tues–Fri 9am–4.30pm, Sun 10am–5.30pm; €2), which, as its title implies, presents the development of the Slovene postal and telecommunications systems – though interesting enough, it would be far more enjoyable with some English captions. The greater part of the castle, however, is occupied by the Centre for the Blind and Partially Sighted – look out for the unique sundial for the blind at the entrance. Opposite the castle stands the neo-Romanesque **Church of St George** (Cerkev Sv Jurij), built in 1865 and unremarkable save for some impressive sixteenth- and- seventeenth-century tombstones along the side chapels.

Puštal

Located on the right bank of the Poljanska Sora River, the peaceful suburb of **Puštal** is a lovely place for a stroll and also contains one of the town's best sights. Crossing the wooden **Hudičeva brv** (Devil's Footbridge), a ten-minute walk south of Spodnji trg, follow the road south until you arrive at Puštal 74, otherwise known as **Nace's House** (Nacetova hiša; to visit call ☎041/769-425 or contact the tourist office; €2; ⓦwww.nacetovahisa.com). Named after its first owner, Ignacij "Nace" Homan, this almost perfectly preserved eighteenth-century Slovene homestead is predominantly of Baroque appearance, though its stone-vaulted cellar and two "black kitchens" (see p.134) are evidence of fifteenth- and sixteenth-century

Hiking and cycling around Skofja Loka

The **Škofja Loka Hills** to the west of town present some terrific opportunities for hiking and cycling. The most popular local excursion is the two-hour **hike to Lubnik** (1025m), reachable via footpaths from Vincarje or from Škofja Loka Castle, passing by the castle ruins and the hamlet of Grabovo. The *Dom na Lubnik* mountain hut at the summit has beds and serves hot food (T04/512-0501; March–Dec daily, Jan & Feb Sat & Sun only). The further west you go, the higher the peaks, culminating in **Stari Vrh**, a small ski resort, and **Blegoš**, the region's highest peak at 1562m – there's a hut here too (T041/212-612; May–Oct daily, Nov–April Sat & Sun only). The 1:50,000 map *Škofjeloško in Cerkljansko Hribovje* (€7) available from the tourist offices, details all routes.

A superb network of **cycling tracks** has now been established in the hills, with routes designed to suit riders of all abilities. The entire track covers an area of some 300km, divided up into twelve stages, with each trail clearly marked by green boards attached to posts. The excellent *Loka's Cycling Track* (€5) map, available from the tourist offices, details all stages, indicating elevation, degree of difficulty and sights along the way. **Bikes** can be rented from the tourist office on Mestni Trg (see p.98).

elements. Its furnishings, including a fine maple-wood table, carved chairs and a ceramic heating stove featuring a motifed-tile from 1417, are all original; take a look, too, at the skilfully crafted iron grilles (*gatri*) adorning the windows.

From the house, head north towards the main road; on the left-hand side is **Puštal Castle** (Puštal Grad), dating from around 1220 and now housing a music school. Two hundred metres east of the castle, a gravelly path breaks off from the main road and spirals steeply up to the simple Baroque **Church of the Holy Cross** (Cerkev Sv Kriš), from where there are wonderful views of the town and castle (you can get the key to the church from the house just below).

Eating and drinking

The best **restaurant**, in a town where there are few, is *Kašča*, housed in the basement of the old granary at Spodnji trg 2 (closed Sun), and which serves tasty stews, such as Kašča pot, to augment its impressive stock of fish and grilled-meat dishes – this is also the place to head to for wine. Two other reasonable places are *Jesharna*, a simple but welcoming pizzeria located across the bridge from the bus station, and *Pr' Starman*, Škofja Loka's most typically Slovene restaurant, just down from the old castle at Stara Loka 22 (closed Sun).

Comfortably the best **drinking** spot in town is *Homan*, whose outdoor terrace – enveloped by a huge linden tree – is a lovely place to relax, day or night.

Around Škofja Loka: Suha and Crngrob

Standing anonymously in a field 2.5km east of town on the outskirts of the village of **Suha** is the diminutive **Church of St John the Baptist** (Cerkev Sv Janez Krstnik), acclaimed for its outstanding medieval paintings. Upon entering this small fifteenth-century church, you are immediately drawn to the stellar rib-vaulted presbytery, coated with stunning frescoes depicting scenes from the life of Christ and the Virgin Mary (surrounded by evangelists, angels and various Apostles peering through columns). The lower panels depict images of the wise and foolish maidens and the holy martyrs, executed by Jernej of Loka. On the inner wall of the triumphal arch is a representation of the Last Judgement. There is no public transport to the village (and buses do not stop on the nearby main road), so if you don't have your own transport hire a bike from the tourist office in town to avoid a long and draining walk. The key to the church can be obtained from no. 32, approximately 150m down from the church.

Crngrob and the Church of the Annunciation

Four kilometres north of Škofja Loka, in the tiny settlement of **Crngrob** (Black Grave), is the fourteenth-century pilgrimage **Church of the Annunciation** (Marijino oznanenje), regarded as one of Slovenia's most significant monuments and distinguished by some matchless frescoes. Completed in the seventeenth century, but originating in the thirteenth century, the church manifests a variety of styles – Romanesque, Gothic and Baroque – though its outward form is predominantly Gothic. The nineteenth-century neo-Gothic columned portico at the western end of the church reveals one of the finest **frescoes** in Slovenia, the partly-effaced *Holy Sunday* (Sveta Nedelja), completed around 1470 by the workshop of Janez Ljubljanski. More than forty scenes portray a series of tasks which good Christians are obliged to do on the Sabbath – pray, assist the sick, and so on; as well as what they should not be doing – gambling, drinking and the like. To the left is *The Passion of Christ*, an earlier work completed by the Friulian masters.

Though on a much larger scale, the church interior is strikingly similar to that of the parish church in Škofja Loka, its shadowy tripartite nave giving way to a sumptuously light chancel supported by six octagonal columns and featuring a delightful pale red-, yellow- and blue-painted rib-vaulted ceiling. Completed by Ljubljana craftsman Jurij Skarnos in 1652, the profoundly ornate **high altar** – the largest Baroque gilded altar in the country – is festooned with almost one hundred statuettes and pillars and rounded off with an oil painting by Leopold Layer. The fabulous organ dates from 1753, and the immense bell-tower, featuring a large fresco of St Christopher on its south wall, was raised to its present height of 62m in 1666. If the church is locked you can obtain the key from the house below (no. 10). The church can be reached via a monotonous, straggling road which extends northwards from Groharjevo naselje in Stara Loka (a 1hr walk). Alternatively, take the Kranj bus and alight at the village of **Dorfarje**, from where it's a twenty-minute walk to the church. If you fancy a rural stopover there is the wonderfully comfortable *Pri Marku* **tourist farm** just down from the church at no. 5 (℡04/513-1626, ⊛www.pri-marku-porenta.si; ❸) – you can even sleep in the hay barn. Refreshments can be had at the *gostilna* just a few paces from the church (closed Wed).

The Selška and Poljanska valleys

The **Selška** and **Poljanska Valleys**, which fan out from Škofja Loka northwest and southwest respectively, are often ignored in favour of the region's more obvious attractions a short way north. This is unfortunate, as there are several lovely villages here and some of the scenery is immensely rewarding. Although there are a few buses serving most of these places, having your own transport will enable you to see a lot more, quickly.

Selca

Twisting its way north out of Škofja Loka, the narrow, flat-bottomed **Selška Dolina Valley** stretches for some 34km between the northern flank of the Škofja Loka Hills and the southern ridge of the forested Jelovica plateau. Twelve kilometres up the valley is the quaint village of **SELCA** (from where the valley took its name), distinguished by the Baroque **Church of St Peter** (Cerkev Sv Petra), rebuilt in 1767 after having been burnt down on two previous occasions; the centrepiece of the church is the high altar, featuring a fine painting by Langus, depicting Christ bestowing power upon Peter.

Železniki

The road continues west for 5km to **ŽELEZNIKI**, the valley's key economic centre. This spindly three-kilometre-long town, made up of several interconnected settlements, has been shaped by its centuries-old iron-smelting industry, which reached its peak here in the seventeenth century when two blast furnaces and more than sixty workshops were operational. Technological advances throughout Europe at the end of the nineteenth century, coupled with the depletion of iron-ore stocks, brought about the demise of the industry and the last furnace was decommissioned in 1902.

The one remaining **blast furnace** (*plavž*), dating from 1826 and the only preserved technical monument of its kind in the country, is situated at the western end of town and stands as a fitting memorial to a bygone era. The town's industrial heritage is thoroughly documented in the **Železniki Museum** (Muzej železniki; June–Aug Tues–Thurs 8am–2pm, Fri & Sat 8am–5pm, Sun 1–5pm; Sept–May Tues–Fri 9am–2pm, Sat 8am–1pm; €2), located opposite the furnace in the **Plavec house**, dating from 1637 and named after the former owner of the furnace. Despite the absence of English captions, the museum is an enjoyable affair, and includes a lovely collection of lace work from Železniki, considered to be the second largest lace centre in Slovenia after Idrija. If you want to see what all the fuss is about, visit the town in mid-July during the **Days of Lace Fair** (Čipkarski Dnevi v Železnikih), a week-long series of lace-related events.

Buses drop passengers off in the centre of town by the **tourist office**, at Trnje 20 (Tues–Fri 9am–noon & 2–5pm, Sat 9am–noon; ☎04/510-2600), which also sells a range of lace products. The only **place to stay** in Železniki is the homely *Kemperle*, located just beyond the public swimming pool in the eastern part of town at Otoki 3 (☎04/514-6084, ✉kemperle@siol.net; ❸). The *Pri Pujsu* **restaurant**, a five-minute walk further east of the *Kemperle* at Češnjica 8, is a decent place to eat, offering a varied mix of casseroles, stews and pasta dishes in warm, countrified surrounds. Better still, and if you've got your own transport, it's worth stopping off at the *Pri Slavcu* (Thurs–Mon) in **Zali Log**, the next village along.

Sorica

Nine kilometres west of Železniki, the road branches off to the right and winds steeply up to the extraordinarily picturesque alpine village of **SORICA**, its smooth undulating pastures spotted with small clusters of houses and dozens of drying racks. Sorica is celebrated as the birthplace of the great Slovene Impressionist painter Ivan Grohar, a sculpture of whom – palette in hand – greets visitors at the entrance to the village; his **birthplace** (Groharjeva hiša; €2) is located beyond the church at Spodnja Sorica 18, and contains a limited collection of his paintings and belongings – the key can be obtained from the *Macesen* restaurant next door, itself a decent enough place for a bite to eat (closed Mon). There are **accommodation** possibilities here in the village, including the *Pintar* apartment just a few paces down from Grohar's house at no. 13 (☎04/519-7055; ❷), and the *Pri Jurju* tourist farm next door at no. 14 (☎04/519-7018; ❷). The road continues onwards and upwards to the Soriška Planina ski resort and beyond to Bohinj. There are just two buses from Sorica to Železniki (Mon–Fri 5.07am & 1.17pm), and one from Železniki to Sorica (Mon–Fri 2.10pm).

Dražgoše and Jamnik

If you have your own transport, a delightfully scenic ride from Železniki – and a good short cut to Kropa (see p.116) – is up and over the **Jelovica Plateau**, a thickly forested highland plain that offered refuge to Partisans during World War II. That didn't, however, stop several ferocious battles taking place here, in particular in the hamlet of **DRAŽGOŠE**, 8km beyond Železniki on the plateau's southern fringe. Forty-one villagers were shot dead and the rest expelled as the village was razed by German troops in January 1942, an event belatedly commemorated by the erection of a brutal-looking concrete monument – though this can't detract from the superlative views of the surrounding lush countryside. Some 10km further on, the diminutive fifteenth-century Church of St Primoz, perched on a slender ridge just outside the village of **Jamnik**, hoves into view. On a clear day, you can easily identify a number of sights spread out below – including Kropa, Radovljica, and the Basilica in Brezje. From Jamnik, it's just 4km down to Kropa by which time you're out of the valley.

The Poljanska Valley

Flanked by the Škofja Loka Hills to the north and the slightly lower Polhov Gradec Hills to the south, the **Poljanska Valley** extends for some 35km between Škofja Loka and the small town of Žiri. Eleven kilometres southwest of Škofja Loka, in the tiny settlement of **LOG**, is the *Gostišče Premetovc*, a magnificent roadside inn accommodating one of the most distinguished restaurants in the region (Tues–Sat 4–9pm, Sun noon–6pm; reservations advised; ☎04/518-6000, ⓔpremetovc@siol. net). The inn also has two immaculately furnished suites (ⓞ).

Five hundred metres beyond the inn, across the bridge on the left, and then along the road to the right, is the **Visoko Mansion**, once the property of the celebrated writer Ivan Tavčar (1851–1923). The mansion (also known as the Tavčar Manor) is now sadly derelict and all there is to see is an enormous bronze sculpture – completed in 1957 by Jakob Savinšek – of a cross-legged Tavčar gazing across

Rupnik Line

Sequenced in an almost vertical chain between Soriška Planina in the north and the small town of Žiri some 50km further south are dozens of bunkers, tunnels, casemates and observation posts built by the Yugoslavs in response to border fortifications constructed by the Italians following the **Treaty of Rapallo in 1920** (see p.330). Although proposals to fortify the border were initially submitted in the mid-1920s, construction work didn't begin until 1937, under the command of its chief architect **Leon Rupnik**, a Yugoslav army general who was later tried and shot in Ljubljana for treason. In the event, the line was neither fully completed – due to the onset of World War II – nor were its existing defences pressed into service.

Many of the fortifications have recently been cleaned up and it's now possible (with a guide) to visit some of them, an opportunity that will almost certainly appeal to adrenaline junkies; the descent into the bunkers and tunnels – some nearly forty metres deep – is quite exhilarating. Moreover, the **hiking** in this region is terrific. The line has been divided into three stages (each stage is roughly a 6–7hr hike, the first is also accessible to cyclists), with a number of different excursions organized by the tourist office in Škofja Loka (☎04/517-0600; see p.98). These range from short two-hour tours (€4), to day-long hikes (€9 per person, €18 with lunch), though tours can be tailored to suit individual or group needs. The Rupnik Line Trail **map** (Po Sledeh Rupnikove Linije; €2), available from the tourist office in Škofja Loka, outlines all three stages.

the field. Born in **Poljane**, the next village along, Tavčar, erstwhile Ljubljana mayor and politician, was considered one of the country's foremost prose writers, basing much of his work on his experiences of life in the valley. His most famous novel, *Visoška Kronika* ("Visoko Chronicle"), charted the lives of the Kalan family who lived in the same house some two hundred years before Tavčar. Beyond the mansion lie the valley's central settlements, Poljane and Gorenja Vas, both pleasant enough but neither worth stopping off for.

Žiri

Twelve kilometres south of Gorenja Vas is **ŽIRI**, a small, quiet town renowned for its lace and shoemaking industries, both of which are well covered in the **Žiri Museum** (Muzej Žiri; May–Oct Sat & Sun 2–4pm; other times by appointment, contact the tourist office; €2). This is located 1km south of the centre at Tabor 2 in the dilapidated former mansion of the Freising bishops. Following World War II the town's various shoemaking industries morphed into the Alpina factory, which now employs around 800 people who manufacture ski boots and a range of other sports footwear for some of the world's top climbers and athletes. Although Žiri is not as large a lace centre as either Idrija or Železniki, the museum's bobbin-lace collection attests to its importance in the town during the first part of the twentieth century. If you wish to have a look at, or purchase, some lace items, pop into the small **Lace Gallery** at Jobstova 29 (Mon–Fri 4.30–7pm, Sat 9am–noon).

Buses drop passengers off in the centre of town, from where it's a two-minute walk to the **tourist information** booth on the main square, Trg Svobode (June–Sept daily 9am–5pm, Oct–May Sat & Sun 9am–1pm); information is also available from the Impulse agency, opposite the main square at Loška 1 (Mon–Fri 9am–noon & 3–7pm, Sat 9am–noon; ☎04/510-5580, ✉impulse-travel@siol. net), whose helpful staff can book **accommodation** on local tourist farms (❷). The *Gostilna Županu*, at Loška 78 (☎04/505-0000; ❸) in the northern part of town, is the sole central source of accommodation here, with a handful of neat, fresh-looking rooms. This is also the best place in town to **eat**, with pizzas, salads and meat dishes constituting the bulk of the menu. For **drinking**, most townsfolk congregate at the pubby *Na Voleriji* on Trg Svobode.

Kranj and around

Despite its reputation as a hard-nosed and gritty industrial centre, **KRANJ**, 10km from Škofja Loka and Slovenia's fourth-largest city, possesses an attractive old city centre severely at odds with its drab surrounds. Positioned on a steep, rocky promontory above the confluence of the Sava and Kokra rivers, between the foothills of the Julian Alps and the western spur of the Kamniške-Savinja Alps, Kranj has been the country's most important industrial city since the end of World War I. It is home to several of Slovenia's major manufacturing industries, including textiles, leather and electronics, which in total employ almost half of the city's population. However, beyond the grimescape of smoking chimneys, the old town possesses a clutch of fine late-Gothic buildings, and the city's strong associations with France Prešeren – he lived, worked and died here – are manifest in an excellent museum. Furthermore, nearby **Brdo Castle** is enjoyable side attraction.

The city's two key events are **Festival Carniola**, two months of street theatre, concerts and workshops at several locations throughout the Old Town from mid-June to mid-August, and **Kranj Nights**, a series of evening concerts at the end of August.

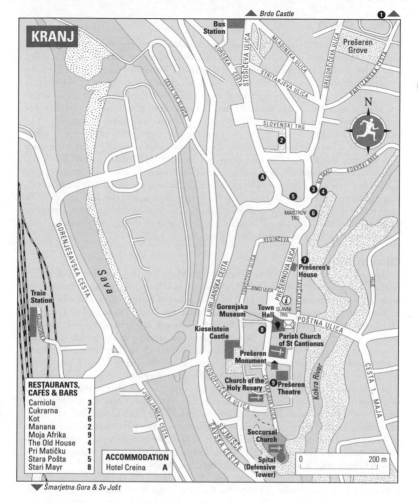

Arrival, information and accommodation

The **train station** is on the west bank of the River Sava, a ten-minute walk from town (or bus #2), and the **bus station** lies 500m north of the old town on Stošičeva ulica. The **tourist office**, at Glavni trg 2 (Mon–Fri 8am–6pm; ☎04/236-3030, Ⓦ www.lto-kokra.si), can arrange **accommodation** on tourist farms (❷) in the villages of **Preddvor**, **Naklo** and **Jezersko**, all a short way north of Kranj – they also have an **Internet** access point. The town's only hotel is the *Creina*, a hideous-looking brick building midway between the bus station and the old town at Koroška cesta 5 (☎04/202-4550, Ⓦ www.hotel-creina.si; ❺) – the rooms, though, are fresh-looking and perfectly agreeable. The **post office** is at Poštna ulica 4 (Mon–Fri 8am–7pm, Sat 8am–noon).

The Town

The town's attractive medieval centre begins at **Maistrov trg**, formerly the site of the upper town gate and once enclosed by the northern section of the city walls. The most obvious legacy of the walls is the **Spital Tower** – one of seven defensive towers incorporated within the walls – and which now forms part of the shop at no. 3. The square, liberally sprinkled with cafés and the hub of all social activity, segues into Prešernova ulica. At no. 7, a memorial plaque above the entrance denotes **Prešeren's House** (Prešerenova hiša; Tues–Sun 10am–6pm; €2). The two-storey building where Prešeren spent the last three years of his life is a fine example of a late-Gothic townhouse, its arcaded gallery uniting what were once two separate dwellings. The first floor has been turned into a superb memorial museum, chronologically presenting phases of Prešeren's life, with manuscripts, diaries and letters, accompanied by excellent explanatory notes. There is also much original furniture to admire, including the bed he died in and the desk and chair he used while working as a lawyer (see box on p.126). Prešeren is buried in **Prešeren Grove** (Prešernov Gaj), a small cemetery 500m north of town, and which has only one other grave, that of another local poet, Simon Jenko.

Glavni trg

Prešernova ulica opens up into **Glavni trg** (Main Square), an elongated square framed by delightful Gothic and Renaissance buildings, the most prominent of which is the **town hall** (Mestna hiša) on the corner of Poštna ulica, and which now accommodates the enjoyable **Gorenjska Museum** (Muzej Gorenjski; Tues–Sun 10am–6pm; €2.5). Its trio of exhibitions kicks off with an above-average collection of archeological finds, notably some outstanding grave goods including ceramic jugs and vessels, and beautifully cut jewellery and figurines. The most recent find is a valuable hoard of Roman tools – probably from a carpenter's workshop and thought to date from 4 AD – discovered in 1996 near Radomlje. The remainder of the museum's collection comprises an interesting assortment of sculptures by Lojze Dolinar (a student of the eminent Croatian sculptor Ivan Mestrovič), and an ethnological exhibition of folk art from Gorenjska, including beautifully crafted chests and cupboards, fifteenth-century frescoes, and a selection of Slovenia's famous beehive panels (see p.114). Have a look, too, at the magnificent Renaissance Hall, sporting a coffered ceiling and two inlaid wooden portals, which is now used as a venue for wedding ceremonies.

Dominating the square – indeed the city skyline – is the glowering **Parish Church of St Cantianus** (Cerkev Sv Kancijan), the most outstanding example of a Gothic hall-church in Slovenia; supported by four immense octagonal columns, its stellar-vaulted central nave is decorated with the *Star of Beautiful Angels* fresco, attributed to the workshop of Janez Ljubljanski, while numerous detailed keystones adorn the arches, most notably Mary and infant Jesus in front of the Triumphal Arch. Other highlights are the modestly fashioned high altar by the serial church architect Ivan Vurnik, and the neo-Gothic stained-glass windows by Kregar. Have a look, too, at the tympanum above the main entrance incorporating a relief of Christ on the Mount of Olives.

Outside the north side of the church is an early Slavonic **ossuary**, containing thousands of neatly stacked bones and skulls of Kranj citizens, thought to have been buried here between the fourteenth and sixteenth centuries but which were only discovered in the early 1970s (you need to ask at the town hall if you want to have a look). On the church's exterior south wall is a small **lapidary** of Roman and medieval tombstones and, beneath, a **fountain** bearing a statue of St John Nepomuk, somewhat bizarrely entangled in an octopus. Across the way, next to an oversized **monument** of Prešeren, is the **Prešeren Theatre** (Prešernovo Gledališče), a bland building which not even Plečnik's arched portico can enliven.

South to Pungert

From here the square narrows into Cankarjeva ulica; halfway down is the **Church of the Holy Rosary** (Cerkev Roženvesnka), a bland Gothic structure entirely reconstructed in 1892, which once served as a Protestant sanctuary during the Reformation. Beside the church is a Plečnik-designed **staircase**; on one side is a characteristic arcade, and in the middle, an unattractive looking fountain, also both by Plečnik. Walking down the stairs brings you to Vodopivčeva ulica (Mohor's Slope), where the lower town gate once stood, and beyond to the Sava River.

Cankarjeva ulica winds up at Trubarjev trg and the southern tip of the promontory known as **Pungert**, which rises up over the confluence of the Sava and Kokra rivers; unfortunately, the **Kokra Gorge**, an inaccessible 30-metre-deep canyon, is largely obscured by trees, though there are some much better views from the Poštna ulica bridge, east of Glavni trg. The horribly graffitied, three-storey **Defensive Tower**, right on the tip, is the only entirely preserved tower within the ancient city walls; at one stage it was adapted for use as a prison and as lodgings. Next to the tower, the late fifteenth-century **Succursal Church** (also called the Plague Church) is dedicated to SS Rok, Fabian and Sebastian in thanks for their intervention against the plague. Unfortunately, Martin Kremser-Schmidt's illustrious painting *Intercessors Against the Plague* (1773) – which until recently ornamented the high altar – has been removed and is currently held within the priest's house. The church is now used for services by the local Serbian Orthodox community.

Retracing your steps back to the Church of the Holy Rosary, head north along Tomšičeva ulica, where you'll pass a restored section of the **city walls**, beyond which is the **Kieselstein Castle** (Grad Kieselstein), formerly a fifteenth-century

△ Kranj

stronghold, later a manor house and now home to several cultural organizations and occasionally used as a venue for outdoor concerts. Continuing along the street, past a series of decaying buildings, you'll eventually end up back at Maistrov trg.

Eating and drinking

The best of a largely disappointing bunch of **restaurants** is *Pr' Matičku*, albeit inconveniently located in a residential area 1km northeast of town at Jezerska cesta 41; it's in a building aping a hunter's lodge, and the menu features a good selection of game dishes (such as medallions of bear, deer and pheasant), alongside the more prosaic pizzas and salads. Of those places in the old town, *Kot*, tucked away in the eastern corner of Maistrov trg, is the most agreeable, serving up very reasonably priced home specials (closed Sun); and *Stari Mayr*, down by the parish church, which, though it may not look like much, has good Slovene food, including cheap daily set menus. *Carniola*, at Gregorčičeva 2, is especially good for ice creams.

What Kranj lacks in decent restaurants, it more than makes up for in **bars** and **cafés**. The loudest and liveliest place in town is *Cafe Manana* at Slovenski trg 7, which features DJ nights at weekends (daily 10am–midnight, Fri & Sat til 4am – they've also got Internet access (free if you buy a drink). Otherwise, the area in and around Maistrov trg is crammed with watering holes, such as the classy and comfortable *Stara Pošta*, up on the fourth floor of the old post office building and sporting a groovy semicircular terrace bar that overlooks the square (daily 11am–midnight, Fri & Sat til 2am); and *The Old House*, a few paces to the north of Maistrov trg at Na Skali 5. Working your way down through the old town, two more very appealing options are *Cukrarna*, a funky, designer-furnished café at Tavčarjeva ulica 9, with an open terrace offering fine views over the Kokra River; and *Moja Afrika* at Cankarjeva ulica 3, an enjoyable, African-themed party bar featuring regular live music.

Around Kranj: Brdo Castle, Šmarjetna Gora and Sv Jošt

Kranj's suburbs present some good opportunities for more solitudinous excursions, the best of which is **Brdo Castle**, while the modest peaks of **Šmarjetna Gora** and **Sv Jošt** offer good walking for those with slightly more energy to expend.

Brdo Castle

Four kilometres northeast of Kranj, near the village of **Predoslje**, is **Brdo Castle** (Grad Brdo), Slovenia's most beautiful and elite presidential residence. Surrounded by 11km of fencing, the estate is no longer reserved exclusively for visits by high-ranking politicians and statesmen – among others, its more recent distinguished guests have included Pope John Paul II, George W. Bush and Vladimir Putin – and now anyone can nose around the castle's stately rooms (groups only here), ramble through the expansive parklands, or even partake in some sporting activities.

As early as 1446, a manor house – under the proprietary of the noble Egkh family (Egkh is German for "brdo" which in English means "hillock") – existed close to, or on the site of, the present castle, though it didn't assume its present form until the sixteenth century. In the mid-eighteenth century, ownership was transferred to the munificent Zois family, who remained in custody of the estate until 1929, after which time it was owned for a short period by the Karadjordjevič Yugoslav royal family. At the end of World War II the estate was nationalized and became one of Tito's many summer retreats – he was particularly enamoured with the place as it afforded him ample opportunity to indulge in his favoured activity of hunting. During this period security was such that a soldier was positioned every 100m, whether the great man was in residence or not. In 1961 Tito issued a decree declaring the estate to the Republic of Slovenia, though this hasn't stopped various members of the Karadjordjevič clan from recently trying to reclaim the property; unsurprisingly, the Slovene authorities have rejected this out of hand.

Even if you don't visit the castle itself (€7) – essentially a brief tour around a handful of rooms, including the magnificent dining room and Tito's trophy room – the grounds (€2) are most definitely worth the short trip from Kranj. Furthermore, you can participate in some horse riding (€12 for a 45min lesson; €20 for a 2hr jaunt around the estate), fishing (€85 per day), or tennis (€7 1hr). Visits to the castle must be booked several days in advance, as must bookings to the sumptuous *Zois* **restaurant** – the catch being that only groups (ten or more) are admitted to both. If you require **information** regarding any aspect of visiting the estate, contact the reception desk at the *Hotel Kokra*, located at the park entrance (℡04/260-1000, 🖰www.brdo.com; ❸); this smoothly run place, with supremely comfortable **rooms**, is almost entirely geared up for conference guests and business groups flying into nearby Brnik airport. If you wish to stay in one of the six Castle **suites**, then count on parting with around €550. Buses #5 and #6 run daily from the bus station in Kranj to the estate every forty minutes or so.

Šmarjetna Gora and Sv Jošt

From Kranj's western suburb of Stražišče, several paths wend their way up to **Šmarjetna Gora** (St Margaret's Hill), a popular forty-minute walk also accessible by car. At the summit is **St Margaret's Church** (Cerkev Sv Marjete), originally dating from 1342, but heavily renovated in 1989; though there's little to see inside, if you want to have a look the key can be obtained from the *Hotel Bellevue* (℡04/270-0070, 🖰www.bellevue.si; ❺), across the car park. This high-class **hotel**, with large, designer-furnished rooms, some with water beds and all with a balcony, also has a good **restaurant** with a pleasant outdoor terrace. There are marvellous views of Kranj, the Alps, and west across to **Sv Jošt**, a higher peak at 847m, and reachable from Stražišče – it's just under two hours from Pot na Jošt. At the summit is the Baroque **Church of St Jošt** (Cerkev Sv Joštu), built between 1735 and 1740 on the site of a former Gothic church. Snacks and drinks are available from the hut a few paces away (closed Mon).

Tržič

From Kranj, hourly buses make the twenty-minute trip north to **TRŽIČ**, a small, somnolent market town holding a handful of satisfying museums and just a stone's throw away from a delightful gorge (see p.112). Although the town has a strong tradition in a number of trades and crafts dating back to the Middle Ages, it was shoemaking that put Tržič on the map, an industry which forms the centrepiece of the **Tržič Museum**, located in the upper reaches of town at Muzejska 11 (Tržiški Muzej; July & Aug Tues–Sun 9am–5pm; Sept–June Mon–Fri 9am–3pm, Wed til 5pm; €2). At the end of the nineteenth century, almost every second house in town accommodated a shoemakers' workshop, though the trade slowly became more industrialized, culminating in the Peko factory – once, one of the most modern footwear factories in Europe, but now a dying industry employing around just two hundred people. Other important town crafts represented in the museum include tanners, wheelwrights, dyers and charcoal-burners.

One hundred and fifty metres south of the Tržič Museum, housed in the former Peko factory building at Koroška 9, is the entertaining **Homogea Museum** (July & Aug Tues–Sun 9am–1pm; rest of year by appointment, contact the tourist office; €2.5). Its permanent exhibition, entitled *Mammoth Hunters*, traces the evolution of man and his environment from four million years ago to the end of the early Stone Age in the form of fossil remains, archeological finds and life-size models. Two hundred metres southeast of the museum at Kurnikova pot 2 – walk south to the church, then along Partizanska ulica and across the bridge – is the **Kurnik House** (Kurnikova hiša; Mon–Fri 11am–noon; other times by appointment, contact the tourist office; €1.5), a beautifully preserved eighteenth-century Gorenjska peasant house named after its original owner, Vojteh Kurnik, who was born here in 1826. Although a wheelwright by profession, Kurnik's true passion was poetry, and in the memorial room dedicated to him, you can see a handful of wood shavings on which he wrote verses while working.

A forty-five-minute walk northeast of Tržič, beyond the tiny settlement of **Čadovlje**, is the fabulous **Dovžan Gorge** (Dovžanova soteska), a protected natural monument owing to its rich deposits of Palaeozoic fossils. Its most distinguishing features are the pyramidal limestone columns on the eastern slopes, and Borova Peč (Pine's bluff) on the western side, though the thrashing Tržiška Bistrica River, bisecting the gorge's steeply pitched sides, is no less impressive. At the gorge entrance you'll pass through a remarkable road tunnel, built at the end of the nineteenth century by Julij Born.

There are no trains to Tržič, but the **bus station** is handily located south of town on Cankarjeva Cesta, from where it's a couple of minutes' walk north to the **tourist office** at Trg svobode 18 (Mon–Fri 9am–5pm, Sat 9am–2pm; ℡04/597-1536, ⓦwww.trzic.si). There's nowhere to sleep in town but the tourist office can book **accommodation** on local tourist farms (❷). The only place of note to **eat** here is the *Pizzeria Pod Gradom*, just up from the Homogea Museum at Koroška 26 (closed Mon), while *Café Spela*, through the passageway next to the tourist office, is the place to head to for a coffee.

Radovljica

The initial urge for most travellers upon reaching **RADOVLJICA**, an expanding little town 21km north of Kranj, is to push straight on to Bled. This is a pity, as it boasts a beautiful square stuffed with some superb Gothic and Renaissance architecture, and one of Slovenia's most surprisingly engaging museums. Built upon a seventy-five-metre-high outcrop above the River Sava, the town came into its golden period during the early Middle Ages when feudal lords, most importantly the Ortenburgs, settled here, building their vast estates. Although Radovljica suffered a lengthy period of stagnation in the eighteenth and nineteenth centuries, the subsequent development of both the highway and railway kick-started the town back into life, and today, despite a population of little more than six thousand, it's a significant administrative and educational centre. With buses every thirty minutes from Bled, just 6km north, it makes for a simple and satisfying half-day trip.

For two weeks in mid-August Radovljica stages the **Festival Radovljica** (ⓦfestival-radovljica.amis.net), one of Europe's foremost festivals of ancient classical music, featuring an international crop of artists – tickets (€10-15) can be bought from the tourist office.

Arrival, information and accommodation

The **bus station** is smack bang in the centre of town on Kranjska cesta, and the **train station** is a couple of minutes south of the centre on Cesta svobode – from

Cave exploration

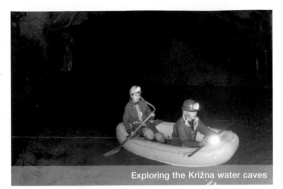

Exploring the Križna water caves

Although caves have been visited since the Middle Ages, it wasn't until the seventeenth century that **systematic exploration** and documentation of Slovenia's caves began. Foremost amongst the scholars of that time was the celebrated Slovene polymath **Janez Vajkard Valvasor**, who explored and wrote extensively on the mysterious subterranean phenomena. However it was only after a visit to Postojna by Emperor Franz Ferdinand in 1819 that caves came into fashion as a mass tourist destination. Today there are around two dozen caves open to the general public, some of which rank amongst Slovenia's most popular **tourist attractions**. A visit to one of these natural wonders could have you traversing an underground canyon, floating on a subterranean lake or even engaging with a cave's animal inhabitants.

Proteus anguinus – the Human Fish

There are an estimated two hundred or so animal species in Slovenia's caves, but none is as enigmatic as **Proteus anguinus**, the Human Fish. This peculiar-looking creature takes its name partly from the Greek sea-god (*Proteus*), and partly from the Latin word for snake (*anguinus*). *Proteus* is a 25cm long amphibian with pigment-less skin, bright red gills and atrophied eyes; it is snake-like in appearance, with two tiny pairs of legs (the front ones have three digits, the rear two – hence the 'human' part of its name) and a flat, pointed fin to help propel itself through water. The fact that the human fish is completely blind matters little, as the creature spends almost all of its one hundred years' existence entirely in the dark. While it usually consumes small animals such as insect larvae, it's not uncommon for *Proteus* to indulge in a spot of cannibalism; conversely, it can go years without food, leaving researchers stumped. The most vexing questions, however, concern its habits of reproduction, which remain, on the whole, a mystery. Although it can be found in many caves throughout the Slovenian Karst, *Proteus anguinus* is normally associated with **Postojna**.

Subterranean
Slovenia

From the magnificent show caves at Postojna and Škocjan to the Ravenska aragonite and Križna water caves, Slovenia boasts some of the finest underground systems in the world. To date, more than seven and a half thousand caves have been catalogued, the majority of which are located in the Karst region in southwest Slovenia.

Visiting Slovenia's caves

Visits to Slovenia's two classic **show caves**, Postojna and Škocjan, take place all year round, with tours usually lasting around ninety minutes; those expecting long walks and steep climbs need not worry, as there are well laid-out paths catering to the less physically inclined, and nothing other than warm clothing and half-decent shoes are required. However Slovenia also offers longer and more **adventurous caving** at places such as Križna, where visitors are kitted out with

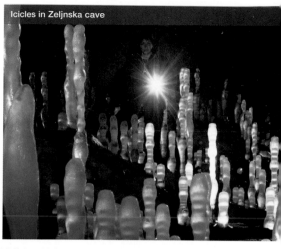

Icicles in Zeljnska cave

flashlight, helmet and boots, and Babji Zob, which requires a reasonable degree of physical exertion. If you fancy a truly authentic cave visit – complete with all the gear (rope, harness and so on) – try your luck with one of the many **caving clubs** located throughout the country, details of which can be found at www.jamarska-zveza.si.

The Karst

An area of particular interest to subterranean enthusiasts lies in southwest Slovenia, where a limestone plateau known as the **Karst** ranks among the country's most fascinating geographical features. The incredible underground formations that characterize this landscape are the result of millions of years of erosion and corrosion of the soluble limestone rock

Karst landscape

by rainwater. The results are rarely anything other than spectacular: weird and wonderfully formed **caves and tunnels,** often with fantastically shaped and richly coloured stalactites (protruding downwards) and stalagmites (protruding upwards), such as those at Postojna; **subterranean rivers and lakes,** like those inside Križna cave; and **deep-sided depressions** (also known as collapse dolines), the best examples of which can be seen at the amazing Škocjan Caves.

Stalagmites and stalactites at Postojna

Slovenia's Top Ten Caves

Škocjan. This awesome natural wonder has an underground canyon that's truly something to behold. See p.193

Križna. A helmet, flashlight and boots are required to visit this magnificent water cave, riddled with lakes, streams and passages. See p.230

Postojna. Slovenia's premier show cave is home to a dazzling array of stalagmites and stalactites. See p.222

Entrance to the Skocjan caves

Vilenica. A beautiful karst cave featuring classic formations, which is also the unlikely setting for a prestigious annual literary festival. See p.192

Babji Zob. Although it's a tough little trek to get here, it's worth it to see this modest cave's highly unusual and rarely seen helictite formations. See p.125

Kostanjevica. Chambers, lakes and dozens of tight passages and staircases characterize this cave, which is inhabited by thousands of southern horseshoe bats. See p.253

Krka. It's one of the smallest caves open to the public, but you will get to see Proteus Anguinus. See p.244

Pekel. The ominously nicknamed "Hell's Cave" features split-level galleries and a lovely subterranean waterfall. See p.279

Ravenska. A relative minnow of a show cave, Ravenska is known for its brilliant white aragonite crystals. See p.187

Pivka. The small and atmospheric Pivka Cave is named after the river that created the neighbouring Postojna cave system. See p.223

here head up Kolodvorska ulica, at the top of which is the **tourist office** (Mon–Fri 9am–7pm, til 6pm in winter, Sat 9am–1pm; ☎04/531-5300). The town's single **hotel** is the miserable and soulless *Grajski Dvor* (☎04/531-5585; Ⓦwww.hotel-grajski-dvor.si; ❺) opposite the bus station. A far better option, 1.5km north of the centre at Gradnikova cesta 2, is the very pleasant and restful *Sport Penzion Manca* (☎04/531-4120, Ⓦwww.manca-sp.si; ❺), which has a pool and tennis court – to get here, head north along Gorenjska cesta (direction Bled), turn right at the traffic lights and walk to the end of Ulica Staneta šagarja, which joins up with Gradnikova cesta. The small **campsite** is located just south of the *Manca* at Obla gorica (☎04/531-5770; June to mid-Sept). Use of the adjoining swimming pool, one of the best in the country and used to host championship events, is free for campers.

The Town

Everything of interest in town is centred on quiet **Linhartov trg** (Linhart Square), the old medieval core framed by a raft of fine Gothic and Renaissance buildings. The square was named in honour of the Slovene dramatist-historian Anton Tomaš Linhart (1756–1795), whose **birthplace** at no. 7 bears a commemorative plaque and bas-relief of people at work and play. Linhart was regarded as Slovenia's most important enlightener, a position reinforced following the publication (in German) in 1791 of his seminal works on the history of Slovenes; moreover, he was credited with writing the first Slovene plays – *Županova Micka* (Mayor's Maid Micka) in 1789, and *Matiček se ženi* (Matiček is Getting Married) in 1790.

The Thurn Mansion and Beekeeping Museum

Continuing eastwards you'll pass several more exceptional buildings – notably the **Renaissance mansion** (Vidičeva hiša) at no. 3 – before hitting upon the **Thurn Mansion** (Thurnov Grad), clearly recognizable by its thickly stuccoed facade and vast spread of coats of arms. Built by the Ortenburg counts in the early Middle Ages, the mansion underwent several reincarnations before it acquired its current Baroque appearance in the eighteenth century. Inside, a magnificent double stairway leads up to the first floor and the quite splendid **Beekeeping Museum** (Čebelarski Muzej; May–Oct Tues–Sun 10am–1pm & 3–6pm; March–April & Nov–Dec Wed, Sat & Sun 10am–noon & 3–5pm; €2.5). Comprising a handful of slickly arranged rooms, the museum presents the development and tradition of Slovenian apiculture from the eighteenth century to the present day. It begins with a collection of hives and wax presses, and by acknowledging the debt owed to the pioneers of beekeeping, such as master apiarists Anton Janša (1734–1773), who published the first treatise on beekeeping, and Michael Ambrošič (1846–1904), the first Slovene to trade in the indigenous Grey Carniolan bee. Next up, and the undoubted high point of the museum, is its collection of over two hundred **beehive panels** – wooden end panels painted with religious, satirical or humorous motifs and scenes – illustrated here in individually themed cabinets (deserters, bandits, religion and so on). Elsewhere, there is an exposition on the **biology** of the aforementioned Carniolan bee, including a live hive and a reconstructed **apiary**. For more on the panels, and beekeeping in general, see the box overleaf. The mansion also houses the **Linhart Memorial Room**, currently closed pending renovation.

Parish Church of St Peter and the Šiveč House

A few paces east of the mansion, in a pretty, irregularly shaped courtyard, stands the **Parish Church of St Peter** (Cerkev Sv Petra), another fine Gothic hall-church, modelled on the parish church in Kranj. The oldest part of the church, the presbytery, dates from the fifteenth century, while the church's Romanesque nave was replaced with its present, late Gothic one in 1495. The Baroque high altar, from 1713, incorporates beautiful sculptural decoration by Angelo Pozzo, as does the white marble altar of St Mary, its sculptures completed by local stonemason Janez Vurnik. Next to the church is the **Priest's House**, assimilated within a neat, recently renovated, late-Gothic arched courtyard (if the church is closed you can obtain the key from here).

The most outstanding building on the square is the muralled **Šiveč House** (Šivčeva hiša) at no. 22, an exceptional example of a Gothic-Renaissance house, and especially noteworthy for its vaulted ground-floor hall and first-floor wood-panelled drawing room – the latter was once the living quarters of a Radovljica burgher family but is now used for weddings. The building also hosts an **art gallery** with rotating exhibitions (daily 10am–noon & 6–8pm; €2). Leaving town en route to Bled, keep an eye out for the former **Savings Bank Building**, on your right at Gorenjska 17, an Art Nouveau edifice notable for its Secessionist-style mosaic of a flowering tree surrounding the entrance.

Eating and drinking

The town is blessed with a trio of first-rate **restaurants**: the best of these is ✳ *Gostilna Kunstelj*, a homely, low-key establishment just west of Linhartov trg at Gorenjska cesta 9, whose Slovene-oriented food is superbly prepared and beauti-

---

A nation of beekeepers

Beekeeping, or apiculture, is one of Slovenia's oldest and most celebrated traditions, originating during the sixteenth century when honey was the principal sweetening agent available and wax an indispensable material for making candles. Bees, in particular the indigenous Grey Carniolan (*Apis mellifera carniolica*) – affectionately known as the "Grizzly" owing to the lining of bright grey hair along its abdomen – have thrived in Slovenia for centuries, attracted to the rich forage afforded by the country's abundant fields of buckwheat and forests of linden, pine and fir. At the tail end of the nineteenth century **bee trading** became a hugely lucrative business, with the export of live bees and their associated products of honey, wax and royal jelly to numerous European countries; today, the country's seven thousand beekeepers produce around two thousand tonnes of honey annually, just about sufficient for domestic requirements.

Bees were traditionally kept in wooden, oblong **hives** called *kranjiči* (Carniolans), neatly stacked together in rows which, if required, could be mounted onto carts and transported; the hives were particularly celebrated for their painted **front panels** (*panjske končnice*), a Slovenian folk art which emerged during the mid-eighteenth century, reaching its acme a century later. Panels were illustrated with colourfully crafted motifs, a practice carried out by both professional and self-taught artists; older motifs typically portrayed biblical or historical happenings, while later paintings depicted moral or satirical, and occasionally profane, images, usually pertaining to peasant life. Many of these were deliciously humorous – such as the local gossip having her tongue sharpened on a grindstone by villagers, or the hunter being pursued by a gun-toting bear – many other panels feature Job, the patron of beekeepers.

Panels had practical functions too, their bright colours supposedly making orientation easier for bees, as well as enabling the beekeeper to distinguish between his many swarms. Whilst there's a good chance you'll see some of the original painted hives on your travels throughout the country – particularly around Gorenjska and the Alpine regions – it's this newer type that is more common.

fully presented; they've got some top-notch wines too. Housed in a five-hundred-year-old building at Linhartov trg 2, *Gostilna Lectar* offers an upscale take on traditional Slovenian meat dishes, as well as buckwheat, mushrooms and dumplings for vegetarians. *Gostilna Avguštin*, at no. 15, serves cheaper standards as well as a more discerning menu of beef, lamb and fish; the seating towards the rear of the restaurant is more comfortable, as is the lovely garden terrace with marvellous views across to Jelovica. For tea or **coffee** pop into *Čajnica*, next to *Avguštin* and if you want to buy some Slovenian wine, head to *Vinoteka Sodček* at Linhartov trg 8 (Mon–Fri 9am–7pm, Sat 8am–noon).

Brezje

A cluster of souvenir stalls, snack bars and an enormous car park welcome you to the small village of **BREZJE**, setting for Slovenia's most important place of pilgrimage, the **Basilica of the Virgin** (Marija pomagaj). Attracting some 300,000 visitors each year, the church began life in 1800 as a chapel, built as an extension to the fifteenth-century **St Vitus' Church**. It first became a site of prayer during Napoleon's occupation of northern Slovenia at the beginning of the nineteenth century, but it wasn't until the French departed that rumours of miracles occurring at Brezje began to spread, fuelling the arrival of tens of thousands of pilgrims from all over Europe. So great was the influx that, in 1900, it was necessary to construct a larger church, the results of which you see today. Around the same time, the Franciscans pitched up and proceeded to build an adjoining **monastery** and have remained the guardians of the church ever since.

Save for Janez Vurnik's stunning **high altar** – adorned with beautifully sculpted cherubs and instrument-playing angels – the interior is actually rather plain; still, this doesn't bother the majority of visitors, most of whom come here to pray at the **altar** of the Blessed Virgin of Help. This much reworked altar – the fourth chapel on the right – contains the church's most renowned piece of work, Leopold Layer's painting of *Mary Help*, framed by a dazzling gold mount designed by Tone Bitenc in 1977. There's also a contribution from Ivan Grohar, who completed the paintings in the third altars on the left and right. In the niche above the southern door is a statue by Boris Kalin, which previously stood at the nearby Otoče train station, and just across the way is a statue of Pope John Paul II, built to commemorate his visit here in 1996.

To get to Brezje from Bled take a **bus** (Mon–Fri 7.20am, 9.20am, 3.20pm and 5.20pm) to the small village of Črnivec, from where it's a ten-minute walk to the village – four buses also make the return trip (8.50am, 10.50am, 12.50pm and 4.55pm).

Begunje

In the tidy little village of **BEGUNJE**, 5km north of Radovljica, thousands of people – including many women and children – were detained, beaten and executed during the German occupation of Gorenjska (1941–1945). During World War II the village's seventeenth-century **Katzenstein Castle** was used as a Gestapo prison; the bare statistics reveal that 849 prisoners were either executed or died here, while a further 5000 were sent away to concentration camps in Austria, Germany and Poland. This grim episode in Slovenian history is vividly documented in the moving **Museum of Hostages** (Muzej talcev; July & Aug Tues–Sun 1–5pm; May–June & Sept–Oct Tues–Fri 9am–2pm, Sat & Sun 1–5pm; March–April & Nov–Dec Wed & Sat 9am–1pm, Sun 2–5pm; €2), housed in a wing of the castle, 200m north of the main bus stop.

Ten preserved cells illustrate the brutal experiences of the hostages confined here for months and years on end, most harrowingly in the form of farewell messages, which the Germans tried unsuccessfully to erase, etched into the walls as they awaited impending death. In one cell there are stakes onto which prisoners were tied before being shot, and in another, objects from Dachau, such as books of the murdered and keys of the guards, as well as more sobering items such as a gas sprinkler and a branch from which prisoners were hung. In the park just across from the museum is a **graveyard** where many of those executed are buried, while just up beyond the graveyard stands a small **chapel**, unmistakably the work of Jože Plečnik (see box on p.62).

Two kilometres north of the village lie the impressive ruins of **Kamen Castle** (Grad Kamen; although not officially open, you can enter the site or, if you want a guide call ☏04/533-3814; free), established by the Ortenburg counts in the twelfth century as a means of defending the Radovljica Plain. Its most extensive period of development, however, came in the fifteenth century, when the still remarkably well-preserved tower and residential palace were constructed. In the early eighteenth century, its function of protecting trade routes, warding off Turkish invaders and quelling peasant revolts was rendered obsolete and it was abandoned. The castle remained in a state of decay until 1959, when work finally began to restore it.

Directly across the road from the main **bus stop** in the centre of the village, the **Avsenik Gallery** (Tues–Sun: summer 10am–6pm; winter 11am–5pm; €1) contains an arsenal of awards dedicated to local folk musician and celebrity Slavko Avsenik – a bigger star in Germany than in Slovenia, apparently; you can also get some basic tourist information here. If you'd like to eat here, head to the reasonable *Avsenik* **restaurant** next to the gallery, though it's all rather hammed up for the tourists (closed Mon). There are hourly **buses** to and from Bled and Radovljica.

Kropa

Settled in a narrow valley below the Jelovica plateau, and flanked by precipitously slanting hills, **KROPA**, 10km southwest of Radovljica, is the place to aim for if you've only time for one excursion. This comely single-street village is renowned for its iron-mining and forging industries, which reached their peak here during the early to mid-nineteenth century, and whose history is relayed in the **Iron Forging Museum**, housed in the **Klinar House** – owned by the eponymous iron baron – at no. 10 (Kovaški Muzej; May–Oct Tues–Sun 10am–1pm & 3–6pm; March, April, Nov & Dec Wed, Sat & Sun 10am–noon & 3–5pm; €2). As impressive as the assemblage of models, bellows and spikes is (there are, incredibly, over one hundred varieties of spike), it's the work of master forger Joša Bertoncelj (1901–1976) which trumps all else here; already forging nails at the age of eleven, Bertoncelj soon graduated to the village's Plamen factory before settling upon a career as an artistic forger, resulting in a quite marvellous collection of wrought-iron gratings, chandeliers, and sepulchral monuments. The second floor illustrates the economic and social conditions under which a blacksmith lived and worked; typically, the smiths and their families would squeeze into the attic, while the first floor was given over to the owner of the foundry. Judging by the salon and its coffered ceiling in this house, it's possible to appreciate just how wealthy some of these owners were.

A few paces north of the museum, at no. 7b, is the **UKO workshop** (Umetniško kovaštvo; July & Aug Mon–Fri 7am–6pm, Sat 9am–noon; Sept–June Mon–Fri 7am–3pm, Sat 9am–noon), a decorative ironwork company set up in 1956 in order to preserve the tradition of manual forging; you can view the masters at work here and buy ironwork products from the neighbouring shop. Heading south towards **Plac**, the very small main square, have a look at the **partisan monument**, comprised of iron figures made at the aforementioned workshop, before crossing the **Kroparica**, a rapid, thrashing mountain stream that once propelled over fifty water-wheels for the bellows and sledgehammers of the foundries, most of which were decommissioned after World War I. A short way south of the bridge is the **Vice Forge** (Vigenjc), the only preserved and operative workshop in Kropa; to view a (free) demonstration, contact the Iron Forging Museum a day or two in advance (℡04/533-6717; English spoken). Just north of the forge, up the slope, is the Gothic **Parish Church of St Leonard** (Cerkev Sv Lenarta), whose cemetery contains some beautifully crafted iron headstones, including the grave of Bertoncelj; there are some lovely views of the village from the terrace. One and a half kilometres south of the village, up on the road to Železniki, stands a fourteenth-century **smelting furnace**, discovered as recently as 1953 when the mountain road to Jamnik was built. Nicknamed the "wolf", it could produce 200kg of iron in one day.

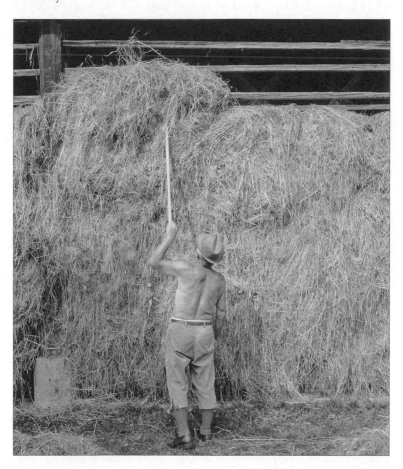

△ Haymaking

The village accommodates two very welcoming **gostilna**: at the extreme northern end of the village, at Kropa 2, is the *Gostilna Pri Jarmu* (closed Wed & Thurs), a pizzeria-style place; and in the centre, 50m south of Plac at Kropa 30, is the cosy *Pri Kovač* (closed Mon), which knocks up some superb local specialities such as Blacksmith's Plate (an assortment of meats) and sour milk and bean soup – they have some excellent wines too. The main **bus stop** is located near the post office, 200m south of the *Pri Jarmu*.

Bled and around

One thousand years old in 2004, **BLED** is by far the country's most popular destination, thanks to its placid fairytale lake and island, dramatically sited castle and snow-tipped mountains. The town itself, which is most densely concentrated to the east of the lake, is thoroughly unspectacular, and there's nothing specific to see. In contrast, the lake – created some 14,000 years ago when water flooded the depression left by a receding glacier – is a natural playground, deluged with skaters during the winter and bristling with row-boats, gondolas and swimmers during the spring and summer months.

The town dates from 1004, when the German emperor Henry II bestowed the castle, and the land between the two Sava rivers, to the bishops of Brixen – who would subsequently rule for the next 800 years. The first visitors to Bled were medieval pilgrims from Carniola and Carinthia, who came to pray at the island church, although mass tourism didn't take long to find its feet. This was in large part thanks to Arnold Rikli, a Swiss-born physician who opened a bathing resort and associated accommodation facilities at Bled in 1855. Between the two World Wars the resort became a popular hideaway for politicians and royalty, with both the Yugoslav royal family, and later, Tito, spending much time here during the summer; even today, Bled is the one place high-ranking officials and diplomats are ushered to when visiting Slovenia. Despite its status as the country's star turn, Bled rarely feels overwhelmed – indeed it can even feel a little bleak outside summer and winter – but if you do fancy a change of pace and a bit of solitude, there are some terrific attractions close by, notably the **Vintgar Gorge**, **Babji Zob Caves** and the **Pokljuka Plateau**. Furthermore, it's a good place to base yourself for hikes into the eastern tranche of the Julian Alps.

Arrival and information

Bled's **bus station** is five minutes northeast of the lake at the junction of Cesta svobode and Grajska cesta. The nearest **train station** to Bled is Bled Jezero (on the Jesenice–Nova Gorica line), located on Kolodvorska cesta, a ten-minute walk northwest of the lake. However, if coming from Ljubljana, you'll alight at Bled-Lesce, 4km southeast of Bled and connected to the town by half-hourly buses. The **tourist office** is located on the lakefront opposite the *Hotel Park* at Cesta Svobode 10 (July & Aug Mon–Sat 8am–9pm, Sun 10am–6pm; June & Sept Mon–Sat 8am–8pm, Sun 10am–6pm; May & Oct Mon–Sat 8am–7pm, Sun 11am–6pm; rest of year Mon–Sat 9am–6pm, Sun 11am–4pm; ☎04/574-1122, ⊛www.bled. si). If you require information on any aspect of Triglav National Park, contact the park's main office, along the northern shore at Kidričeva cesta 2 (Mon–Fri 8am–4pm; ☎04/578-0200, ⊛www.tnp.si). The **post office** is at Ljubljanska 14 (Mon–Fri 7am–7pm, Sat 7am–noon). There is **Internet access** available at the youth hostel, and one expensive terminal at the *Apropos* café in the shopping centre on Ljubljanska cesta (daily 8am–midnight).

BLED

Lesce, C & 5

Vintgar Gorge, Pokljuka Gorge, Bus Station, A, 1, 2 & 3

Sports Hall

Shopping Centre

Festival Hall

Church of St Martin

Swimming Area

Bled Castle

Triglav National Park Office

STRAŽA

Lake Bled

MLINSKA CESTA

Babji Zob & Bohinj

Church of the Assumption

Bled Island

Bled Jezero Train Station

ZA GRADOM

Velika Osojnica

Velika Osojnica

N

0   200 m

RESTAURANTS & CAFÉS
Bistro Arbor 8
Mayer 9
Mlino 10
Okarina 7
Prešeren 4
Pri Planincu 2
Riki 6
Rustika 1
Šmon 3
Topolino 5

ACCOMMODATION
Pension Berc G
Vila Bled J
Bledec Youth Hostel A
Hotel Krim C
Pension Mayer F
Pension Mlino I
Hotel Park D
Pension Pletna H
Vila Prešeren B
Grand Hotel Toplice E

119

Accommodation

As befits Slovenia's premier tourist destination, there is an abundance of **accommodation** in town, from top-class hotels to run-of-the-mill package-type places and homely pensions. The well-run **Bledec Youth Hostel**, a couple of minutes' walk north of the bus station at Grajska cesta 17 (☏04/574-5250; ⓦwww.mlino. si), has spotless three-, four-, five- and seven-bedded rooms, all with bathrooms (€20 per person including breakfast, €18 for IYHF members) – reservations are essential between June and August; it also has laundry facilities (€8), Internet access and a good restaurant.

Camping Bled (☏04/575-2000, ⓦwww.camping.bled.com; April to mid-Oct) – the only **campsite** in Bled itself – is located at the far western end of the lake in a lovely pine-sheltered valley (take any bus heading towards Bohinj and alight at the beginning of Kidričeva cesta). *Camping Šobec* (☏04/535-3700, ⓦwww.sobec. si; mid-April to Sept) – Slovenia's largest campsite – is 2km from Bled-Lesce in the direction of Bled. The site also has half a dozen bungalows, with heating and showers, and each sleeping two to six people (⑥–⑦). With no public transport to the site it's a rather convoluted twenty-minute walk: exiting Bled-Lesce station, walk north towards the crossing, take the second left down Finžgareva ulica for 100m, left again and continue behind the industrial zone for 400m before heading down a gravel track to the right. Both sites are extremely well equipped and maintained, each with a restaurant, supermarket and sporting facilities; *Šobec* also has its own lake for swimming. Despite their vast capacities, both sites fill up very quickly during the summer months.

There is plentiful **private accommodation**, available from several agencies, including Globtour at Ljubljanska cesta 7 (June–Sept Mon–Sat 8am–8pm, Sun 8am–noon & 4–8pm; Oct–May Mon–Fri 8am–3pm, Sat 9am–2pm; ☏04/574-1821, ⓦwww.globtour.si), and Kompas, in the shopping centre at Ljubljanska cesta 4 (same times as Globtour; ☏04/574-1515, ⓦwww.kompas-bled.si). Furthermore, there are quite a few **tourist farms** in the vicinity, the largest concentration of which are located in the villages of **Selo** and **Zgornje Gorje**, southwest and northwest of the lake respectively; you can approach farms directly or book through the above agencies (but not the tourist office).

Hotels and pensions

Pension Berc Želeška cesta 15 ☏04/574-1838, ⓦwww.berc-sp.si. Lovely, family-run place in a renovated nineteenth-century farmhouse, with spacious, cosily furnished rooms – the most restful option in town. ❹

Vila Bled Cesta svobode 26 ☏04/579-1500, ⓦwww.vila-bled.com. Set in its own extensive grounds on the lake's western shore, this is Bled's most characterful and expensive establishment. Rebuilt as yet another country retreat for Tito in 1947, the extraordinary socialist-era rooms have remained largely untouched since the president entertained world leaders here. The hotel also has a wellness centre, its own private beach and boats. Closed Jan–March. ❾

Hotel Krim Ljubljanska cesta 7 ☏04/579-7000, ⓦwww.hotel-krim.si. Firmly in the category of package-tourist hotel, the dark brown rooms at this establishment lack any semblance of quality, but it's one of the cheaper options in town and the jolly

staff do their best to please. ❻

Pension Mayer Želeška cesta 7 ☏04/576-5740, ⓦwww.mayer-sp.si. Located next to the *Berc*, this fine nineteenth-century building has stylish, parquet-floored rooms with large comfy beds and spankingly clean bathrooms; minibar & safe too. Very good value. ❺

Pension Mlino Cesta svobode 45 ☏04/574-1404, ⓦwww.mlino.si. A short walk west of *Vila Bled*, this popular lakeside place has a convivial atmosphere despite the rooms being dated and cramped. Reservations advised. ❺

Hotel Park Cesta svobode 15 ☏04/579-3000, ⓦwww.gp-hoteli.bled.com. This horrible construction blotting the southeastern corner of the lake is Bled's largest hotel; recent wholesale renovation has resulted in a uniform set of smartly furnished rooms, with those facing the lake having a/c. ❼–❽

Pension Pletna Cesta svobode 37 ☏04/574-3702, ⓔpletna@bled.net. The five large and neat rooms in this small, but very good value, pension just 100m east of the *Mlino* all have a balcony with super lake views. They also have bikes, rowing boats and kayaks for hire. ❹

🏃 **Vila Prešeren** Kidričeva cesta 1 ☏04/578-0800, ⓦwww.vila.preseren.s5.net. Handsome nineteenth-century villa accommodating six; it has soothing cream and beige furnished rooms, parquet flooring, elegant bedside lamps, wall pictures and some other neat touches. Top-quality restaurant to boot (see p.123). ❼

Grand Hotel Toplice Cesta svobode 12 ☏04/579-1000, ⓦwww.hotel-toplice.si. Bled's most opulent hotel has magnificently appointed rooms, with antique furniture, large, handsome beds and gold-plated trimmings; the more expensive lakeside rooms have a/c and bed pumps, for that little extra firmness. Houses a thermal pool, jacuzzi and Finnish and Turkish saunas, all free to guests. ❾

Lake Bled

From a visitor's perspective, Bled is essentially the **lake** and all that happens on or around it. The best way to get your bearings is to engage in a circular walk, beginning at the *Hotel Park* and working your way round clockwise, which should take no more than two and half hours.

Bled Castle

Perched high up on a craggy bluff on the north shore is **Bled Castle** (Blejski Grad; daily 8am–7pm, until 5pm in winter; €5 including entrance to the museum), enclosed by a Romanesque wall and spotted with stout-looking parapets, towers and ramparts, just as a castle should be. Originally an eleventh-century fortification, the castle's present appearance dates from the seventeenth century (albeit with further renovations in the 1950s), and is characterized by a lower and upper courtyard. The outstanding feature of the neat upper courtyard is the lovely sixteenth-century **chapel**, decorated with frescoes from around 1700, and containing a fine painting of Henry II conferring the property of Bled on Bishop Albuin.

Adjacent to the chapel is the **museum** (Grajski Muzej), a disappointing and lacklustre affair, not helped by the lack of any decent labelling. However, it starts promisingly, with some fascinating archeological finds from the region, including an interesting coinage exhibition and a stack of Roman gold jewellery; thereafter, the extensive collection of Gothic, Renaissance and Baroque furniture and weaponry does little to evoke the mood of those periods. From the castle terrace there are peerless views – and great photo opportunities – of the lake and island below.

Several paths (marked "Grad") wind up to the castle, each a reasonably stiff fifteen-minute climb; one from behind the swimming area (Grajsko Kopališče) on Kidričeva Cesta, another from the youth hostel on Grajska cesta, and a third from Rikljeva ulica, near the **Parish Church of St Martin** (Cerkev Sv Martina), a neo-Gothic structure built in 1905 on the site of a previous Gothic church; it has sculptures by the ubiquitous Vurnik and frescoes by Slavko Pengov.

If you don't fancy walking around the lake, you can take the **tourist train**, a jump-on, jump-off vehicle that crawls around the lake clogging up the traffic; its starting point is from the sports hall on the lake's east shore (April–Nov; €3 for a day-ticket). Alternatively you can take a ride on one of the **horse-drawn carriages** (*fijaker*), which are parked near the Festival Hall (a thirty-minute jaunt around the lake costs €22 for five people) – longer trips are available too.

Bled Island

During the day, a continual relay of stretch gondolas (*pletnas*) glide back and forth across the water between the shore and **Bled Island** (Blejski Otok), a magically picturesque islet crowned by the exquisite **Church of the Assumption** (Cerkev Sv Marija Božja; daily 8am–dusk). Findings support the theory that there was a settlement here in prehistoric times, while further excavations have revealed the

Activities in and around Bled

Whilst far more challenging hikes can be had in Triglav National Park (see box on p.137), there are some very enjoyable walks in the immediate vicinity of the lake. Velika Osojnica, a 756-metre-high peak at the southwestern corner of the lake, offers the stiffest walk but also the most superlative views; take either the path from Bled campsite (via Ojstrica), or from the main road, Kidričeva cesta (via Mala Osojnica) and allow three hours for a round-trip. A more gentle alternative is a walk up to Straža, a 638-metre-high hill southwest of the *Grand Hotel Toplice*; this is also Bled's very modest **ski slope**, suitable for beginners only. Between December and February a chairlift operates from Pod Stražo, the road above Cesta svobode, to the summit (☎04/578-0530), and during the summer the same hill becomes a 520-metre **sled run** (€4 for one run, €12 for five runs).

Although **swimming** is permitted at various points around the lake (Mlino, Velika Zaka and Mala Zaka, all at the western end), you're better off sticking to the designated, roped-off, area on the north shore underneath the castle, which also has a grassy beach (Grajsko Kopališče; daily mid-June to Sept 8am–7pm; €5 for a daily ticket, €4 after noon). During winter, the lake often freezes over, tempting skaters out onto the ice; however caution should be exercised if you decide to have a go yourself. Although not quite as romantic, you can also try the indoor rink at the sports centre (Športna Dvorana) just to the east of the *Park Hotel* (mid-July to March Mon–Sat 10–11.30am & 4.30–6pm, Sun 4.30–6pm; €3.50, plus €3.50 for skate hire).

Licences for **fishing**, permitted on the lake between April and December, can be purchased from the tourist office (€22 per day). There is **horse riding** at the Hippodrome in Lesce (☎041/675-482); a half-hour lesson, or a one-hour ride (either cross-country or around the track), costs around €15. Also in Lesce, the Alpine Flying Centre at Begunjska cesta 10 (Alpski Letalski Center; ☎04/532-0100, ⓦwww.alc-lesce.si), offers **panoramic flights** around Bled for around €70, and Bohinj for around €120. Slovenia's premier **golf** course, the Bled Golf and Country Club, is located 2km east of town on the Bled-Lesce road at Kidričeva cesta 10 (☎04/537-7711, ⓦwww.golf-bled.si; 18-hole course €55, 9-hole course €35). **Bikes** can be hired from both the Globtour and Kompas agencies, and Promontana (see below); all charge similar rates: €4 for 1hr, €6 for half a day and €10 per day.

Humanfish (☎051/321-383, ⓦwww.humanfish.com) offers an excellent programme of **hikes** in the Julian Alps and Karavanke mountains, including two-day trips to Triglav (€150), as well as a number of easy/moderate (Meadows of Bohinj, Debela Pec; €40) and difficult (Mojstrovka, Prisojnik; €60) day hikes; they also offer biking tours, horse-riding tours (both €40) and a comprehensive winter ski and snowboarding programme. Promontana, just down from the *Hotel Krim* at Ljubljanska 1 (daily: March–Sept 8am–8pm; Oct–Feb 8am–4pm; ☎04/578-0662, ⓦwww.promontana. si), organizes similar hikes, in addition to a number of **river-bound activities** on the nearby Sava Bohinjka River – the following prices are per person based on a group of four, participating in a 2–3hr activity (prices decrease if the group is bigger and, similarly, prices increase if there are fewer than four): rafting (€24), hydrospeed (€30), canyoning (€45) and kayaking (€35).

remains of a pre-Romanesque chapel, as well as a large Slavic cemetery dating from around 9 AD. The present Baroque church dates from 1698, though its most outstanding features are from the preceding Gothic church, namely the remarkably well-preserved **frescoes** on the north and south presbytery walls, depicting scenes from the life of the Virgin, and a wooden statue of the Virgin with Child. The porch on the west side of the church holds more Gothic fresco remains, discovered during the most recent excavations in 1965. The wishing bell, which keeps most visitors amused, was installed in 1534, though a larger bell hangs in the enormous free-standing belfry, itself a hybrid of Gothic and Baroque elements. As well as providing a home to the provost, the **Provost's House** next to the church also functioned as a guesthouse, as did the **hermitage**, the smaller building behind the church.

Predictably enough, a café and souvenir stall have been squeezed onto the island, not that you'll have much time to enjoy them if you come across on a *pletna*. They depart from three locations: down below the *Hotel Park*, near the *Vila Prešeren* (both 30min to the lake) and opposite *Pension Mlino* (15min), though the price is the same whichever location you leave from (€12 per person); departing only when they are full – which means you may have to sit idly for a bit while the *pletnar* solicits custom – you then have thirty minutes on the island to nose around before returning. The alternative is to make your own way across: **rowing boats** can be hired from several points at the western end of the lake (€10 per hour for a three-person boat); it may be harder going, but you won't feel rushed once on the island. Both the *pletna* and rowing boats operate year-round, depending on the weather.

Eating, drinking and entertainment

Bled can count on a number of superb and characterful **restaurants**, a few of which are located within some of the lake's better pensions. Telephone numbers have been given where it's best to make a **reservation**. Conversely, Bled **nightlife** is fairly tame and you'll be hard pushed to avoid drinking in the same venues if you're here for any length of time.

Restaurants

Bistro Arbor Ljubljanska cesta 4 (in the shopping centre). Don't let the unattractive surroundings dissuade you – a big and varied menu, plus good cheap lunch options (€3) should suffice. Daily 9am–11pm.

Mayer Železka cesta 7 ☏04/576-5740. Refined and extremely well regarded restaurant in the pension of the same name, offering a moderate to expensive menu, featuring some good starters (buckwheat, fried cheese) and impressive mains, in particular game and trout. Tues–Fri 5pm–midnight, Sat & Sun noon–midnight.

Mlino Cesta svobode 45. Atmospheric terrace restaurant in the *Mlino* pension, with a commendably adventurous menu featuring horse, shark cutlets and, more teasingly, ox testicles – it also has good veggie options. Also has an a/c indoor restaurant. Daily 9am–10pm.

Okarina Ljubljanska cesta 8. Beautifully appointed restaurant in which to enjoy the wonderful menu of fish, game, tandoori (knocked up by the resident Indian chef), and over a dozen superb vegetarian dishes. Highly recommended. Mon–Fri 6pm–midnight, Sat & Sun noon–midnight.

Prešeren Kidričeva cesta 1. Take your pick from the sumptuously elegant inside restaurant or the beautiful lakeside terrace to indulge in fresh fish from the Adriatic or some of the splendid house

delicacies, such as mushrooms and ostrich – a fairly expensive, but thoroughly enjoyable, dining experience. Daily 11am–11pm.

Pri Planincu Grajska cesta 8. Hugely popular and frenetic inn-style place, serving hearty meat-heavy dishes, notably the juicy Serbian specialities Pljeskavica and Čevapčiči (rissoles of spiced minced meat); a great spot for a beer. Daily 9am–11pm.

Rikli Cesta svobode 15. Located beneath the *Park Hotel*, this seductive-looking place offers a top-class à la carte menu, with heavy emphasis on fish. More modestly, their bright little pizzeria next door serves pasta, noodles and gnocchi. Daily noon–10pm.

Pizzeria Rustika Riklijeva 13. As the name suggests, plenty of rustic trappings, such as dark wooden tables and thick bench seating, in this simple but warm and pleasant pizzeria a short walk down from the youth hostel. Tues–Sun noon–11pm.

Šmon (The Bear), at Grajska 3, is Bled's most enduring café, thanks largely to its prodigious selection of home-made pastries, the best of which is the very creamy Bled speciality *Kremna Rezina*. Daily 7.30am–9pm.

Topolino Ljubljanska cesta 26 ☏04/574-1781. This low-key, slow-food restaurant is Bled's most sophisticated outfit, gorgeously decorated and beautifully lit throughout, with food and wine of the highest quality and prices to match. Wed–Mon noon–11pm.

Drinking

Rather dispiritingly, most of Bled's chief **drinking** venues are located in or around the sprawling, incoherent shopping centre on Ljubljanska cesta; take your pick from *Apropos*, a small cocktail bar and ice-cream parlour; *Café Latino* just across the way, which is good for beer and wines; and *Arbor* (see restaurants), also a popular hangout. All are open til around midnight. The best pub-style place is actually the cosy *Pri Planincu* (see restaurants).

Entertainment and festivals

Bled's key annual event is **Bled Days** (Blejski Dnevi) on the third weekend of July, when three days of fairs and concerts take place along the promenade at the eastern end of the lake; the event culminates in the lighting of thousands of candles on the lake – a memorable sight – and fireworks. Bled's most interesting musical event, the **Okarina Etno Festival**, featuring performances by an eclectic group of world musicians, takes place during the first weekend of August. The **International Music Festival**, at the beginning of July, is a two-week run of classical concerts staged at various venues around the lake, but principally the Festival Hall and St Martin's Church – tickets cost around €7 for each performance (Ⓦ www.festivalbled.com). Then there are the **rowing regattas**, which occur at various dates throughout the year (see box above).

Around Bled

Located within close proximity to Bled are three worthwhile excursions, each of which can be comfortably accomplished within three to four hours: to the north, there are the hugely popular **Vintgar Gorge** and the lesser-visited, but no less impressive, **Pokljuka Gorge**, while to the south, en route to Bohinj, are the fascinating **Babji Zob Caves**. To the northwest, in the village of **Vrba**, you can visit the birthplace of France Prešeren, Slovenia's greatest poet.

Vintgar Gorge

The major attraction in Bled's immediate environs is the **Vintgar Gorge** (Blejski Vintgar; daily mid-April–Oct 8am–8pm; €3), an impressive 1600-metre-long and 150-metre-high defile 4km north of town. The most enjoyable way to get here is to walk, an easy and pleasant stroll along country roads and through a handful of pretty villages: from the bus station join the main road, Prešernova ulica, and head north until you come to Partizanska cesta; continue north along here and after crossing the stream take the left fork (Cesta v Vintgar), continuing towards the village of **Podhom**, from where the gorge is signposted. If the walk is beyond you, there is a daily bus to (10am) and from (noon) the gorge between mid-June and September, leaving from the bus station.

The gorge was actually chanced upon by a local mayor and his cartographer colleague in 1891. So thrilled were they with their discovery that they set up a construction committee in order to seek ways of opening the gorge up to the public, an event that duly occurred two years later. It's since been accessible via a continuous chain of wooden gantries and bridges, suspended from the precipitous rock face, and running the entire length of the gorge to the **Šum Waterfall** (Slap šum) at its northern end; from here you can either retrace your steps and return the way you came, or take the path on the right, returning to Bled via the pilgrimage **Church of St Catherine** and the village of **Zasip**. It can get very damp in the gorge, and if it's been raining, very slippery, so you'd do well to bring some waterproofs and good walking boots. There's a decent *gostilna* near the car park.

Pokljuka Gorge

As an antidote to the hordes that pile up to the Vintgar Gorge, the **Pokljuka Gorge** (Pokljuška soteska), a magnificent fossilized ravine 7km west of Bled, is perfect for those seeking some solitude. Located on the northeastern margins of the **Pokljuka Plateau** – a thickly forested plain at the eastern extremes of the Julian Alps and a world-class venue for cross-country skiing – this dry and narrow trough-like ravine was hollowed out by the former course of the Ribščica River some ten thousand years ago, the retreating glaciers leaving behind the largest fossilized gorge in the country. It's characterized by peculiar dilations – known as "vrtci" ("garden plots") – and a series of natural arches, although its most spectacular feature is the **Pokljuka Luknja** (Pokljuka Window), a 15-metre-high subterranean hall with three natural windows hollowed out of its ceiling. To get here take one of the regular buses from Bled to the village of **Krnica**, from where it's a two-kilometre walk (follow the signs) to the gorge entrance. If you have your own transport, it's possible to drive right to the entrance.

Babji Zob Caves

Completing this trio of natural wonders are the **Babji Zob Caves** (Jama Pod Babjim Zobom), near the village of **BOHINJSKA BELA**, 4km west of Bled. Located beneath **Babji Zob** (Hags Tooth), a formidable-looking, tooth-shaped pillar poised atop a 1128-metre peak, it couldn't be more different to your conventional cave visit – as with Postojna (see p.222) or Škocjan (see p.193) for example. The caves can only be visited on a guided tour, which entails a not inconsiderable one-hour hike up to the cave entrance; thereafter it's a further hour's trek through the complex, before the steep descent back down the hill (approximately three hours in total).

At just 300m long it's not an expansive cave system, but it does possess some unique features, not least several groupings of rarely seen helictites – contorted, sometimes horizontal, calcite deposits, which grow in random directions seemingly defying gravity. Their existence has long confounded experts and remains one of the most vexing speleological questions, though one theory suggests that their form is caused by airflow within the cave.

Tours, which cost €10, take place at 10am on Saturdays between May and September, as well as on Wednesdays and Sundays in July and August at the same time; the

France Prešeren

One of Slovenia's greatest nineteenth-century heroes and indisputably the country's greatest romantic poet, **France Prešeren** did more to advance the cause of the Slovene national consciousness in the nineteenth century than just about any other figure. Born in the village of Vrba in 1800, Prešeren was educated in Ribnica and Ljubljana, before obtaining his law degree in Vienna. Although a lawyer by profession – he spent much of his life working as a clerk in Ljubljana – Prešeren's true vocation was poetry. Underpinned by themes of unrequited love, homeland, friendships and other existential laments, Prešeren's poems combined classical, Renaissance and Romantic elements with traditional Slovene folk customs, resulting in a body of work considered to be the apotheosis of nineteenth-century Slovene language and culture. His most recognized piece of work was the epic *Krst pri Savici* (*Baptism at the Savica*), which explores themes of Christianization in Slovenia, though only one volume of his work, *Poezije doktorja Franceta Prešerna* (*Poems of Doctor France Prešeren*), was published during his lifetime, in 1845.

Through his writing, the liberal-minded Prešeren – along with his peers, and particularly his good friend and mentor Matija Čop – attempted to create an **independent Slovene culture** for townspeople, oriented towards classical Western traditions, whilst he also sought to stimulate national awareness amongst the emerging Slovene middle class. However, he frequently clashed with the government in Vienna over his anti-German sentiments, as well as the Catholic Church, who considered his work immoral.

Prešeren's **personal life** was deeply unhappy: he was a melancholy character, a drunkard and philanderer and had three children out of wedlock. He was particularly depressed by an unrequited love affair with one Julija Primič, whom he first met at the Church of St John in Trnovo, Ljubljana, and by the untimely death of the aforementioned Matija Čop.

From 1846 until his death, from cirrhosis of the liver, on February 8, 1849, Prešeren spent the last three years of his life working in his own practice in Kranj, the city in which he is also buried. His writing aside, Prešeren's legacy is very much alive in other forms – the public holiday on 8 February is celebrated as Prešeren Day (the Day of Slovene Culture), whilst the seventh stanza of *Zdravljica* (*A Toast*), set to music by composer Stanko Premrl, was adopted as the national anthem of the republic in 1991.

meeting point is in front of the Promontana office at Ljubljanska 1, in Bled (☎ 04/578-0660). For the visit, take some warm clothing, waterproofs and a pair of older shoes, as it can get quite muddy. About 3km on from Bohinjska Bela, on the Bohinj road and beside the Bohinjska Sava river (just outside the village of Obrne), the ☀ *Reka Hiša* (☎ 04/576-0340, ⓦ www.actionslovenia.com) is a delightfully welcoming guest house, offering simple but cosily furnished rooms (❺; price includes evening meal). The owners also organise a range of activities and are able to arrange transfers from Bled or Bohinj; otherwise, take any Bohinj-bound bus and alight by the bridge after the second exit for Bohinjska Bela, from where it's a ten-minute walk.

Vrba

VRBA, a tiny village 4km northeast of Bled just off the main road to Kranjska Gora, is famed as the birthplace of France Prešeren, Slovenia's most celebrated poet. Prešeren was sufficiently enamoured with his home village to write:

O, Vrba, happy village, my old home
My father's cottage stands there to this day
The lure of learning beckoned me away
Its serpent wiles enticing me to roam

The solid whitewashed **house** (Rojstna Hiša Prešerna hiša; Tues–Fri 9am–4pm, Sat & Sun 10am–5pm; €2.5), located on the right-hand side of the village as you enter (no. 2), was originally built in the sixteenth century, but partly destroyed by a village fire in 1856. It contains a few original items of furniture, including the poet's cradle, as well as translations of some of his work, but the house is actually more interesting as an architectural monument – most impressive is the traditional "Black Kitchen" (see p.134) preserved in its entirety. As interesting as the exhibition is, you'll learn more about the man and his work at the memorial house in Kranj (see p.108), where he lived and worked for the last few years of his life.

Just up behind the birthplace on a small grassy hill, the Gothic **Church of St Mark** (Cerkev Sv Marko) is worth a look for its sixteenth-century frescoes by the prolific Jernej of Loka – including Christ's Passion and traces of St George doing battle with the dragon – and murals by Friulian masters. The wooden ceiling dates from 1991 when the latest renovation took place. A five-minute walk to the western edge of the village brings you to a sturdy two-hundred-year-old linden tree encircled by sixteen large stones, one for each of the farmhouses that originally stood in the village – it was supposedly also the place where debates between the village representatives would take place. To get here take one of the hourly buses from Bled to Jesenice, which takes a rather convoluted route via Radovljica.

Bohinj and around

Some 20km long and 5km wide, **Bohinj** is the name given to the entire Sava Bohinjka basin southwest of Bled, a region of immense charm and beauty, embracing rugged valleys and mountains, alluring rustic idylls and, best of all, a magical **lake**.

Archeological finds have determined that Bohinj was settled in the late seventh century, a theory given further credence following the discovery of a handful of forges and foundries in the area. Indeed, for many centuries, the smelting of iron was the mainstay of the economy in the region, although eventually, as elsewhere in Gorenjska, competition from more sophisticated European foundries signalled an end to production. As a result, the natives turned to alpine dairy farming, and in particular the mass production of cheese, the quality of which was highly regarded throughout Central Europe. Whilst alpine farming is still practised by small pockets of the community, many more villagers are now becoming engaged in tourism as a means of subsistence.

Bohinj's two key settlements, **Bohinjska Bistrica** and **Ribčev Laz**, suffice for all things of a practical nature, including the main rail and bus connection points, and the tourist offices. By way of contrast, the group of villages northeast of the lake in the upper valley – **Stara Fužina**, **Studor** and **Srednja Vas** – are not only a restful antidote to the often crowded lakeside, but also boast some fabulous indigenous rural architecture. More excitingly, there are some wonderful excursions close at hand, such as the immensely popular **Savica Waterfall** and the beautiful **Mostnica Gorge** and **Voje Valley**, both a short way north of the aforementioned villages. Whilst a fair proportion of visitors come to Bohinj to partake in water-bound activities – on both the lake and the Sava Bohinjka River – many more come to trek the mountains, with the major southerly approach to Triglav via the stunning **Valley of the Triglav Lakes (Valley of the Seven Lakes)** starting here. Bohinj can also count on two spectacularly sited ski resorts, Kobla and Vogel.

Triglav National Park

Abutting the Italian border to the west, within touching distance of the Austrian border to the north, and embracing almost the entire Slovene part of the Julian Alps, **Triglav National Park** (Triglavski Narodni Park) attracts some two million visitors each year. The idea for a national park was first mooted in 1908, a concept partially realized in 1924 with the creation of a "protected nature park" in the Valley of the Triglav Lakes. Proclaimed the Triglav National Park in 1961, the area assumed its present status in 1981, when it also incorporated **Mount Triglav**. The park comprises three distinct sectors: the Bohinj district – which incorporates Bohinj Lake and the greatest concentration of settlements; the Sava Dolinka district to the north, characterized by a series of glaciated valleys; and the Soča district in the west, extending southwards to Bovec and the Soča Valley (see chapter three), and which accommodates the only road passing directly through the park.

The park is home to a wonderful array of **flora and fauna**; its most revered creature is the elusive **chamois** (*Rupicapra rupicapra*), of which some two thousand are believed to roam the grassy mountain slopes. Other significant species include the recently reintroduced **marmot** and **ibex**, whilst sightings of the **golden eagle**, and encounters with **brown bear** – who stray up from the southern forests – are not unknown. However, the possibility of sighting any of the above is slim, as they are all apt to steer well clear of humans. Many of the park's plant species are endemic to the mountains, such as the **Julian poppy** (*Papaver julicum*), most commonly found on scree slopes, and the purple **Zois' bellflower** (*Campanula zoysii*), named after the eighteenth-century Slovene botanist Karl Zois – be warned that most alpine flora here is protected and picking them is an offence.

The park is administered by some twenty professional, and one hundred volunteer, rangers, who are on hand to provide assistance, though there are also information boards haphazardly scattered throughout the park. Otherwise, information can be obtained from the **Triglav National Park Information Centre**, located in the village of Trenta in the Trenta Valley (see p.147), and the park's headquarters in Bled (see p.118).

Bohinjska Bistrica

Routinely given the cold shoulder by travellers keen to reach the star attraction a few kilometres further on, **BOHINJSKA BISTRICA** – 20km southwest of Bled – is Bohinj's main settlement. It is a rather nondescript place, though there's a modest aquapark, as well as a mildly diverting museum and a sprinkling of accommodation including one of Bohinj's two campsites. Furthermore, its **train station** is the closest to the mountains on this side of the Alps, while the **car-train** runs from here to Most na Soči further south (see box opposite). Buses meet trains arriving at the station, which is located ten minutes east of the centre, and link up to Ribčev Laz (see p.132), while the main **bus stop** is located a few paces north of the post office on Triglavska cesta. You can get information at the Bohinj **tourist board office** at Triglavska cesta 30 (mid-June to mid-Sept Mon–Fri 7am–7pm, Sat & Sun 8am–7pm; rest of year Mon–Fri 8am–3pm, Sat & Sun 9am–1pm; ☏04/574-7590). Just across the road at Triglavska 13 is the very commendable *Pension Tripič* (☏04/572-1282, ⓦ www.bohinj.si/tripic; ⑥), which has good-value en-suite rooms, each with balcony. On the western fringe of the village, heading towards the lake, is the *Danica* **campsite** (☏04/572-1055; May–Sept), a well-shaded site backing onto the Sava River, with restaurant and sports facilities.

Just a stone's throw from the tourist board office is the **Aquapark Bohinj** (Vodni park; July–Aug & mid-Dec to March 9am–10pm, rest of year til 9pm; ☏04/577–0210, ⓦ www.vodni-park-bohinj.si), incorporating an indoor pool

(€12 day-ticket, €9 for 3hr), climbing wall, steambath, sauna and fitness centres – there are also bikes for hire (€2 for 2hr, €4 per day). If you have further time to spare, pop into the **Tomaž Godec Museum** (Muzej Tomaža Godca; May–Oct Tues–Sun 10am–noon & 4–6pm; Jan–April Wed, Sat & Sun, same hours; €2) at Zoisova 15 – it's located five minutes west of the post office, down Vodnikova cesta and across the stream. Trained as a leather tanner, Godec was also a champion skier and mountaineer. However, he was best known for his role as one of the founder members of the Slovene National Liberation Movement and as organizer of the 1941 Bohinj uprising. In 1942 he was captured by the Germans and carted off to Begunje (see p.115), before being transferred to Mauthausen where he was execut-ed. The museum was also party to a rather significant piece of history: between March 15 and 18, 1939, in the modest room now dedicated to Godec, the **Central Committee of the Communist Party of Yugoslavia** (CKKPJ) was formed. Fit-tingly, Tito, who was present at the meeting, returned to open the museum some forty years later. The remainder of the museum is given over to a reconstructed leather-tanning workshop – the only one of its kind in the country – with a dis-play of brutal-looking World War I weapons recovered from the Southern Bohinj mountains and an eminently missable archeological display.

Lake Bohinj and around

The largest permanent body of water in Slovenia, **Lake Bohinj** (Bohinjsko Jezero) is utterly different from Lake Bled; its brooding, unerringly calm waters provide perfect theatre to the majestic, steeply pitched mountain faces which frame it. In his epic poem, *Baptism of the Savica*, France Prešeren eloquently described it thus:

> The lake of Bohinj calm in stillness lies,
> No sign of strife remains to outward sight;
> Yet in the lake the fierce pike never sleep,
> Nor other fell marauders of the deep.

Over 4km long, 1km wide, and reaching depths of 45m, the lake is fed by water from the Savica falls, which, in turn, feeds the Sava Bohinjka River at the south-eastern corner of the lake. Mercifully, and unlike Bled, building has been forbidden along the entire lake shore, resulting in a virtually unbroken sequence of trees and grassy banks. Nevertheless, and even more so than Bled, the lake is well geared up for a number of activities, with canoeing, kayaking and windsurfing supplementing the more traditional pursuits of swimming and fishing. Moreover, it's far more likely to freeze over during winter, meaning better opportunities for skating.

The Bohinj Tunnel

Built between 1901 and 1906, the **Bohinj Tunnel** extends for some 6327m (6.3km) between Bohinjska Bistrica and Podbrdo, making it Slovenia's longest railway tun-nel. Introduced in 1999, the **car-train** transports vehicles (car, van or mobile home) through the mountains in a mere ten minutes – as opposed to the one hour it takes to drive across the tortuous road between Bohinj and Baška Grapa, via the village of Sorica. There are six daily trains between Bohinjska Bistrica and Podbrdo, three of which continue to Most na Soči, thirty minutes further on at the southernmost tip of the park – the same number of trains run in the reverse direction (six daily trains from Podbrdo to Bohinjska Bistrica, three of which originate in Most na Soči). From Bohinjska Bistrica to Podbrdo the cost (car and passengers) is €8 one-way, and €11 return. The full journey (Bistrica to Most na Soči) is €11 one-way, €18 return – for bicycles the cost is €2 and €3 respectively (one-way).

2

BOHINJ

N

Mostnica Gorge

Studor & Srednja Vas

Bohinjska Bistrica & Bled

Museum of
Alpine Dairy
Farming

Stara
Fužina

Mostnica

Church
of St John-
the Baptist

Sava
Bohinjka

Pension
Rožič

Pension
Kristal

Hotel
Bohinj

Ribčev Laz

Hotel
Jezero

MK Pizzeria

Hotel Bellevue

Church of the
Holy Spirit

Lake Bohinj

Zlatorog
Campsite

Ukanc

Hotel
Zlatorog

World War I
Cemetery

Vogel
Cable Car

P

P

Sava
Savica River

Mount Vogel

Savica Waterfall & Valley of Seven Lakes

Valley of Seven Lakes

Savica Waterfall & Valley of Seven Lakes

1 km

0

Bohinj is also the location for one of the more unusual alpine festivals; taking place in the second or third weekend of September, the **Kravji Bal**, or "Cows Ball", is a mass booze-up to celebrate the return of the cattle from alpine pastures; taking place near the *Hotel Zlatorog*, happenings include folklore events, various live bands, and of course, much drinking.

Arrival and information

Buses set passengers down just before the lake by the *Hotel Jezero* in Ribčev Laz, from where it's a few steps to the busy **tourist office**, located in the small complex at Ribčev Laz 48 (July & Aug daily 8am–8pm; rest of the year Mon–Sat 8am–6pm, Sun 9am–3pm; ☎04/572-3370, ⍟www.bohinj.si). The **Bohinj Guest Card** (€7), available to anyone staying in one of Bohinj's hotels, rooms or apartments, offers a number of good discounts on local attractions, activities and restaurants – it can be purchased from either the tourist office here or the one in Bohinjska Bistrica, as well as any of the hotels.

You can change money at both the tourist office and in the **post office** (Mon–Fri 8am–9.30am, 10am–3.30pm & 4–6pm, Sat 8am–noon) next door (which offers better rates), and there is **Internet access** at the Pension Rožič (see below).

Accommodation

Lake Bohinj can count on just a handful of **hotels**, and although they generally represent poor value for money during the summer period, prices do drop considerably out of season. Fortunately, there is plentiful **private accommodation** around the lake, particularly in Ribčev Laz and in the villages along the upper valley (Stara Fužina, Studor and Srednja Vas). Be warned though, that during July and August rooms get snapped up very quickly, so it's best to book in advance, or pitch up early in the morning to be sure of finding somewhere. During the summer, expect to pay around €14 per person per night for a room with bathroom, and an additional €5 should you require breakfast; note that for stays of less than three nights you'll have to pay thirty percent more than this; outside peak season, prices are around twenty percent less. An apartment for two people will cost around €35 per night. Bookings can be made through the tourist office or the Alpinum agency, a couple of doors along (☎05/577-8000). The *Zlatorog* **campsite** is located at the southwestern corner of the lake in Ukanc (☎04/572-3482; May–Sept).

Hotel Bellevue Ribčev Laz 65 ☎04/572-3331, ⍟www.alpinum.net. Perched on a hill 800m north of the *Hotel Jezero*, the secluded Bellevue is where Agatha Christie once stayed, the grand old lady commenting that "the lake is far too beautiful for a murder". The hotel retains a pleasant old-style atmosphere, despite the rooms being a little frayed around the edges. For a little extra, you can stay in the room Christie slept in. If you're walking, take the rocky footpath through the wood (5min) instead of the road, which is a gruelling 20min walk. ❻

Hotel Bohinj Ribčev Laz 45 ☎04/577-8000, ⍟www.alpinum.net. Pitched on a small rise across from the tourist office, this alpine-style building offers large and attractive pine–furnished rooms, some of which have glorious views overlooking the lake and across to Mount Triglav. ❽

Hotel Jezero Ribčev Laz 51 ☎04/572-9100, ⍟www.bohinj.si/alpinum/jezero. Just 50m from the water, this is the lake's most prominent hotel,

combining bright, smartly furnished rooms, and older, more modestly sized ones. Pool and fitness suite free to guests; sauna facilities too. ❽

Pension Kristal Ribčev Laz 4 ☎04/577-8200, ⍟www.hotel-kristal-slovenia.com. Located at the entrance to the village, this popular and welcoming pension offers a mix of newer (with Internet access) and older rooms, all simply but smartly furnished. Two rooms for disabled persons. ❹

Pension Rožič Ribčev Laz 42 ☎04/572-3393, ⍟www.pension-rozic.com. Located 100m east of the tourist office, this pension offers rustically styled rooms that are somewhat old-fashioned and boxy, but comfortable enough. Has a reasonable restaurant too (see p.135). ❹

Hotel Zlatorog Ukanc 64 ☎04/572-3381, ⍟www.alpinum.net. Located on the westernmost shore of the lake, Slovenia's first bio-hotel – all the food and drink here is organically produced – is a disappointingly average place, the rooms characterized by dreary brown decor and dated furnishings. The pool is free to guests, but tennis and sauna are extra, while there are also bikes and scooters for hire. ⑤

Ribčev Laz and the Church of St John the Baptist

As well as containing all things of a practical nature, **RIBČEV LAZ** is the location for the lake's outstanding monument, the tiny **Church of St John the Baptist** (Cerkev Sv Janez Krstnik; July & Aug daily 9am–noon & 5–8pm; other times contact the tourist office; €1), one of the most brilliantly frescoed churches in all Slovenia. Located opposite the stone bridge – invariably clogged with walkers and traffic, but offering glorious head-on views of the lake – this chunky, evocative structure has origins dating back to the thirteenth century. Its exterior features a striking **wooden porch**, paved with round river stones in rhomboid style, the middle stones arranged to form the date – 1639 – when it was laid out. Most of the exterior's sixteenth-century frescoes are barely discernible, save for those to the right of the entrance, one of which depicts St John, book in hand, baptizing kneeling persons, and another of St Florian doing what he does best, dousing fires. The south exterior wall bears an oversized St Christopher with the Christ Child on his shoulder. Its Baroque **bell tower**, renovated several times over, features double windows framed with green stone from the Piračica stream, a material common to many church bell towers in the region.

Activities in Bohinj

As in Bled, Bohinj presents some excellent opportunities for a whole raft of activities, on both land and water. Pac Sports, at Ribčev Laz 50 (but located in a hut just below *Pension Rožič*; May Sat & Sun 10am–6pm; June to mid-Sept daily 9am–8pm; ☏041/698-523, ⓦwww.pac-sports.com), offers a comprehensive range of activities including **rafting** (€25), **canyoning** (€40), **hydrospeed** (€30), and **tandem paragliding** (€65 for a 15min flight). They also hire out **canoes and kayaks** for use on the lake (€4 per hour), as do Alpin Sports by the bridge (daily: July & Aug 9am–8pm; May, June & Sept 9am–6pm; ☏04/572-3486, ⓦwww.alpinsport.si). **Bikes** can be rented from a number of places, including Pac Sports, Alpin Sport and the hut opposite the departure point for the excursion boats (see below); all are similarly priced (1hr €4, half a day €11, full day €15). The **Bohinj Horse Centre** (Mrcina Ranč) in Studor, with its stable of Icelandic ponies, offers a varied year-round programme of local treks, with one-hour rides from around €17, half-day trips around €60 and full day-trips around €90 (☏041/790-297, ⓦwww.bombagroup.com). For something a little more relaxing you can take the **excursion boat** (Turistična Ladja) which shuttles up and down the lake between Ribčev Laz and the *Hotel Zlatorog* (June to mid-Sept daily 10am–6pm, every 30min; departures during rest of year dependent upon weather; €9 one-way, €12 return). It's also possible to **fish** on the lake (March–Sept) and in the Sava Bohinjka river (May–Oct), the latter well stocked with brown trout; permits begin at around €22 per day up to €135 for a week for the lake, and €45 (€275) for the river; these can be obtained from the tourist office. **Swimming** is better here than in Bled due to the shallower waters close to the shore – the best areas are at the extreme western end of the lake and the bay-like area to the northeast. Bohinj has two major **ski resorts**, both of which offer easy to moderate skiing: **Kobla** (☏04/574-7100, ⓦwww.bohinj.si/kobla), accessible from the southern part of Bohinjska Bistrica, and the larger **Vogel** ski resort, high above the lake's southwestern corner, which has 26km of ski runs and one of the country's few snowboard parks (☏04/572-4236, ⓦwww.bohinj.si/vogel).

Such is the sheer mass of interior **frescoes** – most of which were painted by the Master of Bohinj – that you may desire a repeat visit just to take them all in, particularly if it's crowded. The Gothic presbytery, dating from around 1440, contains the densest concentration of frescoes; working upwards, the lower walls are painted with singing angels holding up patterned curtains, while the next belt depicts bust-length pictures of holy figures in niches bearing a random selection of items (a lamb, a dragon, a pair of breasts); next up are the Apostles, standing against a background of stage scenery carrying various items of weaponry, above which, in the vaulted compartments, are angels playing instruments. The oldest layer of frescoes – dating from the fourteenth century – are those on the north wall of the nave, featuring just about detectable fragments of scenes of St George and the Dragon, as well as St John the Evangelist blessing the poison (before drinking it and staying alive); adjacent to this, on the north exterior of the arch, are some grisly scenes entitled *St John's Head to Herodius* and *Beheading of a Saint*, the latter featuring St John's headless corpse spewing blood.

The lakeshore walk

The best way to enjoy the lake is to take a leisurely, circular walk around it, which can be completed in around four and a half hours – the route outlined here follows a clockwise fashion. Generally speaking, the **south shore** – alongside which the road to the hamlet of **Ukanc** runs – contains all the historical points of interest, but it's a bit of a grind, and the path is situated away from the lake, elevated above the busy main road. By way of contrast, the rocky, undisturbed **north shore** – accessible only by foot – is uplifting and possesses superior **views** of the lake – if you're short of time take a bus to the *Hotel Zlatorog* and walk the north shore back to Ribčev Laz.

Two kilometres along the road from the stone bridge in Ribčev Laz, just beyond the *Hotel Pod Voglom*, is the **Church of the Holy Spirit** (Cerkev Sv Duh), a compact Baroque structure enclosed within a shallow wall and distinguished by its neat shingle-topped roof. On its north-facing exterior is a large fresco of *St Christopher with Infant Child*, completed by Matija Koželj, who also executed the interior side-altar paintings. Its bonny interior also holds some interesting decoration, including a beautiful crystal chandelier from 1743, and stucco ornaments on the nave and presbytery vaults. If the church is closed the key can be obtained from no. 62, just up the path.

Hereafter, the road continues unexcitingly towards Ukanc, the setting for one of Slovenia's more bizarre alpine festivals (see p.131). Just short of here is the turn-off for the **Vogel cable car** (daily 8am–6pm: May to mid-Oct every half-hour; rest of year hourly; €6 single, €9 return), which can accommodate up to eighty people. Cruising up to the *Ski Hotel* (1537m) in a speedy five minutes, the panorama gradually reveals itself, culminating in memorable views of the lake below and the serried peaks opposite – on cloudless days Triglav is visible. If you fancy an easy to moderate walk, then you can always hike up; one route starts from the *Hotel Bellevue* in Ribčev Laz, and another from Ukanc (both take around 2hr).

One hundred metres beyond the turn-off for the cable car is the Austro-Hungarian **World War I Cemetery**, containing the graves of some three hundred soldiers buried here between 1915 and 1917 following ferocious battles on nearby Mount Krn. From here, the road continues uphill for 4km towards the Savica Waterfall (see p.135); retracing your steps back to the main road, follow it round to the left, past the campsite and the *Hotel Zlatorog*, and continue across the bridge spanning the Savica River. Here, the path splits – the left track heads towards the Savica Waterfall, while the other turns back towards the shore, opening up onto a pleasant grassy expanse popular with bathers and picnickers – the views across to the eastern end of the lake from here are quite splendid. The initial part of the walk along the north shore is characterized by steep slopes of scree, a dry, boulder-strewn channel and densely forested woodland, which, for the most part, meanders tightly along the course of the shoreline. It then opens up into meadowland and a curving shallow bay, one of the best locations around the lake for **bathing** – if you can find a spot. Continuing along the path will bring you back to the bridge and the Church of St John the Baptist.

Stara Fužina, Studor and Srednja Vas

One kilometre north of Ribčev Laz is **STARA FUŽINA**, the largest of the upper valley villages. Located across the bridge, thirty metres up from the *Gostilna Mihovc*, is the enjoyable **Museum of Alpine Dairy Farming** (Planšarski Muzej; Tues–Sun: July & Aug 11am–7pm, Jan–June & Sept–Oct 10am–noon & 4–6pm; €2), an ethnographic repository pertaining to the valley's rich alpine dairy-farming heritage. Thanks to its dense concentration of high-altitude alpine meadows, Bohinj was for centuries the centre of alpine dairy farming in Slovenia, reaching its high point in the late nineteenth century when the introduction of cheese cooperatives substantially increased the lot of farmers and their families. The industry continued to prosper until the 1970s, but following the opening of a modern dairy in Srednja Vas, and the exodus of younger generations to the towns and cities, dairy farming slipped into decline and today it's barely sustained by a handful of older villagers.

Among the more interesting exhibits on display in this abandoned cheese dairy are two huge copper rennet vats, a herdsman's backpack from 1961, containing all the essential items required for a season up in the mountains, and a reconstructed herder's hut. At the eastern end of the village, the **Church of St Paul** (Cerkev Sv Pavel) manifests similar external characteristics to the Church of St John, notably its paved porch, bell tower with stone windows and onion dome, and a more complete fresco of St Christopher – sadly, the frescoes by the main entrance have all but disappeared.

One and a half kilometres beyond the church is the village of **STUDOR**, well known for its splendid double **hayracks**, called *toplars*. While the single stretch type of hayrack (*kozolec*) is more common – and can be found elsewhere in Europe – the double hayrack, consisting of two parallel single hayracks connected by a double-gabled roof (used for storage), is unique to Slovenia; the ones here, dating from the eighteenth and nineteenth centuries, are perhaps the most picturesque grouping of hayracks to be seen anywhere in the country. Heading up into the village you'll pass the Bohinj Horse Centre (see box on p.132), beyond which, at no. 16, is the **Oplen House** (Oplenova hiša; same hours as Alpine Museum; €2), a typical nineteenth-century Bohinj farmhouse, also known as a longhouse because of its unusual arrangement, whereby the living quarters and barn are conjoined under one roof; aside from the typical living room (*hiša*) and "black" kitchen – the latter so-called because of its blackened walls from the open cooking area – the dwelling area consists of a chamber– used primarily as a bedroom, as evidenced by the two impossibly small beds – and an attic. If the house is closed you can get the key from no. 14a next door. **Srednja Vas**, 1km further on, is the upper valley's central settlement, and though there's nothing specific to see, it's a pleasant enough place to stroll around, and the region's best restaurant is located here (see opposite).

Eating and drinking

Aside from the hotel **restaurants**, of which the one in the *Jezero* is the best, there are precious few choices when it comes to eating around here. The *MK Pizzeria*, a few metres up from the tourist office, is the most central place, a busy and enjoyable establishment serving better than average pasta and pizza, while just up the road, the *Rožič* – in the pension of same name – has standard meats and grills. The best places to eat, however, are up in the villages: in Stara Fužina, the *Gostilna Mihovc*, just down from the alpine dairy museum at no. 118, has a simple setup but top-notch, homestyle Slovene food (closed Wed in winter); while the characterful *Gostilna Rupa*, situated at the eastern end of Srednja Vas at no. 87 (closed Mon), is the valley's finest restaurant, with heavy emphasis on pork and fish (worth trying is the delicious Bohinj trout) – during the summer there is live music on Thursdays. *Pizzeria Ema*, a few paces back down from the *Rupa*, is a colourful joint with delicious pasta and pizza and splendid views across to the mountains. The *Hotel Jezero*, and the clutch of **cafés** opposite, is where most people seem to congregate by day and night. During the summer months, there is invariably something going on at either the *Jezero* or *Zlatorog* hotels, usually folk dancing or live music – check at the tourist office.

Hikes and excursions around Bohinj

Beyond the confines of the lake, Bohinj has much to offer walkers of all abilities. The easiest short trek – and the only one accessible by public transport – is the **Savica Waterfall** near the western end of the lake; from here paths break off towards the **Valley of the Triglav Lakes**, an ideal destination for those seeking slightly more physical exertion. To the north of the lake, and accessible from Stara Fužina, is **Mostnica Gorge**, a masterpiece of nature.

Savica Waterfall

Unequivocally the number-one attraction around these parts is the majestic sixty-metre-high **Savica Waterfall** (Slap Savica; April–Oct; 8am–6pm), a forty-five-minute walk along the path (signposted) west of the *Hotel Zlatorog* (this hike can also be done as an extension of the circular walk – see p.133). You can also drive here or, between June and September, take one of the three daily buses from the *Hotel Jezero*. Once you've reached the entrance and paid the path maintenance fee (€3), it's a heavy-going twenty-minute climb up a series of zigzagging steps to the top of the gorge and a small observation hut, invariably crammed with people angling to get a photo in. The falls themselves are spectacular: smooth photogenic ribbons of water tumbling into the circular pool below, before falling away to begin the long journey as the Sava River. To the left, emerging from the same fault, is the subsidiary fall, known as **Mali Savica** (Little Savica). Savica can get murderously busy on a summer's day, which can't help but temper its delights, so to get the most out of it you're best off making an early start. The *Koča pri Savici* hut (☏04/231-2645; April–Oct daily; Nov–March Sat & Sun), by the car park at the entrance to the Savica Waterfall, offers dormitory accommodation and refreshments.

Valley of the Triglav Lakes

The car park also marks the starting point for several superb hikes into the heart of the Triglav National Park – and, if desired, an assault on Triglav itself (see box on p.138). One track forges westwards to the large *Dom na Komni* hut (1520m; 2hr 30min), open year-round (☏04/572-1475); while another spears northwards via the formidable Komarča cliff, a tough and very steep route, aided by iron pegs and rungs. Both then carry on northwards, meeting up at the *Koča pri Triglavskih Jezerih* (1685m; ☏040/620-783; mid-June to mid-Oct), which marks the beginning of the magical **Valley of the Triglav Lakes** (Dolina Triglavskih jezer), also known as the **Valley of the Seven Lakes**.

Hiking in the Julian Alps

The Julian Alps are a hiker's wonderland, its meadows, valleys and mountains carved up by a well-worn nexus of waymarked paths and trails. There are several key **starting points**: **Bled**, furthest from the park's mountainous heart, offers easy to moderate hikes around the eastern spur of the Alps, though there are more demanding walks to be had in the heavily forested **Karavanke** chain bordering Austria to the north. From **Kranjska Gora**, trails head off up into the **Planica** and **Tamar Valleys**, as well as up the **Vršič Pass**, from where further tracks fan out in several directions. A short way east of Kranjska Gora, a trio of valleys – the most prominent being the **Vrata Valley** – provide the starting point for ascents towards Triglav itself; if you're considering tackling the great mountain, consult the box on p.137. The greatest choice of hikes, however, emanate from **Bohinj** in the southeastern corner of Triglav National Park: the lush pastures of the **Fužine highlands** and the **Voje Valley** north of the lake; the **Lower Bohinj** mountains on the south side; the **Komna Plateau** to the west; and up through the **Valley of the Triglav Lakes** to the northwest (which continues towards Triglav), arguably the park's most scenic trek. Unlike in many other European countries, there is no hierarchical system of different signs and colours for **trails**; instead, all paths in Slovenia are marked by a "target", that is, a red circle with a white centre, with intersections and forks indicated by arrows; however, some of the markings are a little inconclusive in places.

The best hiking months are May, June and September, when the weather is at its most dependable and the crowds are somewhat thinner than in the peak summer months; bear in mind that the weather in the mountains can change with alarming rapidity and so the usual provisos apply – sufficient provisions and appropriate clothing and equipment – particularly if you plan to do any high-altitude hiking. If you fancy hooking up with other walkers, a number of **agencies** in Bled and Bohinj (see p.122 & p.135) offer a full range of hikes, from easy to moderate half- or full-day trips such as Debela Peč and the meadows of Bohinj, to more difficult two-day trips up to Triglav (with an overnight stay in a hut). The best up-to-date **maps** are the 1:50,000 editions of *Triglavski Narodni Park* and *Julijske Alps*, published by the Alpine Association of Slovenia (Planinska Zveza Slovenije or PZS; ⊛www.pzs.si). You might also like to consider Roy Clark's pocket handbook *The Julian Alps of Slovenia* (see p.339), which outlines key hikes from Bled, Bohinj, Kranjska Gora, Bovec and Kobarid.

Some key hiking terms

Dolina – valley	**Dom/Koča** – mountain hut
Gora – mountain	**Jezero** – lake
Pot – path/way	**Planina** – high alp/pasture
Sedlo – saddle/pass	**Vrh** - summit

Lined with white limestone cliffs, and rich in alpine and karstic flora, the valley is famed for its beautiful tarns, the lowest and warmest of which is the **Black Lake** (Črno jezero), just above Komarča, while the highest, the **Lake below Vršac** (Jezero pod Vršacem), lies at an altitude of 2000m. The largest and deepest of the seven lakes, the **Great Lake** (Veliko jezero), is approximately midway between these two. The valley is also the setting for Zlatorog, the mythical chamois with golden horns.

Mostnica Gorge and the Voje Valley

Another superb outing is the hike up through the **Mostnica Gorge** (Mostnice Korita), 1km north of Stara Fužina. Two trails – one just before the bridge and one by St Paul's Church – head towards the gorge entrance, before which you cross the stone **Devil's Bridge** (Hudičev Most); follow the path to the right for 400m,

Climbing Triglav

It's said that every Slovene has to climb **Mount Triglav** at least once in their lifetime, but this in no sense means that it's an easy outing. In fact it remained unclimbed until 1778, when a German doctor and three local guides made it to the 2864m summit. The mountain can be approached via several routes:

The **most dramatic approach** – and one not for the inexperienced or faint-hearted – is from the **north**, as Triglav's north face is no less than 1200m high; its central part is for climbers only, but there are fairly tough hiking routes to either side, involving the use of fixed cables. From the *Aljažev Dom* hut (1015m; ☎04/589-1030) at the end of the Vrata valley, continue past a monument to the partisans, and after 45 minutes take the Prag path to the left. At the foot of the north face the Prag, or threshold (a rock cliff), is scaled with the help of metal steps and pegs; thereafter the path winds on up to a small spring, after which you fork right to reach the *Triglavski dom na Kredarici* (2515m; ☎04/202-3181), four or five hours from the *Aljažev Dom*. From the saddle above the hut, a huge painted marker denotes the start of the final ascent; with the aid of steel cables and pegs you should reach the summit in an hour or so. Here you'll find the Aljažev Stolp, or turret, a tiny refuge erected in 1865 that looks like a small space rocket.

The **shortest ascent** is from the **east**, from Rudno Polje (1340m); from here it's about two hours' hike to the Studorski preval (1892m), and another hour to the *Vodnikov dom* (1817m; ☎04/572-3213), from where you continue to *Dom Planika pod Triglavom* (2401m; ☎04/574-4069) and beyond to the summit.

The **most popular route** is from the **south**; from the *Hotel Zlatorog* at the western end of Lake Bohinj, it's a forty-minute walk to the Savica Waterfall, where a path to the right begins the ascent of the formidable-looking Komarča Cliff, a tough climb of 700 metres but fitted with cables. At the top, continue gently uphill in beech trees for a short while before arriving at the Black Lake (Črno Jezero; 1294m) on your left. Soon after, turn left to pass around the lake to the north; after a couple of minutes go straight ahead at a junction, continuing on a slightly rocky path in pine trees, level and then rising for an hour in all. From the top of the White Cliff (Bela Skala) it's an easy fifteen-minute walk through limestone dykes to the *Koča pri Triglavskih Jezerih* (Hut of the Triglav Lakes; 1685m; ☎040/620-783), three to four hours from the *Hotel Zlatorog*. From the hut continue north up the valley and past the Great Lake (Veliko Triglavskih Jezero), reaching the foot of an escarpment after an hour; the route leads steeply up to the right (following a red arrow to Hribarice), reaching the ridge in twenty minutes and the Yellow Lake (Želeno Jezero; 1988m) soon after. Continuing up to the right, you'll pass a turning to the Prehodavici hut (visible not too far to the left), and climb up, partly on scree, for half an hour. In another thirty minutes you reach the Hribarice saddle (2358m), from where the path is reasonably marked for a while; it descends and kinks to the left after about five minutes, then rises a little to reach the Dolič saddle (2164m) in another twenty minutes; from here the *Tržaška Koča na Doliču* (2151m; ☎04/574-4069) is also visible just to the left. The path swings sharply to the right here, and after an hour you'll reach the start of a fairly steep section, after which it takes just five minutes to reach the *Dom Planika pod Triglavom* (2401m), a good place to spend the night. From here the route brings you, in thirty minutes, to the foot of a cliff, where a big red-and-white dot marks the start of the final climb. With the aid of pegs and cables you soon reach a shoulder, where a path leads left and down to the *Dolič* hut. The route to the summit turns right and climbs onwards, reaching the top after another forty minutes.

More detailed information on the various routes can be found in *The Julian Alps of Slovenia* (see p.339); alternatively, any of the park's tourist offices can supply you with in-depth information and maps on Triglav.

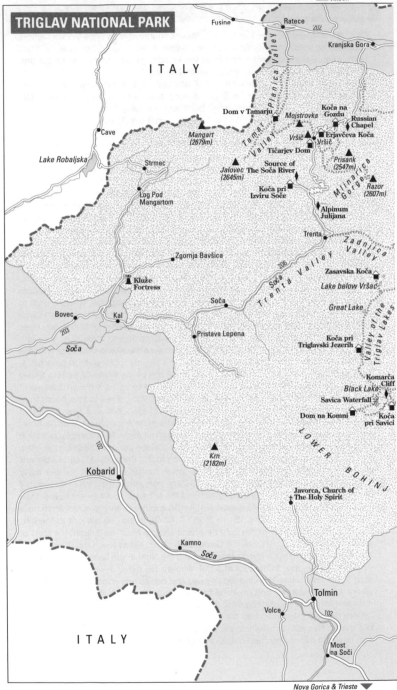

TRIGLAV NATIONAL PARK

▲ Villach

Fusine

Ratece

202

Kranjska Gora

ITALY

Planica Valley

Dom v Tamarju

Koča na Gozdu

Mojstrovka

Russian Chapel

Vršič

Erjavčeva Koča

Mangart (2679m)

Tamar Valley

Tičarjev Dom

Vršič

Lake Robaljska

Strmec

Prisank (2547m)

Jalovec (2645m)

Source of The Soča River

Cave

Koča pri Izviru Soče

Mlinarica Gorge

Razor (2607m)

Log Pod Mangartom

Alpinum Julijana

Trenta

Zadnjica Valley

Zgornja Bavšica

Soča

Trenta Valley

206

Zasavska Koča

Kluže Fortress

Lake below Vršac

Soča

Great Lake

Bovec

Kal

Soča

Pristava Lepena

Valley of the Triglav Lakes

Koča pri Triglavski Jezerih

Komarča Cliff

Black Lake

Savica Waterfall

Dom na Komni

Koča pri Savici

103

203

102

Krn (2182m)

LOWER BOHINJ

Kobarid

Javorca, Church of The Holy Spirit

Kamno

Soča

Tolmin

Volce

102

ITALY

Most na Soči

Nova Gorica & Trieste ▼

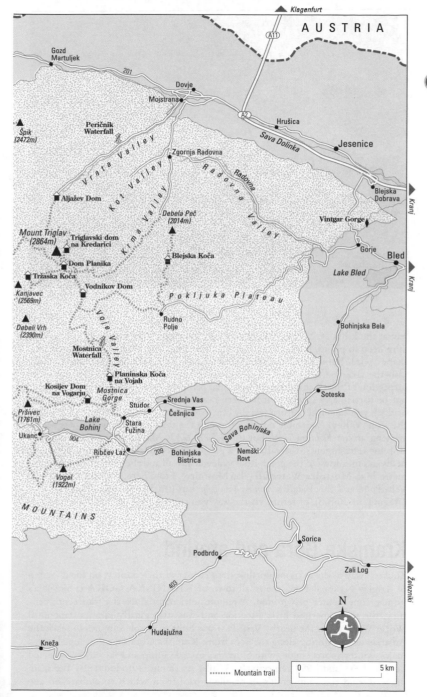

Klagenfurt

AUSTRIA

A11

Gozd
Martuljek

201

Dovje

Mojstrana

Hrušica

Sava Dolinka

A2

Jesenice

Špik
(2472m)

Peričnik
Waterfall

Zgornja Radovna

Blejska
Dobrava

Vrata Valley

Radovna

Radovna Valley

Vintgar Gorge

Kranj

Aljažev Dom

Kot Valley

Krma Valley

Debela Peč
(2014m)

Gorje

Bled

Mount Triglav
(2864m)

Triglavski dom
na Kredarici

Blejska Koča

Lake Bled

Dom Planika

Tržaska Koča

Vodnikov Dom

Pokljuka Plateau

Kranj

Kanjavec
(2569m)

Debeli Vrh
(2390m)

Voje Valley

Rudno
Polje

Bohinjska Bela

Mostnica
Waterfall

Planinska Koča
na Vojah

Kosijev Dom
na Vogarju

Mostnica
Gorge

Srednja Vas

Soteska

Pršivec
(1761m)

Studor

Češnjica

Lake
Bohinj

Stara
Fužina

Sava Bohinjska

Ukanc

904

Ribčev Laz

209

Bohinjska
Bistrica

Nemški
Rovt

Vogel
(1922m)

MOUNTAINS

Sorica

Podbrdo

Zali Log

Železniki

403

N

Hudajužna

Kneža

.... Mountain trail

0   5 km

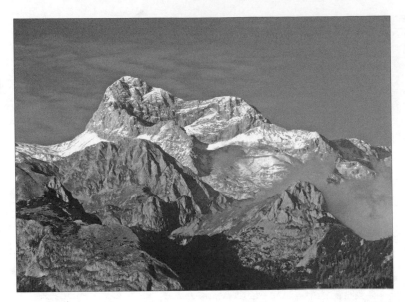

△ Mount Triglav

pay at the kiosk (€2), then take the path to the right. The ravine, 1km long and 20m deep in places, has been smoothly sculpted into all manner of extraordinary shapes, while hundreds of circular hollows, known as river mills, have been eroded into the riverbed, the result of stones spun by whirlpools in the stream; close inspection of the river is possible, as regular paths divert away from the main track, but be particularly careful if it has been raining. At the end of the gorge (by the bridge), you can either return (via the other side), or continue northwards towards the **Voje Valley** – scramble upwards through the trees for twenty minutes before arriving at the *Koča na Vojah* hut (☎04/572-3213; May–Sept), a good place to stop for refreshments; thereafter, it's a pleasant forty-minute walk through open fields and meadows to the precipitous valley headwall and the modest twenty-one-metre-high **Mostnica Waterfall** (Slap Mostnice). From here, you can continue to Velo Polje and the *Vodnikov dom na Velo polje* hut (☎051/607-211; June–Sept) at 1817m (3hr 30min), or return via the way you came.

Kranjska Gora and around

Tucked away in the extreme northwestern corner of the country, on the doorstep of Triglav National Park, the small town of **KRANJSKA GORA** is Slovenia's number one winter playground. A remote settlement since the fourteenth century, the town merited little attention and was strategically unimportant until World War I when the nearby Vršič Pass was built to enable supplies to reach the Austrian army fighting along the Soča front. Kranjska Gora then developed into a major winter sports venue, with Slovenia's first ski jump and ski lifts constructed here in 1934 and 1950 respectively. Whilst its skiing is undoubtedly the main draw, during the summer it's an excellent base from which to embark on any

Skiing in northwest Slovenia

Given its predominantly mountainous terrain, it's not surprising that northwest Slovenia contains the greatest concentration of the country's **ski resorts**, and whilst you won't find the range of slopes that you would in Italy or France, the spectacular alpine scenery, thinner crowds and considerably lower prices are ample compensation. Moreover, Slovenia's ski resorts are uniformly well equipped and extremely safe, although most suffer from a lack of decent après-ski facilities.

Slovenia's largest and best-known ski resort is **Kranjska Gora**, located near the Austrian and Italian borders; however, the skiing here is not particularly exciting, its slopes best suited to beginners and intermediate skiers, which makes it a popular base with families – it is, however, one of only two resorts in the country to host international ski (and ski-jumping) competitions. Consistently rated as one of the most complete, and fashionable, centres in Slovenia – and the most popular resort amongst weekending *Ljubljančani* – is **Krvavec**, some 25km due north of the capital; located at a relatively high altitude, its extensive range of slopes is suitable for skiers of all abilities, moreover, it has a snowboard school, speed-skiing track and a freestyle mogul course. The country's highest-altitude skiing (over 2000m) is at **Kanin**, near Bovec in the Soča Valley. Both this and the centres in Bohinj – **Kobla** and **Vogel** – offer the most spectacular skiing in terms of scenery; the former is the only ski resort in Slovenia accessible by train while the latter possesses the most modern cable car in the country. An increasingly popular centre is **Cerkno**, a well developed and sophisticated resort which has some of the most challenging pistes in the country.

The **season** lasts from December to March, though skiing on the higher pistes, such as Kanin, is often possible until the end of April or beginning of May. Expect to **pay** in the region of €20-25 for a day ski pass and €100-140 for a weekly pass, the latter figure representing the sort of price you'd expect to pay at the more developed resorts. The **Ski Pass Julijske Alps** (€48 for 2 days, up to €140 for a week) covers all the ski centres located within the Julian Alps. Most centres have **ski schools** with English instruction (around €30 for a two-hour individual lesson, and €65 for five, two-hour lessons as part of a group), and offer **ski rental** (around €20 for skis, boots and poles). Telephone numbers for individual centres are given where relevant throughout the guide. For more **information** on skiing (and other winter sports) in Slovenia check out the website ⓦ www.sloveniaski.info, which provides details on resorts, ski trails, ski schools, ticket prices, weather forecasts and so on. Latest ski conditions can be obtained from the Snow Hotline (☏ 041/182-500).

number of hikes, while cyclists will appreciate the extensive network of recently established, and very well-marked, cycle paths.

Arrival and information

The basic **bus station** is just five minutes' walk north of the centre on Koroška ulica – head down Kolodvorska ulica to Borovška cesta, the town's main street. The **tourist office** is in the centre of town at Tičarjeva 2 (Jan-March & June–Sept Mon–Sat 8am–8pm, Sun 9am–6pm; other times Mon–Fri 8am–3pm, Sat 9am–6pm; ☏ 04/588-1768, ⓦ www.kranjska-gora.si), 100m west of which is the **post office** (Mon–Fri 8am–7pm, Sat 8am–noon).

Accommodation

As you'd expect from Slovenia's largest ski resort, there's a healthy stock of **hotels** in town, though the **pensions** here generally offer better value for money. There is plentiful accommodation in **private rooms** (❷) or **apartments** (❸–❺) in the town centre and surrounding villages, which can be arranged through either the tourist office, or the Globtour agency, 150m west of the tourist office at Borovška cesta 92 (July to mid-Sept & mid-Dec to mid-March Mon–Sat 9am–7pm, Sun 9am–noon; other times of the year Mon–Fri 9am–4pm, Sat 9am–noon; ☎04/582-0200, ⒺGlobtour@kranjskagora.com). There are also numerous apartments advertised in the streets east of the bus station.

Hotel Alpina Vitranška 12 ☎04/588-1761, ⓌWww.hit.si. Ignore the portentous exterior and old-fashioned reception area, the rooms are taste-fully decorated, though some are a little boxy. It's well worth paying the minimal extra for the reno-vated rooms. Free use of pools in the *Kompas* and *Larix* hotels. ❻

Pension Borka Borovška cesta 71 ☎04/587-9100. This cheap, downbeat hostel-type place in the centre of town has extremely basic, but clean, double and triple rooms. ❷

Hotel Kompas Borovška cesta 100 ☎04/588-1661, ⓌWww.hoteli-kompas.si. This sprawling complex on the western edge of town accom-modates two categories of room; those in the main building are bright and well furnished, while those in the chalet-type annexe across the way are cheaper, but very dated. There's also a smart indoor pool. ❻–❽

Hotel Kotnik Borovška cesta 75 ☎04/588-1564, ⒺKotnik@siol.net. Housed in a luminous yellow building, this classy, family-run hotel accommodates fifteen large and beautifully designed rooms – the best-value place in town. ❻

Hotel Lek Vršiška 38 ☎04/588-1520, ⓌWww.hotel-lek.si. Located south of town out on the road to Vršič, this polished hotel harbours supremely comfy rooms (with widescreen tv), plus all the other requisite four-star facilities, including a beau-tiful indoor pool, gym and sauna. ❽

Pension Lipa Koroška cesta 14 ☎04/582-0000, ⒺPerkolic@g-kabel.si. Attractive, comfortable pension right next to the bus station; has a lovely restaurant (see p.142). ❻

Hotel Miklič Vitranška 13 ☎04/588-1635, ⓌWww.hotelmiklic.com. Surrounded by baize-like lawns and neatly arranged flowerbeds, this pristine pension, just below the *Alpina* hotel, has well turned out rooms and a terrific restaurant too (see p.142). ❻

Grand Hotel Prisank Borovška cesta 93 ☎04/588-4820, ⓌWww.htp-gorenjka.si. Occupy-ing a central location a few steps west of the tourist office, this big, pink hotel – complete with ultra-modern rooms – is as luxurious as it gets in town. Also houses a good little pizzeria, tearoom and cocktail bar. ❽

The Town

The one key site in town is the **Liznjek House** (Liznjekova hiša; Tues–Fri 10am–4.30pm, Sat & Sun 10am–5pm; closed April and Nov; €3) located 200m east of the *Hotel Kotnik* at Borovška cesta 63. This superbly preserved alpine homestead – once the property of a wealthy local farmer and the largest farm in the village – mostly dates from the late eighteenth century, though its stone ground floor is of seventeenth-century origin. Its interior furnishings are particularly outstand-ing; in one nameless room sits a lovely selection of folk-painted trousseau chests, while in the main living room there is a beautiful corner stove and a lovely, slender grandfather clock. Upstairs is a typically modest bedroom, and a vast attic, once used as storage space and still chock-full with farmers' tools. Opposite the house is the capacious barn, built in 1796 and originally used for storing food and hous-ing livestock; it's now mostly empty, save for some battered old horse carts and grand-looking sleds. Downstairs in the small one-room basement is an exhibition dedicated to the Slovene writer Josip Vandot (1884–1944), whose many stories about the clever shepherd boy, Kekec, endure to this day – many of these were made into films (see p.147).

Three hundred metres west of the Liznjek House, sited on the attractive, square-like portion of Borovška cesta, is the squat, late-Gothic **Church of the Assump-tion** (Cerkev Sv vnebovzetje). The only surviving part of the original church is the stocky, Romanesque bell tower, while the church you see today dates from 1510. There's not an awful lot to see inside, though its exquisite interior does contain one of the most impressive vaulted ceilings in the region and a particularly fine organ, one of the oldest in Gorenjska. West beyond the church are most of the town's hotels and other key facilities, and further west still the ski slopes (see box opposite).

Eating, drinking and entertainment

The town is blessed with a handful of first-rate **restaurants**, the best of which are located within several of the pensions and hotels. Conversely, decent **drinking** establishments are conspicuous in their absence – disappointing, given the town's status as one of the country's premier ski resorts. Most of these restaurants are open daily til 11pm.

Gostilna Cvitar Borovška cesta 83. Housed in a delightful 200-year-old building next to the church, this characterful tavern has some of the best Slovene dishes in town. Its stylish interior has smoking and nonsmoking rooms, while the informal terrace is also an enjoyable place to eat; reasonably priced and top-class service to boot.

Kotnik Borovška cesta 15. Inventively styled place in the *Hotel Kotnik*, with a highly creditable menu featuring fish, game and, unusually, lamb. Also houses a small, rather frenetic, pizzeria.

Lipa Koroška cesta 14. Located in the pension of the same name, this restaurant offers an outstanding international and Slovene kitchen, as well as a superb pizza menu. The winter garden, with its soft green decor and wicker chairs, is the most atmospheric place in town to dine.

Miklič Vitranška 13. As accomplished as the pension it's housed in, this beautiful and classy restaurant offers a more upscale and expensive take on standard beef and fish dishes, as well as a colourful salad bar. The covered outdoor terrace is a delightful place to eat.

Pri Martinu Borovška cesta 61. Enjoyable, vaguely medieval themed restaurant next to the Liznjek House, rustling up healthy portions of solid meat dishes – such as veal stew with buckwheat mush – and some sound veggie options, including dumplings and polenta.

Drinking and entertainment

The town's central watering hole is *Papa Joe Razor*, located in a corner of the once elegant but now defunct *Razor Hotel* at Borovška 83 (daily 9am–5am) – a raucous establishment, it has live music at the weekends and is also a good place for hot snacks, including horse goulash. Other sociable drinking spots are the *Vopa Pub*, next to Globtour at Borovška cesta 99a (open til 1am), and the *Gostilna Cvitar*, while there are a smattering of other, albeit rather uninspiring, cafés along Borovška cesta. If you fancy chancing your arm, as hundreds of neighbouring Italians do each night, then head to the 24-hour casino adjoining the *Hotel Casino Kranjska Gora*, located to the south of town at Vršiška cesta 23. Entrance is €8 (but you get chips to the value of that), and bring some ID, ideally your passport.

West of Kranjska Gora

To the west of Kranjska Gora is the small but beautiful Zelenci Nature Reserve, beyond which is the Planica Valley with its head-spinning ski jumps, and the Tamar Valley, from where a number of paths lead to more challenging peaks.

Zelenci Nature Reserve

Three kilometres west of Kranjska Gora, sandwiched between the ski slopes of Podkoren and the main road to Italy, is the **Zelenci Nature Reserve**, home to an exceptional range of flora and fauna. Located within the reserve is a marsh, which consists of a brilliant emerald-blue, crystal-clear lake, below which cool springs spurt, volcano-like, from limestone sediment called *kreda* – a phenomenon unique to Slovenia. The lake – which is also the source of the Sava Dolinka River, though technically this begins at the Nadiša karst spring up in the Tamar Valley (see oppo-

Activities around Kranjska Gora

The area around Kranjska Gora offers some of the best cycling in the region. The excellent cycling map (*Kolesarski izleti*), available from the tourist office, details some twelve excursions, ranging from gentle (Rateče), to very demanding (Vršič Pass, Belca) routes; paths are clearly signposted at regular intervals, each one indicating relevant turn-off points, distances and length of time to the next destination.

Bikes can be rented from the Julijana agency (daily: mid-June to mid-Sept 9am–noon & 3–9pm; mid-Dec to mid-March, same times except til 7pm; ☎04/588-1325, Ⓦwww.sednjek.si), located in a small hut a few paces west of the *Hotel Prisank*; Šport Bernik, at Borovška 88a (daily: 8am–7pm; winter til 6pm; ☎04/588-1470, Ⓦwww.kranjska-gora.si/sportbernik); and Sport Point, next to the *Hotel Prisank* - all charge around €4 for one hour, €7 for half a day and €12 for a full day. Julijana also organizes **rafting** (€22) on the Sava and Soča rivers, **canyoning** (€25) and **hiking** (€16), so long as there are sufficient numbers (between four and six).

The slopes of **Vitranc** and **Podkoren**, just west of the town centre, offer some 20km of **ski runs** (with five chairlifts and numerous towbars). These accommodate skiers of all abilities, though the proliferation of easy slopes makes it a popular destination for **families and beginners**. Kranjska Gora also has night-time skiing, and between late December and early January, the town welcomes international skiers for the men's World Cup Slalom and Giant Slalom races. **Ski passes** (Vozovnice; around €25 for a day pass, and €140 for a weekly pass) are available from the ticket office at the Alpine Ski Club (Alpski Smučarski Klub), Borovška 99 (daily in winter 8.30am–3.30pm; ☎04/588-5300, Ⓦwww.ask-kg.com). The club's school (Smučarska šola) offers **ski lessons** (around €30 for a 2hr individual lesson, and around €65 for five, two-hour lessons as part of a group); and **snowboarding** lessons (€25 1hr). Both the Alpine Ski Club and Šport Bernik offer **ski rental** (skis, €14 for one day; boots, €7; snowboard, €18). Between December and April (depending on the weather) the Julijana agency offers **tobogganing** (€12) and **motor sleigh** (€22 for 15min on track, €50 for panoramic ride).

site) – can be accessed via a series of carefully constructed walkways from either side of the reserve, while the observation tower provides some lovely overhead views.

As well as harbouring a dense concentration of vegetation – including pygmy willows, alder trees and common cottongrass – the reserve supports some unusual fauna, such as the whiskered bat, sand lizard, the common viper snake, and a rare bird species, the scarlet grosbeak, all of which have been placed on the "Red List" – a list of Slovenia's most endangered species.

The Planica and Tamar valleys

The most enjoyable hike from Kranjska Gora is up the **Planica Valley**, and beyond to the **Tamar Valley** (route no. 3 on the cycling map – see above). Just under 1km beyond the Zelenci Nature Reserve, you come to the grassy lower part of the Planica Valley, the most westerly access point into the Alps. From here, the road ascends steeply up towards the extraordinary **Planica ski jumps** (see box on p.144); a short way north of the last ski jump, you re-enter the National Park, at which point the road gives way to an untidy mess of gravel workings, before continuing as a stony, gently inclining track (used as a cross-country ski track in winter) for about 3.5km up to a lush grassy glade and the *Dom v Tamarju* at 1108m (☎04/587-6055; open all year), which offers beds and good food. The walk up to this point is tremendous, largely for the views of the mighty, razor-sharp peak of **Jalovec** (2645m), due south, and **Mojstrovka** (2366m) to the east. A ten-minute walk west of the hut is the **source of the Nadiža stream**, a powerful karstic

The incredible flying men

Situated at the mouth of the picturesque Planica Valley, 2km west of Kranjska Gora, are the world-renowned **Planica ski jumps**, site of the world's largest ski jump and venue for the longest jump in history. The first of the three jumps located here was built in 1934, on the initiative of **Stanko Bloudek**, engineer, figure-skating champion and the man widely credited with bringing winter sports to a wider Slovenian audience. Not long after its construction (a mere 90m, the longest is a breathtaking 190m), the first record at Planica fell, as the Austrian, **Sepp Bradl**, became the first man to jump beyond the magical one-hundred-metre mark, in 1936. To this day, Planica proudly boasts of holding more ski-jump records than any other venue in the world, not least the current **world record**, held by the Norwegian **Björn Romöeren**, who jumped an astonishing 239m here in 2005.

Slovenes too have a fine pedigree in the sport, gaining their first Olympic medal (a team bronze) in the 2002 Salt Lake City games, while their record-holder is **Rok Benkovič**, who leapt 226m at Planica in 2005. If you've got the energy, take a hike up the stairs located to the side of the jumps and enjoy the extraordinary views. Better still, if you're around at the end of March, then you shouldn't miss the annual World Cup event – celebrated as much for its drinking and music as for its sporting theatrics.

spring which squirts through a small fissure in the rock face before disappearing into underground channels and re-emerging in Zelenci at the base of the valley (see p.142). From the hut, one path heads south up the Tamar Valley to **Jalovec** (2645m; 6hr), and another east to **Vršič** (1611m; 3hr); both contain some very exposed and difficult sections.

East of Kranjska Gora

The small village of **Gozd-Martuljek**, 3km east of Kranjska Gora, is the starting point for hikes into the **Martuljek** group of mountains, a fierce, spectacular range which counts the imperious **Mount Špik** (2472m) among its number, regarded as one of the toughest climbs in the Alps. From the village of **Mojstrana**, a further 10km east, three parallel valleys fan out southwards into the core of the Park, each furrowed with mountain paths heading towards Triglav itself. Adjoining the easternmost of these valleys is the hamlet of **Zgornja Radovna**, which marks the northwestern extremes of the **Radovna Valley**.

Mojstrana and the Vrata Valley

Thirteen kilometres east of Kranjska Gora, just off the fast main road towards Jesenice, is the village of **MOJSTRANA**, the starting point for hikers attempting Triglav's north face (see box on p.138). The most direct road from the village heads southwest up into the **Vrata Valley** ("Gateway Valley"), the largest glacial valley in the northern tract of the Julian Alps and the most direct route to Triglav – consequently, it's often overflowing with hikers and motorists.

Nearing the southern end of the village, the **Triglav Museum Collection** (Triglavska Muzejska Zbirka; May–Oct Tues–Fri 10am–4.30pm, Sat & Sun til 5pm; €3) at Triglavska cesta 50 has some illuminating exhibits pertaining to the National Park and those who have shaped it. One of the park's foremost pioneers was Jakob Aljaž (1845–1927) – parish priest, composer and mountaineer – after whom both the hut at the end of the valley and the rocket-shaped turret (Aljažev stolp) at the top of Triglav are named. In 1895, as competing claims from Germany and Austria for Triglav intensified, Aljaš, a staunch Slovene patriot, purchased the peak for the sum of 1 florin, thus ensuring the mountain remained Slovene property. Other rooms document the work of the Slovenian Mountain Association, the Mountain Rescue Service and the first mountain guides.

Four kilometres beyond the village, two paths branch off up a forest slope (10min) to the **Peričnik Waterfall** (Slap Peričnik), which actually comprises an upper (16m) and lower (52m) fall. Unusually, the falls can be circled – via the narrow, sandy ledge – but wherever you view it from you're likely to get a good soaking from the itinerant spray. The best time to see the falls is in winter when the water freezes into thick curtains of ice.

Six kilometres further north, up an increasingly steep and rugged track (accessible by car) is *Aljažev Dom* (☏04/589-1030; May–Oct), named after the eponymous mountaineer, and the key lodge for hikers en route to Triglav. Ten minutes' walk north of the hut is a **memorial to World War II Partisan fighters**, which takes the form of a carabiner and piton. From here, a couple of paths lead off towards the summit. On a clear day, the views of Triglav's indomitable 1200-metre-high and 3km-wide north face are nothing short of spectacular.

Kot and Krma valleys and Zgornja Radovna

From Mojstrana another road cuts south towards the second and third of the glens which forge into the belly of the National Park. Three kilometres beyond the Kosma Pass (847m), one road branches off into the secluded **Kot Valley**, while the main road continues through the tiny hamlet of **ZGORNJA RADOVNA** and on to the **Krma Valley** which, at 7km in length, is the longest of the glacial valleys in the Julian Alps. In Zgornja Radovna, at no. 25, is the **Pocar Farmhouse** (Pocarjeva Domačija; Fri–Sun 10am–5pm; €2), one of six farms believed to have existed in the hamlet during feudal times. This unusually large seventeenth-century farmhouse consists of a main living area, bedroom – note the date, 1775, inscribed onto the ceiling beam – a "black" kitchen (see p.134) and, upstairs, the attic and granary room. The entire furnishings and contents of the house are all original. The two-storey, part-stone, part-wooden **outbuilding**, previously used for housing livestock and storing hay, now houses a display of farmers' implements and long wooden carts. From the farmhouse, the road east continues down through the **Radovna Valley** towards Bled, some 15km away. For cyclists there is a fairly sedate but attractive path (3hr) from the farmhouse to Krnica near Bled – regular information boards detail local points of interest. At roughly the midway point between Radovna and Bled, in the hamlet of Srednja Radovna, you'll come across the ruins of the Smolej farmhouse – the only building that remained following an attack on the village by Germans in September 1944, in retaliation for the ambush of two of their soldiers.

There are two **campsites** (both open year-round) along the road between Kranjska Gora and Mojstrana; the larger of the two is *Camping Špik* (☏04/ 587-7100), located at the eastern edge of Gozd Martuljek – buses stop in the centre of the village, from where it's a 400m walk east across the river; the small *Kamne* campsite (☏04/589-1105) is located in **Dovje**, a small village settled on the slopes just above the main road 1km east of Mojstrana (buses stop on the main road just outside the site) – it also has two-to-five-bed bungalows ❷–❹). At the road junction is a **monument to Jakob Aljaž**, which has the local hero pointing towards Triglav.

South to the Soča Valley

Linking the Upper Sava and Soča Valleys, the **Vršič Pass** – the highest mountain pass in Slovenia – is one of the most spectacular and scenically rewarding

Mountain huts

Nearly a third of Slovenia's 169 **mountain huts** (Planinarski Domovi) lie within the National Park's boundaries, all managed and maintained by the **Alpine Association of Slovenia** (Planinska Zveza Slovenije or PZS). Huts range from the most basic of refuges (*zavetišče*), often without accommodation or with very few beds and sometimes no running water, to more comfortable places, namely **huts** (*koča*) or **houses** (*dom*), which vary considerably in size, quality and sleeping capacity; expect to pay around €10 for a dorm bed, €15 in a five-to-eight-bed room, and €20 in a twin-bed room – these are the maximum prices for category I huts (classified as a hut more than one hour's walk away from motorized transport) – and typically those around Triglav. A thirty-percent discount is available to UIAA-affiliated members.

Food, available at just about all huts, is usually wholesome, filling and cheap; typical staples include vegetable soup (*zelenjavna juha*; €3), goulash (*golaž*; €5), and tea with lemon (*čaj z limono*; €1.5). Owing to their high-altitude location, the majority of the park's huts are only **open** between June and September, though most of those along the Vršič Pass are open year-round. However, these dates aren't fixed and may deviate by a month either side depending on the weather. All huts take bookings.

trips in the country. Constituting the stretch of road between Kranjska Gora and Trenta – a total of some 25km – the pass is defined by fifty hairpin bends, twenty-four on the Kranjska Gora side, twenty-six on the Trenta side (each bend is numbered and the altitude recorded). Between June and September, four daily buses haul themselves up and over the pass and down to Bovec (44km south of Kranjska Gora), and while there are regular stops at all the huts and villages along the way, this limited service makes it extremely difficult to see much in one day. Hence, it's really only feasible to see many of the places described here if you have your own transport (the road is not suitable for caravans or trailers). The other alternative, of course, is to hike to or between various points. Due to snow drifts and the threat of avalanches, the pass is periodically closed between November and April.

From Kranjska Gora to Vršič

Two kilometres south of Kranjska Gora, in the centre of a large gravel flood plain, is the artificial **Lake Jasna**, a popular excursion spot with the locals but not worth stopping off for. The road then climbs steadily up past the 1000-metre point, reaching, at turn eight (1129m), the **Russian Chapel** (Ruska kapelica), probably the most poignant sight along the pass. Set back 100m from the road, the tiny wood-latticed chapel (which cannot be entered) was built between 1916 and 1917 to commemorate the deaths of over three hundred Russian prisoners of war buried by an avalanche as they constructed the road; thousands more prisoners died from fatigue, starvation and torture during its construction, a few of whom are buried in the small **military cemetery**, set back forty metres from the road just after turn twenty-one.

Beyond this point the road becomes ever more sinuous, passing a couple of mountain huts – *Koča na Gozdu* (℡050/626-641; daily May–Oct, Thurs–Sun Nov–April) and *Erjavčeva koča* (℡051/399-226; all year) – before arriving at **Vršič**, the highest point along the pass at 1611m; if you wish to park, you'll have to pay (€3). There's another hut here – *Tičarjev Dom* (℡050/634-171; May to mid-Oct) – and it's a good starting point for hikes into the surrounding mountains, including **Tamar**, via Vratca (1108m; 3hr 30min), and **Prisank** (2547m; 4hr 30min), though both are hikes of some difficulty.

From Vršič to Trenta

The descent from Vršič to the Trenta Valley is every bit as dramatic as the ascent, with many an unscheduled diversion almost guaranteed – if you have wheels that is. Stationed on an exposed ledge just after turn forty-eight is a fine-looking **monument** to Julius Kugy, the esteemed mountaineer and botanist who pioneered many new routes across the Alps, and whose biography *Alpine Pilgrimage* extolled the virtues of both the mountains and those who climbed them. At the next bend, a road branches off towards the *Koča pri Izviru Soče* (⊕04/586-6070; May–Oct), 2km away, and the source of the Soča River (Izvir Soče). From the hut (which has dorm beds) it's a short, twenty-minute climb up a very rocky and partially secured path to the source – care should be taken on approaching the latter part as it can get slippery; fed by an underground lake, the water emerges from a dark cave before streaking away on its long and eventful journey to the Adriatic, some 136km downriver. If you don't fancy walking that far, you might like to tackle the 20km long Soča Trail (Soča Pot), a carefully tailored path (no bicycles) that follows the course of the river from its source down to Bovec – regular information boards (marked "TNP") line the route indicating various points of interest.

Secreted away in perfect rural isolation just ten minutes' walk west of the hut (signposted) is the wonderful *Kekčeva domačija* pension and restaurant (⊕05/381-1088, ⓔkekec.trenta@siol.net; ❾), named after the legendary Slovenian children's character *Kekec*, the clever shepherd boy, created by the Kranjska Gora-born writer Josip Vandot (see p.141) – the film, *Good luck, Kekec*, was shot here in 1963. The pension has nine beautifully appointed apartments, each with an upstairs bedroom and a downstairs living area and bathroom, while the restaurant (May–Sept) offers delicious homestyle Slovenian cooking.

Back on the main road, 400m south of the junction, is the **Mlinarica Gorge**, another magical masterpiece of nature, which takes the form of immense, overhanging rock faces and an impenetrable ravine, at the head of which is another waterfall; to get here, cross the suspension bridge and follow the footpath to the right around to the gorge entrance. Grafted onto a picturesque hillside 2km south of the gorge is the **Alpinum Juliana** (daily May–Sept 8.30am–6.30pm; €3), Slovenia's only alpine botanical garden. Founded in 1926 by Albert Bois de Chesne, a Trieste merchant and close colleague of Kugy, the garden has a fine collection of flora from the country's various alpine regions, as well as samples from the Pyrenees and Caucasus. The best time to visit is in May following the winter thaws.

Two kilometres further down the road is *Camping Trenta* (⊕041/615-966), the first of four campsites between here and Bovec, all of which are open between May and October. The road continues down the narrow valley and into the village of **TRENTA**, which marks the border of the upper part of the Trenta Valley. The major point of interest here is the **Trenta Lodge** (Dom Trenta), at no. 34, which houses both the **Triglav National Park Information Centre** (daily May–Oct 8am–8pm; ⊕05/388-9330) and the **Trenta Museum** (daily May–Oct 10am–6pm; €4). Beginning with an insightful fifteen-minute multi-vision presentation on the National Park, the museum goes on to explore, in excellent and detailed fashion, the geology and geomorphology of the park, together with displays on its indigenous flora and fauna. The exhibition then peters out somewhat with a rather flat ethnological collection, though there's a reasonably faithful attempt at a mock-up of a Trenta homestead and shepherd's dwelling. The lodge also accommodates a handful of apartments, each sleeping up to five people, with a kitchen and living space downstairs and a bedroom upstairs (❻); the lodge can also arrange private rooms in a house some 300m away (❷). Trenta is also the starting-off point for assaults on Triglav's massive west face, via the **Zadnjica Valley**.

From Trenta to Bovec

Ten kilometres on from Trenta is the village of **SOČA**, consisting of little more than a string of roadside houses and the **Church of St Joseph** (Cerkev Sv Jožef), renowned for Tone Kralj's 1944 painting of the devil, which here bears an uncanny resemblance to Mussolini. There are also a couple of places to stay here: the decent *Gostišče Andrejc* at no. 31 (℡041/332-520; ❹), whose six rooms each sleep up to four people, and the dowdy *Pension Lovec*, 400m further along the road at no. 19 (℡05/388-9305; ❸). Below the village, the powerful current of the Soča river has hollowed out spectacular erosion and abrasion potholes in the limestone rock, creating the fantastic 750-metre-long, fifteen-metre-deep **Velika Korita Gorge** (also called the Soča Ravine), the best views of which can be had from the swing bridge at its upper end. Here, a road branches off left towards the *Klin* **campsite** (℡05/388-9513) and the **Lepena Valley**; the road winds up to *Pristava Lepena* (mid-April to Oct; ℡05/388-9900, ⓦ www.pristava-lepena.com), a self-contained complex incorporating a handful of wooden, cottage-style apartments (❽) at the edge of the forest, a **riding school** (€16 for 50min in riding ring, €20 for 50min trail ride on Lipizzaners), and an expensive, but first-rate, **restaurant** (daily 8am–10pm); guests receive discounted rates for the riding school and free use of the swimming pool and tennis court.

The last point of interest before exiting the park is the **Golobar Telpher Line** (Žicnica Golobar), an odd-looking, but immensely powerful, roadside contraption which was once used to transport heavy goods via overhead cables. Although this one was built in 1931 – one of the few remaining in Slovenia – telpher lines first appeared throughout the region during World War I as a means of supplying the front lines. They were later put to good use by farmers and foresters who used them to transport timber back and forth across the valley. The road descends through the lower Trenta valley and exits the park just prior to Bovec, covered in the next chapter.

Travel Details

Trains

Bled Jezero to: Bohinjska Bistrica (Mon–Fri 6 daily, Sat & Sun 4 daily; 20min); Most na Soči (Mon–Fri 6 daily, Sat & Sun 4 daily; 55min); Nova Gorica (Mon–Fri 6 daily, Sat & Sun 4 daily; 1hr 45min).
Bled Lesce to: Jesenice (every 1–3hr; 15min); Kranj (every 1–3hr; 25min); Ljubljana (every 1–3hr; 1hr); Radovljica (every 1–3hr; 5min); Škofja Loka (every 1–3hr; 35min).
Bohinjska Bistrica to: Bled Jezero (Mon–Fri 7 daily, Sat & Sun 4 daily; 20min); Most na Soči (Mon–Fri 8 daily, Sat & Sun 5 daily; 35min); Nova Gorica (Mon–Fri 8 daily, Sat & Sun 5 daily; 1hr 20min).
Kamnik to: Ljubljana (hourly; 50min).
Kranj to: Bled Lesce (every 1–3hr; 25min); Ljubljana (every 1–3hr; 35min); Radovljica (every 1–3hr; 20min); Škofja Loka (every 1–3hr; 10min).
Radovljica to: Bled Lesce (every 1–3hr; 5 min);
Kranj (every 1–3hr; 20min); Ljubljana (every 1–3hr; 55min); Škofja Loka (every 1–3hr; 30min).
Škofja Loka to: Bled Lesce (every 1–3hr; 35min); Kranj (every 1–3hr; 10min); Ljubljana (every 1–3hr; 25min); Radovljica (every 1–3hr; 30min).

Buses

Bled to: Kranj (hourly; 40min); Kranjska Gora (7 daily; 1hr 15min); Ljubljana (hourly; 1hr 15min); Radovljica (every 30min; 15min); Ribčev Laz for Lake Bohinj (hourly; 40min).
Bohinjska Bistrica to: Ribčev Laz, for Lake Bohinj (hourly; 15min).
Kamnik to: Ljubljana (Mon–Fri every 20–30min, Sat & Sun every 45min–hourly; 40–50min).
Kranj to: Bled (hourly; 40min); Ljubljana (every 30–45min; 50min); Radovljica (every 30min; 30min); Škofja Loka (hourly; 20min); Tržcič (hourly; 20min).
Kranjska Gora to: Bled (Mon–Fri hourly; Sat & Sun 9 daily; 1hr 15min); Bovec (July & Aug 4

daily; 1hr 45min); Ljubljana (Mon–Fri hourly, Sat & Sun 9 daily; 2hr 30min) Radovljica (Mon–Fri hourly, Sat & Sun 9 daily; 1hr 25min).
Kropa to: Radovljica (Mon–Fri 8 daily; 20min).
Radovljica to: Bled (every 30min; 15min); Kranjska Gora (hourly; 1hr 25min); Kropa (8 daily Mon–Fri; 20min); Ljubljana (every 30min; 1hr 15min); Ribčev Laz, for Lake Bohinj (hourly; 45min).
Ribčev Laz (Lake Bohinj) to: Bled (hourly; 40min); Bohinjska Bistrica (hourly; 15min); Ljubljana (6 daily; 1hr 45min); Stara Fužina (Mon–Fri 5 daily; 10min); Studor (Mon–Fri 5 daily; 10min).

Selca to: Škofja Loka (7 daily; 20min); Železniki (9 daily; 10min).
Stara Fužina to: Bohinjska Bistrica (Mon–Fri 5 daily; 15min); Ribčev Laz, for Lake Bohinj (Mon–Fri 5 daily; 10min).
Škofja Loka to: Kranj (hourly; 20min); Ljubljana (hourly; 30min); Selca (6 daily; 20min); Železniki (10 daily; 30min); Žiri (10 daily; 45min).
Tržič to: Kranj (hourly; 20min); Radovljica (Mon–Fri 7 daily, Sat & Sun 2 daily; 30min).
Železniki to: Škofja Loka (Mon–Fri 9 daily, Sat 4, Sun 2; 30min).

NORTHWEST SLOVENIA | Travel details

The Soča Valley to the Istrian coast

CHAPTER 3

Highlights

* **White-water rafting on the Soča** This magical alpine river affords some of the best rafting, kayaking and canoeing in Europe. See p.157

* **Kobarid Museum** Compelling and moving museum documenting the region's World War I mountain battles. See p.162

* **Hiša Franko, Kobarid** Enjoy top-rank comfort and food in this sublime pension/restaurant. See p.161

* **Oldtimer Museum Train** Enjoy the wonderful alpine countryside from the comfort of the Oldtimer. See p.169

* **Goriška Brda** Trek down the cellars of these gorgeous, vineyard-clad hills, which touch the Italian border. See p.175

* **Franja Partisan Hospital, Cerkno** This former World War II hospital has been converted into a moving memorial museum. See p.186

* **Škocjan Caves** Take a trip through this breathtaking cave system, which features the world's largest subterranean canyon. See p.193

* **Church of the Holy Trinity, Hrastovlje** A Romanesque monument, smothered with exceptional fifteenth-century frescoes including the famous *Dance of Death*. See p.195

* **Piran** The coast's most beautiful resort has Venetian Gothic-inspired architecture, Italianate squares and pretty churches. See p.205

△ Seventeenth-century Karst house

The Soča Valley to
the Istrian coast

W hilst northwest Slovenia may possess the lion's share of the country's primary attractions, the thin wedge of land skirting the Italian border – known as Primorska – is unquestionably the country's most diverse region, constituting four geographically distinct areas, namely, from north to south, the Soča Valley, Central Primorska, the Karst, and the Coast.

Crossing over from the Julian Alps or Triglav National Park, your first encounter with this region is likely to be the magisterial **Soča Valley**, whose rugged peaks were the setting for a sustained period of crushing mountain warfare between Italian forces and the Central Powers during World War I – events that are superbly relayed in the museum in **Kobarid**, itself situated close to many of the battle sites. The valley now ranks as the country's premier adventure-sports centre, thanks both to its mountains, which embrace a continuous stream of hikers and skiers all year round, and the amazing **Soča River**, one of Europe's most scenic, chock-full of rafters, canoeists and kayakers during the warmer months.

The valley's alpine peaks eventually give way to the more uniform topography of **Central Primorska**, a region defined primarily by its fertile wine and fruit-growing regions – specifically the **Vipava** and **Brda** hills, located east and west respectively of the bland, modern town of **Nova Gorica**. Central Primorska also incorporates an attractive belt of subalpine countryside (but with peaks still exceeding 1200m), sheltering the relatively little-known and under-visited towns of **Idrija** and **Cerkno**, themselves handy bases from which to take in any number of local sights, chief amongst which is the superb **Franja Partisan Hospital**. Nature asserts itself in spectacular fashion a short way south of here with the **Karst** region, whose star attractions are the jaw-dropping **Škocjan Caves** and the world-famous **Lipica Stud Farm**.

Whilst the **Slovene coast** (all 46km of it) might lack some of the glamour of its more well-heeled Croatian cousin to the south – its beaches are, for the most part, rocky, concrete or grass affairs – there is still much to enjoy. Nearly five centuries of Venetian rule have endowed its towns with some fabulous architecture, not least in its prettiest and most popular resort, **Piran**, although both **Izola** and the coast's largest town and major port, **Koper**, possess a fine kernel of medieval buildings. Those seeking more self-indulgent fare should find **Portorož**, a stone's throw from Piran and the coast's brashest resort, more to their liking. Crowds in this part of Slovenia are rarely an inconvenience, although the major coastal spots

THE SOČA VALLEY TO THE ISTRIAN COAST

▲ Klagenfurt

Kranjska Gora

Mojstrana

Jesenice

A7

ITALY

Udine

Mangart (2679m) ▲

Vršič

Mount Rombon (2208m) ▲

Log Pod Mangrtom

Mount Triglav (2864m) ▲

Lake Bled

Bled

Kluže Fortress

206

Trenta

Bohinjska Bela

Boka Waterfall

Bovec

203

Soča

Soča

TRIGLAV NATIONAL PARK

Kranj

Kanin Ski Centre

Lake Bohinj

Stara Fužina

209

646

Stol (1673m) ▲

Soča Valley

203

Drežnica

Lake Bohinj

904

Bohinjska Bistrica

Breginj

Kobarid

Vrsno

Javorca, Church of The Holy Spirit

Podbrdo

403

Soča

54

102

Tolmin

103

Zakojca

Cerkno Ski Centre

Most na Soči

Baška Grapa Valley

102

Cerkno

Franja Partisan Hospital

Ravenska Cave

210

Cividale

Udine

B R D A

103

Šebrelje

102

Idrijca

Vojsko

Spodnja Idrija

Žiri

Šmartno

Kojsko

Sveta Gora

Vipava

Idrija

Rovte

Dobrovo

Solkan

Medana

Vipolže

Gorizia

Nova Gorica

Klavže Dam

Wild Lake

707

Kromberk Castle

Venice

Palmanova

56

H4

Ajdovščina

Zemono

Vipavski Križ

Vipava

Cervignano

Ronchi

E70

K A R S T

Goče

204

Štanjel

12

Monfalcone

A1

Ljubljana

Pliskovica

Grado

Sežana

A3

Vilenica Cave

Škocjan Caves

Lipica

Divača

405

Lokev

TRIESTE

Adriatic Sea

Muggia

17

Koper

7

Podgrad

Izola

Piran

Strunjan

Portorož

Hrastovlje

Sečovlje Salt-Pans

111

11

208

N

0   20 km

C R O A T I A

Buzet

▼ Pula

▼ Rijeka

can get uncomfortably congested during August; even then, as in other parts of the region, finding accommodation should present few problems.

Getting around the Karst and coastal areas is simple enough, with a healthy stream of **trains** and **buses** serving both. However access up and down the Soča Valley is patchy, the rail line going no further than Most na Soči (midway between Nova Gorica and Kobarid), and bus services are sporadic.

The Soča Valley

Richly textured by history and nature, the **Soča Valley**, skirting Triglav National Park's western boundary and extending all the way down to the flatlands of Nova Gorica, is one of Slovenia's most captivating regions. Although not an immediately obvious destination, the valley has few peers when it comes to sheer, stark beauty; moreover, it boasts one of Europe's most dramatic alpine rivers, the **Soča**, which commands thousands of rafters, canoeists and kayakers to its milky blue-green waters.

During World War I the valley marked the front line – known as the **Soča Front** (or Isonzo Front) – between the Italian and Austro-Hungarian armies who, for two years, engaged in some of the most savage and relentless fighting in the history of mountain warfare, leaving lands ravaged, villages wasted and an estimated one million soldiers and civilians dead. Consequently, the valley is strewn with memorial chapels, abandoned fortifications and dignified military cemeteries.

There are several key settlements sequenced in vertical fashion down the valley's spine: both **Bovec** and **Kobarid**, located in the upper part of the valley (Gornje Posočje), are important tourist hubs, the former, one of the major adventure-sports centres in the country, the latter replete with poignant reminders from the battle front, as attested to in its memorable museum. Further down the valley, the small town of **Tolmin** is worth investigating, not least because of its proximity to the fantastic **Tolminska Gorge** and stunningly located **Church of the Holy Spirit** on Javorca, while a few kilometres further south, **Most na Soči** holds some of Slovenia's most significant archeological sites. **Access** up and down the valley is, however, patchy; the closest rail line passes through Most na Soči, while infrequent buses ply the route between Tolmin and Bovec.

Bovec and around

Situated in a broad basin in the shadow of the Kanin mountain range and the mighty Mount Rombon, the small alpine town of **BOVEC** is one of Slovenia's premier adventure-sports centres, its proximity to the Soča River luring rafters, kayakers and canoeists from all over Europe in their thousands – activities so popular that they have supplanted skiing as the main source of tourist income in Bovec in recent years. For centuries, however, the town and its surrounds were an important centre for animal husbandry, the lofty alpine plateaus ideally suited for high-level pasturing, while the broad valley floor was used for growing hay. The last century was particularly unkind to Bovec: it was burnt down in 1903; massive destruction followed during World War I, when the town was razed and much of the population deported; and more recently,

Bovec was struck by three earthquakes – two extremely powerful ones in 1976 and 1998, and a third, less destructive one, in 2004.

There are several worthwhile attractions within close proximity to Bovec, including the magnificent **Boka Waterfall**, the **Kluže Fortress**, and, right up towards the Italian border, the pretty village of **Log pod Mangrtom**.

Arrival, information and accommodation

All **buses** terminate outside the *Letni Vrt* restaurant on the main square, Trg Golobarskih Žrtev. Just around the corner, in the community centre at no. 8, is the **tourist office** (Jan–May & Oct–Dec Mon–Fri 9am–5pm, Sat & Sun 9am–1pm; June–Aug daily 9am–8pm; Sept Mon–Fri 9am–6pm, Sat & Sun 9am–1pm & 4–6pm; ☏05/384-1919, ⓦwww.bovec.si), which has a good stock of information and maps on the Soča Valley. The **post office** is just up from the tourist office at Slomškov trg 10 (Mon–Fri 8–9.30am, 10am–3.30pm & 4–6pm, Sat 8am–noon).

For private **accommodation** (❷) head to GoTour, located through the passageway next to the Mercator supermarket on the square (Mon–Fri 9am–1pm & 1.30–5pm, Sat 9am–1pm; ☏05/389-6366, ⓦwww.gotourbovec.com). The town's most upmarket accommodation is the *Dobra Vila*, on the eastern edge of town at Mala Vas 112 (☏05/389-6400, ⓦwww.dobra-vila-bovec.com; ❻); its twelve beautifully appointed, and very spacious, rooms are handsomely furnished with big lush beds, televisions with DVD player, and air-conditioning. The town's two main **hotels** are the well-run, neat and agreeable *Hotel Alp* (☏05/388-4000, ⓦwww.alp-chandler.si; ❻), prominently located on the south side of the square, and the *Hotel Kanin* (☏05/388-6021, ⓦwww.hotel-kanin.com; ❼), just behind the *Alp*, which also has a pool. Another option is the *Stari Kovač*, a few paces down from the *Hotel Alp* at Rupa 3 (☏05/388-6699, ⓦwww.starikovac.com; ❺–❼), which possesses five very comfortable and well-furnished apartments sleeping up to four or eight people.

There are four **campsites** located on the southern edge of town, all of which are open between April and October. The closest, and smallest, is the *Polovnik* (☏05/389-6007), 500m southwest of the *Hotel Kanin*. Two kilometres further south (follow the sign for Čezsoča), there are three sites bunched together: the first is *Vodenca* (☏041/620-885); 200m down the hill is *Kajak Kamp Toni* (☏05/388-6454), the best equipped of the sites and frequented almost exclusively by kayakers due to its proximity to the water; and behind there is the smaller *Liza* site (☏05/389-6370).

The Town

As a result of the 1998 earthquake over sixty percent of the buildings in town were seriously damaged, most of which have now been repaired or rebuilt. One of the most affected buildings, and among the first to be repaired, was the **Parish Church of St Ulric** (Cerkev Sv Urh), situated 200m up the hill from the tourist office. Originally a Gothic construction, the present church was rebuilt in neo-Romanesque style in 1734, but underwent substantial reconstruction following heavy World War I damage. Although the interior retains the odd Gothic flourish, notably the portals and triumphal arch, the highlight is the reddish-brown Baroque high altar, made from marble hewn from Mount Rombon, and framed either side by sculptures of St John Nepomuk and St Paul. Unusual features of the church are the niches on the front exterior, containing statues of SS Peter, Paul and Ulric, and the headstones in the surrounding walls, which would indicate that this was the old cemetery – the current one is now located behind the church.

For those keen to learn more about the Soča Front (see box p.162), it's possible to view a **private collection** of World War I weaponry and other objects

Between April and October, the **Soča River** draws watersports enthusiasts from many countries keen to test out one of the most beautiful and challenging white-water rivers in Europe. Sections of the river are graded according to the level of difficulty – from one, the easiest, up to six, the most difficult (which is open only to experienced competition rafters); most trips depart from Boka, 6km west of Bovec, and finish at Trnovo ob Soči, 10km further downriver. A number of agencies located in Bovec and Kobarid offer rafting and a plethora of other river activities, the best of which is X-Point, based in Kobarid at Stresova 1 (℡05/388-5308, ✉x.point@siol.net). The best options in Bovec are: Bovec Rafting Team, located in a small hut a few paces west of the main square (℡05/388-6128, ⊛www.brt-ha.si), and Top Extreme (℡05/330-0090, ⊛www.top.si) – actually 6km south of Bovec in Žaga. Each raft can take up to ten people including one instructor; whoever you go with, expect to pay around €30 per person, which also covers transfers to and from the river and all equipment – just make sure you have swimming gear and a towel. Most of the agencies also offer **kayak** and **canoe** courses (around €60 for one day); alternatively, you can rent kayaks (€22 full-day) and Canadian canoes, which seat two (€30 full-day). Most also offer **hydrospeed** (€35) and **canyoning** (€40). All agencies have similar opening times (July–Sept daily 9am–7/8pm; April, May & Oct weekends only, same times).

Between April and October, the river becomes prime **fishing** territory, richly sourced with brown trout, rainbow trout, the famous marble trout (*Salmo trutta marmoratus*) and grayling. There are two types of licence: the regular one (1 day €50, 3 days €125, 1 week €250), valid for the upper section of the Soča and its tributaries; and the Trophy licence (€70, €180, €360), which covers a three-kilometre stretch of the river in the middle part. These can be obtained from the *Hotel Alp* and the *Klin* campsite in Lepena (see p.148).

At weekends between April and October, Top Extreme offers **bungee-jumping** over the Soča (€40), although this is located in Nova Gorica, some 70km away, as well as Extreme Days, typically a combination of rafting with one other activity (around €60). Depending on where you fly, a twenty-minute **Tandem paragliding** flight with X-point or Top Extreme will cost around €85. **Bikes** (€3 1hr, €10 half-day, €14 full-day) and **scooters** (€10 1hr, €15 half-day, €30 full-day) can be rented from Bovec Rafting team.

retrieved from the battle sites. Amassed by a member of the **1313 Association** (Društvo 13-13) – an ardent group of local historians committed to honouring the men who fought on the Front – this extraordinary collection consists of a stash of weapons (grenades, shells, knives and so on), personal effects (flasks, combs and toothbrushes), and illuminating photographs of some of the battle scenes; to arrange a visit you can either try calling directly (℡05/388–6577) or contact the tourist office. If you want to see where part of the action took place, a signposted path 1km south of Bovec (500m before the turning towards Trenta) leads towards **Ravelnik**, the name given to an area containing a string of huts, caverns and trenches, abandoned following the cessation of fighting; many have been cleaned up and partly reconstructed but are, nevertheless, fascinating to look around. Two kilometres east of Bovec, at the crossroads of the Predel and Vršič roads, is the **Bovec military cemetery** (Vojaško Pokopališče), containing over five hundred headstones of Austrian soldiers killed near Bovec and on Mount Rombon between 1915 and 1917.

If you're looking for an unusual **souvenir** gift, the Galerija Čopi (Mon–Sat 10am–2pm & 5–8pm), on the western side of the square at no. 47, sells a superb range of framed and painted beehive panels.

Ranged high above Bovec to the west, the Kanin mountains offer the highest-altitude skiing in Slovenia (around 2300m), with slopes here for skiers of all abilities. The **Kanin ski centre** is based in the hamlet of **Dvor**, 1km southwest of Bovec (T 05/389-6310, E kanin@siol.net) – holders of five- and seven-day passes can also ski in the resorts of Sella Nevea and Tarvisio across the border in Italy at no extra cost. The modern, four-seater **cable cars** transport passengers to the upper station (station D; 2200m) in thirty minutes (winter daily 8am–4pm nonstop; July & Aug daily 7am–5pm hourly; June & Sept Sat & Sun 8am–4pm hourly; €10 return), but be warned, this ride is not for the jittery. In summer, the sun-bleached rocks and boulders make for a rather bleak scene, but the views on a cloudless day are sensational – there's a basic restaurant at the top too.

If you're not here to ski, or have just come up to have a look around, then there are a number of excellent **hikes** to consider; one of the easiest, though not particularly well-marked, paths is to **Prestreljenik** (2499m; 1hr 30min), with more demanding paths to **Visoki Kanin** (2587m; 3hr 30min) – on a clear day it's possible to see the Adriatic from here – and **Rombon** (2208m; 5hr). The one hut in these mountains is the *Dom Petra Skalarja na Kaninu* (July–Aug daily, June & Sept weekends only; T 041/731-257), a forty-five minute walk south of the upper station. All the above hikes are doable from Bovec itself but, with the exception of Rombon (5hr from Bovec), you should count on an additional four hours at least for each. The excellent 1:50,000 map *Posočje*, available from the tourist office, will help you get your bearings. The X-Point agency (see box on p.157) organizes a number of guided hikes and walks, beginning at the *Alp Hotel* in Bovec – by way of example, a typical full-day hike (8hr) to Krn Lake (including transfers) costs around €30.

Eating and drinking

Bovec can rate three extremely commendable **restaurants**, all of which lean heavily on local food and ingredients; the popular *Letni Vrt* gostilna on the main square, with its huge terrace, has a reputation as a fantastic pizzeria, but this doesn't do justice to its exhaustive menu of fish, game, lamb and local cheeses (closed Tues). More expensive is the warm and classy *Martinov Hram*, 50m west of the square at no. 27, whose grilled Balkan meat and fish dishes are the pick of an outstandingly long and varied menu, which also includes superb vegetarian options. The restaurant in the *Dobra Vila* (see p.156) is a similarly classy affair (closed Thurs) – all three of the above restaurants have excellent wine lists. More basic, but no less enjoyable, *Stari Kovač*, at Rupa 3, has good oven-baked pizzas.

There are disappointingly few **drinking** venues in town, though the *Pink Panter* (daily 5pm–1am), up the hill from the church at Kaninska Vas 7, is the most enjoyable place to sup a beer, while the *Dobra Vila's* cosy conservatory café/bar offers the best coffee (and views) in town. Down in the main square, *Café Plec*, opposite the tourist office (daily 5pm–1am), draws a slightly younger clientele, while the *Hotel Alp's* terrace café is also worth stopping off at and there's a delicious ice-cream parlour here too.

Boka Waterfall

The most popular local attraction is the thundering 106-metre-high and thirty-metre-wide **Boka Waterfall** (Slap Boka), located 6km southwest of Bovec just before the village of **Žaga**. While it's possible to see the waterfall from the main road (albeit at quite some distance), close-up views can be obtained by scrambling along two trails located by the **Boka Bridge** (Most Boka), each offering very different perspectives of Slovenia's highest permanent waterfall: the trail beginning at the west side of the bridge – which provides a head-on view – is the shorter and easier of the two paths, but does involve a fair amount of clambering over boulders; the far more difficult second route, beginning at the east side of the bridge, ascends to a spot above the head of the falls. Emanating from a deep karst spring in the Kanin mountains, the Boka is a stupendous sight, highly dependent upon precipitation and snow-melt from the Kanin plateaus for its massive volume of water – hence the best time to view it is in late spring.

Kluže Fortress

Four kilometres north of Bovec, back inside Triglav National Park on the road towards Log pod Mangrtom and the Predel Pass, stands the formidable-look-ing **Kluže Fortress** (Trdnjava Kluže; July & Aug daily 9am–9pm; June & Sept Mon–Fri 10am–5pm, Sat & Sun til 7pm; €2). Strategically positioned on a steep rock face overlooking the impressive sixty-metre-deep Koritnica gorge, this recently restored chunky grey fortress has seen more than its fair share of action over the years.

Although a wooden fortification was built here in the fifteenth century, it's believed that some kind of fortress existed on this site during Roman times, a theory predicated on the fact that a Roman road ran through the nearby Predel Pass, connecting the northern and southern parts of the Empire. The wooden fortification was supplanted by a stone construction in 1613, during which time it successfully repelled repeated Turkish attacks, before Napoleon's French maraud-ers razed it in 1797. Its current appearance dates from 1882, though the upper part – named Fort Hermann after the hero of the 1809 Battle of Predel – was demol-ished by heavy and sustained shelling during World War I. The interior rooms now house enlightening exhibitions on the Soča Front and the fortress itself while, during July and August, the courtyard makes a fitting venue for re-enactments of battle scenes performed by the 1313 Association, in addition to classical and rock concerts; check with the tourist office in Bovec for events (see p.156).

Log pod Mangrtom and Mangart Mountain

Nestling under the Mangart mountain range 6km north of Kluže is the pretty village of **LOG POD MANGRTOM**, which actually comprises the two adjoin-ing settlements of **Spodnji Log** (Lower Log) and **Gorenji Log** (Upper Log). As if the 1998 earthquake wasn't enough, the village had to contend with an even greater catastrophe during the night of November 16–17, 2000, when a crushing **landslide** – believed to have been caused by a combination of torrential rainfall and significant seismological activity in the area – struck. The landslide began some 1000m further up in the Mangartski mountains and coursed down the val-ley slopes and along the bed of the Predelnica River in a matter of seconds, before smashing into the upper settlement. The impact was such that seven people lost their lives – one person was never found – and a number of houses and farm build-ings were wiped out or irreparably damaged.

At the reconstructed metal bridge, where the devastation is still very much in evidence, the aftermath of the event is documented by several photos pinned to a board. If you have your own transport, you can drive up to the top of the pass, and another reconstructed bridge, to see where the slide began. Just beyond the bridge, the main road continues onwards to Italy, while another – the country's highest mountain road – branches off towards the **Mangart Saddle** (2072m), below which is the *Koča na Mangrtskem sedlu* (☎041/954-761; mid-June to Sept), the only hut in this group of mountains. Two hours' walk from the hut is the magnificent **Mount Mangart** (2679m), Slovenia's third highest peak and known for its reddish-coloured sandstone.

Back in Gorenji Log, the **Parish Church of St Stephen** contains a ceiling fresco by Ivan Grohar, entitled *The Stoning of St Stephen*, and a wooden Gothic statue of Queen Mary dating from the end of the fifteenth century. Midway between the two settlements, just behind the small civilian cemetery, lies a **World War I military cemetery** – one of the few in the region preserved in its original form. It has neat rows of black iron crosses on mounds denoting the final resting places of nearly nine hundred Austrian soldiers killed on Mount Rombon and Mount Čuklja. The monument in the centre of the cemetery features two soldiers, one an Austrian, the other a Bosnian, gazing up to the summit of Rombon. The gravel path just to the side of the cemetery leads up to the entrance of the now disused **Rabelj mining tunnel**, alongside which is an informative outdoor exhibition documenting the tunnel's history from its opening in 1905 to its closure in 1991. Villagers used to travel through the 4km-long tunnel in order to reach the lead and zinc mines at Cave del Predil in Italy, while it was also used to supply the army with troops and materials during World Wars I and II.

There are a couple of **places to stay** in the village: in the lower settlement, the *Motel Encijan* at no. 31 (☎05/384-5130, ⊛www.encijan.com) has basic but pleasant rooms (❸) and apartments (❺), as well as a tennis court; in the upper settlement, the *Gostišče Mangrt* at no. 57 has just three rooms (☎05/388-6024; ❸) – its comely little **restaurant** offers excellent home-style Slovenian cooking, such as the local speciality *Čompe*, a delicious combination of potato, hard cheese and cottage cheese (July & Aug daily 10am–10pm; Sept–June Mon & Wed–Sun 10am–10pm). Unfortunately, there is no public transport from Bovec to Log pod Mangrtom, so if you don't have a car you'll have to cycle, hitch or walk.

Kobarid and around

"A little white town with a campanile in a valley", was how American writer Ernest Hemingway described **KOBARID** in *A Farewell to Arms* in 1929, and though it has retained its pleasantly relaxed air, this good-looking town 21km south of Bovec has had a pretty rum time of it over the years. In October 1917, the nearby Krn mountain range was the chief battleground for one of the war's most decisive military engagements – otherwise known as the Twelfth Offensive – in which the Italians were routed by the combined Central Powers of Germany and Austria, an event superbly documented in the town's gripping museum. The interwar years were defined by nationalist struggles on both sides, but Kobarid (then Caporetto) remained, as did much of the region, under Italian control until the end of World War II.

Although it retains a strong Italianate flavour – the border is just 9km to the west – much of the town's present appearance dates from 1976 following the massive earthquake. Along with its museum, and a superb selection of restaurants, Kobarid's proximity to the Soča River and a stack of other historical and natural sights could quite easily detain you for a day or two.

Arrival, information and accommodation

All **buses** stop opposite the church on the main square, Trg svobode, from where it's a five-minute walk to the **tourist office** at Gregorčičeva 8 (July & Aug daily 9am–8pm, Sept–June Mon–Fri 9am–12.30pm & 1.30–4pm, Sat 9am–1pm; ☎05/389-0000, ⊛www.kobarid.si), which possesses a good stock of literature and maps on

KOBARID map

KOBARID

ACCOMMODATION
Hiša Franko **A**
Hotel Hvala **C**
Kotlar **B**

Bovec

Koren

Lazar

Drežnica

Vrsno

Napoleon's
Bridge

Historical Walk

Statue of
Simon Gregorčič

MARKOVA ULICA

TRG
SVOBODE

Supermarket

Parish Church of
the Assumption

Rafting
X-Point

GREGORČIČEVA ULICA

Italian
Charnel
House

Church of
St Anthony

Kobarid
Museum

MUČENIŠKA ULICA

STREŠOVA

VOLARIČEVA ULICA

GORIŠKA CESTA

PRI MALNIH

Soča

N

**RESTAURANTS,
CAFÉS & BARS**
Bar Cinca Marinca **5**
Gostilna Breza **6**
Hiša Franko **1**
Kotlar **3**
Pri Gotarju **2**
Pri Vitku **7**
Topli Val **4**

0   250 m

Tolmin

the Soča Front. The **post office** is located next to the *Hotel Hvala* on the south side of the square (Mon–Fri 8–9.30am, 10am–3.30pm and 4–6pm, Sat 8am–noon). The tourist office can book **rooms** (❷) both in the town and the villages of Drežnica (see p.165) and Trnovo ob Soči, 5km north. The town's single **hotel** is the beautifully appointed, family-run *Hotel Hvala*, on the main square (☎05/389-9300, ⓦwww. hotel-hvala.si; ❼), whose plush, warm rooms are good value. In addition, there are two first-class pension-style places; on the east side of the square at no. 11, the *Kotlar* (☎05/389-1110, ⓦwww.kotlar-sp/si; ❻) has six simple, but exquisitely furnished, rooms, each with sumptuous designer beds – it also houses a top-floor pool which is free to guests. Located 3km west of town in the settlement of **Staro Selo**, 🏂 *Hiša Franko*, at Staro Selo 1 (☎05/389-4120, ⓦwww.hisafranko.com; ❼), simply oozes class; the highly original and idiosyncratic rooms (some with massage bath) are gorgeously furnished with finely cut drapes, bamboo and other such exotic materials, and each has a safe, minibar and stereo (TV if desired); there's also a handful of older rooms in the building opposite (❸).

The town's two **campsites** (both open March–Oct) are located down by the Soča River, 500m east of town on the road towards Drežnica; *Camp Lazar* (☎05/388-5333), on the west bank of the river, is a small site with good, clean facilities and a ranch-style bar, while the larger *Camp Koren* (☎05/389-1311), across Napoleon's Bridge on the opposite bank, has similar facilities as well as a market. There's also the *Trnovo* campsite (☎05/384-5583; May to mid-Sept), located just above the Soča 6km back down the road towards Bovec in Trnovo ob Soči.

The Town

The centre of Kobarid is essentially the small main square, where the main roads from Bovec and Tolmin, and the road from Italy, converge. From the square, it's no more than five minutes' walk to any of the town's attractions or facilities.

Kobarid Museum

Situated in the lovely two-storey Baroque house at Gregorčičeva 10 (once owned by the naval commander Sergej Mašera), the **Kobarid Museum** (Kobariški Muzej; April–Sept Mon–Fri 9am–6pm, Sat & Sun 9am–7pm, Oct–March Mon–Fri 10am–5pm, Sat & Sun 9am–6pm; €4, ⓦwww.kobariski-muzej.si), memorably evokes the horrors of the Soča Front (see box below). Before viewing the exhibits, you'll get to see a twenty-minute **multi-vision presentation**, containing superbly shot footage of the battles along the Soča Front, and in particular the decisive Twelfth Offensive. The museum's rooms are thematically arranged: up on the first floor, the **Krn Range Room** is represented by a vast map-relief of the Krn mountain range, which illustrates the complex arrangements of the military positions confronting the warring sides. The photographs here, as in most of the rooms, provide an exceptional supplement to the main exhibits. The next room along – the **Black Room** – reflects upon the suffering of the combatant, as graphically illustrated by the pictures of hideously disfigured soldiers; there is also a graffitied door from the military prison in Smast village near Kobarid. The other two rooms on this floor – the **White Room** and **Rear Room** – are given over to themes of mobilization and civilian displacement, and the nightmarish struggle for survival in the mountains during the ferociously cold winter months. As an interesting aside, the two rooms behind the Krn room hold a collection of local archeological finds, the most fascinating exhibits being some delicate bronze statuettes unearthed from Gradič Hill.

The Soča Front (Izonso Front)

When the Italians declared war on the Central Powers in May 1915, the Great War assumed a new and altogether more brutal dimension. This fresh battlefield, part of which extended for some 90km from Mount Rombon, north of Bovec, through Kobarid to a position a short way north of Trieste (Trst) on the Adriatic coast, was known as the **Soča Front** (Izonso Front).

Although the Austro-Hungarians, under the command of the "Soča Lion", General Svetozar Borojevič von Bojna, had already fortified the front, the Italians secured immediate success, capturing Kobarid and the nearby Krn range. More than two years and eleven debilitating and futile offensives later, the two heavily entrenched sides prepared for the denouement. With severely depleted troop numbers, Austrian Emperor Charles I approached the German Kaiser Wilhelm II for reinforcements, and together, they formed the fourteenth Austro-German army. Their breakthrough plan, "Faith in Arms", was based on swiftly coordinated lightning strikes and the element of surprise; in this case, thousands of troops and armoury were quickly repositioned between Bovec and Tolmin.

Effected on October 24, 1917, this **twelfth offensive** – the first counteroffensive by the Central Powers – resulted in the Italian army being pressed all the way back to the Friulian Plain and the Piave River, an episode acknowledged as the greatest single breakthrough of the war and the first successful "blitzkrieg" in the history of European warfare. Fighting continued around the Piave River for another year, the outcome of which was victory for the Italians. With an estimated million fatalities on all sides, a significant number of whom were women and children, the human cost was catastrophic; moreover many thousands more were forced to flee the region, only a fraction of whom returned at the war's end.

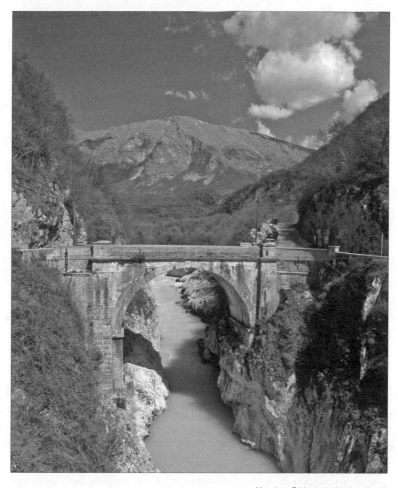

△ Napoleon Bridge over the river Kozjak

On the second floor, the room with the **map–relief** of the Upper Soča region clearly identifies both the positions of the warring troops throughout the valley prior to the Twelfth Offensive, and the awesome volume of military machinery required for this attack; this room leads through to a mock-up **cavern**, in which a wistful young soldier pens one last letter to his father. The central **Breakthrough Room** considers the events pertaining to the critical breakthrough operation of October 24–27, 1917, featuring a hoard of hellish-looking weaponry.

Parish Church of the Assumption

On the south side of Trg Svobode, the ordered **Parish Church of the Assumption** (Cerkev Marijino vnebovzetje) is bestowed with some terrific artwork. The striking red and white marble high altar, designed by Lazzarini in 1716, features a handful of sculpted saints and angels, but is more interesting for what you can't see. Concealed behind the altar picture is a late fifteenth-century statue of the Holy Mother, which is only revealed on special religious occasions or, if you're lucky, upon request; ask at the priest's house opposite the church entrance. To commemorate Pope John Paul II's visit to Slovenia in 1996 (although he didn't actually visit Kobarid) the balcony was blanketed with a beautiful canvas, and is notable for its paintings of several eminent historical characters, including the pope himself. The stained-glass windows were installed as recently as 1995 in order to lighten the church interior. Opposite the church is an oversized **sculpture of Simon Gregorčič** (1844–1906), the beloved Slovenian priest and poet who hailed from nearby **Vrsno** (see p.166).

The Kobarid Historical Walk

For a real flavour of Kobarid's historical, cultural and natural heritage, you should participate in the **Kobarid Historical Walk** (Kobariška Zgodovinska Pot), an enjoyable five-kilometre stroll taking in wartime monuments, abandoned fortifications, bridges and waterfalls. A free leaflet outlining the route, and the key sights along the way, is available from the museum – a gently paced walk, including stops for viewing, should take between three and four hours.

Beginning on the north side of the main square, Trg svobode, a winding road lined with the stations of the cross ascends to Gradič Hill and the **Italian Charnel House**, perhaps the valley's most evocative monument, especially when viewed from afar (note that it's possible to drive up to this point, but no further). The Charnel House – opened in 1938 with Mussolini in attendance – consists of three-tiered octagons tapering upwards towards the **Church of St Anthony**, in itself nothing outstanding. Inside the huge ossuary lie the remains of more than seven thousand Italian soldiers killed during fighting on the Soča Front, the names of whom are engraved onto the slabs of greenish serpentine inside the large niches. From the Charnel House, take the path to the left which forks off into the woods – hereafter, the route is marked with red arrows and the museum logo – and onwards to the remains of the ancient fort of **Tonočov Grad**, unique in that it was occupied continuously from the middle Stone Age, through Antiquity to the Middle Ages; there was also once a significant settlement of some twenty houses and several churches located here. The site is currently a bit of a mess due to ongoing research projects.

From the fort, the path continues down towards the main road, which you should cross carefully, before a knee-jarring descent down to the Soča River – en route you'll pass a section of the **Italian Line of Defence**, one of three constructed by the Italians on the Soča Front during World War I; the trail then continues along a track in the direction of the *Koren* campsite, but you should take the path to the left which opens up into the **Soča Gorge** and a sturdy swing bridge, this one having replaced the original from World War I. From the bridge – where there are terrific views of the gorge and river – it's a twenty-minute walk to most people's favourite part of the circuit, the **Kozjak waterfall** (Slap Kozjak), a graceful, fifteen-metre-high waterfall less impressive for its height than its atmospheric cave-like hall carved out of the surrounding rock. From here, retrace your steps and take the path that forks left up to a **small fortress** and another **line of defence**, scattered with yet more caverns, shelters and observation posts.

The path then cuts inland, passing the campsite and winding up at the **Napoleon Bridge** (Napoleonov Most), an elegant, stone-arched structure connecting the two banks of the river at one of the narrowest and most spectacular points of the gorge. The original bridge was built in 1750 and later named for the eponymous French leader after he marched across it en route to the Predel Pass. The day after World War I was declared, the bridge was blown up by retreating Austrians, though this didn't deter the Italians who first replaced it with a wooden, then an iron bridge, while this one was completed after the war. For the really keen, staff at the Kobarid museum (see p.162) organize a number of excellent **guided tours** – ranging from easy to medium three-hour walks to demanding day-long hikes. For all tours (between €15–20 per hour) call at least one day, but preferably two or three, in advance. Whether on a guided tour or hiking alone, the 1:50,000 *Isonzo Front (From Mount Rombon to Mengore Hill)* map details all the major battle sites and areas of interest throughout the Soča Valley.

Eating and drinking

Few places in the country can boast such a surfeit of distinguished **restaurants** as Kobarid, which may explain why the town is so popular with neighbouring Italians. With one budget exception, the restaurants listed here offer first-class cuisine, exemplary service and an enjoyable atmosphere, though they don't come cheap and reservations are advised. Wherever you eat, it'd be remiss not to try the delicious local speciality, *Kobariški Štruklji*, a sweet dumpling with nut and raisin filling. More predictably, the drinking options in such a small place are very limited, though there are one or two pleasant cafes around the centre.

Eating

Gostilna Breza Mučeniška ulica 17. Secreted away 300m south of the main square, this restful, homely place serves up the most traditional Slovene food in town, including lamb and game; the interior's subtle green colour scheme, wood-beamed ceiling and ceramic stove is complemented by the smart summery terrace. 11am–10pm (closed Thurs).

Hiša Franko Staro Selo 1. Come here if you only have the time to eat in one place in Kobarid. A breathtakingly imaginative menu features dishes such as trout sushi in leek for starters, and mains like thorn rabbit meat with couscous or blueberry pasta with fine bear ragout; try the tasting menu for €45. Wine buffs will be in their element with some 350 bottles to select from. The restaurant itself, with bright orange painted walls, looks fantastic, while the charming, knowledgeable staff will ensure an exquisite dining experience. March–Oct & Dec–Jan Tues–Sun noon–3pm & 7–11pm; also closed Tues throughout Nov & Feb.

Kotlar Trg svobode 11 ☎05/389-1110. Along with the *Topli Val*, this is one of the country's finest fish restaurants, with a menu almost exclusively devoted to seafood from the Adriatic as well as a marvellous wine list. The beautifully lit interior features a curvaceous, nautically themed bar with blue drapings – all in all, superb. Mon & Wed–Sun noon–11pm, until midnight Fri & Sat; closed Wed in summer.

Pri Vitku Pri Malnik 41. For those on a somewhat tighter budget, this small, nondescript place, located in a residential area a ten-minute walk south of town (follow the signs), suffices for the simplest of pizza and pasta dishes. Mon–Fri 11am–midnight, Sat & Sun noon–midnight.

Topli Val Trg svobode 1. Despite now having a serious rival in the *Kotlar*, the classy "Warm Wave" restaurant (in the *Hotel Hvala*) is the town's most established place, with a freshwater and sea fish menu regarded as one of the country's finest – trout salami, mussels and lobster are just some of its specialities. Daily noon–10pm.

Drinking

The best place for a **coffee** is the *Bar Cinca Marinca*, located on the west side of the square next to the *Kotlar*, while the rather arrogantly staffed *Okrepčevalnica Soča*, opposite the *Hotel Hvala*, has a decent **ice-cream** parlour. For a beer make your way to *Pri Gotarju* (daily 6am–11pm, until midnight Fri & Sat) on Markova Ulica, whose flowery garden with wooden bench seating makes for a pleasant summer venue. If you don't mind a little walk, then you could always head down to the lively bar at *Camp Lazar* (see p.161).

Around Kobarid: Drežnica, Vrsno and Breginj

Dramatically situated under the sunny slopes of the Krn mountain range 6km north of Kobarid, the peaceful little village of **DREŽNICA** is renowned for its

Shrovetide Carnival, one of the most enjoyable local events in Slovenia. Taking place at the end of February, it's a kind of mini-Kurent (see box on p.310), starring a procession of masked figures (known as *psti*), who cut a dash through town, visiting houses and causing good-natured mayhem; the day concludes with much drinking and dancing.

Towering over the village is the oversized neo-Romanesque **Church of the Sacred Heart**, which, despite its prominent position, survived remarkably unscathed amidst the fighting in these parts during World War I. Dating from 1911, this church replaced one pulled down a few years earlier and features a capacious, pastel-coloured tripartite nave smothered in frescoes, the most celebrated of which is *The Sacred Heart*, a dual effort by Avgust Černigoj and Zoran Mušič. Note too, above the main entrance, the mosaic representing the Good Shepherd, completed by Kokalj in 1981. The village has some good **accommodation** possibilities – either enquire at the tourist office in Kobarid (see p.160), or wander the narrow streets in search of signs. From the village it's a four-hour hike up to **Mount Krn** (2244m), the valley's most exalted peak and scene of some of the most ferocious battles during World War I. To get to Drežnica from Kobarid, you'll have to cycle, walk or hitch.

While one road snakes up to Drežnica the other winds steeply uphill for 7km to the village of **VRSNO**, known as the birthplace of nineteenth-century priest, poet and national revivalist Simon Gregorčič. Located in the centre of the village at no. 27, the **birthplace** (daily: May–Oct 9am–4pm, Nov–April 10am–3pm; €2) holds his cradle, other original furnishings and some of his works, as well as an ethnological repository downstairs. His descendants still live next door and will be happy to show you around; you can get refreshments in the adjoining café. Gregorčič is actually buried in the village of Smast, back down on the road towards Kobarid.

Until the earthquake in 1976, the village of **BREGINJ**, 15km west of Kobarid, was unique for its highly unorthodox street layout, whereby houses were conjoined in oval fashion, joined to a stable and hayloft and connected by wooden galleries known as *gank*. The one building left standing, or at least not so badly damaged that it couldn't be reconstructed, has been converted into a nameless **museum** (no set times; the key can be obtained from no. 119 behind the museum, although it's better to contact the tourist office in Kobarid first; €2), located in the centre of the village and signposted from the main road. This building, fairly representative of most of the village before the earthquake, comprises three separate, but interconnected, dwellings, each with four, almost identically sized rooms. Although it's not clear when these Mediterranean-style buildings date from exactly, it's believed that they were first inhabited around the beginning of the eighteenth century. The exhibition room has some superb aerial photos, depicting the village as it was both before and after the earthquake – you could easily be forgiven for thinking that these were two different places. To visit here, however, you really need your own transport; there are just two **buses** (Mon, Wed & Fri at 11.10am and 4.55pm) from Kobarid to Breginj and just one return bus on the same days (11.40am), while there is nowhere to stay in the village.

Tolmin and around

Travelling south from Kobarid, the valley flattens out markedly before reaching **TOLMIN** some 14km further on. As the area's administrative centre it's not an especially appealing place – most people come here to catch or change buses. That said, it does conceal a handful of worthwhile sights, and also serves as an excellent jumping-off point for a couple of attractions just inside Triglav National Park a short way north, namely the fabulous **Tolmin Gorge**, and the **Church of the**

Tolmin's Reggae Festival

One of the country's more internationally oriented music events – featuring an impressive line-up of both domestic and international artists – is the four-day **Soča Reggae Riversplash Festival**, which takes place in mid-July down by the banks of the Soča, 3km south of town. Four-day tickets can be bought in advance through Ⓦ www.vinylmaniarecords.si, and cost €45, or on the day for €55 (from the stage only); day-tickets cost €16, but can only be purchased on the day. It's possible to camp here during the festival, but not at any other time of the year.

③

Holy Spirit in Javorca. Furthermore, it's home to one of the country's most exciting and colourful summer music festivals, the **Soča Reggae Riversplash**.

Arrival, information and accommodation

The **bus station** is located in the centre of town on the main through road, Trg maršala Tita. Three hundred metres southwest of here, just beyond Mestni trg at Petra Skalarja 4, is the extremely helpful **tourist office** (July & Aug Mon–Fri 9am–12.30pm & 1.30–8pm, Sat & Sun 9am–1.30pm & 4.30–8pm; Sept–June Mon–Fri 9am–12.30pm & 1.30–4pm, Sat 9am–1pm; ⓣ05/380-0480, Ⓦ www .lto-sotocje.si); they've got one screen for Internet access (free) and can book **private accommodation** (❷) in town and the surrounding villages. They also sell the excellent 1:50,000 *Turistični Zemljevid Kobarid Tolmin* regional map (€6). The **post office** is 100m west of the bus station (Mon–Fri 8am–7pm, Sat 8am–noon).

The Maya sports agency, 100m west of Mestni trg at Ulica Padlih borcev 1 (April–Oct, July & Aug daily 8am–8pm; ⓣ05/381-0060, Ⓦ www.maya-bn.si), offers a welter of **activities**, including the usual water sports plus mountain-bike trips (€30 for one day), adrenaline park (€32 for three hours), and excursions to Dante's Cave (€22; see p.168) – for water-bound activities, expect to pay the same prices as you would do at those agencies in Bovec (see box on p.157). However, if your timing is good and you manage to visit on your birthday, activities are free. **Bikes** can be hired from the VEB shop at Cankarjeva ulica 3, 100m west of the tourist office (Mon–Fri 9am–noon & 2–6pm; €10 for half a day, €14 for day).

The two places to **stay** are located opposite each other on Mestni trg; the friendly *Hotel Krn* (ⓣ05/382-1100, Ⓦ www.hotel-krn.com) has spacious, tidy rooms, as well as a stock of older, rather careworn rooms (❸) – it's worth paying the minimal extra for the former. More agreeable is the lovely lime-green *Pension Rutar* opposite (ⓣ05/380-0500; ❻), which has nine supremely comfortable, air-conditioned rooms, all of which can sleep three.

The Town

Wedged between the *Hotel Krn* and *Pension Rutar* on Mestni trg is the **Tolmin Museum** (Tolminski Muzej; Tues–Fri 9am–4pm, Sat & Sun 1–5pm; €2.5; Ⓦ www.tol-muzej.si), housed in the Coronini Mansion, formerly the home of the noble sixteenth-century Coronini family. The centrepiece of the museum's rich and quite beautifully-presented collection is its treasure-trove of **archeological finds**, excavated from a grave in Most na Soči between 1999 and 2001 (see p.169); the most extraordinary discovery was a clay scyphos (a drinking cup) from Attica in Greece, an exquisite piece featuring one horizontal and one vertical handle, to the side of which is a painted owl. Look out too for the bronze handle of a patera in the form of a ram's head, the ornamented clay pithos (a pottery urn) – which, when discovered, contained charred human remains – and the group of bronze fibulas (a type of clasp), the kind worn by females in the Soča and Bohinj regions.

No less impressive is the **ethnological collection**, pertaining to life in Tolmin from the time of the peasant uprisings of 1713, through to the region's various struggles for identity during the twentieth century. Rounding things off is a collection of valuable fifteenth- to eighteenth-century sacral art, comprising wooden sculptures, paintings, monstrances and a wall painting of *Our Lady of Mercy* (1886), rescued from a house in Breginj following the earthquake in 1976 (see p.166).

Two kilometres south of town, down by the Soča River, is the tiny and undistinguished-looking **German Charnel House** (Nemška kostnica), completed in 1936 from German materials and containing the remains of nearly one thousand German soldiers killed during the Twelfth Offensive (see box on p.162). Beyond the forged grill that divides the space inside, the names of the dead are beautifully engraved mosaic-style on three walls – the key to the house can be obtained from the tourist office or the museum. To get here walk past the tourist office and follow the tarmac road to its conclusion, then take a right turn along the asphalt track.

If you've got further energy to expend, then you might consider tackling **Kozlov Rob**, a 426-metre-high mound located 1km northwest of town, atop which are the substantial remains of a Middle Ages fort. To get to the base of the hill it's a fifteen-minute walk along Brunov drevored, the road which forks left by the Church of St Ulric, itself located a short way north of Mestni trg; from here it's a pleasantly exhausting forty-minute, zigzagging climb to the top. Once you're there, however, it's a bit of a disappointment owing to the thicket of shrubs and weeds smothering the fort – even the views of the town and Soča River are heavily obscured by a shield of trees. Once fortified by four gigantic towers, Kozlov Rob (Goat's Edge) is believed to have originated around the twelfth century, when it was fought over by various factions, including the Venetian and then the Habsburg monarchies. The fort underwent several restoration projects thereafter, the last of which occurred under the auspices of the Dornberg family at the beginning of the seventeenth century, after which time the Corinni family took control and the fort fell into a long-term state of dilapidation; despite periodic excavation works, it has pretty much remained that way ever since.

Eating and drinking

The *Pension Rutar* houses the best **restaurant** in town, offering fresh Italian cuisine and first-class service, all at very affordable prices; alternatively, try the more down-at-heel, inn-style *Pri Kranjcu* at Trg 1 maja 3, 200m east of the tourist office, serving up a reasonable range of local dishes. **Drinking** venues are limited to the occasionally lively *Paradiso*, next to the post office, and the more restful *M Bar*, opposite the tourist office.

Tolminska Gorge, Church of the Holy Spirit and Čadrg

If you have the time and inclination, there are two wonderful excursions to consider in the vicinity of Tolmin, both of which are easily reached by car or foot. Forty-five minutes' walk north of town (it's all signposted), the **Tolminska Gorge** (Tolminska Korita; €2) – the lowest point of Triglav National Park (180m) and its southernmost entry point – is as wild and spectacular as anything the park has to offer. From the entrance, just up from the snack bar, there are several rather confusing signs pointing to various sections of the gorge. However, the best way forward is to head straight along the road and through the tunnel to the vertiginous **Hudičev Most** (Devil's Bridge), looming some 60m above the magnificent ravine. Approximately 500m on from the bridge, just after the bend in the road, is the **Zadlaška Cave**, also known as **Dante's Cave**, for it was here that the poet supposedly found the inspiration for his terrifying inferno images in the *Divine*

Comedy – the caves are closed to the general public, but can be visited on a guided tour through the Maya agency in Tolmin (see p.167).

Backtracking 200m or so down the road, steps lead down to a couple of paths which fork – take the left path down the **Zadlasčica gorge** and after 400m, where the path ends, you'll chance upon the gorge's most bizarre feature, **Glava Medved** (Bear's Head), a huge triangular-shaped boulder wedged between two rock faces. Caution should be exercised here as the paths can get very slippery. Retracing your steps back to the fork, a couple of paths head down to the river; at this point you'll probably get lost among the twisting paths, secret tunnels and swing bridges, but it's all good fun and you're never far from the nearest path out.

From the gorge it's a twenty-minute drive (or a 2hr walk) up a mainly asphalt track that ascends to **Javorca** (571m) – coming by car, you'll have to walk the last 500m or so, as the road is too steep and narrow to continue up. Perched on a panoramic terrace, with resplendent views across the Tolmin Valley, the half-stone, half-wooden **Church of the Holy Spirit** (Cerkev Sv Duha; July & Aug Tues–Sun 10am–5pm; May, June & Sept Sat & Sun 10am–5pm; €2) was built in 1916 by soldiers of the Austro-Hungarian army. Approaching via the stone staircase – which replaced the previous one damaged in the 1998 earthquake – the first thing you'll notice is the remarkably well-preserved coats-of-arms (22 in all), representing the various regions of the Austro-Hungarian Empire. The interior, meanwhile, is striking for its bold Secessionist-style decoration, painted in just four colours, black, blue, white and gold, and the wall-covered wooden panels, onto which the names of nearly three thousand soldiers have been scorched. There is also, somewhat oddly, a small collection of rusting World War I weaponry just inside the church entrance.

From Javorca it's a ninety-minute walk across to the elevated village of **ČADRG** (700m), a unique place in so much as each of the settlement's five houses is a designated ecological (or organic) farm – hence its status as Slovenia's first **ecological village**. The villagers produce large quantities of cheese and other dairy products – made within their small cheese factory – as well as nuts, vegetables and brandy, all of which you can buy. You can stay here too, at the *Pri Lovrču* tourist farm, at no. 8 (☏050/331-232; ❹), which has two apartments, both sleeping four. To get here by car or bike, continue up the road that passes through the Tolmin Gorge, though be warned, it's very narrow and not particularly well-surfaced in places.

Most na Soči

Located on a rocky ledge at the confluence of the Soča and Idrijca rivers 5km south of Tolmin, **MOST NA SOČI** (formerly St Lucija) was one of the most important prehistoric settlements in Slovenia, as evidenced by its exceptional hoard of archeological finds from the Bronze and Iron Ages through to the early Middle Ages. Since the former rector of St Lucija, Tomaž Rutar, began excavations in the mid-nine-

---

The Oldtimer Museum Train

Every Thursday between mid-June and mid-September, the marvellous **Oldtimer Museum Train** (Muzej Vlak) puffs its way between Jesenice, some 12km north of Bled, to Most na Soči, stopping off at Bled and Bohinjska Bistrica along the way – the total journey time is 1hr 30min. It's a fantastic ride, but not cheap; a return fare costs €30, while, for an additional €30, you can partake in a full-day programme, which includes a riverboat ride, guided tour of Kobarid and lunch – bicycles can be taken on the train for no extra charge. Tickets can be booked through the ABC Rent-a-Car office in Ljubljana (☏01/510-4320, ✉infoabc@siol.net), and some of the agencies in Bled or Bohinj.

teenth century, some seven thousand graves and architectural remains including 35 Hallstatt dwellings have been discovered in the surrounding area; further recent digs have unearthed yet more finds, such as, in 2002, some one hundred Iron Age and Roman graves (5 BC–2 AD). You can see a selection of these treasures on display at the Tolmin Museum (see p.167), while other items are kept in Ljubljana, Trieste and Vienna. During the 1970s and 1980s several Hallstatt dwellings were also discovered here, one of which has been partially reconstructed and is now housed in the small **Archeological Museum** (Halštatska hiša; call the tourist office in Tolmin to arrange a visit; €2), located in one room of a school at no. 18, in the centre of town. Disappointingly, neither this nor the remainder of the exhibits has English labelling. For those with a bit more time, the **Cultural and Historical Trail** is a most enjoyable stroll, marking the town's surprisingly rich tapestry of natural and cultural sights, such as burial grounds and settlements, and the extraordinary turquoise-coloured lake. The trail begins at the information point (Plac) next to the petrol station; thereafter all points are marked by information boards, denoted by an owl symbol after the clay scyphos discovered here in 2001.

Next to the museum, the former Gothic, but now Baroque, **Parish Church of St Lucy** (Cerkev Sv Lucija) is worth a glimpse for its exceptional range of artwork by Tone Kralj. Not only did he paint the allegory of St Lucy and the Apostles on the ceiling, but also the eight paintings in the presbytery representing the life and martyrdom of the same saint and the fantastically colourful oil pictures of the Way of the Cross in the nave. For good measure he completed the four wall statues. Much like the private collection in Bovec (see p.157), the **Soča Front Museum** (Mali Muzej Soške Fronte), a few paces west of the petrol station at no. 53, harbours a comprehensive stash of weaponry from both the Italian and Austrian armies – these items were retrieved from the Tolmin region. To arrange a visit call ☎031/699-968, or contact the tourist office in Tolmin (see p.167). Should you wish to **stay** here, the *Hotel Lucija*, in the centre at no. 57 (☎05/381-3290, ⓔinfo@hotel-lucija.com; ⑨), is an accomplished, if unspectacular, place.

Most na Soči is on the rail line between Jesenice and Nova Gorica, and is also the last stop for the **car-train** (see box on p.129) from Bohinjska Bistrica; the station is located across the river 1.5km southeast of town on the road to Idrija – there are sporadic buses into town, which then continue to Tolmin.

Baška Grapa Valley

If you have your own transport, and an hour or two to spare, take a ride through the lovely **Baška Grapa Valley**, which meanders eastwards from Most na Soči joining up with the **Selščica Valley** some 30km distant. Incised with deeply cut slopes onto which dozens of picturesque hamlets and lush vegetation have been neatly grafted, the road snakes along the valley floor in tow with the Bača stream and the scenic rail line.

At the narrow upper end of the valley, the village of **PODBRDO** was once an important frontier post, but is now significant as the southern entrance of the Bohinj tunnel and one of the stopping stations for the car-train (see box on p.129). A few kilometres east of Podbrdo is **PETROVO BRDO**, a tiny hamlet on the mountain-top pass linking the two valleys. The owner of the roadside hut *Planinski Dom na Petrovem Brdu* (☎05/380-8101), which serves limited refreshments and has a few beds, organizes local excursions along the **Rapallo Border Trail**, the one-time border between Yugoslavia and Italy. Established in 1918, and confirmed by the Treaty of Rapallo in 1920 – which effectively annexed the Primorska region to Italy – the border is riddled with deserted fortifications, overgrown bunkers (there's one just yards from the hut) and bomb shelters constructed by the Italians between the two World Wars. Walks, which take in a number of these extraordinary defences (many of which are in the process of being cleaned up), can be improvised to suit whatever time you have, from a short two-hour trip (€9) to a full-day excursion (€20). If you want to know more about visiting the trail, contact the hut or the tourist office in Tolmin (see p.167). Petrovo Brdo is also an excellent starting point for ascents up into the Lower Bohinj mountains; trails lead to **Kobla** (1498m; 90min) and **Črna Prst** (1844m; 4hr), where there's the *Dom Zorka Jelinčiča na Črni prsti* (☏05/380-8260; mid-June to mid-Sept and **Porezen** (1630m; 2hr 30min), and the *Dom Andreja Žvana-Borisa na Poreznu* (☏051/615-245; July & Aug).

Central Primorska

Central Primorska – which roughly covers the block of territory between the southern reaches of the Soča Valley and the Karst region, and the area inland from here – offers a number of exciting and wide-ranging attractions and activities. The one exception is the modern casino town of **Nova Gorica**, which offers little more than the opportunity to make or lose a quick buck, though it does serve as a handy base from which to explore the lovely wine regions of **Goriška Brda** and the **Vipava Valley**. Northeast of here, sheltered amid the deep-sided valleys of the Idrija and Cerklje Hills, the towns of **Idrija** – famed nationwide for its mining and lace – and **Cerkno** – a popular ski town – can both count on enough attractions and activities, particularly in their outlying areas, to make a visit worthwhile.

Nova Gorica and around

Thirty-nine kilometres south of Tolmin, **NOVA GORICA** was built little more than half a century ago following Gorica's (Gorizia) annexation to Italy at the end of World War II. Until this point in time, and despite having been placed under Italian jurisdiction as part of the 1920 Treaty of Rapallo, it had been a predominantly Slovene-speaking community, but following the Paris Peace Treaty of 1947, the city was assigned to Italy leaving the Slovenes without a centre of their own. Undeterred, the local authorities pressed on with the construction of a nascent Slovene Gorica, based upon plans drawn up by the prominent Slovene architect Edo Ravnikar, a keen disciple of Le Corbusier.

Sveta Gora & Goriška Brda

NOVA GORICA

SOLKAN

ITALY

N

Train Station

Bus Station

GORIZIA

Kostanjevica Monastery

Kromberk Castle & 4

Koren

Kanal Koren

Scale Unknown

RESTAURANTS, CAFÉS & BARS
Grajska Klet 4
KGŠ 3
Pecivo 5
Pri Hrastu 1
Vrtnica 2

ACCOMMODATION
Dijaški Dom Nova
  Gorica D
Hotel Casino Park C
Hotel Casino Perla B
Hotel Sabotin A

Although vestiges of antiquity remain, most notably in the northern suburb of Solkan, as well as in the form of one or two other historic structures, its central hub is ultimately too modern to be anything other than charmless. With only its casinos (owned by the ubiquitous HIT group) – upon which the local economy is almost entirely dependent – and the odd splash of greenery to possibly detain you, it's not a place to linger. That said, there are some wonderful diversions close by, most obviously the enchanting **Goriška Brda** wine region northwest of town, the twin attractions of **Sveta Gora** and **Kostanjevica Monastery**, both of which should satisfy those in search of ecclesiastical excitement, and **Kromberk Castle**, out in the suburbs.

Nova Gorica's casinos

As Slovenia's gaming capital, Nova Gorica panders unashamedly to the pretensions of its Italian neighbours, with both the **Perla** and **Park** hotels offering the stock American and French Roulette, Black Jack and Draw Poker games, not to mention a combined total of over one thousand slot machines. Open round the clock, **admission** (you must be 18 or older) to either casino is €5 Friday to Sunday, and free all other days; you should hold on to the admission ticket until you leave the gaming floor. Once inside, you play with tokens (chips) – which can be obtained from the cashier or from automated machines – or cash. If you fancy something a little more relaxing, there's bingo twice a night, each card costing €5. The only regulation as regards dress code is no shorts.

As well as being an important **transport** hub for destinations north into the Soča Valley and south towards the Karst and coast, Nova Gorica is also a key crossing point into Italy, so there's a good chance you'll wind up here at some point.

Arrival and information

The **train station**, a lovely Secessionist pile built in 1906, is located 1.5km west of town on Kolodvorska ulica abutting the Italian border; upon exiting the station turn left and walk for ten minutes, before turning left again at the local border crossing – a further fifteen minutes' walk along Erjavčeva and you're in the centre. The **bus station** is smack bang in the centre of town on Kidričeva ulica, from where it's a five-minute walk north to the **tourist office**, housed in the Cultural Centre on Bevkov trg (Mon–Fri 8am–6pm, Sat & Sun 9am–1pm; ☎05/330-4600, ⓦwww.novagorica-turizem.com). The **post office** is across the road from the bus station at Kidričeva ulica 19 (Mon–Fri 8am–7pm, Sat 8am–1pm). There's free **Internet access** at the student club, *Klub Goriških (KGS)*, located in the town hall on Trg Edvarda Kardelija (daily 8–10am & 11am–5pm), and one screen at the tourist office. **Bikes** (useful if visiting Goriška Brda – see p.175) can be hired from the railway station (Mon–Fri 7am–7pm, Sat 7am–noon; €5 for one day).

Accommodation

There's cheap, clean accommodation in the form of the *Dijaški Dom Nova Gorica*, ten minutes' walk south of the bus station at Streliška pot 7 (☎04/335-4800; ⓦwww .hostel-ng.si; ❶–❷); this enormous **hostel**, offering single, double and triple rooms, is open daily in July and August and at weekends throughout the rest of the year. There's not much in the way of **private accommodation**, but the Lastovka agency (Mon–Fri 1–5pm, Sat 9am–7pm, Sun 10am–7pm; ☎04/333-4400), inside the train station, or the tourist office, can organise rooms.

The town's premier **hotel** is the *HIT Casino Perla* (☎05/336-3000, ⓦwww.hit.si; ❽), a flash glass and steel behemoth located, rather jarringly, opposite several blocks of flats at Kidričeva 7; concealing disappointingly modest rooms, it's patronized in the main by businessmen, as is its less glamorous sister hotel, the *HIT Casino Park*, 100m west of the bus station at Delpinova 5 (☎05/336-2000, same website; ❽). More affordable is the *HIT Sabotin*, a comfortable and decently furnished hotel 2km north of town in the suburb of Solkan at Cesta IX korpusa 35 (☎05/336-5000, same website; ❽); guests of all three hotels receive free entrance to the casinos.

If you have your own transport and don't mind staying out of town, the *Pri Martinovih* **tourist farm** (☎05/395-3190, ⓦwww.binst.si; ❹), 11km north of Nova Gorica in the hamlet of Zagora, is a terrific possibility. This tranquil homestead – signposted from the main road and located at the top of a steep winding road – has five elegantly furnished rooms, some with a balcony terrace.

Kostanjevica Monastery

Fifteen minutes' walk south of town (walk down Erjavčeva ulica and follow the signs), situated atop a small, green hill overlooking Gorizia is **Kostanjevica Monastery** (Kostanjevica Samostan; Mon–Sat 9am–noon & 3–5pm, Sun 3–5pm; €2). Built in 1624, its first custodians were the Carmelites, but following their expulsion in 1781 and a brief period of closure, the monastery was entrusted to the Franciscans, who have remained its guardians ever since.

Most visitors come here to view the tombs of the **French Bourbons**. Exiled from France following the 1830 Revolution in Paris, Charles X sought refuge in various countries, before eventually finding sanctuary in Gorizia under the protection of Count Coronini. His stay, however, was a short-lived one, for barely three weeks after his arrival he died of cholera. The **crypt**, located along a narrow whitewashed passageway under the central aisle of the church, holds the sarcophagi of Charles X and five other members of the Bourbons, including Marie Thérèse Charlotte, daughter of Marie-Antoinette (who was the granddaughter of Austrian Empress Maria Theresa).

Although usually only open to groups, it's worth enquiring about visits to the monastery's beautiful, sixteenth-century, completely renovated **library**, named after Stanislav Škrabec, one of Slovenia's greatest linguists and grammarians, who lived here for more than forty years. The library's most priceless work is Adam Bohorič's delightful pocket-sized book, *Arcticae horulae* (*Winter Hours*), the first Slovene grammar book, written in 1584. The monastery's small, single-nave **church**, which was almost completely destroyed during World War II, is worth a glimpse for its fabulous stuccowork.

Kromberk Castle

Three kilometres east of town in the suburban village of **KROMBERK** is **Kromberk Castle** (Mon–Fri 8am–3pm, Sun 1–5pm; €2), a northern-Italian inspired construction that replaced the original thirteenth-century castle in the early seventeenth century. Despite several reincarnations since – most markedly an almost complete reconstruction following the 1976 earthquake, and a thorough restoration of the interior in the 1990s – the castle has retained its Renaissance appearance. Its **museum collection** is fairly uninspiring, comprising a gallery of old art (Middle Ages to Baroque), and a dour assemblage of period furniture, gloomy portraits and a few abstract pieces by the likes of Spacal and Kralj. Of more interest is the ethnographic section located upstairs on the second floor, which offers temporary thematic exhibitions related to the Goriško region; there's also a small lapidarium on the ground floor.

A much better reason for coming to the castle is to dine in the fine ⭑ *Grajska Klet* **restaurant** on the ground floor (see opposite). If you don't fancy the hike, three buses (Mon–Fri 11.45am, 1.45pm and 3.25pm) stop off en route to Ajdovščina, with just one return bus (Mon–Fri 3.54pm).

Sveta Gora

Positioned atop the 681-metre-high **Sveta Gora** (Holy Mountain), just over 5km north of Nova Gorica, the **Basilica of the Assumption** has been an important place of pilgrimage for centuries. Local legend has it that in 1539 a shepherd girl, Urška Ferligoj, was visited on several occasions by apparitions of the Virgin Mary, an occurrence that precipitated the building of the basilica two years later. A stone slab unearthed during its construction indicated that some form of religious centre has been present on this site since possibly as early as the eleventh century; however it was most likely destroyed by the Turks in the late fifteenth century.

When the church was reduced to a pile of rubble during World War I, authorities initially considered employing Jože Plečnik to undertake a redesign, though, ultimately, the project was taken up by Silvano Barich from Gorizia, as it was ostensibly an Italian concern. The stained-glass windows aside, the church's high, dark and capacious interior betrays little in the way of ornamentation or colour. The high altar, too, is very simple, its only distinguishing feature a picture of the Virgin Mary; originally donated to the church in 1544, the painting (believed to be of Venetian origin) was taken to Gorizia during World War II, later found at the Vatican and returned to the basilica in 1951. Miraculously, the **Chapel of Appearance** – located to the rear of the high altar and containing the original gold wooden statue dating from 1541 – survived the bombing almost completely unscathed. The basilica's **museum** (visits by appointment only) holds fragments from the bombed-out church, and the usual stock of church reliquaries.

A few steps down from the church, in the building housing a rather dull restaurant, is the **Soča Front Museum** (May–Oct Sat & Sun 11am–6pm; €2), displaying a rather tired assortment of artefacts pertaining to the nearby battles fought during World War I – you're best off saving your time and money for the museum in Kobarid (see p.162).

Unfortunately, there are no buses to Sveta Gora so, unless you have your own transport, it's a very steep and exacting walk (roughly 1hr): after passing through Solkan, take the road marked Trnovo/Čepovan (it's a sharp right – the road straight ahead is the Tolmin road) for about 3km, before branching off up the steep and twisting road towards Sveta Gora. From the summit, there are superlative views south across to the Gulf of Trieste and the snow-tipped mountains of the Soča Valley to the north. On the way from Nova Gorica, you'll see the magnificent **Solkan Railway Bridge**, which was, at the time of its construction in 1906, the largest stone arch bridge in Europe, some 85m high.

Eating and drinking

There are depressingly few **restaurants** in town, so you're best off heading to a couple of terrific places on the outskirts. Located 3km east of town, on the ground floor of Kromberk Castle, is the outstanding ✻ *Grajska Klet* (☏05/302-7160; Fri–Tues): tall-backed wooden chairs, lush red carpets and cast-iron chandeliers provide a classy setting for a distinguished and unusual menu, typically featuring *mešani narezek* (cold cuts of ham), *jota* (a local vegetable soup) and *oves sčrno trobento* (oatgrain with black trumpet mushrooms); there's a fine wine selection too, but reserve ahead. Not quite in the same league, but very enjoyable and a good deal cheaper, is *Pri Hrastu*, a one-hundred-year-old inn located at Kromberška cesta 2, just fifteen minutes' walk from the centre on the main road towards Kromberk Castle. For those on a somewhat tighter budget, try *Pecivo*, opposite the *Hotel Park* at Delpinova 16, which doubles up nicely as a café and simple restaurant, or the *Vrtnica* self-service restaurant at Kidričeva 11 (Mon–Fri 7am–6pm).

The liveliest place in town to **drink** is the *KGS* student club (see p.173), which also runs an interesting programme of cultural events, film, and music.

Goriška Brda

Goriška Brda (often just referred to as Brda, which means hill), a small nub of land around 5km northwest of Nova Gorica, is a beautiful region of low, smoothly rounded hills, scattered villages and little white churches, best known for producing some of the country's finest wines. The hills are perfect for fruit growing, too, with the harvesting of cherries, peaches and apricots a major seasonal activity. From the wine aficionado's point of view, the most interesting villages are concentrated in the southernmost part of Brda, namely **Dobrovo** and **Medana**, while the villages of **Šmartno** and **Vipolže** attest to the region's position as an important frontier zone during the Venetian-Habsburg wars.

Whether you're here for the wine or not, Goriška Brda is a wonderful place to explore and, should you choose to stay longer, there's a smattering of accommodation available in several villages. However long you decide to stay, you'll get a lot more out of the region with your own transport, as there is only a very limited, and poorly coordinated, bus service between Nova Gorica and Dobrovo (Mon–Fri school term-time – roughly Sept–June) is only at 12.21pm & 3.25pm, returning at 8.30am, 12.10pm & 1.40pm).

Kojsko and Šmartno

The first major stop travelling from Nova Gorica is **KOJSKO**, a comely little wayside settlement worth a brief stop to view the **Church of the Holy Cross on Tabor** (Sveta Križna Taboru), stationed just above the village. One of the four watchtowers (the other three were burnt down) which once formed part of an ancient fortification here was later rearranged into the church bell tower, a feature common to many churches in these parts. The interior stars a beautifully preserved late-Gothic winged high altar from around 1500.

A couple of kilometres west of Kojsko, a monumentally ugly twenty-three-metre-high **viewing tower** provides a commanding sweep of the surrounding hills, including quite splendid views of **ŠMARTNO**, a superb-looking, fortified village some 2km away. Girdled by partially preserved white-stone walls and watch-towers erected during the sixteenth century, the village is an attractive jumble of crooked, unevenly paved streets lined with crumbling stone houses. In the centre stands the **Church of St Martin** whose fourteenth-century bell tower is another that was converted from a watch-tower; take a look inside at the contemporary, and very colourful, frescoes by Tone Kralj.

Dobrovo

Three kilometres west of Šmartno, **DOBROVO** is Goriška Brda's largest and most heavily populated settlement, as well as the region's principal wine centre. Here, too,

The wines of Goriška Brda

Goriška Brda is the northernmost of the four wine-growing districts that constitute Slovenia's **Primorje** (coastal) region. Thanks to its favourable geographical location and Mediterranean climate and soil, Goriška Brda consistently yields a superlative range of both **red** and **white wines** – one of the few regions in Slovenia to harvest both, though whites account for roughly seventy percent here. Among the former, Cabernet Sauvignon and the lighter Merlot are pre-eminent, whilst of the latter, the ubiquitous Chardonnay (produced all over Slovenia), Beli Pinot, and the dry Briški Točaj (as opposed to the famous sweet Hungarian variety) prevail. The most distinctive white, though, is the golden-yellow Rebula, a widely cultivated, indigenous grape used in the production of *slamno vino* (straw wine). Local **vintners** to look out for include Simčič (☎05/395-9200) and Movia (☎05/395-9510), both in Ceglo, and Prinčič (☎05/304-1272), in Kozana.

If you fancy a spot of **tasting**, there are dozens of cellars in a number of villages to choose from, all well signposted; expect to pay around €6–10 per person for four or five wines, with bread and cheese or *pršut*. You can either contact the cellars directly (a few hours' notice is usually appreciated), or call the tourist office in Dobrovo for further information (see oposite).

The most important of several wine-related events occurring throughout Brda during the year is **Martinmas (St Martin's Day)** on November 11, which is celebrated in grand style throughout the region, topped off with a day of concerts and tasting aplenty within the grounds of Vipolže Castle (see opposite). Otherwise, the biggest and brashest festival in Brda is the **Cherry Fest**, which takes place in Dobrovo during the second weekend of June. Marking the beginning of the cherry season this lively spectacle entails concerts, tastings and much general merriment, climaxing with the parade of the "Cherry Girl".

you will find Goriška Brda's only **tourist office** (Mon–Fri 8am–4pm; ☏05/395-9594, ✉obcina.brda@guest.arnes.si), located in the centre of the village at Trg 25 maja 2, just 100m from where buses stop; the office can assist with enquiries on any aspect of the Brda region, from wine tours and tasting to private accommodation.

Two hundred metres south of the tourist office on Grajska cesta stands **Dobrovo Castle** (Grad Dobrovo; Tues–Fri 8am–4pm, Sat & Sun noon–4pm; €2), a Renaissance-style structure erected around 1600 on the site of an older castle, and not dissimilar to Kromberk Castle near Nova Gorica (see p.174); its cultural history collection is not particularly stimulating, though the gallery of graphic prints up on the second floor by internationally renowned local artist Zoran Mušič (1909–2005) is worth a look. In any case, chances are you'll soon end up sampling wine in the Vinoteka (Tues–Sun 11.30am–9pm), a magnificent stone-vault cellar located in the castle's handsome courtyard. **Bikes** can also be hired from the castle courtyard (€3 for 1hr, €14 for the day).

Alternatively, you could try the **Goriška Brda** winery, a short way north of the castle at Zadružna cesta 9 (🖥www.klet-brda.com), one of the largest wine production cellars in Slovenia. A visit includes some informative spiel about the region's wines, a tour of the cellar – where you'll get the chance to see stunning four-hundred-year-old oak barrels from Bosnia – and a tasting session with snacks (€8 per person for six wines). Wines can be purchased from their on-site shop (daily: Jan–March 8am–5pm, April–Dec 8am–7pm).

Medana and Ceglo

Two further villages worth checking out are **MEDANA** and **VIPOLŽE**, 1.5km and 3.5km south of Dobrovo respectively, the former one of Brda's most prolific winegrowing villages. One of the most highly regarded wineries here is the **Klinec** tourist farm at no. 20 (☏05/304-5092, ✉klinec-medana@s5.net), which has been producing vintages since 1918; there's good food and accommodation available here too (❸). The owners of the farm also organize the **Days of Poetry and Wine Festival** in late August, an international gathering of poets complemented by the requisite quantities of wine. A short walk up the road, at no. 32, the ☀*Belica* tourist farm (☏05/304-2104, 🖥www.belica.net; ❺–❻) is an upmarket establishment with eight decadently furnished, air-conditioned rooms overlooking a gorgeous lawn terrace and with views across to the Friulian hills; they also have tastings, as well as a fabulously classy restaurant, with the pick of the menu a delicious range of home-made salamis, sausages and ribs.

From Medana, the road continues south towards the Italian border; after passing through the village of **CEGLO**, veer eastwards (continuing south will bring you to the local border crossing) and continue up the hill towards Vipolže. Located in the upper reaches of this quaint little village is **Vipolže Castle**, originally an eleventh-century fortification, but later transformed into a handsome Renaissance-style manor house following its appropriation by the Venetians in the seventeenth century. The oaks and cypresses of this once lovely park still flourish, but otherwise it's a wretched site, the castle's bricked-up windows and tumbledown walls the result of heavy bomb damage during World War I, when it was used as a military hospital, and years of subsequent neglect. As some compensation, there are marvellous **views** across the Friulian Plain. From Vipolže, you can return to Dobrovo via the road running parallel to Medana, or take the northeasterly road towards Šmartno.

The Vipava Valley

If the Brda region hasn't sated your thirst for wine, you might like to venture in the opposite direction towards the **Vipava Valley** (Vipavska dolina), the second and largest of Primorje's wine-growing regions. Sandwiched between the thickly forested Trnovo Plateau to the north and the low-lying Karst region to the south, this flat-bottomed valley is raked by lush rolling vineyards which, like Goriška Brda, yield a superb quota of both reds, notably Cabernet Sauvignon and Merlot, and whites; check out the indigenous varieties, Zelen and Pinela.

The valley's continental climate is epitomized by the **burja** (bora), a fiendishly cold and dry wind that whips down from the northern mountain peaks and batters its way through the valley, across the Karst, and down towards the Adriatic. For this reason many of the two dozen or so **wine villages** dispersed throughout the Vipava hills were built in relatively sheltered, south-facing locations, with neither windows nor doors positioned on sides exposed to the wind. The only centres of any meaningful size in the valley are **Ajdovščina** and **Vipava**, unspectacular little towns but both useful as jumping-off points if the villages are your intended target.

The handy little *Vipava Wine Road* leaflet (available from the tourist office in Ajdovščina – see below) outlines a number of villages and cellars you can visit. However, having your own **transport** is pretty much essential here, as public transport is virtually nonexistent.

Ajdovščina

The only centre of any significant size in the Vipava Valley is **AJDOVŠČINA**, a small, plain sort of town, with little to hold your attention save for some extant Roman remains. The compact ancient core of present-day Ajdovščina was once a military encampment called **Castra ad Fluvium Frigidum** (Fortress by the Cold River), built by the Romans around 270 AD as an important link in the defence line of the Empire. Its four-metre-thick defence walls were perforated with fourteen circular towers, of which seven, either whole or partial, remain; the most tangible remnants, including an almost complete tower, lie east of the main square Lavričev trg – other portions of the wall can be detected on the western side of the ancient quarter. There are further exhibits pertaining to the town's ancient past in the small town **museum** (Sat & Sun 1–6pm; €2), five minutes' walk east of the tourist office at Prešernova ulica 24.

More stimulating is the **Veno Pilon Gallery** (Pilonova Galerija; Tues–Fri 10am–4pm, Sat & Sun 3–6pm; free; Ⓦwww.venopilon.com), just across the road from the tourist office at Prešernova ulica 3. A fantastically prolific and versatile artist, Pilon (1896–1970) was amongst Slovenia's foremost expressionist painters, though his repertoire also extended to graphic art and photography. Amongst the most interesting works on display here are sketches completed during his time incarcerated as a prisoner of war in Russia during World War I, and his landscape paintings – mostly motifs from the Vipava Valley – which represented the high point of Slovene modernism in the 1920s. As if that wasn't enough he also starred in Slovenia's first feature film, *Na Svoji Zemlji* (On Our Own Land), and translated a great deal of Slovenian poetry into French.

Arriving at the **bus** or **train** station, located opposite each other on Goriška cesta, it's a five-minute walk northeast to the centre of town and the **tourist office**, housed in a section of a Roman tower at Lokarjev drevored 8 (Mon–Fri: July–Sept 8am–6pm, Oct–June 8am–4pm; ☏05/365-9140, Ⓔtic-ajdovscina@siol.net); they can arrange accommodation on local tourist farms and visits to local wine cellars. Should you desire to stay in town, there's the dreary and overpriced

Hotel Pigal Planika 200m east of the stations at Goriška cesta 25 (☎05/364-4700, Ⓔplanika@pigal.si; ❻).

Vipava and Zemono

From Ajdovščina, hourly buses continue southeast to **VIPAVA**, the valley's second centre some 6km distant. This somnolent little market town, lying under the towering slopes of the Nanos Plateau, somewhat misguidedly styles itself as the Slovene Venice – for no good reason other than that it developed alongside the many karstic springs of the Vipava River. Of course, it's nothing like Venice and, though endowed with a modicum of charm thanks to its generous spread of Baroque architecture and picturesque stone-block bridges, you're unlikely to stay long, if you stop at all.

That said, the **Vipava Winery** at Vinarska cesta 5 (☎05/367-1200), 500m east of the main square where buses drop passengers off, is one of Primorje's major wine cooperatives, and is worth considering if you're unable to reach any of the villages. Its barrique (harvested in barrels) red wines – in particular Merlot and Cabernet Sauvignon – are rated as some of the best in the country. Guided tours and tastings (€5 for five wines) are possible, and there's also a good restaurant (Tues–Sat noon-10pm) and wine shop on site. Otherwise, the friendly little **tourist office**, on the main square at Glavni trg 1 (Tues–Fri 10am–4pm, Sat 9am–1pm; ☎05/368-7041, Ⓦwww.vipavski.dolina.si), can help arrange visits to a number of the local wine cellars. There's nowhere to stay in town, but if you have a car, there's the isolated *Pri Abram* **tourist farm** (☎050/532-002) in the settlement of **Nanos**, on the plateau of the same name.

Occupying a solitary location less than 2km west of Vipava (just off the main road), the Palladian-style **Zemono Mansion** (Grad Zemono; Mon–Fri noon–7pm, Sat 9am–2pm; free) is one of Slovenia's best-preserved Renaissance buildings. Formerly a seventeenth-century hunting lodge, the cross-shaped ground floor, whose walls are blanketed with pastel-coloured landscape murals, is now used principally as a concert venue, and occasionally for weddings. The upper floor, meanwhile, has been rather crudely turned into a home furnishings showroom. More appropriately, the cellar has been converted into the high-class and very expensive *Gostilna Pri Lojzetu* **restaurant**, one of the country's most celebrated slow-food establishments, featuring an innovative menu using specially prepared vegetables, mushrooms and the freshest seafood (☎05/368-7007: Wed–Sun noon–10pm).

Vipavski Križ and Goče

Rising out of the flat plain just 2km west of Ajdovščina, the scenic fortified medieval village of **VIPAVSKI KRIŽ** is one of the few settlements in the valley whose historical importance is greater than its viticultural significance. Its focal point is the **Capuchin Monastery**, built in 1637 and whose **Church of the Holy Cross** harbours a quite beautifully carved dark-wooden high altar, together with a sublime painting of the Holy Trinity, one of the largest Baroque canvases in the country and dating from 1668. Its **library** contains an extensive assortment of books from the fifteenth century onwards. Visits to the monastery are best arranged through the tourist office in Ajdovščina (see opposite). Adjacent to the monastery, on the eastern tip of the village, is the magnificent shell of the ruined fifteenth-century **castle**, erected on the orders of the bishop of Gorica so as to protect the village from Turkish and Venetian raids.

If just one wine village is your limit then make a beeline for **GOČE**, some 5km west of the main trunk road in the southeastern Vipava hills. With streets barely wide enough to squeeze a car through, the village is distinguished by its knot of tightly clustered eighteenth-century sandstone houses, ornamented with Karst-style courtyards and hewn stone portals. You'll have little difficulty tracking down somewhere to sample some wine; there are over sixty **cellars** here, which amounts to one for almost every house. A couple of good ones are Fajdiga at no. 4a and Ferjančič at no. 9.

Idrija and around

The history and development of **IDRIJA**, a town of some seven thousand inhabitants 36km north of Vipava, has been inextricably linked to its mines ever since the discovery of mercury here in 1490. During the eighteenth century, the growth and success of the **mines** – which are now in the process of being closed down for good – spawned a number of other local industries, most importantly forestry and medicine; during this period, the town could justifiably claim to rival Ljubljana as a centre of scientific and technological advancement. **Lace-making** has also played a significant part in shaping the town's identity; originally a seventeenth-century cottage industry, the craft grew to such an extent that Slovenia's first lace school was established here in the late nineteenth century, an institution that still functions today.

Despite its modest size, Idrija can comfortably summon up enough attractions to rate a full day's sightseeing, more if you're looking to explore the surrounding countryside. Within walking distance of town is the mysterious **Wild Lake**, while further afield, the immense **Klavže** water barriers and the fascinating **Partisan Printworks** are no less deserving of a visit.

Arrival, information and accommodation

The **bus station** is centrally located on Lapajnetova ulica, from where it's a short hop to the **tourist office** at Vodnikova ulica 3 (July–Aug daily 9am–6pm; Sept–

Mining in Idrija

In 1490, a local tub-maker, busy soaking his wooden vessel in a spring on the present-day site of the Holy Trinity Church, chanced upon a hitherto unknown substance, **mercury**. He was unable to keep this secret to himself, and locals soon got wind of the discovery; some eight years later work began on the **Anthony Mine Shaft**.

Mercury appeared in the Idrija mine in two forms: as native mercury and cinnabar ore, the former as shimmering silver-grey drops dripping down on to the rock face, the latter a deep red-coloured material, from which the liquid could only be extracted after being burnt at temperatures of 800 degrees. At its peak the Idrija mine yielded some 13% of the world's total mercury output, second only to the Almaden mine in Spain. Working conditions were notoriously bad and, with prolonged exposure to this most toxic of substances, a miner could be expected to work for no more than six or seven years before becoming too ill to continue.

The mine is now in the process of being closed down completely – by 2008 it is anticipated that all fifteen levels will have been filled and sealed once and for all. Several factors have contributed to the mine's demise, namely the lack of rich ore, almost negligible prices on the world market and the increasing use of alternative, environmentally friendly substances.

June Mon–Fri 9am–4pm; ☎05/374-3916, ⓦwww.mestoidrija.si). The **post office** (Mon–Fri 8am–7pm, Sat 8am–noon) is next to the bus station.

There's precious little **accommodation** in town: the small *Dijaški Dom*, up on the hill at Ulica IX Korpusa 6 (just behind the Francisca Mine Shaft), has beds available in summer for around €10 (☎05/373-4070). Otherwise, the only other place to sleep is at the *Gostišče Barbara*, which occupies the second floor of the Anthony Mine Shaft building at Kosovelova ulica 3 (☎05/377-1162); it has two categories of room – four en-suite double rooms with TV and minibar (⑤), and two hostel-style rooms sleeping two to four people, with shared wash/shower facilities (②). Another option, albeit a very expensive one, is the five-star *Hotel Kendov Dvorec*, a splendidly renovated fourteenth-century manor house 4km north of town in **Spodnja Idrija**, at Na griču 2 (☎05/372-5100, ⓦwww.kendov-dvorec.com; ⑨); the immaculate rooms come with antique furniture and linen made from Idrija lace.

The Town

Idrija's handful of terrific sites – all more or less associated with the mining and lace industries, such as the **Mine Shaft**, **Gewerkenegg Castle** and **Lace School** – are broadly contained within the attractive and compact old core on the western side of town, and hence all within comfortable walking distance of each other.

Anthony Mine Shaft

The town's star attraction is undoubtedly the **Anthony Mine Shaft** (Antonijev Rov) whose main entrance building (Šelštev) is at Kosovelova ulica 3. Sunk in 1500, the tunnel shaft (1.5km long and 400m deep) was, after the Almadén mercury mine in Spain, the most productive in Europe, employing around 1300 miners at the height of production.

The visit begins with a twenty-minute **audiovisual presentation** (in English) in the checking room – the place where miners would gather in the early morning hours to be allocated their duties by the Obergutman (a kind of foreman) before heading down into the mine. On the wall at the back of the room is the

Lace-making in Idrija

The art of bobbin **lace-making** first took off in Slovenia in the seventeenth century and, despite having been practised in many towns and rural areas throughout the country, its roots have remained strongest in Idrija, where the craft has been taught in the town's **Lace School** since 1876.

Traditionally, lace-making was practised by most women as a means of supplementing a miner's often very meagre wage – a state of affairs that became even more pressing following the decline of this and other traditional industries (such as iron smelting) in the late nineteenth and early twentieth centuries. The lace-making industry continued apace, with its products sold mainly to the Church, until World War II. After this, however, its popularity waned, only to be revived in the 1980s. Today's lace products are primarily made as gifts and souvenirs.

Idrija Lace (*Idrijska čipka*) takes many forms, from simple flower-based patterns to intricately woven cloths featuring folk or peasant motifs, many of which are technically superb; you can view, and purchase, many such specimens in several of the region's museums and shops. Moreover, the **Lace Festival** in Idrija, and the **Days of Lace Fair** in Železniki (another important regional lace centre), attest to this exquisite handicraft's ongoing importance and enduring popularity.

so-called death clock: before descending into the pit, each miner was obliged to take a number plate which, if not replaced at the end of the shift, indicated that he'd got lost or was in some sort of trouble. Having donned jacket and helmet, you're led along a series of lit galleries and laddered passageways, part of the Main Road which served as the main mine entrance for over two hundred years. Descending to a depth of 100m, you'll pass by several small alcoves in which benches were placed for the miners to take their lunch, items of equipment used to bore through the rock, and a number of life-size puppets of miners – including one of **Berkmandlc**, the pit dwarf, who in return for parcels of food, would tap the walls to indicate to the miners where the richest sources of mercury lay.

The tour winds up at the tiny underground **Chapel of the Holy Trinity**, where miners would pray before the statues of SS Barbara and Acacius (patron saints of miners) for a safe return from their day's work. Scheduled tours, which last around one hour thirty minutes, take place daily at 10am and 3pm, with an extra tour at 4pm on weekends (€5; Ⓦ www.rzs-idrija.si).

Gewerkenegg Castle and the Town Museum

Sited atop a small hill on the western fringe of town, and discernible from some distance thanks to its two cylindrical corner towers and an oddly protruding central clock tower, **Gewerkenegg Castle** (Grad Gewerkenegg) was built by the Acacius Society of Mining Entrepreneurs around 1530 to house the mine administration and other official bodies. Though prevailingly Renaissance in form, the castle was embellished with Baroque appendages in the eighteenth century – including the arcaded courtyard and its rather lurid foliage-style frescoes.

It now plays host to the **town museum** (Mestni muzej; daily 9am–6pm; €3) which, not surprisingly, dotes heavily upon the town's **mining** heritage. An absorbing exhibition begins with an introduction to the Idrija mine, including a depiction of the local tub-maker who kick-started the whole thing. The next three rooms are devoted to all matters geological, and while most people are drawn to the steel ball floating in a bowl of mercury, don't let that detract you from the fine assemblage of fossils, minerals and cinnabar ore deposits on display. Similarly enlightening is the collection of mine maps, land registers, flasks and other objects gathered in the northern Rondel Tower, while the staircase in the southern Mercury Tower has been designed to symbolize the descent down the pit. At the bottom is a Plexiglas cube filled with droplets of mercury.

No less engaging is the exhibition charting Idrija's development in the twentieth century. Aided by some fascinating photographs, there is superb coverage of the town's involvement during the two World Wars, including the first Italian occupation in 1918, which culminated in the Rapallo Treaty (see p.330), thereby annexing part of Slovenia and turning Idrija into a border town; while World War II focuses on the German occupation between September 1943 and April 1945, and its attendant Fascist denationalization policies – the most sobering exhibit is a tree stump upon which two Partisans were beheaded. The last section covers local industry in Idrija and, despite the closure of the mines – you can't fail to miss the enormous hammer and sickle that used to adorn the entrance to the Francisca Mine Shaft (see below) – unemployment is less than one percent here, the lowest in the country.

Inevitably, the town's rich **lace** tradition is well documented with, among other exhibits, a display of work by the winners of the annual bobbin lace competition; the most interesting piece is a sprawling tablecloth, originally made for President Tito's wife, Jovanka Broz, but retained by the museum following his death, and her banishment from political life, in 1980.

The Old Town and the Lace School

Just below the castle, the old town core showcases a couple of significant buildings including the former mine **Granary** on Trg Svetega Ahacija, which was used to store grain and wheat but which now functions as a gallery and library; next to this stands the oldest **theatre** in Slovenia, built in 1769 and now a cinema.

The most impressive building, however, is the lovely Neoclassical Old School (Stara šola) at Prelovčeva ulica 2, which has been home to the town's **Lace School** (Čipkarska šola; Mon–Fri 8am–3pm; €2) since 1876 (see box opposite). The items on display here were completed by students of the school, all of whom attend voluntarily and are mostly aged between six and fourteen; if you ask, you may be allowed to see a lesson in progress. You can also buy lace here, or at one of several **lace shops** dotted around town; the best of these is the Galerija Idrijske Čipke, opposite the school at Mestni trg 16 (Mon–Fri 10am–noon & 4–7pm, Sat 10am–noon). Idrija's major annual event is the **Lace Festival** (Čipkarski Festival) during the last week of August, entailing lace-making competitions, arts and crafts exhibitions and evening entertainment.

The Francisca Mine Shaft and the Kamšt

Up the hill on Bazoviška ulica is the **Francisca Mine Shaft** (Jašek Frančiške; daily, but no set opening times – contact the town museum in the castle; €2), whose former workshops now house a marvellous collection of beautifully restored, nineteenth-century steam-driven pumps, boilers and compressors, most of which were taken out of operation in the 1950s following the introduction of more modern working practices.

Set against a gentle slope just behind the mine shaft is a typically striking, albeit heavily renovated, example of an eighteenth-century **miner's house** (Rudarska hiša). Defined by a high, slender frontage, a sharply pointed roof and neat rows of small, square windows, these houses were traditionally constructed from wood and stone, the external walls made of thick boards daubed with lime-wash, and the rooftops protected with wooden shingles. A miner's house usually comprised three or four floors, in order that several families could be accommodated in the same building – an important consideration during times of overpopulation; moreover, miners could rarely afford their own houses. Today, sadly, you'll do well to spot more than half a dozen such dwellings around Idrija.

There's yet another reminder of Idrija's industrial pedigree 1km southeast of the bus station at the end of Vodnikova ulica. Concealed within the chunky stone-block building is the beautifully preserved **Kamšt** (daily 9am 4pm – if it's closed you can get the key from the Town Museum; €2), held to be the largest wooden waterwheel in Europe, measuring 13.6m in diameter. For more than 150 years, it pumped pit water from a depth of over 200m from the Joseph Shaft.

Eating and drinking

Idrija is bereft of decent places to **eat**, though the two gostilna here are reasonable enough and both serve up the Idrija speciality, *Žlikrofi* – spiced potato balls wrapped in thin pastry. *Gostilna Pri Škafarju*, 50m east of the former granary at Ulica Svete Barbare 9 (Wed–Mon), is fairly plain-looking, but there's a decent menu to choose from, including a handful of horse-meat dishes (including, somewhat disconcertingly, grilled colt); while *Gostilna Kos*, 200m east of the bus station at Tomšičeva ulica 4, veers more towards Italian fare (Mon–Sat). The studenty *Avalon Pub*, at Mestni trg 7, is just about the only place in town to **drink**.

Around Idrija: The Wild Lake and Klavže dams

From the Kamšt a three-kilometre-long trail (Pot ob Rakah) leads south to the brilliant blue-green **Wild Lake** (Divje Jezero), an apposite name for this small body of water that has claimed the lives of several divers attempting to locate the lake's as yet undiscovered source – to date 156m is the deepest anyone has got. What is known is that water flows into the lake from an underground passage, or siphon, reckoned to measure approximately 200m long. The lake itself measures about 65m in length and 30m in width, taking barely fifteen minutes to circle, unless, that is, you happen to be here following snow melt or extremely heavy rainfall, when massive volumes of water are discharged from its depths, flooding the lake to 3m above its normal level. Emanating from the lake is Slovenia's shortest river, the Jezernica, which discharges into the Idrijca after only 55m.

Just as impressive are the precipitous, hundred-metre-high cliffs encircling the lake, whose crevices and ledges shelter a galaxy of alpine **flora**, including several endemic species, such as the Carniolan primrose and hacquetia, the latter named after eminent local surgeon Baltazar Hacquet. Lurking in the lake's depths, and something you won't see, is Proteus Anguinus, the human-fish (see Subterranean Slovenia colour section). If you have your own car, take the Ljubljana road south from Idrija and the lake is signposted after about 1.5km.

Twelve kilometres upstream from the Wild Lake on the Belca River (accessible via an increasingly rutted forest road), is the first of four remaining **dams** (Klavže) in the area. Known locally as the Slovene Pyramids, these superb technical monuments were originally constructed from wood in the sixteenth century, but were replaced by sturdier stone structures in 1770. Their function was to accumulate enough water to enable vast quantities of timber to be floated downriver to Idrija, whereupon the logs would gather in front of a 412-metre-long dam (rake), at which point they would be carted off to the mines (where they were used as supporting structures for the galleries) and smelting plants (for fuel for burning iron ore). The rake remained operational until 1926, when road transportation was deemed more efficient, while the Klavže gradually fell into a state of disrepair. Restored in the 1980s, they now stand as a fitting memorial to a bygone era. There's another dam about 1.5km further upstream and another, also accessible by road, on the Idrijca River, which runs roughly parallel to the Belca.

The most impressive of the renovated dams – completed in 2005 – is located on the Klavžarica river, 8km west of Spodnja Idrija beyond the village of Kanomlja; some 34m long and 8m wide, and constructed from sculpted lime rocks, the **Kanomeljske klavže** was built in 1813 and served the needs of the Idrija mine until 1912. To get here, take a left turn at the village of Spodnji Kanomlja and follow the signs – the last 1km is not suited for cars, but it's a pleasant enough walk anyway.

Partisan Printing Works

Secreted away in an almost impenetrable forest ravine below the Vojsko plateau, 2km north of the tiny hamlet of **Planina** (itself 14km west of Idrija), are several modest wooden cabins which, for a brief period during World War II, functioned as the **Partisan Printing Works** (Partizanska tiskarna; mid-April to mid-Oct 9am–4pm; €2). Operational between September 1944 and May 1945, and with some forty employees, the clandestinely run printworks rolled out between 4000 and 7000 copies of *Partizanski Dnevnik* (*Partisan Daily*) per day, the only daily newspaper to be published by a resistance movement in occupied Europe during the war; over the eight months more than a million copies of the paper were published, as well as stacks of other printed matter.

During the visit, you'll get to see the typesetting room (complete with printing moulds and dozens of original papers), the bindery, kitchen and dining room, the power plant, and the printing room. Purchased for a million lire, the still-functioning printing press was smuggled across from Milan, via Gorica, before being transported, piece by piece, to Vojsko; a demonstration is usually given. Despite numerous German offensives in the vicinity – including one final major assault during the Spring of 1945 in which over 300 Partisans were killed – the printworks was never rumbled. Owing to its extremely remote location, a visit to the printworks requires a little organization and a degree of physical exertion; in the first instance, you should contact the tourist office in Idrija or the Town Museum at Gewerkenegg Castle (see p.182).

Cerkno and around

Located somewhat out on a limb 19km north of Idrija (and 4km off the main Idrija–Tolmin road), the anonymous little town of **CERKNO** was a key centre of Partisan activity during World War II, when a number of military and political bodies, workshops and schools were stationed hereabouts. Life in Cerkno today is played out at a rather more languid pace, and unless you're here for the **skiing** (see box on p.140) or to see either the **Laufarija carnival** in February (see box on p.187) or the **Jazz Festival** in May (see p.186), there's little inducement to linger. That said, it's a good jumping-off spot if you're planning to visit any of the outlying sights, and it also makes a good base for walks into the **Cerkno Hills** (Cerkljansko Hribovje).

If you do find yourself with a bit of time to spare, it's worth a browse around the **Cerkno Museum** (Cerkljanski muzej; Tues–Sun 10am–1pm & 2–6pm; €2), located just off Glavni trg, and across from the post office at Bevkova 12. This engaging exhibition documents the history of the Cerkljansko region from the nineteenth century onwards, with a particularly interesting resumé of events hereabouts during World War II – exhibits include the wedding blouse of Franja Bidovec, founder of the Partisan Hospital (see p.186), and items belonging to writer France Bevk (see p.188) who served with the Partisans. There's also a display of the masks used during the Laufarija Carnival.

Practicalities

Buses arrive and depart from Glavni trg, the small main square around which everything in town revolves. Amenities in Cerkno, however, are negligible; there's no tourist office, though the staff at the *Hotel Cerkno* can furnish you with **information** and help to arrange visits to some of the outlying attractions. The **post office** is 100m west of Glavni trg (Mon–Fri 8am–6pm, Sat 8am–noon). The only **accommodation** in town is the aforementioned hotel, a comfortable, clean and roomy place located a two-minute walk away from the main square at Sedejev trg 8 (℡05/374-3400, Ⓦwww.hotel-cerkno.si; ❻); its large pool is free to guests.

If you don't mind staying a little way outside town, there are two very welcoming possibilities: back out on the Idrija–Tolmin road (at the junction of the Cerkno turn-off) in **Straža**, the *Želinc* tourist farm (℡05/372-4020, Ⓦwww.zelinc.com; ❹) offers very comfortable rooms, with good food to boot; in the other direction, 6km along the road towards the ski centre in the wayside hamlet of **Log**, the great-value *Gostilna Gačnk v Logu* (℡05/372-4005, Ⓔgacnk@cerkno.com; ❹) is a roadside, family-run tavern with nine cosy, wood-furnished rooms; its modern **restaurant** offers a wide choice of exotic game (stag's back, chamois, boar and the like), Serbian meats (*Čevapi* and *Sarma*), and the local Idrijan speciality (*Žlikrofi*). In Cerkno itself, the restaurant in the *Hotel Cerkno* is the best place to dine. The only other option is the rather downbeat *Pri Štruklu* (Tues–Sun) just up from the museum at Platiševa 1, which offers little more than the stock pizzas and grills. The place to **drink** is *Pri Gabrielju* just off the square at Mučnikova 5 (open until 1am). Cerkno is the unlikely setting for an annual **Jazz Festival** (Ⓦwww.jazzcerkno.si), a three-day event in mid-May featuring a surprisingly impressive, and refreshingly diverse, roster of both domestic and international jazz and folk artists.

Around Cerkno

If there's little to excite in Cerkno itself, then the surrounding countryside is well invested with terrific sites, although unless you have your own wheels or aren't disposed to a reasonable amount of walking, reaching them will prove problematic. Best of all is the **Franja Partisan Hospital**, a superbly evocative reminder of Slovenia's Partisan heritage, while less well-known, and hence rarely visited, are the **Divje Babe** and **Ravenska Caves**, both a little way southwest of town; and in **Zakojca** to the north, the writer France Bevk's house. Embracing most of the above, the **Cerkno hills** themselves offer some good hikes.

Franja Partisan Hospital

Dramatically sited in the heart of the spectacular **Pasica gorge** 7km northeast of Cerkno, the **Franja Partisan Hospital** (Partizanska Bolnišnica Franja; April–Sept daily 9am–6pm; March, Oct & Nov daily 9am–4pm; Dec–Feb Sat & Sun 9am–4pm; €3) was built in December 1943 for wounded soldiers of the Ninth Corps of the Slovene Partisan Army. Named after its chief physician Franja Bojc-Bidovec, the hospital remained operational until May 1945, a period during which it treated more than five hundred Partisans, as well as soldiers from Italy, Russia and America.

Comprising thirteen camouflaged **wooden cabins** that housed an operating room, isolation ward, kitchen, X-ray room and several recovery rooms, the complex was protected by bunkers, minefields and machine gun nests pressed into the cliffs above. However, despite the area being shelled by Germans on several occasions, it was never captured. Indeed, its secrecy was such that the wounded were blindfolded before being admitted, food was lowered down the cliff face by neighbouring farm-

The Laufarija

One of Slovenia's more enjoyable Pust (Shrovetide) festivals is the **Laufarija**, staged each year on the Sunday before Ash Wednesday and on Shrove Tuesday in Cerkno's small town square. The central character is the horned **Pust**, made up in a weighty costume of straw, moss and pine branches; as the personification of winter, the Pust is hauled up in front of a court and charged with a litany of barmy crimes – a poor harvest, inclement weather, dodgy roads and so on – before being found guilty and sentenced to summary execution.

The two dozen or so other members of the Laufarija family – each of whom wears one of the distinctive **masks** (*larfe*) carved from soft lime-tree wood – represent either a local trade or craft (baker, butcher, cobbler, and so on), or display certain character traits or afflictions, such as the drunk and his wife, the scabby one, and the sick man with his accordion.

To be honest it's debatable whether even the locals know what's going on, but it's a great deal of fun all the same. If you don't manage to get here for the festival, there's a fine display of the masks worn in the Cerkno Museum (see p.185).

ers, and medical supplies were air-dropped in by Allied forces; note the picture of Winston Churchill in the Invalids Room. Supplies notwithstanding, the hospital was remarkably self-reliant throughout the period of its operation, making its own orthopedic accessories, organizing cultural and educational activities for the wounded and even managing to publish its own bulletin, *Bolniški list (Patient's Bulletin)*.

Despite its relatively remote location, getting to the hospital is not especially difficult, particularly if you have your own transport; the only buses that pass this way are the ski buses from Cerkno in the winter. Seven kilometres along the road east of Cerkno, a road branches north just beyond the tiny hamlet of **Log**; 1km on you come to a car park. From here, a trail (10min) – no disabled access – inclines up the forested gorge, bisected by the babbling Čerinščica stream and hemmed in by overhanging boulders.

The Divje Babe and Ravenska Caves

Two hundred metres above the Idrija–Tolmin road and the Idrijca river, near the village of **Šebrelje**, some 12km west of Cerkno, is **Divje Babe Cave**, one of the most important Palaeolithic sites in Slovenia. Whilst digging near the cave entrance in 1995, excavators stumbled across the femur of a young cave bear – nothing particularly revelatory in itself – but this one had been perforated with four holes (two complete, two partially worn away), giving it a flute-like appearance. Researchers in Canada calculated the four-inch bone to be around 45,000 years old, possibly more, thus dating from the Mousterian period, time of Neanderthal man. On the assumption that the holes were made by human hands – the most plausible explanation given that no teeth marks were detected on the bone – it can lay fair claim to being the oldest known **musical instrument** in Europe. The flute currently resides in the National Museum in Ljubljana. Getting here really does entail having your own transport; otherwise, you can take a Cerkno–Tolmin bus and alight at the roadside hamlet of Stopnik; however, from there, you've still got a long (about 3km) and steep walk along the road up to Šebrelje. To arrange a visit contact the Local Tourist Board at Bevkova 9 (☎05/373-4645), or the *Hotel Cerkno* (see p.186).

Chanced upon by a local farmer in 1832, the **Ravenska Cave** (Ravenska jama), high up in the village of **Ravne Pri Cerkne**, 7km southwest of Cerkno, is known for its clusters of brilliant white aragonite crystals, spidery-like formations that owe their shape and colour to the high levels of magnesium present in the soil.

The crystals here are amongst some of the finest specimens of aragonite to be found anywhere in Europe. The cave itself is something of a minnow in Slovene terms, measuring just over 350m in length, of which you'll get to see about 100m; there's no need for sensible shoes, as walkways have been constructed, but bring a jumper as the temperature is around just eight or nine degrees.

In theory, the cave is not officially open, though in practice visits can be arranged if you show enough interest – contact either the local tourist board at Bevkova 9 (℡05/373-4645), or the *Hotel Cerkno* (see p.186). If you don't have transport and are considering walking, there's a very satisfying circular hike from Cerkno to the cave, via the village of **Zakriž** (4hr).

Zakojca and the Cerkno Hills

Approximately 20km north of the Ravenska Cave, and rather more difficult to reach (but still accessible by road or several marked paths), is the tiny village of **ZAKOJCA**, birthplace of children's novelist France Bevk (1870–1970). The immaculately restored **homestead** (Domačija Franceta Bevka; no set times; €2) where Bevk also spent much of his youth is a fairly simple dwelling; the downstairs space comprises a living room *(hiša),* two small bedrooms, a "black" kitchen (see p.134) and a small stable for livestock, while the first floor attic, where he wrote his earliest works, has been transformed into an exhibition space, with family photos, books and personal effects.

The house is a ten-minute walk from the *Pri Flandru* tourist farm (where you'll have to go first to get the key) in the centre of the village at no. 1 (℡05/377-9800, Ⓔinfo@kmetija-flander.si; ❸) – this is a good place to **stay** if you're planning to spend a day or two hiking in the surrounding hills, and there's terrific home-cooking on offer too. From Zakojca, you could tackle the highland area's highest peak, **Porezen**, which tops at a very respectable 1630m (2hr); just below the summit is the *Koča na Poreznu* mountain hut (℡05/377-6275; June–mid-Sept). Porezen can also be attempted from the Franja Partisan Hospital (3hr). If you're considering any sort of hiking in the hills, consider buying the 1:50,000 *Idrijsko In Cerkljansko* map.

The Karst

A dry, rocky, and thickly forested limestone plateau, scattered with ancient stone villages, the Karst is famed for its subterranean wonderland of rivers and streams, hollows, depressions and caves, which have fired the imagination of travellers for centuries – none more so than those at **Škocjan**. Just a few kilometres west of Škocjan is the Karst's second major draw, the world-famous **Lipica Stud Farm**, home of the magnificent Lipizzaner horses, and another fine cave at **Vilenica**. Of the villages, the obvious draw is **Štanjel**, whose bleached-white stone houses and wonderfully disparate range of sights are a delight.

Whilst here take the opportunity to sample the local culinary delights, in particular the delicious air-dried *pršut* ham, which complements perfectly a glass of **Kraški Teran**, a spiky, cherry-red wine that acquires its deep aroma and colour from the iron-rich *terra rosa* soil peculiar to this region.

Štanjel

Contender for most picturesque village in the Karst, if not Slovenia, the medieval hilltop settlement of **ŠTANJEL**, situated 28km southeast of Nova Gorica, is the archetypal Karst village. Most likely the site of a Halstatt settlement, the prominent limestone hill was fortified around the twelfth century, gradually evolving across several gently curving, south-facing terraces, a layout modelled on the plans of the ancient Etruscan towns. Its textbook stone houses are delightful, and there's more than enough to warrant a few hours' exploration.

The Village

The best place to start is the **Castle** (Grad Štanjel), located through the main **entrance tower**. Erected by the counts of Koblenz in the sixteenth century, upon the foundations of an older, medieval castle, there is now little to see except for a battered shell, the result of heavy pounding during World War II. There's redemption, however, in the renovated residential wing of the castle, which houses the **Lojze Spacal Gallery** (Galerija Lojzeta Spacala; April–Oct Tues–Fri 10am–2pm, Sat & Sun 10am–6pm; Nov–March Tues–Fri 11am–2pm, Sat & Sun 11am–5pm; €2, including entry to the Karst House – see opposite), a brilliant collection of abstract paintings, prints, woodcuts and tapestries by the eponymous, Trieste-born artist. Spacal was profoundly influenced by the surrounding landscape, as is evident in his extensive use of Karst motifs and colours – greys and whites representing stone, and reds representing the soil.

Štanjel's most visible symbol, courtesy of its smooth steeple shaped like a bishop's hat, is the **Church of St Daniel**. Its most interesting interior features are a marble tomb etched with a relief of Daniel and the lions, a relief of the castle as it once supposedly looked, and paintings of interlocking crosses on the presbytery walls; if the church is locked contact the tourist office (see 190).

From the church it's a few paces east to the six-hundred-year-old **Karst House** (Kraška Hiša; €1.5), a superb example of vernacular architecture, constructed entirely from stone, including the roof and gutters. The downstairs space would have been used for keeping livestock, with the living quarters located upstairs, into which a family of typically five or six members would squeeze; both floors now hold a modest ethnological collection. The house has the same opening times as the gallery (see above), from where the key must be obtained first.

In the southeastern corner of the village, a few hundred metres and a couple of terraces below the Karst house, is the **Ferrari Garden**, designed by internationally renowned architect and town planner (and former mayor of Štanjel) Max Fabiani, but named after his brother-in-law, Enrico Ferrari. This winsome little park was designed as an adjunct to the now abandoned Ferrari Villa (which rises above the eastern edge of the park), incorporating traditional Karst features – terraces, stone retaining walls and stairways – and foreign elements, such as a pavilion, oval pool and a delicate, balustraded stone bridge, the inspiration for which was undoubtedly the author's earlier work in Vienna. The park had a more utilitarian function, however; in order to counter the chronic water shortages in the Karst region, Fabiani designed a water supply system using a series of ditches, storage tanks, pipes and irrigation channels, all integrated within a complex system, thus providing the villa and surrounding buildings with their own source of running water.

From the garden there are expansive views across the Karst towards Italy and the hills of the Vipava Valley. You can also follow a marked footpath (Fabiani Path) south towards the village of **Kobdilj**, Fabiani's birthplace.

Practicalities

Trains actually stop in Kobdilj, the next village along, though it's only a fifteen-minute walk into Štanjel itself; **buses** stop on the main road opposite the principal entrance to the village. The **tourist office** (Mon & Wed–Sat 11am–4pm, Sun 2–5pm; ☎05/769-0056, ⓦhttp://vodnik.kras.carso-com), located in the new block of buildings a few paces up from the bus stop, can arrange **private accommodation** in apartments (❸) in Štanjel, and on tourist farms in nearby villages. For coffee and light refreshments, make a beeline for the pleasant café in the castle courtyard (Tues–Sun 10am-6pm).

There are a couple of further accommodation possibilites between Štanjel and Sežana. About 10km southwest of Štanjel, in the small isolated village of **Pliskovica**, is the terrific ⚐ *Pliskovica* **youth hostel** at no. 11 (☎05/764-0250; ⓦwww.pliska.org; ❶). A preserved heritage site, this beautifully restored four-hundred-year-old farmstead accommodates six- to fourteen-bed dorms, all with shared bathroom facilities; there's also an information point, bike hire, laundry and Internet – and it's possible to camp here. However, without a car or bike, you'll struggle to get here, as there are only two buses from Sežana (Mon–Fri 10.40am & 3.30pm). Easier to reach is the *Škerlj* **tourist farm**, 12km south of Štanjel on the main road towards Sežana, in **Tomaj**, at no. 53a (☎05/764-0673, ⓔskerlj. tomaj@siol.net; ❸); comfortable rooms are complemented by good food and hospitality – they've also got bikes for hire.

Sežana and Divača

If you're heading to Lipica or the Škocjan Caves, there's a good chance you'll pass through either **Sežana** or **Divača** at some point, as both towns are on the rail line from Ljubljana and the bus route to the coast or Trieste. Although there are a couple of mildly diverting things to see in these small towns, they're more useful from a practical point of view, with information, accommodation and refreshments available. If you do find yourself waiting for a connection in **SEŽANA** (5km north of Lipica), you could make the fifteen-minute walk north along Partizanska ulica – the town's main through road – to view the well-turned-out **Botanical Gardens** (Botanični Park; Mon–Fri 7am–3pm; €2). Alongside the gardens (behind the civilian cemetery) is a World War I **cemetery,** holding some fifty neatly tended graves.

The **train** and **bus** stations are situated just 200m apart on Kolodvorska ulica; inside the bus station building the small and helpful **tourist office** (Mon–Fri 8am–4pm; ☎05/731-0128, ⓔtic.sezana@siol.net) can advise on private **accommodation** and other aspects of visits to Lipica or the Škocjan caves. Conveniently situated between the two stations is the bright and clean *Hotel Tabor*, at Kolodvorska 4 (☎05/734-1551; ⓔhotel.tabor@siol.net; ❺). You can **eat** well at the *Carvallino* pizzeria and spaghetteria, Partizanska ulica 25.

DIVAČA, 6km east of Lipica, is a less-enticing option but there is a worthwhile diversion here, as well as a couple of cheap accommodation possibilities. In the centre of town, at Kraška cesta 26, the **Škrateljnova House** (Škrateljnova domačija; Sat 10am–noon & 3-5pm, Sun 10am–1pm; €1) houses a small exhibition on Slovenia's first major female film star, **Ita Rina** (1907-1979), but is actually far more interesting from an architectural point of view; a marvellous example of vernacular architecture, this seventeenth-century homestead claims to be one of the oldest houses in the Karst region. On the first weekend of July a selection of old Slovene films are staged in the back yard.

Both the **train** station (with a handful of left-luggage lockers) and the main **bus** stop are on Trg 15 Aprila from where it's a five-minute walk up the road to the grim and gloomy *Pension Risnik* (℡05/763-0008; ❷) located opposite the petrol station; a far better option is the bright and clean *Malovec*, 200m north of the *Risnik* along Kraška cesta at no. 30a (℡05/763-1225; ❸). The *Orient Express*, just across the road from the *Malovec* at Kraška 67, is a lively and colourful **restaurant/bar**, serving up salads, grills and meat platters alongside a great selection of light and dark beers brewed on site. If you are planning to visit the Škocjan Caves from Divača, and don't fancy walking, an alternative is to hire **bikes** (April–Oct €2 for 1hr, €10 for the day, €22 for the weekend) at the train station.

Lipica

After Postojna and Lake Bled, Slovenia's most emblematic tourist draw is **Lipica** (ⓦ www.lipica.org), birthplace of the famous white Lipizzaner horse. Located 6km south of Sežana and just 2km from the Italian border, the Lipica estates were acquired by the Austrian Archduke Karl (son of Emperor Ferdinand I) in 1580. He established the stud in order to breed horses for the Spanish Riding School in Vienna, as well as the Royal Court stables in Graz. That the Lipizzaner has survived at all is remarkable; the breed was evacuated to southern Hungary during Napoleon's occupation in the late eighteenth century, divided by the Italians and Austrians during World War I and seized by the Germans during World War II. Today the horse is bred at half a dozen European stud farms and widely throughout the United States. Here at Lipica there are around four hundred horses divided between show, competition and riding horses, and some three hundred more around Slovenia in private hands – thus it is estimated that Slovenia is home to around one-fifth of the world's Lipizzaner.

A tour of the **stud farm**, which entails little more than a visit to the stables and riding halls, is not in itself that enthralling, though you do get the opportunity to see these magnificent creatures close up. **Tours** take place throughout the year (daily: Jan–March & Nov–Dec 11am, 1pm, 2pm and 3pm; April–June & Sept–Oct hourly 10am-5pm (except noon), plus extra shows at 9am & 6pm on Sat & Sun; July & Aug hourly 9am–6pm, except noon; €8). To really make your visit worthwhile, try and coordinate it with a presentation of the **Classical Riding School** (April–Oct Tues, Wed, Fri & Sun at 3pm; €14); whilst nothing as grand as the shows put on at the Spanish Riding School in Vienna, it's still quite something to see, the riders all tof-

The Lipizzaner

Despite competing claims from Austria and Italy over the geographical origin and lineage of the **Lipizzaner** (Lipicanec), the original stud was established at Lipica in 1580 by the then governor of the Slovene territories, Habsburg Archduke Karl. Horses of Spanish, Arabian and Berber stock were bred with the tough and muscular local Karst horse, thus creating the Lipizzaner strain. As a result of such fastidious breeding, Lipizzaner are comparatively small in stature – 14.3 to 15.2 hands – with a long back, short, thick neck, and a powerful build. Born dark or bay coloured they do not turn white until the age of five or six, though their coat is in fact grey, a colour that only manifests itself when the horse sweats. These distinctive physical traits are complemented by a beautiful sense of balance and rhythm, a lively, high-stepping gait and an even temperament. With such qualities, it's little wonder that the Lipizzaner have for centuries excelled at **carriage driving** and as **show horses** – performing the bows, pirouettes and other manoeuvres that delight dressage cognoscenti as well as the average punter.

fed up in period costume while the horses go about performing their well-crafted exercises.

The school offers a number of **riding** programmes (all 50min long), from rides out in a guided group (€16), to group or individual classes with an instructor (€22/€35), and dressage (€45). For real enthusiasts, there are a host of week-long riding courses. Reservations are required for all lessons. Between April and October it's also possible to go **carriage-riding** (daily 3.30pm and 4.30pm; €40 per carriage for 1hr, maximum 4 people).

Practicalities

If you don't have your own **transport**, getting here will be difficult; the only buses which head this way are the school ones, during term-time only (Mon–Fri at 11.45am, 12.25pm, 1.30pm and 3.50pm, with return buses at 8.30am and 2.50pm) – otherwise you'll have to hitch or take a taxi (€6), which can be booked through the tourist office in Sežana (see p.190).

Neither of the two **hotels** located within the complex, the spacious and comfortable *Maestoso* (☎05/739-1580, ✉info@lipica.org; ❼), or the downbeat and shabby *Klub* (same number and email; ❻), are likely to appeal, or are particularly good value for money – and in any case they're more interested in catering to groups. If you do plan to stick around the area, you're best off staying in Sežana or Divača (see opposite). Within the Lipica estate there are several sporting and leisure amenities available, including a casino, tennis (€6 per hour; free to hotel guests), and a nine-hole golf course, Slovenia's only year-round course (☎05/734-6373; €22 for nine holes/€30 for eighteen).

Vilenica Cave and Lokev

Two kilometres east of Lipica is the **Vilenica Cave** (Jama Vilenica), a relative minnow in comparison to Slovenia's better known and more glamorous show-caves, but certainly no less attractive for it. Reputedly the first cave in the country open to the public, way back in 1633, it wasn't until 1963, when the local caving club took it upon themselves to clean up the galleries and install electric lighting, that tourism really made its mark here. The walk of some four hundred metres takes in numerous galleries, home to a wondrous array of weird and fantastically shaped stalagmites and stalactites, many stained a rich rust-red colour owing to the surrounding Karst soil. Tours (€6), which last one hour, take place on Sundays throughout the year (May–Oct 10am, 3pm, and 5pm; Sept–April 3pm). Each year, the largest hall in the system, the Dance Hall, hosts the **Vilenica Festival**, a prestigious international literary gathering each September.

Just two kilometres on from Vilenica in the village of **LOKEV**, there's yet more delightful Karst architecture on view; the most outstanding building here is the **Tabor Tower**, a cylindrical stone edifice built in 1485 by the Venetians as a defence against the Turks and which later served as the town granary. Its three floors now accommodate a **private war museum** (Bojaški muzej; Wed–Sun 9am–noon & 2–6pm; €3), with memorabilia from both World Wars. Crammed into every conceivable space, there's a wealth of stuff on display, including the uniform of the commander of the Austrian forces on the Soča Front, Svetozar Borojevič (the Soča Lion), and stacks more accoutrements from the various warring sides; there's a fine display of photos too, including one of Mussolini during his visit to the Postojna Caves in 1938.

Škocjan Regional Park

Located 5km south of Divača in the belly of the **Škocjan Regional Park**, the **Škocjan Caves** are the country's most memorable natural attraction, a breathtaking complex of passages, chambers, collapsed valleys and, reputedly, the world's largest subterranean canyon. Measuring around 5800m in length, the caves were formed by the **Reka River** (River River), which begins its journey from springs deep below Snežnik mountain 50km southeast of the cave near the Croatian border. At the village of Škocjan, not far from the cave entrance, the river sinks underground for the first time, briefly reappearing at the bottom of two collapsed dolines, before vanishing again into the mouth of the cave. It re-emerges some 40km later at the Timavo springs north of Trieste. The park also embraces three tiny villages, **Škocjan**, **Betanja** and **Matavun**, the last of which is where the cave reception is located.

Little was known about the caves until the sixteenth century, when the first maps of the system were printed. After that, more thoroughgoing accounts were offered in several seminal seventeenth- and eighteenth-century works, most notably Valvasor's *Glory of the Duchy of Carniola* and Gruber's *Hydrological Letters from the Carniola*.

Although parts of the cave had already been discovered, and several paths cut, during the early nineteenth century, it wasn't until around 1840 that the first systematic explorations of the main cave took place, when Giovanni Svetina from Trieste managed to penetrate some 150m downstream. Other pioneering explorers followed, but the most important explorations were left to **Anton Hanke**, a Czech mining engineer, and two colleagues who, between 1884 and 1890, progressed to the fourteenth waterfall along what is now known as the Hanke Canal – in the process stumbling upon several more chambers. A few years later four locals entered the cave proper for the first time. Electricity was installed in 1959 and the caves were given UNESCO World Heritage status in 1986.

The Caves

After purchasing your ticket from the booth in the reception area (tours daily: June–Sept hourly 10am–5pm; April, May & Oct 10am, 1pm and 3.30pm; Jan–March & Nov–Dec 10am & 1pm; €12, tours last approx 1hr 30min; Ⓦ www. park-skocjanske-jame.si), join the crowd milling around by the tables and wait for the guides to appear. From here, you'll be escorted to the cave entrance down in the **Globočak Valley** (Dolina Globočak), some ten minutes' walk away. Heading along the one hundred and thirty-metre-long, artificially created tunnel, you enter the cave proper, the first part of which is called the **Silent Cave** (Tiha jama); at this point, you'll break off into different groups, depending on which language you speak.

Discovered around 1904, and totalling some 500m, the Silent Cave comprises several smaller chambers, each modestly decorated with stalagmites and stalactites, though neither the first, the **Paradise Cave**, nor the second, the **Calvary**, is particularly well endowed, having been subjected to earthquakes and floods aeons ago. More impressive is the one hundred and thirty-metre-long and thirty-metre-high **Great Hall** (Velika dvorana), whose most celebrated formations are the 250,000-year-old Giant stalagmite, and a ribbed dripstone stalactite dubbed the Organ, because of its resemblance to a pipe organ and the sounds it emits when tapped.

Beyond here the cave widens, the temperature drops and the low rumbling of the **Reka River** can be heard; this marks your entry into the magnificent **Murmuring Cave** (Šumeča jama), a three hundred-metre-long, sixty-metre-wide and

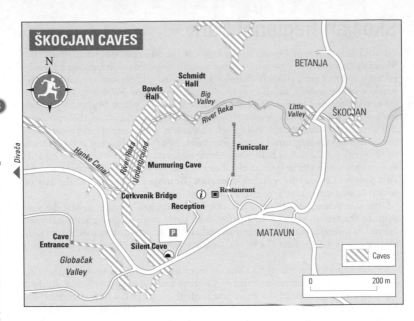

one hundred-metre-high subterranean gorge carved out by the Reka – it is, quite simply, the most fantastic creation imaginable. From here you walk along a narrow ledge incised into the great shafts of limestone rock, towards the vertiginous forty-five-metre-high **Cerkvenik Bridge** (Cerkvenikov most), under which the Reka flows before continuing its course along the **Hanke Canal** towards further, larger chambers (accessible only to speleologists). The bridge was rebuilt in 2003, replacing the original Hanke Bridge – dating from 1933 – which itself replaced the **Cat's Footbridge**, the remains of which can be detected 20m higher, just below the ceiling.

From the bridge, the path continues upstream along the side of the gorge for several hundred metres, through the **Bowls Hall** – so-named because of its circular limestone troughs – and towards the **Schmidt Hall** (Schmidlova dvorana), the yawning, natural cave entrance which emerges into the collapsed **Velika Dolina** (Big Valley); from here it's a short walk to the funicular, which transports you the 150m back to the top.

The Park

If you've still got time, you might want to trek the **Educational Trail**, a scenic two-kilometre-long footpath, which more or less circles the two collapsed valleys, **Velika Dolina** (Big Valley) and **Mala Dolina** (Little Valley); you can pick up a leaflet from the reception area, from where the trail begins and ends. Alternatively, you could just do part of the walk taking you as far as the tiny Karst hamlet of **Škocjan**, a ten-minute walk from the reception area, where two renovated stone barns house a modest collection of implements and artefacts pertaining to the park's archeological and ethnological heritage (daily June–Oct 11am–5pm, at other times enquire at the information booth; €1.5, free if visiting the cave). The most interesting items are the maps and sketches illustrating the discovery of the cave, one of which was drawn by Valvasor, and an old ladder used for lowering cavers down into the depths. The 1:6000 *Regijski park Škocjanske jame* map outlines further walks in the park.

Practicalities

Without your own **transport**, getting to the caves will entail a fair bit of walking: the nearest train station is in Divača, some 5km to the northwest by road (see p.190), but 3km (1hr) if walking from the station – you can, though, hire **bikes** from here (see p.191); the caves are signposted from the station. If travelling by bus, you may be able to get the driver to set you down by the access road (just off the Ljubljana–Koper highway), from where it's a more manageable 1.5km to the caves.

Next to the ticket booth is a café-cum-**restaurant**, where you can get drinks and simple meals (daily 9am–8pm).

Hrastovlje

Thirty-one kilometres south of Divača, in the upper Rižana River Valley – which roughly separates the Karst plateau from the coastal hinterland – **HRASTOVLJE** would be just another pretty, yet inconsequential, Istrian village, were it not for the Romanesque **Church of the Holy Trinity** (Sveta Trojica), whose exceptional spread of late-medieval frescoes mark it out as a cultural monument of the highest rank.

The Church

Sited on an exposed, shallow rise, and concealed within a thick, ten-metre-high, grey-stone wall, the **Church of the Holy Trinity** was built sometime between the twelfth and fourteenth centuries, although the wall was a sixteenth-century addition, erected to provide a place of refuge for the locals against marauding

△ Dance of Death fresco, Hrastovlje

The Dance of Death

The **Dance of Death** is not unique to Hrastovlje and can be found in many countries throughout Europe, from England to Estonia, although the only other one in Istria is in the village of Beram, in Croatia. Thought to have derived from a thirteenth-century literary genre called Vado Mori ("I prepare myself to die"), the artistic genre of the Dance of Death originated as **La Danse Macabre** at the Cemetery of the Innocents in Paris around 1424. More often than not painted (or carved) on the outside walls of cloisters and ossuaries, or church interiors, the composition of the dance, and the number of characters involved, varied from place to place.

In this one in Hrastovlje, a cast of eleven characters – which include the pope, a king and queen, bishop, burgher, cripple, and a child – are escorted by skeletons towards the narrator (the twelfth skeleton), who sits on a stone throne, waiting with shovel and pick at his feet, and hand poised on the coffin lid. There's some wonderful detail to admire, such as the painting of the usurer who – deciding it's not his time to go – tries to bribe the skeleton by offering a purse, seemingly impervious to the idea that not even the rich can circumvent a fate that awaits us all.

Turks. Constructed from stone-cut square blocks, with a typical Istrian stone-slab roof, this beautifully compact church is even smaller than you might have imagined from outside the wall. The inside, comprising a simple tripartite nave, is completely unfurnished.

Taking almost ten years to complete, the **frescoes** were executed by the master Istrian painter Johannes de Castua (Janez Kastav) at the end of the fifteenth century, although they weren't discovered until the 1950s, concealed under several layers of whitewash. Far and away the most celebrated and complete painting is the *Dance of Death*, or *Dance Macabre* (see box above), on the lower half of the south wall; with its powerful images alluding to the inevitability of death, this fresco pretty much surpasses any other specimen of medieval iconography in Slovenia. Cast your eye downwards and you'll see some decorative **Glagolitic inscriptions**, an ancient Slav script which originated in the ninth century as a means of converting Slavs to Christianity.

The remaining frescoes depicting numerous biblical scenes take some digesting, so it's worth focusing your attention on a select few: represented in fifteen scenes immediately above the *Dance of Death* is the cycle of Christ's Passion, while, on the opposite, north wall, the Three Kings come bearing gifts for Mary, who is seated upon a gold throne with Infant Child. On the ceilings of the north and south aisles, the calendar year is represented by scenes (note there are fourteen) of seasonal activities – hunting, harvesting and so on – and local customs, and is unique in that it is believed to be the only case of a secular cycle in a Slovene Gothic church. The apses are decorated with portraits of the Apostles, and scenes from the Crucifixion and the crowning of Mary.

To help you negotiate your way around this tangle of paintings, there's a taped commentary available in English. In theory, the church does have set opening hours (daily 8am–noon & 1–5pm; €2), but you'd do well to phone ahead first just in case; the key holder, Rihter Rozana, can be contacted on ☏031/432-231.

Practicalities

Getting to Hrastovlje is not easy. The closest that **buses** get is 6km north, in the village of **Črni Val** just off the main highway to Koper. The alternative is **train**, though, rather hopelessly, there's just one train stopping here each day; the 5.55am from Ljubljana (7.47am from Divača), arriving in Hrastovlje at 8.20am, with the one return train to Divača/Ljubljana departing from Hrastovlje at 7.28pm (7.12pm from Koper). The station is actually located in the village of **Dol**, 1.5km southeast of Hrastovlje; exiting the station, take a left down the path towards the main road, from where it's around a twenty-minute walk to the church. A return trip by **taxi** from Koper will cost around €30.

The Istrian Coast

Sandwiched between the Gulf of Trieste and the Croatian coast, the Slovenian seaboard packs a surprisingly large amount into its short 46km stretch, harbouring a rich complement of historical sights amongst the more traditional beach-related pursuits. Whilst its proximity to Italy ensures that it receives a healthy number of vacationing Italians, this also means that certain places can get a little mobbed at the height of summer. By way of contrast it's largely avoided by Slovenes, most of whom prefer to holiday along Croatia's Dalmatian coast. That said, in places, it possesses an abundance of charm, not least in **Piran**, a protected cultural monument and the coast's most seductive spot. **Koper**, too, possesses a fabulously appealing old town, much at odds with its prevailingly industrial backdrop; edging down the coast, the pretty little fishing town of **Izola** is worth a minor diversion, while **Portorož** – the coast's main beach resort, just a stone's throw from Piran – will appeal to those seeking more hedonistic fare. More generally, the beaches along the coast, such as they are, are invariably rocky or concrete affairs, though you might find the odd sandy spot if you're lucky.

The basis for much of the coast's fabulous cultural legacy is overwhelmingly Italian – indeed, its handful of towns wouldn't look out of place on the other side of the Adriatic – thanks to nearly 500 years of **Venetian rule** that preceded the region's incorporation into the Austro-Hungarian Empire, and, eventually, the Yugoslav Federation.

This northern part of Istria didn't actually become a part of Yugoslavia until the **1954 London Agreement**, which finally resolved the problem of post-World War II territorial boundaries between Italy and Yugoslavia. Until then, this bitterly disputed area of the Adriatic had been divided into two zones, known as the Free Territory of Trieste – Zone A (which included Trieste), and Zone B (which included Koper); the agreement subsequently assigned Zone A to Italy and Zone B to Yugoslavia. However, neither side was entirely appeased, as both lost what they considered to be historic pieces of territory, a fact recognized by the Italians who refused to ratify the agreement, at least until the 1975 Treaty of Osimo, which did little more than review and reaffirm the original agreement. Although many Italians resettled in their homeland following the 1954 Agreement, many towns have retained significant communities.

Getting around is simple enough, with buses and ferries shuttling up and down the coast, and, if you're looking to push on to Trieste or the Croatian Istrian towns, there are frequent bus connections.

Koper

Easily reached by train from Ljubljana, and just 20km from Trieste, **KOPER** (Capodistria in Italian) is the first major stop along the coast. At first glance it's an unenticing spectacle, little more than a messy jumble of cranes, tower blocks and wasteland. However, within this gritty outer shell lies a beautifully preserved medieval core, embracing an attractive lattice of paved alleys, Italianate squares and a stack of fine cultural monuments.

Believed to have originated as Aegida in around 3 BC, the town – at that time an island – acquired several identities before the Venetians assumed control in the late thirteenth century. Thanks to its maritime industries, the town's economy remained in rude health until the beginning of the eighteenth century, when both Trieste and Rijeka (in Croatia) were proclaimed free ports and an already bleak situation was further compounded by the opening of the Vienna–Trieste rail line in 1857. Following the 1954 London Agreement, the town experienced a surge of development, with the advancement of a new port and an extension of the rail line to Koper, thus reaffirming the town's status as the coast's most important economic and political centre. Today, not only is it Slovenia's largest coastal town and chief maritime port, but it also services the shipping needs of Austria and Hungary.

Arrival and information

The **train** and **bus** stations are located next to each other in a wasteland 1.5km southeast of town, from where it's a dull walk along Kolodvorska Cesta to the centre; alternatively, regular buses shuttle passengers into town, and then onwards to Izola, Portorož and Piran. The **tourist office** is located inside the Praetorian Palace on Titov trg (June–Sept Mon–Sat 8am–8pm, Sun 10am–8pm; Oct–May daily 9am–5pm; ☎05/664-6403, 🌐www.koper-tourism.si). The **post office** is in the old town on Muzejski trg (Mon–Fri 8am–7pm, Sat 8am–noon), and there's **Internet access** at the *Pina Bar*, Kidričeva ulica 43 (Mon–Sat 9am–11pm, Sun 5–11pm).

Accommodation

The Kompas agency, at Pristaniška ulica 17 (Mon–Fri 8am–7pm, Sat 8am–1pm; ☎05/663-0582, 📧kompas.koper@siol.net), has a good stock of **private accommodation**, including rooms (❶) and apartments (❸–❺) – note that there is a surcharge for stays of less than three nights with any private accommodation. There are no **campsites** in Koper, though there are several elsewhere along the coast; these are detailed in the relevant sections.

Those on a budget should head to the student **hostel** *Dijaški Dom Koper* at Cankarjeva 5 (☎05/662-6250, 📧ddkoper-recepcija@guest.arnes.si; ❶), located 100m east of the cathedral; it has one-, two- and three-bed rooms (all with shared wash and shower facilities) available during July and August, and a handful at weekends during the rest of the year. The town has rather limited **hotel** possibilities; the most central is the *Hotel Koper* at Pristaniška 3 (☎05/610-0500, 📧info@terme-catez.si; ❹), a stylish place with big, airy rooms, frequented in the main by busloads of package tourists; part of the same hotel group is the *Žusterna*, located out on the road to Portorož at Istrska 67 (☎05/663-8000, 📧zusterna@terme-catez.si; ❼) – this colourful, frenetic place has cool, air-conditioned rooms, some of which have a balcony, while all guests receive free use of the seven pools in the adjoining Aquapark (as do those staying at the *Hotel Koper*). Buses stop by the swimming pool opposite. The *Vodišek*, located in a barren spot midway between the stations and the town centre at Kolodvorska 2 (☎05/639-2468, 🌐www.hotel-vodisek.com; ❼), has neat and functional rooms, all with air-conditioning.

Carpaccio trg and Kidričeva ulica

As good a place as any to start your exploration of the old town is **Carpaccio trg**, just behind the old **salt warehouse**. In the centre of this peaceful little square, named after the Venetian painter, is the spindly **Column of St Justin**, erected to commemorate the famous naval victory against the Turks at Lepanto in 1571, in which a Koper galley participated. From here, Kidričeva ulica inclines gently eastwards past the redundant churches of **St Nicholas** (1594) and the **Holy Trinity** (1735). A little further up on the right is a splendid **Venetian-Gothic townhouse** – one of several such buildings in town – sporting a protruding upper floor and check-painted facade. Opposite here is the **Totto Palace**, whose facade bears a relief of a lion with an open book; traditionally, this was meant to symbolize peace, as opposed to a closed book which symbolized war; similar reliefs adorn many other prominent buildings along the coast.

A few paces along at no. 19 is the fine, sixteenth-century Mannerist-Baroque **Belgramoni-Tacco Palace**, whose interior is palpably more interesting than the **Regional Museum** housed within (Pokrajinski Muzej; Tues–Fri 10am–6pm, Sat 9am–1pm; €2). This insipid collection of art and cultural history merits only the briefest of visits, though it's partially redeemed by a decent archeological collection, the highlight of which is a collection of animal reliefs, and a copy of the *Dance of Death* fresco from Hrastovlje (see p.195). Housed in the pavilion next to the lapidarium, containing sculptures of Apostles and prophets, is a marginally more interesting exhibition of contemporary history, which pertains to Slovene Istria's role before, during and after the two World Wars. The most illuminating aspect of this exhibition, however, is Tone Kralj's gruesome painting, *Rapallo*, in which a woman is savaged by hideous-looking creatures.

Titov trg and around

Continuing eastwards, Kidričeva ulica opens up into **Titov trg** (Tito Square), laid out in the fifteenth century and once the fulcrum of the old city. The square's stunning synthesis of Gothic, Renaissance and Baroque styles is superbly encapsulated in the **Praetorian Palace** (Pretorska palača), Koper's most enduring symbol, whose battlements look like a stage backdrop for a Renaissance drama. Equally as impressive is its facade, randomly plastered with reliefs and busts – the most striking of which is the black bust of Nicola Donato, praetor of Koper between 1579 and 1580. Although there was a building here in the thirteenth century (which was subsequently destroyed), the foundations for the current palace were laid down in the fifteenth century, when the Gothic left wing and the Renaissance right wing were constructed; its Baroque elements were added during further seventeenth-century renovations. Following the 1797 downfall of the Venetian Republic, whose governors had used the palace as their main headquarters, the palace fell into a state of long-term decline; first the Austrians moved into the adjacent **Armoury building** (previously an arms dump, but which has recently been restored to accommodate part of the new University of Primorska), then successive town authorities snubbed it in favour of alternative buildings. Its handsomely restored interior is now used almost exclusively for council and mayoral functions as well as weddings; free guided tours are possible, though really there's not a whole lot to see.

Opposite the palace, the fifteenth-century **Loggia** (Loža), with its striking Gothic-style lancet arches, has been the town's most popular meeting place ever since philosophers and artists gathered here for chinwags in the seventeenth century – its first coffee house, *Caffe della Loggia*, established in 1846, is now the *Loggia*, which remains the most swish **café** in town; the statue of the Madonna in the corner pillar was placed there to commemorate the 1554 plague. The Loggia's upper floor houses a **gallery**, which holds different exhibitions each month (Galerija Loža; Tues–Sat 11–5pm, Sun 11–1pm; €1.5).

The **Cathedral of the Assumption** (Stolnica Marija vnebovzetja; 7am–noon & 3–7pm) on the east side of the square is believed to be the fifth or sixth church on this site, though much of this present one has eighteenth-century origins. Its exterior is an odd amalgam of Gothic lower storey and Lombardy-style upper storey, the latter part completed a century later than the lower part. By way of contrast, its vast interior, endowed with some glorious works of art and furnishings, is mostly of Baroque appearance; particularly worth paying attention to is the central nave's magnificent Rococo pulpit, designed by Lorenzo Ferolli in 1758, and, in the presbytery, the finely carved olive-wood choir pews and the gold-plate-encrusted bishop's throne, dating from 1730. The major works of art were completed by Vittore Carpaccio, the most outstanding of which is *The*

Enthroned Madonna with Child and Saints from 1516. Pressed into the cathedral's south side is the formidable **city bell tower** (daily 10am–1pm & 3–5pm; €3), a fifteenth-century structure which once doubled as a lookout; climb the 43m to the top and you'll understand why – the views of the town, coast and hinterland are tremendous. Situated on the cathedral's north side is one of the coast's oldest sacral monuments, the twelfth-century Romanesque **Rotunda of John the Baptist**.

Trg Brolo, a leafy, triangular square just east of the cathedral, showcases some terrific Venetian-Baroque architecture, the most eye-catching of which is the **Brutti Palace** on the north side, whose facade is attractively ornamented with relief images from the Old Testament – the building now functions as the town library. On the east side of the square at no. 4 is the several-times rebuilt **Fontico**, a former grain warehouse studded with rich heraldic decoration completed by Lombardian stonemasons. Tucked in just behind the Fontico is the crumbling, fourteenth-century Gothic Church of St Jacob (Cerkev Sv Jakob), which cannot be entered.

South and east of Titov trg

Back on Titov trg, pass through the portico under the Praetorian's Palace and take a stroll down Čevljarska ulica (Shoemaker's Street), which took its name from the profession which was practised here for several centuries. Probably the single prettiest street in the town, Čevljarska ulica preserves a happy ensemble of two- and three-storey shuttered buildings, variously housing tenements, shops and galleries. At the end of the street cross Župančičeva ulica, and continue down the steps passing the pink-chequered façade of the Almerigogna Palace into Gortanov trg. This square segues into Staničev trg, which in turn brings you out to the main road ringing the old town, a rather sobering return to the twenty-first century.

By taking a left turn at the junction of Čevljarska ulica and Župančičeva ulica, you'll wind up at Prešernov trg (Prešeren Square), a pleasant, elongated space, in the centre of which stands Ponte's Fountain; built in 1666, the fountain is furnished with a small, Plečnik-style bridge – *"ponte"* is Italian for bridge – and, at the bottom, four masks from whence water spouted until 1898. South of the fountain is the triumphal arch-style Muda Gate (Vrata Muda), built in 1516 and the last of the city's twelve town gates; note, on the inner arches, two reliefs of a blazing sun with the shape of a face, which is the city coat-of-arms.

Housed in another exceptional Venetian-Gothic house east of town at Gramšijev trg 4, is the **Ethnological Museum** (Etnološki Muzej; March–Oct; Tues–Fri 10am–6pm, Sat 9am–1pm; €2), one of the most enjoyable museums on the coast, though it's sadly little visited due to its rather isolated location. For the most part, the collection focuses on the Istrian cultural landscape, with particular emphasis on the art of stonecutting and stonedressing, industries which first took wing in the region during the seventeenth century. The pick of the museum's collection is its assemblage of skilfully hewn stone-cut **portals**, commonly found at entrances to courtyards and houses; many portals were traditionally ornamented with floral patterns, sacral symbols and other motifs and reliefs, though few have been preserved. More superb stonemasonry can be seen in a partial reconstruction of a **shepherd's hut**, typically used to store farming tools and arable crops but also useful as a form of shelter during extremes in temperature; and a portion of a **dry-stone wall**, a prevalent feature of the Istrian landscape. To round off this engaging collection, there is a presentation of a Koper **kitchen**, at the centre of which is a hearth, surrounded by some exquisite copper, glass and china food-preparation items garnered from the Veneto and Friuli regions, and which date from the nineteenth and twentieth centuries.

Eating and drinking

Disappointingly, Koper has a meagre selection of **restaurants**; the best is *La Storia*, a friendly trattoria-style place adjoining the *Hotel Koper* – the large covered terrace is a congenial place from which to take your pick from a generous and inexpensive menu featuring pasta, risotto, gnocchi and fish. Another convivial place is *Slovenski Hram*, located a short walk northeast of Prešernov trg at Ulica Talcev 8, which serves up salads, pasta, meat and fish, as well as a very strong veggie menu (Mon–Sat noon–10pm). More basic, but no less enjoyable, is *Istrska Klet* at Županičičeva ulica 39, which has filling domestic fare and wines straight from the barrel (Sun–Fri 7am–9pm). Far more straightforward and clinical is the fish restaurant, *Skipper*, located 100m north along the road running behind the beach at Kopališko Nabrežje 3, though it does have some fine views overlooking the water. Otherwise, you can pick up goods from the lively **market** by the shopping centre (Tržnica) on Pristaniška, which also has a couple of very tempting ice-cream parlours.

Similarly, **drinking** venues are thin on the ground. The grooviest spot around is *Pub Carpaccio* (daily 5pm–1am), on the square of the same name, an English-style place with split-level flooring and a good selection of beers. Both its setting, on Titov trg, and its choice of drinks, mark the *Loggia Café* out as the place to indulge in coffee (see p.200). Otherwise, there are plenty of run-of-the-mill cafés along Pristaniška ulica and on the north side of the shopping centre across the road.

Festivals and Activities

The **Primorsko Summer Festival**, throughout July and August, is a series of open-air theatrical performances (and occasionally dance and music) taking place in several towns along the coast, but principally here and in Izola and Portorož. Some of the more unusual venues include a catamaran, a disused railway tunnel and the Sečovlje saltpans (see p.212). Otherwise, the main summer event is **Koper Nights** on the last weekend of July, featuring theatrical and musical performances and an epic fireworks display.

The town's small, tidy beach is located between the pier and the Marina on Kopališko Nabrežje (daily 8am–8pm; €3), while further fun can be had at the Aquapark, located by the *Žusterna* (see p.199); it has a total of seven indoor and outdoor pools (daily 9am–9pm; weekdays €6 for 2hr, €11 all day; weekends €8 for 2hr, €15 all day).

Izola and around

Jutting out to sea on a rounded promontory 6km south of Koper, **IZOLA** is a busy little fishing town and one of the country's fastest-growing tourist destinations. Though most visitors come here for the beaches, Izola possesses an endearing old town core, whose narrow, sloping streets and pastel-coloured tenements delight in all their crumbling charm.

Numerous local ruins bear testament to the long-standing presence of the Romans hereabouts, not least in Simon's Bay, where the ancient port of Heliaetum was located – it's said that, at very low tide, parts of the ancient pier are still visible. First mentioned in historical sources in 972 AD as Insula, the town enjoyed a brief period of autonomy before becoming a satellite of Venice in 1280, which it remained until the Republic's downfall in 1797; around the same time, both the town wall and its two gates were pulled down, and the town (hitherto an island) was finally connected to the mainland. Thereafter, the town acquired the northern Adriatic's largest fishing fleet, as well as a number of fish canneries, the first of which opened in 1879. While tourism has since supplanted the industry as the main source of income, the town's fishing tradition remains alive and kicking.

One of the best events along the coast is the **Izola Film Festival** at the end of May, a five-day run of colourful and wide-ranging world films, some of which are screened in the open-air on Manzioli trg.

Arrival and information

The town's main **bus stop** is on Trg Republike, from where it's a 50m walk west to the small and helpful **tourist office** at Sončno nabrežje 4 (June–Sept Mon–Sat 9am–9pm, Sun 10am–5pm; Oct–May Mon–Fri 9am–7pm, Sat 9am–5pm; ℡05/640-1050). Between April and October, the *Prince of Venice* catamaran offers day-trips across to Venice and back, departing from the pier by the fishing port, opposite Veliki trg; tickets (the schedule changes monthly; around €70) can be purchased from the tourist office or from the Bele Skale agency (see below). Trg Republike is also where the **post office** is located (Mon–Fri 8am–7pm, Sat 8am–noon).

Accommodation

Several agencies can arrange **private accommodation**, the most convenient of which is Bele Skale (July–Aug Mon–Sat 7am–7pm, Sun 8am–noon; Sept–June Mon–Fri 7am–6pm, Sat 7am–noon; ℡05/640-3555, ⓦwww.beleskale.si), right next to the bus stop. The cheapest place to **stay** in town is the *Hotel Riviera* (℡05/641-7159; ❷), a somewhat misleading name for this large student dorm located on the waterfront, 200m south of the tourist office at Prekmorskih brigad 7; the rooms, available between June and August and at weekends during the rest of the year, come with or without shower facilities. The *Hotel Marina* in the centre of town on Veliki trg (℡06/660-4100, ⓔmarina@belvedere.si; ❼), is a considerable step up in class, with variously sized air-conditioned rooms, some of which have large balconies with sea views. Located amidst a pine grove atop a bluff 2.5km west of town is the *Belvedere Hotel* (℡05/660-5100, ⓦwww.belvedere.si), which has good-looking rooms (❼) and apartments (❻–❽) housed within several brightly coloured villas. There is also a **campsite** (April–Oct) within the grounds; buses doing the Koper–Portorož route stop outside the entrance. These same buses also stop outside Izola's other campsite, the *Jadranka*, which is wedged between the noisy main road and its own bit of beach 1km east of town (℡05/640-2300; April–Oct).

The Town

Everything of interest in Izola is located within the confines of the old town. From **Trg Republike** head north to Kristinov trg, past the small market, and then left up Smrekarjeva ulica for about 100m before taking a right turn down Alme Vivode. Just before the church, a passageway leads to the **Railway Museum** (Muzej Parenzana; Tues–Sun 10am–5pm; €3), which contains a staggering assortment of model trains assembled from all over the world. Its chief exhibit, however, is a model replica of the Parenzana Line, once the most important transport link between Central Europe and Istria; built in 1902 by the Austrians, the line ran between Trieste and Poreč (in Croatia), passing through Koper, Izola and Portorož along the way, until 1937 when Mussolini pulled the plug and closed it. The locomotive that used to chug up and down the line is stationed at the town's eastern entrance by the Jadranka campsite. Meanwhile, the line – passing through settlements, hills, vineyards and all the old tunnels – has recently been transformed into a **cycle** and **recreation track**; ask at the tourist office for more information.

From the church, take a left, and then another left, onto Gregorčičeva ulica; after about 300m you come to the town's most important architectural set piece, the **Besenghi degli Ughi Palace**, distinguished by its pale blue, stucco-ornamented wrought-iron grilles. Its interior, too, is festooned with stuccowork, but is especially worth viewing for its first-floor salon, furnished with a fine wooden balcony and illusionist ceiling piece – the palace is now home to a music school. The street to the side of the building, Bruna ulica, slopes upwards to the much remodelled sixteenth-century **Church of St Maurus** (Cerkev Sv Mavricij), whose dark yet impressive clutch of paintings do little to lift the air of gloom; the mighty **bell tower**, visible from all over town, was built in 1585.

From the church, head down Garibadjeva, then Krpanova, which brings you to Veliki trg and the waterfront. From Veliki trg walk south past the **Municipal Palace**, whose Gothic frontage bears another relief of a lion with an open book, and round to Manzioli trg, a bright little square on which stands the **Church of St Mary** (Cerkev Sv Marija), whose oldest parts date from the ninth century. Directly opposite the church is the recently restored Venetian late-Gothic **Manzioli Palace**, which now houses the town's Italian centre. Walking down Koprska ulica and Ljubljanska ulica, two pleasant streets that curl southwards towards Trg Republike, you'll notice a disproportionate number of **artists' workshops and galleries**; these were set up a few years ago on the initiative of the town authorities, who decided to rent out these previously empty buildings for free in the hope of rejuvenating the area – evidently, this was a highly successful strategy.

Izola has a couple of good **beaches**, both of which are free: one of the best along the coast is at **Simon's Bay**, a blue flag beach 1.5km west of the centre. The rocky beach north of Veliki trg, which also has a grassy area, is less developed.

Eating and drinking

The most convivial **place to eat** is *Gušt*, just south of Trg Republike at Drevored 1 Maja, serving up over thirty varieties of pizza, steaming plates of pasta and spaghetti, soups and salads (open until 1am Fri & Sat) – it's also a good place to drink. Of those restaurants along the waterfront, the best is *Parangal* at Sončno nabrežje 20, a refined, beautifully decorated place, with a spot-on fish menu. Next door, the *Wall Pub* is the liveliest spot for a beer (open until midnight), while the *KT1* cybercafe, opposite the market on Kristinov trg, is a chilled-out place with **Internet access** (Mon–Sat 8am–midnight, Sun 3–11pm). Izola can also boast two of the coast's better **clubs**: *Gavioli* (Fri & Sat; entrance around €10-15) out in the industrial zone east of town, and the cheaper *Club Belvedere* (daily; entrance around €5) in the grounds of the *Hotel Belvedere*.

Strunjan

A few kilometres along the coast from Izola is **STRUNJAN**, a small, yet widely dispersed settlement, part of which has been turned into a **nature reserve**. All Koper–Piran buses stop just off the main road, from where it's a three-hundred-metre walk west towards the pleasant Strunjan **campsite** (☎05/678-2076). Five hundred metres further on, in a wonderfully secluded spot facing the bay, is the *Salinera* complex, which has **accommodation** in the form of a very comfortable hotel (◎) and some lovely, well furnished apartments, sleeping three to six people (◎–◎) – both are open between April and September (☎05/676-2502; ⓦwww.salinera.si); there's also a decent bathing area here (€4). Retracing your steps back to the abandoned saltpans, where the brackish water now supports a wide range of fauna, walk north along the narrow path to another, busier, beach (€3), to the west of which is **Giuseppe Tartini's Villa**, once the Tartini family home (see p.207) but now off-limits to visitors.

North of the large **Stjuža lagoon**, which backs onto the beach, a path trundles up to the top of the cliffs, passing the Church of St Mary and a small snack bar along the way. Unique along the Adriatic for its distinctive layers of Flysch sediment – composed of sandstone, marl and turbidite – the most prominent feature of this stretch of coastline is **Cape Ronek** (Rtič Ronek) at its northernmost point, which harbours what few sub-Mediterranean species exist in the region, such as myrtle and strawberry trees. Below, in the **Bay of St Cross** (Zaliv Sv Križa), the large bed of seaweed shelters fan-mussels, sea dates and crabs. From the cliff top several paths wind down to the rocky beaches below, popular with naturists.

Piran

Located on the tip of a long, tapering peninsula that projects like a lizard's tail into the Adriatic, **PIRAN** – the most Italianate of the coastal towns – is simply delightful. Having retained its compact medieval shape and character, the town is a tangle of arched alleys and tightly packed ranks of houses, fantastic Venetian-inspired architecture and exquisite little churches.

PIRAN

Punta Lighthouse
Punta Madona
St Clement's Church
Bathing Area
Cliff Wall
ADAMIČEVA ULICA
St George's Church & Museum
Belfry
Baptistry
PRESERNOVO
GREGORČIČEVA
A
TRG 1 MAJA
TRUBARJEVA ULICA
VERDIJEVA
Venetian House
St Mary of the Snows
2
NABREŽJE
Town Hall
1
i
3
Tartini's House
4
PARTIZANSKA
St Peter's Church
Duka Gallery
5
TARTINIJEV TRG
St Francis's Church
ST JENKOVA
D
ROZMANOVA ULICA
N
Aquarium
6
KIDRIČEVO NABREŽJE
C
Sergej Masera Maritime Museum
Gulf of Piran
Piran Port
CANKARJEVO NABREŽJE
ŽUPANČIČEVA ULICA
TOMŠIČEVA ULICA

RESTAURANTS, CAFÉS & BARS
Da Noi   2
Kavana Galerija   1
Mario's   4
Pizzeria Batana   5
Pri Mari   7
Stara Gostilna   3
Café Teater   6

ACCOMMODATION
Hotel Fiesa   B
Hotel Piran   C
Hotel Tartini   D
Hostel Val   A

0   150 m

Ferry Pier

Bus Station

DANTEJEVA ULICA

B & Campsite

Portorož & 7

Major urban development first occurred during the seventh century following the fall of the Roman Empire, when Piran became a heavily fortified "castrum". Under Venetian rule, which began here in 1283, the town's physical appearance changed considerably, as further town walls were erected to supplement the existing ones – which at that time encompassed the western Punta district at the end of the promontory. Economically too, the town was in good shape, thanks in no small measure to its three **saltworks** – in Sečovlje, Strunjan and Lucija, of which only the first is still operational. A prolonged period of decline ensued thereafter, first under the Habsburgs, and then, between the two World Wars, the Italians. However, the development of nearby Portorož as a popular health resort, and the construction of the Lucija–Piran rail line, last operational in 1956, led to an increase in visitors to the town. Whilst relations with Italy are today on a somewhat better footing, ongoing disputes with Croatia over fishing rights in the Bay of Piran are doing little to ameliorate an already fraught relationship between the two countries.

Arrival and information

The **bus station** is located on Dantejeva ulica, from where it's a pleasant 400m walk past the bustling little fishing harbour to Tartinjev trg, the main square. Located on the square's west side, by the town hall, is the **tourist office** (July & Aug 9am–1.30pm & 3–9pm; rest of year Mon–Fri 9am–4pm, Sat 10am–2pm; ℡05/673-0220, Ⓦwww.portoroz.si). The **post office** is located on Cankarjevo nabrežje (Mon–Fri 8am–7pm, Sat 8am–noon), and there is **Internet access** here on the third floor of the student centre at Župančičeva 14 (daily 1–9pm). **Bikes** can be rented from the *Da Noi* bar on Prešernovo nabrežje (€2.50 for 1hr, €18 for the day), particularly useful if you're thinking of heading to the saltpans in Sečovlje. There are a few companies around the harbour offering **boat trips** up and down the coast, such as the **Marconi**, which offers cruises down to Rovinj (around €25) and Brioni (around€50) in Croatia – your best bet, however, is to contact one of the agencies here (such as Maona) or in Portorož.

Accommodation

Piran can count on less than a handful of places to stay, which may force you to opt for **private accommodation**. If this is the case, head to Maona, midway between the bus station and the main square at Cankarjevo nabrežje 7 (daily: July & Aug Mon–Sat 9am–8pm, Sun 10am–noon & 5–8pm; April–June & Sept–Oct Mon–Fri 9am–5pm; ℡05/673-4520, Ⓦwww.maona.si). Alternatively, try Turist Biro opposite the *Hotel Piran* (June–Sept daily 9am–1pm & 4–8pm; Oct–May Mon–Fri 10am–1pm & 4–6pm; ℡05/673-2509, Ⓦwww.turistbiro-ag.si).

Budget travellers should make their way to the *Val* **hostel**, secreted away amongst an atmospheric warren of alleys at Gregorčičeva 38a (℡05/673-2555, Ⓦwww.hostel-val.com; ❷); it has spotless two- three- and four-bedded rooms with shared shower facilities, and there's also laundry and Internet access. The *Hotel Tartini* on Tartinjev trg (℡05/671-1000, Ⓦwww.hotel-tartini-piran.com; ❸) is one of the coast's most elegant **hotels**, featuring stylish and colourful air-conditioned rooms with ultramodern fittings, small TV and minibar; it's worth paying the minimal extra for a sea- or square-facing room. Across the square, the waterfront *Hotel Piran* at Stjenkova 1 (℡05/676-2100, Ⓦwww.hoteli-piran.si; ❼–❽) is another smart hotel, with polished, spacious rooms and bathrooms; if you can get one, try to bag a sea-facing room. The only other hotel hereabouts is the beachside *Hotel Fiesa*, 1km east of town in Fiesa (℡05/671-2200, Ⓦwww.hotel-fiesa.com; ❽); it's a comfortable place with good facilities, though it's not a quiet area with the beach below and a rather noisy games room next door; adjoining the hotel is the cramped Fiesa **campsite** (℡05/674-6230) – the quickest way to get here by foot is to follow the coastal path that runs east from the Church of St George.

The Town

Tartinjev trg

The town's most obvious point of reference is **Tartinjev trg** (Tartini Square), whose striking, marble-surfaced oval interior features a bronze statue of the acclaimed violinist Giuseppe Tartini (1692–1770), after whom the square is named. At its entrance, on the southeastern corner, are two fifteenth-century **stone flagpoles** bearing several Latin inscriptions and reliefs of St Mark with the lion symbol, and St George, the town patron.

The building on the square's west side is the old **court house**, adjacent to which is the **town hall**, dating from the late nineteenth century and distinguished by four graceful pillars, the lower parts of which are beautifully ornamented; in the central axis is the ubiquitous lion relief with an open book (see p.199). Continuing in a clockwise fashion, the stunning ruby-red Gothic **Venetian House** (Benečanke hiša) at no. 10 is the oldest preserved building on the square, a fifteenth-century edifice showcasing some outstanding stonemasonry, exemplified by its superb corner balcony. The relief under the windows on the second floor bears the inscription "Lassa pur dir" ("Let them talk"), a retort to gossiping townsfolk disapproving of a wealthy merchant's romantic liaisons with a local girl. About 50m further south, up the small flight of steps, is **Tartini's House** (Tartinijeva Hiša; daily: June–Aug 9am–noon & 6–9pm; Sept–May 11am–noon & 5–6pm; €2), where the musician was born in 1692. After being schooled in Koper, Tartini left Piran for Padua, in Italy, and remained there for the greater part of his life, composing, teaching and performing, before later devoting himself to theoretical and pedagogical issues. He is buried alongside his wife in Padua. One room of the birthplace has been converted into a small memorial room containing one of his four violins – the whereabouts of the other three are unknown – his death mask, and scores of books, diaries and letters.

Opposite Tartini's house is **St Peter's Church** (Cerkev Sv Petra), unremarkable save for the **Crucifix from Piran**, one of three such medieval masterpieces on the eastern Adriatic (the others are in Split, in Croatia, and Kotor, in Montenegro). This much-restored polychrome sculpture, a beautifully mournful Christ nailed to a tree-shaped cross, is believed to have been completed some time in the fourteenth century, though its creator is unknown. Unfortunately, owing to previous incidents of theft and vandalism, most of Piran's churches are closed, or can only be viewed through metal grilles. However, if you wish to visit any of them contact the tourist office.

West of Tartinjev trg

Heading west from Tartinjev trg through the dense lattice of arched alleys, you'll wind up at **Trg 1 Maja** (First of May Square), once the heart of the town but now a pleasantly scruffy space framed by peeling Baroque edifices. Located under the square's vast elevated deck and guarded by allegorical stone statues of law and justice is a stone rainwater cistern, built in 1776 following a drought in order to conserve water; at the rear, the two statues of babies – one holding a pot, the other a fish – once connected surrounding gutters with the cistern. Classical concerts are regularly held here during the summer.

Picking your way west through the maze of streets will eventually bring you out at the very tip of the peninsula and the **Punta lighthouse**, behind which is the sadly decrepit **Church of St Clement** (Cerkev Sv Zdravja), also known as the Church of Our Lady of Health on account of the role it played during the plague which swept across Istria in the seventeenth century; the interior can only be seen through the grilles or by attending mass. The lively promenade east of here is the location for the town's main (concrete) **bathing area** and a handful of places to eat and drink. It is also one of the coast's best **diving** areas – if you fancy a spot of diving, Sub-net, along the promenade at no. 24 (℡05/673-2218, Ⓦwww.sub-net.si), offers a comprehensive programme; expect to pay around €40 for a two-hour dive. En route back to the square take a look at the fine Gothic **Dolphin Gate** (Dolfinova vrata) in Savudrijska ulica, and, if you've time, pop into the **Duka Gallery**, close by at Partizanska 2 (Atelje Duka; Mon–Sat: June–Aug 9am–1pm & 6–10pm; Sept–May 9am–1pm & 4–7pm), which has a marvellous display of pottery and ceramic art; you can even see items being made, many of which are for sale.

Church of St George and around

Crowning a commanding spot on a steep rise to the north of town is the temple-like **Church of St George** (Cerkev Sv Jurija), originally built some time around the twelfth century, but whose present appearance dates from 1637. It's a classic example of a simple Baroque hall-church, lined with seven mighty altars, each laden with paintings by Venetian and Dutch artists; the second altar on the left also incorporates a large sculpture of St George slaying the dragon. Take a look too at the cream and gold church organ, a magnificent specimen designed in 1746 by the Venetian master organ builder Peter Nakič. The unusually long and deep presbytery, which can still be viewed during the period of closure, boasts the largest oil on canvas painting in the country, a colourful depiction of the martyrdom of St George (1844); by way of contrast, the other two paintings here, *Mass of Bolsensa* and *The Miracle of St George*, are rather dull.

Displayed within the small **church museum** (Župnijski Muzej; daily 11am–5pm; €1.5), which is actually more interesting than it sounds, is a glittering hoard of church treasures, including bejewelled chalices, reliquaries and staffs, though the most memorable piece is a marvellous silver-coated sculpture of St George and the dragon. One floor below are some well-preserved archeological remains from an eighth-century Roman temple and a section of the church as it was in the fourteenth century; look out for the protruding bones in the corner. The sacristy, held in the basement, is especially interesting for its superb pictures illustrating the restoration process of the Crucifix from Piran, now in St Peter's Church (see p.207), and a four hundred-year-old wooden model of St George's Church thought to be the oldest of its type in the country. Between the church and **Baptistry** – where a large Roman sarcophagus can be viewed – is the monumental **belfry** (same times as museum; €1), a fine-looking structure built in 1609 and modelled on the campanile in St Mark's Square, Venice. If you thought the views from the church terrace were impressive, then you'll be wowed by the sensational vista of the Adriatic from atop the 46-metre-high tower.

South of here, amongst the tightly knit web of streets are a cluster of beautiful little churches. At the corner of Istrska and Bolniška, the delightfully named **Church of St Mary of the Snows** (Cerkev Marija Snežna) features a marvellous Baroque altar and two broad canvases depicting the Annunciation and other scenes from the life of the Virgin Mary. Opposite here is the fourteenth-century, but much remodelled, **Church of St Francis**, whose impressive gallery of paintings would be even more valuable had the most important one – *Mary with all the Saints* by Vittore Carpaccio – not been taken to Italy in 1940. It's an issue that still rankles with Slovenes, many of whom insist that this and other valuable Renaissance works be returned to Slovenia (these are collectively known as "Istria's Jewels", some of which are currently on display in Rome); not surprisingly, the Italians have steadfastly resolved to keep them. The adjoining **Minorite Monastery** incorporates a bright atrium (*Križni Hodnik*, or

Passage of the Cross), entered via a lovely stone-carved portal; the acoustics in the atrium are splendid, so try and catch a concert here if you can.

From Korpusa ulica (back up by St George's Church), one path heads down towards a rocky beach and onwards to the small bay at **Fiesa** 1km away (look out for falling rock and debris from the cliff face, which strangely isn't protected), the other uphill towards Mogorn Hill – which is also accessible from Tartinijev trg via Rožmanova ulica. Ranged across the top of the hill is a two-hundred-metre stretch of the old **town walls**, completed between the late fifteenth and early sixteenth centuries and perforated with seven inspiring-looking towers; at the southern end of the wall stands the Gothic **Rašpor Gate** (Rašporska vrata). The walls, now connected by specially constructed walkways and stairs, offer the best photo opportunities in town.

South of Tartinjev trg

Housed in the battered old building to the west of the marina is the **aquarium** (Akvarij; mid-June to Aug daily 9am–10pm; April to mid-June & Sept 10am–noon & 2–7pm; €2.5), which accommodates a rather desperate assortment of marine life in its depressing tanks.

Occupying the splendid nineteenth-century **Gabrielli Palace**, on the opposite side of the marina, is the **Sergej Mašera Maritime Museum** (Pomorski Muzej Sergej Mašera; Tues–Sun: July & Aug 9am–noon & 6–9pm; Sept–June 9am–noon & 3–6pm; €2.5), named after the naval commander, whose destroyer, *Zagreb*, was blown up off the Croatian coast during World War II. The highlight of this eminently enjoyable collection, which charts Slovenia's seafaring exploits, is its outstanding ensemble of eighteenth-century model ships – originally built as teaching aids for future naval officers and nautical engineers – made in the Gruber workshop in Ljubljana; one model in particular to look out for is the Austrian warship, *Emperor Charles VI*. On the ground floor there is a fine, and cleverly presented, display of underwater archeological finds from the Slovene Istrian coast, consisting mainly of Roman amphorae, fragments of earthen vessels and lead tiles and hoops; there's also an informative ethnological saltworks collection, which will especially appeal if you're thinking of visiting the saltpans in Sečovlje (see p.212).

Eating and drinking

Most people are drawn to the row of uninspiring, rather samey and very expensive seafood **restaurants** lining the waterfront promenade west of the *Hotel Piran*. You're better off searching around the back streets, where there are much better value establishments, such as *Stara Gostilna*, 50m north of the *Hotel Piran* at Savudrijska 2 – this secluded place, with a pleasant little conservatory restaurant and pavement dining, has a rather limited menu, but the food is of a very high standard. *Pizzeria Batana*, housed in the old courthouse by the marina front, is a standard pizzeria but its agreeably tatty terrace is an enjoyable place to eat, while *Mario's*, across the square by Tartini's house, is a more traditional gostilna which does a good line in moderately priced meats and grills. Heading out of town, just beyond the bus station at Dantejeva ulica 17, is *Pri Mari*, another simple and cosy gostilna-style place offering lots of great pasta dishes, risottos and Mediterranean salads, in addition to the stock fish dishes.

The town's most popular **drinking** spot is *Café Teater*, next to the theatre by the waterfront; as lively a place as this can be – the views are excellent too – the beer is ridiculously expensive and the staff rather brusque. A far better bet is *Da Noi* on Prešernovo nabrežje, whose neat outdoor drinking terrace is complemented by a cool, indoor cellar-style bar (both of these open until 1am). For a decent cup of coffee in relaxing surrounds, head to *Kavana Galerija*, just off Tartinjev trg.

Portorož and around

Situated in its own sunny sheltered bay just 2km south of Piran, **PORTOROŽ** (Port of Roses) is Slovenia's major beach resort. While it may feel like stepping into a cold shower after Piran's charm, it's a likeable enough place, and despite possessing all the customary trappings of your average seaside resort, it's by no means a brash place; moreover, the beaches are clean, safe and well maintained, and there's enough going on here to keep activity-seekers happy.

The town's modern appearance belies a history dating back to the thirteenth century, when Benedictine monks from the nearby monastery of St Lawrence cured a range of diseases using the local mineral-rich brine and mud from the saltpans, the same health-inducing properties that led to the development of Portorož as a popular resort in the nineteenth century. The resort's first hotel – originally intended to accommodate the military – went up in 1830, followed by the once magnificent *Palace Hotel* in 1912, built in expectation of a visit by Emperor Franz Jozef. Whilst the town remains a popular health and treatment centre, most visitors to Portorož today come here for the more traditional **beach** diversions.

Arrival and information

From Piran it's a gentle thirty-minute **walk**, via the Bernadin complex, to Portorož. The main **bus stop** is located midway along Obala, the main coastal strip, though buses doing the loop between Piran and Koper stop at regular intervals along here. The **tourist office** is housed in the large building across the road from the bus stop at Obala 16 (July & Aug 9am–1.30pm & 3–9pm; Sept–June 10am–5pm; ☎05/674-2220, ⓦwww.portoroz.si). The **post office** is at K Stari cesta 1, just down from the *Hoteli Palace* (Mon–Fri 8am–7pm, Sat 8am–noon), and there is **Internet access** at the *Heineken Pub*, Obala 14. The beaches aside, everything of interest is located along Obala. **Bikes** can be rented from the Istriana agency (see below).

Accommodation

As befits Slovenia's major beach resort, Portorož is awash with **hotels**, though most are managed by small groups of companies, resulting in a characterless uniformity to the majority; furthermore, there is nothing which could remotely be termed budget. This being the case, your best bet is **private accommodation**, for which the most efficient agency is Istriana, conveniently located by the main bus stop (June–Sept daily 9am–9pm; Oct–May Mon–Sat 9am–4pm; ☎05/674-0360, ⓦwww.istriana.si); they have the best stock of both rooms (❶–❷) and apartments (❸–❼), all of which are priced according to category and distance from the sea – they also have an online booking facility. Otherwise, Maona at Obala 14b, is a useful backup (daily June–Aug Mon–Sat 9am–8pm, Sun 10am–1pm & 5–8pm; Sept–May Mon–Fri 9am–5pm; ☎05/674-0363, ⓦwww.maona.si). With any agency, it's almost always assumed that you'll be staying for at least three days, so if you aren't, expect to pay thirty percent more. Out of season, prices drop considerably. The town's large **campsite** is located 2km south of the main bus stop in the small suburb of Lucija (☎05/690-6000; May–Sept).

Hotels

The village-like **Bernardin complex** on the western edge of town (midway between Portorož and Piran) incorporates three contrasting, but all very expensive, places: the *Grand Hotel Bernardin* (☎05/695-0000, ⓦwww.h-bernardin.si; ❾), a monstrous-looking building sloping down to the sea, but which has quite spectacular rooms and sea views and all the attendant facilities of a five-star hotel;

the very well-appointed *Histrion* (same ☎ as *Grand*; ❽); and the unfortunately named, but extremely comfortable, *Vile Park* (same ☎ as *Grand*; ❻) – guests of all three receive free entry to the Waterpark located in the complex (see opposite).

The almost identical *Riviera* (☎05/692-0000, ⓦ www.lifeclass.net; ❾) and *Slovenija* (same contact details as *Riviera*) at Obala 33 are two of the more characterful hotels along the main strip; the former has an authentic Thai Massage Centre. Of the cluster of Metropol-owned hotels at Obala 77 (towards Lucija), the roadside *Lucija* (☎05/690-3000, ⓦ www.metropolgroup.si; ❼), and the *Roža* (☎05/690-2000; ❻), behind, are the only ones with any semblance of charm – guests of these hotels receive free use of the tennis courts and the swimming pool, both of which are located opposite the *Lucija*. At some point, you're bound to pass the gutted **Palace Hotel** on Obala, a once grand establishment but now stripped of its dignity and awaiting its fate.

The beaches

The main **beach**, an incongruous mix of sand, grass and concrete, is clean and well maintained, with lifeguards dispersed along the shore and a wide range of facilities available. Parasols and sunbeds can be rented (€4), as well as cabins and safes (same price plus €5 deposit). Inevitably, it can get tremendously crowded when it's hot, though there's usually enough space to go around; otherwise you could head to one of several **private beaches** – in effect those owned by the hotels – the best of which are those in front of the *Grand Hotel Bernardin* (€5) and the *Hotel Slovenija* (€3). All these designated beaches are roped off and it is forbidden to swim outside the boundary. There are other spots along the beachfront (essentially concrete banks) where you can bathe without restriction.

There are activities aplenty to be had on the main beach. The **water sports centre** in the central kiosk offers, among other activities, water-skiing (€30) and jet-skiing (€50 for 30min). The Laguna Waterpark in the Bernardin Complex has a beautiful **swimming pool** (€7 for 2hr, €13 for the day), with a great section for kids, and Turkish and Finnish saunas (€10 for 2hr). There's also a good pool opposite the *Metropol Hotel* (daily 8am–7pm; €4), next door to which are **tennis** courts (€8 for 1hr). The Terme Palace **spa**, located within the *Hoteli Palace* at Obala 43 (☎05/696-9001, ⓦ www.hoteli-palace.si), houses some five different centres, each offering a huge range of treatments and therapies – the centre also accommodates two thermal pools and two whirlpools. From the main pier, a number of boat companies solicit custom for **excursions** around the bay and to other destinations along the coast, including Poreč in Croatia and Trieste in Italy.

Seča

If you want to leave the crowds behind, take a stroll over to **Seča**, 2km south of town. Dispersed throughout the western end of this knobbly peninsula is the **Former Viva Sculpture Park** (accessible via the road behind the campsite or via a set of steps partway through the campsite), one of several such sculpture parks in Slovenia (each park demonstrates works of art made from a different material). This particular grouping, opened in 1961, consists of over one hundred greying, weather-worn pieces carved from stone; though the odd piece might interest, a better reason for coming here is for the views back to Portorož and the sea. On the other side of the peninsula are the famous Sečovlje saltpans (see p.212).

Eating, drinking and entertainment

Obala is lined with an endless succession of indistinguishable **restaurants**, pizzerias and snack joints, few of which stand out. One restaurant worth trying, how-

△ Sečovlje Saltworks, Primorska

ever, is *Staro Sidro*, 100m east of the Maona agency at no. 55; it's a restful, rather old-fashioned place, but its fish, the mainstay of a reasonably pricey menu, comes highly recommended. Away from here, there are a couple of decent places worth venturing to, the best of which is *Tomi*, 500m north of the main bus stop, just by the bend in the road at Letoviška 1; accommodating both a smart interior and a sunny, canopied terrace, the strong menu features fish – including exotic starters such as truffles and crab – and stomach-busting, meat-heavy Serbian dishes. Half-way up the hill towards Piran, at Vilfanova 10, is *Miranda*, a low-key restaurant with a tidy, straw-covered terrace from which to enjoy the sea views; the food, a good mix of fish and meat dishes, is not bad either. The best place to stock up on provisions is the Market Lucija (daily 6am–midnight) by the *Metropol Hotel*.

By the standards of your average coastal resort, nightlife in Portorož is pretty tame. Cruising Obala is your best bet for **drinking** spots, though again, there's nowhere particularly outstanding. You could also try the Bernardin complex to the west of town, where there are a reasonable selection of eateries and bars – the best of these is the *News Café*, a capacious American-style saloon bar. Also look out for happenings – usually films and concerts – at the **open-air theatre** (Portorož Avditorija), behind the bus station at Senčna pot 12.

Sečovlje saltpans

Located right along the border with Croatia, some 3km south of Portorož, are the **Sečovlje saltpans** (Sečoveljske soline; Ⓦ www.soline.si), once the most extensive saltpans in Slovenia, but now a designated Regional Park. Although salt is still harvested in the northern section of the park (Lera), this larger southern part (Fontanigga) – traversed by vast grids of canals, dykes and pools – has been out of commission since the late 1960s.

From the main road (for how to get here see opposite), a long, dusty track runs alongside the Dragonje River, which marks the border between Slovenia and Croatia. After the first kilometre or so – by which point you'll probably have

Salt of the earth

Salt harvesting has been practised along the Slovenian coast since the first salt-pans were introduced in Piran some time in the fourteenth century. Although the pans remain at Strunjan, Sečovlje is now the only place where harvesting still takes place, albeit on a much smaller scale than in its heyday during the first half of the last century, when over 40,000 tonnes of salt were yielded annually – today around 2,000 tonnes are harvested each year.

The **saltpans** are supplied by seawater funnelled along several large channels, before settling in dammed crystallization basins lined with "petola" (artificially grown crust consisting of algae, gypsum and clay), a method used so as to prevent the salt mixing with sea mud and other sediments. The water is then slowly removed with the aid of large wind-powered pumps, while the remainder evaporates in the sun as the salt crystallizes. After being drained and washed, the salt would – in days of yore – be carted off to large warehouses (*skladišča soli*) sited along the coast, before being distributed; there's a good example of one of these (now disused) warehouses in Portorož, near the Bernardin complex.

Saltpanners' (*solinarji*) dwellings – inhabited by the entire family, but only during the harvesting season (April to September) – were extremely modest, comprising a large downstairs storage room and, upstairs, living quarters, divided into a couple of bedrooms and a joint living and kitchen area; the most important aspects of the building, however, were the windows and doors, positioned on both sides of the house so that changes in the weather could be carefully observed.

despaired at the monotony of the walk – dozens of deserted saltpanners' houses inch into view. It makes for an eerie sight, dozens of stark, crumbling, grey-stone houses randomly strewn across the pancake-flat landscape. A further 3km down the track, it comes as some relief to see the **Saltworks Museum** (Muzej Solinarstva; daily 9am–1pm & 2–7pm; €3), easily spotted as this comprises the only two intact buildings in the park, having been completely renovated for the purposes of housing the museum. As interesting as the exhibits are, including a store of salt-making equipment and techniques and, upstairs, a mock-up of a saltpanner's living quarters, more fascinating is the detailed explanation of the salt-making process given by the helpful guide (see box above).

Amongst the most important heritage sites in the country – it is, along with the Škocjan Caves, on the Ramsar List of internationally protected wetlands – the rich, salt-impregnated soil supports a wide variety of saltwater (halophytic) **flora**, sheltering over forty species of plant, many of which feature on the "Red List" (Slovenia's list of endangered plant and animal species), and a range of land vertebrates, including *Suncus etruscus*, a tiny shrew alleged to be Europe's smallest mammal. **Bird-life**, too, is prominent; the warm, sub-Mediterranean climate and abundance of food in the basins attracts large numbers of migratory birds, such as the common coot and great cormorant, while herons, gulls and egrets have established themselves as permanent residents.

If you haven't got your own transport, **getting here** is tricky and time-consuming: your best bet is to take the *Solinarka* boat (July and August only), which departs from the Bernardin Complex (see p.210) at 9.15am, Portorož at 9.30am and Piran at 9.45am every day; the trip, which includes entrance to the museum, lasts around four hours (☏031/653-682, ✉poropat@siol.net; €11). Otherwise, the nearest you can get by bus (there are none direct to the pans) is the village of Sečovlje itself, some 1.5km before the border crossing, though you'd do just as well jumping on a Croatia-bound bus and getting off at the border crossing; either way, take your passport as a precaution, as you will have to pass through Slovenian customs. One hundred metres beyond the crossing (but before the Croatian border – you are now in "no man's land"), a sign on your right points to the museum.

Travel details

Trains

Divača to: Koper (4–7 daily; 50min); Ljubljana (5–8 daily; 1hr 30min); Postojna (4–7 daily; 35min); Sežana (13 daily; 10min).

Koper to: Divača (5–7 daily; 50min); Ljubljana (5–7 daily; 2hr 30min); Postojna (5–7 daily; 1hr 30min).

Most na Soči to: Bled Jezero (4–7 daily; 1hr); Bohinjska Bistrica (4–7 daily; 50min); Jesenice (4–7 daily; 1hr 15min); Nova Gorica (4–7 daily; 40min).

Nova Gorica to: Ajdovščina (2 daily; 40min); Bled Jezero (4–7 daily; 1hr 30min); Bohinjska Bistrica (4–7 daily; 1hr 15min); Jesenice (4–7 daily; 1hr 50min); Most na Soči (4–7 daily; 40min); Sežana (3–5 daily; 1hr).

Sežana to: Divača (13 daily; 10min); Ljubljana (7 daily; 1hr 35min–2hr); Nova Gorica (4–6 daily; 1hr).

Buses

Ajdovščina to: Ljubljana (Mon–Fri 8 daily, Sat & Sun 3 daily; 1hr 20min); Nova Gorica (Mon–Fri hourly, Sat & Sun 3 daily; 40min); Postojna (Mon–Sat hourly, Sun 3; 40min); Vipava (Mon–Sat hourly, Sun 2; 10min).

Bovec to: Kobarid (Mon–Fri 5 daily, Sat 2, Sun 1; 35min); Kranjska Gora (June & Aug 4 daily; 1hr 45min); Tolmin (Mon–Fri 5 daily, Sat 2, Sun 1; 1hr 10min).

Cerkno to: Bovec (2 daily; 1hr 15min); Idrija (Mon–Fri hourly, Sat 5, Sun 3; 25min); Ljubljana (Mon–Fri 4 daily, Sat & Sun 3 daily; 1hr 25min); Tolmin (Mon–Fri 3 daily; Sat & Sun 2 daily; 40min).

Divača to: Koper (Mon–Fri 9 daily, Sat & Sun 2 daily; 1hr 15min); Ljubljana (Mon–Fri 7 daily, Sat & Sun 4 daily; 1hr 45min).

Idrija to: Bovec (1 daily; 1hr 30min); Cerkno (Mon–Fri hourly, Sat 6, Sun 4; 25min); Ljubljana (Mon–Fri 8 daily, Sat 6, Sun 4; 1hr 15min); Tolmin (Mon–Fri 4 daily, Sat 2, Sun 1; 1hr).

Kobarid to: Bovec (Mon–Fri 5 daily, Sat & Sun 3 daily; 35min); Tolmin (Mon–Fri 6 daily, Sat & Sun 3 daily; 30min).

Koper to: Ljubljana (5 daily; 2hr 20min); Piran (every 20–30min; 25min); Postojna (6 daily; 1hr 20min).

Nova Gorica to: Ajdovščina (Mon–Fri hourly, Sat 6, Sun 4; 40min); Bovec (Mon–Fri 4 daily, Sat & Sun 2 daily; 1hr 15min); Kobarid (Mon–Fri 4 daily, Sat & Sun 2 daily; 50min); Ljubljana (Mon–Fri 10 daily, Sat & Sun 6 daily; 2hr 30min); Postojna (Mon–Fri 10 daily, Sat 6, Sun 3; 1hr 10min); Tolmin (Mon–Fri 7 daily, Sat 4, Sun 4; 40min); Vipava (Mon–Fri hourly, Sat & Sun 5 daily; 45min).

Piran to: Koper (every 20–30min; 25min); Ljubljana (5 daily; 2hr 40min); Postojna (6 daily; 1hr 40min).

Sežana to: Ajdovščina (Mon–Sat 1 daily; 40min); Divača (Mon–Sat 1 daily; 15min); Ljubljana (Mon–Fri 2 daily, Sun 1; 1hr 40min); Nova Gorica (Mon–Fri 4 daily, Sat & Sun 2 daily; 1hr 10min); Štanjel (Mon–Fri 5 daily; Sat & Sun 1 daily; 30min); Postojna (Mon–Sat 3 daily; 40min).

Tolmin to: Bovec (Mon–Fri 4 daily, Sat & Sun 2 daily; 1hr 10min); Cerkno (Mon–Fri 3 daily, Sat & Sun 2 daily; 40min); Kobarid (Mon–Fri 4 daily, Sat & Sun 2 daily; 30min); Most na Soči (Mon–Fri 6 daily, Sat & Sun 2 daily; 15min); Nova Gorica (Mon–Fri 6 daily, Sat & Sun 2 daily; 40min).

International trains

Divača to: Pula (1 daily; 2hr 45min).

Sežana to: Trieste (1 daily; 1hr 40min); Venice (2 daily; 2hr 30min).

International buses

Koper to: Trieste (10 daily; 1hr).

Southern Slovenia

CHAPTER 4

Highlights

✳ **Postojna Caves** Vast chambers and dazzling formations in one of the world's truly great cave systems. See p.222

✳ **Predjama Castle** Visit Slovenia's most dramatically sited castle, and discover the legend of Erasmus Lueger. See p.224

✳ **Lake Cerknica** Europe's largest intermittent lake is another of Slovenia's great natural wonders. See p.228

✳ **Križna Water Cave** Discover cave-bear bones and over a dozen lakes in one of Europe's finest water caves. See p.230

✳ **Walking in Kočevjski Rog** Explore Slovenia's finest expanse of forest, and catch some wildlife along the way – mind the bears though. See p.237

✳ **Kayaking on the Kolpa River** The beautiful, twisting, Kolpa River is a great spot for kayaking and other water sports. See p.238

✳ **Pleterje Monastery** Visit the atmospheric church and grounds of Slovenia's only functioning Carthusian monastery. See p.251

✳ **Repnice wine cellars** Down a few glasses of wine in unique cellars hewn from sand. See p.257

△ Postojna caves

Southern Slovenia

The three regions comprising southern Slovenia: Notranjska, Dolenjska and Bela Krajina, offer an attractive mix of darkly forested hills, karstic rock formations, river valleys, castles, monasteries and spas, not to mention several outstanding wine-producing regions. Moreover, and with very few major centres of population in the region, there are opportunities aplenty for hiking, cycling and other leisurely pursuits.

The province of **Notranjska** encompasses an expanse of terrain extending south from the Ljubljana marshes to the Croatian border, bound by Primorska and the Karst to the west and by the Velika Gora hills to the east. Characterized by karst fields, underground rivers and thickly forested limestone hills and plateaus pocked by innumerable cave systems, its most celebrated attractions are the astonishing **Postojna Caves** and the majestically sited **Predjama Castle**. Largely ignored by most travellers, Notranjska's lesser-known sites include **Lake Cerknica**, Europe's largest intermittent lake, and the wonderful **Križna Water Cave**. Pressed up hard against the Croatian border, the **Snežnik Mountains** offer some of the country's best non-alpine hiking.

The thick forests of Notranjska extend eastwards into the neighbouring province of **Dolenjska**, the largest of the three regions and the one possessed of the lion's share of southern Slovenia's historical sites. Its westernmost flank centres around the towns of **Ribnica** and **Kočevje**, close to both the massive forests of Velika Gora and **Kočevski Rog**, and the **Kolpa River Valley** on the Croatian border, the latter offering an exciting complement of fantastic scenery and superb walking, cycling and adrenaline-fuelled sports.

The only town of any real size is **Novo Mesto**, a handy base from which to take in any number of local attractions, foremost of which is the beautiful **Krka River Valley**, which extends northwest to the village of **Muljava**, itself just a few kilometres from the ancient **Stična Monastery**. Following the course of the Krka River eastwards from Novo Mesto brings you to **Otočec Castle**, the secluded **Pleterje Monastery** and the sleepy island town of **Kostanjevica na Krki**. Beyond here the road and river continue to **Brežice**, setting for one of the country's most celebrated classical music festivals; **Čatež**, the country's largest spa centre; and the **Bizeljsko wine region**, perhaps the most appealing of Posavje's four winegrowing centres.

Quietly tucked away in the far southeastern corner of the country and bound by the forests of Kočevjski Rog to the west and the Croatian border to the south and east, is **Bela Krajina**. It is easily the smallest of southern Slovenia's regions, a gentle landscape where hilly slopes raked with lush vineyards descend to flatlands strewn with the region's famous white birch trees.

Today, viticulture and fruit growing are the main agricultural activities in this region, and it's these, along with strong folk traditions, that entice any visitors the region receives. Of the province's two main towns, **Črnomelj** and **Metlika**, the latter is more appealing by dint of its architecture and museums as well as its proximity to the fabulous Gothic pilgrimage shrine of **Tri Fare** (Three Parishes) and some lovely **wine villages**.

Getting around by **public transport** is more difficult here than in any other part of the country, so it's the one region where having your own wheels is particularly advantageous; trains serve relatively few places outlined in this chapter, whilst local bus services are patchy at best.

SOUTHERN SLOVENIA

Notranjska and Western Dolenjska

Most visitors to **Notranjska** head straight to Slovenia's number one tourist attraction, the **Postojna Caves**, and follow that with a visit to the nearby **Predjama Castle**, perched miraculously halfway up a cliff. However, the region contains other, less-visited subterranean delights in the form of the **Pivka and Black Caves**, a mere stone's throw from their more famous counterparts. To the north of the caves, a worthwhile diversion en route to or from Postojna/Ljubljana is the **Bistra Technical Museum**; containing a massive collection of agricultural and industrial machines, trams, carriages and cars, this is a must for any vehicle enthusiast.

South of Postojna, the **Snežnik mountains** offer both tremendous hiking and the opportunity to spot some of Slovenia's most spectacular, and aggressive, wildlife. Further east, the **Rakov Škocjan Regional Park** presents more rambling possibilities. Close by is one of Slovenia's most unusual landmarks, the extraordinary **Lake Cerknica** – by winter a lake, by summer a field; permanent, though underground, lakes can be explored at **Križna Water Cave**, where skeletons of prehistoric cave-bears have been discovered. Finally, for the less energetic, **Snežnik Castle** offers lovely landscaped gardens and a fine art collection.

Although the main towns in **Western Dolenjska** are nothing special, they are useful jumping-off points for **Velika Gora** and the stunning virgin forests of **Kočevjski Rog**. If you find yourself with time to kill, **Ribnica** has a fine woodenware tradition in evidence in the town's museum and at the annual fair, and in nearby Nova Štifta lies one of Slovenia's main pilgrimage churches. Furthermore, **Kočevje**, once home to the country's German-speaking minority, contains Slovenia's first parliament building. Straddling the Croatian border south of Kočevje, the beautiful **Kolpa Valley** is the region's centre for river-based activities, all of which can be organized from the valley's main village, **Osilnica**.

Postojna and around

The town of **POSTOJNA**, 66km south of Ljubljana, would be an eminently forgettable place were it not the location of one of Slovenia's most popular tourist attractions, the amazing **Postojna Caves**, whose vast chambers and dazzling formations have been pulling in the punters for nearly two centuries. Despite its role as Notranjska's administrative and economic centre, the town itself is pretty much devoid of character and you'll not want to hang around once you've visited the caves and the **Predjama Castle** (see p.224), just a few kilometres away. Indeed, just about the only other distinction the town has is that it's home to one of the country's largest army barracks, acquired in 1945 following the annexation of Primorska to Italy. Located on the main road and rail routes to the coast, the caves are easily managed as a half-day trip from Ljubljana, or as a stop-off en route to the coast itself.

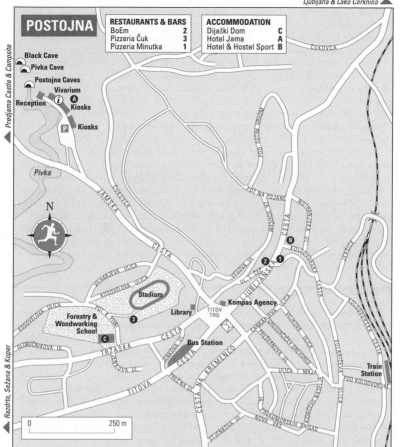

Arrival, information and accommodation

From the **bus station** on Titova cesta, it's an easy five-minute walk to the main square, Titov trg, while the **train station** is less conveniently located 1km southeast of town on Kolodvorska cesta – from the station exit, take the stairs down to Pod Kolodvorom, then walk along Ulica 1 Maja until you reach the main square. The **tourist office** (May–Sept daily 9am–6pm; ☎05/720-1610, ⓔtd-tic. postojna@siol.net) is somewhat inconveniently located out by the caves; in town itself the Kompas agency at Titov trg 2a (April–Oct Mon–Fri 8am–7pm, Sat 9am–1pm; Nov–March Mon–Fri 8am–5pm, Sat 9am–1pm; ☎05/721-1480, ⓔinfo@kompas-postojna.si) can provide all the information you need. There's **Internet access** in the library, 100m behind the defunct *Hotel Kras* on Trg Padlih borcev (July & Aug Mon & Wed 10am–6pm, Tue, Thu & Fri 7am–3pm; rest of year Mon–Fri 7.30am–5.30pm, Sat 7am–noon; free), and the **post office** is at Ulica 1 Maja 2a, just south of the main square (Mon–Fri 8am–7pm, Sat 8am–noon).

There's a decent spread of budget **accommodation** in town; the *Hotel & Hostel Sport* at Kolodvorska 1 (☎05/720-2244; Ⓦwww.sport-hotel.si) – actually more hostel than hotel – is a simple, clean and colourful place offering singles, doubles, and multi-bedded rooms (❶–❸) – they've also got bikes for hire (€10 per day), and Internet access. Cheaper still, but far more basic, is the *Dijaški Dom* in the Forestry and Woodworking School at Tržaška cesta 36 (☎05/726-5291), which has triples all with shared bathroom (€13 including breakfast). Postojna's only conventional hotel is the *Jama* (☎05/728-2400; ❺; April–Oct), a concrete monstrosity located near the cave entrance, which caters mainly to groups. Alternatively, you can take a **private room** through the Kompas agency who have a good stock in town and the surrounds (❷). Finally, if you've got your own transport, the *Hudičevec* tourist farm, 10km west of town just outside the village of Razdrto (☎05/703-0300; Ⓦwww.hudicevec.com; ❷), offers warm, homely rooms and its own organically grown food – the farm (it's signposted) stands in a field just off the main road.

Scenically located in a pine forest 4km north of the cave (go 1.5km along the road to Predjama, take a right and the site is 2.5km further on) is the large *Pivka* **campsite** (☎05/720-3993; April–Oct), which also has simple four-bed bungalows with bathrooms (❺), a handful of which have kitchens (❻). During July and August the full rate is applicable, regardless of the number of people staying; at other times, it's half-price. If you don't fancy walking here (there are no buses), you can order a taxi at Kompas.

Postojna Caves

Located an easy walk (1.5km) northwest of town along the road to Predjama, the 19km of tunnels, chambers and passages which constitute the **Postojna Caves** (Postojnska jama; Ⓦwww.postojna-cave.com) lie under the slopes of a broad karstic limestone plateau on the eastern fringes of the Postojna basin. Millions of years of erosion and corrosion by the Pivka River, coupled with abundant rainfall seeping through the cave's permeable limestone ceilings, has created a fantastic jungle of stalactites and stalagmites, Gothic-like chiselled columns and translucent stone draperies.

Although parts of the cave had been continually visited since the Middle Ages, it was Valvasor (see p.242), inevitably, who first reported upon this immense grotto, commenting, "in some places you see terrifying heights, elsewhere everything is in columns so strangely shaped as to seem like some creepy-crawly, snake or other animal in front of one". The caves were pronounced open to tourists on the occasion of a visit by Emperor Franz Ferdinand in 1819, the first in a long line of distinguished visitors to Postojna. Within six years of his visit, the caves had been illuminated with oil lamps and professional guides had been employed. The famous cave train, meanwhile, entered service in 1872, a rather crude model in which tourists were shunted along in hand-pushed wagons. These carriages were superseded by gas-powered trains in 1914, themselves replaced by the electric version (used today) in 1959.

The Cave Tour

Tours take place throughout the year (Jan–March & Nov–Dec daily 10am, noon & 2pm plus 4pm on Sat & Sun; April & Oct every 2hr 10am–4pm; May–Sept hourly 9am–6pm; €16), but to get the most out of your visit, particularly if you're here in the summer months when the place can get swamped with groups, try and make one of the first or last tours of the day. Dress warmly, as it can get quite chilly.

After purchasing your ticket, assemble with everybody else by the entrance and wait for the signal to board the **cave train**, which whisks you along 2km of preliminary systems before the tour proper begins. As the train hurtles forth keep an eye out for several interesting features: a shaft of blackened walls, the result of a Nazi fuel dump blown up by Partisan saboteurs during World War II; the **Congress Hall**, a beautifully lit chamber so-named following the staging of a Speleological Congress here in 1965; and the **Curtain**, a transparent, wafer-thin formation precariously angled on a sloping wall.

Alighting at the **Great Mountain** (Velika Gora), you'll break off into the group of your chosen language before the guided tour begins, which amounts to around one hour of walking. The most impressive formations in this vast hall – a forty-five-metre-high stone-block mound formed when the ceiling collapsed and which, in time, became smothered in calcite – are the so-called **Natural Curtains**, whose shape and colour is akin to that of dried tobacco leaves. Crossing the **Russian Bridge**, built in 1916 by Russian prisoners of war, you enter the most enchanting part of the system, a series of chambers collectively known as the **Beautiful Caves** (Lepe jame), whose names are suggestive of some of the lustrous formations and colours on display, such as the **Spaghetti Hall**, with its dripping, needle-like formations, the calcium-rich **White Hall**, and the **Red Room**, stained a rich ochre by iron oxides. Continuing in a circuitous route, you pass back under the Russian Bridge through several more chambers, one of which, the **Winter Chamber** (Zimska dvorana), is home to the two formations that have become symbols of the cave: one called the **Pillar**, and another dubbed **Brilliant**, the latter on account of its dazzling snow-white colour and peculiar shape, which resembles something like a stack of giant cauliflowers. The main attraction in the next gallery has less to do with the formations on display and more to do with the contents of the large tank located in the centre, which contains **Proteus Anguinus**, the largest permanent cave-dwelling vertebrate known to man (see the Subterranean Slovenia colour section). The tour concludes a little further on in the **Concert Hall** (Koncertna dvorana), the largest open space in the system, and which, you are told, can hold some 10,000 people – the odd concert is still held here. From here you return to the entrance by train.

You can see more Proteus Anguinus, as well as other cave flora and fauna – such as crickets, beetles and spiders – in the Speleobiology Station, or **Proteus Vivarium** (daily: Jan–March & Nov–Dec 9.30am–2.30pm plus Sat & Sun til 4pm; April & Oct 9.30am–4.30pm; May–Sept 8.30am–6.30pm; €6 or €19 with entrance to caves), a short walk back down from the cave entrance by the row of kiosks. The exhibition is housed inside the Gallery of Signatures, so-called because of the many signatures scrawled over the cave walls, the oldest of which (no longer visible) is thought to date from 1213. You'll do well, though, to spot more than a handful of these tiny creatures, as most are apt to hide themselves away.

Pivka and Black Caves

If you'd rather avoid the crowds, then more low-key subterranean alternatives are the **Pivka Cave** (Pivka jama) and **Black Cave** (Črna jama). The entrance to the former is via a sixty-metre-deep collapsed chasm near the Pivka camping ground, some 4km north of the main Postojna entrance (follow the signs to the camp). Descending nearly three hundred steps, the route then follows a specially constructed walkway cut into the wall just above the level of the Pivka River. Beyond an iron door and a short tunnel is the Black Cave (also known as the Magdalena Cave), a modestly sized, dry gallery, which takes its name from the large amount of black calcite present. From here, another, much longer, man-made tunnel links the cave with one of the main chambers in Postojna; this last part is generally not accessible to tourists, though it might be worth asking. If you wish to visit these caves, you should contact the ticket office at the Postojna Caves two or three days in advance (€8).

Eating and drinking

Eating options in Postojna are very limited. By some distance the best place is *Pizzeria Minutka*, a five-minute walk northwest of the main square at Ljubljanska cesta 14; aside from the usual range of pizzas and fresh salads, this very pleasant restaurant offers a superb choice of Serbian stews, such as *Prebranac* (oven-baked beans), and grilled meats, notably *Čevapi* and *Pljeskavica*, both served with *Lepinja*, a deliciously doughy bread – the service is good too. Otherwise, *Pizzeria Čuk*, slightly out of the way near the sports park at Pot k Pivki 4 (head along Tržaška cesta for 200m then turn right), is a popular and decent alternative. If you're out by the cave there is a cluster of typically tacky tourist eateries to choose from. Opposite *Minutka*, the café-cum-bar *BoEm* is about as exciting as it gets for **drinking**.

Predjama Castle

Second only to Postojna as the region's main tourist attraction is the fabulously dramatic **Predjama Castle** (Predjamski grad; daily: Jan–March & Nov–Dec 10am–4pm; April & Oct 10am–6pm; May–Sept 9am–7pm; €6), 9km north of the caves in the village of the same name. Pressed into a huge cavern, hollowed out of the high, flat rock face over the karstic swallow hole of the Lokva stream, its setting is as unforgettable as it is improbable. Stopping here in 1802 en route to Italy, the German architect Karl Schinkel recalled "it was with the wildest bravery that man was ordered to settle in this place. There is nothing more stirring than to look upon the castle, wondrously composed of tower-like structures which, built under the dark vault of the cavern, need not their own ramparts, as the dark cavern's huge bulk hangs far beyond them."

Amongst its many aristocratic residents, the most infamous was the castle's last owner, knight and brigand **Erasmus Lueger** (see box on p.226), who inhabited the castle during the second half of the fifteenth century, and whose life – in particular the manner of his death – has intrigued historians for centuries.

With origins dating back to around the twelfth century, the castle manifests a number of styles, from Romanesque through to Gothic, although its predominant form is Renaissance following heavy renovation in the sixteenth century. With a total of some fifteen rooms, as well as numerous passageways, galleries and alcoves, all condensed into five floors, there's much to see, though little of what's on display is original. Before you start, take one of the useful accompanying leaflets to guide you through the numbered rooms. On the second floor, keep an eye out for a portrait of the suitably gruff Erasmus (one of the few pictures of him known to exist), and the cupboard in the dining room – made by an inmate who spent four years in a local prison using just his pocket-knife. Located on the same (third) floor where Erasmus came to grief is the tiny castle **chapel**, containing a fifteenth-century Gothic pietà. Next door is the chaplain's room, from where he could witness the punishments being meted out in the torture chamber one floor below. From the natural apertures on each floor there are fine panoramas of the flower-speckled Vipava Valley ahead.

At the very top of the castle – across the drawbridge and up some uneven steps – lie the ruins of the Cave Castle, beyond which is the **secret natural passage**; tours of the latter are possible during the summer, but you should call a couple of days in advance. Easier to visit is the **cave under the Castle** (Jama pod Predjamskim gradom), which extends for some 13km (much of it still unexplored) to the Vipava Valley, though only around 700m of walking is possible for the casual visitor. Bar the odd stalactite, there's not an awful lot to see, but it's one of the few caves around that hasn't been artificially lit, so it's quite good fun wandering around with torches. Scheduled tours, lasting forty-five minutes, take place

△ Prejdama Castle

between May and September (11am, 1pm, 3pm & 5pm; €6 or €10 if combined with the Castle); contact the ticket office in the castle. If you're around in August try and make it for the annual **jousting tournament**, which takes place on the narrow strip of grass just below the castle on the last, or second to last, Sunday of that month.

Bistra Technical Museum

Twenty-two kilometres southwest of Ljubljana, close to the small settlement of Vrhnika in the tiny hamlet of Bistra, is the former **Bistra Monastery**, a large complex that is now home to the **Technical Museum of Slovenia** (Muzej Techniški Slovenije; July & Aug Tues–Fri 10am–6pm, Sat 8am–5pm, Sun 10am–6pm; March–June & Sept–Nov Tues–Fri 8am–4pm, Sat 8am–5pm, Sun 10am–6pm; €4). The museum is divided up into several departments, though such is the size of the place you're best off making a beeline for a select few, particularly if time is short. As interesting as the voluminous displays of textiles, forestry, agriculture and engineering are, it's the massive road vehicle department – comprising a magnificent collection of pre-World War II automobiles, carriages (including a fine Ljubljana tram from 1901), bicycles and tractors – which demands greatest attention.

The highlight of the collection is some two dozen cars given as gifts to Tito by various government offices and heads of state, and which were used for his many travels throughout Yugoslavia and abroad, including India and Burma; there are some splendid models on display, notably a magnificent Rolls Royce Silver Wraith, a Mercedes Benz (from the Croatian Home Office), and an armour-plated 1937 Packard Twelve, presented to Tito by Stalin in 1945 – ironically, just three years before Yugoslavia's expulsion from Cominform. There's also a 1953 Fiat Zastava, just one of Tito's many hunting vehicles. Before making the trek back, pick up some refreshments from the gostilna next door.

Although undoubtedly worth a special visit from Ljubljana, the museum is more conveniently done as a trip en route to Postojna. Moreover, without your own

The death of Erasmus Lueger

The beginning of what proved to be a rather sticky ending for **Erasmus** began after he killed one of the Austrian emperor Frederick III's kinsmen, in revenge for the decapitation of a friend. Hot on his heels as he fled to Predjama was the governor of Trieste, Caspar Ravbar, whose mission it was to capture Erasmus. For more than a year Ravbar and his men laid siege to Predjama, attempting to starve out its defenders. However, Ravbar hadn't reckoned on a **secret natural passage**, located beyond the castle walls, through which came a constant supply of fresh food that Erasmus would occasionally hurl down into the valley to taunt his besiegers. Finally betrayed by a double-dealing servant, Erasmus's **death**, when it finally came, was an ignoble one. The poor fellow was blasted to bits by a large projectile while settling down to answer nature's call. Local legend has it that he is buried under the linden tree, supposedly planted by his girlfriend, next to the **Church of Our Lady of Sorrows**, just down from the castle.

transport, getting here is fairly time-consuming; take one of the regular buses from Ljubljana (stand 29 at the bus station) to Vrhnika, and alight by the *Hotel Mantova* in the centre; from here, it's a signposted three-kilometre walk along a winding country road to the museum – however, many cars travel this road, so there's a good chance of hitching a ride.

South of Postojna: the Snežnik Mountains

Thirty-three kilometres south of Postojna, and just 11km from the Croatian border, the nondescript market town of **ILIRSKA BISTRICA** holds no specific appeal, but it's a good place from which to strike out into the wonderful **Snežnik Mountains**, a densely forested karst plateau cloaked in spruce, beech, fir and dwarf pine, and traversed by a number of well-marked trails, including a section of the European footpath E6. From Ilirska Bistrica, it's a good three-hour walk to **Sviščaki** (1242m), where the *Dom na Sviščakih* (☎051/222-212) has a handful of beds available between June and mid-September as well as at weekends throughout the rest of the year; from here it's a further two-hour trek to the cone-like **Mount Snežnik**, where there are more beds at the *Koča na Velikem Snežniku* (☎050/615-356; May–Oct Sat & Sun, Aug daily). Usually topped with snow until late spring, Slovenia's highest non-Alpine mountain (1796m) offers fantastic views of the Alps to the north, and the Croatian seaboard, dotted with its many islands, to the south. From Mount Snežnik, the path continues to **Mašun** (1024m; 4hr), where there's good food served (daily 8am–10pm), and down through the Leskova Valley towards Snežnik Castle (see p.231). If you have a car, you could drive to Sviščaki and walk to Snežnik from there – from Sviščaki, the deteriorating mountain road continues to Mašun (13km), before descending to Snežnik Castle. If you're doing this route in reverse – from Snežnik Castle – you could drive to Mašun and walk to Snežnik from there. The plateau also shelters numerous large mammals, including lynx, wolf and a growing bear population – sightings of all three are not uncommon.

In Ilirska Bistrica, the **tourist office**, just 100m northeast of the bus station (itself located 400m south of the train station) at Gregorčičeva cesta 2 (Mon–Fri 8am–3pm, plus Sat in summer 9am–noon; ☎05/710-1384, ⓔrazvojni.center@siol.net), can organize **private accommodation** if you wish to stick around.

East of Postojna

The area east of Postojna is blessed with several first-rate attractions. The first of these is the **Rakov Škocjan Regional Park**, an enjoyable walking spot from where it's a short distance to the small town of **Cerknica**, of little interest itself but which is close to one of the counry's most extraordinary geographical features, the intermittent **Lake Cerknica**, sometimes lake, sometimes field. East and south of here respectively is the must-see **Križna Water Cave** and **Snežnik Castle**, the latter tucked away under the shadow of the Snežnik Mountains. This is lovely cycling country, and there are a few places in Postojna from where bikes can be hired. This is just as well, as public transport around this relative backwater is extremely limited; without your own transport, careful planning is required, particularly if you wish to see more than one of these places in the same day.

Rakov Škocjan Regional Park

A couple of kilometres north of Postojna, the secondary road running parallel to the main E70/E61 Ljubljana–Koper highway breaks off sharply to the right in the direction of Cerknica. After a further 5km, the road passes the **Rakov Škocjan Regional Park**, a small, lush karst valley popular with local walkers. There's an easy, well-marked, circular trail around the park, which should take no more than a couple of hours to complete.

The park's focal point is the short, well-defined **Rak Gorge**, which begins at the **Small Natural Bridge** (Mali Naravni Most) – the first of two stunning natural rock bridges sited at either end of the gorge – just below which lurks the **Zelške Cave** (Zelške Jama) and the Rak Spring, from whence the babbling **Rak River** emerges. The river, which carries water from Cerknica Polje to the Planina Polje, winds its way down the gorge to the immaculately cut arch of the **Great Natural Bridge** (Veliki Naravni Most), underneath which is the **Tkalca Cave** (Tkalca Jama). On the far side of the bridge a crumbling heap of stone ruins, including parts of a stone altar, are all that remain of the **Church of St Kancijan**. During periods when the river is low, or completely dry, it is possible to explore both cave entrances, but caution should be exercised as it's likely to be slippery. Located in the heart of the park is the *Hotel Rakov Škocjan* (℡01/709-7470, ⓦwww .h-rakovskocjan.com; ❺), a small and cosy lodge-style residence with warm, pine-furnished rooms – there's also a restaurant and café here, as well as bikes for hire (€3 for 1hr, €10 per day).

Cerknica and Lake Cerknica

Approximately 4km kilometres east of Rakov Škocjan, the town of **Cerknica** is the jumping-off point for **Lake Cerknica** (Cerkniško Jezero), an enormous karst *polje* (or field) that is also Europe's largest intermittent lake.

Cerknica and Slivnica Plateau

CERKNICA town is a drab place, enlivened only during the **Pust Festival** each February – one of Slovenia's better organized carnivals – but it does offer a smattering of accommodation, useful if you're planning to spend a day or two anywhere in the vicinity of the lake. There is a **train station** 4km northwest of Cerknica in **Rakek**, which may be a more feasible option if you don't mind walking or hitching the rest of the way, given the paucity of buses to Cerknica. The **bus station** is on Čabranska ulica, from where it's a short walk to the rather useless **tourist office**, located next to the post office at Cesta 4 maja 51 (Mon–Fri 8.30am–3pm; ℡01/709-3636, ⓔzzt@postojna.si). They might be able to help out with private rooms but otherwise, *TeliCo*, 500m east of the tourist office up the hill at Brestova 9 (☎01/709-7090, ✉vilma.telic@guest.arnes.si; ❸), has a couple of **rooms** with great views out towards the lake. Pretty much the only place in town to eat is the *Valvasorjev hram* **restaurant** opposite the tourist office, which knocks up cheap, good food in a roomy, if rather unatmospheric, cellar bar.

Cerknica is also the starting point for trails to the **Slivnica Plateau**, ranged across the lake's northern shore. If the lake looks impressive from ground level, the views from atop its highest peak, **Velika Slivnica** (1114m; 2hr from Cerknica), are superlative; Velika Slivnica is also known as witch mountain, owing to its associations with witchcraft hereabouts in the Middle Ages. Once at the top, you can partake in some refreshments at the *Dom na Slivnici* (☎01/709-4140) just below the summit, which also has beds available year-round (Oct–April Sat & Sun only).

Lake Cerknica

There are several ways to approach a visit to Lake Cerknica, but what you see, and how you see it, will largely be determined by which time of the year you visit, and which mode of transport, if any, you use. The most direct route across the lake (or field) is via an unsurfaced north–south road that shaves the lake's western shore. Beginning at **Dolenje Jezero**, a small village 2km south of Cerknica, the road bisects a group of sink holes, before passing by the small wooded island of Gorica and continuing southwards to **Otok** (Island) which, when the lake is full, magically becomes the country's sole inhabited island. From Otok you can either head back in a northerly direction via the forest road which skirts the western shore of the **Zadnji kraj inlet**, or take the longer route along the lake's eastern shore through the settlements of Laze, Gorenje Jezero, Lipsenj and Žerovnica, winding up at Grahovo on the main road.

The disappearing lake

Although the so-called **"disappearing lake"**, located about 2.5km south of Cerknica, had been the subject of much postulation and fascination on the part of researchers and explorers long before Valvasor's time, it was left to the great polymath himself to unravel the lake's eccentricities, concluding as he did: "I think there is no lake so remarkable either in Europe or in any other of the three corners of the world...no lake has as many exceptional features". As a result of his efforts, which included the publication of a map of the lake in 1689, Valvasor was granted honorary membership of the Royal Society in London. There were other significant contributions too, most notably from the botanist Balthazar Haquet and the Jesuit Tobijas Gruber, both of whom offered thoroughgoing accounts of the lake's extraordinary hydrological functions.

The lake functions thus: once water from the Slivnica and Bloke Plateaus to the east, and the Javornik mountains to the west, enters the permeable limestone surface of the lakebed, it begins to percolate through the lake's many sink holes, into the subterranean area, and when more water enters the lake than can be depleted, the waters of the main channel, the Stržen (itself fed by a number of tributaries and streams), overflow and the shallow lake is created, sometimes in a matter of days. At its fullest, the lake can extend for some 10km in length and nearly 5km in width – that's roughly three to four times the size of Lake Bohinj, Slovenia's largest permanent body of water. The disappearing act takes a little longer, usually between three and four weeks. There have been numerous, hitherto unsuccessful, attempts at human intervention over the years – either to prevent the lake filling (in order to grow more hay for livestock), or, conversely, to preserve a permanent body of water (in order to prolong the fishing season and encourage tourism).

As a rule the lake is usually present between October and June, and at its most voluminous during spring, following snowmelt from both the Snežnik and Slivnica plateaus. During this period, the lake becomes a vast playground for a multitude of **activities**, the most popular of which is fishing – pike, tench and chub are the main stock here – as well as swimming, rowing, windsurfing, and even skiing and skating when it's cold enough. With over two hundred species of bird, including corncrake, lapwing and field lark, either migrating or nesting amongst the wide expanse of reeds, the lake is something of a haven for birdwatchers.

The most enjoyable way to see the lake is on a **bike**, which can be rented from *TeliCo* in Cerknica (see opposite), and from the *Hotel Sport* (see p.22) in Postojna. Alternatively, the family at Dolenjske Jezero 50a organizes jollies around the lake by **horse and cart** (1hr; €3 per person in a small group). Should you wish to **stay** near the lake, the house next door has one clean and spacious apartment sleeping between two and five people (℡01/709-1932, ✉marija.leskovec-k@siol. net; ❸). If you plan to spend any length of time around the lake, arm yourself with a copy of the 1:25,000 *Notranjska Cerkniško jezero* map, which outlines a good range of walks and cycle routes in the area.

Museum of Lake Cerknica

For a better understanding of the lake's peculiarities, you should pay a visit to the **Museum of Lake Cerknica** (Muzej Cerkniškega Jezera; €4) in **Dolenje Jezero** (no. 1e). The centrepiece of this family-run museum is an enormous 1:2500-scale **map-relief** of the lake and its surrounding features, constructed by the museum's indefatigable owner over the course of three years. By way of the lake's most salient features – tributaries, springs, sink holes, as well as settlements and roads, and complemented by live recordings of bird and other animal sounds – the map illustrates how the lake performs and what it looks like during both dry and wet periods.

There's also a twenty-five-minute slide show, featuring some beautifully shot images of the lake in its various guises, and a collection of tools and implements traditionally used by local fishermen – wooden skates, nets, baskets and the like – as well as models of the long wooden canoes (*drevak*) that were used, until the 1970s, for transporting cattle and other livestock across the lake. In theory the museum is only open to visitors at 3pm on Saturdays, but if you call in advance a visit should be possible at other times (☎01/709-4053, ⊛www.jezerski-hram. si). In any case, the adjoining café-cum-bar (open daily except Tues; 1–10pm) is a useful place to stop off for **refreshments** en route to the lake.

Križna Water Cave

Utterly different from Postojna and that ilk of cave, the eight-kilometre-long **Križna Water Cave** (Križna jama), 12km southeast of Cerknica, is one of the world's great lake caves, and *the* cave to visit in Slovenia if it's a more authentic caving experience you're after. Entering the cave via a small aperture hollowed out of the rock face, you immediately descend into a rocky, dry gallery, also known as the **Bear's Corridor** (Medvedji rov) owing to the many cave-bear (*ursus spelaeus*) that sheltered here thousands of years ago. The first cave-bear excavations – carried out some 130 years ago – uncovered around two thousand fossil remains from over one hundred animals, mainly mandibles, skulls and other bone fragments; there are still many fragments, typically part of a jaw or a tooth, embedded within the rock, some of which you'll see as you walk around. There's also an almost-complete cave-bear skull on display, next to a much smaller skull of a brown bear; the difference in size is striking, though this will be of little comfort should you have the misfortune to encounter one in the surrounding forests, which is by no means improbable. Less alarmingly, the cave is home to a large number of bats, drawn here by the relatively warm temperature of around 8°C.

First explored in 1926, the chain of 22 lakes that comprise the **Lakes and Stream Passages** (Jezerski rov) is, should you decide to go this far, the undeniable high point of a visit to Križna. Separated by calcite barriers, the lakes are fed with water from the nearby Bloke Plateau, via a number of springs in the eastern part of Lake Cerknica; a group in excess of four persons cannot go any further than the first lake, but smaller groups can venture to the thirteenth and most decorative of all the lakes, the **Calvary** (Kalvarija), a wonderful grotto comprising a huge mound of collapsed material and a shimmering array of stalactites and stalagmites, many of which lie submerged under water. Beyond the Calvary the cave splits, one branch leading to **Mud Passage** (Blata rov), the other to the **Coloured Passage** (Pisani rov), both of which can only be visited by professional cavers.

Visits to the cave take place at 3pm on Sundays between May and September, and should be arranged at least two or three days in advance – visits at other times may be possible by arrangement; trips just to the dry part (including a paddle on the first lake) cost €5 per person, whereas a trip across the lakes to the Calvary – allow around four hours – costs €30 per person if there are two of you, €26 each if there are three, and €23 each if there are four people. Bear in mind, though, that after a period of heavy rainfall it's usually not possible to advance beyond the first lake. All equipment – helmet, flashlight and boots – is supplied by the **cave guide**, Alojz Troha, who lives in the tiny village of Bloška Polica, at no.7 (☎04/163-2153; ⑳www.kovinoplastika.si/gsk/krizna-jama/kriznaje.html), approximately 1km north of the turning off the main road towards the track which leads to the cave (it's signposted).

Snežnik Castle

Sitting in the middle of a luscious landscaped park of chestnut trees and silky lawns, some 7km south of Križna Jama and just beyond the village of **Kozarišče**, is **Snežnik Castle** (Snežnik Grad; mid-April–Oct Wed–Fri 10am–noon & 3–6pm, Sat & Sun 10am–6pm; €4), a handsome, three-storey Renaissance building impressively girdled by ramparts, towers and a high grey wall.

Entered via a graceful stone-arch bridge spanning a small brook, the castle was originally the thirteenth-century domain of the Aquileian patriarchs, and their subjects the Snežniški lords, after which time the castle changed hands on many occasions. As a result of a court assessment in 1832 the castle was recovered from the heavily-in-debt Lichtenberg family and declared a lottery prize; however, its winner, a Hungarian blacksmith, opted for a cash prize instead, leaving the entire estate up for grabs. Snapped up by Prince Oton Schönburg at an auction in 1853, the castle remained under the ownership of the family until World War I, when it was appropriated by the state. Although there's not a great deal to see inside, the castle was fortunate enough – unlike many other castles in Slovenia during World War II – to retain most of its original nineteenth-century bourgeois furnishings and other works of art, the pick of which is an exotic hoard of deities, sphinxes and pharaohs in the Egyptian Room. Located in one of the former dairy buildings across the way from the castle is a small information point (mid-April to Oct Wed–Fri 10am–noon & 3–6pm, Sat & Sun 10am–1pm & 2–6pm) and the **Dormouse Hunting Museum** (Lovski Polharski muzej; same times; €2), where you can learn more about one of Slovenia's more unusual customs. A unique tradition in Notranjska, the dormouse (*polh*) has long been hunted for commercial purposes – its fur for caps and its fat for machine oil – though it's also something of a culinary speciality in these parts. The first Saturday after 25 September, known as **Dormouse Hunting Night** (Polharska noč), is given over to a frenzied night of hunting activity. The grounds around the castle are a lovely spot for a picnic, with or without dormice.

Without your own transport getting here is awkward: the closest you can get by one of the few buses heading this way is the village of **Stari Trg**, 4km north of Kozarišče – from here there's little option but to hitch a ride or walk. The castle is also the main starting point for **hiking trails** and **cycle routes** up into the Snežnik plateau (see p.226), while those with a car can take the mountain road, which winds its way across the plateau to Ilirska Bistrica.

From Lake Cerknica to Ribnica

From Lake Cerknica the road heads eastwards across the **Bloke Plateau** – a flat, wide, and largely featureless karst plateau whose abundant streams feed Lake Cerknica and Križna Cave to the southwest. The name of the plateau gave rise to one of Slovenia's most enduring cultural symbols, the **Bloke skis**; these short, fat skis, made of beech or birch wood and bound to the foot by a leather strap, were used principally as a means of transportation across the snowy plateau during winter. Valvasor, for one, was suitably impressed, proclaiming: "they descend into the valley with incredible speed…one such strip of wood is strapped under each foot, they take a stout cudgel into their hands and push it into their armpit, and use it as if it were some sort of a rudder to slide off…no less swift than those who use skates in Holland to glide on ice". Whilst skiing as a sport all but died out here after World War I, the plateau is now a popular cross-country skiing venue. Some 25km beyond the plateau's unremarkable main settlement, Nova vas, is Ribnica.

Ribnica and around

Pitched in the centre of a lovely flat-bottomed river valley, between the pine-beech covered ridges of Velika Gora and Mala Gora some 40km south of Ljubljana, **RIBNICA** is an idyllic, diminutive town known throughout Slovenia for its woodenware, pottery and witchcraft. Like many other towns and villages in the Dolenjska region, Ribnica suffered mercilessly at the hands of the Turks during the fifteenth century: records recount some 27 raids in all though, ironically, it was as a result of these incursions that the town's woodenware, or *suha roba* (dry goods), industry flourished. In order to kick-start the local economy, Emperor Frederick III issued a decree allowing peddlers from Ribnica, Kočevje and surrounding areas to trade freely throughout the Austrian territories. Such was their aptitude for a good sell, however, that these indomitable characters began to trade as far afield as Africa and Asia. Ribnica is a good place to break up a journey en route to the forests of Kočevje and other attractions further south.

The Town

Pretty much everything of interest (and of a practical nature) lies along, or just off, the town's main street, **Škrabčev trg**, a fetching thoroughfare preserving a neat ensemble of grey, cream and white two-storey tenements. Running parallel to the main street is the slender Bistrica River, spanned by three exquisite stone bridges, each of which crosses over to **Ribnica Castle** on the left bank. Originally built around the tenth or eleventh century, it later assumed a Renaissance form, though all that remains now – two defensive towers linked by a residential passageway – is the result of the building having been occupied, and subsequently wrecked, during Word War II. More commonly known as the **Cultural Activists' Park**, the surrounding grounds feature busts and memorial stones of prominent local achievers such as Jakob Gallus (composer) and Stanislav Škrabec (linguist; see opposite).

Now a cultural centre, the castle holds the collection of the **Ribnica Town Museum** (May–Oct 10am–1pm & 4–7pm; €2.5), a hit-and-miss affair, but worth a visit to view its Woodenware Collection. This activity was traditionally split into nine or ten branches, each branch – for example, frame making, vessel making, wickerwork and sieve making – linked to a particular household, village, or type of wood (typically pine, beech or lime-tree wood). Although somewhat haphazardly arranged, there's much to admire here, from wicker baskets, drinking vessels and farm tools to less orthodox items such as mousetraps, ski-shoes and backpacks, plus all the appliances used for making these items, every single one of which was handmade. There's also a tidy little collection of ceramic goods from nearby Dolenja Vas, the valley's principal pottery centre. The best time to see the full array of products is at the **Ribnica Fair**, held each year on the first Sunday in September, which entails much buying and selling of wares along the main street.

The museum's other exhibitions merit just a brief look: the first documents the lives of those emigrants who left Dolenjska, mainly for North America, during the late nineteenth and early twentieth centuries in search of a more fruitful life; while the second features a group of mock-up implements and nasty-looking contraptions – gallows, spiked chairs and the like – used in the torture and killing of witches in these parts between the fifteenth and eighteenth centuries.

A short walk east of the castle, across the river and midway along Škrabčev trg, stands the **Parish Church of St Stephen** (Cerkev Sv Štefan), the third church on this site, built in 1868. Its drab exterior was given a sharp contemporary twist shortly after World War II by Slovene architect Jože Plečnik (see p.62), who designed the crown-like steeples atop the twin bell towers – an odd, but effective, amalgamation of triangular arches, spiked cones and pillars. Originally designed for an unnamed cathedral, this was Plečnik's last ever project, though it was actually completed by one of his students after his death. Its interior stars a ceiling painting of the Holy Trinity, a couple of sculptures of St Peter and St Paul, and some terrific paintings by the likes of Langus and Koželj, although, unfortunately, Ivan Grohar's wonderful painting *St Stephen the Pope*, which once adorned the high altar, is no longer on show; however, you will get to see it if you're here at Easter when it's brought out specially. If the church is closed, call in at the priest's house next door (no. 15). The **Steklíček House**, opposite the church at no. 26, is where Slovenia's most esteemed poet, France Prešeren (see box on p.126), was schooled between 1810 and 1812.

Located 1km south of town in Hrovača (no. 42), is the town's most enjoyable diversion, the **Škrabec Homestead** (Škrabčeva Domačija; no set opening times so contact the tourist office; €2), ancestral home of the Škrabec family for more than two centuries. Widely regarded as the country's premier nineteenth-century linguist, Stanislav Škrabec (1844–1918) published his first work in 1870 – a text on the vocal properties and dialect of Slovene literary language and writing – followed by a number of other important treatises, critiques and religious texts. Moreover, he taught several languages at a monastic school in Gorizia. The renovated house comprises the traditional setup of "black" kitchen, living room and bedroom, each room having retained its outstanding original furnishings. The thoroughly modern-looking barn, formerly used for threshing wheat and millet, displays a number of objects made from glass, clay and, of course, wood.

Practicalities

Although there is a rail station at Ribnica, this line nowadays carries only freight traffic. All **buses** stop outside the church on Škrabčev trg, from where it's a two-minute walk to the **tourist office**, on the same street at no. 40 (Mon–Fri 9am–3pm; ☎01/836-9335, ⓦwww.ribnica.si).

There's no **accommodation** in town, but a couple of possibilities exist just outside: 4km south of town in the village of Prigorica, *Pension Izlaty* at no. 115 (☎01/836-4515; ❸), has six boxy rooms sleeping between one and three persons; buses en route to Kočevje stop 50m from the pension opposite the church. A more rural alternative is the *Boltetni* tourist farm (☎01/836-0208; ❷), located on the edge of a forest in the tiny village of Dane (no. 9) 4km west of town, and hence only really accessible by car.

You'll fare marginally better if you're looking for somewhere to **eat**: *Gostilna Mihelič*, opposite the church at Škrabčev trg 22 (Tues–Sat 9am–10pm, Sun til 4pm), can sustain you with a decent range of fish, grills and salads, as well as dumplings and cottage cheese dishes for vegetarians; and, in a similar vein, but slightly more cheerful, is the *Pri Pildarju* at no. 27. The oddly named *Pub Hotel* (there is no hotel), just around the corner on Kolodvorska ulica, is a surprisingly lively place, equally good for a daytime coffee or late-night beer (daily until midnight, Fri & Sun until 2am). The **post office** is at Kolodvorska ulica 2 (Mon–Fri 8am–7pm, Sat 8am–noon), a few metres from the *Pub Hotel*, and there's **Internet access** in the library next to the tourist office (Mon–Fri 9am–7pm, Sat 8am–1pm).

Nova Štifta

Six kilometres west of Ribnica in the tiny hamlet of **Nova Štifta**, at the foothills of Velika Gora, the **Church of the Assumption** (Vnebovzetje Device Marije) is one of Slovenia's foremost pilgrimage churches, a fine-looking Baroque structure built between 1641 and 1671 and noteworthy for its unorthodox octagonal form and unusual arcaded portico embracing the south and east facades.

Its interior, meanwhile, would ordinarily be considered unremarkable were it not for the blisteringly colourful, gold, red and green wood-carved altars, ornamented with dazzling spiral columns. Around a century after the church was built, the **Holy Steps** (Sancta Sanctorum) were constructed on the north side in order to allow greater numbers of pilgrims into the church; unfortunately, the steps are now out of bounds, though you can just catch a glimpse of them, and the frescoes lining the side walls, through the windows. As the church is usually kept locked, it's best to call before you set off (℡01/836-9943), although there should be someone with the key in the monastery building adjacent. Without your own **transport**, the only way to get here is to hitch or walk, neither of which is an especially appealing option.

Kočevje and around

From Ribnica, hourly buses trundle south to **KOČEVJE** (some 16km distant), whose first inhabitants were German settlers way back in the fourteenth century, the result of a policy of systematic colonization introduced by the then ruling Ortenburgs – the name Kočevje is actually derived from the German word Gottschee, the name of the region (and the German-language speaking, Slovene, minority) during the interwar years. Historically, Kočevska (the name of the region) has always been a sparsely populated area, the legacy of poor transportation links, a programme of mass resettlement of the majority ethnic German population towards the end of World War II, and the closure of a large part of the region for military purposes following the end of the same war – a regulation that was lifted following independence in 1991. Although the town itself is not particularly appetizing, its proximity to **Kočevski Rog**, the country's finest uninterrupted expanse of forest, and the **Kolpa Valley** on the Croatian border, means that there's a good chance you'll pass through here if either of these places are your intended destination.

The Town

As hard as it is to imagine, a castle stood on the site of the present main square, Trg Zbora Odposlancev, until as recently as World War II, when it was obliterated and its remains removed. From the **World War II monument to freedom** in the centre of this same square, it's a short walk to the enormous Neo-Gothic **Parish Church of St Fabian and St Sebastian**, completed in 1903 and announced by two searing sixty-five-metre-high spires. Inside, the bright and beautiful paintings of the Holy Trinity on the presbytery ceiling, the twenty-four old men of Israel underneath, and the kings and angels to the side, were executed by Slavko Pengov in 1932, while the large wooden statue of Saint Jernej next to the high altar was completed by popular local sculptor, Stane Jarm, a native of Osilnica (see p.239).

If you've got some time to pass, then head to the **Kočevje Regional Museum** (Pokrajinski Muzej Kočevje; Mon–Fri 9am–3pm, plus Wed 4–6pm, Sat 9am–noon; €2.5), a ten-minute walk east of the main square at Prešernova 11. Of particular interest – indeed of some historical importance for Slovenes – is the building itself: built in 1937, the **Šeškov House** (Šeškov Dom) staged the Assembly of the Delegates of the Slovene Nation in October 1943, the first elected parliament in Slovenia's history. The only remaining original feature of the hall is the heavily pockmarked bright red insignia above the stage, which reads "Narod si bo pisal Sodbo Sam" ("The people will make their own judgement"). The walls of the hall are now framed with a fine selection of sketches and drawings by Dolenjska native **Božidar Jakac**, an artist whose work you'll come across time and again in this region; completed during the sessions of the 1943 assembly, his drawings depict local landscapes, portraits and the lives of the Rog inhabitants – notably the Partisans, for whom he acted as pictorial chronicler.

The museum's core exhibition deals with the plight of the **Kočevje Germans** who, until the Italian occupation during the winter of 1941–42, had been the region's majority population for some 600 years. The effect of the occupation was catastrophic; most of the population was relocated into homes of previously deported Slovenes in the lower Posavje region (which was then under German control), more than half of the 170 or so German-speaking settlements in the region were abandoned, demolished or renamed, whilst nearly one hundred churches were razed. The absence of English captioning, however, makes this part of the museum a frustrating and frankly rather dull experience.

Practicalities

The **bus station** is 200m south of the main square, Trg Zbora Odposlancev (abbreviated to TZO on signs), location for pretty much everything else of a practical nature, including the **tourist office** at no. 18b (April–Aug Mon–Sat 8am–6pm; Sept–March Mon–Fri 8am–3pm, Sat 8am–1pm; ℡01/895-4979, Ⓔinfo@kocevje.si). Opposite is the town's sole **hotel**, the very reasonable and pretty good value *Valentin* (℡01/895-1286, Ⓦwww.hotel-valentin.com; ❺). Less conveniently located out by the Rudnik Lake, 1km northeast of town, the rather downbeat *Pension Jezero* (℡01/895-2230; ❸) is a cheaper alternative.

Eating possibilities are dreadfully unexciting, with options limited to a couple of pizzerias: *Pizzeria Luigi*, just across from the bus station, is a bright place with a decent spaghetti menu, or there's the larger but wholly characterless *Pizzeria Briški*, a few paces along from the *Hotel Valentin*. For a daytime or evening **drink**, the colourful and loungy *Kavarna*, on the main square, is a good spot (Fri & Sat til 1am), and also on the square, *Café Medo* has a superb choice of cakes and pastries.

Brown bears

The majority of Slovenia's estimated six hundred or so brown bears are to be found in the heavily forested regions of southern Slovenia, and in particular, those forests surrounding Kočevje and Snežnik.

The country's indigenous brown bear population was almost decimated during the nineteenth century, thanks to intensive farming, deforestation and excessive hunting practices. But stricter environmental protection standards since the end of World War II have contributed to a sharp increase in their number over the past few decades, numbers that were boosted during the wars in Bosnia in the early 1990s when many bears sought to escape their disturbed habitats. Today around one hundred bears are culled each year, while small numbers are regularly transferred to France, Spain and other European countries in order to repopulate certain areas.

The most likely time to see bears – not that you really want to – is from March to June, and during October and November. In any case, you'd do well to follow the cardinal rules: store food and rubbish properly, make sure bears know you're there (make lots of noise as you're walking along), and, clearly, do not approach them – also watch out for fresh tracks, diggings and droppings. In the unlikely event of a direct encounter, stay calm, do not engage in direct eye contact and try to back off slowly speaking in a low, monotone voice – under no circumstances should you run. If the bear decides to attack, the situation is truly grim, though playing dead – curling up into a foetal position and protecting your head – is commonly known to be the most effective method of survival.

△ Kocevje Forest

Kočevski Rog

One of the country's most secluded karst landscapes, **Kočevski Rog** is a massively forested thirty-five-kilometre-long mountain range bordering Kočevje to the east, and extending in a northwest–southeast direction (a typical Dinaric range) towards the Kolpa River and Croatian border. During World War II Kočevski Rog offered perfect sanctuary for Partisan activities, sheltering military and political offices, workshops, hospitals, printing presses and schools. The centre of operations was **Baza 20** (Base 20), which consisted of some 26 wooden shacks occupied by members of both the Central Committee of the Communist Party of Slovenia, and the Executive Committee of the Liberation Front. At the height of operations, nearly two hundred people were ensconced here, including twenty senior commanders, although Tito only visited once, when the war was over.

As an attraction it can't compare with the Franja Partisan Hospital near Cerkno (see p.186), but if you want to see inside a couple of the huts (save for some bunk beds and a small exhibition there's not much to see), contact the tourist offices either in Kočevje (see p.235) or Dolenjske Toplice (see p.246). Baza 20 is sited on the eastern ridge of Kočevski Rog, and is actually easier to get to from the small town of Dolenjske Toplice, at the foot of Rog, than it is Kočevje. From Dolenjske Toplice take the road south for 1km to Podturn, then head up the mountain road to the car park, a further 7km distant; from here it's a fifteen-minute walk through the forest to Baza 20. There's also a small **restaurant** by the car park.

It was in these forests, too, that several thousand anti-communist forces – mostly members of the notorious Slovene Home Guard (Domobranci) returned by British military authorities at the war's conclusion – were summarily executed and dumped into limestone pits. The existence of these **mass graves** remained a secret until 1975, when the dissident writer and politician, Edvard Kocbek, revealed the grim details in an interview to a Trieste newspaper. It was only recently, however, that the victims of these "silent killings" were acknowledged, with the passing of the 2003 War Graves Act, which effectively made provision for the management and marking of burial sites at the appropriate spots.

Kočevski Rog offers some of the best non-alpine hiking in the country and, though not especially demanding, the walks here are no less enjoyable. You'd do well, however, to stick closely to the trails; not only are you likely to get completely lost if you stray, but it's not inconceivable that you'll encounter brown bear, a large number of whom inhabit these parts – as do lynx, wolf, boar and red deer. Not surprisingly, Kočevksi Rog is a popular destination with functionaries and hunters. The circular **Rog Footpath** (Roška Pešpot) – somewhat ominously marked out by bear paws – totals some 60km. While it's unlikely you'd want to tackle the whole thing as this would take around three days, you can easily do parts of it; one possibility is to drive to the highest point, **Veliki Rog** (1099m), where's there's a viewing tower, and hike a section of the trail from there.

Three kilometres south of Veliki Rog is **Rajhenavski Rog**, one of Kočevski's six **virgin forests** – there are a total of fourteen in the country. The trees here are manifestly higher, thicker, and older (four and five hundred-year-old trees are not uncommon) than those of your average forest, whilst strictly administered rules forbid the cutting or removal of any trees, dead or alive; moreover, as protected and preserved areas, virgin forests are strictly off-limits to the general public, though trails are laid out around the periphery. The best known of the forests' trees, and the symbol of Kočevski Rog, is the **Queen of Rog**, a magnificent fifty-metre-high, five hundred-year-old fir sited 2km south of Rajhenavski Rog. There are beds at two **forest huts**; Luža at the northernmost point of the path (approx 16km from the start in Kočevje), and at Podstene, 2km south of the Queen of Rog.

An excellent alternative to the above is the Stojna Highland south and west of town, in particular the popular trail which leads up to **Mestni Vrh** (1034m; 1hr) and the ruins of **Friedrichstein Castle** (970m), built in the early fifteenth century but abandoned around 1650. The dated but still useful 1:50,000 *Kočevsko* map, available from the tourist office, is an essential aid if you plan to take any hikes in these forests.

The Kolpa Valley

The main Ljubljana–Ribnica–Kočevje road continues south towards the stunning **Kolpa Valley**, a contorted, gorge-like river valley named after the beautiful 120-kilometre-long **Kolpa River** (Kupa in Croatian), which forms the border with Croatia. For the most part, the valley remains well off the main tourist track, thanks both to the popularity of more-established destinations further north and the paucity of public transport hereabouts. This is, though, wonderful driving and cycling country, and if you have wheels or are prepared to hitch then you could do a lot worse than spend a day taking in the scenery, partaking in any number of water-bound activities, or just resting up at one of the many delightful riverside picnic spots. Although quite different in character and temperament to the Soča River, the Kolpa, with its picturesque rapids and dams, is a big draw for adventure-sports enthusiasts, while swimmers and bathers flock to its warm waters in the summer months.

Before you reach the border, it's worth taking a minor detour to the dramatically sited ruins of the thirteenth-century **Kostel Castle**, perched atop a lofty promontory about 20km south of Kočevje, and just 6km shy of the Petrina border crossing. The castle is currently undergoing extensive renovation works (and hence, partly closed off), but you can scramble up to the entrance, a great spot from which to soak up the magnificent views. A good time to visit is at the end of August, when the **Tamburanje Festival**, a showpiece for local folk bands, is staged in and around the castle's grounds.

Sport and activities

As far as **activities** go, there's just about everything on offer in the Kolpa valley, most of which is available between April and October – be sure to call at least a day in advance to organize. Activities include rafting, kayaking, hydrospeed and canyoning, each costing around €20 per person for a three- to four-hour trip; in addition, there's an Adrenaline Park (€15–€50 depending upon activity and length of time), as well as archery (€12 for 1hr), paintballing (€20 for 3–4hr) and tennis (€6 for 1hr). Guided hikes are also possible upon request, and there are bikes for hire (€8 for half a day, €12 per day). If you've got your passport, you could also hike to the **source of the Kolpa** in Croatia, which should take around five hours round trip.

The Upper Kolpa Valley

The valley is at its most impressive between the tiny hamlet of **Dol** – some 26km east of the Petrina border crossing – and the village of Osilnica, 20km west of the same crossing, a stretch known as the **Upper Kolpa Valley** (Zgornja Kolpska Dolina).

Approximately 10km west of the border crossing, just beyond the village of Srobotnik (stop off at the small parking bay), a short gravel path sneaks its way up to the redundant **Church of Saint Anne** (Cerkev Sv Ana); the church is closed but the stupendous views are more than ample compensation. Back on the road, shortly after the church, the entrance to the uppermost part of the valley – **Osilnica Valley** (Osilniška Dolina) – is marked by a hulk-sized **wooden statue** of the local mythological folk hero **Peter Klepec**, whose feats of strength and daring against the Turks are the stuff of legend in these parts. A further 4km on from here, the village of **GRINTOVEC PRI OSILNICI** is the starting point for an energetic hike up to the formidable bluff of **Loška stena** (875m; 5hr).

The first building you see upon entering the village of **RIBJEK**, some 2km on from Grintovec and sited almost directly beneath Loška stena, is the preposterously pretty roadside **Church of St Egidius** (Cerkev Sv Egidija), the valley's most important historical monument. Built around 1680 but substantially renovated a few years ago, this dinky Renaissance structure manifests some absorbing detail: whitewashed walls, painted window frames, shingled gable roof and portico and a flat bell tower. Its interior, meanwhile, stars a wood-coffered ceiling and elaborately carved wooden altars dating from around the same time. If the church is locked the key can be obtained from no. 2, just a few paces away.

Osilnica

At the confluence of the Kolpa and Čabranka rivers, 3km beyond Ribjek, **OSILNICA** is the valley's largest settlement, and pretty much the end of the line as far as things to see and do are concerned. Aside from harbouring most of the valley's practical facilities, the reason you're most likely to wind up here is to have a crack at one of the many sports and activities on offer. A good time to be in the village is on the last Saturday in July (**St Peter's Day**), a day of live music, food and drink in honour of the mythical local hero, Peter Klepec.

The helpful little **tourist office** is located on the small main square at no. 16 (Mon–Fri 8am–3pm; ☎01/894-1594, ⊛www.osilnica.si); if it's closed, pop across the road to the municipal building (Občina), where someone will be able to help. Whilst here, it's quite likely that you'll end up at Kovač Tourism and Sports, a large family-run affair five minutes' walk away at Sela 5 (☎01/894-1508, ⊛www.kovac-kolpa.com), as this is virtually where everything in the village happens. **Accommodation** is present in the form of two ⚓Kovač-run hotels: a lovely and very comfortable residence (④); and, across the road, a hostel-like place, with doubles and triples (②). If you'd rather **camp**, there's a small area near the hotel. Kovač also rents out apartments (located next to the tourist office) sleeping between four and six people (③). The classy ⁂ **restaurant** offers superb home-style cooking and the terrace is a splendid place to eat in the summer months.

A short walk uphill from the tourist office, at no. 19, is the **Stane Jarm Gallery**, named after the sculptor who was born here in 1931. He used wood as his principal medium (see also his dramatic sculpture of Saint Jernej in the Parish Church in Kočevje, p.234), and the small gallery is chock-full of the master sculptor's haunting, rigidly cut faces; contact the tourist office if you wish to visit.

Eastern Dolenjska and Bela Krajina

The eastern half of Dolenjska holds the majority of its sights. These are by and large ranged along the **Krka River**, which emanates from a cave near the village of the same name and flows eastwards towards the Croatian border, joining up with the mighty Sava River near Brežice. Approximately midway between Ljubljana and the beginning of the Krka, both **Stična Monastery** and **Bogenšperk Castle** are well worth visiting, despite each being fairly awkward to reach.

From its source, the Krka continues east towards the ruins of **Žužemberk Castle** and **Soteska Manor**, before turning north just prior to the atmospheric little spa town of **Dolenjske Toplice**. A little further on, **Novo Mesto** hoves into view; comfortably southern Slovenia's largest town, it merits a leisurely half-day visit. East of Novo Mesto, the river continues a course past the beautifully set **Otočec Castle**, and the delightfully slumberous town of **Kostanjevica na Krki**, itself close to another of Slovenia's ancient monasteries, **Pleterje**. The region's easternmost attractions are the small market town of **Brežice**, and the country's largest spa centre in **Čatež**.

Bela Krajina acquired its name – meaning White Carniola, derived partially from the ubiquitous birch tree, and the white costumes worn by its inhabitants, the **Bela Kranjci** (White Carniolans) – during the fifteenth century, when the lands were incorporated into the province of Carniola. Its frontline position ensured that, around the same time, the region's towns and villages suffered a fair battering at the hands of the Turks, whose unremitting drive up through the Balkans also led to an influx of Croat and Serb refugees and renegades (Uskoks) from Bosnia. A period of cultural and economic efflorescence eventually gave way to regional decline, as the closure of many important industrial plants was compounded by a catastrophic bout of phylloxera at the end of the nineteenth century, which destroyed almost all the region's vineyards. Much of the local population was forced to emigrate, mainly to North America, whilst those that remained continued to engage in traditional cottage industries as a means of eking out a living. Its two main towns, **Črnomelj** and **Metlika**, are fairly low-key places but are convenient for the more interesting sites close at hand.

Stična Monastery

Some thirty kilometres southeast of Ljubljana, just off the Ljubljana–Novo Mesto highway near the village of **Ivančna Gorica**, stands **Stična Monastery**. Slovenia's oldest monastery, it was established in 1136 as part of the European network of Cistercian monasteries. Within a few years of its foundation Stična had assumed the role of Dolenjska's chief centre of culture and learning, with several important religious manuscripts having been drawn up in the monastery's scriptorium; these are now kept at the NUK library in Ljubljana and the Austrian National Library in Vienna.

The thick walls and towers you see today were erected as a result of repeated Turkish raids during the fifteenth century, a period of otherwise relative prosper-

△ Stična Monastery

The
Great Outdoors

There are few more active nations in Europe than Slovenia, where abundant mountains, forests, hills, rivers and lakes offer unlimited potential to indulge in a wide range of outdoor pursuits: from hiking the lush meadows and valleys of the Julian Alps, cycling amidst the rolling hills and forests of Dolenjska, rafting and kayaking the thrashing Soča River, or climbing Mount Triglav, Slovenia's highest mountain – the permutations for adventure are endless.

Hitting the Slopes

Skiing was first popularized in Slovenia in the seventeenth century, when natives took to the broad open spaces of the Bloke Plateau in Notranjska. Slovenes today are no less enthusiastic and alpine skiing remains the nation's number one sport. Uniformly well-equipped, efficient and safe, Slovenia counts more than fifteen major **resorts** (and many smaller ones), the best equipped and most popular of which are Kranjska Gora, a good family resort and international competition venue near the Austrian border, Krvavec, near Kranj (very popular with weekending Ljubljančani), Cerkno, in Primorska, and Pohorje, on the outskirts of Maribor – this the country's largest skiing area. A number of resorts (such as Krvavec, and Vogel, near Lake Bohinj) also offer good **snowboarding** facilities, and **cross-country skiing** is another Slovene institution, the main venue here being the Pokljuka Plateau near Bled. For more detailed information on skiing in northwestern Slovenia, see the box on p.140.

Skiing at Kranjska Gora

Mountain climbing in the Julian Alps

Scaling the peaks

Slovenia is traversed by over seven thousand kilometres of marked paths, and for the majority of **climbers and hikers**, the main destination is the **Julian Alps**, at the heart of which is **Mount Triglav** (2864m), the country's highest peak. Along with the Julians, the **Karavanke Mountains** and the **Kamniške-Savinja Alps** (both of which count numerous peaks topping the 2500-metre mark) offer the country's most varied and challenging climbs and hikes. For the less energetic, there's more **moderate walking** in the non-alpine tracts of the Pohorje Massif near Maribor, and the Snežnik hills south of Postojna along the Croatian border, while there's also gentler rambling territory south of Triglav National Park in the sub-alpine hills of Cerkno and Idrija, and in the deep forests of Dolenjska. For more details on hiking in Slovenia see p.136.

Horsing around

As the home of the Lipizzaner it's perhaps not surprising that Slovenia displays a deep-rooted attachment to all things equine. Whilst the most obvious destination for equestrians is Lipica (see p.190), there are dozens more **horse riding centres** throughout the country, many sited in fabulously scenic locations. Most offer some form of recreational (trail) and arena riding, and a range of classes and courses – some also offer carriage rides; three of the most established centres are Pristava Lepena in the gorgeous Trenta Valley (there are Lipizzaner here too), the Kaval Centre at Prestranek near Postojna, and the Brdo estate just outside Kranj.

Horse riding

Casting a line

Slovenia offers some of the finest freshwater **fishing** in Europe, its abundant rivers, streams and lakes richly sourced with many different species of fish. The Soča river is renowned for its bountiful reserves of grayling and trout – brown trout, rainbow trout, and, above all, the highly prized marble trout. Elsewhere, the Kolpa, Krka, Sava Bohinjka and Unica rivers have healthy stocks of pike, perch, chub and eelpout. Of the lakes, fishing from boats is permitted at Lake Bohinj and the intermittent Lake Cerknica. The main fishing season lasts approximately from April to October, although this can vary slightly depending upon the water levels. Permits are required, and they don't come cheap (expect to pay €20–40 for a daily permit); details on obtaining permits are listed throughout the guide.

Fisherman on the Krka river

Slovenia's top 5 adrenaline rushes

Slovenia is geared up in a big way for **adventure sports and activities**, in particular around its rivers, which attract enthusiasts from all over Europe each summer.

Paragliding

• **White-water rafting** Whether on the fast, foaming waters of the Soča river, or the calmer, warmer stretches of the Kolpa, this is the country's most popular adventure sport.

• **Canyoning** The ultimate adrenaline experience, involving abseiling down ravines and waterfalls, jumping into pools and sliding through mountainous rivers.

• **Hydrospeed** Descending the rapids face down on a small polyurethane raft, this pursuit is the most extreme of all water activities.

• **Kayaking** Paddling solo or in a pair, Slovenia's rivers allow for thrilling white-water kayaking experiences.

• **Tandem Paragliding** A head for heights is all that's required for spectacular bird's-eye views of Slovenia's phenomenal natural scenery.

Kayaking

Daredevil Slovenes

In recent years Slovene alpinists have a gained a world-class reputation, thanks in no small part to the daredevil deeds of several **extreme athletes**: foremost amongst these is climber **Tomaž Humar**, who has made over 1500 ascents, over fifty of which have been first ascents, including the indomitable South Face of Nepal's Mount Daulaghiri. Not to be outdone is the mountaineer and extreme skier **Davo Karničar**, who has skied down the highest mountain of every continent, including an amazing descent of Mount Everest in 2000 – the first man to do so. No less remarkable have been the exploits of ultra marathon swimmer **Martin Strel**, who holds several world records for long-distance swims; in 2000, he swam the entire length of the Danube River in 58 days, and in 2004 swam the Mississippi River (the first man ever to do so) in 68 days; next up is the Amazon in 2007. Ironically, the name of his home town, Mokronog, translates as 'Wet Feet'.

ity for Stična. Dissolved by Emperor Joseph II in 1784 as part of his sweeping reforms, the monastery remained defunct until 1898, at which point it was revived by Cistercians from the monastery at Bodensee (Lake Constance). It is currently home to eleven monks (including the abbot), and whilst not as asocial as Pleterje Monastery (see p.251), the monks at Stična remain strictly governed by the motto of Saint Benedict, "*Ora et labora*" ("Pray and Work"), and so must devote themselves to between six and eight hours of prayer each day, whilst all meals are taken in complete silence. A visit to Stična entails a **guided tour** (Tues–Sat 8.30am, 10am, 2pm & 4pm, Sun 2pm & 4pm; €4) of the monastery's religious museum, the church and cloister.

The nearest **train station** is in Ivančna Gorica (on the Ljubljana–Novo Mesto line), about 2.5km south of the monastery, whilst buses can set you down on the highway running parallel to the rail track. If you need to stay, there's **accommodation** at the homely Grofija tourist farm, about 1.5km southeast of the monastery in the village of Vir pri Stični, at no. 30 (T01/787-8141, E tk.grofija@volja.net; ❷).

The Slovene Religious Museum

On the north side of the courtyard (to the right as you enter), the two-storeyed, Renaissance-era **Old Prelature**, formerly the monastery's administrative centre, now houses the **Slovene Religious Museum**; its first floor is a treasure trove of monastic riches – antique furniture, liturgical vessels, vestments and so on – while the second floor (entitled Christianity in Slovenia) chronicles the many disparate groups and movements that have shaped the development of the Slovene Church throughout the centuries, including Protestants, Jesuits, Capuchins and Ursulines. The museum's impressive art and cultural history section has fresco remains by the renowned fifteenth-century artist Janez Ljubljanski, paintings by Langus and Metzinger, and a typically exuberant chalice designed by architect Jože Plečnik as a gift for Simon Ašič, a former abbot who also happened to be one of Slovenia's most eminent herbalists; you can purchase some of his medicinal herbs and teas from the shop by the entrance.

The Abbey Church and Cloister

Adjacent to the Prelature, the twelfth-century **Abbey Church** betrays few signs of its Romanesque origins, having been extensively reworked in Baroque style during the seventeenth and eighteenth centuries. Its vast, white tripartite nave is fairly naked, save for a larger than usual number of side altars – one for each priest to pray to – although there are some fine artistic treasures to admire, most notably the fourteen Stations of the Cross painted by Fortunat Bregant in 1766; a marble tabernacle by Plečnik; and some beautifully worked tombstones – look out for the red stone tombstone of Abbot Jacob Reinprecht, the chief architect of the church's present Baroque appearance.

Abutting the church at the heart of the complex is the thirteenth-century Gothic **cloister**, a splendid rib-vaulted space complete with lancet windows and several layers of just about discernible frescoes, the best of which are those by master painter Janez Ljubljanski in the north wing. Elsewhere, look out for the figural keystones in the western wing depicting human faces, and the two superbly restored bifora (double-arched windows), the cloister's most obvious Romanesque remains. On the south side of the cloister, the **refectory's** pink vaulted ceiling is decorated with some marvellous stuccowork (it's forbidden to enter, but you can see it from the doorway), as is the ceiling of the **Upper Tower**, located on the opposite side of the Prelature; the compositions on the latter depict scenes from the Crucifixion and Last Judgement, as well as images of the four Church Fathers.

Bogenšperk Castle

Surrounded by the densely forested Dolenjska hills some 20km north of Stična, close to the large village of Šmartno pri Litiji, **Bogenšperk Castle** (March–Oct Fri 9am–5pm, Sat & Sun 10am–5pm; Nov–Feb Sat & Sun 9am–5pm; €2) is a descendant of a twelfth-century medieval fortification, though the present structure dates from around 1511. Built by the lords of Wagen (Wagensperg is German for Bogenšperk), the castle is synonymous with the great polymath Janez Vajkard Valvasor (see box below), who lived and worked here between 1672 and 1692, during which time he compiled his immense opus *The Glory of the Duchy of Carniola.*

The building is a classic Renaissance-era chateau featuring three cylindrical towers and a partly arcaded inner courtyard. The interior, meanwhile, has been refurbished – the castle's entire contents were plundered at the end of World War II – so as to evoke the atmosphere of Valvasor's day. His **library** (at least that's the assumption, based on the fact that it's the largest room in the castle) is now used as a wedding venue, while the old hunting room contains an odd, and rather mundane, mishmash of exhibits: hunting trophies, geological and folk-costume displays, as well as an exposition on seventeenth-century witch trials, a subject Valvasor wrote about in his aforementioned work. Of greater interest are the two rooms packed with fascinating maps and sketches, including original works by Valvasor and eminent Slovene cartographer Peter Kosler, and a cylinder printing press of the type Valvasor used – the original is in Mainz, Germany. Valvasor's **study**, which we know to be his because of the four marble pillars to which he referred in his writings, contains the museum's principal exhibit, an original copy of *The Glory of the Duchy of Carniola.* Indeed, the castle retains just four of Valvasor's books: one other is kept in Zagreb, whilst the whereabouts of the other two is unknown.

Bogenšperk is not the easiest place to get to; if you're coming from Ivančna Gorica, you'll have to get here under your own steam, be it by bike or car. By **public transport** you must take a bus or train from Ljubljana as far as Litija, though from here it's still another 6km slog uphill to the castle.

Janez Vajkard Valvasor

Arguably Slovenia's greatest scholar, **Janez Vajkard Valvasor** – historian, topographer and ethnologist – was born in Ljubljana in 1641 of a noble family from Bergamo in Italy. Following extensive travels throughout Europe and North Africa, Valvasor purchased Bogenšperk in 1672, assembling a rich library and establishing important graphics and printing workshops within the castle. Having devoted his entire life to research, he spent the next fifteen years compiling and writing his monumental baroque topography *The Glory of the Duchy of Carniola*, four illustrated encyclopaedic volumes weighing in at 3532 pages. In it, Valvasor offered the first thoroughgoing presentation of the then province of Carniola, as well as several neighbouring provinces, expounding upon the region's extraordinary natural phenomena, such as the caves at Postojna and Škocjan, and the disappearing Lake Cerknica, as well as extolling the virtues of the people who shaped these lands. Following the book's publication, Valvasor lectured to the Royal Society in London on the miraculous workings of the lake, an occasion that saw him rewarded with a fellowship from the society. However, such was the debt accumulated by Valvasor during the process of compiling and publishing the book, that he was eventually forced to sell both the castle and all its contents. He died, destitute, in the town of Krško in 1693.

Trebnje

Back on the main Ljubljana–Zagreb E70 highway, 18km east of Stična (it's also on the Ljubljana–Novo Mesto rail line), it's worth stopping off at the small town of **TREBNJE** to visit the **Gallery of Naïve Artists** (Galerija Likovnih Samorastnikov; no set opening times so contact the tourist information office – below; €3), the only museum of its kind in the country. Modelled on the famous Hlebine school in northern Croatia, the gallery presents an outstanding collection of naïve art principally from Slovenia and other countries of the former Yugoslavia, but also from Africa, Asia and Latin America. The origins of self-taught painting in Slovenia can be traced back to the popular nineteenth-century folk art of beehive panel painting (see p.114), itself believed to have derived from the widely practised discipline of painting farm furniture and glass. These wonderfully authentic expressions of indigenous peasant culture later manifest themselves in the colourful world of the naïve painters during the 1930s and 1940s.

The pictures here – painted on wood, canvas or glass – are typically fresh and vibrant, occasionally kitsch or sometimes just plain bizarre, but in nearly all cases touch upon themes pertaining to everyday village life; there are also some wonderfully bucolic landscape paintings, such as *Eve* by the Bosnian Sekula Dugandič, and *Two Blooms*, by eminent Croatian village painter Ivan Rabuzin. Works by Slovenian artists to look out for include scenes from the Kurent by Boris Žohar, and several portraits by Irena Polanec. If you're here at the end of June there's a week-long festival starring international artists working live inside the gallery.

The museum is in the centre of town on Goliev trg – from the **train station** on Kolodvorska ulica, walk up to the main road, turn left and continue for some 150 metres. The **bus station** is next to the church, which is opposite the museum, as is the small **tourist office** (Mon–Fri 9am–3pm; ☎07/304-4717, ✉tictrebnje@volja. net). A simple, but decent place to **eat** here is *Gostilna Šeligo*, 150m back down from the tourist office on the corner of Kolodvorska ulica and Goliev trg. If you're looking to **stay** hereabouts, there's the classy *Gostilna Rakar* (☎07/346-6190, ✉gostilna.rakar@siol.net; ❻), 3km southeast of town in the village of Gorenje Ponikve, at no. 8; it offers a dozen or so very tidy rooms as well as a handsome restaurant (closed Tues).

The Krka River Valley

The **Krka River Valley** is one of the country's most picturesque valley regions, yet it's little visited by tourists, many of whom inadvertently bypass it travelling on the main road or rail routes just to the north. The valley's defining feature is its wide, languid river, richly stocked with brown trout, pikeperch and grayling; issuing forth from a spring in the Krka Cave, it continues beyond the valley's lower reaches to Novo Mesto, and then onwards to Brežice where it discharges into the Sava River. The Krka is also known for its attractive calc-tufa falls and rapids, step-like waterfalls composed of porous rock formed from calcium carbonate, which you can see at regular intervals along the entire stretch of the river. Natural attractions aside, there's much of historical importance to see within the valley, including castle remains at **Žužemberk** and **Soteska**, the village of **Muljava** – birthplace of one of Slovenia's great writers – and, at the tail end of the valley, the quaint spa town, **Dolenjske Toplice**.

Muljava and the source of the Krka

Due south of Ivančna Gorica, on the other side of the highway, **MULJAVA** is an attractive little village known throughout the country as the birthplace of popular Slovene novelist and journalist Josip Jurčič (1844–1881), the man credited with writing Slovenia's first full-length novel *Deseti Brat* (*The Tenth Brother*), in 1866. The house in which he was born (Jurčičeva Domačija; Tues–Sat 8am–noon & 2–5pm, Sun 2–5pm; €3), and lived in until the age of twelve, was built by his grandfather in 1826 and is as interesting for its architectural detail – a traditional "black" kitchen, living room, bedroom and cellar – as it is for the memorabilia on display pertaining to Jurčič's life. In the garden stands a beehive, furnished with the traditional painted panels, while to the rear of the house there's a granary and a Krjavelj Hut, a timber shack dwelling usually inhabited by a *bajtar* – a poor villager. The house, at no. 11, is signposted from the main square.

Each year, on two or three consecutive weekends at the end of June/beginning of July several of Jurčič's works are staged in the fabulous natural amphitheatre located at the edge of woodland behind the house; tickets (around €6) can be purchased one hour before each performance. Muljava also marks the starting point for the very scenic and very popular **Jurčičeva Pot walk;** named after Jurčič, the walk (3–4hr) winds up at the lovely little medieval settlement of Višnja Gora (550m) some 15km further north.

One section of the walk takes in the village of **Krka**, 2km south of Muljava, and the **source of the Krka River** (Pri Izviru), another 2km further on. The source (a seventeen-metre-deep siphon lake) is actually located inside the small, 200-metre-long **Krka Cave** (Krška jama), an unexciting spectacle with none of the spectacular formations you'd find in Slovenia's better-known caves; it does, however, hold a specimen of Proteus Anguinus (the Human Fish – see the Subterranean Slovenia colour section). To visit you should head to the kiosk located 200m before the entrance,

△ Krka River

from where you will be escorted to the cave and given a short guided tour; although opening times can be erratic, the cave is usually open daily between 9am and 6pm (4 or 5pm in winter), but it's best to call in advance to make sure (☎041/276-252; €2).

Žužemberk Castle and Soteska Manor

The valley's major settlement is the market town of **ŽUŽEMBERK**, which is dominated by the formidable bulk of **Žužemberk Castle** (July & Aug Fri 9am–7pm, Sat & Sun 10am–6pm; free), much of which was razed during World War II; although a programme of renovation has been ongoing for years, the restoration of the five huge towers and bastions aside, you'd hardly notice. Dramatically sited on a steep bank high above the Krka River and buffered by a thick clump of trees which slope down to the water, the original castle dates from the thirteenth century, with piecemeal development over the ensuing centuries, including the aforementioned towers, as well as defensive walls, arcades and vaulted cellars, most of which you can still see.

Today, the castle's large inner courtyard is the atmospheric venue for summer concerts and plays, all of which are usually free; the key event is the **Market Town Days Festival** in mid-July, a weekend of medieval jousting, exhibitions, food and craft stalls and the like. To find out what else is on, contact the municipal building (Občina) opposite the castle at Grajska trg 33 (Mon–Fri 8am–4pm; ☎07/388-5180, ✉obcina.zuzemberk@zuzemberk.si). In the centre of this main square is a fine little cast-iron fountain, forged at the ironworks in the nearby village of Dvor and worth a look for its splendidly crafted animal heads from whence water spouts. For the best views of the castle, walk down to the river and across to the opposite bank; standing on the bridge gives you head-on views of the calc-tufa falls.

The town's position on the Krka allowed for the extensive development of water-powered installations during the sixteenth and seventeenth centuries, most commonly iron foundries and sawmills. At one stage there were around forty of the latter lining this stretch of river, though by the end of the twentieth century most had ceased functioning. The Zajčev Mill, located a little way upstream near Prapreče, is the only mill still in operation and can be visited if you contact the municipal building (see above). The Krka River is also popular with water-sports enthusiasts; canoes and kayaks (€3 per hour) can be rented from the *Koren* tourist farm, down by the river at Dolga Vas 5 (☎07/308-7260, ✉turizem_koren@volja. net; ❷) – they also have one- to four-bed **rooms**, camping space, and offer solid home-cooked food.

Some 9km downriver from Žužemberk are the less complete ruins of **Soteska Manor** (Dvorec Soteska), built between 1664 and 1689 by Duke Jurij Gallenberg but which, for the greater part of its existence, was the domicile of the Auersperg counts. Today, a fairly unbroken outer shell incorporating two of the four original corner towers and the entrance gate are all that remain of the manor following its destruction in 1943 by Partisan units, an act of deliberate sabotage carried out in order to prevent German troops from appropriating it.

From the former entrance to the manor, a path cuts across the main road towards a field (formerly a walled-in park), in the centre of which stands the park pavilion, otherwise known as the **Devils Tower** (Hudičev turn); its empty interior is illuminated with murals of mythological figures, pillared architecture and other fantastical compositions painted by the Almanach workshop in the seventeenth century. Before the manor's destruction, the path was lined with three stone portals, one of which – and it's a particularly fine piece of craftsmanship – marks the entrance to the field. If you wish to see inside the tower, contact the tourist office in Dolenjske Toplice (see p.246).

Dolenjske Toplice

Just where the river turns sharply in the direction of Novo Mesto is **DOLENJSKE TOPLICE**, a classic, neat and orderly spa town, whose elegant Habsburg-era buildings give it an authentic *fin-de-siècle* ambience. Exploited since medieval times for curative purposes, the town's springs were first channelled into a bathhouse by Ivan Vajkard, a member of the Auersperg family, in the seventeenth century, although it wasn't until the late nineteenth century that Dolenjske Toplice (then called Strascha Toplitz) prospered as a fashionable, modern spa resort, utilized to treat a wide range of disorders and illnesses. During both World Wars the resort was pressed into action as an emergency military treatment centre and hospital.

The town's main **thermal pools** are part of the super-modern Balnea Wellness Centre (Mon–Thurs & Sun 9am–8pm, Fri & Sat 8am–11pm; weekdays €7 for 3hr, €10 day & weekends €9 for 3hr, €12 day), which has both indoor and outdoor (May–Sept) thermal pools, complete with water massages, waterwalls and geysers, as well as an array of saunas and baths. Elsewhere, the modern complex inside the *Kristal/Vital* hotels (see below) houses three pools (€10 for three hours, free to hotel guests). If you fancy doing something a little more energetic than wallowing, pop into the K2M agency, 100m south of the tourist office at Pionirska cesta 3 (Mon–Fri 9am–4pm, Sat 9am–1pm; ☎07/306-6830, ⓦwww.k2m.si); they organize rafting (€16 per person for 2hr30min) and kayaking (€25 per person for 3hr) on the Krka, and you can also rent canoes (€12 per day) and bikes (€4 per hour, €10 per day).

Practicalities

Buses stop off along Zdraviliški trg, the town's main street and from where nothing is more than a ten-minute walk away. From the bus stop it's just metres to the **tourist office** at no. 8 (Mon–Fri 10am–5pm, Sat 10am–noon & 3–6pm, Sun 10am–noon; ☎07/384-5188, ⓦwww.dolenjske-toplice.si), and the **post office** at no. 3 (Mon–Fri 8–9.30am & 10am–5pm, Sat 8am–noon).

Facing each other across Zdraviliški trg's southern, square-like portion, are the town's two, almost identical spa **hotels**, the lime-green *Kristal* and the pink *Vital* (☎07/391-9400, ⓦwww.krka-zdravilisca.si; reception for both is in the *Vital*; ❼); whilst neither is particularly spectacular, they do possess the comforts you'd expect from a luxury spa hotel. Aside from these there's more than enough accommodation to go around: 200m east of Zdraviliški trg at Ulica Maksa Henigmana 15, the *Gostišče Račka* (☎07/306-5510; ❸) has a handful of perfectly decent rooms plus a couple of apartments or, alternatively, take your pick from one of the many private rooms (❷) advertised throughout town; either the tourist office or the K2M agency can help out if you're struggling to find a place. The town's small and tidy **campsite** is nicely located at the northern end of Zdraviliški trg, at the foot of the wooded slopes by the Sušica stream (☎07/391-9400; May–Sept).

For eating, the town's main **restaurant** is the vaguely countrified *Gostilna Rog* at Zdraviliški trg 22, though for a similar menu and at similar prices you can dine under the huge chandeliers of the rather more refined *Kristal Hotel* restaurant; there's also the *Gostišče Račka*, which serves stock pizza and pasta dishes. Coffee is best at the *Bistro Rožek*, the small circular building in between the *Kristal* and *Vital* hotels, while the *Illy Pub* next to the K2M agency is a more heads-down drinking venue.

Novo Mesto

As Dolenjska's cultural and religious centre since the Middle Ages, **NOVO MESTO** (New Town) is quite comfortably the largest town in southeastern

NOVO MESTO

ACCOMMODATION	
Hotel Krka	A
Ravbar Apartments	B

RESTAURANTS, CAFÉS & BARS	
Črni Baron	6
Gostilna Don Bobi	7
Gostišče Kos	1
Loka	5
Lokal Patriot	2
Pri Slonu	3
Pri Vodnjaku	4

Slovenia. Continuously settled since the Bronze Age – as attested to by the numerous archeological sites hereabouts – Novo Mesto was granted city rights in 1365, thereafter evolving into a prosperous market town and trade centre and, following the establishment of a collegiate chapter around the same time, a centre of ecclesiastical importance too. In recent times, Novo Mesto has established itself as one of the country's leading industrial heartlands, home to the major pharmaceutical enterprise Krka, and the highly productive vehicle manufacturer Revoz (a subsidiary of Renault), formerly the largest plant in Yugoslavia.

The town's sights are few, but its personable old core, attractively sited on a rocky promontory in a hairpin bend of the Krka River, does possess a couple of noteworthy monuments, while its museum keeps a first-rate collection of archeological treasures; moreover, it's handy as a springboard for the many attractions – rivers, castles, spas and monasteries – close at hand.

Most of the out-of-town sights are situated along the E216 (west from Novo Mesto) and E419 (east from Novo Mesto) roads, both of which run south of and parallel to the main E70 Ljubljana–Zagreb highway. However, without your own transport, you will have to rely on a modest bus service in order to reach them, as most buses travel the highway; moreover, the rail line from Ljubljana follows the same course as the highway, although only as far as Novo Mesto, before continuing south into Bela Krajina.

Arrival, information and accommodation

The **bus station** is on Topliška Cesta, a ten-minute walk southwest of the town centre, whilst there are two **train stations** – the main one, Novo Mesto, is 800m west of town on Ljubljanska cesta, while the second one, Center, is on the north side of Šmihelski bridge, just five minutes' walk into town; all trains stop at both stations, so alight at Center. The **tourist office** (June–Sept Mon–Fri 9am–6pm, Sat 9am–noon; Oct–May Mon–Fri 8am–3pm, Wed til 5pm; ℡07/393-9263, ⓦwww.novomesto.si) is presently secreted away by the side of the Občina (municipal) building at Novi trg 6, though plans are afoot for a move to the Old Town. The **post office** (Mon–Fri 7am–8pm, Sat 7am–1pm) is on Novi trg, and there's **Internet access** at the library, Rozmanova ulica 26 (Mon–Fri 8am–7pm, Sat 8am–1pm; free), and in the Planet Tuš complex opposite the bus station (daily 10am–8pm; €2 for 1hr).

The town's sole **hotel** is the outrageously overpriced *Krka* on Novi trg (℡07/394-2100, ⓦwww.krka-zdravilisca.si/en/hotel_krka; ❾), a self-styled business hotel with well-turned-out rooms including minibar, safe and air-conditioning. A far better alternative is the family-run *Ravbar apartments* (℡07/373-0680, ⓦwww.ravbar.net), a fifteen-minute walk east of the bus station at Smrečnikova ulica 15–17, which has eight apartments sleeping two to six people (❸–❺) and a couple of rooms (❷), all of which are large, modern and immaculately kept.

The Town

Most things of a practical nature are in or around modern and charmless Novi trg, whilst the city's main sights – the Chapter Church, Franciscan Church and Town Museum – are a short walk east in the Old Town.

Chapter Church and Dolenjska Museum

Commanding the summit of Kapiteljski hrib, a five-minute walk from Novi trg up Dalmatinova and then Kapiteljska Ulica, the **Chapter Church of St Nicholas** (Cerkev sv Miklavza) is the town's oldest monument. Encompassing a chequered mix of Gothic, neo-Gothic and Baroque elements, the most striking thing about the church is its fifteenth-century presbytery, constructed at a peculiar seventeen-degree angle to the nave. Inside, the church is possessed of some outstanding works of art, most notably the high-altar painting of *St Nicholas* by Tintoretto, one of the country's most celebrated church paintings and, allegedly, one of only two of the Venetian master's works in Slovenia. Elsewhere, look out for the copy of *Maria Pomagaj* (*Mary Help*) in the first altar on the left and several works by Metzinger adorning other altars. To the right of the presbytery a flight of steps leads down to a chilly, Gothic-vaulted **crypt**, the only one of its kind in the country and somewhat unusual in that there's actually no one buried here as it was built rather as a support for the presbytery which was constructed on a slight down slope. The crypt is usually locked, but if you want to have a look try calling at the provost's house just across from the church.

Housed in a complex of several buildings a short walk down from the church at Muzejska ulica 7, the **Dolenjska Museum** (Dolenjski muzej; April–Oct Tues–Sat 9am–5pm, Sun 9am–1pm; Nov–March Tues–Fri 9am–4pm, Sat & Sun 9am–1pm; €3) keeps one of the finest stockpiles of archeological treasures in Slovenia. The core of the collection comprises grave finds unearthed from hundreds of burial sites on the slopes of Marof and Mestne njive, two modest rises located a short way north of the town centre. The earliest artefacts, from the late Bronze Age (the so-called Urnfield culture), comprise a superb display of large ceramic urns, into which the remains of the deceased, together with their personal belongings – bronze needles, jewellery, beads and the like – were placed.

The **Hallstatt** period (the early Iron or late Bronze Age, approximately 8th–4th BC) is represented by more vessels and jewellery, including earrings, bracelets and anklets, as well as several pieces of armour – the star exhibits are a beautifully well-preserved Bronze Age helmet and breast plate. The most impressive items, however, are the specimens of **Situla Art**, bronze buckets, or pails, ornately embossed with festive or hunting scenes, a collection which represents the greatest achievement in prehistoric art in Slovenia. The larger grave urns from the Celtic period were somewhat more sophisticated, suggesting that the deceased were from a higher social rank. Rounding off this veritable treasure trove is a hoard of Roman grave goods, typically cups, coins, wine pitchers and oil lamps, as well as a stash of Roman legionary weapons. The remainder of the museum, comprising ethnological and modern history collections is, by comparison, distinctly underwhelming.

Glavni trg and around

From the museum a number of narrow alleyways descend through town to cobbled **Glavni Trg** (Main Square). Actually more street than square, this is the city's focal point, once the haunt of merchants and craftsmen but today profiled with two rows of handsome townhouses, variously accommodating public buildings, shops and the odd café or bar. The square's most striking feature is its elegant arcades, although its most prominent building, located midway down the left-hand side at no. 6, is the grey, mock-Renaissance **Town Hall** (Rotovž), built in 1905.

Lurking just behind the Town Hall on Frančišk trg (accessed via Jenkova ulica) stands **St Leonard's Franciscan Church** (Frančiškanska cerkev sv Lenarta), whose elegant, mustard-coloured neo-Gothic gabled facade dating from around 1880 was just one of the church's many piecemeal additions following a fire in 1664. From the original church, built in 1472 as a place of refuge for Franciscan monks from Bosnia (who had initially sheltered at the Tri Fare Parish in Metlika, see p.265), only the Gothic presbytery was retained, although its wooden altars were lost and replaced with the current neo-Gothic editions. The adjoining **monastery** boasts a fine library with some superb incunabula, a tiny prayer book from 1450, and a psalm book made from animal skin and featuring Gothic and Baroque text dating from 1418 (visits to the monastery are possible by prior arrangement only; contact the tourist office).

At the square's southern end, just above the picturesque **Breg** embankment (turn right just before the bridge), the **Božidar Jakac House** (Jačkev Dom; Tues–Fri 9am–4pm, Sat & Sun 9am–1pm; €2) holds the eponymous artist's largest collection of sketches and drawings outside Kostanjevica (see p.252); there's also a terrific selection of watercolours and oils depicting town scenes and local landscapes. Formerly a hotel, this building was actually the house of his father – Jakac was

Cviček

Whilst in Novo Mesto, it would be remiss not to try the local speciality, **Cviček** (pronounced tsveechek), one of the country's most distinctive and unusual wines. Cultivated only here in southeast Dolenjska, Cviček is produced from a blend of red and white grapes – said to be more than a dozen, but this is considered an exaggeration – giving it a cranberry-juice-like appearance. Despite its dry, rather sour taste, it's a surprisingly refreshing wine, made all the more drinkable thanks to its low alcoholic content of around nine percent. Whilst most Cviček is produced for home consumption, it's the first drink you'll be offered in the local restaurants and bars.

born 100m further up the street in what is now the *Breg* restaurant. Crossing the **Kandijski Bridge** (Kandijski Most) gives you some lovely views back to Breg and the bright orange-tiled rooftops of the Old Town.

Eating, drinking and entertainment

The town is somewhat lacking in decent places to **eat**, although a most welcome addition is *Loka*, a good-looking place down by the river (under the Šmihelski Bridge) offering a classy Slovene and international menu – there's a terrific outdoor terrace in the summer, though the mosquitoes can be a nuisance here. Otherwise there's the cosy, cellar-like cavern *Gostilna Don Bobi*, out on the busy main road Kandijska cesta (no. 14), which knocks up steaming plates of pastas; or *Črni Baron* at Muzejska 3, whose lunchtime *malica* is worth dropping by for. Although inconveniently located 1.5km out on the road towards Otočec at Šmarješka cesta 26, the stylish *Gostišče Kos* is worth a visit for its inventive menu of mushroom, steak and fish dishes and, for vegetarians, buckwheat and *štruklji* (fruit dumplings).

Similarly, exciting **drinking** venues are few and far between, though a couple of places in the Old Town, the pubby *Pri Vodnjaku* at the top end of Glavni trg, and the old-style café *Pri Slonu* (At the Elephant) a short walk away at Rozmanova ulica 22, are both enjoyable venues; otherwise, there's an indistinguishable spread of cafés on Novi trg. The student club, *Lokal Patriot*, in the Občina building (on the opposite side to the tourist office), offers a varied mix of club nights, film showings and rock and jazz concerts, occasionally starring some of Slovenia's top acts (Mon–Fri 7am–midnight, Sat 5pm–2am).

Otočec Castle

Picturesquely sited on an elongated, tree-covered island in the middle of another attractive stretch of the Krka river, 7km east of Novo Mesto, is **Otočec Castle**. Surrounded by dozens of tiny islets and the Krka's distinctive calct-ufa falls, the country's only island castle was originally occupied by the knights of Otočec during the thirteenth century, thereafter passing through the hands of various noble families. Fortified with walls and four chunky towers during persistent fifteenth-century Turkish raids, the castle was purchased in 1560 by Ivan Lenkovič, commander of the Austrian Empire's Vojna Krajina region, during which time it acquired its present, largely Renaissance appearance, albeit heavily renovated following extensive World War II damage.

The castle now functions as one of Slovenia's few five-star **hotels**, the *Hotel Grad Otočec* (☏07/307-5165, ⓦ www.krka-zdravilisca.si/en/otocec; ❾), whose apartment-style rooms are fitted out with extravagant period furniture and enormous bathrooms with oversized baths. The hotel's understated yet elegant **restaurant**, complete with waiters in rather daft medieval get-up, offers superb fish (red trout and pikeperch), as well as more exotic dishes such as ostrich steak, and avocado dumplings with octopus; suffice to say, it doesn't come cheap. If your wallet can't stretch to a meal, then settle for a coffee in the courtyard café.

There's more accommodation back across the main road (under the bridge on the other side of the highway) in the shape of the *Hotel Šport* (same contact details as the *Grad Otočec*; ❺), whose bland exterior belies some good-looking and comfortable rooms; they've also got cheaper, en-suite bungalows (❹) and motel rooms (❸) opposite. Guests of both hotels receive complimentary use of the thermal pools in Šmarješke Toplice (see opposite), and there's an adjoining **tennis centre** with indoor and outdoor courts (€20 & €6 respectively). The small and grubby **campsite** (☏07/307-5168; May–Sept) is located a few hundred metres east of the castle on the river's south bank.

There's a smattering of other accommodation hereabouts, the best of which is the fabulous 🌲 *Šeruga* **tourist farm**, located in an isolated wooded area some 3km south of Otočec (just off the main road to Kostanjevica) at Sela pri Ratežu 15 (☎07/334-6900, ✉turist.kmetija.seruga@siol.net; ❷); its ten homely, yet modern, rooms are complemented by exceptional home cooking and local wines. Back on the main road, 2km further east at Ratež 48, the roadside inn *Gostilna Vovko* also has a handful of good-value rooms (☎07/308-5603; ❸), but if you're heading this way anyway don't pass up the opportunity to try out its terrific **restaurant** (Tues–Sat 10am–10pm, Sun 11am–4pm), which specializes in fantastically tasty and filling grilled meat dishes.

During the first or second weekend of July, Otočec is awoken from its slumber thanks to the staging of the **Rock Otočec Festival** (🌐www.rock-otocec.com), the country's largest rock gathering featuring the biggest names from Slovenia and the ex-Yugoslav republics, as well as the odd big name international outfit. Tickets cost around €18 for a one-day pass, and around €40 for a three-day pass, while there are free buses to/from Novo Mesto for the duration of the festival.

Šmarješke Toplice

From Otočec, five daily buses (Mon–Fri) make the short trip to **ŠMARJEŠKE TOPLICE** some 5km to the northeast. Although far smaller and more low-key than Dolenjske Toplice (see p.246), Šmarješke Toplice has been a spa centre of sorts since the eighteenth century, only developing into a serious resort after World War II, when it served the needs of ailing Communist Party members. It now counts five thermal pools – two indoor and three outdoor, averaging 32°C (€9). Even if you don't plan on taking a dip, the park is a good place for a gentle stroll or a picnic.

Accommodation comes in the form of three conjoined hotels located at the heart of the complex, itself a short way north of the village (☎07/384-3400, 🌐www.krka-zdravilisca.si/en/smarjeske); the most upmarket of the three (all ❼) is the *Vitarium*, with huge, immaculately furnished rooms and heated bathroom floors, while the *Šmarjeta* and *Toplice* are both clinical and characterless. Although the hotels are primarily concerned with serious therapy treatments, they also offer all manner of health and fitness facilities. In addition to the regular pools (free of charge to hotel guests) there are steam baths, saunas and massage pools. A much cheaper alternative is the *Domen Pension* (☎07/307-3051; ❸), located 1.5km back down the road towards Otočec at Družinska Vas 1.

Pleterje Monastery and Skansen

Beautifully set in a secluded valley at the foot of the Gorjanci forests, **Pleterje Monastery** is Europe's easternmost Carthusian monastery, and the only one of Slovenia's four charterhouses still functioning. Shut off from the outside world by a formidable 2600-metre-long, three-metre-high enclosure wall, the monastery has endured a chequered history, one not that dissimilar to that of Stična (see p.240). Founded in 1407 by Count Herman II of Celje, Pleterje was fortified during the fifteenth century in advance of Turkish raids, before its dissolution and subsequent appropriation by the Jesuits at the end of the sixteenth century. Following the reforms of Emperor Joseph II, the monastery was disbanded again in 1784, only to be repurchased and rebuilt by the Carthusian order in 1899.

While the main church is open to visitors, the rest of the monastery (cloisters, courtyards, the new monastery church, orchards and meadows) is strictly out of bounds, and it's unlikely that you'll get to see one of the fifteen monks that live here. Rooted in the anchorite traditions of Early Christianity, the Pleterje monks live according to a precisely defined schedule, completely devoted to prayer (liturgy and meditation) and work (both study and manual labour). While here, make time to visit the **Skansen** (see below), located just down from the monastery.

Church of the Holy Trinity

Rated as one of the best-preserved examples of early French Gothic in Central Europe, the single-nave **Church of the Holy Trinity** (built in 1420) is astonishingly simple and, though almost completely devoid of furniture or ornamentation, is possessed of some wonderfully subtle detail. Entering through the low, stone rood-screen which separates the nave and chancel, have a look up at the splendid cross rib-vaulted ceiling, embellished with numerous bosses bearing a range of motifs, and the seventy or so clay vessels (also known as acoustical pottery) spotted along the walls. You can't really miss the high altar, a smooth slab of grey stone placed upon two stone stools. On the exterior the badly pockmarked wall was the result of heavy shelling during World War II.

You can learn more about the Carthusian order by watching the informative, twenty-five-minute **presentation** set up in the sacristy to the side of the church. Information and tickets (€2.5) for this can be obtained from the monastery **shop** (Mon–Sat 7.30am–5.30pm), located just down from the church; they've also got a terrific stock of wines and brandies produced at the monastery's own distillery – take your pick from juniper (*brinovec*), pear (*hruška*), and plum (*slivovka*) – as well as honey and propolis (another bee-produced substance).

The Skansen

Spread out across a lovely green field at the bottom of the road leading up to the monastery is a fabulous little **Skansen,** or open-air museum (Pleterje Skansen; April–Oct Tues–Sun 10am–6pm; €3 with monastery, €2 museum only), whose handful of buildings, representing a typical farmyard from this region, were relocated partly in order to draw visitors away from the monastery itself. As well as its classic thatched wooden houses, fully equipped with authentic domestic furniture, the complex includes a threshing floor, fruit and flax dryer, and a superb double hayrack; you can also buy pottery and ceramics.

Time and energy permitting, you can partake in the **Pleterje Way**, a circular footpath that skirts the hills above the monastery, and which affords views of the complex you wouldn't normally get to see; allow around ninety minutes to complete it. Unless you've got your own transport, getting here entails taking a bus to Šentjernej (6km west of Kostanjevica along the road to Novo Mesto), from where it's a 3km walk south to the monastery.

Kostanjevica na Krki

Compacted into a tight loop of the Krka River, the island settlement is one of the country's smallest towns, a once thriving commercial centre with its own mint but now a rural backwater, possessed of a ghostly charm. From the main bus stop on Ljubljanska cesta, it's a five-minute walk north to the bridge, which in turn leads you onto the tranquil, palette-shaped island, comprised of two main streets that join to form a circle around a cluster of buildings in an advanced state of decay. Aside from a couple of small Gothic churches sited at either end, there's actually very little to see or do in this part of town, but if you've got an hour to spare following a visit to the out-of-town attractions, it's definitely worth taking a leisurely stroll around.

The Božidar Jakac and Jože Gorjup galleries

A fifteen-minute walk southwest of town (head down Ljubljanska Cesta and follow the signs) is the former **Cistercian Monastery**, founded in 1234, disbanded in 1784 and largely destroyed during World War II. All but completely renovated now, there are some interesting masonry fragments – vaulted ribs, keystones and so on – from the previously damaged church in the **lapidarium**, located in the eastern arcaded passage of the monastery's immense three-sided cloister. The cloister's numerous rooms now accommodate the **Božidar Jakac Gallery** (Galerija Božidar Jakac; April–Oct Tues–Sun 9am–6pm, Nov–March 9am–4pm; €3) which, with the works of no less than eight of Slovenia's most prominent artists to plough through, requires no little stamina.

The most obvious place to start is the collection by the versatile Jakac, whose prolific stock of prints and graphics, many of which document his time spent with the Partisans, are complemented by some exquisite pastels and oils, featuring land or townscapes from both Slovenia (*Hayrack*) and Prague, where he studied – keep an eye out for the lovely *Midnight Mass on Hradčani*. After Jakac, make a beeline for the rooms holding the extensive collections of the Kralj brothers, France and Tone, both key figures in the interwar Slovene avant-garde but whose later works veered towards the realm of Socialist Realism. Tone's later work, in particular, is biased towards themes of war, revolt and daily peasant life (*Black Gold*). Family portraits feature heavily too, such as the disturbing *My Mother*, which depicts their mother standing over her dead pilot brother's body.

Of the other artists, try not to miss the fabulously creative bronze sculptures of Janez Boljka, whose work evolved from sculpting simple motifs from Ribnica, to more adventurous subject matter, such as the animal kingdom (*Bull*, *Chimpanzee*) and the human form – in particular, eminent Slovenes (*Ivan Cankar and his Muse*, *Rihard Jakopič Seated*); there are further sculptures (and oils) by France Gorše and Jože Gorjup – Gorše also specialized in portraits of noteworthy Slovenes, such as Primož Trubar. Worth a peek, too, is a rather dusty collection of Old European Masters (German, Italian and Flemish) from Pleterje Monastery. The monastery's gardens are used to exhibit some one hundred oak-wood sculptures, otherwise known as the **Former Viva** (Living Form), one of several such sculpture parks around Slovenia, each of which demonstrates works of art made from a different material.

If you've still got the appetite, there's more work by some of the same artists at the **Jože Gorjup Gallery**, housed in the primary school of the same name at Gorjanska ulica, 2200m east of the bridge. Take a look at the wall on the side of the school's gym building, which features a brilliant mosaic of the 1573 Battle on Krško Plain, in which the counts do battle with peasants amidst a fierce snowstorm.

Kostanjevica Cave

One and a half kilometres southeast of town, in a small wooded area bound by a stream, is **Kostanjevica Cave** (Kostanjeviška Jama), the largest and most impressive of Dolenjska's cave systems. Speleologists were first drawn to the possibility of the cave's existence following a flood in 1937, after which time systematic exploration uncovered numerous other shafts, chambers and lakes. Fifty-minute guided tours of the old part of the cave take in approximately 250m of the 1800m discovered to date, beginning at the sixty-metre-long entrance tunnel. Beyond here a series of tight passages and staircases wend their way through several chambers, past two lakes, the **Watershed Cavern** (Razvodna dvorana) and the **Intermittent Lake** (Presihajoče jezero – see p.228), and up to the **Cross Cavern** (Križna dvorana). The tour winds up at the **Stalactite Cavern** (Kapniška dvorana), a relatively narrow hall that, true to its name, is replete with dozens of shimmering stalactites, the tallest of which, the pillar, stands twelve metres high. The remainder of the cave is accessible only to experienced cavers. There are bats here, too, lots of them, including the southern horseshoe bat, which is found only in this cave. **Visits** (€5) take place every two hours between 10am and 6pm each day in July and August, and at the same times but only at weekends between April and June, and September and October.

Kostanjevica na Krki practicalities

The main **bus stop** is opposite the *Green Bar* on Ljubljanska cesta, from where it's a five-minute walk to the island and the **tourist office** at Talcev ulica 20 (℡07/498-7108); however, the office is often closed for no apparent reason, so you may or may not get lucky. The *Gostilna Žolnir*, 500m north of St James Church, across the bridge at Krška cesta 4 (℡07/498-7133, ⓦwww.zolnir-sp.si; ❸), doubles up as the only place in town to **sleep** and the best place to **eat**. There's similarly fine food at the rustically styled *Kmečki Hram*, back on the island at Oražnova ulica 11 (closed Mon).

Brežice

The town of **BREŽICE**, a moderately important regional economic and cultural centre, sits at the confluence of the Krka and Sava rivers in the middle of the hill-fringed Krško Plain 15km east of Kostanjevica na Krki. Granted its town charter in 1354, Brežice retains a distinctive, small-town atmosphere, its single concession to grandeur a fine Renaissance Castle now housing a very good museum. Beyond this one major sight there's little else to see or do here, but if you want to make good use of a night's stopover you have the option of several not too distant trips; the **Čatež Spa** and **Mokrice Castle** a few kilometres to the south, and the **Bizeljkso wine region** to the north, though the latter is served by just a few buses.

Arrival, information and accommodation

From the **bus station**, around 800m east of town on Cesta Svobode, it's a ten-minute walk to the centre: head south along Cesta Svobode, then right down Bizeljska Ulica, past the Water Tower to the main street Cesta prvih borcev. Less conveniently, the **train station** is located 2.5km north of town on Trg Vstaje, in the village of Šentlenart; buses depart from the station forecourt every thirty minutes on weekdays, and every two hours on Saturdays until 2.30pm) – there are none on Sundays. If walking, exit the station, turn left and follow the road around; you'll eventually end up on Cesta prvih borcev. There's no **tourist office** here, but there is a small one at the Čatež spa complex, 3km southeast of town (see p.256). The **post office** is on Trg Izgnancev (Mon–Fri 7am–7pm, Sat 7am–noon).

Decent **accommodation** in the town centre is limited to the comfortable *Splavar* pension at Cesta prvih borcev 40a (℡07/499-0630, ⓦwww.splavar.si; ❹), whose tidy, air-conditioned rooms also offer WiFi Internet access. Much cheaper, and much gloomier, are the handful of three-bedded, hostel-style rooms (shared bathrooms) at the *Gostilna Berdnik*, a short walk up from the post office at Cesta bratov milavcev 39 (℡07/496-1161; ❷). Another option, south of town, across the bridge and near the traffic lights, is *Gostilna Les* (℡07/496-1100, €g.les@siol. net; ❸), which has a mix of older, somewhat careworn rooms, and much smarter, newer rooms – they've got a very creditable pizzeria.

Brežice Castle and the Posavje Museum

Prominently positioned at the extreme southern end of the town's long and attractive main street, Cesta prvih borcev, the foundations of present-day **Brežice Castle** were laid in 1529, when it was also fortified with robust, red-tiled conical towers. Following its purchase by the counts of Attems in the seventeenth cen-

The Brežice Festival

One of the country's most celebrated musical and cultural events, the **Brežice Festival** (mid-June to mid-Aug) is an outstanding series of ancient and Baroque music concerts, featuring some of Europe's finest musicians. Whilst the majority of concerts are staged here in Brežice – many in the superb Knight's Hall – many other concerts take place throughout Slovenia, mostly in first-rate venues such as Bogenšperk Castle, the Monastery Church in Kostanjevica na Krki, and Fužine Castle in Ljubljana. Tickets (€10-25), available from the Festival Box Office at Cesta prvih borcev 5 (☏07/499-1050), usually go on sale at the beginning of May; for more information consult the website ⊛www.festivalbrezice.com, which has full programme details.

tury, the castle underwent a major style renovation – the courtyard was arcaded with Tuscan columns and several of its most important spaces, such as the stairway, chapel and, most famously, the Knight's Hall, were decorated with splendid Baroque frescoes.

The castle is now home to the **Posavje Museum** (Posavski Muzej; Mon–Fri 8am–2.30pm, Sat & Sun 10am–2pm; €2), as comprehensive a regional museum as you'll come across; there are useful information sheets in each room to guide you. The first ten of the museum's twenty or so rooms are given over to archeological and ethnological collections: the former is crammed with ancient skeletons, weapons, jewellery, and equine equipment extricated from over four hundred Celtic graves at Dobova on the Croatian border. The latter documents life in the Posavje region, with due prominence given to wine-making, featuring a weighty display of viticultural implements including two large wine presses.

Located in two small vaulted rooms in the northeastern tower is a small medieval history section documenting the Slovene and Croatian peasant struggles of the sixteenth century, as well as items and literature related to the Reformation in Dolenjska; the key exhibit, and the museum's most precious item, is the Dalmatin Bible from 1584, the first complete translation of the Bible from German into Slovene. Of the 1500 copies originally printed, only around eighty survive. The several rooms constituting the Baroque Art collection are taken up with portraits of the aristocracy, some fine sacral art (paintings by Metzinger and wooden sculptures) and, best of all, a magnificent eighteenth-century wooden sled made in Vienna and donated to Brežice by Empress Maria Theresa.

The museum's centrepiece is the **Knight's Hall** (Viteška dvorana), awash with typically florid Italian Baroque paintings featuring scenes from classical myth and legend, the arts and sciences and portraits of the Attems family; the hall is now used for weddings, high-level state functions and as one of the principal venues for concerts of the Brežice Festival.

Eating and drinking

Given its modest size, the town has a surprisingly healthy number of places to **eat and drink**. The most accomplished place is the cool ⚜ *Ošterija Debeluh Hram* restaurant and wine bar at Trg Izgnancev 7 (closed Sun), whose attractive pastel painted walls and chunky wooden tables and chairs make it an enjoyable place to tuck into the very juicy Balkan grills – the bar has a terrific selection of wines from the local Bizeljsko region (see p.257). Otherwise, there's the popular *Santa Lucia* at Cesta prvih borcev 15, whose bright walls are a bit much, but the Italian food on offer is good (daily until 1am). The two most popular drinking venues in town are the *Jazz Club*, opposite the post office at Trg Izgnancev 2 (daily til midnight), and *Rafters Pub*, part of the *Splavar* pension (see opposite). The most original place, though, is *Aquarius* with four small circular floors inside the enormous pink Water Tower on Bizeljska ulica (daily til 1am). The bright *Kavarna*, just down from the castle at Cesta prvih borcev 14, has a good selection of **coffees and teas** to indulge in, alongside some delicious cakes (Mon–Fri 7am–8pm, Sat 7am–2pm).

Čatež

From Brežice, hourly buses (five on Saturdays) run the 3km southeast (across the Sava) to **ČATEŽ**, Slovenia's largest and most popular **spa centre** (Terme Čatež; ⓦwww.terme-catez.si). Hot springs were first discovered at Čatež in 1797, only to be flooded by the Sava, then rediscovered some fifty years later, around which time the first private spa – a basic wood cabin and pool – was built by Father Edvard Zagorc. A fledgling resort in the 1920s, offering numerous therapies and treatments to a wide variety of disorders, Čatež only really began to develop as a serious spa centre in the 1960s, with the construction of the first large pools and hotels. Today this more or less self-contained village, incorporating restaurants, shops, a bank and post office, is as much a recreational park as it is a therapeutic and treatment centre.

Water and sauna parks

The huge **water park** (daily April to mid-Oct 9am–8pm; weekdays €8, weekends €10) comprises some nine thermal pools and bathing areas (average temperature 30ºC), some with wave machines, waterfalls and slides. If it gets a bit cool, there's indoor action at the *Toplice*'s modern Thermal Riviera (daily 9am–9pm; weekdays €10, weekends €11), which has a multitude of slides, wave pools, whirlpools and water massage machines; guests of the *Toplice* have unlimited free use of this pool, while guests of the other two hotels have free usage once a day.

If you fancy sweating off a few pounds, then the **sauna park** (weekdays €10, weekends €13), also inside the *Toplice*, incorporates eight different saunas – the Indian sauna, Salt sauna and Finnish Aroma sauna, to name but three. If that's not enough, the spanking new **spa and wellness centre** inside the *Hotel Čatež* accommodates a plethora of modern and exotic massages and treatments. There are more activities in the shape of indoor and outdoor tennis (€5–10 per hour), badminton (€6 per hour) and squash (€7 for 45min).

Practicalities

The **tourist office** (June–Sept Mon–Sat 7am–8pm, Sun 7am–2pm; Oct–May Mon–Fri 7am–6pm, Sat 9am–4pm, Sun 9am–2pm; ⓣ07/493-6777, ⓔturizem-brezice@siol.net) is located opposite the *Hotel Toplice* (see below). Unless you're here for more than a few days, it's unlikely you'll need or want to stay on site. If you do, the complex incorporates three pricey **hotels**; the *Čatež* (ⓣ07/493-5022; ❸), an attractive atrium-style building with exquisitely appointed rooms, and the more expensive *Toplice* and *Terme* (ⓣ07/493-6700; ❾) hotels, both of which offer similarly luxurious rooms – the former also has rooms in a 1920s Swiss-style chalet. At the eastern end of the complex, alongside the clean and well-equipped **campsite** (ⓣ07/493-6000; March–Oct), is the holiday village, which has dozens of large, two- and four-bed apartments (❻–❼).

The only places to **eat** are the hotel restaurants, but there are several cafes sprinkled around the complex, where you can grab a snack.

Mokrice Castle

At the end of the secondary road which runs parallel with the E70 highway to Zagreb, 8km southeast of Čatež, stands **Mokrice Castle**, a beautifully proportioned

Renaissance chateau which once functioned as a defensive outpost against the Turks. Today, and like Otočec Castle (see p.250), it has been converted into a luxury **hotel**, the *Grad Mokrice* (℡07/493-6700, ✉mokrice@terme-catez.si; ❾), and very posh **restaurant**; those staying longer than one night receive free use of the pools at Čatež. During the golf season (April–Oct) there are some superb-value golf **apartments** (❾) available, each sleeping up to four people.

Both the restaurant and the long and hilly eighteen-hole **golf course** (℡07/457-4246; 18 holes €38 or €46 at weekends, 9 holes €25 or €30 at weekends, plus €10 for club hire – fifty percent discount for guests staying at the hotel here and the hotels at Čatež Spa) are popular with the moneyed middle classes, a good number of whom make the short trip up from Zagreb. For those with neither the time nor wallet for a meal or a round of golf, you can take a stroll around the impressively manicured lawns of the stately landscaped English Park, whose pear-tree orchards provide the fruits for the fiery local brandy, *Viljamovka*. There's more affordable **accommodation** out along the road to Mokrice in Dvorec, at the super-modern and very smart *Penzion Čateški Dvorec* (℡07/499-4870, ⓦwww .cateski-dvorec.com; ❺), which also has a sauna, wine cellar and **restaurant**.

Bizeljsko-Sremič wine region and Podsreda Castle

Tracking the Croatian border, the road heading north out of Brežice heads up through the **Bizeljsko–Sremič wine region**, renowned for its characteristic blended wines, such as the dry whites *Bizeljčan* and *Sremičan*. Although the odd **bus** trundles this way (Mon–Fri, 4 daily), it's difficult to get the most out of the region unless you've got your own wheels. Wine can be sampled anywhere where you see the sign *vinska klet* (wine cellar) of which there are many; however, to be sure of getting a visit in, it's best to call in advance – reckon on paying around €5 for three or four wines, a little more for sparkling wine.

The wine road doesn't really begin until the village of **Stari Vas**, some 10km north of Brežice, where you can sample sparkling wines at the *Istenič* cellar at no. 7 (℡07/495-1559); they've also got a comfortable little pension on site (❸). Two kilometres further up the road, there's more tasting and nicer accommodation at the countrified roadside inn *Pri Peču* (℡07/452-0103; ❸; restaurant closed Tues.

From the *Istenič* cellar, a footpath (Pot k Repnicam) winds its way across the shallow hills up to the village of **BREZOVICA**, some 5km distant. Spotted around this area are some 150 unique cellars called *repnice*, small sand caves hewn from the surrounding flint-stone hills, their walls and ceilings wonderfully patterned with obliquely laid layers of sand. *Repnice* were traditionally used for the storage of turnips (*repa* means turnip) and other produce, before local vintners discovered that the caves' climatic conditions (a constant 7–11°C) and humidity were ideal for the maturing and storage of wine. Around thirty *repnice* are still in use today, the greatest concentration of which are in Brezovica itself; particularly worth trying are *Kovačič* at no. 29 (℡07/495-1091), *Kelhar* at no. 31 (℡07/495-1551), which was dug out in 1825 and, most impressively, *Najger* at no. 32 (℡07/495-1115) – all three are located approximately 1.5km from the main road up the hill.

The next village along is **Bizeljsko** itself, the region's main settlement, where there's one excellent cellar, the *Klet Pinterič*, at no. 115 (℡07/495-1266), and the well regarded *Gostilna Šekoranja* (no. 72; closed Mon), a real old-fashioned eatery serving up heavy Slovene fare such as smoked bacon, thick homemade sausages and black pudding. Beyond here, the road gently ascends to **Bistrica ob Sotli**, whereupon a branch road cuts west to the village of **PODSREDA**, above which looms the resplendent **Podsreda Castle** (April–Oct Tues–Sun 10am–6pm;

€2.5). Originally a thirteenth-century fortification, its fine Romanesque core remains splendidly intact, although systematic and comprehensive renovation work on the interior has left few visible traces of its former state, with just the old medieval kitchen and single-cell jail remaining from the original building. Its empty rooms are now used almost exclusively as exhibition and gallery spaces, and there are currently collections devoted to glassworks and prints.

The castle can be reached by road (5km from Podsreda) or, if you're walking, via a steep trail (45min) beginning south of the village – look for the signs to Levstikov Mlin (Levstikov Mill) and the trail starts there.

Kumrovec

With your own transport, and an hour or so to spare, you could make an interesting little diversion across the border into **Croatia** and the village of **KUMROVEC**, about 2km distant. In the centre of the village is the superb **"Old Village" Museum** (Staro Selo Muzej; daily April–Sept 9am–7pm, Oct–March til 4pm; €3, plus €1 for a guiding map), a gathering of well-preserved late nineteenth- and early twentieth-century peasant dwellings, most of which contain ethnological exhibitions pertaining to the various trades – Blacksmiths, Cartwrights, Potters and the like – which sustained the region (Zagorje) during this period. The museum's most important house is the one just a few steps beyond the entrance, otherwise known as the **birthplace of Josip Broz Tito**, who was born here on May 7, 1892. The neat, brickwork house contains a modest assortment of mementoes and personal effects, along with photos of Tito with esteemed heads of state. Outside is a fine bronze statue of the great man.

Bela Krajina

Of the region's two towns, **Črnomelj** and **Metlika**, the latter, with its fetching architecture and two impressive museums, is more deserving of a visit. The best of Bela Krajina, however, is to be found in the surrounding countryside, amidst the birch trees and vineyards. History and culture buffs can get their kicks at the **Mithraeum shrine** at Rožanec, near Črnomelj, and the fabulous **Three Parishes Pilgrimage Centre** at Rosalnice, near Metlika; those seeking more relaxing fare should make a beeline for the **Lahinja Landscape Park** or the numerous wine villages sprinkled around the region. To combine a wine-tasting session with an overnight stay, head for **Drašiči** with its pleasant vineyard-clad surrounds.

Črnomelj

Sitting plumb in the geographical centre of Bela Krajina, 45km east of Kočevje, **ČRNOMELJ** is both the capital, and the largest, of the province's towns. Frankly, though, it's not much to get excited about, and the only reason you might contemplate a visit here is to indulge in the town's marvellous folklore **festival** in June, or to use it as a springboard for visits to surrounding attractions.

Unlike many settlements in the region, Črnomelj was spared widespread devastation by the Turks, owing to its naturally strong fortifications, although its strategic importance was stripped away in the mid-sixteenth century following the erection of a fort and the relocation of the command of the military frontier across the border in Karlovac, Croatia. Its decline continued for several centuries thereafter, though its fortunes were partially revived following the opening of the Novo Mesto–Karlovac rail line in 1914.

Bela Krajina's rich folk-music heritage is joyously celebrated each year here in the form of the **Jurjevanje** (St George's Day Festival), which features a tremendous, and usually very accomplished, line-up of both local and international folkloric groups and dance troupes. Usually taking place during the third weekend of June, it's a great opportunity to see rarely used folk instruments – such as the *tamburica*, *bisernica* (lute) and *berdo* (contrabass) – being played live.

Arrival, information and accommodation

The town's **train station** is located 1km due north of the centre on Železničarska cesta, from where it's a twenty-minute walk due south to the Old Town core. More conveniently, all **buses** stop on the main square, Trg Svobode, from where it's a quick hop across the road to the **tourist office**, located inside the castle building at no. 3 (Mon–Fri 8am–3.30pm, Sat 9am–noon plus Sun 9am–noon in summer; ☏07/306-1142, ✉turizem@crnomelj.si); they can advise on private accommodation and local tourist farms. The **post office** is some 500m north of here on Kolodvorska ulica (Mon–Fri 7am–7pm, Sat 7am–noon).

Town **accommodation** is scant: there are dorm beds available in July and August in the *Dijaški Dom*, 400m north of the tourist office at Otona Župančičeva 7 (℡07/306-2160; €12); *Gostišče Muller*, south of the main square, and along the road below the bridge at Ločka cesta 6 (℡07/356-7200, ⓦwww.gostilna-muller .si; ④) has four large, modern, spotless and reasonably priced rooms; whilst the town's only hotel, the *Lahinja* (℡07/306-1650; ④), 200m from the train station on the main road Kolodvorska cesta, is old, tired and only recommended as a last resort.

The Town

What little there is of interest is centred on an elongated promontory in a tight loop of the Dobličica and Lahinja rivers to the south of town. Consuming the eastern side of the main square, Trg Svobode, is the town's rather low-key **castle**, originally built in the twelfth century but rebuilt, modified and tinkered with by numerous owners over the years, the result being that it doesn't much look like a castle at all now, instead just another regular building on the square. There's little of interest to see, inside or out, and even the small **town museum** (same hours as the tourist office; €1), offers not much more than a weary collection of local photographs, though there are a few drawings by Božidar Jakac (see p.252) to admire. A few paces south of the castle, at the beginning of Ulica Staneta Rozmana – the main traffic thoroughfare – the Baroque **Church of St Peter** is fairly standard issue, but look out for an oversized fresco of St Christopher on the exterior west wall. Perched above the confluence of the two rivers at the end of Ulica Mirana Jarca, the street running parallel to Ulica Staneta Rozmana, is the late-fifteenth-century **Church of the Holy Spirit**, now finally in the process of being restored to something like its former glory.

Eating and drinking

Eating options are fairly minimal, though the *Gostišče Muller* (see above) has a cracking, rustically styled restaurant, with a generous choice of seafood dishes, game, and some good veggie options (closed Mon). The quiet and pleasant *Kavarna Črnomeljska*, under the bridge at the end of Ulica Staneta Rozmana, has good coffee and thick hot chocolate, while the *Piccolo Bar*, down some steps directly opposite the Church of St Peter, is a bit of a smoky den, but does for a beer. Wine buffs should check out the *Črnomaljska Klet* wine cellar, next to the church at Ulica Mirana Jarca 2 (℡07/306-1100, or contact the tourist office), where you can partake in some tasting of the regional wines (around €4 for four or five wines); you can buy bottles here too.

Excursions around Črnomelj

If Črnomelj is bereft of sights, there's enough a short drive away to keep you occupied for a few hours: north of town in the village of Rožanec is the **Mithraeum**, one of the country's most outstanding Roman monuments, while to the south, en route to the Kolpa River, the **Lahinja Landscape Park** and the border village of **Vinica** are each worth a visit.

Rožanec and the Mithraeum

Just after the village of Lokve, beyond a couple of Romany settlements, a left turn takes you up to the smaller village of **Rožanec**; from the parking place, a signposted path leads you across the rail track, and up into a chestnut forest, at the edge of which is a small, picturesque hollow. Hewn into the rock face of one wall is the **Mithraeum** (Mitrej), a second-century Roman shrine dedicated to the invincible sun god Mithras.

The centrepiece of the rock-cut relief (first excavated in 1921) is the sacrifice of the bull, which has Mithras kneeling on, and plunging a dagger into, its back. The spilling of the bull's blood supposedly gave rise to the plant kingdom, while its semen gave rise to the animal kingdom, the latter represented here by the presence of a dog, a snake and a scorpion. The sacrificial scene is accompanied by personifications of the sun and the moon (light and darkness), as well as two priests, Cautopates and Cautes. The inscription, meanwhile, is an address to Mithras from three brothers (Nepos, Prokulus and Firminus), appealing for health and prosperity. The Mithraeum's presence at this particular site is unsurprising given that a Roman road once ran from Črnomelj to Semič, a small town some 5km further north, at which point it divided with one road continuing to Emona (Ljubljana), the other towards present-day Novo Mesto. A copy of the relief is held in the Bela Krajina Museum in Metlika. For more on Mithraism, see the box on p.310.

Lahinja Landscape Park

A couple of kilometres south of Črnomelj – along the road to Vinica and the Kolpa River – you'll pass another Romany settlement, 7km beyond which is the **Lahinja Landscape Park**, a protected area of fields, marshy groves, streams and karstic springs. The park can be accessed from any one of several hamlets clustered in or around its boundary, though the best and most convenient point of entry is at **Pusti Gradac**, the park's northernmost settlement, located up a minor (gravel-track) road 1.5km beyond the village of **Dragatuš** (see below); if you're travelling by bus get the driver to set you down on the main road, from where it's a fifteen-minute walk.

Pusti Gradac also happens to be the park's most culturally well-endowed patch: not only have several extremely important archeological finds been unearthed here – including a remarkable gold coin featuring an imprint of Hungarian King Matthias Corvinus (which dates from around the fifteenth century) – but it's also the site of one of the country's few remaining working **water-mills**. The mill still operates according to traditional methods, its grinders powered by an impressively large water-wheel, itself propelled by waters from the nearby Lahinja River. Demonstrations of the mill are organized by the Klepec family, who live in the house next door at no. 10 (℡07/305-7660, ✉klepec@siol.net). They can also provide information and assistance on the park and its facilities, as well as arrange two- to four-hour-long **guided tours** of the park (€2.5); in theory these tours are only available to groups, but arrangements can be made for individuals as long as you contact the family at least a day or two in advance. There's also **accommodation** here in the renovated family house near the mill, which can sleep between three and six people (❷–❸). A leisurely circular walk around the park takes around three hours.

Vinica

There's more comfortable accommodation in Dragatuš, at the *Pri Štefaniču* tourist farm (℡07/305-7347, ✉stefanic@siol.net; ❸), which also possesses a very accomplished restaurant – the *Župančičev Hram* – named after the poet, playwright and essayist Oton Župančič, who was born in the small fishing village of **VINICA**, 10km further south right on the Croatian border. Along with Ivan Cankar, Župančič (1878–1949) was regarded as the principal exponent of the so-called *Moderna* movement, a Slovene literary trend which appeared at the end of the nineteenth century, and which was closely aligned to the tenets of Slovene national and socio-historical identity; his principal contribution was a collection of poetry entitled *Čaša opojnosti*

(Intoxicating Cup). A prolific wordsmith, Župančič also wrote and translated numerous plays (including Shakespeare), composed poems for the Partisan press, and wrote many children's stories; above all he is known to every Slovene as the creator of the children's character, *Ciciban*. His **birthplace** is located on the main road in the centre of the village at no. 9 (get the key from no. 6, opposite; €1.5); on display, albeit in Slovene only, are copies of his work, his death mask and a beautiful sketch portrait completed by Božidar Jakac just two years before Župančič's death. He is buried at Žale cemetery in Ljubljana. A short way beyond the house is the derelict sixteenth-century **castle**, which now offers little more than terrific views across the Kolpa towards Croatia.

There are two beautifully located **campsites** down by the river on the southern fringe of the village, close to the border crossing: by far the better of the two is the clean, green and spacious *Katra* (☎07/364-6034; ✉katra@siol.net), but if that's full, you might have to settle for the grubby *Kolpa-Vinica* (☎07/306-4018) right next door; both are open between May and September.

Metlika and around

Pressed up hard against the Croatian border just 15km northeast of Črnomelj, **METLIKA** is Bela Krajina's second centre of population. It's a mellow town, but palpably more interesting than its neighbour, thanks to a couple of fine museums, some lovely architecture, and a strong viticultural tradition.

Founded in the thirteenth century when the province (then an important frontier region) was known as Metlika March, it acquired its town rights and developed into a prosperous medieval centre the following century. However, as one of Austria's border strongholds it found itself at the sharp end of Hungarian, then Turkish, attacks – it was razed no fewer than sixteen times. Almost entirely gutted by fire in 1705, its historic centre was swiftly rebuilt, although it received another battering at the hands of its Italian occupiers during World War II, which makes the survival of its attractive old core all the more remarkable.

The town's principal annual happening is the **Spring Wine Festival** (Vinska Vigred) on the third weekend of May, a booze-fuelled three days of wine-related events taking place throughout the Old Town's three squares.

Arrival, information and accommodation

The **bus station** is located by the main crossroads at the southern entrance to town, from where it's a fifteen-minute walk to the Old Town; the **train station**, meanwhile, is 1km southeast of the same crossroads, on the road towards the Croatian border crossing on Kolodvorska ulica. The small, and very helpful, **tourist office** is located in the Old Town at Mestni Trg 1 (May–Aug Mon–Fri 9am–4pm, Sat 9am–noon; Sept–April Mon–Fri 8am–3pm, Sat 9am–noon; ☎07/363-5470, ⊛www.metlika.si). The **post office** (Mon–Fri 7am–7pm, Sat 7am–noon) is located in the small complex across the road from the bus station.

The town's only **hotel** is the *Bela Krajina*, an awful place with depressing, dishevelled rooms, located just down from the old town on the main through road, Cesta Bratstva in Enotnosti (☎07/305-8123; ❸). The nearest **campsite**, *Podzemelj ob Kolpi* (☎07/306-9572; May–Sept), is 7km southwest of town, just off the main Črnomelj–Metlika road down by the Kolpa River – the waters are good for swimming here; buses heading in either direction can drop off on the main road, from where it's about 1km to the site. Five hundred metres prior to the campsite, at Podzemelj 17, the *Gostišče Veselič* has a handful of very small, basic rooms available (☎07/306-9156; ❷), in addition to a pretty accomplished **restaurant**.

The Town

Everything of interest in Metlika is located within the confines of the **Old Town**, sited on a low elevation between the main thoroughfare, Cesta Bratstva in Enotnosti and the River Obrh, and reached via Ulica na Trg, opposite the *Hotel Bela Krajina*. On the north side of **Trg Svobode**, the largest and most central of the three irregularly shaped squares which form the backbone of the Old Town, stands the neat, triangular-shaped **Metlika Castle**, whose vaulted tracts house the **Bela Krajina Museum** (Belokranjski muzej; Mon–Fri 9am–5pm, Sat & Sun 10am–2pm; €2.5), one of Slovenia's finest regional museums. Following an informative fifteen-minute video presentation on the region, the collection kicks off with an impressive haul of Bronze and Iron Age artefacts – vessels, armour, jewellery and the like – and a stash of Roman finds, many of which were unearthed from Pusti Gradac south of Črnomelj (see p.258); there's also a copy of the Mithraic relief at Rožanec on display (see p.260). The most enjoyable part is the section devoted to the region's inhabitants, Bela Kranjci, and features a fine display of homespun attire, as well as items and artefacts pertaining to the traditional cottage industries practised hereabouts, typically pottery, spinning, weaving, cart- and barrel-making and an exhibition of one of the more delicate Slovenian folk-arts, Pisanice (egg-painting).

The development of viticulture – as important to the local economy today as agriculture was prior to World War II – is also given due prominence, as is the role of local societies and associations in Bela Krajina during the nineteenth and twentieth centuries. Foremost amongst these was the Metlika Fire Brigade, whose heroics are documented in the **Firefighting Museum** (Slovenski gasilski muzej; Mon–Sat 9am–1pm, Sun 9am–noon; €1.5), in the building next to the castle. Opened upon the occasion of the Metlika firefighting brigade's centenary anniversary in 1969, the museum proudly displays an assortment of photographs, awards, helmets and uniforms, klaxons and other memorabilia. Best of all, though, are the old firefighting machines – the oldest of which is a model from Cerknica dating from 1836 – located in both this building and the pavilion opposite.

Trg Svobode segues into **Mestni Trg**, an elongated square bound by an attractive blend of beige, cream and mint-coloured buildings, the most distinguished being the neo-Gothic **Town Hall** at no. 24. Positioned atop the building is a slightly askew town coat-of-arms, featuring two ravens perched either side of a castle tower – no doubt on the look-out for rampaging Turks. The bottom end of the square is consumed by the box-like **Church of St Nicholas** (Cerkev Sv Nikolaj), a uniform Baroque structure resurrected in 1759 following a fire some fifty years earlier. The statues of St Nicholas and the pope adorning the high altar were carved by an unknown sculptor, while the frescoes were executed by the Friulian Domenico Fabrio. Just behind the church stands the **Commandery** (Komenda), the one-time residence of the knights of the Teutonic Order, but which is now an old people's home; its impressive size is best appreciated from below the Old Town.

Eating and drinking

Eating options in Metlika are thin on the ground, to say the least, and you may well spend more time drinking in the local wine cellars than you had initially intended – the Old Town, in particular, is disappointingly devoid of life. The only place here is the *Gostilna Bartusu*, at Mestni trg 6, which offers a short and simple menu. Otherwise, you'll have to make the trek to *Gostilna Budački*, awkwardly located in a residential area out near the train station at Ulica Belokranjskega odreda 14; the food's good though, featuring a decent grill menu and fish from the nearby Kolpa. Two places to sample the local **wine** are the *Grajska Klet* café, inside the castle courtyard, and *Vinoteka Pinot*, a cramped cellar bar a few paces along from the tourist office at Trg Svobode 28 (Mon–Sat 8am–11pm, Sun 8am–noon).

For a more sophisticated bout of wine-appreciation, *Vinska Klet Metlika*, across the road from the bus station, arranges organized visits of their extensive cellars with a

---

Wine villages

The triangle of land between Metlika and the pretty wine villages of **Drašiči**, **Vinomer** and **Radovica** to the northeast is classic Krajina countryside, swathes of copse-like *steljniki* – birch tree and fern – set against the backdrop of soft, gently sloping vineyards. The majority of wines cultivated here are blends, the trademark one being *Metliška Črnina*, a rich, velvety and very dark red; others worth trying include the lighter reds, *Modra Portugalka* and *Modri Pinot* and, if you're prepared to spend that little extra, the sparkling white *Metliška Penina*.

Of the aforementioned villages, Drašiči (6km northeast of Metlika) offers most to the wine connoisseur, with a number of cellars providing tasting: a good one for starters is the *Simonič* tourist farm at no. 56 (☏07/305-8185); otherwise, take your pick from the many cellars advertised – these can be approached direct or, alternatively, contact the tourist office in Metlika, who will happily fix something up for you. The 1:50,000 *Bela Krajina* map, available from either of the tourist offices, should help you navigate your way around the villages.

tasting session to boot; they are, though, heavily inclined towards groups, so you may end up having to pay the group rate even if there are only a couple of you (☎07/363-7000). There's a shop here too (Mon–Fri 8am–3pm, Sat 7am–noon).

The Three Parishes Pilgrimage Centre

Two kilometres east of Metlika in the village of **ROSALNICE**, the **Three Parishes Pilgrimage Centre** (Tri Fare) – comprising three fourteenth- and fifteenth-century Gothic churches – is the region's most outstanding ecclesiastical monument. From the few historical documents that existed, it was ascertained that the original churches were likely to have been built by the Knights Templar some time during the twelfth century. Following the arrival of a group of refugee Franciscan monks from Bosnia shortly after the completion of the middle church in the fifteenth century, the complex evolved into an important pilgrimage site. It reached its apogee a century or two later when followers of many different faiths, including Orthodox, journeyed here on a regular basis.

The largest and oldest of the three churches, the **Lady of Our Sorrows** (Žalostna Mati božja) features a superb Gothic interior with Baroque appendages, decorated with a splendid array of frescoes: the presbytery is covered with scenes from the New Testament, the side walls with images of the Apostles and, on the triumphal arch, scenes representing the Ten Commandments. The main altar is ornamented with a fine statuette of Mary with Seven Swords (the Seven Sorrows), the story of which is relayed in the middle church, while the Rococo side altars – dedicated to St John Nepomuk and St Francis of Paola – are no less impressive. Of the three churches this is the only one where Mass is still held.

Next to Our Sorrows, the **Ecce Homo Church** (Glej človek) is the smallest of the three and the only one possessed of a bell tower. It, too, boasts a marvellous Gothic presbytery and high altar, but the show-stealer is its cupola ceiling, painted with wildly colourful frescoes depicting the story of Mary's Seven Sorrows. Completing the trilogy is the poorly preserved **Church of Our Lady of Lourdes** (Lurška Devica Marija), almost completely devoid of colour or ornamentation. Its singular highlight is the neo-Gothic high altar featuring a statue of Mary of Lourdes, whilst it's just about possible to detect the fragments of a fresco of the Crucifixion, from around 1500.

There is a **train station** in Rosalnice, one stop along the line from Metlika, but few trains actually stop here and you're just as well-off walking: the most direct route is along Cankarjeva cesta, which begins from a point some 100m north of the main crossroads in the south of town (on Cesta Bratstva in Enotnosti), and winds its way to the village. If you plan to visit the churches, make sure you call the tourist office in Metlika in advance (see p.262), so that arrangements for the keys can be made.

Travel details

Trains

Brežice to: Ljubljana (Mon–Fri hourly, Sat & Sun 6 daily; 1hr 30min–2hr).
Črnomelj to: Ljubljana (Mon–Fri 6 daily, Sat & Sun 3 daily; 2hr 10min–2hr 45min); Metlika (Mon–Fri 8 daily, Sat & Sun 3 daily; 20min); Novo Mesto (Mon–Fri 8 daily, Sat & Sun 3 daily; 45min–1hr).

Metlika to: Črnomelj (Mon–Fri 7 daily, Sat & Sun 3 daily; 20min); Ljubljana (Mon–Fri 5 daily, Sat & Sun 3 daily; 2hr 30min–3hr); Novo Mesto (Mon–Fri 7 daily, Sat & Sun 3 daily; 1hr–1hr 15min).
Novo Mesto to: Črnomelj (Mon–Fri 9 daily, Sat & Sun 3 daily; 45min–1hr); Ljubljana (Mon–Fri 10 daily, Sat & Sun 4 daily; 1hr 20min–2hr); Metlika (Mon–Fri 8 daily, Sat & Sun 3 daily: 1hr–1hr

15min); Trebnje (Mon–Fri 12 daily, Sat & Sun 4 daily; 20min).

Postojna to: Divača (every 40min–1hr 30min; 30min); Koper (5–7 daily; 1hr 30min); Ljubljana (every 40min–1hr 30min; 1hr); Sežana (hourly–1hr 30min; 45min).

Buses

Brežice to: Bizeljsko (Mon–Fri 4 daily; 30min); Ljubljana (Mon–Fri 4 daily, Sat & Sun 3 daily; 2hr 30min); Novo Mesto (Mon–Fri 6 daily, Sat & Sun 3 daily; 50min).

Cerknica to: Ljubljana (Mon–Fri 8 daily, Sat & Sun 2 daily; 1hr 15min); Stari Trg (Mon–Fri 7 daily, Sat & Sun 2 daily; 25min).

Črnomelj to: Metlika (Mon–Fri 4 daily; 25min); Novo Mesto (Mon–Fri 4 daily; 50min); Vinica (Mon–Fri 10 daily; 35min).

Dolenjske Toplice to: Novo Mesto (Mon–Fri 10 daily, Sat 4 daily; 20min); Žužemberk (Mon–Fri 3 daily; 30min).

Kočevje to: Ljubljana (Mon–Fri hourly, Sat & Sun 6 daily; 1hr 30min); Ribnica (Mon–Fri hourly, Sat & Sun 6 daily; 30min).

Kostanjevica na Krki to: Brežice (Mon–Fri 7 daily, Sat & Sun 2 daily; 25min); Ljubljana (Mon–Fri 4 daily, Sat & Sun 2 daily; 2hr 30min); Novo Mesto (Mon–Fri 8 daily, Sat & Sun 2 daily; 35min).

Metlika to: Črnomelj (Mon–Fri 5 daily; 25min); Novo Mesto (Mon–Fri 2 daily; 25min).

Novo Mesto to: Brežice (Mon–Fri 6 daily, Sat & Sun 3 daily; 50min); Črnomelj (Mon–Fri 1 daily; 50min); Dolenjske Toplice (Mon–Fri 12 daily, Sat 3 daily; 25min); Kostanjevica na krki (Mon–Fri 8 daily, Sat & Sun 3 daily; 40min); Ljubljana (Mon–Fri 5 daily, Sat 4, Sun 2; 1hr 10min); Metlika (Mon–Fri 3 daily; 25min); Otočec (Mon–Fri 7 daily, Sat 3; 15min); Šmarjeske Toplice (Mon–Fri 7 daily, Sat 3; 15min); Trebnje (Mon–Fri 6 daily, Sat & Sun 3 daily; 30min); Žužemberk (Mon–Fri 1 daily; 40min).

Postojna to: Ajdovščina (Mon–Fri 11 daily, Sat & Sun 5 daily; 40min); Ilirska Bistrica (Mon–Fri 6 daily; 40min); Koper (Mon–Fri 6 daily, Sat & Sun 4 daily; 1hr 15min); Ljubljana (Mon–Fri hourly, Sat & Sun 7 daily; 1hr); Nova Gorica (Mon–Fri 10 daily, Sat & Sun 6 daily; 1hr 10min); Piran (Mon–Fri 6 daily, Sat & Sun 4 daily; 1hr 40min); Sežana (Mon–Fri 3 daily; 40min).

Trebnje to: Ljubljana (Mon–Sat 3 daily, Sun 2; 45min); Novo Mesto (Mon–Sat 4 daily, Sun 2; 30min).

International trains

Postojna to: Pula (1 daily; 3hr); Rijeka (2 daily; 1hr 35min); Trieste (1 daily; 2hr); Venice (3 daily; 3hr).

International buses

Novo Mesto to: Zagreb (1 daily; 1hr 20min).

5

Eastern Slovenia

CHAPTER 5

Highlights

* **Logar Valley** Gorgeous alpine valley in the heart of the Kamniške-Savinja Alps, ideal for a number of leisurely pursuits. See p.285

* **Lent Festival, Maribor** Fantastically lively and colourful two-week gathering, featuring street theatre, music and dance all over town. See p.303

* **Pohorje Massif** Skiing, cycling and hiking are just three sporting possibilities on this thickly wooded plateau. See p.294

* **Ptuj** Slovenia's oldest and prettiest town, stuffed with remnants of its Roman and medieval past, and famed as the home of the Kurent Carnival. See p.303

* **Church of the Virgin Mary, Ptujska Gora** Sublime Gothic church featuring the masterful *Virgin with Mantle* misericordia. See p.310

* **Ljutomer Wine Road** Spend the day cycling through the rolling, stepped vineyards of this beautiful wine road. See p.313

* **Prekmurje** Quaint villages, churches, farmhouses and storks characterize Slovenia's distinctively flat northeastern region. See p.314

△ Ljutomer-Ormoz Wine Road

Eastern Slovenia

Taken as a whole, eastern Slovenia receives relatively few visitors, as most people are content to stick to the more celebrated attractions west of Ljubljana. This is a shame, as there's some enticing countryside and a wealth of interesting sites to explore, whilst many towns and villages host excellent spring and summer festivals of classical music, drama, folk music and dancing, as well as carnivals. The region's history is certainly writ large: **Štajerska**, the country's largest province, was formerly part of Austrian Styria prior to World War I, whilst **Koroška** was once the centre of the oldest Slovene state, Karantanija, from the seventh century, and later part of the former Habsburg duchy of Carinthia. This was divided amongst Austria, Italy and Yugoslavia following the collapse of the Austro-Hungarian Empire in the early twentieth century – indeed, it's still sometimes referred to as Carinthia. Whereas Koroška and Štajerska came under the sway of the Austrians, **Prekmurje**, in many ways the country's most distinctive region, if only for its flatness, was subject to around a thousand years of Hungarian rule before being divided between Hungary and the new Yugoslav state in 1920.

Beyond the smattering of small-scale industrial settlements of central Štajerska lie **Maribor** and **Celje**, the second- and third-largest cities in Slovenia respectively. Whilst both offer a smattering of culture, neither can match the historic resonance of **Ptuj**, Slovenia's oldest and most appealing town, which is also a short ride away from the stunning Gothic Church of the Virgin Mary in **Ptujska Gora**. As much as anything else, though, eastern Slovenia is known for its spas – notably **Rogaška Slatina**, the country's oldest and most quintessential spa town – and its wine. Štajerska harbours the largest of the country's three wine-growing regions, **Podravje**, which comprises six districts, each yielding a superb range of predominantly white wines. The one route to seek out if you're being selective is the beautiful **Jeruzalem wine road** ranged along the Croatian border. The region's main activity centre, however, is the **Pohorje Massif**, a broad, arcing plateau which extends some 50km west from the foothills of Maribor, and offers plentiful opportunities for recreational pursuits, including two of the country's largest and best-equipped ski resorts.

Lying to the west of the Massif and bordering Austria to the north, **Koroška**, Slovenia's smallest region, marks a return to the alpine peaks of the Karavanke and Kamniške-Savinja Alps to the west. The mining and iron-working towns of the region, which for years sustained the region's economy, are now largely redundant and offer little in the way of specific appeal, although they do make useful bases for forays into the surrounding hills and mountains, which are mapped out with an excellent series of hiking and cycling routes. The one town here that merits a visit, however, is the region's economic and cultural centre, **Slovenj Gradec**.

Spread across the edge of the Pannonian basin, bordering Austria, Croatia and Hungary, **Prekmurje** is the country's easternmost province and the polar opposite of mountainous western Slovenia. It's also the least visited, yet its mellow tranquillity offers a surprisingly enchanting mix of neat, flower-bedecked villages, such as **Bogojina**, **Filovci** and **Beltinci**, ancient churches, as at **Martjanci** and **Selo** and lush, green countryside, whose flat, wide open spaces provide the ideal terrain for cyclists with an aversion to hills. Although sparsely populated – the only settlements of any conspicuous size are **Murska Sobota** and **Lendava** – Prekmurje is one of the most multifarious regions in Slovenia, populated with a large Hungarian minority as well as the country's largest Roma community.

Transport links in this part of the country are pretty good: the main rail line to Budapest serves quite a few places, with many destinations easily reached from the capital and a well-integrated system of buses and trains linking remoter towns and villages.

Celje and around

From Ljubljana, several main roads – the fastest of which is the A1 highway – head eastwards to **CELJE**, which lies at the heart of the **Lower Savinja Valley** (Spodnja Savinjska Dolina), a predominantly flat, fairly densely populated landscape raked with vast hop plantations and wheat fields and punctuated by the occasional industrial enterprise.

Slovenia's third-largest city after Ljubljana and Maribor, though with a population that still just barely tops the fifty thousand mark, Celje derives its name from the Roman settlement, Celeia, a key administrative centre of the Roman province of Noricum. Economically and culturally the town peaked in the Middle Ages under its overlords, the counts of Celje, who, for three centuries, staked their claim as one of Central Europe's foremost ruling dynasties – one of their last acts before the Habsburgs assumed control was to award Celje its town rights in 1451. As in much of the Štajerska region, Celje faced formidable Germanizing pressures during the late nineteenth and early twentieth centuries, culminating in German occupation during World War II, during which time the town was heavily bombed by Allied planes. Despite its heavy industry, modern-day Celje is not an unattractive place, and worthy of a full day's sightseeing thanks to its clutch of impressive churches and buildings, and one of the largest castles in the country.

Aside from Celje, the area's sites are relatively few, though there's an impressive **Roman necropolis** west of Celje, in Šempeter, and you could spend an entertaining couple of hours in the towns of **Velenje** and **Laško**, located a short way north and south of Celje respectively.

Arrival and information

Both the **train** and **bus stations** are smack-bang in the centre of town, the former just across the road from Krekov trg, the latter 400m north of here; you'll also find left-luggage facilities at the bus station (Mon–Fri 6am–8pm, Sat 7am–2pm; around €2). From the train station it's a short hop across the road to the very helpful **tourist office**, located inside the striking Celje Hall (Mon–Fri 9am–5pm, Sat 9am–1pm; ☏03/428-7936, ✉tic@celje.si). The **post office** (Mon–Fri 8am–7pm, Sat 8am–1pm) is on Krekov trg and there's cheap **Internet access** at *Cyber Café Stane*, next to the Metropol cinema at Stanetova ulica 17a (Mon–Fri 8am–9pm, Sat 9am–9pm, Sun 2–8pm).

Accommodation

There is a limited stock of **private accommodation** in town, which can be booked through the tourist office, and a **student dorm** (Dijaški Dom) about 500m west of the centre at Ljubljanska 21 (☏03/426-6600), which has one- two- and three-bed rooms available throughout the year (€12 per person including breakfast). Celje is poorly served with **hotels**, there being just four uninspiring and almost identically priced places in town.

The two most central hotels are the *Evropa* (☏03/426-9000, ⓦwww.hotel-evropa .si; ❺) on Krekov trg, which has clean, modern and comfy rooms on the first two floors (those on the third floor are abysmal and not much cheaper anyway); and

Ⓐ, Dijaški Dom, Student Dorm & Šempeter ◀

▶ Castle

Theatre

Ⓒ
Church of
St Mary's

Market

❺
Stari Pisker Prison

National Hall

TRG CELJSKIH
KNEZOV

**Museum of
Modern History**

❽

Celje Regional
Museum

GLAVNI
TRG

**Train
Station**

KREKOV TRG

Ⓓ
ⓘ
**Celje
Hall**

Josip Pelikan
Gallery

SLOMŠKOV
TRG

**St Daniel's
Church**

Savinja

City Park

Bus
Station

Ⓑ

P

**RESTAURANTS,
CAFÉS & BARS**

Branimir	2
Café Gallus	5
Gostilna Amerika	1
Kljub	4
Leonardo	8
Local	6
Metropol	3
La Temporada	7

ACCOMMODATION

Astor	A
Evropa	D
Štorman	B
Turška Mačka	C

0 ————— 200 m

St Cecilia's Church

BREG

N

▼ Church of St Nicholas

Novo Mesto & Laško ▼

the *Turška Mačka* built on the site of an inn of the same name at Gledališka ulica 7 (☏03/548-4611, ✉turska.macka@siol.net; **❹**), whose corridors and rooms are ominously gloomy. Popular with visiting business folk, the *Hotel Štorman*, a nine-storey block opposite the bus station at Mariborska cesta 3 (☏03/426-0426, ✉recepcija.storman@siol.net; **❺–❼**), has a mixed bag of rooms, though most are smoothly furnished and colourful enough, if a little poky. Located 1km north of the centre on the road to Šempeter, the *Hotel Astor* at Ljubljanska 39 (☏03/545-2350, Ⓦwww.astor-hotel.net; **❹–❺**) is a low, motel-style building concealing a mix of modern, renovated rooms and older, somewhat shabby, smelly rooms.

The City

The castle aside, all the main sights – churches, squares and museums – are compacted together in the **Old Town**, itself bounded by the Savinja River to the

273

south, the railway line to the east and a chain of main streets to the north and west. The best way to take in the town is to follow a roughly circular route from pedestrianized Krekov trg, opposite the train station, through to Prešernova ulica, down Muzejski trg and along the riverside promenade to Glavni trg.

Krekov trg and around

Facing the busy main street on Krekov trg is **Celje Hall** (Celjski Dom), a red and cream brick building erected in 1906 as a cultural centre for the town's German citizens – various events are still staged here and it's also the location for the tourist office. Further along the street, where Krekov trg segues into Prešernova ulica, take a short diversion down Stanetova ulica for a quick glance at the **Bank of Celje** building, whose curving balconies and distinctive pillar and column motifs are instantly recognizable as the work of the great Slovene architect, Jože Plečnik (see box on p.62).

A two-minute walk south of Krekov trg at Razlagova ulica 5, the **Josip Pelikan Gallery** (Tues–Fri 10am–2pm, Sat 9am–noon, Sun 2–6pm) holds an extensive number of the photographer's images, mostly studio portraits, mountain landscapes (he was a mountaineer himself) and pictures of Celje and surrounds. The gallery is actually part of the glass photo studio in which Pelikan (1885–1977) worked – he lived in the building next door – so there's plenty of his original equipment on display too.

Museum of Modern History and Stari Pisker Prison

Just beyond the pedestrianized portion of Prešernova ulica, the former town hall, at no. 17, now accommodates the **Museum of Modern History** (Muzej Novejše Zgodovine; Tues–Fri 10am–6pm, Sat 9am–noon, Sun 2–6pm; €2.5), an enjoyable and imaginatively presented trawl through twentieth-century Celje. Contained within a series of cabinets are numerous items relating to different subject matter, such as education, work and war, as seen through the eyes of three fictitious characters, each from a different generation. Upstairs, the "Streets of Craftsmen" is presented as a number of mock-up workshops representing goldsmiths, clockmakers, milliners, tailors and so on, that thrived throughout the region during the interwar period. There are further such models of the main square, Glavni trg, and the northeastern working-class suburb of Gaberje, which is now a sprawling industrial zone. The museum also incorporates **Herman's Den** (Hermanov Brlog), the only dedicated children's museum in the country, although it's really been designed with school groups in mind. Not that that'll bother kids, as there are plenty of gadgets and gizmos to keep them entertained, as well as a small play area to mess around in while the parents go off and enjoy the rest of the museum in peace.

Across the road, beyond the door at Prešernova 20, is the **Stari Pisker Prison** (Tues–Fri 10am–2pm, Sat 9am–noon, Sun 2–6pm), where, during World War II, 374 civilian prisoners were executed by occupying German forces. The courtyard where the shootings took place is now a memorial yard, with the names of those killed identified on one wall alongside a bronze relief, while the old torture chamber now contains various items from that time, including clothing, shackles, farewell letters and objects made by prisoners – note, too, on the wall, several photos of the shootings, which were taken by Josip Pelikan (see above). During Slovenia's ten-day war of independence in 1991 a large number of Yugoslav army soldiers were briefly held here, while today the prison functions as a young offenders centre. In order to visit you should call in at the Museum of Modern History first – tickets for that museum are also valid for the prison.

Wedged between two modern administrative buildings on the same side of the street is the fourteenth-century, but several times rebuilt, **Church of St Mary**

The counts of Celje

For more than three hundred years the **counts of Celje** ranked amongst the great Central European ruling dynasties. The dynastic line began with Gebhard I de Saun in 1130, before it morphed into the lords of Žovnek in the thirteenth century and the counts of Celje in 1341. As their status and wealth grew, the counts established their own court system, minted their own money and built castles and churches around the Savinja region. They reached the zenith of their powers under the reign of Hermann II around the end of the fourteenth century, a period during which they extended their sphere of control outside Slovenia into neighbouring lands, at the same time establishing important ties with other European ruling aristocratic houses. Raised to the rank of dukes of the province in 1436, the counts were, for a short period, the equal of their great adversaries and former feudal overlords, the Habsburgs. Their sudden demise followed Ulrich II's assassination by his long-time Hungarian adversary, Laszlo Hunyadi, in Belgrade in 1456.

(Cerkev Sv Marijina), an unprepossessing structure no less dour on the inside than it is on the outside. The church chapel once kept the tombs of the counts of Celje, whose skulls are now on display in the Regional Museum (see below). The street continues up to the grandly named **Trg Celjskih knezov** (Dukes of Celje Square), a large irregularly shaped space dominated by the late nineteenth-century, neo-Renaissance **Narodni Dom** building (National House), now the headquarters of the town council.

Celje Regional Museum

From the square's southern end, take the second left onto Muzejski trg, and part-way along you come to the arcaded Old Manor House, now home to the **Celje Regional Museum** (Pokrajinksi Muzej Celje; Tues–Sun 10am–6pm; €4). If you only see one thing in this museum (quite frankly, there's not much else really worth seeing), make it the **Celje Ceiling**, a dramatic, illusionist tempera painting discovered under another wooden ceiling in 1926. Completed around 1600 by an unknown author (the piece has been attributed to Almanac, although this is disputed), this splendid Renaissance composition comprises eleven fields or panels featuring the four seasons, four gods, two battle scenes, and, in the central panel, a tangle of pillars and columns rising upwards to an imaginary sky. As a measure of protection, the room is kept in a permanent state of near darkness.

The remainder of the museum is taken up with several rooms of not very exciting furniture garnered from all over Slovenia, including Biedermeier, Baroque, Rococo, the odd painting and a bit of sculpture. The one minor saving grace is the room given over to the deeds of the counts of Celje, its star exhibit a glass cabinet holding eighteen of the counts' grisly skulls, including that of its last ruler Ulrich II, easily identifiable as it's the one with the jaw missing. To the rear of the museum, on a small grassy patch by the riverfront, is an open-air **lapidarium** featuring a few weatherbeaten Roman stone blocks.

Slomškov trg, Glavni trg and the City Park

From the Celje Regional Museum, continue along the promenade, past a section of medieval walls, to cobbled **Slomškov trg**, a small square named in honour of the saint, Anton Slomšek – there is statue of him nearby (see box, p.299). Standing in the middle, the fourteenth-century **Abbey Church of St Daniel** (Cerkev Sv Danijel) is the town's most impressive ecclesiastical monument. Invested with some outstanding Gothic architecture, including a fine rib-vaulted ceiling and a towering arch at the entrance to the presbytery, the church also features numerous high-quality wall frescoes, most notably in the **Chapel of Our Lady of the Sorrows**, which also keeps a fifteenth-century pietà of the Sad Madonna. The chapel dedicated to Slomšek was added in 2000, one year after his beatification in Maribor.

From Slomškov trg a narrow path leads through to **Glavni trg**, a lovely square flush with Baroque and Renaissance buildings, and a convivial place to enjoy a drink during the warmer summer months. In the centre stands **St Mary's Column**, adorned with statues of SS Rok, Joseph and Florian. Heading north out of the square brings you to the intersection with Krekov trg and Prešernova ulica.

For a bit of peace and quiet, head across the river to the **City Park** (Mestni Park), a tranquil green expanse where you can ramble, play tennis or skate (in winter) in the recreation centre. Also on this side of the river is the **Church of St Cecilia** (Cerkev Sv Cecilija), reached via a long covered walkway (though it's often closed), and, further up the hill, the **Church of St Nicholas** (Cerkev Sv Miklavž); although this, too, is almost always closed, there are some superlative **views** of the castle opposite.

The Old Castle and around

Once the largest fortification in the country, the windswept ruin of Celje's **Old Castle** (Stari Grad; daily summer 9am–9pm, winter 10am–5pm; free) sits atop a four-hundred-metre rise 2km southeast of town. Originally a twelfth-century structure, the castle acquired its present layout in the fourteenth century during the rule of the counts of Celje, who reinforced the walls and invested the interior with residential quarters; ad-hoc additions followed, before its eventual demise and descent into ruin during the seventeenth century. Although there are vestigial Romanesque and Gothic remains, years of systematic and extensive renovation have quashed much of the castle's historical charm; nevertheless it remains an impressive site, particularly when viewed from afar. Whilst here it would be remiss not to climb the enormous **Friedrich Tower** (Friderikov Stolp), originally a four-storey defence tower built by the counts in the fourteenth century but now a roofless structure offering stupendous **views** of the rust-red and orange tiled town rooftops, and the hump backed hills of the Lower Savinja Valley. The castle stages a regular programme of medieval themed events throughout the summer; check with the tourist office. To reach the castle, head through the underpass by the train station and follow the signs; beyond the football stadium, the quickest walking route is to cut through the woods and rejoin the road at the top, from where it's a further 1km or so (40 min). If, after that walk, you're in need of refreshments, the *Tlačan* gostilna just down from the castle offers drinks and simple meals (closed Mon).

The castle is also a good starting point for several short to medium length **hikes** in the area, with signposted trails to Celjska koča (651m; 2hr 30min or 1hr 30min), Svebotnik (700m; 2hr) and the delightful little hill village of Svetina (679m; 2hr 30min). If you are planning to do some walking, pick up a copy of the 1:50,000 *Celjska Kotlina* **map**, available from the tourist office. At the last of these, just above the beautiful Gothic Church of Mary of the Snows, there's an excellent mountain chalet, the *Almin Dom* (☎03/780-3000, ⓔsvetina@almindom.com), which has spotless and very comfortable pension-style **rooms** (❹), as well as dorm beds (❶). There's a very accomplished **restaurant** here too, worth visiting even if you're not planning to sleep over. The chalet can also be reached by car (or bicycle) from Celje; heading east out of town, look for signs to the industrial zone of Store, and follow the road south from there up to Svetina. On a good day, there are views as far as the Zagrebačka Gora mountains in Croatia.

Eating and drinking

There are very few really decent **restaurants** in town; the best is *La Temporada* at Savinova ulica 9, a comfortable Mexican place with dark red and bright yellow painted walls and a brick vaulted ceiling, serving up the usual suspects – between 11am and 5pm they offer a good selection of *malica* dishes (bargain two- or three-course set meals) for €4. Although a bit depressing looking, *Istrska Konoba*, in the *Turška Mačka* hotel, is a decent seafood restaurant, and has fresh fish flown in daily from the Croatian coast. Although a little way north of the centre at Mariborska cesta 79, opposite the huge Interspar building, the oddly named *Gostilna Amerika* is worth trekking to for its huge portions of southern Balkan specialities such as bean stews, *čevapi* (rolls of minced meat), and *ražnjiči* (a combination of meats on a skewer). All four of the hotels offer decent lunchtime *malica* menus.

Celje has a healthy sprinkling of cafés, pubs and clubs to choose from. Of the town **cafés**, take your pick from the restful *Café Gallus*, secreted away in a passageway just off Ljubljanska cesta (daily 9am–11pm, Sun till 2pm); *Leonardo* on Gosposka ulica, whose mouthwatering selection of cakes and pastries are quite likely to draw you in (Mon–Fri 8am–9pm, Sat 8am–4pm); or the loungey café inside the Metropol art-house cinema (kino) at Stanetova ulica 17.

For evening drinking your first stop should be *Kljub*, a real underground den on the corner of Cankarjeva ulica and Aškerčeva ulica, which has frequent live rock evenings. Alternatively, there's *Local*, a long, coolly lit cellar bar attracting a mixed crowd enjoying the regular DJ nights of jazz, funk, soul and swing – it's located through a small passageway opposite the National Hall on Prešernova ulica. No less enjoyable is the roomy, pub-like *Branimir* at Stanetova ulica 27.

Entertainment

The **Slovenian People's Theatre** (Slovenski Ljudsko Gledališče), just behind the *Turška Mačka* hotel at Gledališka ulica 5 (box office Mon–Fri 9–11am & 5–7pm, plus 60min prior to each performance), is one of the best professional theatres in Slovenia; bear in mind, though, that it shuts down for most of July and August. The theatre is also the venue for the **Days of Comedy** festival in February, though surmounting the language barrier might prove a little tricky. The town puts on a couple of other festivals, foremost of which is **Summer in Celje**, a two-month programme of small concerts and gigs at various venues around town, while **medieval-themed events** (markets, jousting and the like) take place on a regular basis up at the castle during the summer months; enquire at the tourist office for information on any of the above.

Sports fans should head to the enormous Petrol Sports Arena complex (which incorporates the new national football stadium) on Opekarnitska cesta 1.5km north of town, to watch the men's **handball** team; as regular European Champions League participants, Celje Pivovarna Laško is Slovenia's best handball team, and arguably the country's finest team in any sport. Games, played between September and May, are big events here which means tickets (around €10) can be difficult to come by (check with the tourist office).

Šempeter and the Roman Necropolis

Approximately 12km west of Celje along the main road running parallel to the A1 highway, the small urban settlement of **ŠEMPETER** is the setting for a **Roman Necropolis** (Rimski Nekropoli; April–Sept Tues–Sun 10am–6pm, Oct Sat & Sun 10am–4pm; €3). One of the most important archeological sites in this part of Europe, the necropolis, excavated and reconstructed over a fifteen-year period

△ Roman Necropolis

during the 1950s and 1960s, served as a burial ground for the nobles of Celeia (Roman Celje) until it was swamped by floodwaters from the Savinja River around 270 AD. Four marble mausolea, emblazoned with relief portraits of the families they commemorate, as well as scenes from classical mythology, were re-erected, and dozens more plinths, columns and fragments were unearthed.

The largest and grandest of the four monuments is the **Spectatii** family tomb, its members represented by three headless statues; the funerary plinths are arrayed with mythical figures and various seasonal scenes, whilst the head of Medusa juts out over the gable. The most arresting tomb is that of the **Ennii** family, depicted here by three shallow relief portraits of the mother, father and daughter, Kalendina, though curiously there's not one of the son, Vitulus. On the front-facing plinth there's a fine relief of *Europa Riding the Bull* and, on the Baldachin ceiling, sculpted caskets bursting with rosettes. By way of contrast, the other two mausolea are less fanciful: the altar-shaped tomb of **Vindonius** – understood to be the oldest of the four – features reliefs of *Hercules and Alcestis* and, on the side panels, two hunters, one with a hare draped around his neck, the other carrying a shepherd's staff and a basket of birds. Built in the form of a chapel, the tomb of **Secundinii** is largely devoid of ornamentation. More detailed information about the site can be obtained from the tourist office.

To get here take one of the hourly **buses** from Celje, alight in the centre, and backtrack 100m to the traffic lights; from here walk up Ob rimski nekropoli towards the church, opposite which is both the necropolis and the small **tourist association office** (April–Oct Tues–Sun 10am–6pm; ☎03/700-2056, ⓦwww. td-sempeter.si). From Šempeter, buses continue west along the main road, stopping after 2km at the road which branches south to the village of **Dolenja Vas** (which is actually part of **Prebold**). At no. 147 the private little *Dolina* **campsite** (☎03/572-4378, ⓔkamp.dolina@siol.net; April–Oct) also has three simple rooms (❷) and two apartments (❹). Some 800m further on from here, at Graščinska ulica 9, the

Garni Šport Hotel (☏03/703-4060, ⓦwww.garnisporthotel.com; ⑤) has comfortable, clean and warm rooms.

Hell's Cave

If you don't manage to get down to the Karst region, you can content yourself with a visit to the **Pekel (Hell's) Cave** (Jama Pekel), the only one open to tourists in the Štajerska region. Located 5km north of Šempeter, across the main A1 highway near the tiny hamlet of **Podlog**, this atmospheric little cave takes its name from the devilish figure carved into the rock face above the entrance. Inside, it's split between two levels; the first, lower gallery tracks the Peklenščica (Hell Stream) past several lakes towards a small subterranean waterfall. Thereafter it's a steady climb to the stalactite-infested upper gallery, and then onwards to the exit, located some 40m higher than the entrance. Fifty-minute **tours** of the cave (€5) take place hourly from 9am to 6pm between April and September, and at weekends only in March and October till 5pm; however, check with the tourist office in Šempeter first (see opposite); they can also advise on how to reach the cave if you're not sure. If you don't have your own transport, **bikes** (€5 per day) can be hired from the *Dolina* campsite (see opposite).

Laško

Eleven kilometres south of Celje, the small spa town of **LAŠKO** has been brewing beer since 1825, and is today one of the two largest breweries in the country – the Union brewery in Ljubljana is the other – and formerly one of the largest in Yugoslavia. Visits to the **brewery** (*pivovarna*), which take in the filtration and bottling plants, a modest museum and a spot of sampling, are usually only available for groups, but if you call well in advance it should be possible to arrange a tour (☏03/734-8000 or contact the tourist office).

However, there's more to Laško than just beer. Known to have existed since Roman times, the town's thermal springs have been attracting a more contemporary crowd since 1854 when the first formal baths were built. Today the **Laško spa** (Zdravlišče Laško), a ten-minute walk north of the tourist office at Zdravilišče cesta 4 (☏03/734-5111, ⓦwww.zdravilisce-lasko.si), is a thoroughly modern complex with superb indoor and outdoor thermal baths, comprising a therapeutic pool, massage whirlpool and children's pool (daily 9.30am–10pm; weekdays €7 for 3hr, €9 all day; weekends €8 for 3hr, €10 all day); in addition there's a sauna centre and massage facilities.

The town's **Beer and Flowers Festival** (*Pivo-Cvetje*) in early/mid-July is one of the most enjoyable provincial events in the Slovene calendar, four manic days of music, sports and games, flower displays and, of course, lots of beer.

The town's **train** and **bus stations** are positioned side by side on Trg Svobode on the west bank of the Savinja River, and just a few paces from the friendly **tourist office** (Mon–Fri 8am–5pm, Sat 8am–noon; ☏03/733-8950), housed in a modern glass building by the bridge. The spa complex boasts two very accomplished, albeit identical, **hotels** (⑥) – ask for a riverside room. Better still, the hugely stylish and excellent value *Hotel Savinja*, across the river in the old part of town at Valvasorjev trg 1 (☏03/734-3030, ⓔstorman.savinja@siol.com; ⑤), has ten large and fantastically luxurious rooms. Back across the bridge, opposite the tourist office, the *Hotel Hum* (☏03/573-1321, ⓦwww.askerc-sp.si; ④–⑤) possesses a mix of upgraded modern rooms and more down-at-heel older rooms.

Beautifully set on the slopes of Mount Hum (583m) 1km north of town is **Tabor Castle** (Grad Tabor), whose two renovated towers – one round, one square – now accommodate a wedding hall and **restaurant** (daily 11am–11pm, Sun til 10pm).

The latter is seriously posh and expensive, but the food is exemplary, featuring an exotic menu of meats and fish (deer, duck, cuttlefish and lobster) alongside some intriguing local specialities such as beer soup and beer mousse. More affordably, the very enjoyable *Pivnica Pačnik* (closed Sun), housed in a lovely sky-blue building 200m north of the *Hotel Savinja* on Aškerčev trg, offers delicious beer sausages; and in the basement of the *Hotel Savinja* there's a traditional *pivnica* (daily noon–midnight, till 2am Fri & Sat) serving up beer and snacks. From the castle there's a well-marked footpath to the top of Mount Hum, where you'll be rewarded with some splendid views (45min).

Velenje

Opened with great ceremonial pomp in 1959, **VELENJE**, 24km northwest of Celje and well connected by both bus and train, is Slovenia's youngest town. Formerly known as Titov Velenje – the Yugoslav president Tito visited here no less than four times, on one occasion with Brezhnev – modern-day Velenje was designed as a model industrial workers' town, characterized by a uniform series of grim high-rise apartments and wide streets broken up by the odd splash of greenery. Today, Slovenia's fifth largest city is still sustained by major industry, including coal mining, which employs around two thousand people, and the major domestic appliances producer, Gorenje, which employs more than five thousand people. Amidst this oddly appealing Socialist-Realist aesthetic are two worthwhile attractions: the town castle and museum, and the coal mining museum.

Velenje Castle and the Coal Mining Museum

Sited on a high, rounded hill above Velenje's small, almost forgotten, Old Town quarter is the beautifully renovated **Velenje Castle** (Velenjski Grad), most of which dates from the sixteenth century. The castle now houses the **town museum** (Tues–Sun 9am–5pm, €2.5), which comprises several disparate but interesting exhibitions: the most enthralling section is the collection of African art donated to the museum by Czech-born sculptor František Foit, who spent more than twenty years living in and travelling around the continent. During this time he accumulated some terrific stuff, most of which is on display here, including jewellery, furniture, musical instruments, tribal masks and puppets, as well as some of his own wood-carved sculptures. The two other major exhibitions are those on twentieth-century Slovene art, featuring big-hitters such as Pilon, Kralj, Mihelič and Tisnikar, and an exposition on the region in Medieval times, comprising lots of sacral artwork, a reconstruction of a seventeenth-century house, and items culled from the area – look out for an exquisite, and extremely rare, ivory watch. A couple of rooms are also given over to the development of Velenje post World War II though, for the most part, it's little more than a shrine to socialist-era figureheads such as Tito and Edvard Kardelj, busts and pictures of whom adorn several of the rooms. The castle can be reached via a path just across from the bus station and by road from the old part of town.

Coal has been excavated at the **Velenje Coal Mine** in Škale, 1.5km north of town, since the mid-eighteenth century, although it was the drilling of the main lignite layer around a century later that really put the town on the map. Although the mine remains operational, it's possible to visit certain parts of it as part of an organized **tour** (daily 9.30am–5pm; €9). The ninety-minute visit – enlivened by audiovisual presentations and puppets of assorted mine characters – takes in sections of both the old and new mine shafts, the latter first used after World War II; you also get to partake in a hearty miner's lunch in the underground canteen. Once done you can view the **coal mining exhibition** (price included in the tour ticket, or €2 for exhibition only).

Unless you have your own transport, it's a good thirty-minute walk to the mine; from the Old Town, head north up Cesta Talcev, cross the rail tracks and continue along Kidričeva cesta, which loops round and becomes Koroška cesta. However, in order for an ad-hoc visit to take place, there needs to be a minimum of seven people, so you should ring in advance to see when tours are scheduled (☎03/587-0997).

If you've got a moment to spare, pop over to Titov trg, opposite the *Hotel Paka*, to see the oversized **monument of Tito** – one of very few statues of the former Yugoslav president remaining in Slovenia.

Practicalities

The **bus station** is located to the south of town on Šaleška cesta, at the intersection of the Celje and Slovenj Gradec roads, whilst the **train station** is 1km northeast of here, just off Cesta Talcev near the industrial zone. The very informative **tourist office** is located inside the enormous red sports centre behind the bus station (Mon–Fri 8am–6pm, Sat & Sun 9am–1pm & 3–6pm; ☎03/896-1860, ⓦwww.velenje-tourism.si) – they've also got bikes for rent.

There are three decent **places to stay** in town, the best of which is the *Hotel Ražgoršek*, below the castle on Stari trg (☎03/898-3630, ⓦwww.hotelrazgorsek.com; ❻), whose brazenly colourful – if slightly over the top – rooms are fashioned in Baroque style, with plush carpets, oversized paintings and gold trimmings. Near the bus station, at Rudarska 1, is the clinical yet pleasant *Hotel Paka* (☎03/898-0700, ⓦwww.hotelpaka.com; ❻); and about 400m east of the bus station at Kopališka cesta 1, the upmarket, nineteenth-century *Vila Herberstein* (☎03/896-1400, ⓔvila.herberstein@siol.net; ❻) possesses seven large rooms furnished in period style. The best **eating** option is the fanciful restaurant inside the *Ražgoršek* hotel.

Koroška

From Velenje, two roads forge their way into the heart of **Koroška**, a mountainous, heavily forested region abutting the Austrian border, crossed by three river valleys and scattered with isolated highland farmsteads and small valley settlements. One road heads north up the Mislinja Valley to the pretty town of **Slovenj Gradec**, and beyond to **Dravograd**, whilst the other road straggles across a mountain pass northwest to the ex-mining towns of **Črna na Koroškem** and **Mežica**; the former is also a key starting point for forays into the heart of the Koroška mountains themselves.

Slovenj Gradec

In stark contrast to Velenje, the spruce little town of **SLOVENJ GRADEC**, 27km further north in the Mislinja Valley and the largest settlement in Koroška, preserves a delightful medieval core, one not that dissimilar to Kamnik (see p.92) or Škofja Loka (see p.97). The town is renowned for its rich cultural heritage, thanks to the likes of prominent Slovene artists, Bogdan Borčič and Jože Tisnikar, and the Austrian composer Hugo Wolf, all of whom were born here.

The Town

Everything of interest is located along **Glavni trg**, a wide, smoothly curving street that forms the heart of the town's beautifully preserved historic medieval core. The town's two principal sites are located inside the former town hall building at no. 24; on the first floor is the **Koroška Gallery of Fine Arts** (Koroški Galeriji Likovnih Umetnosti; Tues–Fri 9am–6pm, Sat & Sun 9am–noon & 3–6pm; €2.5), one of the largest and most progressive art centres in the country. The gallery dotes almost exclusively on the works of artists from Koroška, namely Franc Berneker, the first modern Slovene sculptor, Bogdan Borčič, painter of brightly coloured abstract pieces – though several darker works were influenced by his time spent in Dachau – and Jože Tisnikar, whose overwhelmingly bleak and moody paintings, defined as "dark modernism", undoubtedly owe much to the time he spent in a hospital pathology department. The gallery is also an important venue for guest exhibitors.

Installed in the cells of the former town prison (last used during World War II by the Germans) across the courtyard is a fine little **archeological collection** (Arheologija Krajine; same times; €2), whose finds, from the Mislinja, Mežica and Drava valleys, span several periods: the earliest exhibits include cave-bear remains, a bone harpoon, and Stone and Iron Age tools, whilst from the Roman and Slavic period there is a stack of grave goods (signet rings and bronze fibula brooches) and, from the Middle Ages, tiles and clay pots; further treasures – ceramics, coins and jewellery – were unearthed in 2000 during the building of a new school.

Situated in a recess directly opposite the town hall, the thirteenth-century, but several times rebuilt, **Parish Church of St Elizabeth** honours the Hungarian princess Elizabeth. The interior showcases an abundance of Baroque extravagances, most notably a sumptuously overblown high altar – the central painting of Elizabeth was executed by the Baroque workshop of Franz Strauss – and a richly gilded pulpit. Also keep your eye out for numerous liturgical items, Gothic knight's tombstones, and, to the right as you enter, a painting of St Anton Slomšek (see box on p.299), completed in 2000. The interior of the neighbouring **Church of the Holy Spirit** is beautifully ornamented with a fine array of fifteenth-century frescoes – although the church is usually closed, there is a small peephole in the door through which you can see some of the artwork, but for a closer look contact the tourist office.

Practicalities

The town's **bus station** is on Pohorska cesta, from where it's a ten-minute walk south to Glavni trg. The helpful **tourist office** (May–Sept Mon–Fri 9am–6pm, Sat & Sun 9am–noon; Oct–April Mon–Fri 8am–4pm; ☎02/881-2116, ⓦwww.slovenj-gradec.si) is located on the ground floor of the old town hall halfway along Glavni trg at no. 24; they can also arrange private **accommodation**, which may be your preferred choice given that the town is possessed of just one hotel, the very ordinary *Slovenj Gradec*, (☎02/884-5285; ❺), a short walk up from the tourist office at no. 43. Somewhat oddly located out at the small airport 3km south of town on the road to Velenje, *Gostišče Aerodrom* (☎02/885-0500, ⓔinfo@aerodrom-sg.si; ❻) has smart, sunny air-conditioned rooms, bungalows sleeping three people (❺), and spaces for camping.

The only worthwhile place to **eat** in town is *Sedmica*, a pizzeria/spaghetteria opposite the tourist office, though if you've got wheels a better option is *Gostilna Murko* on the northern outskirts of town (on the road to Dravograd) at Francetova cesta 24 (Mon–Sat 8am–10pm, Sun 10am–5pm). Adjoining *Sedmica* is the appealing *Mestna kavarna* **coffee house**.

Dravograd, Šentanel and Jamnica

Eleven kilometres north of Slovenj Gradec and just 4km shy of the Austrian border, the old market town of **DRAVOGRAD** sits at the junction of Koroška's three valleys – the Drava, the Meža and the Mislinja – as well as several key road routes and the Maribor–Klagenfurt rail line. Although it's likely that the only reason you might end up here is to take an onward connection, there are a couple of minor sights worth checking out if you've got an hour or so to spare, both of which lie across the river in the old town core.

Some 50m along the main street, Trg 4 julija, in the basement of the municipal town building at no. 7, is a World War II **Gestapo prison** (Muzej Zbirka Gestapovski; Mon–Fri 8am–2pm; free), whose half a dozen dingy, cobwebbed cells now display a dusty collection of uniforms and artefacts belonging to both the captives and their captors. The Gestapo controlled the prison on two occasions, the first time between the beginning of the occupation and July 1941, and the second time between January 1944 and the end of the war. Five minutes' walk further along the street stands the attractive twelfth-century **Church of St Vitus** (Cerkev Sv Vid) one of the few Carinthian-style Romanesque structures remaining in this region, and unusual in that it features a bell tower at its eastern end – it's usually closed so if you'd like a look, contact the tourist office.

The **train** and **bus stations** are just 200m apart, on the south bank of the river near the bridge. The **tourist office** (May–Sept Mon–Fri 10am–5pm; ☎02/871-0285, ✆info@dravograd.si) is across the road from the Church of St Vitus in a vaulted underpass at Trg 4 julija 57. Fifty metres on from here at Koroška cesta 48 is the town's one **hotel** (and just about the only place to eat), the very dull *Hesper* (☎02/878-4440, ⓦwww.hesper.si; ⑤).

From Dravograd, one road (and the rail line) threads its way through the scenic Drava Valley eastwards to Maribor some 60km away, whilst the road west passes through the uninteresting towns of **Ravne na Koroškem** (the "capital" of Koroška) and **Prevalje**. About 2km beyond Prevalje, a road branches off up towards the villages of **ŠENTANEL** (4km distant) and **JAMNICA** (7km distant), two picturesque mountain settlements known for their abundance of **tourist farms** (all ❷): two of the best in Šentanel are *Ploder* at no. 3 (☎02/823-1104, ✆kmetijaploder@hotmail.com), and *Marin Miler* at no. 8 (☎02/824-0550, ✆marin@koroska.org) – the latter has a terrific gostilna too; and in Jamnica, there's the large *Koroš* tourist farm (☎02/823-1106, ✆franc.stern@volja.net).

Mežica and Črna na Koroškem

A short way south of Prevalje is the town of **MEŽICA** where, up until a few years ago, lead and zinc had been mined for over three hundred years. Although organized mining began here way back in 1665, it wasn't until Napoleon's arrival in 1809 – and his subsequent occupation of the nearby Austrian mine areas, which forced the Austrians to look elsewhere for new sources of ore – that intensive, heavy-duty production took place. Further modernization of the mine during the early twentieth century saw the introduction of electricity in addition to pneumatic drilling methods, though the gradual depletion of ore reserves after World War II led to a decline in production and the mine finally closed in 2000. Part of it, however, was kept open for **tours** (Tues–Sun: April–Oct 11am & 3pm; Nov–March 11am; ☎02/870-0180, ⓦwww.podzemljepece.com; €7). Kitted out with jacket, helmet and light, you clamber aboard the very small and rickety mine train (not for the claustrophobic), which transports you 3.5km along a shaft into the heart of the mine complex, the area known as Moring. During the one-hour tour you walk through numerous large galleries on two levels (there are twenty in total, each approximately 30m apart), where you'll get to see the calling room, where miners would gather at the beginning of the shift before dispersing to their stations, various mining equipment and machinery preserved *in situ* and a series of audiovisual demonstrations.

After resurfacing, head to the adjacent **mine museum** (Tues–Sun: April–Oct 9am–5pm, Nov–March 9am–3pm; price included in the mine ticket), where you can view a fine display of minerals and fossils, mine survey maps and mapping instruments and a mock-up miner's home, a typically cramped living space which would be expected to accommodate up to eight members of the same family.

For something a little more adventurous, you can participate in **underground bike rides** through a section of the mine; the first part of the ride is from the *Hotel Club Krnes*, in the old mining settlement of **ČRNA NA KOROŠKEM** (see below), to the mine entrance, before the descent into the mine and through 5km of illuminated tunnels constructed for the transportation of lead ore and waste materials – you also get to see the mine museum before returning to the hotel. Tours (€20 for two to four people, €18 for five to eight people) take place at 10am daily except Monday, but in any case you should call the *Hotel Club Krnes* first.

During the mine's heyday, most of the population of this sedate little town, 7km south of Mežica in the Upper Meža Valley, were also employed at Mežica, as well as in the local ironworking, forestry and timber industries. For the visitor, Črna is chiefly of interest as a springboard for onward ventures into the mountains, and there are several tourist facilities here. If you've got some time to kill, there are a couple of minor collections to nose around: across from the bus stop, the **ethnological museum** (€2) comprises a modest assortment of everyday household items and farming implements used by local peasants; hewn into the rock face a few metres from the bus station, the **mining museum** (closed Nov–April; €2) presents mine trucks, drilling equipment and tools used in the Mežica mine before its closure.

To view either collection contact the helpful **tourist office** (June–Sept Mon–Fri 8am–6pm, Sat 9am–1pm; Oct–May Mon–Fri 8am–3pm, Sat 9am–1pm; ☎02/870-3066, ✉pkm@siol.net), just around the corner from the **bus stop** at Center 100. The town's one **hotel**, which is a five-minute walk south of the tourist office at Center 153, is the *Hotel Club Krnes* (☎02/870-3060, ✉krnes@siol.net; ❶–❷); this friendly, cyclists' hotel offers very basic, but perfectly acceptable, hostel-style accommodation in singles, doubles and apartments, and you can camp

Cycling and hiking around Črna na Koroškem

The mountains encircling Črna na Koroškem, also known as King Matjaž Park in all the tourist material, offer some of the best **cycling** in the country, with around 500km of marked trails; at present there are five circular routes – with a further five in the pipeline – each of which is marked out by yellow animal footprints. Everything you need to know about cycling in the region can be obtained from the *Hotel Club Krnes* (see above), where you can also **rent bikes** (€15 per day) and get repairs done. As well as organising guided mountain bike tours, the hotel arranges climbing and kayaking excursions – check out ⊛www.mtbpark.com for more details.

From Črna there are a number of good **hiking** possibilities, the most popular of which is the trek northwest up to **Mala Peca** (1731m; 3hr 15min), just below which is the *Dom na Peci* hut (April–Oct daily, Nov–March Sat & Sun only; ☎02/823-8406); fifteen minutes' walk from the hut is the **cave of King Matjaž** (Matjaževa jama), the alleged sleeping place of the mythological folk hero named after the Hungarian king, Matthias Corvinus – there's a bronze statue of Matjaž inside the cave entrance. From the hut, you can continue via one of two paths towards Kordeževa glava (2125m) and the Austrian border. From Črna there are shorter hikes, too, including one trail north to the year-round *Koča na Pikovem* hut (992m; ninety minutes), and another trail south to **Najevska Lipa** (1hr 45min), the site of an enormous Linden tree, alleged to be one of the largest trees in Slovenia. Whatever activity you plan to undertake, you'll find the 1:50,000 *Koroška* map (€7) available from the tourist office, a useful aid.

here too. They've also got a bike shed and test track in the garden. If you're look-ing for something to **eat**, try one of the several gostilna dotted around town, the most central of which is *Rešer*, directly opposite the tourist office at Center 101.

Črna is also known throughout Slovenia for its **Snow Castle Festival**, staged 6km from town up at Pod Peca on the last weekend of January, and which sees over a hundred teams compete to see who can design the highest, grandest or most dazzling ice castle. How long these constructions remain intact is, naturally enough, dependent upon the weather, though most are still standing about a week or so after the event.

The Upper Savinja Valley

Named after the **Savinja River**, which flows from the heart of the Kamniške-Savinja Alps, down through Celje and beyond to Zidani Most, where it joins the Sava River, the **Upper Savinja Valley** (Zgornja Savinjska Dolina) is a pristine landscape of towering alpine peaks, river valleys and undulating slopes. The terri-tory it covers extends roughly from between the aforementioned Alps to Letuš, a small village just north of Šempeter.

The region's settlements are mainly large villages and a couple of small towns and, as picturesque as some of them are, such as the administrative centre of **Mozirje**, they're not really worth a special visit. In any case, the chances are that you'll be keen to push on to the wonderful **Logar Valley** and the surrounding hills and mountains, where there are ample opportunities for hiking, climbing, cycling and other activities.

The Logar Valley

The region's siren draw is the extraordinarily beautiful **Logar Valley** (Logarska dolina), a seven-kilometre-long alpine valley situated along the western margins of the Upper Savinja in the cradle of the Kamniške-Savinja Alps. Formed during the Ice Age, the U-shaped glaciated valley manifests a level, green valley floor covered with flower-speckled meadows and beech woods, enclosed by step-like cliff sides riddled with glacial boulders, waterfalls, springs, streams and a majestic wreath of jagged grey peaks, most of which top 2000m.

From the entrance to the valley (between April and October there's a €5 charge for cars), it's about 2km to a cluster of tourist facilities, including an information hut and a couple of hotels (see overleaf), beyond which point the road continues for a further five kilometres up to the head of the valley and Logarska's most popu-lar site, the ninety-metre-high **Rinka Waterfall** (Slap Rinka); if you're walking, there's a trail (6km long) to the waterfall beginning approximately 1km along the road after you've entered the valley. Although the mountains look formidable, they can be traversed via a trail which starts at Rinka and climbs to **Okrešelj** (1396m), where there's a hut (☎03/838-9070; May–Oct), before continuing to **Kamniško Sedlo** (1864m) and another hut (☎051/241-639; mid-June to mid-Oct); from here the trail continues down to Kamniška Bistrica (see p.96).

The valley's small **information hut** (May–Oct daily 8am–6pm; ☎03/838-9004, ⓦ www.logarska-dolina.si), located 2km along the valley road from the point of entry, has a mine of information on the valley and its surrounds, and can book private accommodation in the region. Also on offer here are three-hour guided walks of the valley (€25 for a group of up to ten people), as well as a number of other activities, including **horse-riding** (€12 for a 1hr guided tour), **rock climbing** (€15 for 2hr), and **archery** (€10); there are also **bikes** for hire (€3 for 1hr, €10 for 4hr plus).

Out of season, you can get information at the alpine-style *Hotel Plesnik* (☎03/839-2300, ⓦwww.plesnik.si; ❾) across the road; this extremely comfortable, and very expensive, place also has a pool and sauna, but it's not as homely as the neighbouring *Vila Palenk* (same ☎ as *Plesnik*; ❻), which has some rooms with a fireplace, lovely if you're here during the winter. Otherwise, there's plenty more affordable accommodation elsewhere throughout the valley: 500m along the road from the *Plesnik* is the *Plesnik* tourist farm (☎03/838-9009, ⓔnina.plesnik@cmok.si; ❸), and, another 500m further on from here, the smart *Pension Na Razpotju* (☎03/839-1650, ⓔrazpotje@sol.net; ❻). Back down in the opposite direction, roughly midway between the valley entrance and the *Hotel Plesnik*, there's the small *Juvanija* tourist farm (☎03/838-9080; ⓔjuvanija@email.si; ❸), with just four rooms.

The one major approach to Logarska is via the road from **Ljubno ob Savinji**, a small town located 34km east of Kamnik and 26km northwest of the Ljubljana–Celje highway. Logarska can also be reached from Črna na Koroškem (see p.284), via a relatively short (20km), but difficult and mostly unsurfaced, mountain road – the road actually emerges in Solčava from where it's a short drive to Logarska. Indeed, unless you've got your own **transport**, getting to Logarska will prove difficult; although there are a handful of (weekday) buses from Celje and Velenje to Ljubno ob Savinji, Luče and Solčava (the nearest settlements to Logarska), only one of these continues to Logarska, and even then, that's only between April and October (10.45am from Luče & 11.06am from Solčava).

Around the Logar Valley

Whilst most cars and buses pile into Logarska, the two glaciated valleys flanking Logarska Dolina, **Robanov Kot** to the east and **Matkov Kot** to the west (and just a couple of kilometres from the Austrian border), are no less magnificent, and should appeal to those seeking more solitudinous recreation. The only accommodation in either valley is the *Govc-Vršnik* tourist farm in Robanov Kot, at no. 34 (☎03/839-5016, ⓔgovc.vrsnik@siol.net; ❸).

The nearest settlements to Logarska are the villages of **Solčava**, 4km to the east, where there's a **tourist office** (daily: July & Aug 9am–6pm, April–June & Sept–Oct 9am–4pm; ☎03/839-0710), and **LUČE**, 10km further along the same road, which also has a tourist office (same times; ☎03/839-3555). Luče is the best place to stock up on provisions (there are a few shops, a bank and post office here) prior to heading on to Logarska; there's **accommodation** in the form of the *Pension Raduha* at no. 67 (☎03/838-4000, ⓔinfo@raduha.com; ❹), which also has a good **restaurant**, and the beautifully sited *Spodnji Jerovčnik* tourist farm (☎03/584-4087, ⓔrebeka.kumer@volja.net; ❸), located 1.5km south of Luče in the hillside hamlet of Krnica – follow the signs for Podvolovljek. The only **campsite** in the area, *Camp Smiča* (☎03/584-4330, May–Sept), is located 1km back out along the road towards Solčava by the Savinja River.

East of Celje

The region east of Celje is dominated by spas, the best known of which are **Rogaška Slatina** and **Olimia**, the former once one of Europe's grandest resorts, the latter a relatively recent addition to the scene. There is also a brace of cultural diversions to enjoy – the Skansen-like **Rogatec open-air museum** near Rogaška Slatina, and **Olimje monastery**, not far from the Olimia spa.

Rogaška Slatina

Thirty kilometres east of Celje, **ROGAŠKA SLATINA** was built around several mineral-rich springs (Donat, Styria and Tempel) discovered during the sixteenth century, and was once one of the most fashionable spa resorts in Central Europe – some of its more illustrious visitors included the Habsburg ruler Franz Jozef, the French Bonapartes, and King Karađorđevič of Serbia.

Arrival, information and accommodation

The town's **train station** is on Kidričeva ulica, some 500m south of town, while the **bus station** is closer to the centre on Celjska cesta, from where it's a five-minute walk to the main square Zdravíliški trg. The **tourist office** (April–Oct Mon–Fri 9am–7pm, Sat 9am–noon & 4–7pm; Nov–March Mon–Fri 9am–4pm, Sat 9am–noon; ℡03/581-4414, ⊚tic.rogaska@siol.net), easily visible on the southwestern corner of the square, can arrange private **accommodation** if you can't afford, or don't fancy, one of the many hotels in town. By some distance the grandest of these are the *Grand Hotel Rogaška* (❾), *Styria* and *Strossmayer* (both ❽), adjoining each other on the square's eastern side (reception for all three is in the *Grand* ℡03/811-2000 ⓦwww.terme-rogaska.si); all three are supremely comfortable, with big square beds, thick pile carpets, and gowns and bottled water supplied. There are more affordable options on Celjska cesta, the town's other main street, running adjacent to Zdravíliški trg; the *Slovenija* (℡03/811-5000; ❻), a large yellow building 100m north of the tourist office, and the good-value *Slatina* (℡03/818-4100, ⊚info@hotelslatina.com; ❼), a short walk further along, which also has some apartments (❾). The **post office** (Mon–Fri 8am–6pm, Sat 8am–noon) is next to the bus station.

If you so wish, you can jump on a **tourist train** (*turistični vlak*), one of which runs to Rogatec (Tues, Thurs & Sat; €5 return; 30min), the other to the Olimia spa and onwards to Olimije monastery (Wed, Fri & Sun; €5; 1 hour); both depart from outside the tourist office. **Bikes** can be rented from the *Sava* and *Donat* hotels, both located at the northern end of Zdravíliški trg (€10 for the day).

The Town

Despite the addition of a couple of beastly looking hotels, the town has managed to preserve its quintessential spa ambience. This is particularly true around its central square, **Zdravíliški trg**, a broad, immaculately kept landscaped park neatly framed by gravel walkways and grand buildings, the pick of which is the stately **Zdravíliški Dom** (now the *Grand Hotel Rogaška*), one of the finest Neoclassical buildings in the country.

Although its curative properties have long been used to treat a wide range of disorders – typically for those with gastrointestinal complaints and metabolic problems – the water is tapped first and foremost for commercial purposes, and you'll find many bottled waters from Rogaška in bars and restaurants throughout the country; in its purest form, however, it is incredibly metallic, and hence barely drinkable. You can sample the magnesium-laden Donat mg, the spa's most famous water, and others, in the large **pump room** (daily 7am–1pm & 3–7pm; €1.5) located at the northern end of Zdravíliški trg near the **Temple**, an oval pavilion sitting on top of the spa's main spring; head towards reception, grab a cup and away you go.

The main therapeutic baths, as well as all the treatment centres, are located in the Terapija building adjoining the pump room. However, casual visitors tend to make a beeline for the **Riviera swimming complex** (Termalna Riviera; daily

9am–8pm, Fri & Sat til 11pm; €8 for the day, €6 after 3pm), indoor and outdoor pools located halfway along Celjska cesta; guests of some hotels receive free entry to these pools so check with yours.

The lovely, mint-coloured building at the southern end of Zdravíliski trg, dating from 1904, houses a **glass showroom** where you can buy, or just view, some beautiful cut-glass and lead crystal pieces (Mon–Fri 9am–6pm, Sat 9am–1pm). There's another shop (Mon–Fri 8am–7pm, Sat 8am–noon) out by the **Glass Factory** (Steklarska šola) 2km south of town; tours of the factory are possible by prior arrangement – contact the tourist office.

Eating and drinking

The town's eating and drinking options are not bad at all; the pick of the **restaurants** is *Sonce* (Mon–Sat 9am–11pm, Sun 11am–5pm), a short walk beyond the Riviera pool complex on Celjska cesta, with a menu heavily skewed towards fish from the Dalmatian coast, but where you can also find other, rarely found delicacies such as horsemeat and ostrich – they've got a fine stock of wines here too. Back down the street at no. 6, the cute little cellar pizzeria, *La Gondola* (daily noon–11pm, Fri & Sat til 1am), also has some good salads and pasta dishes; or there's *Bohor*, near the bus station on Kidričeva ulica, a good old-fashioned place serving standard grills. The most enjoyable of the several **cafés** in town is the cool *Café Attems* (open til 1am), housed in the building at the bottom of Zdravíliski trg (see above); alternatively there's *Central Café* a few paces away, or the cosy *Teater Café*, housed inside the undistinguished cultural centre opposite *La Gondola*.

Rogatec Open-Air Museum

Regular buses and some trains make the short trip east to the ancient little market village of **ROGATEC**, known for its delightful **Open-Air Museum** (Muzej na Prostem Rogatec; March–Oct Tues–Sun noon–7pm; €2.5), a modest gathering of vernacular architecture from Štajerska's sub-Pannonian plain. Standing either side of the entrance gate are the **forge** and **general store** (*Lodn*), the former a single-room building built from sandstone in 1930, and stuffed with tools and semi-finished products, the latter a typical Rogatec grocer's store, furnished with a counter surrounded by weighing and measuring machines, containers and jars full of goodies. The museum's central space is taken up by the early nineteenth-century wooden **house** which once belonged to the local poet Jože Šmit from the nearby village of Tlake. Comprising a traditional setup of *lojpa* (entrance hall), *kuhna* ("black" kitchen) and *hiša* (living room), this type of house had unusual sleeping arrangements: whilst young, the children would sleep with their parents in the larger bedroom, but once grown-up, the girls would move to another bedroom, which had smaller windows barred with an iron cross, in case of any unwanted male visitors; the boys, meanwhile, had to make do with the barn.

The double **hayrack** is of the type found all over Slovenia, though, curiously, this one was taken from the village of Prišlin in Croatia. There's also a working well, a beehive, and a thatched-roof pigsty, which doubles up as a storage rack for turnip and carrot leaves, used as fodder for the swine during winter months. To the rear of the museum the old **winegrowers house** now serves as a catering centre. Regular workshops are held here during the summer, whereby you can watch, or participate in, such pursuits as bread making, corn braiding and nail forging. Next door to the museum is the Strmol **riding centre** (℡070/279-249), offering trail riding and regular lessons (around €12 per hour for either).

The museum is a little awkward to get to; from the train station, head due north using the church as a marker; at the main road turn right and walk to another road junction where you should turn left following the signs for Ptuj. The museum is about 1km along the road from here. Buses from Rogaška usually stop at the *Gostilna Jelša*, from where you must backtrack until you reach the road junction – again, from here, follow signs to Ptuj.

Podčetrtek and Olimia Spa

A somewhat more contemporary spa resort than Rogaška Slatina is **Olimia** in the border village of **PODČETRTEK**, 15km south of Rogaška Slatina. The spa (daily 8am–8pm, Fri until 9pm, Sat until midnight; Mon–Fri €7 for 3 hours, €9 for the day; Sat & Sun €8 for 3hr, €10 for the day; ⓦ www.terme-olimia.com), actually located just under 1km northeast of Podčetrtek, is essentially geared towards long-stay and package tourists – most day-trippers head to the water park a short way to the north (see below). However, if you want to stay, there's plenty of **accommodation** here (all ⓣ 03/829-7000), all of which is of a uniformly high standard: the upmarket and very pricey *Sotelia* (❾) and *Breza* (❽) hotels – the latter has its own pool; the *Rosa* apartments (❼–❽); and the *Vas Lipa* tourist village, comprising two dozen apartment buildings holding four separate units each, and sleeping two to five people (❺–❼); there's a restaurant, supermarket, hairdressers and so on in the village too; guests of all three receive free entrance to the pools and the water park.

There are more thrills and spills less than 1km further north of the spa at the large **Water Park Aqualuna** (daily May–Sept 9am–8pm; €10). Spread across a field next door is the large and well-equipped *Natura* **campsite** (ⓣ 03/829-7833; mid-April to mid-Oct), guests of which receive free entry to the water park. Back out on the main road, opposite the campsite, *Gostišče Ciril* (ⓣ 03/582-9109, ⓔ gostisce.ciril@siol.si) is a hostel-style place offering no more than cheap beds (❶) and simple food; indeed there are several places offering private rooms along this stretch of road.

△ Olimje

From a distance, the much-remodelled twelfth-century **Podčetrtek Castle** high above the village looks very impressive, but on closer inspection it is, sadly, nothing of the sort. Ravaged by looters and now littered with debris and crumbling masonry, it's a depressing site and you're best off just admiring it from afar. The village itself holds little of interest, though is useful for practical means: there's a **tourist office**, in a small hut at Škofja Gora 1 (Mon–Sat 8am–4pm, Sun 9am–noon; ☏03/810-9013, ✉tic@podcetrtek.si), and on the main road opposite the entrance to the village, the *Aparthotel Pirc* (☏03/818-3802, ✉chorus@email. si), which has large, modern and well furnished rooms (❸) and apartments (❹–❺), as well as a restaurant and pizzeria.

If you're coming by **train** (Podčetrtek is on the Celje–Imeno line), then make sure you get off at the appropriate stop: for Podčetrtek get off at the station of the same name; for the spa it's "Atomske Toplice" (this is the old name for the spa); and for the campsite and water park, it's "Podčetrtek Toplice". **Buses** also stop in all three places.

Olimje Monastery

From Podčetrtek, a smooth, winding valley road snakes through some gorgeous countryside to **Olimje Monastery**, 3km to the southwest. Originally built as a castle in 1550, on the site of a former fortification possibly dating from the eleventh century, the building was acquired by Pauline monks from Lepoglava, Croatia in 1663. They proceeded to convert it into a monastery, enlarging the premises and augmenting it with a church. Modifications continued apace up until the order's dissolution in 1782, when the monks were redispersed to various monasteries throughout Croatia. The Minorite order returned here in 1990.

Tacked on to the left-hand side of the monastery, the **Church of the Assumption** was completed in 1675 by the monks as part of the monastery's rebuilding programme. Preceded by two jet-black and gold marble altars – the one to the left holds a painting of Christ's Passion, the one to the right honours St Paul the Hermit, regarded as the founding father of the monastery – the small presbytery is almost entirely filled by an immense three-tiered golden altar, finished with several paintings and a dozen statues of saints. The side chapel, dedicated to St Francis Xavier and featuring a majestic, caramel-coloured late Baroque altar, was a later addition (1766) to the church. Note, too, the fine upright organ in the choir loft.

Reputedly the third-oldest preserved pharmacy in Europe, after ones in Paris and Dubrovnik, the Pauline **pharmacy** (daily 10am–noon & 1–6pm; €1.5), located on the ground floor of the left round tower as you face the monastery, was founded in the mid-eighteenth century, functioning until 1782 when the monastery was disbanded. There's now little left in the way of fittings and fixtures or pharmaceutical goods (these were all removed when the monastery was dissolved), but its frescoes – executed around 1789 by local painter Anton Lerchinger, and depicting SS Cosmas and Damian, patron saints of physicians and pharmacists, eminent physicians Aesculapius and Paracelsus and scenes of Christ healing – are worth the small entrance fee. If it's not open, ring the bell on the door a few paces along the cloister.

Just behind the monastery is the most fantastic **chocolateria** (daily 10am–5pm) where you can indulge your wildest sweet-toothed fantasies with an eye-popping selection of the finest chocolates, all of which are produced in the factory to the rear of the shop.

There are a couple of places to **sleep** and **eat** along the road between Podčetrtek and the monastery; approximately midway between these two points, the roadside *Gostišče Haler* pub and brewery (Pivovarna Haler) brews its own beer (*Haler Pivo*) on the premises, the perfect foil for its bistro, which features a selection of beer dishes alongside a more sophisticated à la carte menu (both daily until 10pm). Located in a separate building just to the rear of the pub, the *Pension Katja* (☎03/812-1202, ⓔinfo@haler-sp.si) has some very smart, modern rooms (❸) and apartments (❸–❺), sleeping four to six people; there's also a small basement swimming pool, sauna and gym.

The *Gostišče Amon* (☎03/818-2480, ⓦwww.amon.si), 1.5km further on, was one of the first private **wineries** in the country and is renowned for its Laški Rizling and Chardonnay; tasting costs around €5 for four or five wines. The **restaurant** (daily until 10pm) is of the highest order, with specialities of the house including roast duck and oyster mushrooms, and baked snails, while the interior looks great – almost all the fittings and fixtures have been recycled from old wine presses, hence the chunky oak tables and chairs. They've also got four great-value rooms (❸), each of which overlooks the nine-hole **golf course** (☎03/810-9066; €15 for 9 holes).

If you don't have your own wheels, you'll have to walk, which is no great hardship as it's a very enjoyable short trek. If you'd like to do more extensive **walking**, pick up a copy of the 1:18,000 *Podčetrtek* map from the tourist office which maps out several local walks between one and four hours long, one of which is the walk to Olimje.

From Celje to Maribor

There are several worthwhile sites between Celje and Maribor, most of which are easily reached by public transport. Just off the main highway, the charming little town of **Slovenske Konjice** lies close to the enchanting ruins of **Žiče Monastery**. A few kilometres further on, the small spa town of **Zreče** is the jumping-off point for the ski and sports resort of **Rogla**, which nestles at the heart of the **Pohorje Massif** mountain range.

Slovenske Konjice

Nineteen kilometres northeast of Celje, just off the main highway to Maribor, is **SLOVENSKE KONJICE**, the self-styled town of "Wine and Flowers", owing to recent triumphant efforts in Europe-wide floral competitions and a strong tradition of wine-making. The centre of town is shaped by Stari trg, a lovely, gently inclining street framed by a neat kernel of yellow, apricot and lime-green townhouses, and bisected by the Gospodična (Miss) stream, itself straddled by a series of tiny wooden bridges.

At no. 15, the **Riemer Gallery** (Mestna Galerija Riemer; Tues & Thurs noon–3pm, Wed til 4pm, Fri & Sat 10am–noon; €2) is a private collection of art and period furniture amassed by wealthy local businessman Franc Riemer. As impressive as his collection of Old Masters, paintings by Ivana Kobilica and sketches by Rihard Jakopič are, the show-stealer is a fourteenth-century fresco of the Crucifixion, retrieved from Žiče Monastery in 1996, and held to be the only fresco from the monastery still in existence. Fifty metres further up the street on the opposite side, at no. 24, is a **wine shop**, where you can partake in some tasting (around €3 for three wines) – however, as there are no regular opening hours, you should contact the tourist office to arrange a session.

There's tasting of a very different kind further north at the **Trebnik Manor House** (Dvorec Trebnik; Mon–Fri 10am–6pm, Sat & Sun 10am–5pm), located up beyond the **Church of St George** (Cerkev Sv Jurij). The one renovated part of this otherwise dilapidated building has been transformed into a herbal shop and gallery, displaying and selling a range of products such as honey, oils, creams, shampoos and brandies, all of which have been cultivated from the beautifully tended herb garden to the rear of the manor. There are free brandy-tasting sessions, though an acquired palate is most definitely required. In the barn next door to the shop sits a fine, but poorly maintained, collection of old carriages; ask at the shop if you wish to have a look. From behind the manor house, it's a two-hour walk up a marked path to **Konjiška Gora**, from where there is a superlative panorama of the town and vineyards below, and the Pohorje Massif in the distance.

Practicalities

The **bus station** is located on Liptovska cesta, from where it's just a couple of minutes' walk north to Mestni trg and beyond (across the bridge) to the centre of town, which is essentially the main street, Stari trg. About two-thirds of the way along Stari trg, at no. 27, is the **tourist office** (Mon, Tues & Thurs 7am–3pm, Wed 7am–4pm, Fri 7am–2pm, Sat 9am–1pm; ℡05/759-3110), a friendly little place, although there's scant information available. The town's one **hotel** is the welcoming, but ultimately plain and not particularly good-value, *Dravinja* (℡05/759-3110, @hotel-dravinja@siol.net; ❺), down by the bridge on Mestni trg.

The town's one truly outstanding **restaurant**, the ⚡ *Zlati Grič*, is a fifteen-minute walk north of the centre, planted amongst the impossibly lush Škalce vineyards; the Slovene food and wine on offer is of a high standard, but really it's a place to come and enjoy the setting. To get here from Mestni trg, walk through the small park-like area to the traffic lights, cross the road and walk up Škalska cesta, from where it's a further ten minutes. There are few other places to **eat or drink** in this quiet town; the *Beli Konj* (White Horse) at the lower end of Stari trg (no. 6) is a colourful and energetic pub, or there's the slightly more laid-back *Tattenbach* café next to the Riemer Gallery. The smart little *Patriot* bar, in the **Youth Club** (Mladinski Center) north of Stari trg, behind the fire station at Žička 4, occasionally has live music at weekends – they've also got free **Internet access** upstairs in the club proper.

Žiče Monastery

Fringed by ancient woodland in the isolated splendour of the Valley of St John, some 12km southwest of Slovenske Konjice, lie the mist-swathed ruins of **Žiče Monastery** (Žička Kartuzija; March–Nov Mon–Fri 10am–6pm, Sat & Sun 9am–7pm; Dec–Feb Sat & Sun 9am–4pm; €2). Founded around 1160 by Otakar III of Traungau, the margrave of Styria, Žiče was the first of four Carthusian monasteries to be chartered on Slovenian territory, and fairly prospered until its dissolution under the reforms of Joseph II in 1782. Although part of the complex has been renovated (and work is ongoing), the rest is pretty much as it was, including the twelfth-century Romanesque **Church of St John the Baptist**, now hollowed out – its vaults and roof collapsed around 1840 – but still exuding a befitting sense of authority. A healing place of repute during the thirteenth century, Žiče remained an important medicinal centre for locals and travellers alike until the monastery's dissolution; there's now a reconstructed **apothecary** (closed in winter) on the site of the old one, offering the opportunity to sample some powerful home-made herbal brandies. The small, grass-covered mounds just behind the pharmacy were the former monks' cells.

Standing at the entrance to the monastery is the *Gostišče Gastuž*, dating from 1464 and reputedly one of the oldest guesthouses in Central Europe; it's now a

△ Žiče Monastery

very good **restaurant**, which also has excellent wines (Wed–Fri 10am–7pm, Sat & Sun 10am–8pm), and downstairs a small inn-style room where you can get tea and mulled wine. Getting to Žiče entails taking a local bus from Slovenske Konjice to the village of **Špitalič**, 2km shy of the monastery, and then it's a gentle walk from here.

Zreče

From Slovenske Konjice hourly buses make the short five-kilometre journey north to the small industrial town of **ZREČE**, a relatively recent addition to the country's growing number of spa resorts. The spa aside, there's nothing else of interest here, though you may find yourself passing through if Rogla and the Pohorje Massif are your intended destinations. The **Terme Zreče spa** has an excellent complement of facilities, including indoor and outdoor therapeutic and recreational pools (daily 9am–9pm, Fri & Sat til 10pm; €8 for 3hr, €10 for the day), with temperatures ranging between 28 and 36°C, sauna and solarium facilities (Mon–Thurs 11am–9pm, Fri–Sun 10am–10pm), gym and a Thai massage centre (Mon–Sat 10am–noon & 3–9pm).

The spa also accommodates the very modern *Dobrava Hotel* (☏03/757-6000; ❽), and, more appealingly, the *Terme Zrece Villas* (❻–❼), a series of lodge-like apartments located 200m across the park on the edge of the forest, which sleep two to six people. Aside from the *Dobrava*, there are a couple of places opposite the **bus station**, itself adjacent to the spa: the pension-like *Zvon* (☏03/757-3600, ✉info@hotelzvon.com; ❻), and the almost identical *Smogavc* next door (☏03/757-6600, ✉hotel@smogavc.com; ❺). Both offer good-looking rooms with all mod cons and are also decent places to eat. There's a small **tourist office** (Mon–Fri 7am–3pm, Thurs til 2pm, Sat 9am–noon; ☏03/759-0470; ✉tic.zrece.

lto@siol.net) two minutes' walk from the bus station inside the small shopping mall (PTC Tržnica) at Cesta na Roglo 11j.

The two best **places to stay**, however, are located out of town, and are really only reachable if you've got your own transport. Three kilometres north of Zreče on the road up to Rogla, in the tiny hamlet of **Loška Gora**, the *Hotel Pod Roglo* (☎03/757-6800, ⓦwww.hotelpodroglo.com; ❺) has beautifully warm, colourful rooms fitted with plush carpets and large beds. They also brew their own beer on the premises, which complements the large, buzzy pizzeria here superbly – at weekends there's live music in the adjoining pub (open Fri & Sat only). A couple of kilometres southwest of town in the hillside village of **Križevec**, the *Urška* tourist farm at 11a (☎03/576-2180, ⓔtk.urska@siol.net; ❸) offers cosy rooms, delicious home cooking and charming hospitality. There are several other tourist farms scattered around the hills between Zreče and Rogla.

Rogla and the Pohorje Massif

From Zreče the road zigzags steeply for 16km to **Rogla** (1517m), one of Slovenia's premier ski and sports resorts sited on the eastern margins of the **Pohorje Massif**, a fifty-kilometre-long, sparsely populated plateau, arcing between Dravograd in the west and Maribor in the east. Geologically, the massif is an extension of the Alps, although physically it's quite different, a series of gently rounded ridges – few peaks top 1500m – riddled with peat marshes and small swampy lakes, and where the only settlements are isolated farmsteads and tiny upland churches. The massif was once home to sawmills, forges and *glažute* (glass-making workshops), but it is now tourism that rules the roost, with ski runs, hiking paths and other recreational facilities complemented by a good number of mountain huts and tourist farms.

Rogla's extensive **sports facilities** – an outdoor stadium, huge sports hall and swimming pool – are frequently used by Slovenian and Croatian Olympic teams, but all are available for use by the general public when they're not in residence; some sample prices (hourly rates) include: badminton €10; tennis €15; squash €9 (45min); gym €9; and swimming €6. Despite all these facilities, it's **skiing** that's the real draw. The resort possesses two package-type **hotels** (☎03/757-7100) within one building, the comfortable *Planja* (❻) and the slightly less expensive *Rogla* (❼), as well as modern chalets (❺) sleeping up to four. Although the main restaurant is for hotel guests only, there is the comely inn-style *Stara Koča* in the same building, serving up wholesome, filling meals, and there's also good food at the *Koča na Jurgovem* mountain hut, sited at the top of the Jugovo chairlift a few kilometres east of the *Planja*. In winter there's a **ski bus** from Zreče to Rogla (and return) six times a day.

Maribor and around

Located at the easternmost foothills of the Pohorje Massif, **MARIBOR** is Slovenia's second city of culture, commerce and education. Yet despite its position as such, the city remains small, with a modest population of around 100,000, about a third that of the capital. Despite lacking Ljubljana's sophistication and cultural appeal, Maribor still offers much to enjoy; the prevailing industrial sprawl is countered by an incoherent, yet appealing, Austrianie old core, patchworked with an elegant confection of architectural styles, colourful squares and streets, monuments and churches. Furthermore, if you tire of the city, there's plenty to see and do on the outskirts, including a couple of enjoyable wine roads to the north, and

Rogla, in the heart of the Pohorje Massif, and **Mariborsko Pohorje**, further east on the doorstep of Maribor, are consistently rated two of the best **ski and snowboard** resorts in the country. Rogla has around 12km of ski trails, most of which are suited to intermediate skiers, though there are a few slopes for the less experienced. You can also take a ride on a **snowmobile** here (€4 for a circular track ride, or €50 for a safari with a guide). At 1347m, Mariborsko Pohorje is a slightly lower mountain range, but has one of the largest capacities of all Slovenia's ski resorts, with more than 60km of trails, almost half of which are beginners' slopes. It also claims to have the longest night-time (floodlit) slope in Europe. Moreover, it possesses far more tourist facilities, particularly accommodation, than Rogla. The ski season at both resorts usually runs from December to March, and the presence of snow cannons along the main runs ensures that it's possible to ski throughout this period, regardless of snowfall. **Day passes** at both cost around €25 and **weekly passes** around €125. The main piste at Mariborsko Pohorje is also the venue for the women's World Cup slalom race, the "Golden Fox", at the end of January, an event not to be missed if you're in the region around this time.

Skiing aside, the massif also has some excellent **hiking**. The trails on Rogla are numbered from PP1 to PP7, and range in distance from just a few kilometres to more than thirty. If you're short on time, there's a nice and easy 45-minute walk north from the *Planja* hotel to the *Koča na Pesku* mountain hut (1386m), which has accommodation and food available year-round (☎031/415-612). From here you can either continue northwest to the beautiful **Lovrenc Marsh Lakes** (Lovrenška jezera; 1hr), and then further onwards to *Ribniška Koča* hut (1507m; 2hr), where there's more accommodation (☎02/876-8246; closed April & Nov); or east to **Osankarica** (1193m) and the *Dom na Osankarica*, where there are refreshments only – the trail continues east to the **Black Lake** (Črno jezero), one of the largest lakes in the massif. The 1:25,000 *Zreče* map, available from the tourist office in Zreče (see p.293), marks out a number of hiking and cycle routes around both Zreče and Rogla.

the Pohorje Massif to the south, where it's possible to ski, hike or partake in any number of other sporting and adventure activities.

Some history

The seeds of present-day Maribor were sown around the **twelfth century**, when the Carinthian duke, Spanheim, instructed a fort to be built (known as Marchburg, later Marburg and eventually Maribor) on Piramida, a low hill to the north of town, in order to protect the town from Hungarian raiders from Pannonia. During the **fourteenth century**, a large and diligent Jewish population established important commercial ties with major European cities, Milan, Prague and Dubrovnik; unfortunately their expulsion from the city in 1497, in addition to Hungarian and Turkish sieges, fires and recurrent plague epidemics, led to a sudden and long-term decline in the city's fortunes. The key to its revival in the **nineteenth century** was the arrival of the rail line from Vienna in 1846 (which would later be extended to Ljubljana and Trieste), together with the relocation of the seat of the Lavantine diocese from St Andraz in Austria to Maribor. Meanwhile, the establishment of a raft of major cultural and financial institutions further heightened the city's importance around this time.

Ongoing nationalist struggles between the city's German and Slovene populations towards the end of the nineteenth century culminated in outright warfare at the tail end of **World War I** following German attempts to incorporate the city into Austrian lands. However, a resounding defeat for the Germans at the hands of the Slovenes, led by

MARIBOR

City Park

N

① & Three Lakes

Aquarium

Ljudski Stadium

National Liberation Museum

Trg Generala Maistra

Castle & Regional Museum

Vinag Wine Cellar

TRG SVOBODE

GRAJSKI TRG

St Mary's Church

VOLMERJEV PREHOD

TRG BORIŠA KRAIGHERJA

Maribor Theatre

University

SLOMŠKOV TRG

Cathedral Church of St John the Baptist

ROTOVŠKI TRG

Town Hall

National Hall

GLAVNI TRG

Plague Monument

TRAFFIC ISLAND

ŽIDOVSKA ULICA

St Alosius's Church

Jew's Tower

Judicial Tower

Synagogue

Old Vine

Water Tower

Drava

RESTAURANTS, CAFÉS & BARS

Ancora	5	Kibla	12
Čajnica	3	Novi Svet pri Stolnici	8
Ilich	2	Šamsara	13
Gostilna pri Treh Ribnikih	1	Štajerc	4
		Stari Grill	11
Gril Ranca	15	Takos	14
Jazz Klub Satchmo	6	Tildos	7
KGB	10	Toti Rotovž	9

ACCOMMODATION

Hotel Bajt Garni	E
Garni Hotel Tabor	D
Hotel Orel	B
Hotel Piramida	A
Hostel Uni	C

0   100 m

④ Bus & Train Stations

▼ *Maribor Pohorje,* **④** & **⑤**   ▼ *Ptuj*

General Rudolf Maister, resulted in the incorporation of Slovenian Styria into Slovene lands, and the establishment of the present-day border with Austria. Despite Maribor's assimilation into the **Kingdom of Yugoslavia**, German expansionist tendencies continued and the city eventually succumbed to German forces during **World War II**, with the mass expulsion of thousands of Slovenes and the demolition of nearly half of the city's buildings. As one of the most industrialized cities in the former Yugoslavia, Maribor was amongst the hardest hit by the **break-up of the federation** in 1991, the sudden loss of important inter-republic trade resulting in tremendous economic hardship and high levels of unemployment. Today the city is more or less back on track thanks largely to a booming local wine trade and its proximity to one of the largest ski resorts in the country.

Arrival and information

The **bus** and **train stations** are handily located just 400m apart on Partizanska cesta, from where it's just a ten-minute walk into the city centre, and the **tourist office**, located near the Church of St Mary at Partizanska cesta 6 (Mon–Fri 9am–6pm, Sat 9am–1pm; ☎02/234-6611, ⓦwww.maribor-tourism.si). The main city **post office** is at Slomškov trg 10 (Mon–Fri 8am–7pm, Sat 8am–1pm), but there's another next to the train station (same times). There's free **Internet access** at the *Kibla* multimedia centre in the Narodni Dom at Ulica Kneza Kozlja 9, and at the office-like *KIT* Cyber Café (Mon–Fri 9am–10pm, Sat 8am–1pm) on Glavni trg, which has printing and scanning facilities.

Accommodation

The city centre is poorly served with **places to stay**, but there are further possibilities in Zgornje Radvanje, at the foot of the **Maribor Pohorje** ski resort 7km southwest of town; for purposes of convenience these are included along with the city hotels here. To get to any of the places in Zgornje Radvanje, take bus #6 from the train station to its last stop, which is the cable car station. The hotels at the top of Pohorje itself are listed on p.303.

Whilst they cannot book **private accommodation**, the tourist office can advise on places to stay. The city's **youth hostel** (Dijaški Dom; ☎02/480-1710; ❶; July & Aug only), is inconveniently located out in the southeastern suburb of Pobrežje at Železnikova ulica 12; take bus #3 to the cemetery stop. A second hostel option is the *Uni Hostel* at Gosposka 30, which is actually part of the *Hotel Orel* just around the corner; the hostel is mostly occupied by lecturers and students, but does have a limited number of beds available between June and August (☎02/250-6700, ❶).

Hotel Arena Pot k mlinu 57, Maribor Pohorje ☎02/614-0950, ⓔinfo.arena@sc-pohorje.si. A great location right at the bottom of the piste, this is a reasonable option with large, perfectly fine, if dull, rooms – ask for a room overlooking the slope. ❺

Hotel Bajt Garni Radvanjska 99 ☎02/332-7650, ⓔinfo@hotel.bajt.com. Extremely pleasant, family-run place across the river en route to Pohorje, with fairly simple, but modern and bright rooms – they've got a laundry too. Bus #6. ❹

Hotel Habakuk Pohorska cesta 59, Maribor Pohorje ☎02/300-8100, ⓔhabakuk@termemb. si. Featuring all the luxuries you'd expect of a five-star hotel, the *Habakuk*, just across from the cable car station, simply oozes class; fantastically comfortable, richly furnished rooms, indoor and outdoor pools, sauna and fitness facilities. ❾

Garni Hotel Tabor Ulica heroja Zidanška 18 ☎02/421-6410, ⓦwww.hoteltabor.podhostnik.si. Frequented by sporty types using the neighbouring facilities, this decent place, 200m north of the *Bajt*

Garni, has boxy, but modern two-, three- and four-bed rooms. Take bus #6 to stop Tabor (direction Uzpenjača). ❺

Gostišče Janez Ciril-Metodova 4 ☎02/420-4404. Great-value pension 1km west of the centre across the river near Koroški most. Doubles, triples and one quad available. Take bus #4 along Valvasorjeva ulica and alight at the junction with Ruška cesta. ❹

Hotel Orel Grajski trg 3 ☎02/250-6700, ⓔorel@termemb.si. Overpriced place with run-of-the-mill, rather dank, rooms, though the location does compensate somewhat. ❼

Hotel Piramida Ulica heroja Šlandra 10 ☎02/234-4400, ⓔpiramida@termemb.si. Very much the city's business hotel, this is an expensive, charmless place with disappointingly bland rooms. ❽

Pohorska Kavarna Ob Ribniku 1, Maribor Pohorje ☎02/614-1500, ⓦwww.potocnik.si. Clean, bright and modern pension with nine two- and three-bed rooms located about 500m before the cable car. Excellent value, and a good coffee house too. ❹

The City

Almost all of the city's sights are grouped around the city's three principal squares – **Grajski trg**, **Slomškov trg** and **Glavni trg** – and the Lent waterfront district on the north bank of the **Drava River**. Beyond these areas, possibilities exist for more leisurely diversions, such as the city park and lakes to the north of town, and a small island retreat and spa complex out to the west. There's nothing of interest to see on the residential, south side of the Drava, and the only reason you might need to cross the river is to visit the huge shopping mall, or if you're heading out to the ski resort in **Maribor Pohorje**. Wine aficionados, meanwhile, can content themselves with a visit to one of the city's outlying wine roads.

Grajski trg and around

Although not especially interesting itself, the best place to start a walking tour of the city is **Grajski trg** (Castle Square), so-named after the fifteenth-century town **castle** on the square's northeastern corner. Inside the entrance to the castle (and the museum), on Grajska ulica, is a wonderfully fanciful Rococo staircase, ornamented with sculptures by **Jožef Straub**, more of whose work is contained within, whilst the ceiling is strewn with stuccoed swirls and vines.

Most of the castle's rooms are now taken up with the **Maribor Regional Museum** (Muzej Pokrajinski; Tues–Sun 10am–5pm; €2.5); there are excellent guiding handouts in English in each room. Following the standard display of archeological bits and bobs, the ethnological section presents some fine rafts and cargo boats – of the type that used to dock along the Drava waterfront in the nineteenth century – beautifully painted chests and wardrobes, beehive panels and the famous *pust* masks from Ptuj. No less absorbing is the cultural history section, and in particular its voluminous collection of costumes representing the multifarious regions of Slovenia – the most celebrated piece of attire, however, is a military uniform that belonged to Tito.

The upper floor is mostly given over to the history of Maribor, and although much of it is not that stimulating, the displays of locally produced wrought ironwork and glassware are worth a lengthy pause. There's some impressive artwork here too, the best of which is the group of smooth humanist sculptures by Jožef Straub (1721–1783), Slovenia's leading exponent of Baroque sculpture. Facing the square, the **castle chapel** (Grajski kapeli), built some time around 1660, is a copy of the Santa Casa church in Loreto, its blackened interior so small it barely seats twenty people.

Looming large over the square to the east is the massive red-brick **Franciscan Church of St Mary** (Cerkev Sv Marija; daily 6am–noon & 3–7.45pm), commissioned by Viennese architect Richard Jordan in 1903 and built at the same time as the Franciscan monastery complex behind. The only concession to grandeur inside the capacious and gloomy interior is the high altar, featuring four statues in niches and some contemporary, almost cartoonish, wall paintings, completed by Catholic priest and artist Stane Kregar, one of Slovenia's foremost post-World War II church painters.

Heading south, Grajski trg funnels down to Vetrinjska ulica, a busy pedestrianized thoroughfare whose houses are now mainly ramshackle and medieval, occasionally slicked up as shops and stores but mainly dark and crumbling – memories of an earlier, more fanciful past, when the street served as a major route for traffic en route from Vienna to Ljubljana; the standout building is the richly stuccoed, mint-coloured Vetrinje Mansion at no. 16, dating from 1725.

Back on the square, Grajski trg merges into Trg Svobode, a large, nondescript space containing little of note save for an ugly, bulbous-shaped bronze memorial to Partisans killed during World War II, and the Vinag wine cellar on the east side, at no. 3. Trg Svobode segues into grassy Maistrov trg, from where it's another five-minute walk to the **National Liberation Museum** (Muzej Narodne Osvoboditve; Mon–Fri 8am–6pm, Sat 9am–noon; €2.5), housed in a handsome late nineteenth-century terracotta and grey villa at Ulica heroja Tomšiča 5. The most interesting exhibits, of what is otherwise a slapdash offering, are those items pertaining to Slovenia's struggle for independence in 1991, including objects left by the retreating Yugoslav army and the jacket worn by Igor Bavčar, head of police during the Ten-Day war.

The City Park

The broad, lamp-lined promenade across the road from the museum marks the entrance to the **City Park** (Mestni Park), a large, well-groomed expanse of greenery laid out in 1872 and carved up by concrete strips of pathway. For kids, there's a rather downbeat **aquarium-terrarium** (Akvarij-Terarij; Mon–Fri 8am–7pm, Sat & Sun 9am–noon & 2–7pm; €3) located on the park's east side, its tanks filled with the usual suspects, including fish, snakes, lizards, turtles and spiders. Beyond here the park tapers towards the slender chain of the **Three Lakes** (Trije Ribniki). If you fancy a slightly more strenuous walk, take the path that peels off of Ribniška ulica (the road skirting the park's eastern side), and continue uphill through the almost vertically pitched vineyard to **Piramida** (386m), at the top of which is a tiny chapel; from here there are fine views of the bright red and terracotta-coloured rooftops of the city, and the broad slopes of the Pohorje mountains in the distance.

Slomškov trg

Named after St Anton Slomšek (see box, below), **Slomškov trg** is the largest, greenest and grandest of the city's three squares, endowed with some venerable old buildings and site of Maribor's premier ecclesiastical monument. The lumpish **Cathedral Church of St John the Baptist** (Cerkev Sv Janez Krstnik) was originally built as a single-naved Romanesque structure in the twelfth century, though later modifications gave it its present, predominantly Gothic and Baroque appearance. The highlight of what is otherwise a rather plain interior is the splendid Gothic presbytery, featuring exquisitely carved choir stalls inlaid with reliefs showing scenes from the life of the patron saint. The north side **Chapel of the Holy Cross** holds the tomb of the beatified Slomšek, while the stained-glass windows depicting images of Pope John Paul II were crafted on the occasion of his second visit to Maribor, in 1999 – his first visit was in 1996. There's further homage to Slomšek in front of the church, in the form of a large bronze statue.

Anton Slomšek

Bishop, poet and scribe, **Anton Martin Slomšek** was born in the small parish of Ponikva, near Celje, in 1800. Ordained in 1824, just three years into his theological studies, Slomšek took his first Mass in Olimje that same year, before returning to his studies in Celovec. He spent the next few years devoting his time to the development of Slovene schooling – in particular Sunday schools – in rural areas, and writing prayer and hymn books; by the time of his death, Slomšek had had some fifty books published.

His greatest achievement, however, was to transfer the seat of the Lavantine diocese from St Andraz, in Austria, to Maribor, thus uniting all Styrian Slovenes in one diocese, as well as affecting an upgrade in the status of the parish church to a cathedral. Slomšek was also instrumental in setting up the Catholic Society of St Hermagoras (Družba Sv Mohorja), a publishing house established in 1851 in order to help Slovenes read and write. His second great contribution was the establishment of Maribor's Theological High School in 1859, the forerunner to today's university. Slomšek died in 1862, and was beatified by the pope in September 1999.

The neo-Renaissance bulk at the square's western end is the former City Savings Bank, now the **university building**. Of a similar ilk, but appreciably smaller, is the splendid, pea-green-coloured **post office** (Pošta Slovenije) building at no. 10 on the square's south side. Although aesthetically less pleasing, the one other building of note is the **National Theatre**, adjacent to the university on the north side. From the square's southeastern corner, a narrow path leads into the lovely arcaded courtyard, Rotovški trg, and then into Glavni trg.

Glavni trg and around

Bounded on one side by a sweep of elegant buildings, and on the other by one of the city's busiest thoroughfares, cobbled **Glavni trg** is a fine-looking Renaissance square that functioned as the city's market area during the Middle Ages. Standing in the centre of the square, and arguably one of the finest monuments of its type in Central Europe, the **Plague Monument** was originally raised in 1681 as a memorial to the thousands that perished during the great plague. This second version was erected in 1743, its smooth column topped with a gold-leaf statue of Mary, and its base with six saintly intercessors, the entire project masterfully sculpted by **Jožef Straub.**

Opposite, at no. 9, the Renaissance **town hall** was originally built in 1515, though reworked several times over before it attained its present appearance, featuring an exquisite Venetian stone balcony emblazoned with a two lion-relief and the city coat of arms; underneath and to the right of the town hall is *Toti Rotovž*, one of the city's best restaurants. Recessed between two buildings on the opposite side of the road is the former Jesuit **Church of St Aloysius.**

A short walk east of Glavni trg, **Židovska ulica** (Jewish street) was the centre of the Jewish ghetto during the Middle Ages, its focal point the now beautifully restored **synagogue** (Sinagoga; Mon–Fri 8am–noon) at no. 4. The first Jewish presence in the city was recorded around 1290, at around the same time the synagogue was built, but, following a decree in 1496 banishing Jews from Maribor, the synagogue was converted into a Catholic Church. It operated as such until it was closed down under the reforms of Emperor Joseph II at the end of the eighteenth century; thereafter it functioned variously as a factory, warehouse and residential quarters. A decade-long renovation programme, during which four wooden boxes containing the remains of ancient skeletons were unearthed, has restored the synagogue to something like its former glory, and it's now used as a cultural centre and exhibition venue.

Erected in 1465, the **Jews' Tower** (Židovski stolp), just across from the synagogue, was once an integral part of the city's defence walls – it's now a photographic gallery (Mon–Fri 10am–7pm, Sat 10am–1pm) – as was the immaculately restored sixteenth-century **Water Tower** (Vodni stolp) down by the river.

Lent

Across the busy main street, Koroška ulica, several alleyways slope down to the **Drava River** and the **Pristan** (Pier) district, or, as it's more commonly known, **Lent** (Port). Until the construction of the railways in the 1860s, the Drava was the city's principal transport artery, and Lent the main docking station for the hundreds of rafts and small cargo vessels that would stop here en route to the Danube and the Black Sea. Today, it's a bustling promenade and *the* place to kick back with a beer on summer evenings.

Lent's star attraction, and the city's most celebrated symbol, is the 400-year-old **Vine** (Stara Trta), reputedly the world's oldest. The vine still yields the evocatively titled *Žametna Črnina* (Black Velvet), thirty-five litres of which are harvested each year, although, unfortunately, this is usually bottled up for visiting dignitaries. Two of the city's main events, the pruning of the vine, and its ceremonial harvesting, take place here in March and October respectively.

A five-minute walk further west along the embankment stands the rotund, whitewashed **Judicial Tower** (Sodni stolp), though this name is something of a misnomer given that it was erected as a defensive bastion in 1310; this present structure dates from 1830. Up behind the tower, Vojašniški ulica (Army Street) and Vojašniški trg (Army Square) – essentially one and the same – are scattered with a shabby fusion of half-wrecked buildings, one of which, the former **Minorite Church and Monastery**, once functioned as a barracks and warehouse, though it's now defunct and decaying. Just beyond here is Vodnikov trg and the city's open-air market-place. The best views of Lent can be garnered from **Glavni most** (Main Bridge), an elegant, rich-red structure completed in 1913.

Terme Fontana and Maribor Island

About 3km west of the centre (bus #15), the **Terme Fontana** spa and recreation complex at Koroška cesta 172 (daily 9am–10pm, Fri till 11pm; ☎02/234-4100) offers a raft of activities – swimming (€8 for 4hr, €10 for the day), sauna and solarium, gym facilities and aerobics. A further 1.5km along the road, a left turning leads to **Maribor island** (Mariborski Otok), a pleasant rambling and bathing spot in the summer; if you don't fancy taking to the Drava, there's a large outdoor pool in the centre of the island (daily June–Sept 9am–8pm; €3).

Eating, drinking and entertainment

What Maribor's **restaurant** scene may lack in quantity, it makes up for in quality, with a select core of excellent and diverse places to eat. On summer evenings, the **cafés and bars** of the Lent waterfront spill out onto the street with the hectic atmosphere of a mass open-air bar. Otherwise, there are several excellent bar-cum-club places scattered elsewhere throughout town.

Restaurants

Ancora Jurčičeva ulica 7. Large and buzzy pizzeria with split-level flooring, which also incorporates a popular, but very smoky, pub. Daily 9am–midnight, Fri & Sat til 1am.

Gostilna pri Treh Ribnikih Ribniška 3. Though not quite in the same league as *Novi Svet*, this inn-style restaurant out by the Three Lakes is, nevertheless, an enjoyable place to sample fish dishes. Good set menus (€6–15), including one for vegetarians. Daily 11am–10pm, Sun 11am–8pm.

Gril Ranca Dravska 10. Fast-food Balkan style, with a menu exclusively devoted to gut-busting Serbian meats, *Čevapčiči* and *Pljeskavica*, all for around €4. Mon–Sat 8am–11pm.

Novi Svet pri Stolnici Slomškov trg 5. In the style of a Dalmatian *konoba* (pub), this superb, homely restaurant – with fishing gear strung along the walls – has fresh fish flown in daily from the Adriatic. They've a fine wine list too. Located on the corner of Slomškov trg and Rotovški trg. Mon–Sat 9am–midnight, Sun 9am–9pm.

Samsara Slovenska cesta 1. Despite its bland location inside the Kolosej (cinema) building, this neat and colourful restaurant offers a very decent choice of well-cooked and stylishly presented Italian food; the wines aren't bad either. Mon–Fri 9am–8pm, Sat 9am–2pm.

Štajerc Vetrinjska ulica 7. Rather restrained, orderly place, but one which does an unusual line in beer-infused dishes – soup, sausages and risotto – in addition to Slovene specialities such as buckwheat, polenta and *Štruklji*. Daily 11am–10pm.

Stari Gril Glavni trg 5. In the same vein as *Gril Ranca*, this cosy little place serves hunks of juicy beef with raw onion and *kajmak* (cheese) wedged inside a deliciously doughy *lepinja* (bread roll) – sit down or takeaway. Daily 8am–10pm.

Takos Mesarski prehod 3. Located down a narrow passage on the south side of Glavni trg, this cool, understated restaurant offers well-cooked and well-presented Mexican dishes. The place takes on a clubby feel as the evening wears on. Mon–Thurs 11am–midnight, Fri & Sat til 2am.

Toti Rotovž Rotovžski trg 9. Top-class restaurant boasting three separate kitchens; Slovene (Pohorje steak, boar, chamois and pheasant); Japanese (sushi, vegetable tempura), and Thai (red/green curry, steamed shrimps, fish with coconut milk or chilli). The fantastic cellar bar (where you can also eat) rocks to live music at weekends. Mon–Fri 9am–midnight, Sat 9am–2am.

Cafés and bars

Čajnica Slovenska 4. Charming and cosy tea-house with the complete range of world teas – you even get given a timer to tell you when your brew is ready. Mon–Fri 7am–10pm, Sat 9am–2pm & 5–10pm, Sun 10am–5pm.

Ilich Slovenska 6. Not only does this well-frequented café offer the best range of coffees and cakes in town, it's also the most relaxing place to while away an hour or so. Daily 7am–9pm.

KGB Vojašniški trg. Located opposite the Minorite church on a ramshackle square just west of Lent, this small, but brilliant underground cellar bar/club (check out the fantastic door as you enter) is the funkiest place in town, with regular live music to boot. A guaranteed good time. Daily 7pm–2am, Fri & Sat til 4am.

Kibla Ulica Kneza Kozlja 9 (inside the Narodni Dom). Cool and relaxing Internet café, bookshop and multimedia centre all rolled into one – the centre is highly regarded for the quality of contemporary art exhibitions staged here. See ⓦwww.kibla.org for programme and events. Mon–Fri 9am–10pm, Sat 4–10pm.

Satchmo Jazz Klub Strossmayerjeva ulica 6. Good-time jazz club with a top-class rota of gigs, though the summer programme is irregular – count on around one gig every two weeks during this period; otherwise, ideal for a bout of mellow drinking. See ⓦwww.jazz-klub.si for programme. Mon–Fri 9am–2am, Sat 7pm–3am, Sun 7pm–midnight.

Tildos Slomškov trg. Energetic, youthful place just across from the university building; just a few paces along from *Tildos* is *Toto Café*, another good little drinking spot, though rather less raucous. Both open daily till midnight.

Entertainment

The highly regarded **Slovenian National Theatre** (Slovensko Narodno Gledališče, SNG) on Slomškov trg stages a regular top-class diet of plays, opera and ballet; theatre tickets cost around €10–15, operatic and ballet performances around €16–20 (box office Mon–Fri 10am–5pm, Sat 10am–1pm and 1hr before each performance; ⓦwww.sng-mb.si). The **Puppet Theatre** (Lutkovno gledališče) at Rotovški trg 1 (☎02/228-1970), puts on performances, in Slovene, every Saturday at 10am (€3; closed July & Aug).

Maribor Pohorje

From Maribor bus #6 runs regularly to Zgornje Radvanje, 7km southwest of town at the foot of the popular ski resort, **Maribor Pohorje**. The last stop is at the **cable car** station (vzpenjača; April–Nov hourly 7am–9pm, Dec–March nonstop 7am–10pm; €7 return), from where the small four-seater cabins transport skiers and hikers to the upper station (1040m) on **Bolfenk** in fifteen minutes. A short walk from the station, inside the completely renovated Church of St Bolfenk, which burnt down in 1950, is a small **tourist office** (Wed–Sun: May–Oct 9.30am–4.30pm, July & Aug 9.30am–5.30pm, Nov–April 10.30am–3.30pm; ☎02/603-4211, ⓔbolfenk@siol.net). A couple of rooms in the church have been given over to exhibitions, one on the geology of the mountain, the other on the history of the Golden Fox ski race. Between May and September classical concerts (free) are held in the presbytery every Sunday at 10am.

Aside from **skiing** (see box, p.295), there are plenty more exciting activities on offer at the **Adrenaline Park** (Adrenalinski Park), which is not a park as such, but rather the collective name for a range of **activities** taking place at different locations around the mountain. Take your pick from mountain biking (€30 for a 4hr trip, €42 for an all-day trip), summer tobogganing (€5 per hr), paintballing (€18 per person – minimum group of six required), and horse-riding (€10 for 1hr, €45 for 5hr). For more information on the park and the activities on offer, contact the Sports Centre (Športni Centre Pohorje) in Maribor, at Mladinska ulica 29 (☎02/220-8825; ⓦwww.pohorje.org), or the tourist office at Bolfenk (see above). Pohorje offers terrific woodland **cycling**, with numerous cycle paths carv-

Maribor festivals

Maribor puts on a great range of festivals and events throughout the year, the biggest and best of which is the **Lent Festival** at the end of June/beginning of July. Second only to Ljubljana's Summer Festival in size, this is arguably Slovenia's most exuberant gathering, comprising two fabulous weeks of street theatre, modern and classical dance and jazz, popular and serious music along the waterfront and in the squares and streets around town. The Lent Vine is the site of the **Pruning of the Vine** at the beginning of March, and the **Embrace of the Vine** in October, the latter entailing the harvesting of the grapes, though both are actually little more than excuses for a good old jolly-up.

Musically, there's the **National and International Choir Competition**, staged in the Maribor Union Hall in April, and at the end of August the **No Border Jam Festival**, a gathering of international punk acts, with performances in the Pekarna complex. For kids (and adults too), the terrific **International Puppet Festival** runs throughout July and August and features a huge variety of acts from all over Europe.

The **Golden Fox** (Zlata Lisica) slalom race on the slopes of Maribor Pohorje at the end of January is one of the country's major sporting occasions, attracting the world's top women skiers, not to mention some 25,000 spectators, for a weekend of top-class sporting action and lots of drinking. For more details of these events contact the Maribor tourist office.

ing their way across the massif. There's a free cycle map outlining numerous trails, while another useful aid (whether hiking or cycling) is the 1:50,000 *Pohorje* **map** – both of these are available from the tourist offices in Maribor and Bolfenk.

There's stacks of **accommodation** on top of the mountain: beside the cable car station the *Hotel Bellevue* (☎02/603-6506; ❷) is a grubby, shambles of a place with hostel-style rooms, though just behind here the *Bolfenk Apartments* (☎02/603-6500; ❻–❽), sleeping between four and eight people, offer considerably more comfort; of a similar standard is the *Pension Martin* (☎02/603-6510), 500m southwest of the *Bolfenk*, which has both rooms (❸) and apartments (❼). Approximately 2km along the road to **Areh**, the *Aparthotel Pohorje* (☎02/603-6700, ⓦwww .aparthotel-pohorje.com) offers a range of excellent apartments sleeping two to four people (❺–❻) – the restaurant here is by far the best place to eat. In Areh itself, a further 4km distant, there's the very basic *Hotel Areh* (☎02/603-5040; ❸), and the *Ruška koča* **mountain hut** (☎02/603-5046; €16) just across the field and open all year. There's another hut, the *Mariborska koča* (☎02/603-2731), forty-five minutes' walk from the church at Bolfenk (or one hour from *Ruška koča*).

Across from the mountain hut is the **Church of St Areh**, a simple, late seventeenth-century Baroque building, which is now in a rather sad state of decrepitude; if it's closed, get the key from the hut. Hourly **buses** (9am–4pm) from Bolfenk to Areh depart from the car park next to the cable car station. Note that the road goes no further than Areh.

Ptuj and around

If you've only got time to visit one place in eastern Slovenia, make it **PTUJ**. Set 26km southeast of Maribor on the broad, flat Drava Plain between the Slovenske Gorice and Haloze hills, Ptuj is the oldest continuously settled site in Slovenia and is historically the most important settlement outside Ljubljana. The town and its surrounds are run through with two thousand years of history, its squares, streets

Maribor's wine roads

Maribor is one of the **Podravje** wine region's six wine-producing areas, and counts two **wine roads** with the **Kamnica** road to the west, and the more-visited **Malečnik** road to the east. Although a couple of reds are produced here (Žametna Črnina and Modri Pinot), this is overwhelmingly white wine territory – Laški and Renski Rizling, Chardonnay and Sauvignon, as well as the blended Mariborčan. One of the region's best wineries is at the *Joannes* tourist farm (the Protner winery) in the small hamlet of **Vodole** (no. 34), in Malečnik (℡02/473-2100), where you can also sample grilled blood sausages with sauerkraut. Although having your own wheels is certainly an advantage, it is feasible to walk at least part of these routes from Maribor. The 1:50,000 *Podravje* map, available from the tourist office in Maribor, should help you negotiate your way around.

If you have neither the time nor the means to head out into the countryside, make your way to the **Vinag Wine Cellar** in Maribor at Trg Svobode 3, one of the largest cellars in Central Europe; its 2.5km of tunnels hold some 150 wooden, concrete and aluminium barrels, with a storage capacity of some seven million litres. For a **tour** of the cellar and a **tasting** session (€6 for four wines), you should contact them a day or two in advance (℡02/220-8113, ⓦwww.vinag.si). You can also buy their wines at the adjoining shop (Mon–Fri 9am–7pm, Sat 9am–1pm).

and buildings rampant with architectural and archeological riches – Romanesque and medieval townhouses, built-in Roman monuments and tombstones, and ancient Mithras shrines. Moreover, Ptuj is home to the wonderful Shrovetide **Kurent Carnival**, Slovenia's most famous, and entertaining, folkloric event. Though not the easiest to reach without your own transport, two further places worth venturing to are the beautiful Church of the Holy Virgin in **Ptujska Gora**, and the **Haloze wine region**, bordering Croatia to the south.

Some history

Settled as far back as the late **Stone Age**, and later populated by the **Celts**, Ptuj began life around 69 AD, when a **Roman** legionary camp was established on the south bank of the Drava River. The result of expansion across the river was the creation of a self-governing, civilian entity called Poetovio, which functioned as a major staging post linking the Roman provinces of Pannonia and Noricum. Occupied successively by **Avars**, **Magyars** and then **Slavs**, Ptuj received its town rights in 977 AD, at which point it passed into the hands of the **Salzburg** archdiocese, whose members grew rich from the trade between Pannonia and the Italian peninsula. During the **Middle Ages**, the town developed around the solidly fortified castle, and established itself as a commercial centre of some considerable importance. Until the death of **Frederick XI** in 1438, the town remained under the jurisdiction of the Ptuj nobility, vassals of the Salzburg archdiocese, though subsequent incursions by the Turks, and wars with the Hungarians, undermined the town's development. It recovered sufficiently to re-establish itself as a small provincial town, which it remains to this day.

Arrival and information

Ptuj's **train station** is 500m northeast of the centre on Osojnikova cesta, the **bus station** 200m nearer town on the same road. From both stations, continue down Osojnikova to the junction with ulica Heroja Lacka: a right turn here lands you straight in the centre. The **tourist office** is at Slovenski trg 5 (Mon–Fri 8am–5pm, Sat 8am–noon; ℡02/779-6011, ⓦwww.ptuj-tourism.si), though you can

Mithraic Shrines ◀   Terme Ptuj Spa & Campsite   ▶ Bus and Train Station

PTUJ

**RESTAURANTS,
CAFÉS & BARS**

Amadeus	2
Café Bo	3
Café Evropa	7
Café Orfej	5
Čajni Kotiček	4
Kitajski Vrt	8
Old Irish Pub	6
Perutnina Ptuj	1
Ribič	9

ACCOMMODATION

Garni Hotel Mitra	B
Kurent Youth Hostel	A
Hotel Poetovio	C

get the same information at the welcoming **Centre for Free Time Activities** (CID), located just across from the bus station in the modern building at Osojnikova 9 (Mon–Thurs 8am–6pm, Sat 10am–1pm; ☎02/780-5540, ⓦwww.cid. si); they also offer **Internet access** (free), as does the town library at Prešernova ulica 35 (Mon–Fri 8.30am–7pm, Sat 8am–1pm, €1 per hour). The **post office** is opposite the Minorite church at Vodnikova ulica 12 (Mon–Fri 7am–7pm, Sat 7am–1pm). **Bikes** can be hired (€2 for 1hr, €8 for the day) from Terme Ptuj (see overleaf), worth considering if you're without wheels and you'd like to visit either the Mithra Shrines (see p.310) or the Haloze wine region (see p.311).

Accommodation

There's precious little in the way of town **accommodation**, with just two hotels, a hostel and a campsite, though there are a smattering of private rooms around town too – the tourist office can advise on this, as well as accommodation on local tourist farms (❸). The excellent ⚓ *Kurent* **youth hostel**, at Osojnikova 9 (☎02/771-0814, ⓔyhptuj@csod.si), has modern and colourful rooms sleeping between two and six people, each with its own washing and shower facilities (€16 per person; there's a discount for IYHA holders); they've also got laundry facilities.

Of the town's two **hotels**, by far the better is the refurbished ⚓ *Garni Hotel Mitra* at Prešernova ulica 6 (☎02/787-7455, ⓦwww.hotel-mitra-fm.si; ❻), whose rooms are a model of elegance and taste. By way of contrast the rooms in the dour *Hotel Poetovio*, on the edge of the Old Town at Vinarski trg 5 (☎02/779-8201; ❹), lack any semblance of style or character, but they are fairly priced. The town's best **private accommodation** is the restful *Šilak*, a renovated 300-year old house down by the Drava river at Dravska ulica 13 (T 02/787-7447, E rooms.silak@siol. net; ❸–❹), which has a handful of extremely comfortable and stylish rooms and apartments.

Two kilometres east of town across the river, the **Terme Ptuj spa** at Pot v Toplice 9 (T 02/749-4100, W www.terme-ptuj.si) has an adjoining **campsite** (open year round) and spacious, well-furnished **apartments** (❻) sleeping up to six, as well as more basic **bungalows** (❹) sleeping up to three. Guests staying in any of this accommodation receive free, unlimited use of the spa's pools.

The Town

Ptuj is a compact town and a leisurely half-day should be enough to cover the main sights, although you could quite easily use up the best part of a day admiring the wealth of architectural detail. Pretty much everything of interest is located on or just off the two main squares, **Mestni trg** and **Slovenski trg**, and the old main street, **Prešernova ulica**, which curls under the base of the castle-topped hill.

Mestni trg and around

The ideal place to start is fourteenth-century **Mestni trg** (Town Square), a charming little square ringed by several stately buildings, the most prominent of which is the muddy-green **Town Hall**, a large neo-Gothic German pile raised in 1907 on the site of a late-Renaissance structure built by the Dominicans in 1571. Remnants of this earlier building are still just about visible in the form of a pair of dragon reliefs and a reclining nude on one of the corner prominences. The colourful, heavily stuccoed eighteenth-century **corner house**, opposite at no. 2, is now the popular *Café Evropa* (see p.309); above the entrance is a slender corner niche holding a statue of Mary with Child. At the heart of the square, the regulation **plague column**, featuring a posturing St Florian dressed in military attire, is a copy, erected in 1993.

There's more architecture to admire along Krempljeva ulica – the street heading south from Mestni trg – notably at no. 1, whose peeling and cracked paintwork can't detract from some marvellous stuccowork, and in particular, the beehive relief between the windows on the prominence. At no. 7, the entrance to the old **Court House** is framed by a superb sixteenth-century Renaissance portal, either side of which sit a pair of lions holding escutcheons. West from Mestni trg, up Murkova ulica, check out the portal with griffins at no. 2, and the Patrician Mansion, opposite at no. 1. At its top end, Murkova ulica opens up into Slovenski trg.

The Minorite Church

Krempljeva ulica segues into Minoritski trg, site of the late thirteenth-century **Minorite Monastery** (Minoritski Samostan), which, unlike the majority of Slovenia's monasteries, wasn't closed down under the reforms of Emperor Joseph II at the end of the eighteenth century. Instead, it continued to prosper as a centre of learning until World War II, when it was confiscated by the Germans, then bombed by the Allies. The most feted part of the complex is the first-floor **summer refectory**, thanks to its thickly stuccoed ceiling, decorated by Italians Quadrio and Bettini, and oval and rectangular panels depicting scenes from the lives of the monastery's patrons, SS Peter and Paul. The prize exhibit in the monastery's richly stocked **library** is one of three original copies of the New Testament translated into Slovene by Primož Trubar in 1561 – the other two reside in the National Library in Ljubljana, and in Vienna. If you wish to visit the monastery, contact the tourist office.

The adjoining Church of St Peter and St Paul was one of Slovenia's greatest ecclesiastical losses during World War II. The only part of the church to survive the raids was the presbytery, slightly shortened after the war in order to accommodate, rather insensitively, a post office on the site of the bombed-out nave. Look out for the beautifully worked relief of a lamb on a keystone by the high altar, and the gargoyle-like animal heads on the exterior buttresses. Reconstructed in 2005, the nave stands in stark contrast, a large, austere space worked over in glass and marble.

A short walk east along Dravska ulica – the street running parallel to the river – brings you to the bulky Drava Water Tower (Drava stolp), the largest of six former defensive towers that once formed the core of the town's fortification system; contrary to popular legend the stone balls built into the upper section of the walls were not those fired by Turks, but rather were placed there by local enthusiasts who had a penchant for this kind of architecture. The tower's two floors now function as the France Mihelič Gallery (Miheličeva galerija; Tues–Sun 10am–1pm & 4–7pm; €2), holding a selection of works by the graphic artist as well as other rotating exhibitions. During the Middle Ages Dravska ulica was known for its butcher's shops and tanneries, as indicated by the numerous portals embedded with the traditional tanners' symbols of a bucket with two crossed scrapers.

Slovenski trg: the Town Tower and St George's Church

The centre of triangular-shaped **Slovenski trg** is dominated by the chunky, five-storey **Town Tower** (Mestni stolp), originally a sixteenth-century bell tower, then a seventeenth-century watchtower, before retiring gracefully in the eighteenth, when it was embellished with an onion-bulb spire. Embedded within the tower's lower reaches are numerous civil and military tombstones, relief votive slabs and sacrificial altars, though the most impressive tombstone is the freestanding **Orpheus Monument** in front of the tower (it's covered up in winter). Cut from Pohorje marble, the thick rectangular column commemorates Marcus Verus, former mayor of Poetovio, although during the Middle Ages it was used as a pillory, whereby petty criminals were chained to iron rings fastened to the bottom of the block – the poor state of the inscriptions is down to the wear and tear caused by the chains.

Outwardly austere, the twelfth-century Gothic **Church of St George** (Cerkev Sv Jurij) conceals some exceptional works of art. The first thing you see as you enter is a small glass cabinet on the left, containing a fragile and rather foppish-looking fourteenth-century wooden **sculpture of St George** nonchalantly slaying a dragon. From here proceed into the central nave, arranged with incongruously placed frescoes, altars and chapels, such as the **Crucifixion**, framed with an elaborately decorated banner, immediately to the left, and opposite, the **Altar of the Three Kings**, featuring a relief of the Coronation of St Mary inside a Baroque casing. The church's most renowned piece of work, **Laib's winged altar**, is positioned to the rear of the south aisle; dating from around 1460, the gilded paintings depict, in the centre, Mary's death, and to the left and right respectively, St Hieronymous with a church model in one hand and a book in the other, and St Mark writing the Gospel held by a lion. Of the several chapels dotted around the church, the most important is the **Chapel of Our Lady of Sorrows** at the end of the north aisle, the centrepiece of which is a fifteenth-century stone pietà sculpture. Just to the right of the chapel, a splendid, high lancet-arch fronts the bright fourteenth-century cross-vaulted presbytery, and a magnificent long choir, lined either side by two long rows of oak-wood pews ornamented with figures of animals.

Prešernova ulica

The Old Town's central artery, **Prešernova ulica**, is an attractive, peaceful thoroughfare, lined with tightly packed ranks of medieval townhouses, almost every single one furnished with a Renaissance stone portal or some other beautifully crafted feature. For starters take a look at house no. 1, whose corner prominence is supported by a so-called Parlerian mask, a black painted head of a grinning, curly-haired man; and, opposite, at no. 4, the Romanesque Bratonič house, the oldest tenement along the street and which now accommodates the tourist office. Before continuing, take a quick look down **Jadranska ulica**, and in particular nos. 4 and 6, the facades of which are decorated with *Kurent*-style masks worked in flat relief (see box p.310).

Back on Prešernova, beyond the colourful neo-Baroque *Garni Hotel Mitra* at no. 6, the house at no. 16 is notable for some marble fragments jutting out of the passageway wall, which, on closer inspection, reveal themselves to be parts of dedication blocks or tombstones – there are more complete blocks embedded into the back wall of the run-down courtyard. On the opposite side of the road, at no. 27, take a peek inside the courtyard, where there's another grey marble relief, this one of a prostrate, headless lion. The building on the corner of Prešernova and Cafova ulica used to be the **Small Castle** (Mali Grad), and the seat of the lords of Ptuj who held their court here; it now functions as the town library.

The Dominican monastery and Archeological Museum

A few paces on from the Small Castle, the **Dominican monastery** (Dominikanski Samostan) stands in a small park-like area on Muzejski trg, its bright pink facade hung with spidery stuccowork and pocked with five niches containing statues of saints. Unlike the Minorite monastery less than 500m away, the Dominican monastery, founded in 1230, was forced to disband as part of Joseph II's reforms in 1786, after which time it was used alternately as a barracks and a residential building, before eventually falling into a state of disrepair.

The monastery is now home to the town's **Archeological Museum** (daily: mid-April to Nov 10am–5pm; €3), an impressive hoard of archeological treasures held within several separate areas of the building. Begin with the monastery's gloriously dishevelled **cloisters** – painted with early fourteenth-century frescoes (restored during the interwar period) and vaulted around a century later – and which are now cluttered with an array of statuary and fragments, some of which were brought across from the demolished Minorite church after World War II. The **small archeological collection** on the upper floor comprises a fabulous store of Celtic and Roman grave finds, mostly urns and vessels, but also gold jewellery, exquisite bronze and clay statuettes and oil lamps. The **lapidarium**, meanwhile, contains a matchless collection of marble and sandstone sarcophagi, statues and busts, mosaic floors and beautiful votive altars dedicated to various deities. There are also memorials from Mithra shrines II (in the church crypt) and IV (see box, p.311). The **old refectory** now keeps a modest collection of Celtic and Roman coins (also look out for the clay piggy banks), but is more interesting for its gorgeous vaulted and stuccoed ceiling – not dissimilar to that of the summer refectory in the Minorite monastery, and similarly painted with venerated saints.

Ptuj Castle and Regional Museum

Lording it over the flutter of red roofs and cobbled streets below, **Ptuj Castle** (Grad Ptuj) is the town's showpiece attraction. It began life around 69 AD when the inhabitants of Roman Poetovio built a fortress and temple atop this very hill. The oldest archives date the present structure to some time in the twelfth century, when the castle was owned by the archbishops of Salzburg, who in turn leased it to the lords of Ptuj. Fortified ahead of anticipated Turkish raids in the sixteenth century, the castle was further modified in Baroque fashion during the seventeenth century.

Whether approaching from the path opposite the monastery, or via Grajska ulica, a narrow street just off Prešernova ulica near the *Garni Hotel Mitra*, you enter the castle grounds through the thick-set **Charles portal**, which opens up into the lower courtyard, once the location for the castle stables and military outbuildings, but now empty save for a weatherbeaten statue of a one-armed St Florian dousing yet another fire – the views from this platform, however, are fantastic. Walk on up through the fine Renaissance **Peruzzi portal** into the immaculate inner courtyard, enclosed by a horseshoe-shaped, three-tiered **residential palace**. Before entering the museum take a look at the splendid, red Salzburg marble tombstone of Frederick IX, the last lord of Ptuj, embedded into the wall on the left-hand side of the courtyard.

The castle's **regional museum collection** (daily: May to mid-Oct 9am–6pm, plus July & Aug Sat & Sun 9am–8pm; mid-Oct to April 9am–5pm; €3) comprises a mixed bag of exhibitions. The first rooms, stuffed full of period furnishings, tapestries and paintings, are not especially enthralling, though there's much fine stucco-work to admire. More stimulating are the colourful displays of *Kurenti* masks and associated carnival paraphernalia (see box on p.310), and a fascinating section on musical instruments; supplemented by sound recordings, the exhibition charts the history of Ptuj's military and town brass bands, though more intriguingly there are some Greek and Roman artefacts, including a tibia fragment believed to have been used as a pipe to be played at funerals, social dances and the like. After your visit, you can savour the marvellous views of the Drava River, and Haloze Hills beyond, or have a coffee in the small courtyard café.

Eating and drinking

The town counts on just two really decent **restaurants**: *Ribič* (Mon–Thurs 10am–10pm, Fri & Sat 10am–midnight, Sun noon–6pm), down by the river at Dravska ulica 9, has a menu almost exclusively devoted to fish, but it doesn't come cheap – the riverside terrace is a wonderful place to dine in summer. The other is *Amadeus* (Mon–Sat 11am–11pm, Sun noon–4pm) at Prešernova 36 (opposite the library), a warm, classy place offering an upscale take on Slovene standards, including a terrific steak menu, and unusually appealing vegetarian options, all at slightly more affordable prices. Otherwise, there's *Kitajski Vrt*, a reasonable, if not wholly authentic, Chinese place opposite *Ribič*, and *Perutnina Ptuj (PP)* on Novi trg, a canteen-style joint which knocks up fast, filling and cheap daily specials for around €4 (Mon–Fri 8am–6pm, Sat 8am–1pm).

Whilst Ptuj's **nightlife** is, predictably enough, fairly tame, there is no shortage of cafés around town: indisputably the number one hangout is *Café Evropa* on Mestni trg, by day a fairly relaxed place for coffee, by night a noisy, frenetic bar. If it's too busy, head up to the *Old Irish Pub* on Murkova ulica. More sedate options, but equally good places for a daytime or evening drink, are the comfortable and loungey *Čajni Kotiček*, also on Murkova ulica; *Café Bo*, at Slovenski trg 7; and *Café Orfej*, at Prešernova ulica 5. The quaint little coffee house in the *Garni Mitra Hotel* is well worth a visit. It's also worth checking out what's going on at the Centre for Free Time Activities (see p.305), as it occasionally stages the odd gig in its basement bar.

If you haven't time to visit the Haloze winegrowing region (see p.311), the next best option is to call in at the **Haloze wine cellar** at Vinarski trg 1 (☎02/787-9810); although it's usually full of tour parties, individual visits (around €3) are

One of the oldest, most unusual and celebrated folklore events in the Slovene calendar is the **Kurent**, a kind of fertility rite and celebration of the awakening of Spring confused together, which takes place in the ten days up to Shrove Tuesday (late February/early March). Wearing spooky masks made of sheepskin and feathers with a coloured beak for a nose, white beads for teeth and long, bright red tongues, the *Kurenti* proceed from house to house, warding off evil spirits with the incessant din from the cowbells and other instruments tied to their weighty costumes. Leading the procession is the Devil (*Hudič*), pitchfork in hand and wrapped in a net to symbolize his capture: behind the *Kurenti*, the ploughers (*Orači*) pull a small wooden plough, scattering sand around to represent the sowing of seed, whilst the other participants smash clay pots at their feet in return for good luck and health.

Although several similar carnivals, known as *pust*, take place in other towns throughout Slovenia – most famously in Cerkno and Cerknica – and in neighbouring countries such as Hungary and Croatia, most are pale imitations of the events that take place here in Ptuj.

possible so long as you call in advance – this incorporates a fifteen-minute film presentation, a tour of the labyrinthine cellars (complete with sound and light effects) and a sampling session. There's also a shop here (Mon–Fri 7am–7pm & Sat 7am–noon).

Mithra Shrines

Approximately 1km west of town, across the river in **Zgornji Breg**, the **Mithra III Shrine** is one of four shrines in Ptuj dedicated to the sun god and warrior Mithra. The Mithras III shrine, housed in a small pavilion just off Mariborska cesta (it's signposted), dates from 3 AD and comprises the remains of a three-naved temple, around which are scattered sacrificial altars carved with votive inscriptions. The plate on the far wall is a copy of an altar relief of the sacrificial bull from the Mithraeum in Osterburken, in Germany, though there are a few surviving fragments from the original in the right-hand corner. The rest of the room is neatly arranged with dedication blocks, chunky slabs of marble carved with reliefs from the Mithras cult – his birth from a rock, his slaying of a bull, and another that depicts him shooting water from a rock with an arrow. The most impressive stone, however, is the one positioned in front of the main altar, which depicts two figures taking an oath over the fire on the sacrificial altar.

A twenty-minute walk southwest of Mithra III, across a dusty field in the tiny settlement of **Spodnja Hajdina**, a smaller building holds the remains of the **Mithra I Shrine**, discovered in 1898 and considered to be the oldest of the Mithra temples located in the Roman Empire's northern province; this one dates from around the second half of the second century. The most interesting of the dozen or so haphazardly arranged stone dedication blocks are statues of Mithras dragging the sacrificial bull, and a snake coiled around a torso emerging from a rock mass. Both temples are usually closed, but the keys can easily be obtained from the neighbouring houses, the numbers of which are given on the respective doors.

Church of the Virgin Mary

In the village of Ptujska Gora (twelve kilometres southwest of Ptuj along the road to Rogatec), the Gothic **Church of the Virgin Mary** (Cerkev Sv Marija) ranks alongside the churches at Brezje and Sveta Gora as one of the country's premier

Mithraism

Mithraism, the ancient religion of Mithras the sun god, is believed to have originated in Persia, before spreading west during the time of the Roman Empire. However, it was never officially recognized as a Roman religion, in all probability because the Romans believed that Mithraism consisted of elements of the religion of their bitter enemies, the Persians. For this reason the first Mithras shrines, such as those in Ptuj, were built outside town boundaries. By the second half of the third century, however, Mithraism – with Ptuj as one of its leading centres – had almost established itself as the state religion, rivalling Christianity as the dominant faith. However, with Emperor Constantine's ascension to the throne in the fourth century, Mithraism, along with other pagan religions, was outlawed and most of its temples destroyed.

Little is known of its rituals and believers, although it's likely that meetings took place within confined religious communities, dominated exclusively by male members; Initiates were typically imperial administrators, slaves of the customs administration or soldiers, and would number around one hundred. Members would be grouped and divided into several ranks, ranks that were depicted in relief. Although stone dedication blocks and relief depictions of Mithras were widely distributed throughout the Roman Empire, few match the calibre of those in Ptuj. There's another excellent Mithraeum shrine in Rožanec, near Črnomelj (see p.260).

pilgrimage destinations. Built some time around 1400, the church's beautifully cool interior manifests some outstanding Gothic architecture, most notably in the form of the three arches which presage the tripartite nave, whose aisles are separated by smooth slender columns. But nothing in this, or any other church in Slovenia, comes close to the splendour of the **high altar**, a majestic, towering work of art whose focal point is the *Virgin Mary with Mantle* relief, which features seven angels lifting a dusky green cloak to reveal ranks of some eighty figures, each carved in remarkable life-like detail; mingling amongst the cast of the rich and the poor are several of the counts of Celje. So compelling is this piece that it somewhat detracts from the rest of the altar's ornamentation, most notably some extraordinary sculptural work.

To the right of the high altar, in the southern aisle, the canopied **Celje Altar** pays further homage to the counts of Celje, its baldachin ceiling and pillars beautifully ornamented with sculpted flowers, animal figures and the counts' coats-of-arms. Also worthy of close inspection are the frescoes depicting scenes from Christ's Passion by John Bruneck, located under the organ loft, and a fine statue of St James standing on the console of a pillar in the southern aisle. To get here take one of the five daily buses (hourly during school term-time) heading to **Majšperk**, and alight on the main road just below the church, from where it's a five-minute walk.

Haloze Hills

Rearing up from the iron-flat Drava Plain south of Ptuj, the **Haloze hills** present further opportunities to sample Slovenia's fine wines. Extending for some 30km east, from the village of Makole (just beyond Ptujska Gora), along the Croatian border to Zavrč, the Haloze are divided into two diverse landscapes – the Vinorodne (winegrowing) region to the east, and the Gozdnate (forested) region to the south and west, both regions spotted with solitary farms, orchards and hamlets.

Although the many cellars here can be visited independently – the clearly visible brown and yellow signs denote what each cellar has to offer – you can, alternatively, head to the friendly and accommodating Halo Agency (☏02/795-3200, ⒺInfo@halo.si) in the village of **CIRKULANE**, situated a couple of kilometres south of **Borl Castle**, now a neglected station perched high above the Drava 12km southwest of Ptuj. Located in the centre of the village across from the church, the agency can provide information on the region, arrange accommodation in holiday homes (⑤), and organize guided visits to a selection of the cellars; many of these produce their own goat's cheese, bread and pastries, and other homemade treats. Between Monday and Friday there are three daily buses (hourly during school term-time) from Ptuj to Cirkulane, but otherwise there's no public transport around the region itself, so you'll need your own wheels.

Ormož

Pressed up hard against the Croatian border 23km east of Ptuj, **ORMOŽ** was the setting for some of the heaviest fighting between Slovene units of the Territorial Defence and Yugoslav Federal forces during the Ten-Day War of Independence in 1991. Nothing quite so animated happens here these days and, in truth, the town has very little to commend it, but it is the starting point for ventures up into the Ormož hills winegrowing region (see below). If you do find yourself with half an hour to spare, the recently renovated town **castle** (Mon–Fri noon–3pm, Sat 10am–2pm; €1), a short walk up from the bus station, showcases a few rooms containing a selection of items and furniture, as well as a sprinkling of frescoes, whilst there's a modest gallery of local art.

The **bus station** is smack-bang in the centre of town, and the **train station** about 500m beyond the castle right on the border crossing point. The **tourist office**, a five-minute walk up behind the bus station at Kolodvorska ulica 11 (Mon–Fri 9am–5pm, ☎02/741-5707), can assist with visits to local wine cellars. Should you really need to stay, the town's single **hotel** is the dreadfully ordinary, and horribly brown, *Ormož* (☎02/740-1121, ✉hotel.ormoz@siol.net; ❸) opposite the bus station.

The Ljutomer wine road

Extending from Ormož in the south to Ljutomer in the north (see opposite), the eponymous **wine road** is the smallest of Podravje's six winegrowing districts, yet it possesses a high density of viticultural sites. Vying with the Goriška Brda region in Primorje for the title of Slovenia's most beautiful wine-producing region, this fabulously picturesque and sunny landscape is shaped by horizontal rows of curving, terraced vineyards set against the backdrop of *Klopotec*, wooden wind-powered rattles designed to scare off birds and, according to local superstition, to drive snakes out of the vineyards. Of the predominantly white wines harvested here, the smooth and slightly sweet Beli Pinot is regarded as the finest, followed by Laški Rizling – one of the few Slovenian wines to find its way into British supermarkets – Šipon and Traminec, whilst the blended wines, Jeruzalemčan and Ljutomerčan are popular alternatives. The numerous **cellars** lining the route are marked by brown and cream signposts – although you can call in on the off-chance, most prefer advance notice of your arrival.

The midway point of the route is the delightful little hilltop village of **JERU-ZALEM**, so-named after crusaders visiting here in the thirteenth century became so enamoured with the wine and the people that they decided to name the settlement after the holy city. At the centre of the village is the Baroque **Church of Our Lady of Sorrows**, whose painting of Our Lady of Sorrows on the high altar is a late seventeenth-century copy of the original, which was brought here by the aforementioned crusaders, but later stolen. Look out, too, for the imprint of a horse hoof which, according to local legend, was left here by one of the marauding Turks during seventeenth-century raids. Just across from the church is the **tourist office** (daily; summer 10am–7pm, winter 10am–4pm; ⓦwww.jeruzalem.si), which is a more than useful source of advice on the best cellars to visit. Just beyond the village, heading towards Ljutomer, there's an **observation tower**, from where there are superlative views of the surrounding hills – on a clear day it's possible to see as far as Lake Balaton in Hungary.

The route is made for **cycling**, and you may not have much choice anyway, as what buses that do travel between Ormož and Ljutomer, and vice versa, take the main road running parallel to the east, passing through Ivanjkovci. If you're planning to cycle the entire route, you should allow for around four to five hours, a little more, of course, if cellar-hopping is on the agenda. The stretch between Jeruzalem and Ljutomer is slightly tougher going than the stretch between Jeruzalem and Ormož, which flattens out markedly after Vinski Vir. **Bikes** can be hired at the tourist offices in both Jeruzalem and Ljutomer.

Ljutomer

LJUTOMER, the economic and cultural centre of the region, is the last town before you cross the Mura River into Prekmurje. Although it's unlikely you will need, or should want to stay here, there are a couple of interesting diversions; it also has excellent rail connections, including the Budapest–Venice InterCity train, which passes through here once a day. The wine connections aside, the town is best known for its horse racing, having staged trotting races since 1874. Today, the **hippodrome** – located around 500m northwest of the town's main square, Glavni trg – stages some ten **horse-trotting races** a year. These usually take place on Sundays and public holidays between April and September (approx €5), but check with the tourist office (see below) first for schedules. If you can't manage to get here for a race day, you can still visit the track and stables, whilst you may also get to see the horses in training; the tourist office should be able to fix something up for you.

Otherwise fairly limited, the small **town museum** (Mon–Fri 8am–3pm, €2), located in the town hall on Glavni trg, is worth visiting to view some original footage of the first-ever films to be produced in Slovenia, *People Leaving the Church* and *The Fair at Ljutomer*, which were shot by Karol Grossmann in 1905 (see p.342). There's also an interesting exhibition on the so-called "Tabor Movement"; between 1868 and 1870, numerous groups of young intellectuals living in Slovene ethnic territories initiated regular mass open-air forums (*tabors*) to publicize and rally support for a united Slovenia, whose very existence as a national group around that time appeared seriously threatened. Although they were subsequently banned by Vienna, the influence of the *tabors* continued to be felt in later years whenever questions concerning the Slovene national movement were raised.

Practicalities

All the town's practical facilities are located within fairly close proximity to each other: Ljutomer has two **train stations**, Ljutomer, and the smaller Ljutomer Mesto, where you should alight for the town centre. This is located on Rajh nade ulica, from where it's a ten-minute walk south to the **bus station** and the town centre. The **tourist office** is about 400m west of the bus station at Jureša Cirila 4 (Mon–Fri 8am–4pm; ☎02/584-8333, ⓦwww.lto-prlekija.si), though it's actually located inside the courtyard of the town hall building on Glavni trg. As well as supplying information on the Ljutomer wine road (see opposite), the helpful staff here can arrange private **accommodation** along the route, and rent out **bikes** (€8 per day). Glavni trg is also the site for the town's only **hotel**, the very grey and really rather depressing *Hotel Jeruzalem* (☎02/581-1211; ❹); as well as the only place in town worth **eating** at, the *Galileo* pizzeria/spaghetteria, which is located inside the courtyard of the town hall building.

Prekmurje

Cut off by the fast-flowing Mura River to the south, and bounded on the remaining three sides by the Austrian, Hungarian and Croatian borders, **Prekmurje** (Pomurje to Slovenes) is a region quite apart from the rest of the country. Known as Slovenia's bread-basket, it is, for the most part, a relentlessly flat landscape, carved up by grids of smooth green fields, picturesque villages and little white churches. Prekmurje's relative isolation is rooted in over a thousand years of Magyar rule, a situation that changed only after World War I when it was incorporated into Yugoslav lands, although there was another brief period of Hungarian imposition during World War II. Physically, economically and culturally distanced from the rest of the country prior to World War I – there was no bridge crossing the Mura until 1924 – Prekmurje is still regarded by many Slovenes as something of a backwater. However, thanks largely to Hungary's long-term rule, Prek-murje remains one of Slovenia's most ethnically diverse regions, embracing a sizeable Hungarian minority, as well as the country's largest Roma community. Prior to World War II it also accounted for over half of the country's Jewish population.

Prekmurje has one of the richest culinary traditions in Slovenia, and you shouldn't leave without trying *bograč*, a steaming goulash pot of mixed meats, onions and potatoes, or its most famous product, *gibanica*, a delicious sweet pie stuffed with cottage cheese, poppy seeds, walnut and apple.

There's a fairly regular **bus service** linking the region's only two towns, **Murska Sobota** and **Lendava**, via most of the villages in between, including **Martjanci**, **Bogojina** and **Beltinci**. However, services are dramatically reduced (if non-exist-ent) at weekends, so try and coincide a visit with a weekday. Alternatively, and if you've got the time and inclination, the best way to explore the region is by bike (see box, p.317).

Murska Sobota

Located in the geographical centre of Prekmurje, **MURSKA SOBOTA** is the largest settlement in the province, a one-horse town where nothing very much ever happens. However, it is the region's main road and rail hub, so there's a good chance you'll wind up here if you're planning to explore the surrounding coun-tryside. The town developed alongside the Ledava River, in the plains north of the Mura River, during the eleventh century, and was almost immediately incor-porated into the Hungarian state, under whose administration it remained until 1920. Another, brief period of Hungarian control during World War II was ended by the Red Army, who liberated the town in April 1945.

With the reopening, in 2001, of the rail line between Puconci, a few kilometres north of Murska Sobota, and Hodoš, on the Hungarian border, the town once again found itself the first major stop, in Slovenia, for intercity trains travelling from Budapest to Ljubljana. If you do have an hour or two to spare while waiting for buses to the outlying villages, there's a very worthwhile museum, as well as a pleasant park to laze around in.

Arrival, information and accommodation

Both the **bus** and **train stations** are centrally located, the former on Slomškova ulica, the latter to the east at the end of Ulica Arhiteka Novaka. The **tourist** office (Mon–Fri 9am–5pm, Sat 8am–noon; ☏02/534-1130), located inside a roadside booth, is midway along Slovenska ulica, near the junction with Trg Zmage, though it's of limited help, and you'll get far more out of the tourist office in Moravske Toplice, 7km northeast of town (see p.316). The town's one **hotel** is the slightly overpriced *Diana* at Slovenska ulica 52 (☏02/514-1200, ✉recepcija@zvezda-diana.si; ❻), which has slick rooms with cool blue furnishings and large beds; there's also a pool, sauna, solarium and gym. The **post office** is on the south side of Trg Zmage (Mon–Fri 7am–7pm, Sat 7am–1pm), and there's free **Internet access** in the new town library across from the bus station (Mon–Fri 8am–7.30pm, Sat 8am–2pm).

The Town

The town's only real point of interest, and its saving grace, is the **Regional Museum** (Pokrajinksi muzej; Mon–Fri 9am–5pm, Sat 9am–1pm; €2.5), housed inside an eighteenth-century Renaissance mansion in the centre of the leafy **City Park** west of the town's main square Trg Zmage (Victory Square). The museum's fifteen or so rooms (there are comprehensive English captions) offer an impressive and thorough narrative of life in the town and the wider Prekmurje region from prehistory to the present. Selected highlights from the earliest periods include Roman burial mounds and the remnants of a medieval forge discovered in Grad na Goričkem in 1990. The medieval period is further represented by some superb Gothic architecture, including a stone tabernacle and other sculptural pieces, as well as some fresco fragments. Trades and crafts, such as shoemaking, milling and wheel-making, all make an appearance, though the greatest emphasis is on pottery, one of the region's most important nineteenth-century cottage industries, and a tradition that just about survives to this day in old potters' settlements such as Filovci (see p.318). The last few rooms document the town's liberation by the Red Army in 1945, including a short film of the unveiling of the Liberation Monument on Trg Zmage, erected on August 12, 1945, less than two months after the Red Army left Murska Sobota; the exhibiton concludes with a slightly tacky presentation pertaining to contemporary life in the region.

On the opposite side of City Park stands the slender, whitewashed neo-Gothic **Evangelical Church**. Although there's little in the way of traditional church ornamentation, its paintwork is striking, the cream-coloured walls splattered with geometric patterns of burgundy, green and blue; note the presbytery, too, which, unusually, is carpeted.

Eating and drinking

There's little choice here when it comes to **eating and drinking**, though the lively *Zvezda* on the southeastern corner of Trg Zmage doubles up nicely as a restaurant and pub; worth trying is the game (particularly the chamois) and goulash, whilst there's a good selection of light and dark beers on tap, all brewed on-site (open until 1am Fri & Sat) – before you enter, take a look at the stuccoed reliefs of moustachioed men on the facade. One other place worth considering is *Rajh no 1* (closed Mon), located on the bottom floor of an apartment block on the corner of Lendavska ulica and Cvetkova ulica, which offers deliciously simple spaghetti, salad and pasta dishes at rock-bottom prices.

If you're prepared to travel for your food, then make tracks for the *Rajh* restaurant (Tues–Sat 10am–11pm, Sun 10am–4pm), 5km south of town in the village of **Bakovci**; neither the building nor the interior particularly flatter, but the food here, including pheasant, lamb and goose, as well as Serbian specialities such as *Sarma* (minced meat wrapped inside cabbage leaves), is exceptional. It's located at the very beginning of the village, at Soboška ulica 32.

Martjanci

Heading north out of Murska Sobota along the road to Moravske Toplice, it's worth taking a moment to stop off at the roadside **Parish Church of St Martin** in the village of **MARTJANCI**. Distinguished by an elegant high belfry, the church was designed and painted by Janez Aquila, a frequent contributor to religious monuments in the Prekmurje region. Arguably the most beautifully frescoed church in Prekmurje, its gorgeous, cross-ribbed vaulted presbytery is smothered with some fine paintings – Apostles (including the *Masters of the Apostles*), saints and prophets, as well as a painting of the author himself (supposedly one of the oldest self-portraits known to exist in European art). On the inner wall of the triumphal arch there's a fabulous fresco of George and the Dragon. The simple high altar, meanwhile, featuring a statue of St Martin, is the work of Jože Plečnik, a modest contribution by the architect in comparison to his work at Bogojina (see p.318).

Moravske Toplice

From Martjanci, buses continue for a further 3km to **Moravske Toplice**, dominated by the **Terme 3000 Spa** (Ⓦwww.terme3000.si), a sprawling, ultra-modern

Given the region's predominantly flat terrain, **cycling** around Prekmurje is a joy, and there's an excellent network of well-marked and well-maintained cycle paths to choose from. Moreover, with no two villages more than a few kilometres apart, there are plenty of opportunities to rest up before pushing on to the next destination. If you do plan to do some cycling, there's plenty of information and materials to assist. The best place to start is the excellent Bike Center (☎02/512-2186; ☒www. pomurjeonbike.com), whose shop is located within the grounds of the Terme 3000 spa in Moravske Toplice; as well as **renting bikes** (€10 per day), they also organize bicycle excursions – the website outlines ten routes throughout the region. The Cycling Around Prekmurje pamphlet, available from the tourist office in Moravske Toplice, details eight, each one indicating sights of interest, places to sleep and eat, as well as bike rental and repair shops; the 1:75,000 Pomurje map (€7) is also a useful aid. Bikes can also be rented (€2 per hour, €10 per day) from the tourist office, though these are not as good as those at the Bike Center.

complex incorporating one of the largest recreational centres in the country. Starting out in the 1960s, when thermal springs were discovered during a search for oil, the spa now comprises some twenty separate indoor and outdoor bathing areas featuring water and air massage pools, geysers and waterfalls, a diving pool, wave machines and enormous water slides (daily 9am–9pm; daily ticket €11, after 3pm €7, after 6pm €5).

There's plenty of accommodation on site, though neither of the (spa's) two adjoining **hotels** is particularly inspiring: the shiny four-star *Ajda* (☎02/512-2200; ❼) and the very similar but slightly cheaper *Termal* (❻). A far more pleasant alternative is the lovely thatched-roof, Prekmurje-style **bungalows** (❻) sheltered amongst trees on the opposite side of the complex (reception is in the *Ajda* hotel); or the huge *Prekmurska Vas* complex adjacent, which has newer **apartments** sleeping between two and five people (❻–❽) – reception is across the road. There's an excellent year-round **campsite** here too (☎02/512-1200). Guests of all the above accommodation receive free access to the spa pools.

Bikes can be rented from the Bike Center (€10 per day; Mon–Sat 9am–6pm, Sun 10am–2pm; ☎02/512-2186), located in a wooden hut near the campsite entrance. There's also **tennis** (€5 for 1hr) and an eighteen-hole **golf course**; green fees (€25 for 9 holes, €35 18 holes) must be paid at the reception in the *Ajda* Hotel.

The **tourist office** (Mon–Sat 8am–6pm, summer til 8pm, Sun 8am–2pm; ☎02/538-1520, ☒www.moravske-toplice.com) is situated amongst the small complex of shops as you enter the village (if coming by bus backtrack 200m from the bus stop at the entrance to the spa); they can assist in finding **private accommodation** (❷) in the area, of which there is plenty, and there are bikes for hire (see above). The *Flisar* tourist farm, 4km northwest of Moravske Toplice at Dolga ulica 216 (☎02/538-1320, ✉tur.kmetija-flisar@siol.net; ❷), is a terrific rural retreat, combining homely accommodation with fabulous domestic cooking. Likewise, there's the *Tremel* tourist farm (☎02/545-1017, ✉info@kmetija.tremel.si; ❷), a lovely renovated farmstead located further north in the village of Bokrači, at no. 28 (from Murska Sobota follow signs for Hodoš, then Sebeborci).

Around Moravske Toplice

Three of Prekmurje's most interesting villages – **Bogojina**, **Filovci** and **Beltinci** – are located between Moravske Toplice and Lendava, whilst another, **Selo**, is sited a short way to the north of Moravske Toplice near the Hungarian border. If you don't have your own transport, it's not difficult to hop from one village to the next using local bus services, although this is more difficult at weekends due to drastically reduced services.

Bogojina, Filovci and Beltinci

BOGOJINA, some 5km east of Moravske Toplice, is the location for what is perhaps Prekmurje's best-known church, the **Church of the Ascension** (Cerkev Vnebovhod). Visible from miles around – owing to its slight elevation above the rest of the village – the church was redesigned by Slovenia's greatest architect, Jože Plečnik (see box on p.62), between 1925 and 1927, and clearly manifests his trademark characteristics, from the high cylindrical tower to the columns, pillars and fanciful oddments gracing the interior. At the heart of this bright, single-nave hall-church is a monumental black marble column, from which four equally striking vaults emanate, built to help support the beautiful oak timber ceiling. In typically idiosyncratic fashion, Plečnik furnished the church with numerous flamboyant accessories, such as the ceramic plates and jugs ornamenting the ceiling and high altar. The village itself is exceptionally pretty, and it's an enjoyable fifteen-minute walk from the bus stop on the main road to the church, past rows of colourful Prekmurje-style farmhouses – L-shaped homesteads built on narrow strips of land perpendicular to the traffic routes.

The so-called *črna keramika*, or **black pottery**, industry, flourished in several villages hereabouts from the late eighteenth century onwards, and especially in **FILOVCI**, 2km further along the road from Bogojina. In the centre of the village, at no. 29 – walk across the small bridge and beyond the church – the Bojnec family offers pottery demonstrations in their workshop; they've also got a shop selling a wide range of earthenware. There is usually somebody at home, but to be sure you're best off contacting the tourist office in Moravske Toplice first.

If you're around during the last weekend of July, then don't miss the **Beltinci International Folklore Festival**, which takes place in the large village of **BELTINCI**, about 10km south of Bogojina – it is actually easier to reach the village via the faster road from Murska Sobota to Lendava. For over thirty years this superb festival has consistently attracted a high-calibre roster of both domestic and foreign folk groups, musicians and dance troupes, who perform over four days on several stages in the village's large and leafy manor park – Saturday is generally reckoned to be the best day. It's also a great opportunity to try out some traditional Prekmurje dishes at the many stalls spread out around the grounds.

The focal point of the park itself is the seventeenth-century L-shaped **Manor House**, now mostly decrepit and decaying, but which does house, in opposing corners on the gound floor, a **tourist office** (Mon–Fri 8am–1pm; ☎02/541-3580, ✉beltinci.info@siol.net), and the *Grajskem Stolpu* **restaurant**, a tidy and friendly place offering regional specialities (Mon–Sat 8am–10pm, Sun 7am–4pm).

Selo

From the village of **Tešanovci**, a kilometre or so east of Moravske Toplice, a road breaks left and climbs slowly up to the scattered settlement of **SELO**, some 10km distant. Standing in a field below the main road is the pinkish **Chapel of St Nicholas** (Rotunda Sv Nikolaj), a superb Romanesque rotunda built in the mid-thirteenth century. Its interior is adorned with some exceptional, albeit badly effaced, wall paintings, the upper half covered in scenes from the Adoration of the Magi and the Passion Cycle, and the dome smothered with evangelical symbols. To gain entrance to the church, you will need to call in at the roadside **information hut** (April–Oct daily 9am–5pm), whereupon someone with the key will escort you. Located 1km back along the road (before the church), the roadside gostilna, *K Rotundi* (Mon–Sat 11am–10pm, Sun 10am–4pm), is one of the region's best **restaurants**; as well as the standard Prekmurje specialities, it's known for its game and roast goat dishes.

Lendava and around

Wedged into the southeastern corner of Prekmurje, 31km from Murska Sobota and just a stone's throw from the Croatian and Hungarian borders, **LENDAVA** (Lendva in Hungarian) is Slovenia's easternmost town and also one of the largest bilingual settlements in the country, its sizeable Hungarian minority accounting for around a third of the town's population. Despite this harmonized ethnic union, it's a fairly low-key place, its relative isolation ensuring that few visitors make it to this remote little corner of the country.

Lendava's major **festival** is the *Bogračfest* on the first weekend of September, a culinary affair where dozens of teams line up along Glavna ulica to prepare the tastiest, meatiest goulash, accompanied by lots of wine and music.

Arrival, information and accommodation

Arriving at the **bus station** on Kolodvorska ulica, make your way across the ugly concrete square towards the *Hotel Elizabeta*, through the small complex of shops to the park; take a right here, up past the Ljubljanska bank to the triangle in the middle of the road. At this point turn left and you'll find yourself on Glavna ulica, location for the **tourist office** at no. 38 (Mon–Fri 8am–6pm, Sat 9am–2pm, Sun 9am–1pm; ☎02/578-8390, ⓦwww.lendava-turizem.si) – the helpful staff here can organize visits to several of the outlying attractions.

Aimed at nonexistent business travellers, the **hotel** *Elizabeta* (☎02/577-4600, Ⓔelizabeta.termelendava@siol.net; ❼) is a gleaming glass block at Mlinska ulica 5 (though it's actually sited on the aforementioned square) – the rooms are perfectly fine and comfortable, albeit pricey. The only other hotel hereabouts is the unattractive and absurdly overpriced *Lipa* (☎02/577-4100, ⓦwww.terme-lendava. si; ❸), which is actually part of the Lendava spa complex 1km south of town at Tomšičeva 2; more appealingly, they've got good-looking apartments sleeping two to four people (❺–❼), and a few spaces for **camping**.

The Town

The town's major attraction is the **castle**, reached via a steep path next to the **Parish Church of St Catherine**, midway along the main thoroughfare, Glavna ulica. Although a fortification of sorts stood here as early as the twelfth century, the present castle was rebuilt by the noble Hungarian Esterházy family between 1712 and 1717, remaining within their possession until the beginning of World War II. It now houses a modest **museum** (Mon–Fri 9am–4pm, Sat 9am–2pm; €2), containing a rather ordinary collection of Bronze Age artefacts, weaponry from battles with the Turks, and a small ethnographic collection.

The only other two sites of note are located on the opposite side of Glavna ulica near the town park. Built in 1866, the **synagogue** (Mon–Fri noon–4pm, Sat & Sun 9am–1pm) on Župančičeva ulica was cleared out, along with the town's several-hundred-strong Jewish population, during World War II. Thanks to the recent completion of a decade-long rebuilding programme, it has been restored to something like its former self, and now accommodates a few exhibits – mainly photo documentation and religious items – from the pre-World War II period. Sadly, there is no longer a Jewish community in town. After a decade of protracted wrangling over finances, the extraordinary building in the park opposite – designed

Slovenia's Roma

Most of Slovenia's estimated seven thousand **Gypsies**, or **Roma**, many of whom settled in the country following the wars in Croatia and Bosnia, live in small, scattered settlements throughout Prekmurje, such as Črenšovci, near Lendava, and Pušča, on the western outskirts of Murska Sobota. The majority of the remainder of the Roma community live in southeast Dolenjska and Bela Krajina. Although the lot of the Roma in Slovenia is considerably better than that of those in many other countries of the former Eastern Bloc – Slovenia is one of the few European countries that have included the Roma in the constitution – discrimination is still commonplace. Moreover, living conditions remain, on the whole, substandard, with many settlements still lacking basic infrastructure, whilst standards of education are low and unemployment remains unacceptably high.

While the rights of the Roma community are not nearly as well protected as those of the country's Hungarian and Italian minorities, the situation is improving. In recent years, the state has made concerted attempts to integrate them into the majority culture. The most significant piece of legislation, adopted in 2002, allowed for Romany community representatives to be elected to local councils in more than twenty municipalities. The Roma community, too, have made concentrated efforts to organize themselves into coherent groups, such as the Union of Roma of Slovenia (the country's major Roma organization), which was formed in 1991 following Slovene independence. Amongst its many activities, it publishes the magazine *Romano Them* (*Romany News*), as well as producing Roma plays and numerous other publishing and theatrical initiatives.

by the renowned, and controversial, Hungarian architect **Imre Makovecz** – has finally been converted into the town's cultural centre, the centerpiece of which is a fine theatre, with Slovene and Hungarian productions sharing equal billing.

Nestled amongst the winegrowing **Lendava Hills** (Lendavske Gorice), less than 1km southeast of town, is the **Church of the Holy Trinity** (Cerkev Sv Trojian), a standard Baroque issue built in 1728. The church is notable, however, for holding the grisly, mummified body of local warrior Mihael Hladik, slain by the Turks in 1603, but whose immaculately preserved body – take a peek if you wish – was miraculously discovered in a casket during construction of the castle chapel in 1728. If you wish to visit the church contact the tourist office, and a member of staff will accompany you. If you fancy a wallow, head over to the **Terme Lendava Spa** (daily 7am–8pm, Fri & Sat til 11pm; €8 for day-ticket, €6 after 1pm), 1km south of town at Tomšičeva 2; one of the country's warmest spas, it has two indoor and three outdoor (May–Sept) pools, with temperatures between 29 and 37 degrees.

Eating and drinking

The *Domačija* **restaurant**, opposite the *Hotel Elizabeta* on Mlinksa ulica, is pretty much the only place to eat in town, but really only suffices for a cheap and filling lunch (Mon–Sat 7am–8pm). The best spot for a drink is the *Theatre Café* inside the cultural centre (daily 8am–9pm), while there's also good coffee, and free **Internet access**, at *Banffy* (Mon–Sat 7.30am–9pm, Sun 8am–noon), a lovely, restful spot just along from the tourist office on Glavna ulica. **Wine** buffs may care to visit the Cuk Wine Cellar at Lendavske Gorice 217 (☎02/575-1815), a lovely little hillside cellar 1km southeast of town on the fringe of the Lendava Hills; contact the tourist office if you're interested in some tasting (about €6 for five wines). They've also got a handful of rooms (**③**) and apartments (**④**) if you wish to stop over.

Velika Polana and Črenšovci

If you've got your own transport, there are two villages of interest a short way from Lendava. **VELIKA POLANA**, around 10km west of Lendava, is one of Europe's officially designated **stork villages** thanks to the dozen or so storks that pitch up here and in some of the neighbouring villages each spring. Attracted by the abundance of food, especially frogs and toads, to be found in the nearby marshes and swamplands, the storks usually return to the same nest (improbably bulky constructions perched atop telegraph poles or chimneys) they occupied the previous year. The female will usually lay between three and five eggs, then incubate them for around five weeks before they hatch in July or August. The offspring normally fledge at around eight or nine weeks. Whether kicking back in their nests, or skulking around the local fields foraging for food, these birds offer irresistible photo opportunities.

Around five kilometres further west of Velika Polana, the dusty little community of **Kamenci**, actually an adjunct of the village of **ČRENŠOVCI**, is home to one of the largest **Roma settlements** in Prekmurje. A few members of this community of around one hundred have joined forces with the tourist office in Lendava to offer organized visits, which include a programme of entertainment featuring traditional Roma music and dance. There is also a small **Gypsy Museum** here, the first and only one of its kind in the country.

Travel details

Trains

Celje to: Laško (every 45min–2hr; 10min); Ljubljana (every 45min–2hr; 1hr–1hr 40min); Maribor (every 45min–2hr; 45min–1hr 10min); Podčetrtek (Mon–Fri 5 daily; 45min); Rogaška Slatina (Mon–Fri 6 daily; 45min); Velenje (Mon–Fri 9 daily, Sat 2; 50min).
Dravograd to: Maribor (Mon–Fri 5 daily; 1hr 40min).
Ljutomer to: Ljubljana (Mon–Fri 6 daily, Sat & Sun 3 daily; 3hr 10min); Murska Sobota (Mon–Fri 9 daily, Sat & Sun 3 daily; 20min); Ormož (Mon–Fri 8 daily, Sat & Sun 3 daily; 25min).
Maribor to: Celje (every 45min–2hr; 45min–1hr 10min); Dravograd (Mon–Fri 5 daily; 1hr 40min); Ljubljana (every 45min–2hr; 1hr 45min–2hr 45min).
Murska Sobota to: Ljubljana (Mon–Fri 6 daily, Sat & Sun 3 daily; 3hr 30min); Ljutomer (Mon–Fri 9 daily, Sat & Sun 3 daily; 20min); Ormož (Mon–Fri 9 daily, Sat & Sun 3 daily; 45min); Ptuj (Mon–Fri 7 daily, Sat & Sun 4 daily; 50min–1hr 10min).
Ormož to: Ljubljana (Mon–Fri 8 daily, Sat & Sun 3 daily; 2hr 50min): Ljutomer (Mon–Fri 8 daily, Sat & Sun 3 daily; 25min); Murska Sobota (Mon–Fri 9 daily, Sat & Sun 3 daily; 45min); Ptuj (Mon–Fri 12 daily, Sat & Sun 5 daily; 25min).
Podčetrtek to: Celje (Mon–Fri 6 daily; 45min).
Ptuj to: Ljubljana (Mon–Fri 8 daily, Sat & Sun 3

daily; 2hr 30min–3hr); Murska Sobota (Mon–Fri 7 daily, Sat & Sun 4 daily; 50min–1hr 10min); Ormož (Mon–Fri 12 daily, Sat & Sun 5 daily; 25min).
Rogaška Slatina to: Celje (Mon–Fri 5 daily; 45min).
Velenje to: Celje (Mon–Fri 9 daily, Sat 2; 50min).

Buses

Celje to: Laško (Mon–Fri 9 daily, Sat 5; 15min); Ljubljana (Mon–Fri 11 daily, Sat & Sun 4 daily; 1hr 30min); Maribor (Mon–Fri 10 daily, Sat & Sun 4 daily; 1hr 15min); Murska Sobota (2 daily; 2hr 30min); Rogaška Slatina (Mon–Fri 8 daily, Sat 4, Sun 3; 40min); Slovenske Konjice (Mon–Fri hourly, Sat & Sun 4 daily; 25min); Velenje (Mon–Fri hourly, Sat 5, Sun 2; 25min); Zreče (Mon–Fri 8 daily; 25min).
Črna na Koroškem to: Dravograd (Mon–Fri hourly, Sat 8, Sun 4; 45min); Maribor (3 daily; 1hr 50min); Slovenj Gradec (Mon–Fri hourly, Sat 8, Sun 4; 50min); Velenje (Mon–Fri 6 daily, Sat & Sun 4 daily; 50min).
Dravograd to: Celje (1 daily; 1hr 10min); Črna na Koroškem (Mon–Fri every 30min–hourly, Sat 8, Sun 5; 45min); Maribor (Mon–Fri 9 daily, Sat & Sun 6 daily; 1hr 15min); Slovenj Gradec (Mon–Sat every 30min–hourly, Sun 8; 20min); Velenje (Mon–Fri every 45min–hourly, Sat & Sun 6 daily; 40min).

Lendava to: Črenšovci (Mon–Fri 10 daily; 25min); Maribor (Mon–Fri 4 daily, Sat 2; 1hr 40min); Murska Sobota (Mon–Fri hourly, Sat 2; 40min); Moravske Toplice (Mon–Fri 6 daily, Sat 1; 15min).
Ljutomer to: Murska Sobota (Mon–Fri 8 daily; 40min); Ormož (Mon–Fri 5 daily; 30min).
Maribor to: Celje (Mon–Fri 8 daily, Sat & Sun 4 daily; 1hr 15min); Dravograd (Mon–Fri 9 daily, Sat & Sun 6 daily; 1hr 15min); Ljubljana (Mon–Fri 6 daily, Sat & Sun 4 daily; 2hr 30min–3hr); Ljutomer (Mon–Fri 3 daily, Sat & Sun 1 daily; 1hr 20min); Murska Sobota (Mon–Fri every 30mins, Sat 7, Sun 3; 1hr 10min); Ormož (Mon–Fri 4 daily, Sat & Sun 1 daily; 50min); Ptuj (Mon–Fri every 45mins–hourly, Sat hourly, Sun 6; 30min) Radenci (Mon–Sat every 30–45mins, Sat 8, Sun 6; 1hr); Slovenske Konjice (Mon–Fri 8 daily, Sat & Sun 3 daily; 50min).
Moravske Toplice to: Bogojina & Filovci (en route to Dubrovnik) (Mon–Fri 8 daily; 10min); Lendava (Mon–Fri 3 daily; 30min); Murska Sobota (Mon–Fri 10 daily; 10min).
Murska Sobota to: Bakovci Mon–Fri 8 daily; 15min); Beltinci (Mon–Fri every 20–30min, Sat 5, Sun 2; 15min); Bogojina (Mon–Fri 9 daily; 20min); Filovci (Mon–Fri 9 daily; 25min); Lendava (Mon–Fri hourly, Sat & Sun 3 daily; 40min); Ljutomer (Mon–Fri 8 daily; 40min); Maribor (Mon–Fri hourly, Sat & Sun 5 daily; 1hr 10min); Moravske Toplice (Mon–Fri 10 daily; 10min); Radenci (Mon–Fri every 20–30mins, Sat 7, Sun 5; 15min).
Ormož to: Ljutomer (Mon–Fri 7 daily; 30min); Maribor (Mon–Fri 2 daily, Sat 1; 50min); Ptuj (Mon–Fri 8 daily, Sat 4; 30min).
Podčetrtek to: Bistrica ob Sotli (Mon–Fri 6 daily; 25min); Celje (Mon–Fri 5 daily; 45min); Rogaška Slatina (Mon–Fri hourly, Sat 4 daily; 20min).
Ptuj to: Ljutomer (Mon–Fri 2 daily; 1hr 10min); Maribor (Mon–Sat every 30min, Sat 9, Sun 6; 30min); Ormož (Mon–Fri 9 daily, Sat 1; 30min); Ptujska Gora (5 daily; 20min); Rogaška Slatina (Mon–Fri 1 daily; 1hr 5min).

Rogaška Slatina to: Celje (Mon–Fri 9 daily, Sat & Sun 3 daily; 40min); Maribor (Mon–Fri 3 daily; 1hr 10min); Podčetrtek (Mon–Fri hourly, Sat & Sun 4 daily; 20min); Ptuj (Mon–Fri 1 daily; 1hr 5min); Rogatec (Mon–Fri 8 daily, Sat & Sun 3 daily; 15min).
Rogatec to: Celje (Mon–Fri 6 daily, Sat 2; 50min); Ptuj (Mon–Fri 1 daily; 1hr 20min); Rogaška Slatina (Mon–Fri 4 daily, Sat 2; 15min).
Slovenj Gradec to: Celje (1 daily; 45min); Dravograd (Mon–Fri every 45min–hourly, Sat & Sun 10 daily; 20min); Ljubljana (2 daily; 2hr); Maribor (2 daily; 1hr 20min); Velenje (Mon–Fri every 45min–hourly, Sat & Sun 10 daily; 25min).
Slovenske Konjice to: Celje (Mon–Fri hourly, Sat & Sun 4 daily; 25min); Ljubljana (Mon–Fri 8 daily, Sat & Sun 5 daily; 2hr 15min); Maribor (Mon–Fri 8 daily, Sat & Sun 3 daily; 50min); Zreče (Mon–Fri every 45min–hourly; 10min).
Velenje to: Celje (Mon–Sat hourly, Sat 5, Sun 3; 25min); Črna na Koroškem (Mon–Fri hourly, Sat 6, Sun 4; 50min); Dravograd (Mon–Fri hourly, Sat 6, Sun 4, 40min), Ljubljana (Mon–Fri 3 daily, Sat & Sun 2 daily; 1hr 30min); Slovenj Gradec (Mon–Sat hourly, Sun 6; 25min).
Zreče to: Celje (Mon–Fri 8 daily, Sat & Sun 1 daily; 25min); Slovenske Konjice (Mon–Fri hourly, Sat & Sun 4 daily; 10min).

International trains

Maribor to: Graz (4 daily; 1hr 15min); Vienna (3 daily; 3hr 45min).
Murska Sobota to: Budapest (2 daily; 5hr 15min).

International buses

Lendava to: Čakovec (Croatia) (Mon–Sat 1 daily).
Ptuj to: Zagreb (Mon–Sat 1 daily).
Maribor to: Graz (Mon–Fri 1 daily at 7.20am).

Contexts

Contexts

The historical framework

Although recorded history of the area now covered by Slovenia begins with the arrival of the Romans, archeological finds suggest that this territory was already settled in the **Paleolithic** and **Neolithic** eras. The most intriguing discovery from the Paleolithic era was a bone flute unearthed from a cave in Šebrelje near Cerkno in 1995, whilst the most compelling evidence of the existence of a Neolithic culture comes from the Ljubljana Marshes south of the capital. Here, the inhabitants built wooden huts on stilts, made coarse pottery and raised livestock.

The early Iron Age, or **Hallstatt**, period (eighth to fourth centuries BC) coincided with the arrival of the region's first identifiable peoples – Illyrian-speaking tribes, possibly called Veneti, who settled in the Alpine region. The major Hallstatt settlements were located in Most na Soči and throughout the region of Dolenjska, as indicated by some superb archeological finds in these areas, such as armour, jewellery and *situlae* (ornately embossed pails, or buckets). More generally, this was a period of great economic and cultural advancement. Around the third century BC the Hallstatt cultures were superseded by the Celts who, led by the Norics, established a protostate called **Noricum**, the centre of which was located in the eastern Alps, whilst a second centre was established in the area of present-day Celje, then called **Celeia**.

The Romans

Noricum was subsumed into the Roman Empire around 10 BC, which more or less marked the beginning of **Roman occupation** in this territory. Settled by colonists from Aquileia (a small town in the Gulf of Trieste established by the Romans in 181 BC), Emona (Ljubljana) was the first Roman town to develop on the territory of present-day Slovenia, followed by Poetovio (Ptuj) and Celeia (Celje). Trade, administration and culture grew up around these garrison towns and spread along the roads constructed to link the imperial heartland with Pannonia and beyond. Some of the country's best-preserved **Roman remains** are still to be found in and around these towns, including vestigial ruins in Ljubljana, a wealth of monuments in Ptuj, and a superb Roman necropolis in Šempeter, just outside Celje. The most significant legacy of the Roman occupation was the partition of the Byzantine and Roman spheres – the Eastern and Western empires respectively – into separate civilizations, a division that would later result in a critical split between the Eastern Orthodox and Roman Catholic churches. The disintegration of the Roman Empire in the fifth century corresponded with a series of incursions into the region by a multitude of warring tribes, such as the Huns, Ostrogoths and Lombards, and the all-powerful **Avars**, a Turkic people from Central Asia whose empire survived well into the eighth century, before it was crushed by the Franks.

From the first Slav state to Habsburg rule

Although there is no definitive record as to when, or from where, the ancestors of today's Slovenes first entered the territory of present-day Slovenia, the most widespread theory is that migrating Slav tribes (loosely divided into two different, but related, groups, Slaveni and Antes) arrived from the Carpathian Basin in the middle of the sixth century. As Avar power waned, these tribes, along with others (including the great Kingdom of Samo), united into a loose confederation, resulting in the first Slav political entity, the **Duchy of Karantanija**, whose centre was located somewhere near present-day Klagenfurt just across the border in Austria. This brief period of autonomy lasted until 745 AD, when the Duchy was subsumed into the Carolingian Empire of the Franks, thus subjecting the Karantanian Slav population to a Germanic domination that would continue for several centuries more. Around the same time, an influx of western missionaries and the establishment of a formal church paved the way for the **Christianization of the Slovenes**.

In the tenth century, the Magyars, led by the feared Arpad clan, invaded and settled in the Slovenian regions of Pannonia. Before they were able to advance any further, however, they ran into the imperial forces of the German king, Otto I, who promptly routed them in a counter-offensive just outside Augsburg in 955 AD. German victory instigated the reorganization of Karantanian territory into frontier marches, namely, Carinthia (Koroška), Carniola (Kranjska), Styria (Štajerska), Gorica (Goriška) and Bela Krajina, the boundaries of which would essentially remain the same for the next thousand years.

The first chartered towns on Slovene territory – Kamnik, Piran, Ptuj, Škofja Loka, and the capital Ljubljana – began to develop a short while thereafter, around the beginning of the twelfth century. By the fourteenth century there would be some 27 towns and countless other market towns in Slovene lands, many of which developed trade and crafts industries as an adjunct to agricultural activity. Cultural life during this period, meanwhile, was mostly centred around the newly established monasteries, such as the Carthusian orders at Pleterje and Žiče, and the Cistercian orders at Kostanjevica and Stična. Although primarily schools for the education of the clergy, they also served a wider educational purpose, functioning as key centres of learning for intellectuals, musicians and so on. Meanwhile, the prominent ruling entities of this time – the Bamberg, Spanheim and Premysl dynasties – were confronted with the spectre of the Habsburgs who, by 1270, had already established a stronghold in the eastern Alps and would soon rule across most of the Slovene lands.

Habsburg rule, Turkish invasions and the Reformation

The **Habsburg dynasty** established its first feudal holdings in Slovene lands (the provinces of Carniola, Gorizia, Istria, Carinthia and Styria) in 1282, holding sway across most of the territory until the end of World War I, whilst small geographical areas in the eastern and western peripheries were governed by Hungary and Venice respectively. The only serious political rivals to the Habsburgs at this time were the **counts of Celje**, an aristocratic dynasty who, through a combination of fortuitous politics and skilfully arranged marriages into distinguished European feudal houses, managed to acquire great swathes of territory and wield tremendous influence across Slovene lands. Whilst the assassination of Count Ulrik II in Belgrade in 1456 nullified this particular threat, the Habsburgs now had to contend with other problems.

Having already conquered much of the Balkan peninsula in the first half of the fifteenth century, the **Ottoman Turks** resumed their advance north towards Slovene lands around 1470. Despite repeated raids, which reached their peak during the reign of Sultan Suleyman I "the Magnificent" (1520–66), the defining moment was the **Battle of Sisak** in 1593, where the Turks were crushed by combined Habsburg-Croatian forces, an episode which effectively put the lid on Turkish aspirations in Habsburg-occupied lands.

The economic pressures engendered as a result of these assaults, coupled with the transformation of the old feudal tax system into less favourable forms, precipitated a series of violent and widespread **peasant revolts** throughout Slovene lands. The most famous of these was the 1573 uprising, during which some ten thousand Slovene and Croatian peasants (*puntarji*) participated. In the event, the rebellion was crushed and its leader, Matija Gubec, met a somewhat ignominious fate (crowned with a red-hot metal rod in Zagreb Cathedral), while the peasants were bound to perpetual serfdom. The prevalence of serfdom and other local agricultural policies meant that there was little other economic activity to speak of around this time, though pockets of proto-industrialization existed in parts of the country, for example, the Idrija mercury mine and the forges in Kropa.

The **Germanization** of culture, education and administration had been a key policy of Habsburg rule since the tenth century, yet despite this, Slovenes managed to preserve both their language and cultural identity. This was largely down to **Protestant reformers** such as **Primož Trubar** (the "Slovene Luther"), who wrote and published the first book in the Slovene language, and **Adam Bohorič**, who compiled the first Slovene grammar book, which was also the first grammar book in a Slav language. It would, however, be another two centuries before written Slovene would be appropriated for secular use. Having seen off the Turks, the Austrians, under Archduke Ferdinand, turned their attention to the religious revolts taking place throughout Habsburg lands, and by the end of the century the **Counter-Reformation** was in full swing. The ensuing period of recatholicization and absolutism resulted in a lengthy spell of political, economic and cultural regression for Slovenes.

The eighteenth century: reform and the Enlightenment

Prospects looked decidedly brighter at the turn of the eighteenth century owing to strong economic growth and modernization, manifest in the development of manufacturing industries – forges in Bohinj and Jesenice, textile mills in Ljubljana, improved transport links between Vienna and Trieste (via Maribor, Celje and Ljubljana) and the declaration of Trieste as a free port. These developments were taken a stage further under the centralized, state-building reforms of **Maria Theresa** and her son **Joseph II** during the second half of the century: judicial reforms were introduced, primary schooling was made compulsory and religious tolerance was decreed. More tendentiously, German replaced Latin as the language of government business, a move that caused some alarm amongst the emerging national groups, many of whom preferred to use their own language.

Led by the cultural innovator **Baron Žiga Zois** and a small coterie of Slovene intellectuals (the so-called "Zois Circle"), the **Slovene Enlightenment** (roughly 1760–1820) was the first sustained period of cultural advancement since the work of the sixteenth-century Protestant reformers. This celebrated group featured the historian/playwright **Anton Linhart**, poet/journalist **Valentin Vodnik** – founder of the first Slovene newspaper, *Ljubljanske Novice* (*The Ljubljana News*)

– and the priest, **Marko Pohlin**, whose 1768 publication, *Kranjska gramatika* (Carniolan Grammar), was the forerunner to a modern Slovene literary language. In addition, theatres in Ljubljana, Maribor and Celje were built, public and private libraries became the focus for Slovene cultural life, and the establishment of assorted professional and cultural societies and institutions, including the Philharmonic Music Society (1794) and the literary and linguistic society, Academia Operosorum, affirmed Slovenia's integration into the circle of cultured European nations. It was also a time of great **Baroque** extravagance, particularly in the fields of architecture, painting and sculpture. Nowhere was this more so than in Ljubljana, which acquired several beautiful churches, church paintings and buildings. Leading Baroque contributors included the painters Valentin Metzinger and Giulio Quaglio, architect Andrea Pozzo, and sculptor Francesco Robba, whose Fountain of the Three Carniolan Rivers in Ljubljana is one of the finest specimens of Baroque-era artwork in the country.

The nineteenth century: nationalism and reform

Following **Napoleon's** dissolution of the Venetian republic in 1797, the French were drawn into several wars against the Austrians, culminating in a hard-fought victory for the French at Wagram in 1809. Subsequent to this, Napoleon cut the Austrians off from the Adriatic and created a quasi-ethnic state, stretching from Graz in Austria down to the Bay of Kotor in Montenegro, a region known as the **Illyrian Provinces**. Over the next four years, and with Ljubljana designated as the provinces' administrative centre, Slovenes enjoyed a series of liberating French reforms, the most important of which was free use of the Slovene language in administration and schools. Following Napoleon's disastrous defeat at the hands of the Russians in 1813, and the subsequent collapse of the French Empire, Slovene territory was reincorporated into the Habsburg domain and all the old political and feudal systems were restored. Nevertheless, four years of French rule was long enough for Slovene intellectuals to be made aware of their ethno-national identities; moreover the inclusion of Croats, as well as a minority Serb population, within the same state gave rise to the notion that some form of common Slav union might one day be realized. These embryonic national sentiments were powerfully reinforced through the work of Slovenia's pre-eminent Romantic poet and greatest-ever literary figure, **France Prešeren** (see box, p.126), who not only refashioned Slovenian as a literary language but raised it to the level of other European languages. It was no surprise, therefore, when Prešeren's poem, *Zdravljica* (*A Toast*), was adopted as the Slovene national anthem in 1991.

The **1848 Revolution** was the catalyst for tremendous upheaval across continental Europe, including Austria, where the tenets of absolutism and serfdom had reigned since the demise of the Illyrian provinces in 1813. Fired by the literary brilliance of Prešeren and the pedagogic reforms of **Anton Slomšek** (the bishop of Maribor), **Slovene nationalism** became increasingly vocal around this time, culminating in calls for a **United Slovenia programme** (*Zedinjena Slovenija*), whose prime objectives were to unite all ethnic Slovene territories within one autonomous region and to promulgate the use of the Slovene language. In the event, no such programme was ever realized, though its basic tenets informed much of Slovene political life well into the next century. By and large though, most Slovenes remained committed to Austria and few envisaged a future outside the Habsburg Empire.

According to the terms of the **Compromise of 1867**, the Habsburg state became the **Dual Monarchy of Austria–Hungary**, whereby the two became constitutionally separate entities, albeit with the same Habsburg ruler, Franz Jozef – emperor in Austria and king in Hungary. In practice this meant shared common foreign and defence policies, but internally, each was governed by its own constitution. As a result of the compromise most Slovenes remained within Austria, though a small, yet significant, number were incorporated into Hungarian and Italian sectors. Around this time Slovenes began to make important strides politically, organizing themselves into distinct and identifiable political groupings, and by the end of the century three core parties had been established: the liberal **National Progressive Party**, the conservative, or clerical **Slovene People's Party**, and the socialist **Yugoslav Democratic Party**. Each of these parties presented alternative political philosophies, but they collectively espoused a common commitment to some form of pan-Slavism, or **Yugoslavism**, a political concept that had initially taken root earlier that century. However, despite adopting broadly nationalist agendas, which were largely premised upon the United Slovenia programme of some years earlier, all three parties remained firmly committed to their Austrian overlords, aware that they were too small and there were too few of them (even with their Slav allies) to go it alone. Instead, they concluded that **Trialism** – the notion that a third element, a South Slav component, would be created within the Habsburg Empire – could be the only possible framework for any form of Slovene self-determination. The latter part of the century was also a time of cultural efflorescence for Slovenes, manifest in the establishment of **reading societies** (*čitalnice*), the **Slovene Literary Society** (Slovenska Matica) and other gazettes, and the **Sokol** (Falcon) association, a patriotic gymnastic society which advocated the cult of the healthy body as well as Slavonic brotherhood.

In the two decades prior to World War I, Slovene political life became increasingly preoccupied with the idea of Yugoslavism, and while most Slovenes ostensibly remained loyal to Austria, there were those who felt increasingly uneasy with regard to Austria's domestic and foreign policies, and in particular its progressively cosy alliance with Germany. Championing the Yugoslav cause was the celebrated novelist **Ivan Cankar**, who posited that some form of linguistic and cultural merging was both practical and desirable. Cankar was closely associated with the avowedly anti-Austrian student organization **Preporod** (Rebirth), who, along with other South Slav groups, including the ultra-nationalist Young Bosnian movement from Sarajevo, advocated an independent Yugoslav state. Following the **assassination of Archduke Franz Ferdinand** in Sarajevo in 1914 by Gavrilo Princip (a member of the Young Bosnians), Austria declared war on Serbia. Within a matter of days, Europe's major alliance systems had been activated – Germany joined forces with Austria, whilst their opponents, who supported Serbia, were the Entente powers of Russia, France and Britain.

World War I and the Kingdom of Serbs, Croats and Slovenes

During the formative stages of **World War I**, Slovenes fought in several arenas on behalf of the Austrian crown, including the Serbian and Russian fronts, though the prospect of fighting fellow Slavs appealed to few Slovenes and defections were common. The single most important factor affecting Slovenia during the course of the war was the **1915 London Pact**, under the terms of which Italians were persuaded to join the Entente forces in return for promises of land populated by Slovenes and Croats. Galvanized into action, Slovenes pitched in with the Austrians along the western, **Soča front**, which extended for some 90km from Mount Rombon, near Bovec, along the course of the Soča river down to a position just north of Trieste on the Adriatic coast. The Soča Front was one of the bloodiest battlegrounds of the entire war, with catastrophic losses on both sides, though particularly for the Italians who were routed during the famous twelfth and final offensive in the Krn mountain range above Kobarid in October 1917.

With an increasingly mutinous Slovene military, and the Habsburg Empire on the verge of collapse, a group of South Slav delegates, led by Slovene Anton Korošec, presented the **May 1917 declaration** to Vienna demanding the creation of an autonomous, democratic Slav state within the Habsburg monarchy. The demand was dismissed, but support for a unitary state continued apace and in October 1918, Serb, Croat and Slovene political leaders convened in Zagreb to form the **National Council**, at the same time declaring their independence from Budapest and Vienna. Little more than a month later, on December 1, 1918 in Belgrade, Serbian Prince Alexander Karađorđević declared the establishment of the **Kingdom of Serbs, Croats and Slovenes**, which also incorporated the territories of Bosnia, Montenegro and Macedonia.

At the end of the war, Slovenia's ethnic territory was subject to widescale dismemberment: whilst the greater part of Slovenia was incorporated into the kingdom, a significant portion of southern Carinthia was ceded to Austria and, under the terms of the **1920 Treaty of Rapallo**, almost a third of Slovene territory – which included the economically important cities of Trieste and Gorizia – was annexed to Italy. The first few years under Italian jurisdiction were bearable, but the situation worsened considerably following Mussolini's ascent to power: political and cultural institutions were banned, public use of the Slovene language was abolished (except in Catholic churches), and all Slavic geographical names were Italianized. Whilst large numbers of Slovenes chose to emigrate during this heightened period of Italian irredentism, many more established political, social and cultural organizations and underground movements, in order to fight for minority rights – some, such as the terror group, **TIRG** (Trst, Istra, Reka, Gorica), had several of its members executed.

For Slovenes living within the new kingdom, the situation was not much better than it was for those in Italy or Austria, and certainly not what they had in mind when they cast their lot with that of their fellow southern Slavs. The centralistic **1921 Vidovdan Constitution**, which established a parliamentary, constitutional monarchy for the kingdom, with Belgrade as its capital and Karađorđević as head of state, immediately buried any aspirations Slovenes (and other constituent groups within the state) may have had for political autonomy. Although traditional liberties were largely protected by the constitution, the rights of liberals and communists were frequently infringed and the king wielded almost absolute power. Years of political chaos – ineffectual governments, high-profile assassinations and persistent attempts to undermine Serb rule – culminated in the suspension of the constitution in January 1929. A **royal dictatorship** was imposed and the Kingdom of Serbs, Croats and Slovenes was recast as the **Kingdom of Yugoslavia**, ostensibly to foster Yugoslav political unitarism but which was ultimately a disaster for all non-Serbs. Increasingly violent nationalist strains began to emerge amongst the constituent groups, particularly in Croatia, where the ultranationalist, proto-fascist **Ustaše** movement were particularly prominent – it was they who masterminded the assassination of King Alexander Karađorđević in Marseille in 1934. Authority, thereafter, passed to Prince Paul, whose regime merely escalated anti-Serb sentiment.

Another organization opposed to the unitary Yugoslav state was the **Communist Party of Yugoslavia** (CPY), which, from the time of its formation in 1919 until the mid-1930s, had remained a largely underground movement, with many of its congresses held abroad and most of its activity supervised from Moscow. With the appointment, in 1937, of **Josip Broz Tito** as its leader, the party began to reorganize itself into a federation of national units – hence the birth of the **Communist Party of Slovenia** (CPS). Of immediate concern to Slovenia was the menacing presence of Italian Fascism and German imperialism, for both Italy and Germany had territorial designs on Slovene lands.

World War II

Whereas in World War I Slovenia and the other Slav states found themselves embroiled in combat from the very start, it was over eighteen months after the start of **World War II** before Yugoslavia (and by implication, Slovenia) became involved. By this time much of continental Europe had already fallen under the sway of Germany and Italy. After initially being cowed into joining the Axis powers' orbit, Yugoslavia renounced the decision following a governmental coup, a decision they paid for on April 6, 1941, when Germany blitzed Belgrade. The king fled in exile to London and within a matter of days the country had capitulated. For its part, Slovenia was partitioned between Germany, which claimed the northern and eastern areas, Hungary, which took Prekmurje, and Italy, which annexed the rest. While the Italians were more or less sympathetic to Slovenes, allowing them a measure of cultural autonomy, those in the German and Hungarian occupied territories were subject to aggressive denaturalizing policies – arrests, torture, execution and deportation.

In response, **resistance groups** took up arms almost immediately. Organized by the CPY, with Tito as chief military commander, a **Yugoslav Partisan resistance** movement was established. In Slovenia, the **Liberation Front** (OF – Osvobodilna Fronta) was formed, organized and controlled by the CPS and comprising Christian Socialists, the liberal Sokols and leftist intellectuals, as well as party members. The Liberation Front was broken up into smaller Partisan units, dispersed throughout the cities and countryside – circumstances, however, dictated that in the early stages at least, the Slovenes and Tito's Partisans were mostly detached from each other. The Slovene Partisan army continued in a fairly independent manner until 1944, when they joined forces in a wider pan-Yugoslav resistance movement, which had by now received official recognition from the Allies. By this stage Tito had already moved to establish a provisional government, the **Anti-Fascist Assembly for the National Liberation of Yugoslavia** (AVNOJ), which laid down the principles for the eventual Yugoslav state. For the most part, the terms of the programme – one of which made provision for a republic's right to self-determination (this was later dropped) – were welcomed by the Slovenes, as confirmed by their participation at the second AVNOJ meeting in Jajce, Bosnia, in 1943.

Communist resistance was complicated by conflicting political ideologies within Slovenia, which manifested itself in the emergence of several armed organizations. The most prominent of these was the **Home Guard** (Domobranci), a major anti-Communist organization formed in Ljubljana in September 1943 with the approval and assistance of the Germans. Their resistance, however, didn't last long. Faced by overwhelming Partisan force, the Guard was forced to retreat into Austrian Carinthia, where they were met by the British and disarmed as German collaborators. Following their repatriation to Slovenia and the waiting Partisans, thousands of guardists and anti-Communist civilians (estimates suggest up to ten thousand in total) were executed and thrown into pits close to the Liberation Fronts' wartime headquarters in the forests of Kočevski Rog in southern Slovenia. The grisly secrets were only revealed to the wider Slovene public some thirty years later, when politician and writer Edvard Kocbek spilled the beans in an interview with a Trieste newspaper.

Having finally driven the occupying forces from Slovene territory in May 1945, the Partisans liberated Trieste that same month, but just two months later the Western Allies issued an ultimatum requiring Yugoslav forces to leave. At the 1946 Paris Peace Conference the region was partitioned into two zones: Zone A (Trieste and hinterland), controlled by the Allies, and Zone B (Slovene coast and Istria), controlled by Yugoslavia. The **1954 London Agreement** restored Zone A to Italy, thus bringing an end to a bitter and long-standing dispute, though many Italians returned to Italy, as others had done at the end of the war.

The second Yugoslavia: Tito and socialism

Following the émigré government's recognition of Tito as *de facto* leader, **elections** were held towards the end of 1945, though these were something of a foregone conclusion, given that the only party standing was the **People's Front**, an organization dominated by the Communist Party. Following these elections, the monarchy was abolished and in November the **Federal People's Republic of Yugoslavia** was proclaimed, comprising six federal republics – Serbia, Croatia, Bosnia, Macedonia, Montenegro and Slovenia.

Power was now incontrovertibly held in the hands of the Communists, who sought to emulate the Soviet model of control, a system shaped by central planning, nationalization of property and ideological conformity – this also included a substantial amount of **forced industrialization** throughout the entire country, although the speed with which this was done created numerous problems, not least the decline in agricultural practices, as individual and large institutional landowners were expropriated without compensation. A critical rift over political and ideological differences between the Soviet Union and Yugoslavia in 1948 resulted in the latter's **expulsion from the Cominform**, the Soviet-controlled organization of European Communist countries. The split effected an almost immediate (albeit cosmetic) change in name of both the Communist Party of Yugoslavia, renamed the **League of Communists of Yugoslavia** (LCY), and the Communist Party of Slovenia, renamed the **League of Communists of Slovenia** (LCS).

More importantly it presented Tito with an opportunity to fashion his own, alternative brand of Communism, one that featured a mix of socialist and capitalist ideals. The basic institution at the heart of "Titoism", as it was known, was a system of **workers' self-management** which, as the slogan, "Factories to the workers!", suggested, vested greater power in the hands of the workers. Such an approach, however, was open to the possibility of dissent, which duly occurred in the form of strikes and political criticism, particularly in Slovenia. In the international arena, meanwhile, Tito manoeuvred carefully, his policy of **non-alignment** enabling Yugoslavia to secure prestigious international endorsement. Meanwhile, those party members suspected of collaborating with Stalin (known as "Conformists") were immediately purged and packed off to concentration camps, such as the notorious Goli Otok ("Bare Island") camp in the Adriatic. With regard to this there were few dissidents on the Slovene side, the Slovene Communists well aware that supporting a federal Yugoslav republic was their only option, especially given that such a Yugoslavia would support Slovenia's claims to ethnic territory in Italy and Austria.

The 1960s and 1970s

Yugoslavia in the 1960s was characterized by strong economic growth and improved living conditions, particularly for Slovenes, many of whom could travel freely abroad, a liberty denied to citizens of most other countries in the Eastern bloc, including many within the Yugoslav federation itself. That said, Slovenes, and to a lesser degree, Croats, were becoming increasingly resentful at the federal bureau's centrally planned means of redistribution, whereby money was siphoned off to support the less wealthy republics in the federation, thereby stifling economic development for the likes of Slovenia. The so-called **Road Affair** of 1969 was indicative of such problems. Having solicited funds from the World Bank for the development of its road network – in order to better facilitate trade with neighbouring countries and increase tourism opportunities – the federal authorities redistributed the money to road projects in other republics instead, triggering widespread public protests throughout Slovenia. The federal bureau merely dismissed the protest as nothing more than the work of a bunch of renegade Slovene nationalists. In any case, the Road Affair signalled the end of the **liberalization movement** of the 1960s, whose members had pushed for major market economic reforms throughout Yugoslavia. Fearful of losing control, the conservative Communists purged the party of its stronger liberal elements, before turning their attention to those in other institutions – universities, intellectual journals and the media.

Numerous **constitutional amendments and changes** repeatedly brought to the surface old arguments about decentralization and the need for greater autonomy within the federation, with Slovenia invariably at the forefront of these disputes. The **1974 constitution** went a stage further than previous ones, in that it not only gave more autonomy to the provinces of Vojvodina and Kosovo, but it also made provision for each republic to assume greater responsibility for its own internal affairs. However, the issue of centralism versus federalism, a recurring theme since the formation of the Kingdom of Serbs, Croats and Slovenes back in 1918, remained at the forefront of Slovene and Yugoslav political life up to and following **Tito's death** in 1980.

The 1980s

With the death of its founding father, the federal construct began to fall apart in dramatic fashion: Yugoslavia had racked up enormous foreign debt and unemployment, inflation had reached unacceptably high levels and **inter-republic relations** were at an all-time low. Of particular concern were the worsening relations between the Serbs and the Albanian majority in the autonomous province of Kosovo in southern Serbia, where riots in 1981 were followed by further draconian anti-Albanian measures, culminating in the annulment of the province's autonomy in 1989. On the domestic front, in 1986, Milan Kučan was elected president of the League of Communists of Slovenia, who were by now struggling to reconcile the political and ideological doctrines of the Yugoslav League of Communists with the increasingly widespread pluralistic inclinations pervading Slovenian society around this time.

In particular it was the emergence of **avant-garde and alternative movements** (also known as new social movements) – foremost amongst these were the arts collective **Neue Slowenische Kunst** (New Slovene Art), one of whose members was the legendary punk rock group Laibach, see p.344 – that paved the way for the democratization of Slovene society. No less influential were the counter-cultural **magazines** *Nova Revija* (New Review) and *Mladina* (Youth; see box on p.34), both of which provided broad-based platforms for cultural and intellectual expression and exchange, as well as political dialogue and debate. In *Nova Revija's* infamous issue no. 57 (February 1987), the magazine published "Contributions to a Slovene National Programme", a collection of papers that outlined provisions for Slovenian self-determination (this essentially echoed and amplified the content of *Revija 57*, a document which had appeared exactly thirty years earlier). Despite intense pressure from the federal government, the Slovene authorities refused to acquiesce to Belgrade's demands for those responsible to be prosecuted. *Mladina*, meanwhile, continued to provoke with its fearless and often humorous attacks on key groups and individuals within the Yugoslav federation, and articles on social taboos such as homosexuality and World War II massacres. In 1988, three of the magazine's members, along with an officer, were hauled up before a military court on trumped-up charges of betraying state secrets (widely believed to be a plan for military intervention in Slovenia), an affair known as the **Ljubljana Four Trial**. Conducted entirely in secret and in Serbo-Croatian, the trial was considered unconstitutional by most Slovenes, and served only to radicalize political opinion towards Belgrade. The trial, and the mass rallies that it inspired, represented the last hurrah for these movements, which became increasingly marginalized thereafter.

The fall of the Berlin Wall in November 1989 set in motion a chain of events which convulsed Eastern Europe, culminating in the bloody overthrow of Ceaușescu in Romania. These events, though, had little direct effect on Yugoslavia, which was readying itself for its own, spectacular implosion.

The road to independence

At the fourteenth and final Congress of the Yugoslav League of Communists in January 1990, Slovenian calls for absolute independence for the respective Communist parties were given short shrift by the Serbs. In response, the Slovene delegation walked out of the assembly, an incident that effectively spelt the end of the Yugoslav Communist Party. Just three months later, in April 1990, the country's first ever multiparty elections were won by the coalition Demos Party (Democratic Opposition of Slovenia), whilst **Milan Kučan**, the reformed Communist leader of the Party of Democratic Renewal (SDP) – formerly the League of Communists of Slovenia – was sworn in as president. Immediately after the elections, a number of constitutional amendments were implemented, thus paving the way for eventual separation from the Yugoslav federation.

The one remaining obstacle was Serbia which, with Slobodan Milošević in charge and championing a greater Serbia, now had control of four of the eight votes on the federal presidency (those of Vojvodina, Kosovo and Montenegro, in

The Ten-Day War

Even as Slovenes were celebrating the declaration of independence in Ljubljana on the night of June 26, the Serb-dominated **Yugoslav army** (JNA) had begun manoeuvring tank units towards Ljubljana's Brnik airport, and some thirty border posts that Slovenia had taken over following the declaration. The well-drilled Slovenian defence comprised the Territorial Defence (which itself was removed from the JNA's jurisdiction in a constitutional amendment the previous year) and the police, and was orchestrated by Minister of Defence Janez Janša – ironically one of those implicated in the Ljubljana Four Trial three years earlier.

As Slovene soldiers and officers began **deserting** the Yugoslav army in droves, the first strikes took place, though the capture of Brnik and threatened assault on the capital itself never materialized. In the end, there were few major clashes, with the majority of engagements being small-scale skirmishes at key traffic points and border positions. Nevertheless, and much to the surprise of the Yugoslav army – as well as neutral observers and many Slovenes themselves – the Slovene forces proved themselves to be more than competent adversaries, forcing around 2500 JNA troops to desert or **surrender**, whilst many more were captured. Following a flurry of diplomatic activity and several attempts to mediate by European Union representatives, the ten-day conflict was brought to an end on July 7, following the brokering of the Brioni Agreement, which provided for an **immediate ceasefire** and **withdrawal** of the Yugoslav army. Moreover, it stipulated that Slovenia put its declaration of independence on hold for a further three months. In human terms, the price was relatively low: officially, 21 Slovenes (military and civilian) were killed and a further 100 wounded, whilst 39 Yugoslav troops were killed and around 160 wounded.

The reason for Belgrade's confused and rather diffident policy in Slovenia was unclear, though most analysts concurred that it was based on an (ill-founded) assumption that a short, sharp show of force would be enough to cow the Slovenes into submission – failing that, they could resort to a policy of escalation. Their humiliating climb-down, meanwhile, was attributed to the fact that Serbia had no strong territorial or ethnic claims to Slovenia.

addition to its own), prompting Slovenes, somewhat mischievously, to coin the phrase "Serboslavia". Undaunted, Slovenia pressed on, and in December that year a **plebiscite for independence** was held, the result of which was an overwhelming 88 percent vote (the turn-out was 93 percent) for a split with the federation. Six months later, on June 25, 1991, the Slovene Parliament passed a constitutional law declaring independence, thus triggering the **Ten-Day War** (see box, above). Slovene independence was formally recognized by the European Union on January 15, 1992, and the country was officially admitted into the United Nations on May 22.

The 1990s

Whilst the war continued to savage effect for another four years in Croatia and Bosnia, Slovenia was facing up to the **difficult transition** from communist to market economy. Despite possessing an already relatively sound economy – especially compared to its former federal partners – Slovenia still faced considerable problems, namely, rising unemployment, low salaries and high inflation, whilst additional strains were being placed upon the economy as a result of the influx of refugees fleeing the chaos in Croatia and Bosnia. The task of economic restructuring was further complicated by the necessary imposition of **trade barriers** with the other republics, hitherto its most important markets. Moreover, potential foreign investors were frightened off by the perceived political risks associated with the ongoing **hostilities in the region**. It was for this very same reason that tourist numbers remained well below the levels the country experienced prior to the war, when it was one of the most popular destinations in Yugoslavia. However, the introduction of a **new currency** (the *tolar*), coupled with reforms in the banking and public service sectors, and the creation of new institutions, gradually smoothed the path to economic stability.

Slovenia's first **multiparty elections** as an independent nation took place in December 1992, by which stage internal discord within the Demos coalition had seen that party disband. Of the eight parties to win seats in the ninety-member parliament, it was the reform-oriented centre-left Liberal Democratic Party, led by the introverted yet competent **Janez Drnovšek** (he was also president of the Yugoslav Federation from May 1989 to May 1990), who secured the greatest number of votes (22 percent), followed by the centre-right Slovene Christian Democrats. Drnovšek himself was elected head of the coalition government. That same month saw the popular and avuncular Kučan returned as president, thus cementing his considerable standing in Slovene politics. Four years down the line, the 1996 elections yielded similar results, with the Liberal Democrats once again topping the polls, leaving Drnovšek to form a coalition government with seven other parties, despite the clear ideological differences between them. However, as in 1992, the overriding agenda was economic and political modernization. In November the following year, the unassailable Kučan was re-elected president for a second and final term.

One of the key issues dominating the political agenda was **Europe**, and in particular Slovenia's prospective membership of both NATO and the European Union, organizations to which the country had aspired since 1994. With high hopes going into the Madrid summit in June 1997, Slovenia was somewhat dismayed to find itself omitted from the invitation list. This sense of grievance was compounded when Hungary, Poland and the Czech Republic formally joined NATO in March 1999, just as the alliance was preparing to launch strikes on Serbia following the collapse of diplomatic talks aimed at ending the escalating violence in Kosovo. Whilst relations with Serbia had more or less normalized by this stage, most Slovenes shed few tears over the country's plight, regarding the bombing campaign as just desserts for the events of 1991. Yet the bombing cast yet another long shadow over the region, precipitating, amongst other things, another alarming drop in visitor numbers to the country.

Europe and the New Millennium

Since the early 1990s, Slovenia was always regarded as one of the outstanding candidates for EU accession amongst the central and east European countries, which was in part a reflection of the country's relatively strong economic and political standing. The invitation to open accession talks following the Madrid summit went some way to making up for the NATO snub. In fact these talks were arguably of greater importance to Slovenia, given the wider opportunities, particularly from an economic perspective, that potential membership afforded. Obstacles remained, however, not least a simmering feud between Slovenia and **Italy** (one of the more influential EU members) over disputed property rights, and in particular

△ Ptuj Town Hall displaying Slovenian and EU flags

the issue of **restitution of property** to Italian owners who had emigrated from Yugoslavia after World War II, an issue Slovenes claimed had been resolved in 1983 following the Treaty of Rome.

Relations with **Croatia** have been no less troubled in recent years, with disputes over the question of outstanding debt of the Zagreb branch of Slovenia's now defunct Ljubljanska Bank, as well as questions over the rights and responsibilities pertaining to the Krško nuclear reactor in southern Slovenia, which was built to provide energy for both republics. By far the thorniest issue concerns the long-standing dispute over **sea borders** in the Bay of Piran. The initial problem arose because no sea border ever existed during the time of Yugoslavia, and neither was one defined once the two countries had seceded from the federation. Following a series of incidents in the disputed waters, the situation reached crisis point in the summer of 2003, when Croatia unilaterally announced its intention to declare an Exclusive Economic Zone (EEZ), a move vehemently opposed by Slovenia, who argued that it would be impossible to create such a zone if the boundaries of the territorial waters hadn't been defined. Moreover, any such zone would effectively invalidate Slovenia's right to access international waters. Despite much diplomatic activity, including the issuing of various codes of conduct, and attempts at bilat-eral border agreements, a final solution appears to be as far away as ever. Slovenia's recent accession to the EU, which has entailed the imposition of tighter border controls between the two countries, has done little to ameliorate this fraught relationship. By way of contrast, relations with Serbia have improved immeasurably since the conflicts of some years earlier, a fact confirmed by the resumption of bilateral relations in 2000.

During **parliamentary elections** in October 2000, the ruling Liberal Democrats, with Drnovšek still firmly in command, once again eased to victory, their third in succession. Two years later, in December 2002, the **presidential elections** saw an end to the decade-long Kučan-Drnovšek union, for Kučan was obliged to stand down having served the maximum two terms allowed in the constitution. His retirement paved the way for Drnovšek as his successor, though not before a closer than expected run-off against the independent candidate, Barbara Brezigar. Drnovšek's elevation, meanwhile, opened the door for a new prime minister, a post duly taken up by finance minister and vice-president of the senior coalition party (Liberal Democrats), Anton Rop. Rop was immediately assigned the task of forming a new government from a broad-based coalition of four parties.

On the international front, final accession negotiations to both NATO and the EU were wrapped up at the tail end of 2002, with referendums held the following March. As predicted, support for the former was far from overwhelming, though a 66 percent "yes" vote was much higher than anticipated; support for the EU, meanwhile, was more or less unequivocal, with the "yes" camp accounting for almost 90 percent of the vote. **NATO membership** was finally confirmed in March 2004, and was followed just over a month later, on May 1st, by the country's **admission into the European Union** alongside nine other central-eastern European countries.

Other key political subjects came to the fore in 2004, the most controversial of which was the issue of the so-called '**erased**', some eighteen thousand citizens from other countries of the former Yugoslavia (mainly Bosnia and Serbia) who were removed from the population registry after the country obtained independence in 1992. Having declined the offer of citizenship at the time, most of the erased immediately lost their jobs, in addition to being stripped of any health and pension rights they may have been entitled to. In a highly charged referendum in April 2004, Slovenes decided overwhelming to deny full citizenship rights to the erased, a decision that prompted many observers to suggest that nationalism was still alive and kicking in the region.

Parliamentary elections in October later that year – the fourth since independence, and one that also saw the lowest-ever turnout – resulted in a surprisingly comfortable victory for the opposition Slovenian Democratic Party (SDS) over the Liberal Democrats, the first time that the latter had been ousted since independence. Anton Rop was replaced as prime minister by **Janez Janša**, a former member of the League of Communists, but best known as one of the defendants in the infamous Ljubljana Four Trial in 1988 (see p.334), which resulted in his imprisonment for six months. Following his release, Janša helped found the Slovenian Democratic Union (SDZ), after which he became defence minister, a position he held during the ten-day war of independence.

EU membership, meanwhile, has had little direct impact on the general population, most of whom are largely apathetic about their country's newly acquired status. Slovenia did, though, claim a minor coup when it became the first of the ten new member states to **introduce the euro currency**, in January 2007. More generally, the economy remains buoyant, with a strong industrial base and greater numbers of tourists visiting the country than ever.

Books, maps, film and music

There's a real dearth of books about Slovenia in the English language, in every genre. What recent titles there are – particularly travelogues and historical or political publications – tend to revolve almost exclusively around the other countries of the former Yugoslavia. Slovenia's literary heritage, however, is strong, and whilst there's little available in translation, there are several impressive anthologies to choose from. Likewise, in film and music, Slovenia has yielded some terrific, and influential, artists and producers in recent years; unfortunately, with the exception of one or two, few are known beyond the country's borders.

Books, maps and literature

The number of publications dedicated to the break-up of Yugoslavia is considerable, yet in most cases there is scant coverage of Slovenia's involvement in the conflict. Whilst you'll find some reference to Slovenia in the titles below, you may also find the following excellent reads in their own right, and well worth dipping into if you're travelling more widely around the region: Misha Glenny *The Fall of Yugoslavia*; John Allcock *Explaining Yugoslavia*; John Lampe *Yugoslavia as History*; Branka Magas & Ivo Žanič *The War in Croatia and Bosnia-Herzegovina 1991–1995*; and Leslie Benson *Yugoslavia: A Concise History*.

Jill Benderley and Evan Craft *Independent Slovenia* (MacMillan). Enjoyable and wide-ranging collection of essays pertaining to the country's historical development up to and including independence. The most interesting accounts are those which chart the development of the so-called new social movements of the 1980s (trade unions, women's organizations and the local punk scene), all of which helped fashion a strong and independent civil society in the run-up to independence.

Janez Bogotaj *Handicrafts of Slovenia* (Rokus). Beautifully illustrated work covering Slovenia's rich tradition of crafts, including ceramists, potters, lace-makers, weavers and glass painters.

Justi Carey and Roy Clark *The Julian Alps of Slovenia* (Cicerone Press). Useful pocket-sized book detailing over fifty trails throughout the Julian Alps, with treks starting from Bled, Bohinj, Bovec, Kobarid and Kranjska Gora. Although essentially a guide to the French/Italian/Swiss Alps, Kev Reynolds' *Walking in the Alps* (Cicerone Press) also features a short chapter on hiking in the Julian Alps.

John Corsellis and Marcus Ferrar *Slovenia 1945: Memories of Death and Survival after WWII* (IB Tauris). Sympathetic and superbly accomplished account documenting the fate of the large Catholic, non-Communist Slovene migrant community (including members of the anti-Communist Home Guard) both during and after World War II.

Aleš Debeljak *Twilight of the Idols; Recollections of a lost Yugoslavia* (White Pine Press). Better known for fiction and poetry (see p.341), the Slovene novelist turns his attention here to politics in this critical reflection on the disintegration of Yugoslavia, though his portrayal of the Serbs as outright aggressors is overly subjective.

📖 **James Gow and Cathie Carmichael** *Slovenia and the Slovenes* (Hurst). This is the most thoroughgoing assessment of twentieth-century Slovenian history currently available. The introductory chapter sets the tone with an illuminating overview of the country, and is followed by very readable accounts of Slovenia's cultural, economic and political maturation; the book concludes with a revealing insight into the events surrounding the country's drive for independence and the Ten-Day War.

Andrej Hrausky and Janez Koželj *Architectural Guide to Ljubljana* (Rokus). Insightful guide to one hundred of the capital's buildings, from its castles and churches to its many Baroque and Secessionist splendours, as well as most of the projects conceived by Slovenia's greatest urban planner, Jože Plečnik. For more on Plečnik, try the more detailed *Plečnik's Ljubljana*, and *National and University Library, Ljubljana*.

Tine Mihelič *Mountaineering in Slovenia* (Cordee). Excellent and easy-to-follow guide to tackling Slovenia's most important summits, in the Julian, Kamnik and Savinja Alps, and the Karavanke mountains. Complete with diagrams and lots of shiny pictures.

📖 **Alexei Monroe** *Interrogation Machine* (MIT Press). Thoroughgoing and fascinating insight into the workings of the provocative avant-garde Slovene collective NSK (see p.334), the most famous and controversial component of which was the rock band Laibach.

Julij Nemanič and Janez Bogataj *Wines of Slovenia* (Rokus). This comprehensive handbook, featuring some beautifully illustrated pictures, is the definitive guide to the country's wines (with ratings for each) and wine growing districts; a must for anyone serious about Slovenian wine.

David Robertson and Sarah Stewart *Landscapes of Slovenia* (Sunflower). Regional books with small maps and photos detailing easy to moderate walks, mostly covering the western half of Slovenia, as well as half a dozen car tours.

Nigel Thomas *The Yugoslav Wars: Slovenia and Croatia 1991–95* (Osprey). Authoritative and well-illustrated guide – including some rare photos – documenting the roles played by the various combatant armies on Slovenian and Croatian territory during the wars of the early 1990s.

Slavoj Žižek and Glyn Daly *Conversations with Žižek* (Polity Press). In this entertaining series of conversations, the renowned Slovene theorist elaborates on various aspects of popular culture and politics, including topics such as Marxism, Nazism, and the films of Stanley Kubrick; a far more accessible introduction to the mindset of Žižek than his other work.

Maps

Most tourist offices can give you a basic town or city map, but for more detailed ones, and regional maps, expect to pay around €5-6. If you haven't bought maps in advance of your trip, you're best off trying the bookshops in Ljubljana (see p.83).

Country maps (Freytag & Berndt, and the GeoCenter Euro Map of the Dalmatian Coast and Croatia, which also covers Slovenia; both 1:300,000): the latter is particularly useful if you're thinking of combining the two countries.

Hiking maps (Triglav National Park, the Julian Alps, and the Karavanke mountains; 1:50,000): published by The Alpine Association of Slovenia (Planinska zveza Slovenije; PZS), you can order these directly from PZS, or obtain them from tourist offices and

bookshops.
Tourist Road map (turistična
avtokarta; 1:270,000): published by
the national motoring organization
AMZS, this is the best road map currently available.

Literature

Although written records in Slovenian appeared as early as the tenth century, **Slov-enian literature** began to systematically develop during the **sixteenth–century Reformation**. This development was thanks to leading reformers Primož Trubar (writer of the first Slovene book, the primer *Abecedarium*, in 1550), Jurij Dalmatin (the first Slovene translation of the Bible, in 1584), and linguist Adam Bohorič, whose *Arcticae horulae* (Winter Hours) was the first Slovene Grammar book, written in Latin and published the same year as Dalmatin's Bible. Around a century later Janez Vajkard Valvasor (see box, p.242) wrote and published (in German) the *Glory of the Duchy of Carniola*, a seminal work that synthesized the country's history, sights and peoples in one encyclopedic, four-volume work; to this day it remains the single most important document written about the Slovene lands.

It was during the period of **romanticism** in the early nineteenth century that Slovene literature reached its first peak, thanks to the poet France Prešeren (see box, p.126), the most iconic literary figure in Slovenia's history. Very little of Prešeren's work has been translated into English, but the audio CD, *Sonnets of Unhappiness*, is a beautifully read collection (by Vanessa Redgrave, Katrin Cartlidge and Simon Callow) of the poet's key works. The next writers to make their mark were the **realists**, led by the playwright Josip Jurčič, whose enduringly popular *Deseti Brat* (*The Tenth Brother*) was the first full-length Slovene novel to be pub-lished (1866) – an abridged version is available in English. Literary trends at the start of the twentieth century were shaped by the so-called **Moderna movement**, whose main representatives were Oton Župančič and Ivan Cankar, the second of whom is regarded as Slovenia's finest prose writer. A prolific and highly politicized essayist, novelist and polemicist, Cankar was also one of the first to champion a southern Slav union.

The coexistent movements of expressionism and social realism that had domi-nated both the artistic and literary landscape prior to, and just after, World War II eventually gave way to western literary trends, notably **symbolism and exis-tentialism**. Foremost amongst these writers was the dissident politician and ex-Partisan Edvard Kocbek, whose opposition to Communist ideology and socialist repression manifested itself in a short-story collection, *Strah in pogum* (*Fear and Courage*), and the diaries *Tovarišija* (*Comrades*) and *Listina* (*The Document*) – it also landed him a spell in prison. Similar critiques of the resistance movement were the preserve of other commentators at that time, too, including Dane Zajc and Tomaž Šalamun, the doyens of Slovene postwar poets.

Prominent amongst the **new generation** of writers are essayist and poet Aleš Debeljak – *The City and the Child* is one of his best volumes of poetry; post-mod-ern fiction writer Andrej Blatnik, whose collection of short stories, *Skinswaps*, is a good introduction to his work; and poet and gay rights activist Brane Mozetič. Given that there's only a limited amount of Slovenian **literature in translation**, you're best off starting with one of the several excellent anthologies available: *A Bilingual Anthology of Slovene Literature* includes poems and prose by a panoply of Slovenia's literary greats, from Trubar and Prešeren to Kocbek and Šalamun, while *The Imagination of Terra Incognita; Slovenian Writing 1945–1995* is the best available anthology of essays, poems and fiction by authors from the second half of the last century. A useful reference book is *Key: Slovenia: Contemporary Slovenian Literature in Translation*.

Film

Cinematography in Slovenia made its mark as early as 1905, with the short documentaries *The Fair at Ljutomer* and *People Leaving the Church*, shot by the pioneer of Slovene film, Karol Grossman. The development of the industry continued apace after World War II, a golden period for Slovene film thanks to the state-financed Triglav Film house, which produced several classics, such as *Kekec*, Jože Gale's enduringly popular 1952 film about a clever shepherd boy, and France Stiglič's 1956 film, *Dolina Miru* (*Valley of Peace*). Despite the fact that, on average, around just five films a year are made in Slovenia – one of the lowest outputs amongst central-eastern European countries – a fine crop of movies have been released in recent years; predictably, few of these films ever make it beyond their own country or the occasional art film festival in western Europe. By far the most successful and celebrated of these – it was actually a joint Belgian-French-Italian-Slovenian project, and shot in the village of Bač near Postojna – was the Oscar-winning (Best Foreign Film 2001) *Nikogaršnje ozemlje* (*No Man's Land*) by Bosnian director Danis Tanović. Featuring a Bosnian and a Serb as the two protagonists trapped together in a trench somewhere between enemy lines, it's an acute, compassionate, and darkly comic dissection of a pitiless conflict, and without doubt one of the most affecting movies ever made about the Yugoslav wars. Another recent landmark Slovenian film, and winner of the prestigious Golden Lion award at the 2001 Venice Film festival, *Kruh in Mleko* (*Bread and Milk*) is the outstanding debut film by young director Jan Cvetkovič, a brooding social commentary on the effects of alcoholism and alienation in small-town Slovenia. Other films to look out for include Damjan Kožole's *Rezervni deli* (*Spare Parts*), a gritty, sobering drama about human trafficking across Slovenia; the humorous *Kajmak in marmelada* (*Cheese and Jam*), which explores race, immigration and happiness in contemporary Slovenia – directed by and starring the respected Bosnian actor Branko Djurič (also the lead actor in *No Man's Land*); and *Varuh meje* (*Guardians of the Frontier*), a creepy, atmospheric tale of sexual discovery down on the Kolpa river.

Slovenia stages a couple of excellent **film festivals** each year: the Festival of Slovenian Film in Celje during September, and the Ljubljana International Film Festival (LIFFe), which takes place in the capital in November (see p.82).

Music

As in other spheres of the arts and culture, Slovenia's musical heritage is surprisingly strong, manifest in ancient **folk** traditions and a **punk/rock** scene that, during the 1980s, spawned some of the most exciting and controversial music in the former Yugoslavia. Whilst Slovenia has few **jazz** artists of its own, the genre has a small, yet devout following, as evidenced by the increasing number of bars with live music and a world-class summer jazz festival in Ljubljana. In general there's no shortage of music events, chief amongst which are the **world music** festival, Druga Godba, and Rock Otočec, which invariably attracts a strong international line-up; moreover, there are countless folk gatherings and **classical** music concerts staged around the country each summer.

Folk music

Whilst **Slovenian folk music** (Ljudska Glasba) generally belongs to the alpine, Austro-Bavarian cultural sphere, the best and most authentic song and dance emanates from the rural towns and villages of Bela Krajina and Prekmurje. The most traditional forms of Slovenian folk music are based on age-old folk literature and poems; this music would usually be performed for both ritual and entertainment functions (weddings, family holidays and religious ceremonies), and utilizes instruments such as the *okarina* (clay flute), *trstenka* (panpipe), *drumlja* (Jew's Harp) and the *gudalo*, a small clay pot over the top of which a pig's bladder is stretched – the bass sound emitted is made by rubbing the straw rod which extends up through the membrane. Although its role in everyday life has largely diminished you are likely to come across traditional music during local festivals.

Some of the best Slovene folk music in recent years has come out of the small village of Beltinci in Prekmurje, in particular from the remarkable **Beltinška Banda Kociper**, a kind of Mitteleuropean Buena Vista Social Club, whose members, playing the fiddle (a stock Prekmurje instrument), violin, clarinet, cimbalom, double bass and accordion, have been delighting audiences for more than half a century. The baton has now been passed down to a new generation of musicians from the same village, namely the four-strong **Marko Banda**, and the ten-strong, teenage **Mlada Beltinska Banda**. Other folk musicians to listen out for include the stunning all-female vocal group **Katice**, who specialize in interpreting classic harmonies from the Rezija mountain valley region on the Italian side of the Julian Alps; **La Zonta**, who perform traditional Istrian dances using bagpipes, fiddle and accordion; and the soloist **Tomaž Podobnikar**, whose repertoire extends to the dulcimer and the amazing singing saw.

No self-respecting gathering is complete without some form of **dancing** which, like songs, varies greatly from region to region. The oldest dances developed in Bela Krajina during the sixteenth century and were heavily influenced by the Uskoks, bands of renegades from Serbia and Croatia who fled the Turks and settled in the region. The most popular dance is the *kolo*, an energetic, circular group dance performed to both musical and vocal accompaniment. The dances of Prekmurje are less exuberant affairs – typical is the *tkalecka* (weaver's dance), a kind of skipping dance whereby handkerchiefs are waved under the knees (reminiscent of an English Morris dance) – whilst those of Primorska are of an altogether more refined bent, having been established in bourgeois circles.

Although not strictly folk, Slovenia's best-known band, at least outside their own country, are **Terra Folk**, a group of four academically and classically trained musicians, whose free-ranging repertoire of Balkan, Gypsy, Folk, Klezmer, Irish and classical pretty much defies any standard form of categorization. Featuring an eclectic set of violin, flute, guitar, drums, accordion and double bass, Terra Folk's reputation has largely been built upon their entertaining live shows, which combine ebullient musicianship with a roguish sense of humour. Their biggest accolade to date came at the 2003 World Music Awards in London, when they scooped the Audience Award, while that same year they also delighted audiences at the Edinburgh Fringe Festival. The group tours incessantly, and devote much of their schedule to playing in the UK as well as their homeland, so there's a good chance of catching them live somewhere. Another fine live prospect is the marvellous six-piece ensemble **Katalena**, another slightly unorthodox outfit who marry traditional folk forms with souped-up jazz and blues to beautiful effect.

C

Rock and pop

Although a number of creative bands emerged throughout Yugoslavia in the 1970s, Ljubljana was the first of all the Yugoslav cities to develop an authentic, home-grown musical scene of its own. In particular, it was the emergence of a local punk subculture in the late 1970s, alongside other so-called new social movements, that set the tone for the next few years. The most prominent of the first generation of punk bands were **Pankrti** (The Bastards). They, like the majority of punk groups and their followers at that time, were deemed a threat to civil society by the authorities, who attempted to associate the movement with Nazism; concerts were prohibited, persecution by the police was commonplace, and spurious accusations against punks abounded in the media. Dismantled by the state in the early 1980s, the punk scene was eventually supplanted by other social movements, most notably an avant-garde collective called **Neue Slowenische Kunst** (New Slovene Art, or NSK), whose core members were the visual artists Irwin, the theatrical group Sestre Scipion Nasice, and the rock group Laibach.

Conceived in the industrial mining town of Trbovlje in 1980, shortly after Tito's death, **Laibach** produced some of the most uncompromising music and art ever to come out of the former Yugoslavia. Following an interview on national television in June 1983 – six months after the band's original singer and spokesman, Tomaž Hostnik, committed suicide – Laibach were summarily banned from appearing in public. The authorities argued that the band's use of the German language (Laibach is the German name for Ljubljana, and was used during both Habsburg rule and the Nazi occupation) and their apparent appropriation of Nazi images was just a cover for the resurgence of fascism. Laibach, meanwhile, maintained that rather than espousing totalitarianism, they were in fact exposing its ugliest facets. Ostracized, the group embarked on the "Occupied Europe Tour" later that year, a tour that took them to countries on both sides of the Iron Curtain and exposed them for the first time to audiences outside their own country. In 1987, Laibach marked the lifting of the ban with a series of homecoming gigs (the "Bloody Ground-Fertile Soil" tour) in several Yugoslav cities, including Zagreb and Belgrade. Returning to Belgrade two years later, the group delivered a typically incendiary speech, warning against the inflammatory rhetoric of Slobodan Milošević, alongside a screening of a 1941 German propaganda film on the bombing of the Serbian capital.

Since their eponymously titled debut in 1985, Laibach have released more than a dozen albums. Their earlier recordings were wilfully experimental, avant-garde exercises, which drew heavily upon the electronic minimalism of Kraftwerk and DAF – as a result they do not make for easy listening. Towards the end of the 1980s the group moved towards a more overt and accessible rock sound (though still remaining faithful to their trademark militant Wagnerian soundscape), thanks in part to their predilection for doing cover albums, namely the Beatles' *Let it Be*, and the Stones' *Sympathy for the Devil*, neither of which will sound quite the same again once you've heard Laibach's version. The group returned to familiar ground with the 1994 release, *NATO*, which pointedly anticipated the expansion of western influence in the region, and included covers of Status Quo's *You're in the Army Now* and Pink Floyd's *Dogs of War*, while 1996's metal-driven *Jesus Christ Superstars* marked another shift in musical direction. After a seven-year hiatus, Laibach returned in 2003 with *WAT* (We Are Time), as direct and aggressive a record as any previously released and one that marked a return to the heavy techno/industrial rhythms of earlier albums.

Although few bands of note have emerged since Laibach's heyday, Slovenian **popular music** has undergone something of a revival in recent years. Spearheading the charge is the youthful, six-piece band, **Siddharta**, whose melodic brand of stadium rock has made them the most successful and popular home-grown outfit since Laibach – interestingly, *B-Mashina*, a track from the band's second album, *Nord*, was covered (in English) by Laibach for their last album, *WAT*. Other current popular acts range from mainstream pop groups (**The Elevators** and **Big Foot Mama**), to dance and techno-inspired performers like the multi-rooted **DJ Umek**, a regular on the European tour circuit. Two stalwarts of the Slovenian music scene are the singer-songwriter **Vlado Kreslin**, who has kept legions of fans in thrall for nearly two decades with his folksy brand of guitar-based rock, and the perennially popular poet and songwriter **Zoran Predin**, who first came to prominence some twenty years ago as the founder of the rock group Lačni Franz (Hungry Franz). In addition to writing film and theatre scores, Predin now spends most of his time collaborating with other artists, such as **Šukar**, Slovenia's outstanding Romany group, with whom he has recorded an album of gypsy music.

One of the most memorable music groups in recent years was a drag trio from Ljubljana called **Sestre** ("Sisters"), who caused a storm of controversy in Slovenia when they were selected – in somewhat dubious circumstances – to represent the country at the 2002 Eurovision Song Contest (dressed as air-stewardesses). Whilst the group is unlikely to go down in the annals of Slovenian popular music, this fractious affair did at least reignite the debate over gay rights in Slovenia.

Discography

The following list is merely a pointer to some of the recordings available, a few, but not many of them, internationally; rooting around stores and record shops in Slovenia will yield the many more CDs that don't have international distribution.

Folk music

Katalena *(Z)godbe* (RTV Slovenija). Luscious sounding album of traditional songs from Slovenia's multifarious folk regions – Prekmurje, Istria and Bela Krajina, as well as the Rezija Valley in Italy. Whilst remaining faithful to their folk roots, the two subsequent releases, *Babje Leto* and *Kmečka ohcet* (Dallas), feature a denser, rockier sound.

Mlada Beltinska Banda *Prekmurje Musical Heritage* (KUD Beltinci). Traditional folk music from the Prekmurje region, as performed by the young Beltinci Band.

Modern Folk Music in Slovenia Volumes I & II (Folk Slovenia Cultural Society). This enjoyable two-disc set is the best introduction to Slovenia's contemporary folk artists, including the female vocal group Katice, Styrian folk trio Kurja Koža, and the Marko Banda from Prekmurje.

Slovenian Folk Songs (RTV Slovenija). Four-disc set of narrative folk music recorded on-site by the Institute of Ethnomusicology in Ljubljana. Drawing upon themes of heroes, legends and love, this voluminous collection brings together poems, songs and instruments from the country's multifarious regions. The excellent sleeve notes help make some sense of it all.

Terra Folk *StereoFolk Live* and *Jumper of Love* (Music Net). Packed with their trademark effervescent tunes, the band's first two releases are both live outings, recorded in clubs across Slovenia. The third (studio) album, *N'taka*, is in a similar vein and features the gorgeous female voices of Katice.

Rock/popular music

Laibach The band's earliest works are cassette-only affairs, and very difficult to get hold of. Otherwise, selected albums available on CD include: *Laibach* (Ropot, 1985); the double box-set *Rekapitulacija 1980–1984* (this is a remastered, redesigned edition of the 1985 original released on the Hamburg independent label, Walter Ulbricht; Mute, 2002); *Nova Akropola* (Cherry Red, 1987); *Opus Dei* (Mute, 1987); *Krst Pod Triglavom* (the soundtrack to NSK's theatre performance that same year; Sub Rosa, 1987); *Let it Be* (Mute, 1988); *Sympathy for the Devil* (Mute, 1990); *Nato* (Mute, 1994); *Jesus Christ Superstars* (Mute, 1996); *The John Peel Sessions* (recordings from two sessions, in 1986 and 1987, with the legendary British DJ; Strange Fruit, 2002); and *WAT* (Mute, 2003). For an overview, there's the best of package, *Anthems* (Mute, 2004), which also contains a superb forty-page booklet.

Siddharta *ID*, *Nord* and *Rh-* (Menart). Released between 1999 and 2003, these are the band's three albums to date. A limited edition English version of the third, and best, album, *Rh-*, is also available.

Romany

Šukar *Prvo Ti* (*First Snow*; Nika) and *En Concert 1990–2002* (Etno Karavana). Whilst the best Romany music from the former Yugoslav republics is largely the preserve of musicians from Serbia and Macedonia, these two offerings (the second a live album) by Slovenia's standout Romany group – a young, five-piece tamburica ensemble from Ljubljana – feature sumptuous reworkings of traditional gypsy dance songs and ballads. *Mentol Bombon* is an album of songs recorded with singer songwriter, Zoran Predin.

Language

Language

Slovenian

A lthough the earliest written records in Slovene date from around 1000 AD, it has existed as a literary language since the middle of the sixteenth century, when the first printed books – including a translation of the Bible – came into being. Today it's spoken by nearly two million people within Slovenia, and around half a million more outside the country's borders. Slovenian is a Slavic language, a branch of the Indo-European linguistic family, and is most closely related to Croatian and Serbian, with which it shares quite a few identical words and phrases.

Whilst attempting the odd word or phrase of **Slovenian** will be appreciated, and can be a fun experience in itself, generally speaking there will be little call for it, as the standard of English amongst Slovenes – especially the young – is exceptionally high. Many older generation Slovenes speak Serbo-Croatian (as it was formerly called), whilst Italian is widely spoken in the Primorska region, and Hungarian in Prekmurje. Regional variations of Slovene abound, and the language is characterized by nearly fifty dialects and subdialects.

Basic grammar

Slovenian is grammatically complex with **six cases** for nouns, adjectives and pronouns, three genders (masculine, feminine and neuter) and four verb tenses (although only three are used in everyday language). Besides the singular and plural in the Slovene grammar, the dual number is also used (for two persons or objects): for example, not only *gora* (mountain) and *gore* (mountains), but also *dve gori* (two mountains). Matters become very complex when one considers special endings for gender, numbers and different cases. In Slovenian the prepositions are important because the forms or the following noun, pronoun and adjectives are dependent on them. Slovenian has no articles (such as "a" or "the") and the gender of the word is defined by its ending. The script is Roman and there are 25 letters, the speciality being s, c, z with a caron (a small "v" or hook) on top of each, which indicates sh, ch and zh sounds.

Pronunciation

Slovenian has free stress – it may fall on any syllable of a word. Like English, there are different values for vowels; vowels can be stressed or unstressed, long or short, open or closed, with further subtle variations in the pronunciation. The Slovenian consonants are mostly pronounced as they are spelt. Letters not included below are pronounced as in English.

A short a as in cat, long a as in father
C ts as in bats
Č ch as in church
D d as in dog (dan), t as in sit (grad)

E short e as in met (več), ea as in pear (mleko)
I short i as in hit (ris), long ee as in been (sin)
J y as in yet

L l as in leap
O short o as in hot (voda), long o as in short (sok)
R r pronounced with the tip of the tongue like a Scottish "r"

Š sh as in shop
U oo as in foot (kruh)
V v as in vat (voda), w as in word (avto)
Ž zh as in measure

Words and phrases

Slovenian distinguishes between formal and informal means of address. The formal (polite) way is very often used. The informal way is used among friends and people you know well. In the phrases below the polite form of address has been used.

Basics

Yes	Ja
No	Ne
I am from	Sem iz
...Britain/Ireland/ America/Canada/ Australia/New Zealand	...Velike Britanije/ Irske/Amerike/Kanade/ Avstralije/Nove Zelandije
Slovenian	Slovensko
Slovenian person	Slovenec (male)/ Slovenka (female)
Slovenian language	Slovenščina
Do you speak...?	Govorite...?
English	Angleško
German	Nemško
French	Francosko
What's your name?	Kako ti je ime?
My name is	Ime mi je
I (don't) understand	(Ne) Razumem
Please	Prosim
Excuse me	Oprostite
Two beers, please	Dve pivi, prosim
Thank you (very much)	Hvala (lepa)
You're welcome	Prosim / ni za kaj
Hello (informal)	Živijo
Goodbye	Nasvidenje
See you later (informal)	Adijo
Good morning	Dobro jutro
Good day	Dober dan
Good evening	Dober večer
Good night	Lahko noč
How are you?	Kako ste?

Could you speak more slowly?	Lahko govorite počasneje?
What do you call...?	Kako se reče...?
Please write it down	Lahko prosim napišete
Hurry up!	Pohitite!
Entrance	Vhod
Exit	Izhod
Arrival	Prihod
Departure	Odhod
Open	Odprto
Closed	Zaprto
Free admission	Prost vstop
Toilet	Stranišče / WC (women's – ženske, men's – moški)
Shop	Trgovina
Market	Trg
Hospital	Bolnica/bolnišnica
Pharmacy	Lekarna
Police	Policija
Caution/beware	Previdno/pozor
Help!	Na pomoč!
I'm ill	Bolan (bolna) sem
No smoking	Kajenje prepovedano
No bathing	Kopanje prepovedano
Where is/are?	Kje je/so?
What?	Kaj?
Why?	Zakaj?
When?	Kdaj?
Who?	Kdo?

Accommodation

I'd like/we'd like	Rad(a)**/radi bi	Do you have a student discount?	Ali imate študentski popust?
when speaker is male	**rad	Is everything included?	Je vse vključeno v ceno?
when speaker is female	**rada	Is breakfast included?	Ali je zajtrk vključen v ceno?
How much is it?	Koliko stane?	Full Board	Polni penzion
Per night	Na noč	Half Board	Pol penzion
Per week	Na teden	Can we camp here?	Ali lahko tukaj kampiramo?
Single room	Enoposteljna soba	Can I see the room?	Ali lahko vidim sobo?
Double room	Dvoposteljna soba	I have a reservation	Imam rezervacijo
Rooms for rent	Sobe/oddaja sob	The bill please	Račun prosim
Hot (cold) water	Topla (mrzla) voda	We're paying separately	Plačamo posebej
Shower	Tuš		
It's very expensive	Zelo drago je		
Do you have anything cheaper?	Ali imate kaj cenejšega?		

LANGUAGE | Words and phrases

Getting around

Where's the...?	Kje je...?	When does the next train/bus leave for...?	Kdaj odpelje naslednji vlak/avtobus v...?
Campsite	Kamp	Do I have to change trains?	Ali moram prestopiti?
Hotel	Hotel	Towards	Proti
Railway station	Železniška postaja	On the right (left)	Na desni (levi)
Bus station	Avtobusna postaja	Straight ahead	Naravnost
Bus stop	Avtobusno postajališče	(Over) There/here	Tam/tukaj
Inland	Notranji promet	Where are you going?	Kam greste?
International	Mednarodni promet	Is that on the way to...?	Ali je to na poti v...?
Is it near (far)?	Ali je blizu (daleč)?	I want to get out at...	Rad(a) bi izstopil(a) v...
Which bus goes to...?	Kateri avtobus pelje v...?	Please stop here	Prosim ustavite tukaj
A one-way ticket to... please	Enosmerno vozovnico za... prosim	I'm lost	Izgubil(a) sem se
A return ticket to...	Povratno vozovnico za...	Arrivals	Prihodi
Can I reserve a seat?	Ali lahko rezerviram sedež?	Departures	Odhodi
What time does the train/bus leave...?	Kdaj odpelje vlak/avtobus...?	To/from	V/iz
		Change	Prestop

Numbers

1	Ena		10	Deset
2	Dva		11	Enajst
3	Tri		12	Dvanajst
4	Štiri		13	Trinajst
5	Pet		14	Štirinajst
6	Šest		15	Petnajst
7	Sedem		16	Šestnajst
8	Osem		17	Sedemnajst
9	Devet		18	Osemnajst

19	Devetnajst	150	Stopetdeset
20	Dvajset	200	Dvesto
21	Enaindvajset	300	Tristo
30	Trideset	400	Štiristo
40	Štirideset	500	Petsto
50	Petdeset	600	Šesto
60	Šestdeset	700	Sedemsto
70	Sedemdeset	800	Osemsto
80	semdeset	900	Devetsto
90	Devetdeset	1000	Tisoč
100	Sto	Half	Pol
101	Stoena	Quarter	Četrt

Time, days and dates

Either the 24 or 12-hour clock is used. When the 12-hour clock is used, "in the morning" (*dopoldan*), or "in the afternoon" (*popoldan*), is usually added. Halves and quarters are used: 4.30 is either *štiri trideset* or *pol petih* (half five), the latter being more common; 4.15 is either *štiri petnajst* or *četrt čez štiri* (quarter past four). Duration is expressed by the prepositions *od* (from) and *do* (to). To ask the time, say: *Koliko je ura?*

Day	Dan	Thursday	Četrtek
Week	Teden	Friday	Petek
Month	Mesec	Saturday	Sobota
Year	Leto		
Today	Danes	January	Januar
Tomorrow	Jutri	February	Februar
The day after tomorrow	Pojutrišnjem	March	Marec
Yesterday	Včeraj	April	April
The day before yesterday	Predvčerajšnjim	May	Maj
In the morning	Zjutraj	June	Junij
Before noon	Dopoldan	July	Julij
Noon	Opoldan	August	Avgust
Afternoon	Popoldan	September	September
In the evening	Zvečer	October	Oktober
At midnight	Ob polnoči	November	November
At night	Ponoči	December	December

Sunday	Nedelja	Spring	Pomlad
Monday	Ponedeljek	Summer	Poletje
Tuesday	Orek	Autumn	Jesen
Wednesday	Sreda	Winter	Zima

Food and drink

Basics

Bedro	Leg	Dunajsko	Vienna-style (deep fried in breadcrumbs)
Dober tek!	Bon appétit!	Dušeno	Steamed

Gorčica/senf	Mustard
Kis	Vinegar
Kisla smetana	Sour cream
Kruh	Bread
Kuhano	Boiled
Malo krvavo	Underdone/rare
Maslo	Butter
Med	Honey
Na žaru	Grilled
Na zdravje!	Cheers!
Ocvrto	Fried
Pariško	à la Parisienne (deep fried without breadcrumbs)
Pečeno	Baked
Poper	Pepper
Praženo	Roasted
Prsi	Breast
Sladkor	Sugar
Smetana	Cream
Sol	Salt
Žemlja / Štrucka	Bread roll
Zapečeno	Well done (fried)

Soups (juhe) and stews (enolončnice)

Fižolova juha	Bean soup
Gobova juha	Mushroom soup
Goveja juha	Beef broth
Jota	Sauerkraut soup
Kisla juha	Sour soup
Krompirjeva juha	Potato soup
Mineštra	Minestrone (mixed vegetable stew)
Paradižnikova juha	Tomato soup
Prežganka	Soup made by browning flour on lard and adding water
Ribji brodet	Istrian fish soup
Ričet	Barley and pork broth
Telečja obara	Veal stew
Zelenjavna juha	Vegetable soup

Appetizers – cold or hot (predjedi – hladne ali tople)

Jetrca	Liver
Narezek	Slices of cold meats

Olive	Olives
Pašteta (jetrna, račja, ribja)	Pâté (liver, duck, fish)
Pršut	Dry-cured Italian ham/ smoked ham
Rižota	Risotto
Sir (kozji, kravji, ovčji)	Cheese (goat, cow, sheep)
Šunka	Ham
Tatarski biftek	Raw mince with spices spread on toast
Testenine	Pasta

Salads (solate)

Salads are usually served with vinegar and oil (vegetable, olive or pumpkin). Other dressings often include yogurt. Many restaurants have salad bars.

Fižolova solata	Bean salad
Hobotnica v solati	Octopus salad
Krompirjeva solata	Potato salad
Kumarična solata	Cucumber salad
Mešana solata	Mixed salad
Motovilec	Lamb's lettuce
Paradižnikova solata	Tomato salad
Radič	Radicchio
Rdeča pesa	Beetroot
Regrad	Dandelion
Sezonska solata	Fresh salad or whatever is in season
Zelena solata	Lettuce
Zeljnata solata	Cabbage salad
Šopska solata	Mixed tomatoes, cucumbers, red/ green peppers and cheese

Fish dishes (ribje jedi) & seafood (morski sadeži)

Brancin	Seabass
Lignji	Squid
Losos	Salmon
Morski list	Sole
Ocvrta riba	Fried fish
Orada	Dorada
Oslič	Variety of cod
Postrvi	Trout

Rakci	Prawns
Sardele	Anchovies
Skuša	Mackerel
Škampi	Shrimps
Školjke	Mussels
Tuna	Tuna

Meat dishes (mesne jedi)

Čevapčiči	Minced meat, grilled in rolled pieces
Divjačina	Venison
Dunajski zrezek	Wiener schnitzel
Golaž	Goulash
Gos	Goose
Govedina	Beef
Goveji zrezek	Rumpsteak
Jagnjetina	Lamb
Kranjska klobasa s kislim zeljem	Sauerkraut with sausage
Mesne kroglice	Meatballs
Meso na žaru	Assorted grilled meat
Ovčetina	Mutton
Perutnina	Poultry
Piščanec	Chicken
Polnjene paprike	Peppers stuffed with meat and rice
Puran	Turkey
Raca	Duck
Sarma	Cabbage stuffed with meat and rice
Svinjina	Pork
Svinjski kotlet	Pork chop
Telečja (svinjska) krača	Veal (pork) shank
Telečja (svinjska) pečenka	Roast veal (pork)
Telečji zrezek	Roast cutlet
Teletina	Veal
Vampi	Tripe
Zajec	Rabbit
Žrebickov zrezek	Horse steak

Sauces (omake)

Gobova omaka	Mushroom sauce
Paradižnikova omaka	Tomato sauce
Sirova omaka	Cheese sauce
Smetanova omaka	Cream sauce

Tatarska omaka	Sauce made of mayonnaise, mustard, garlic and parsley
Vinska omaka	Wine sauce

Accompaniments (priloge)

Ajdovi ganci	Buckwheat porridge
Krompir	Potatoes
Kuhan	Boiled
Pečen	Roasted
Pire	Mashed
Pommes frittes (pomfri)	French fries
Krompirjevi cmoki	Potato dumplings
Kruhovi cmoki	Bread dumplings
Riž	Rice
Testenine	Pasta
Kuhana zelenjava	Boiled vegetables
Žlinkofi	Slovene type of ravioli

Vegetables (zelenjava)

Artičoka	Artichoke
Beluši/šparglji	Asparagus
Brstični ohrovt	Brussels sprouts
Bučke	Courgette
Čebula	Onions
Česen	Garlic
Cvetača	Cauliflower
Fižol	Beans
Gobe	Mushrooms
Grah	Peas
Hren	Horseradish
Jajčevec/melancana	Aubergine/eggplant
Korenje	Carrots
Koruza	Sweetcorn
Krompir	Potatoes
Kumara	Cucumber
Paprika	Red/green peppers
Paradižnik	Tomato
Peteršilj	Parsley
Por	Leek
Rdeča pesa	Beetroot
Redkev	Radish
Repa	Turnip
Špinača	Spinach
Zelena	Celery
Zelje	Cabbage

Fruit (sadje) and nuts

Ananas	Pineapple
Breskev	Peach
Češnja	Cherry
Ribez	Currant
Grozdje	Grapes
Hruška	Pear
Jabolko	Apple
Jagoda	Strawberry
Lešnik	Hazelnut
Limona	Lemon
Lubenica	Watermelon
Malina	Raspberry
Mandelj	Almond
Marelica	Apricot
Melona	Melon
Oreh	Walnut
Pomaranča	Orange
Sliva	Plum
Figa/smokva	Fig

Desserts (sladice)

Gibanica Pastry filled with apples, cheese and poppy seeds baked in cream

Palačinke z orehi, čokolado ali marmelado Pancakes with walnuts, chocolate or jam

Potica (orehova ali pehtranova) Cake (walnut or tarragon)

Štruklji (ajdovi, orehovi ali sirovi) Rolls (buckwheat, walnut or cheese)

Zavitek (jabolčni ali sirov) Strudel (apple or cheese)

Drink

Pivo	Beer
Sok	Juice
Vino (belo, rdeče)	Wine (white, red)
Voda	Water
Mineralna voda	Mineral water, usually with gas

Glossary of Slovenian words and terms

Avtobusna postaja	Bus station		Jezero	Lake
Avtobusna postajališče	Bus stop		Kmečki turizem	Farm tourism
Avtocesta	Highway		Letališče	Airport
Banka	Bank		Mestna hiša	Town hall
Bolnica	Hospital		Mesto	Town, city
Center	Centre		Morje	Sea
Cerkev	Church		Most	Bridge
Cesta	Road		Nakupolvani center	Shopping centre
DDV	Goods tax, equivalent to VAT		Otok	Island
			Plaža	Beach
Denar	Money		Ploščad	Platform (at the station)
Dolina	Valley			
Gostilna	Inn		Pokopališče	Cemetery
Gora	Mountain		Polje	Field
Gozd	Forest		Pošta	Post office
Grad	Castle		Pristanišče	Port
Hiša	House		Reka	River
Hrib	Hill		Restavracija	Restaurant
Jama	Cave		Samostan	Monastery

355

Sejem	Fair	**Trg**	Square, market
Slap	Waterfall	**Ulica**	Street
Šola	School	**Vas**	Village
Toplice	Spa or mineral baths with therapeutic properties	**Vodnjak**	Fountain
		Vozni red	Timetable (bus and train)
Trajekt	Ferry	**Vrt**	Garden
Trgovina	Shop	**Železniška postaja**	Railway station

Small print and

Index

A Rough Guide to Rough Guides

Published in 1982, the first Rough Guide – to Greece – was a student scheme that became a publishing phenomenon. Mark Ellingham, a recent graduate in English from Bristol University, had been travelling in Greece the previous summer and couldn't find the right guidebook. With a small group of friends he wrote his own guide, combining a highly contemporary, journalistic style with a thoroughly practical approach to travellers' needs.

The immediate success of the book spawned a series that rapidly covered dozens of destinations. And, in addition to impecunious backpackers, Rough Guides soon acquired a much broader and older readership that relished the guides' wit and inquisitiveness as much as their enthusiastic, critical approach and value-for-money ethos.

These days, Rough Guides include recommendations from shoestring to luxury and cover more than 200 destinations around the globe, including almost every country in the Americas and Europe, more than half of Africa and most of Asia and Australasia. Our ever-growing team of authors and photographers is spread all over the world, particularly in Europe, the USA and Australia.

In the early 1990s, Rough Guides branched out of travel, with the publication of Rough Guides to World Music, Classical Music and the Internet. All three have become benchmark titles in their fields, spearheading the publication of a wide range of books under the Rough Guide name.

Including the travel series, Rough Guides now number more than 350 titles, covering: phrasebooks, waterproof maps, music guides from Opera to Heavy Metal, reference works as diverse as Conspiracy Theories and Shakespeare, and popular culture books from iPods to Poker. Rough Guides also produce a series of more than 120 World Music CDs in partnership with World Music Network.

Visit www.roughguides.com to see our latest publications.

Rough Guide travel images are available for commercial licensing at www.roughguidespictures.com

Rough Guide credits

Text editor: Sarah Eno
Layout: Dan May
Cartography: Amod Singh
Picture editor: Nicole Newman
Production: Aimee Hampson
Proofreader: Stewart Wild
Cover design: Chloë Roberts

....

Editorial: London Kate Berens, Claire Saunders, Geoff Howard, Ruth Blackmore, Polly Thomas, Richard Lim, Alison Murchie, Karoline Densley, Andy Turner, Keith Drew, Edward Aves, Nikki Birrell, Helen Marsden, Alice Park, Sarah Eno, David Paul, Lucy White, Ruth Tidball, Jo Kirby, Joe Staines, Duncan Clark, Peter Buckley, Matthew Milton, Tracy Hopkins; **New York** Andrew Rosenberg, Steven Horak, AnneLise Sorensen, Amy Hegarty, April Isaacs, Sean Mahoney, Ella Steim
Design & Pictures: London Simon Bracken, Dan May, Diana Jarvis, Mark Thomas, Jj Luck, Harriet Mills, Chloë Roberts; **Delhi** Madhulita Mohapatra, Umesh Aggarwal, Ajay Verma, Jessica Subramanian, Ankur Guha, Pradeep Thapliyal, Sachin Tanwar, Anita Singh

Production: Katherine Owers, Aimee Hampson
Cartography: London Maxine Repath, Ed Wright, Katie Lloyd-Jones; **Delhi** Jai Prakash Mishra, Rajesh Chhibber, Ashutosh Bharti, Rajesh Mishra, Animesh Pathak, Jasbir Sandhu, Karobi Gogoi, Amod Singh, Alakananda Bhattacharya
Online: New York Jennifer Gold, Kristin Mingrone, Cree Lawson; **Delhi** Manik Chauhan, Narender Kumar, Shekhar Jha, Rakesh Kumar, Chhandita Chakravarty, Amit Kumar, Amit Verma, Rahul Kumar
Marketing & Publicity: London Richard Trillo, Niki Hanmer, Louise Maher, Jess Carter; Anna Paynton, Nikki Causer; **New York** Geoff Colquitt, Megan Kennedy, Katy Ball; **Delhi** Reem Khokhar
Custom publishing and foreign rights: Philippa Hopkins
Manager India: Punita Singh
Series editor: Mark Ellingham
Reference Director: Andrew Lockett
PA to Publishing Director: Megan McIntyre
Publishing Director: Martin Dunford

SMALL PRINT

ROUGH GUIDES

Publishing information

This second edition published January 2007 by **Rough Guides Ltd**,
80 Strand, London WC2R 0RL
345 Hudson St, 4th Floor,
New York, NY 10014, USA
14 Local Shopping Centre, Panchsheel Park,
New Delhi 110017, India
Distributed by the Penguin Group
Penguin Books Ltd,
80 Strand, London WC2R 0RL
Penguin Putnam, Inc.
375 Hudson Street, NY 10014, USA
Penguin Group (Australia)
250 Camberwell Road, Camberwell,
Victoria 3124, Australia
Penguin Books Canada Ltd,
10 Alcorn Avenue, Toronto, Ontario,
Canada M4V 1E4
Penguin Group (NZ)
67 Apollo Drive, Mairangi Bay, Auckland 1310,
New Zealand
Cover concept by Peter Dyer.

Typeset in Bembo and Helvetica to an original design by Henry Iles.

Printed and bound in China.

376pp includes index

A catalogue record for this book is available from the British Library

ISBN 1-84353-725-7

ISBN 13: 9781843537250

Help us update

We've gone to a lot of effort to ensure that the second edition of **The Rough Guide to Slovenia** is accurate and up to date. However, things change – places get "discovered", opening hours are notoriously fickle, restaurants and rooms raise prices or lower standards. If you feel we've got it wrong or left something out, we'd like to know, and if you can remember the address, the price, the time, the phone number, so much the better. We'll credit all contributions, and send a copy of the next edition (or any other Rough Guide if you prefer) for the best letters. Everyone who writes

to us and isn't already a subscriber will receive a copy of our full-colour thrice-yearly newsletter. Please mark letters: "**Rough Guide Slovenia Update**" and send to: Rough Guides, 80 Strand, London WC2R 0RL, or Rough Guides, 4th Floor, 345 Hudson St, New York, NY 10014. Or send an email to **mail@roughguides.com**
Have your questions answered and tell others about your trip at
www.roughguides.atinfopop.com

Acknowledgements

A big, special thank you to: Sarah, for her skilful and diligent editing, extreme patience and wholehearted enthusiasm; Tatjana Radovič for continued help and friendship; Mary Stuart-Miller (the UK Slovenian Tourist Office) for her invaluable assistance and kindness; Renata Kosi and Vesna Čuček at the Association of Slovenian Tourist Farms for their huge support; Špela Jurak for fine tuning the language section and other bits and pieces; Sabina Žibert in Čatež; Petra Stušek at the Ljubljana Tourist Board; Nika Božič and Ian Middleton in Ljubljana; Joanna Chandler in Bovec; Gaby Lukič in Murska Sobota; Tomaž Lukančič in Žiri; Jurij Šarman in Ptuj; Miha Mlinar in Most na Soči; Karin Tomažič in Brussels; Majda Dolenc, Brina Čehovin, Eva Ferlič and Rebeka Kumer at the Slovenian Tourist Board in Ljubljana.

Thanks are also due to:
Ljuba Bagar in Nova Gorica
Sabina Banjlč and Mirna Tabak in Maribor
Zvone Ciglič in London
Petra Čuk in Bled
Janez Fajfar in Bled

Boštjan Gombač from Katalena
Zoran Grom at Rokus Publishing
Janko Humar in Tolmin
Saša Jereb in Škofja Loka
Clive Judge and Myrna Santos in Bohinjska Bela
Bene Kavčič in Žiri
Zvonka Korošac in Kočevje
Jana Kovač in Ljubljana
Marko Koščak and Matjaž Pavlin in Novo Mesto
Dejan Luzar in Kobarid
Liljana Ošterbenk and Eva Štravs Podlogar in Bled
Ana Roš and Valter Kramar in Kobarid
Brett and Russell Smith in Leamington Spa
Lili Šeruga in Sela pri Ratežu
Mojca Špiler in Kranj
Joško Štajer in Postojna
Jaka Terpinc at the *Slovenia Times*
Ana Tušar at Slovenian Railways
Vesna Valentinčič in Deskle
The boys and girls at ISIS in Greenwich
And most importantly, Biljana and Luka James

Readers' letters

Thanks to all those readers of the first edition who took the trouble to write in with their amendments and additions. Apologies for any misspellings or omissions.

Natalie Holmes, Stephen Roe, Dave Tootell, Ivan Valencic, Amna Whiston, Ian Williamson,

Peter Moody, Alex Bugeja and Rob & Margaret Wiscombe.

Photo credits

ROUGH GUIDES

SMALL PRINT

Index

Map entries are in colour.

INDEX

Map symbols

maps are listed in the full index using coloured text

-----	International boundary	Monastery
---	Chapter division boundary	Synagogue
	Motorway	Museum
	Road	Castle
	Pedestrianized street	Fortress
	Steps	Monument
-----	Footpath	Mansion/stately home
	Railway	Statue
	Funicular railway	Gate
•---•	Cable car	Garden
■ ■ ■	Wall	Airport
	Bridge	Accommodation
	Mountain trail	Restaurant
/	\\	Hill	Boat transfer
	Mountains	Bus stop
▲	Mountain peak	Parking
	Cave	Hospital
	Waterfall	Tourist office
	Saltpan	Post office
	Border crossing	Market
	Mountain refuge	Stadium
	Skiing	Building
	Ruins	Church
	Lighthouse	Park
	Campsite	Cemetery
	Point of interest	Marshland
	Church (regional maps)	Beach